KT-143-749

The USBORNE SCIENCE ENCYCLOPEDIA

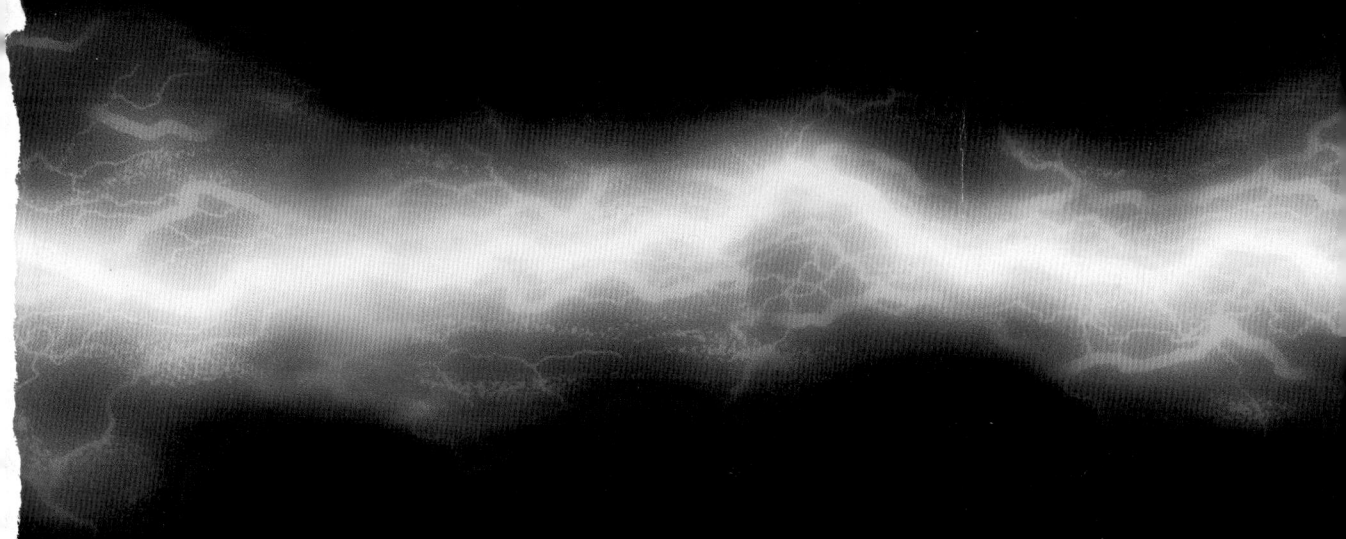

Usborne Publishing is not responsible and does not accept liability for the availability or content of any website other than its own, or for any exposure to harmful, offensive or inaccurate material that may appear on the Web. Usborne Publishing will have no liability for any damage or loss caused by viruses that may be downloaded as a result of browsing the sites it recommends.
Usborne downloadable pictures are the copyright of Usborne Publishing Ltd. and may not be reproduced in print or in electronic form for any commercial or profit-related purpose.

To access all the website described in this book, go to www.usborne-quicklinks.com and enter the keyword "science".

This edition first published in 2009 by Usborne Publishing Ltd,
Usborne House, 83-85 Saffron Hill, London EC1N 8RT, England.

www.usborne.com

Copyright © 2009, 2002, 2000 Usborne Publishing Ltd. The name Usborne and the devices ⚲ ⚲ are Trade Marks of Usborne Publishing Ltd. All rights reserved. No part of this publication may be reproduced, stored in a retrieval system or transmitted in any form or by any means, electronic, mechanical, photocopying, recording or otherwise, without the prior permission of the publisher.

Printed in UAE

The USBORNE SCIENCE ENCYCLOPEDIA

Kirsteen Rogers, Laura Howell, Alastair Smith,
Phillip Clarke and Corinne Henderson

Designed by Ruth Russell, Karen Tomlins,
Chloë Rafferty, Candice Whatmore and Jane Rigby

Digital illustrations by Verinder Bhachu

Digital imagery by Joanne Kirkby

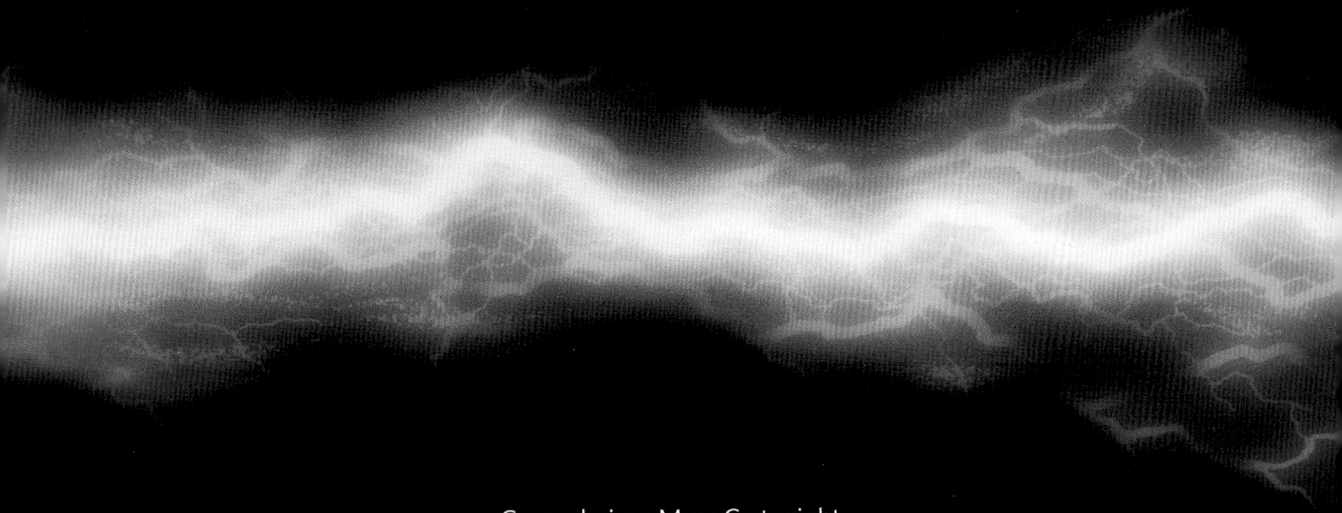

Cover design: Mary Cartwright

Consultants: Dr Margaret Rostron, Dr John Rostron, Dr Tom Petersen,
Elaine Wilson, Dr Roger Trend, Stuart Atkinson, Mark Beard

Internet researcher: Jacqueline Clark
Editorial assistant: Valerie Modd

Senior designer: Ruth Russell
Managing editor: Judy Tatchell

INTERNET LINKS

The Usborne Quicklinks Website is packed with thousands of links to interesting and informative websites. To visit the recommended sites for this book, go to **www.usborne-quicklinks.com** and enter the keyword "**science**". Then enter a page number to find the links for that page.

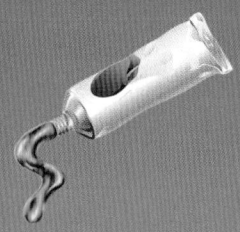

Internet links

Go to
www.usborne-quicklinks.com
and type in the keyword "science" for links to websites recommended in this book.

Always follow the internet safety guidelines on the Usborne Quicklinks Website.

USBORNE QUICKLINKS

For homework, research or just for fun, the Usborne Quicklinks Website saves time and takes you straight to relevant and reliable websites. You'll find links to sites with:

- Homework help
- Video and sound clips
- Quizzes and exercises
- Educational games

The recommended websites are regularly reviewed and updated, but please note, the content of a website may change at any time and Usborne Publishing is not responsible for the content of any website other than its own.

DOWNLOADABLE PICTURES

Many of the pictures in this book can be downloaded from the Usborne Quicklinks Website and used in schoolwork or projects. Look for the pictures marked with a ★ symbol – these are pictures that can be downloaded.

To download pictures, follow the instructions on the left to go to the internet links for this book, then enter the page number of the picture you want to download.

The pictures are the copyright of Usborne Publishing and may not be used for any commercial or profit-related purpose.

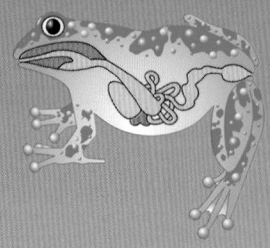

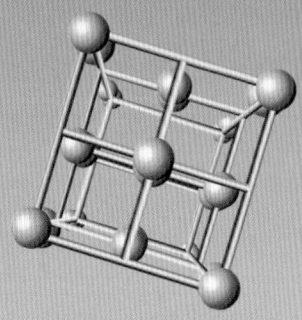

INTERNET SAFETY

When using the internet, make sure you follow the internet safety guidelines displayed on the Usborne Quicklinks Website.

- Children should ask an adult's permission before using the internet.
- Never give out personal information, such as your name, address or telephone number.
- If a website asks you to type in your name or email address, children should check with an adult first.

CONTENTS

MATERIALS

10 Atomic structure
14 Molecules
16 Solids, liquids and gases
18 Changes of state
20 How liquids behave
22 How gases behave
24 The elements
26 Elements in the Earth
28 The periodic table
30 Metals
32 Groups of metals
34 Alloys
36 Iron and steel
38 Main metals and alloys
40 Corrosion
42 The discovery of metals
44 Recycling metals
46 Hydrogen
48 The halogens
50 Carbon
54 Sulphur
55 Phosphorus

MIXTURES AND COMPOUNDS

58 Mixtures
60 Separating mixtures
62 The air
66 Compounds
68 Bonding
72 Water
76 Chemical reactions
80 Oxidation and reduction
82 Electrolysis
84 Acids and bases
88 Salts
90 Crystals
92 Organic chemistry
96 Alkanes and alkenes
98 Crude oil
100 Polymers and plastics
102 Using plastics

ENERGY, FORCES AND MOTION

106 Energy
110 Heat
112 Heat transfer
114 Radioactivity
116 Nuclear power
118 Forces
122 Dynamics
124 Friction
126 Motion
130 Gravity
132 Pressure
134 Simple machines
137 Work and power
138 Floating
140 Ships and boats
142 Flight
144 Aircraft design
146 Engines
150 Cars and motorbikes

EARTH AND SPACE

154 The universe
156 Galaxies
158 Stars
162 The Sun
164 The inner planets
166 The Earth and Moon

168 The outer planets
172 Space debris
174 Space exploration
178 The early Earth
180 Earth's structure
184 The atmosphere
186 Life on Earth
188 Seas and oceans
190 Rivers
192 Weather
194 Climate
196 World population
198 Earth's resources

LIGHT, SOUND AND ELECTRICITY

202 Waves
204 Wave behaviour
206 Sound
208 Musical instruments
210 Sound reproduction
212 Electromagnetic waves
214 Light and shadow
216 Colour
218 Light behaviour
220 Lenses and mirrors
222 Optical instruments
224 Cameras
226 TV and radio
228 Electricity
232 Magnetism
236 Electronics
238 Digital electronics
240 Computers
244 Telecoms
246 The internet

PLANTS AND FUNGI

250 Plant cells
252 Stems and roots
254 Plant tissue
256 Inside older plants
258 Leaves
260 Leaf structure
262 Movement of fluids
264 Plant food
268 Plant sensitivity
270 Flowering plants
274 Seeds and fruit
278 New plants from old
280 Water plants
282 Flowerless plants
284 Fungi
286 Fighting for survival
288 Plant lifestyles
290 Plants and people
292 Natural cycles
294 Classifying plants

ANIMAL WORLD

298 Animal cells
300 Body structure
302 Body coverings
304 Moving in water
306 Flying and gliding
308 Moving on land
310 Feeding
312 Teeth and digestion
314 Breathing
316 Internal balance
318 Sending messages

320 Animal senses
324 Creating new life
328 Life cycles
330 Ecology
332 Food and energy
334 Balance in nature
336 Conservation
338 Evolution
340 Classification

HUMAN BODY

346 The skeleton
348 Muscles
350 The circulatory system
352 Teeth
354 Digestion
356 Food and diet
358 The respiratory system
360 Energy for life
362 Balancing act
364 The nervous system
366 The brain
368 Skin, nails and hair
370 Eyes
372 Ears
374 The nose and tongue
376 Reproduction
378 Growing and changing
380 Genetics
382 Gene technology
386 Fighting disease
388 Medicine

SCIENCE FACTS AND LISTS

394 Research on the Web
396 Revision questions
404 Units of measurement
406 Measuring nature
408 Geometrical shapes
409 Laws and symbols
410 Earth and space facts
412 Scientists and inventors
416 Key dates in science
418 A-Z of scientific terms
436 Index
447 Answers

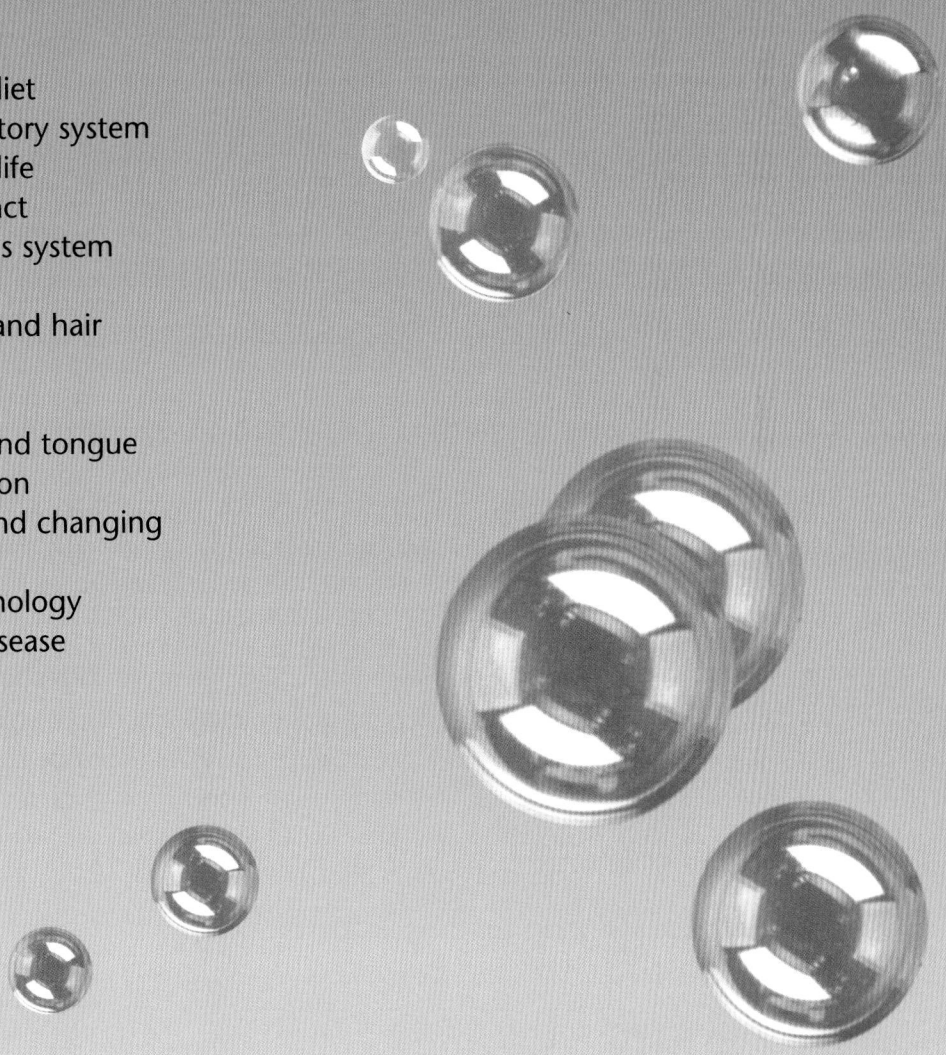

MATERIALS

ATOMIC STRUCTURE

Atoms are the tiny particles of which everything is made. It is impossible to imagine how small an atom is. A hundred million atoms side by side would measure only 1cm, and a sheet of paper, like the ones that make up this book, is probably a million atoms thick.

SUBATOMIC PARTICLES

Atoms are made of smaller particles called **subatomic particles**. In the middle of every atom is its **nucleus**. The nucleus contains two types of subatomic particles, called **protons** and **neutrons**.

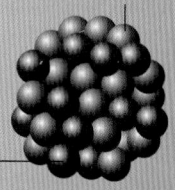

Protons and neutrons form the nucleus of an atom.

Subatomic particles of a third type, called **electrons**, move around the nucleus. The electrons exist at different energy levels, called **shells**, around the nucleus. Each shell can have up to a certain number of electrons. When it is full, a new shell is started.

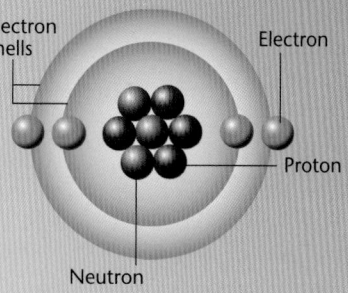

Scientists now think that protons and neutrons are made of even smaller subatomic particles, called **quarks**.

This diagram uses coloured balls to represent the parts of an atom and illustrate the relationships between them.

In the middle of the atom is the nucleus. It is made of protons (shown in pink) and neutrons (shown in purple).

Most of an atom consists of empty space between the particles.

Electrons are trapped by their attraction to protons, which are in the nucleus. They whizz around the nucleus at different levels, called shells.

The two electrons shown in green exist in the first shell of this atom. Those in blue are in the second shell.

Electron

ELECTRICAL CHARGES

The subatomic particles that make up an atom are held together by electrical charges. Particles with opposite electrical charges are attracted to one another.

The protons have a positive electrical charge and the electrons have a negative charge. Neutrons have no electrical charge, so they are neutral.

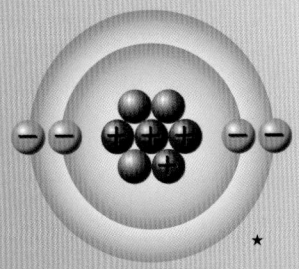

Proton: positive electrical charge.

Electron: negative electrical charge.

Neutron: no electrical charge.

An atom usually has an equal number of positively charged protons and negatively charged electrons. This makes the atom itself electrically neutral.

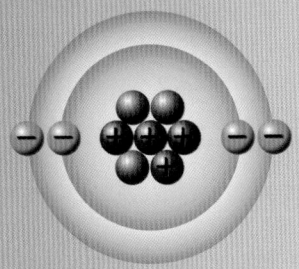

This atom is electrically neutral.

It has four protons.

It has four electrons.

Its three neutrons have no effect on its electrical charge.

REPRESENTING ATOMS

Although atoms are often represented by diagrams like the main picture, scientists now believe that the electrons are held in cloud-like regions around the nucleus, as in the **electron cloud model** below.

Electron cloud model

Electrons can be anywhere within their cloud, at any time. Sometimes they even move outside it.

ELECTRON DENSITY

In the picture below, different colours show different levels of density of electrons in a group of atoms. The turquoise areas show where the electrons are most dense.

This is a picture of what you might see through an extremely powerful microscope.

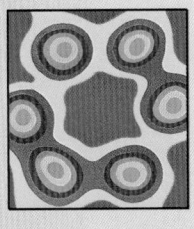

Internet links

To find out more about atoms, go to **www.usborne-quicklinks.com** and type in the keyword "science".

There you'll find links to websites where you can:

- Take a look inside an atom
- See how incredibly tiny atoms are
- Find out more with online activities

Go to Usborne Quicklinks for links to hand-picked websites on hundreds of subjects.

ATOMIC NUMBER

Atoms of different substances have different numbers of protons in their nucleus. The number of protons in the nucleus is called the **atomic number**.

The atomic number of an atom indicates what substance it is.

An atom usually has an equal number of protons and electrons, so the atomic number also shows how many electrons it has.

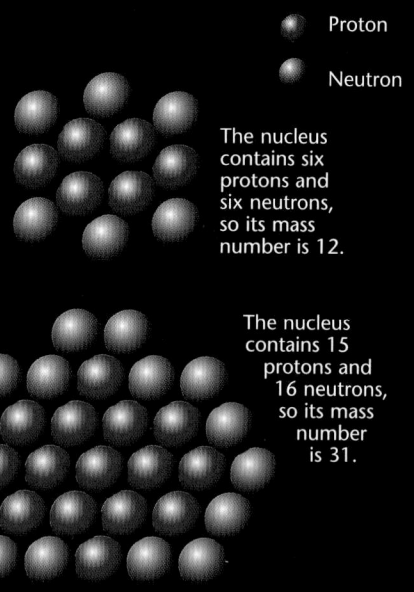

MASS NUMBER

The more protons and neutrons an atom has, the greater its mass (the measurement of the amount of matter in the atom). The total number of protons and neutrons in an atom is called its **mass number**.

Electrons are left out of the mass calculation as they add so little to the mass of an atom.

A machine called a **mass spectrometer** can be used to help identify atoms by sorting them by mass.

This type of machine is called a **cyclotron**, a device which scientists use to break atoms apart. Machines like this have enabled research into the nature of atoms, and the particles of which they are made.

Cyclotrons are used in certain industries. Manufacturers use them to create particular types of plastics. In hospitals, they are used to create radioactive isotopes to treat cancer patients.

ISOTOPES

Most atoms exist in a number of different forms, called **isotopes**. Each form has the same number of protons and electrons, but a different number of neutrons. So all the isotopes of an atom have the same atomic number, but they have different mass numbers.

The mass number of the isotope of an atom is written beside its name. For instance, carbon-12 has six protons and six neutrons.

These examples show the three isotopes of carbon.

Proton

Neutron

$^{12}_{6}C$

Carbon-12 has six neutrons and six protons.

$^{13}_{6}C$

Carbon-13 has six protons and seven neutrons.

$^{14}_{6}C$

Carbon-14 has six protons and eight neutrons.

★

Isotopes have different physical properties but their chemical properties are the same. Most of the atoms in an **element** (a substance made up of only one type of atom) are a single isotope, with small amounts of other isotopes.

ANCIENT IDEAS

The idea that everything in the universe is made up of atoms is not a new one. Philosophers in Ancient Greece, 2,500 years ago, believed that matter was made up of particles that could not be cut any smaller. The word "atom" comes from the Greek word atomos, which means "uncuttable".

The theories of Aristotle, an Ancient Greek philosopher, influenced atomic science for centuries.

Aristotle (384-322BC)

ATOMIC THEORY

The term "atom" was first used by the British chemist, John Dalton, when he put forward his **atomic theory** in 1807.

Dalton suggested that all chemical elements were made of very small particles, called atoms, that did not break up when chemicals reacted. He thought that every chemical reaction was the result of atoms joining or separating. Dalton's atomic theory provided the basis for modern science.

John Dalton (1766-1844)

Dalton used symbols to represent one atom of each element or substance.

Examples of Dalton's symbols

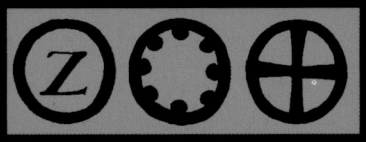

Zinc Mercury Sulphur

EARLY MODELS

Early in the twentieth century, scientists began to make models of atoms.

Ernest Rutherford (1871-1937) showed electrons with a negative electric charge circling a positively charged nucleus.

Rutherford's model

Niels Bohr (1885-1962) showed a model with electrons following specific orbits. In 1932, James Chadwick (1891-1974) showed the nucleus made of particles called neutrons and protons.

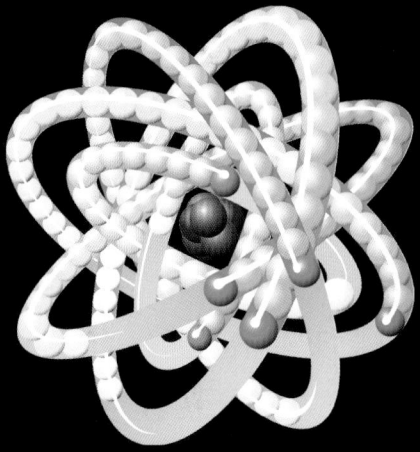

This model of an atom, which is also shown larger on pages 10-11, is based on models by Rutherford, Bohr and Chadwick.

Internet links

To find out more about atoms, go to **www.usborne-quicklinks.com** and type in the keyword "science".

There you'll find links to websites where you can:

- Examine different types of atom
- Learn curious atomic facts

MOLECULES

Atoms are rarely found on their own. They usually cling, or bond, together to form molecules or large lattice structures. A **molecule** is a group of atoms that are bonded together to form the smallest piece of a substance that normally exists on its own. Molecules are much too small to be seen with the naked eye.

SHELLS AND BONDING

Most atoms have several shells of electrons*. The first shell of an atom can hold two electrons. The second and third shells can hold eight, although some atoms can hold up to 18 electrons in their third shells. When a shell is full, the electrons start a new shell. An atom is particularly stable when it has a full outer shell of electrons.

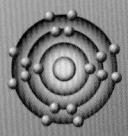

An argon atom has three full shells of electrons. It is a stable atom.

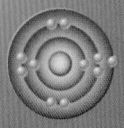

A sodium atom is unstable. It has only one electron in its third shell.

Atoms bond together in order to become stable. They do this by sharing electrons, or by giving up or taking electrons from another atom in order to achieve a full, or fuller, outer shell. Two hydrogen atoms, for instance, bond together to make a hydrogen molecule. They share their electrons, giving each atom a full outer shell. (For more about bonding, see pages 68-71.)

Two hydrogen atoms

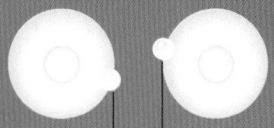

Hydrogen molecule

Each atom has a full shell of two electrons, so it is stable.

* *Electrons, 10.*

This is a model of a molecule of DNA, a complicated chemical compound found in the cells of all living things.

WATER MOLECULE

A water molecule consists of two different elements: hydrogen and oxygen. The two hydrogen atoms share electrons with the oxygen atom, so each has a complete shell. The oxygen atom uses two electrons (one from each hydrogen atom) to complete its own outer shell. All the atoms become stable.

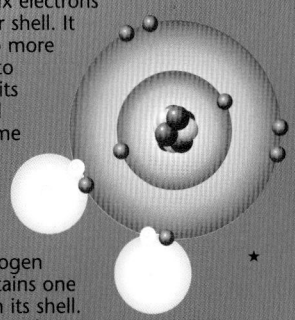

The oxygen atom contains six electrons in its outer shell. It needs two more electrons to complete its outer shell and become stable.

Each hydrogen atom contains one electron in its shell. They each seek one electron to complete their shells and become stable.

CHEMICAL FORMULAE

An atom's name can be shown by a symbol (its **chemical symbol**). This is usually the first letter or two of its name in English, Latin or German.

O	The symbol for oxygen
Au	The symbol for gold, from the Latin word aurum
Fe	The symbol for iron, from the Latin word ferrum
K	The symbol for potassium, from the German word kalium

A **chemical formula** shows the atoms of which a substance is made and in what proportions. For example, each molecule of carbon dioxide is made up of one atom of carbon and two atoms of oxygen, so the formula for carbon dioxide is CO_2. The figure "2" shows the number of oxygen atoms in the molecule.

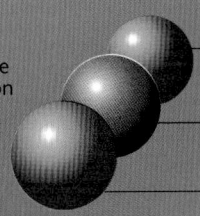

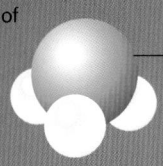

MODELS OF MOLECULES

When studying molecules, scientists often use models to represent them. There are two main types: ball-and-spoke models and space-filling models.

In **ball-and-spoke models**, the bonds that hold the atoms together are shown as sticks.

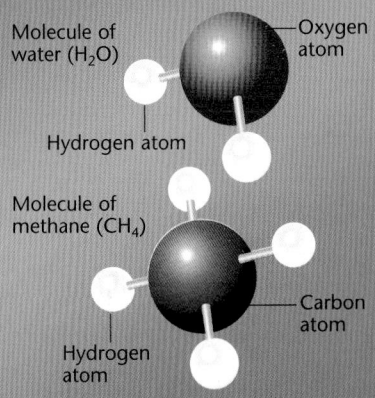

In **space-filling models**, atoms are shown clinging together.

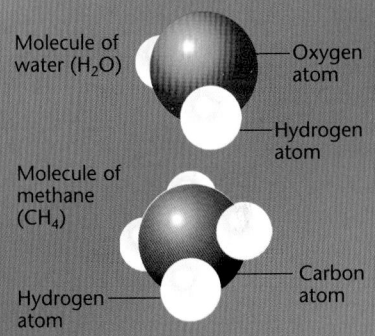

Neither model looks like an actual molecule, but they are simple ways of showing the atoms that form the molecule.

Internet links

To find out more about molecules, go to **www.usborne-quicklinks.com** and type in the keyword "science".

There you'll find links to websites where you can:

- Play a molecule game
- Take part in interactive lessons

SOLIDS, LIQUIDS AND GASES

Most substances can exist in three different forms: as solids, liquids or gases. These are called the **states of matter**. A solid has a definite volume and shape. A liquid has a definite volume, but its shape changes according to the shape of its container. A gas has neither shape nor volume. It will move to fill the space available.

THE KINETIC THEORY

The theory that explains the properties of solids, liquids and gases is called the **kinetic theory**. It is based on the idea that all substances are made up of moving particles. It explains the properties of solids, liquids and gases in terms of the energy of these particles.

Heating a substance gives the particles more energy, enabling them to move around faster and change from one state to another. (See Changes of State, pages 18-19).

Like many scientific theories, the kinetic theory has never been proved. It provides an explanation, though, for how solids, liquids and gases are seen to behave, and why substances change from one state to another.

Movement of particles in solids, liquids and gases

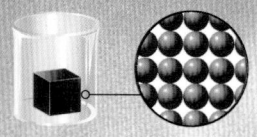

The particles in a solid have the least energy and cannot overcome the attraction between one another. They vibrate, but stay where they are.

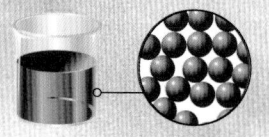

Heating a solid gives the particles more energy so they can escape from each other. The solid melts and becomes a liquid.

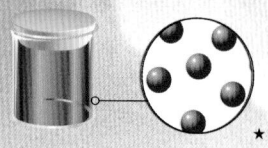

The particles in a gas have even more energy. They easily move far apart and spread out through the available space.

This is a geyser. Water heated to boiling point under the ground turns from a liquid to a gas (steam) and shoots out of a crack. You can find out more about what causes geysers over the page.

BROWNIAN MOTION

The movement of particles in liquids and gases is known as **Brownian motion**, named after a British biologist, Robert Brown (1773-1858). In 1827, Brown observed how tiny grains of pollen moved around randomly in a liquid, but he could not explain what caused this movement.

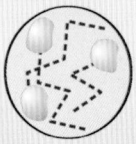

Random movement of particles in a liquid

The German-born scientist Albert Einstein (1879-1955) later explained that the movement of particles in a liquid or gas is caused by the particles being hit by the invisible molecules of the fluid in which the particles are floating.

MEASURING SUBSTANCES

Volume is the amount of space occupied by a solid or liquid. It is measured in cubic metres (m^3).

You can calculate the volume of a rectangular solid using this formula:

Volume = Length x Breadth x Height

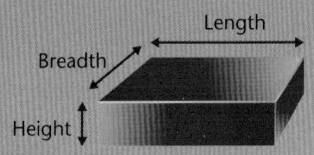

The volume of a liquid can be found by pouring the liquid into a measuring cylinder marked with a scale.

The volume of an irregularly shaped solid is measured by finding how much liquid it displaces, using a Eureka can.

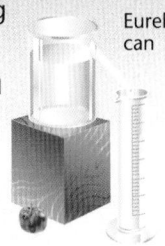

1. Eureka can is filled with water to base of spout.

2. Object is put into Eureka can.

3. Volume of displaced water is measured.

The **mass** of a solid, liquid or gas is the amount of matter it contains. This is measured in kilograms. Mass is different from **weight**, which is a measure of the strength of the pull of gravity* on an object. Mass is measured by weighing a substance and comparing its mass with a known mass.

Density is the mass of a substance compared with its volume. For example, the same volumes of cork and metal have different densities because the mass of the metal is much greater than that of the cork. Density is found by dividing the mass of an object by its volume, and it is measured in kilograms per cubic metre (kg/m^3).

$$\text{Density} = \frac{\text{Mass}}{\text{Volume}}$$

The density of a liquid is measured using a **hydrometer**. The hydrometer floats near the surface in a dense liquid, as only a small volume of liquid needs to be displaced to equal the weight of the hydrometer (see Why Things Float, page 138).

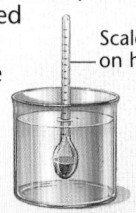

See for yourself

You can do an experiment to find the volumes of irregularly shaped solids without using a Eureka can.

You will need a measuring jug, a cake mixing bowl and a washing-up bowl.

First, put your mixing bowl inside the washing-up bowl. Then carefully fill the mixing bowl with water up to the brim.

Now take the object that you want to measure and hold it just on top of the water's surface. Let the object sink into the water. Water will slop over the side of the mixing bowl and be caught in the washing-up bowl.

Take the mixing bowl out of the washing-up bowl. Now pour the water from the washing-up bowl into the measuring jug. The volume of water is equal to the volume of the object.

Internet links

To find out more about solids, liquids and gases, go online at **www.usborne-quicklinks.com** and type the keyword "science".

There you'll find links to websites where you can:

- Find out how gases mix
- Try virtual experiments
- Test yourself with an online quiz

Go to Usborne Quicklinks for links to hand-picked websites on hundreds of subjects.

* *Gravity, 130-131.*

CHANGES OF STATE

An ice cream melts and becomes a liquid in the heat of the Sun.

A substance changes from one **state of matter**, that is solid, liquid or gas, to another, depending on its temperature and pressure. When something changes state, heat is produced or lost as the energy of its particles is increased or decreased. Different substances change state at different temperatures.

The heat from a flame melts candle wax, but the wax sets as it drips away from the flame and cools.

MELTING AND BOILING

When a solid is heated, its temperature rises and its particles gain energy until it reaches its **melting point**. The particles now have enough energy to break away from their neighbours so the solid melts.

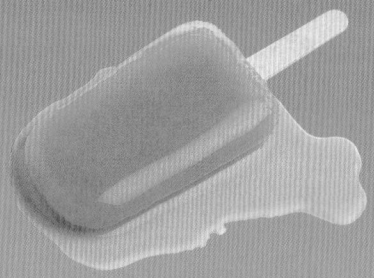

This ice melts at a lower temperature than pure water ice because orange juice has been added to it.

Further heat causes the temperature of the liquid to rise until it reaches its **boiling point** and the particles break free of each other completely. The liquid becomes a gas.

Some substances, for example carbon dioxide, change from gas to solid, or solid to gas, without passing through a liquid form. This is called **sublimation**.

The temperature at which a substance melts or boils changes if it contains traces of any other substances. For instance, ice (the solid form of water) melts at 0°C. Adding salt to the ice lowers its melting point.

When steam cools down, it turns back into water.

GEYSERS

Geysers are jets of boiling hot water and steam that shoot out from the Earth's crust.

They occur when water under the ground is heated by hot rocks and begins to boil.

As the water turns to steam, the pressure builds up in the channels between the rocks. The geyser then erupts, shooting a jet of steam and water high up into the air.

How geysers occur

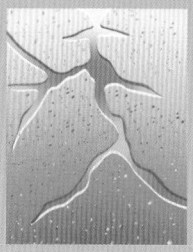

Water flows into cavities between the rocks under the ground.

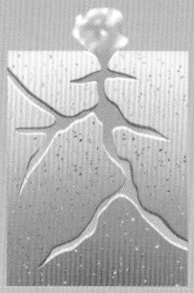

Pressure builds as the water heats and expands. Eventually, it turns to steam.

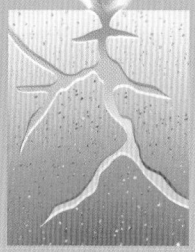

The pressure builds until boiling water and steam shoot out of a crack in the ground.

CONDENSATION

When a gas cools down enough, it **condenses**, becoming a liquid. This is because as it cools down, its particles lose energy and are unable to stay as far away from each other.

Condensation

Water vapour in the air in a room condenses on a cold window. Droplets of water are formed on the inside of the window.

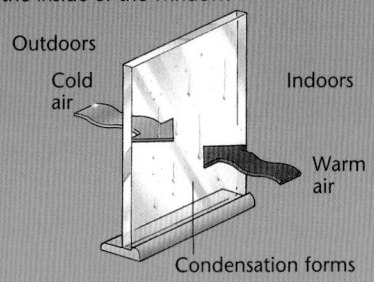

FREEZING

When a liquid cools enough, it sets or **freezes**, becoming a solid. Its particles lose further energy and are unable to overcome the attraction between each other.

When tiny droplets of water in the atmosphere freeze, they sometimes join together in beautiful patterns of crystals and form snowflakes like these.

PRESSURE

Air pressure has an effect on the melting or boiling point of a substance. The air naturally presses down on the Earth with a force called **atmospheric pressure**. At sea level, this is described as **one atmosphere**, or **standard pressure**.

At sea level, pure water boils at 100°C.

Higher up, the atmospheric pressure is less. It is easier for the particles in liquids to escape into the air, so their boiling points are lower.

At the top of Mount Everest (8,850m above sea level), where the pressure is less than one atmosphere, pure water boils at 71°C.

WATERLESS PLANET

The surface of Mars is dry. Scientists think that this is because the atmospheric pressure is very low, so any water immediately boils away.

Most of Mars is covered by a reddish dust.

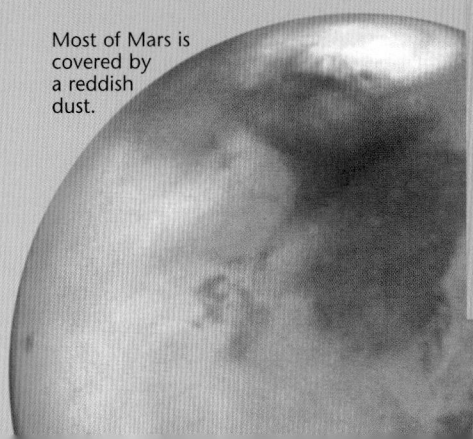

SOLID LIQUID OR GAS?

Whether something is classified as a solid, liquid or gas depends on its state at room temperature (20°C).

Mercury melts at -40°C. It is a liquid at room temperature.

Chlorine boils at -35°C so is a gas at room temperature.

See for yourself

Fill a metal container with ice cubes. Stand it in a warm place and leave it for a few minutes. Then look at the container. You will see drops of water on the outside of it.

Water molecules in the warm air lose energy and slow down when they are cooled by the ice. They stick to each other, forming water droplets.

Droplets of water on the side of the can

Internet links

To find out more about states, go to **www.usborne-quicklinks.com** and type in the keyword "science".

There you'll find links to websites where you can:

- Watch animated tutorials
- Get instructions for experiments
- See photos of intricate snowflakes, and learn how they form

Go to Usborne Quicklinks for links to hand-picked websites on hundreds of subjects.

HOW LIQUIDS BEHAVE

A **liquid** has a definite volume but it flows and changes shape to fill its container. The particles in a liquid are fairly close together, but have more energy than the particles in a solid, so are free to move about (see *The Kinetic Theory*, page 16).

The particles in water (like all liquids) are free to move about.

EVAPORATION

Some of the molecules on the surface of a liquid have more energy than others, and they escape, or **evaporate**, into the air. Liquids are evaporating all the time, even when they are not being heated.

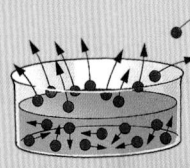

These particles have enough energy to escape, or evaporate, from the surface of the liquid to form a vapour.

RATE OF EVAPORATION

The **rate of evaporation** increases with any one or a combination of the following:

- an increase in temperature.
- a decrease in pressure. For instance, water evaporates more quickly at the top of Mount Everest, where the atmospheric pressure is less, than it does at sea level.
- the immediate removal of the vapour from above the liquid by a flow of air. This is why washing hung out to dry on a windy day dries more quickly than on a still day.
- an increase in surface area. For instance, a spilled drink will evaporate or dry up more quickly than the same drink in a glass.

COOLING DOWN

When a liquid is evaporating, its temperature falls because the average energy of the molecules that are left in the liquid has fallen.

SURFACE TENSION

The molecules in a liquid are attracted by all the other liquid molecules around them. The ones on the surface, though, are not pulled upwards because there are no liquid molecules above them. They are more attracted to the other liquid molecules than to the air.

This sideways and downwards attraction at the surface creates a force called **surface tension**. It makes a liquid seem to have a "skin".

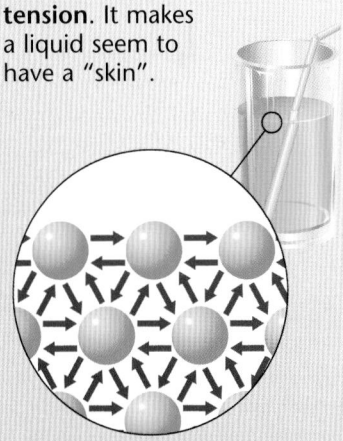

Molecules at the surface are attracted to each other, and to those below them. This creates surface tension.

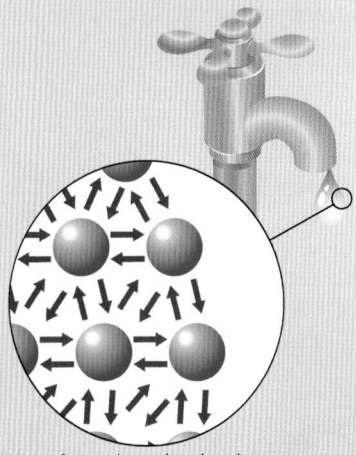

Water forms into droplets because surface tension pulls inwards from all sides, keeping the molecules together.

The drips on these leaves form because surface tension pulls molecules of rainwater together.

STRETCHY SKIN

As a result of surface tension, a liquid's surface is like a stretchy skin, strong enough to support very light objects, such as dust or even insects.

Pond skaters can walk on the surface of water as they are not heavy enough to break the skin-like surface tension.

COHESION

Cohesion happens when molecules of one substance are more attracted to each other than to a substance they are touching. Surface tension is an example of this. Molecules at the water's surface try to stay together rather than move towards the air above.

ADHESION

When molecules of a liquid are more attracted to a substance they are touching than to each other, **adhesion** occurs. The liquid adheres (sticks) to the other substance. Water does this when it touches the sides of a glass.

See for yourself

To see how surface tension can support certain objects, try this quick activity.

Fill a container with water. Put a needle on a small piece of tissue paper and lay it gently on the water.

The tissue soon becomes waterlogged and sinks, but the needle stays afloat, supported by surface tension.

Look closely and you will see that the needle actually dents the water's surface.

Internet links

To find out more about liquids, go to **www.usborne-quicklinks.com** and type in the keyword "science".

There you'll find links to websites where you can:

- Find recipes for making big bubbles
- Investigate the power of soap

Go to Usborne Quicklinks for links to hand-picked websites on hundreds of subjects.

HOW GASES BEHAVE

A **gas** is a substance that has no definite volume or shape. Its particles have enough energy to spread far apart from each other and fill the space available.

DIFFUSION

The molecules in a gas have enough energy to break free of the forces between them (see *The Kinetic Theory*, page 16). They spread out to fill the available space. This is called **diffusion**.

During diffusion, molecules move from an area where they are in higher concentration to one where their concentration is lower. Diffusion stops when the molecules are evenly distributed.

Smells, such as the scent of flowers, are gases that travel through the air by diffusion.

Molecules of a light gas

Molecules of a heavy gas

Molecules of these two gases diffuse together over time. Light gases diffuse faster than heavy ones.

This scientist is taking samples of gases emerging from holes in the side of a volcano. Some of the gases are harmful, so the scientist has to wear a breathing mask.

The set-up below shows how two gases mix by diffusion. A jar of air is turned upside down on top of a jar of bromine, which is heavier than air.

After fifteen minutes, the air and bromine in the jars become mixed by diffusion as their molecules spread through the two jars.

PRESSURE, TEMPERATURE AND VOLUME

Gases exert a push on things that they are contained in. This push, called **pressure**, is felt in all directions. It is the rate at which molecules in a gas hit the sides of its container.

Any change in pressure, temperature, or the container's volume will cause a change in the molecules' behaviour.

If the volume of a gas at a constant temperature is decreased, for example by reducing the size of its container, the pressure of the gas increases. This is because the gas molecules hit the walls of the container more frequently.

When heated, the molecules in a gas gain energy, move around faster and become even further apart – the gas expands and becomes less dense. This is why hot-air balloons float – the air inside them is less dense than the air around them.

If a gas is heated but is not allowed to expand, then its pressure increases. This is because the molecules in the gas gain energy, move around more quickly and hit the walls of the container more frequently.

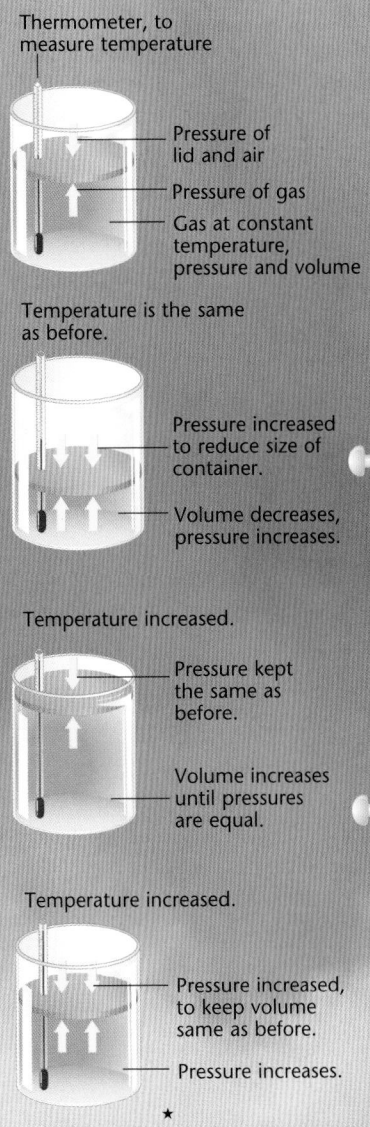

Under the ground, volcanic gases become extremely hot. The pressure builds and builds until they shoot out of cracks and holes in the ground.

Balloons stretch as air spreads out to fill them.

See for yourself

Next time you use a balloon pump, see how it uses pressure to fill the balloon with air.

1. When you pump the handle, the volume of the pump's chamber is decreased so the air pressure inside it is increased.

Chamber

2. Air shoots out of the nozzle, into the balloon.

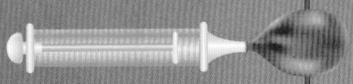

3. A valve in the pump prevents air from being sucked back out of the balloon.

4. Pressure inside the balloon increases so it stretches and expands. Its volume increases.

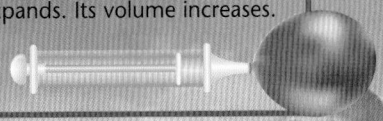

Internet links

To find out more about gases, go to **www.usborne-quicklinks.com** and type in the keyword "science".

There you'll find links to websites where you can:

- Investigate how gases behave, with information and experiments
- Watch animations that explain gas pressure and diffusion

Go to Usborne Quicklinks for links to hand-picked websites on hundreds of subjects.

THE ELEMENTS

An **element** is a substance that contains only one kind of atom – the tiny particles of which all substances are made. For example, sulphur, helium and iron are elements: they contain only sulphur, helium or iron atoms and they cannot be broken down into simpler substances.

GROUPING ELEMENTS

So far, 111 elements have been discovered, but only 90 occur naturally on Earth. Elements can be sorted into metals, non-metals and semi-metals and arranged in a table, called the periodic table, which is shown on pages 28-29.

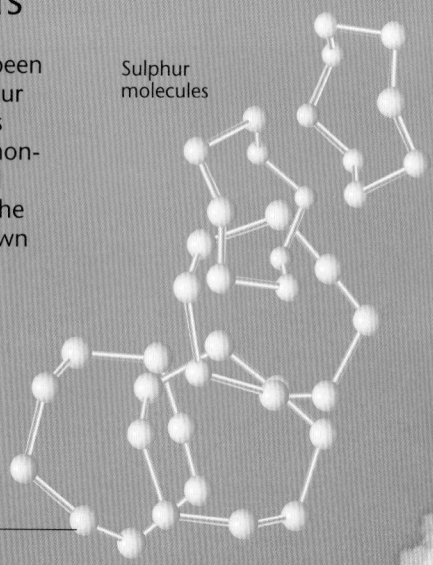

Sulphur is one of the 90 elements that occur naturally on Earth. It is a non-metal. Its molecules, as shown in this diagram, form irregular ring shapes consisting of eight sulphur atoms.

The Space Shuttle relies on burning elements to blast it into space. It burns the non-metal hydrogen (stored in the red-brown coloured external fuel tank) and powdered aluminium metal (stored in the two white rockets).

METAL ELEMENTS

Over three-quarters of all the elements are **metals**. Most of the metal elements are dense and shiny. They have many uses as they are strong, but can be easily shaped. They are also good conductors of heat and electricity. Metals are usually found combined with other elements in the Earth's crust (see pages 26-27).

These chocolate eggs are wrapped in thin aluminium foil to keep them fresh. Aluminium is the most common metal on Earth.

Here, aluminium is rolled into a long, thin sheet. It can be re-shaped easily without breaking because its atoms, which are closely packed, slide over each other.

NON-METALS

There are 16 naturally occurring **non-metal** elements. All (apart from graphite, a form of carbon) are insulators – poor conductors of heat and electricity.

At room temperature, four non-metals (phosphorus, carbon, sulphur and iodine) are solids, and bromine is a liquid. The other 11 non-metals are gases.

Non-metals

Hydrogen	Sulphur
Helium	Chlorine
Carbon	Argon
Nitrogen	Bromine
Oxygen	Krypton
Fluorine	Iodine
Neon	Xenon
Phosphorus	Radon

SEMI-METALS

Semi-metals, also called **metalloids**, can act as poor conductors, just like non-metals. They can also be made to conduct well, like metals. Because of this, semi-metal elements are called **semiconductors**. There are nine semi-metals (see list, right). They are all solids at room temperature.

Semi-metals

Boron	Antimony
Silicon	Tellurium
Germanium	Polonium
Arsenic	Astatine
Selenium	

The semi-metal germanium is used to make transistors* like this one. They are used in radios.

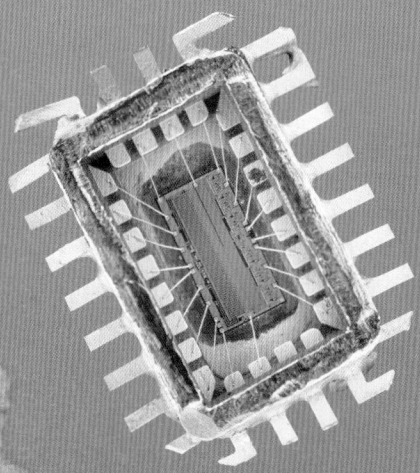

Silicon is used to make integrated circuits* such as this one. Microscopic pathways in the circuit conduct and block electrical pulses.

See for yourself

Finding out how well a substance conducts heat can help to identify whether it is a metal or a non-metal. Try the experiment below.

You will need several long objects such as a metal spoon, a wooden spoon and a plastic ruler. Put a smear of cold butter near the end of each object.

Place the objects in a mug filled with warm water.

As the heat travels up the object, it melts the butter. You should find that the butter melts on the metal things first, because metals are better conductors of heat than non-metals. Eventually, the warmth of the rising air melts the butter on all the objects.

Internet links

To find out more about elements, go to **www.usborne-quicklinks.com** and type in the keyword "science".

There you'll find links to websites where you can:

- Find illustrated element facts
- Test yourself with an online quiz
- Watch animated tutorials

Go to Usborne Quicklinks for links to hand-picked websites on hundreds of subjects.

* *Integrated circuits, 239; Transistors, 237.*

ELEMENTS IN THE EARTH

The outermost layer of the Earth is called the **crust**. Most of it is made of only five elements. It is rare for these elements to occur alone, though some, like gold, do. More often they are found together as combined substances called **compounds**. The pure and combined elements found in the crust are called **minerals**. Minerals that contain metals are called **ores**.

Some minerals, such as this chalcedony, can be polished to make beautiful decorative objects.

COMMON ELEMENTS

Oxygen is the most common element in the Earth's crust. It often occurs combined with silicon, the second most common element, and with aluminium and iron, the commonest metals.

This pie chart shows the proportions, by mass, of the five main elements in the Earth's crust.

MINERAL FORMATION

Most minerals are formed when hot **magma** (molten rock that contains dissolved gases) pushes up from deep below the Earth's crust, cools and solidifies.

The conditions in the place where magma cools determine which type of mineral forms. Geometric shapes called **crystals** form when minerals cool slowly. The cooling process can be so quick, though, that the mineral has no time to crystallize. A kind of shiny black glass, called obsidian, forms in these conditions.

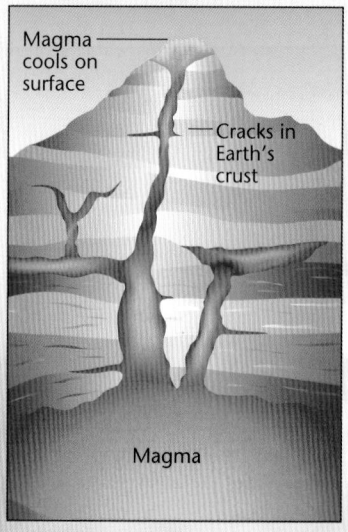

Molten magma is less dense than the surrounding crust. It rises up through cracks and cools to form minerals.

This picture shows huge clumps of shiny black obsidian jutting out of its surrounding rock.

MINERAL GROUPS

Minerals are divided into groups according to the elements which make them up. Minerals made of a single element are called **native elements**.

Pure silver on a piece of rock

This rock contains specks of pure gold.

Diamonds are crystals of pure carbon. Most are found in a rock called kimberlite, which forms under great heat and pressure.

Silicates, which contain **silica** (silicon combined with oxygen), are the largest group, making up 92% of minerals in the crust.

Beryl is a silicate made up of the elements silicon, oxygen, aluminium and beryllium.

Carbonates are minerals that contain elements combined with carbon and oxygen. They are the most abundant minerals after the silicates.

Smithsonite is zinc carbonate.

Malachite is copper carbonate. It is often polished and used in jewellery.

Halides are a group of minerals which contain halogen* elements.

Rock salt (halite) is formed when salt water evaporates.

Sulphides are a group of minerals that contain elements combined with sulphur.

Sphalerite is made of zinc and sulphur. Most of the world's zinc is mined from this mineral.

See for yourself

Rocks are made up of a mixture of minerals. If you look at a rock with a magnifying glass, you can sometimes see the different minerals in it.

Magnified piece of granite

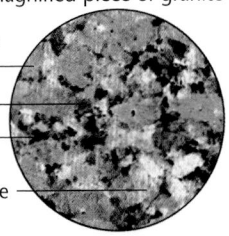

Phosphates are minerals formed when phosphorus reacts with oxygen and other elements.

Turquoise is a semi-precious mineral which is a phosphate of aluminium and copper.

Many elements combine with oxygen in the crust to form the group of minerals called **oxides**.

Haematite is a red iron oxide used to produce iron. This type is called "kidney-stone" because of its shape.

There are a number of other mineral groups containing oxygen. These all have names ending in "ate". The first part of their names (see below) show the other elements involved.

Mineral group	Element
Arsenates	Arsenic
Borates	Boron
Chromates	Chromium
Molybdates	Molybdenum
Nitrates	Nitrogen
Sulphates	Sulphur
Tungstates	Tungsten
Vanadates	Vanadium

Internet links

To find out more about elements, go to **www.usborne-quicklinks.com** and type in the keyword "science".

There you'll find links to websites where you can:

- Find a guide to the Earth's minerals
- Investigate ways to identify minerals
- Discover more with online activities

Go to Usborne Quicklinks for links to hand-picked websites on hundreds of subjects.

* *Halogens, 48.*

THE PERIODIC TABLE

The **periodic table** is an arrangement of the elements placed in order of increasing atomic number (the number of protons in the nucleus). Each element is represented by a box containing its chemical symbol, atomic number and relative atomic mass (see far right). Some versions, such as the one shown here, also give the elements' names. New elements are added when they are discovered.

Structure of an atom

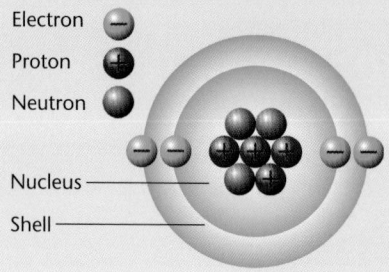

READING THE TABLE

The table is arranged into rows and columns. Looking at the table you will see that it has numbered rows (called **periods**) and columns (**groups**).

PERIODS

Each period is numbered, from 1–7. The atoms of all the elements in one period have the same number of shells, which contain electrons. For example, elements in period 2 have two shells and those in period 3 have three.

Moving from left to right across a period, each successive element has one more electron in the outer shell of its atoms. This leads to a fairly regular pattern of change in the chemical behaviour of the elements across a period.

GROUPS

Each group has a Roman numeral, from I-VIII. Elements in the same group have the same number of electrons in their outer shell. This means that, chemically, they behave in similar ways.

Period number — 1

Group number — I II

1	
1 H Hydrogen 1.0	

Hydrogen is the lightest element. It has an atomic number of 1. It is not a metal so it is placed separately.

	I	II							
2	3 Li Lithium 6.9	4 Be Beryllium 9.0							
3	11 Na Sodium 23.0	12 Mg Magnesium 24.3							
4	19 K Potassium 39.1	20 Ca Calcium 40.1	21 Sc Scandium 45.0	22 Ti Titanium 47.9	23 V Vanadium 50.9	24 Cr Chromium 52.0	25 Mn Manganese 54.9	26 Fe Iron 55.8	27 Co Cobalt 58.9
5	37 Rb Rubidium 85.5	38 Sr Strontium 87.6	39 Y Yttrium 88.9	40 Zr Zirconium 91.2	41 Nb Niobium 92.9	42 Mo Molybdenum 96.0	43 Tc Technetium (98)	44 Ru Ruthenium 101.1	45 Rh Rhodium 102.9
6	55 Cs Caesium 132.9	56 Ba Barium 137.3	71 Lu Lutetium 175.0	72 Hf Hafnium 178.5	73 Ta Tantalum 180.9	74 W Tungsten 183.8	75 Re Rhenium 186.2	76 Os Osmium 190.2	77 Ir Iridium 192.2
7	87 Fr Francium (223)	88 Ra Radium (226)	103 Lr Lawrencium (262)	104 Rf Ruther-fordium (267)	105 Db Dubnium (268)	106 Sg Seaborgium (271)	107 Bh Bohrium (272)	108 Hs Hassium (277)	109 Mt Meitnerium (276)

The relative atomic masses for unstable, radioactive* elements are shown in brackets.

The elements with atomic numbers 57-70 belong to period 6.

The elements with atomic numbers 89-102 belong to period 7.

57 La Lanthanum 138.9	58 Ce Cerium 140.1	59 Pr Praseo-dymium 140.9	60 Nd Neodymium 144.2	61 Pm Promethium (145)	62 Sm Samarium 150.4	63 Eu Europium 152.0
89 Ac Actinium (227)	90 Th Thorium 232.0	91 Pa Protactinium 231.0	92 U Uranium 238.0	93 Np Neptunium (237)	94 Pu Plutonium (244)	95 Am Americium (243)

Key

Each element has a separate box in the periodic table containing the information below.

50	Atomic number
Sn	Chemical symbol
Tin	Name
118.7	Relative atomic mass

* *Radioactivity, 114-115.*

SIMILAR BEHAVIOUR

On this periodic table, all elements that behave more-or-less in similar ways have the same coloured background. The colour-coding is explained here.

Non-metals
Mostly solid or gas, and non-shiny. Melt and boil at low temperatures.

Semi-metals
Also called metalloids, these have a mixture of the properties of metals and non-metals.

Metals
All are solid (except mercury, a liquid). Generally, they are shiny and have high melting points.

Transition metals are mostly hard and tough. Many are used in industry or jewellery.

Inner-transition metals are rare and tend to react easily with other elements, which makes them difficult to use in their natural state.

			III	IV	V	VI	VII	VIII
								2 He Helium 4
			5 B Boron 10.8	6 C Carbon 12.0	7 N Nitrogen 14.0	8 O Oxygen 16.0	9 F Fluorine 19.0	10 Ne Neon 20.2
			13 Al Aluminium 27.0	14 Si Silicon 28.1	15 P Phosphorus 31.0	16 S Sulphur 32.1	17 Cl Chlorine 35.5	18 Ar Argon 39.9
28 Ni Nickel 58.7	29 Cu Copper 63.5	30 Zn Zinc 65.4	31 Ga Gallium 69.7	32 Ge Germanium 72.6	33 As Arsenic 74.9	34 Se Selenium 79.0	35 Br Bromine 79.9	36 Kr Krypton 83.8
46 Pd Palladium 106.4	47 Ag Silver 107.9	48 Cd Cadmium 112.4	49 In Indium 114.8	50 Sn Tin 118.7	51 Sb Antimony 121.8	52 Te Tellurium 127.6	53 I Iodine 126.9	54 Xe Xenon 131.3
78 Pt Platinum 195.1	79 Au Gold 197.0	80 Hg Mercury 200.6	81 Tl Thallium 204.4	82 Pb Lead 207.2	83 Bi Bismuth 209.0	84 Po Polonium (209)	85 At Astatine (210)	86 Rn Radon (222)
110 Ds Darmstadtium (281)	111 Rg Roentgenium (280)							

Transition metals

Inner-transition metals

64 Gd Gadolinium 157.2	65 Tb Terbium 158.9	66 Dy Dysprosium 162.5	67 Ho Holmium 164.9	68 Er Erbium 167.3	69 Tm Thulium 168.9	70 Yb Ytterbium 173.1
96 Cm Curium (247)	97 Bk Berkelium (247)	98 Cf Californium (251)	99 Es Einsteinium (252)	100 Fm Fermium (257)	101 Md Mendelevium (258)	102 No Nobelium (259)

Elements 57-70 are called the **lanthanides** or **rare earths**.

Elements 89-102 are called the **actinides** or **radioactive rare earths**.

RELATIVE ATOMIC MASS

Relative atomic mass is the average mass number of the atoms in a sample of an element. (The mass number is the total number of protons and neutrons in a nucleus.) Moving through the periodic table, elements are progressively heavier. For example, hydrogen (relative atomic mass: 1) is the lightest element. Ruthenium (101.1) is over a hundred times heavier.

GROUPS WITH NAMES

Some of the groups in the periodic table have names. For example, the metals in group I are all alkali metals and group II are alkaline earth metals. The elements in group VII are halogens and group VIII (sometimes called group 0) are called noble gases.

DIFFERENT VERSION

An alternative version of the periodic table shows it split into 18 groups rather than eight. This is achieved by treating each column in the transition metals section of the table as a separate group, numbered from 3-12. In this version, all groups are referred to by ordinary numbers, not Roman numerals.

Internet links

Go to **www.usborne-quicklinks.com** and type "science" to find out more about the periodic table.

There you'll find links to websites where you can:

- Play a periodic table game
- Discover the periodic table's origins

METALS

All the metal elements share certain properties. For example, they are shiny and they conduct electricity. They are classified according to the way they behave. For instance some, such as potassium and sodium, are very reactive and react violently with water and air, while others, such as gold, do not react at all.

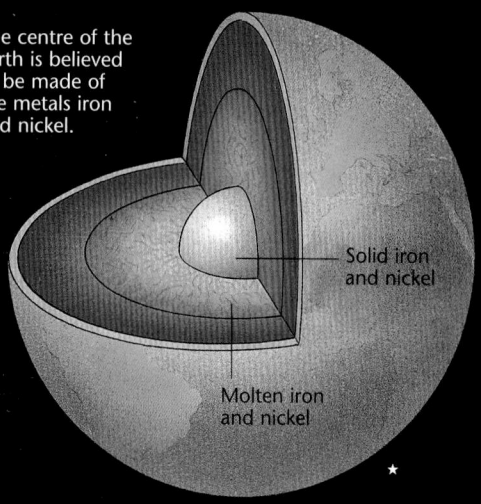

The centre of the Earth is believed to be made of the metals iron and nickel.

Fireworks contain metal compounds that burn with brilliant colours.

PROPERTIES OF METALS

All metals, except for mercury, are solid at room temperature (20°C) and they are good conductors of electricity and heat. They are shiny when cut, and some, such as iron and nickel, are magnetic.

Metals that can be pulled out to make wire are described as **ductile**. Those that can be beaten flat are described as **malleable**.

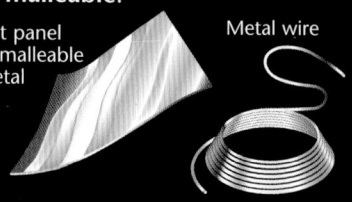

THE REACTIVITY SERIES

The **reactivity series** is a list of metals showing how reactive they are. The position of each metal is decided by observing how they behave during reactions involving other metals. For instance, more reactive metals pull oxygen from less reactive metals.

Reactive metals are difficult to separate from the minerals in which they are found, while the least reactive metals can be found as pure metals.

Sodium and potassium are stored in oil as they react violently with air and water.

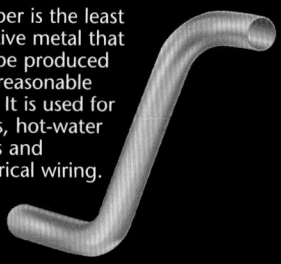

Copper is the least reactive metal that can be produced at a reasonable cost. It is used for pipes, hot-water tanks and electrical wiring.

Reactivity series

Most reactive
Potassium
Sodium
Calcium
Magnesium
Aluminium
Zinc
Iron
Tin
Lead
Copper
Silver
Gold
Platinum
Least reactive

See for yourself

Metals conduct electricity, so a simple way to test whether something is made of metal is to see if you can pass an electric current through it. You can see this for yourself, using a simple electrical circuit.

You need:
3 pieces of insulated copper wire, each 20cm long
4.5 volt battery
3.5 volt bulb and holder

Using one wire, twist one end around a battery terminal and the other around one of the bulb holder's terminals. With a second wire, twist one end around the remaining terminal of the bulb holder. Twist one end of the third wire around the remaining battery terminal. (You can use sticky tape to hold the wires in place.)

Carry the equipment around your home, touching the free wire ends to one object at a time. If the wires touch metal, electricity will flow through it and the light bulb will shine.

CAUTION
Never use mains electricity for this experiment. It will kill you.

FLAME TESTS

When some metals burn, they produce distinctive coloured flames. Burning a substance can be used as a way to test for the presence of a particular metal. The substance is held in a flame on a piece of unreactive platinum wire.

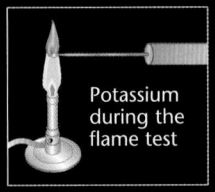

Potassium during the flame test

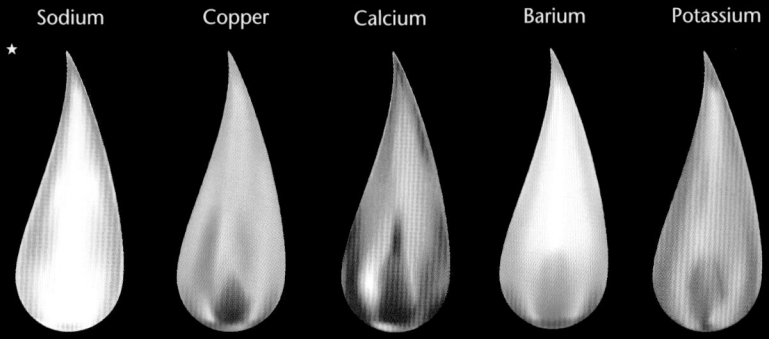

Internet links

To find out more about metals, go to **www.usborne-quicklinks.com** and type in the keyword "science".

There you'll find links to websites where you can:

- Play a fireworks game
- Explore the properties of metals

Go to Usborne Quicklinks for links to hand-picked websites on hundreds of subjects.

GROUPS OF METALS

Metals can be grouped according to their chemical properties and the way they behave. There are five main groups of metals, called noble metals, alkali metals, alkaline earth metals, poor metals and transition metals. The noble metals are also transition metals.

The copper in this ore has not reacted with any other elements. Copper is a noble metal.

NOBLE METALS

Noble metals are those that can be found as pure metals, not as part of compounds, in the Earth's crust. These metals are copper, palladium, silver, platinum and gold.

The noble metals are all unreactive (see The Reactivity Series, page 30). They do not easily combine with other elements to form compounds.

Because they are unreactive, noble metals do not easily corrode and they are used for jewellery and coins. Gold is very unreactive and ancient gold objects are still shiny.

This ancient Greek gold mask was untarnished when it was found.

ALKALI METALS

The **alkali metals** are six very reactive metals, including sodium and potassium, that form group I of the periodic table. They have low melting points – potassium melts at 64°C – and they are soft and can be cut with a knife. They form alkaline* solutions when they react with water, which is why they are called alkali metals.

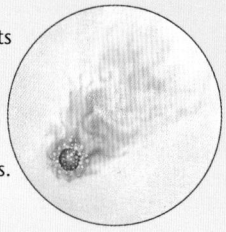

Potassium reacts violently with water, giving off hydrogen that bursts into lilac coloured flames.

ALKALINE EARTH METALS

The **alkaline earth metals** are six metals, including magnesium, calcium and barium, that form group II of the periodic table. These metals are found in many different minerals in the Earth's crust. For example, calcium is found in calcite, which forms veins in limestone and chalk.

Alkaline earth metals are not as reactive as the alkali metals and they are harder and have higher melting points.

This shell contains large amounts of calcium, in the form of calcium carbonate.

Magnesium is found in chlorophyll, the green pigment needed by plants for photosynthesis.

** Alkaline, 85.*

The frame of this bike is made mostly from titanium, a very light and extremely strong transition metal.

TRANSITION METALS

The **transition metals** can be regarded as typical metals. They are strong, hard and shiny and have high melting points. They are less reactive than the alkali and alkaline earth metals.

Iron, gold, silver, chromium, nickel and copper are all transition metals. They are easy to shape and have many different industrial uses, both on their own and as alloys (see next page).

POOR METALS

The **poor metals** are a group of nine metals: aluminium, gallium, indium, tin, antimony, thallium, lead, bismuth and polonium. They are grouped to the right of the transition metals in the periodic table.

Poor metals are, in general, quite soft, and are not much use on their own. Many are used to make more useful substances, though.

Aluminium is one of the least dense metals. Lead, on the other hand, is very dense and is used in hospitals as a barrier against radiation and X-rays.

See for yourself

Many tooth fillings are made using mercury, a transition metal. A mercury-based filling (called **dental amalgam**) is inexpensive, hard wearing and easy for dentists to press into shape. Fillings made with mercury are a dull, light grey colour.

You might also notice that some people have fillings or even an entire tooth made of a noble metal, particularly gold. Gold is used as a filling because it is harder wearing than a mercury filling, so it will last longer. Entire teeth are made of gold because it is practically unbreakable.

Internet links

Go to **www.usborne-quicklinks.com** and type in the keyword "science" to find out more about metals.

There you'll find links to websites where you can:

- Explore gold and copper mines in Australia
- Discover more about groups of metals from the periodic table

Go to Usborne Quicklinks for links to hand-picked websites on hundreds of subjects.

ALLOYS

An **alloy** is any mixture of two or more metals, or a metal and another substance. Alloys are made because they combine the properties, such as lightness or strength, of the different metals which make them up.

Stainless steel, such as that used for cutlery, is an alloy of steel, nickel and chromium.

This ship's propeller is made of bronze, an alloy of copper and tin. The bronze has been strengthened further by adding manganese.

ADDING STRENGTH

In pure metals, the atoms are arranged tightly in rows. The rows can slide over each other and this makes the metal soft. Sudden pressure, however, can cause cracks to form across the rows, making the pure metal brittle.

Arrangement of atoms in pure metal

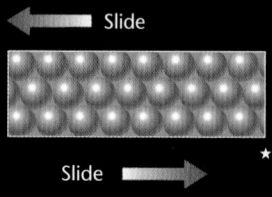

When another metal is added, its atoms help to strengthen the first metal. It does this by holding the parts of the metal together, so stopping its rows from sliding over each other.

Arrangement of atoms in an alloy

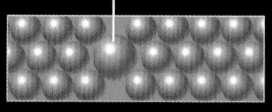

Atoms cannot slide

Bronze is often used in ship building, because it is highly resistant to corrosion by sea water.

ALLOY PROPERTIES

An alloy's properties depend on exactly what it is made of. Steel, for example, which is an alloy of iron and carbon, combines strength with ease of use. It can easily be worked into different shapes in a forge. It can also be melted without releasing poisonous fumes.

Steel's hard-wearing properties are increased by adding manganese. Steel-manganese alloys are used for industrial cutting equipment.

Railway tracks are made of steel strengthened with manganese.

Some pure metals, such as gold and silver, are good at resisting corrosion, so they are ideal for use outside. But they are very expensive. Some alloys are just as good at resisting corrosion, yet are much cheaper to produce. Brass, an alloy of copper and zinc, is a good example.

Some alloys, such as bronze, a mixture of copper and tin, are easily shaped, even at room temperature. Because of this, bronze has been used for thousands of years to make decorative objects.

Ancient Greek bronze sculpture

STRONG, LIGHT ALLOYS

Like steel and brass, alloys of aluminium and magnesium, for example duralumin, are strong and corrosion resistant. But they are also much lighter. They are used for aircraft and bicycle frames.

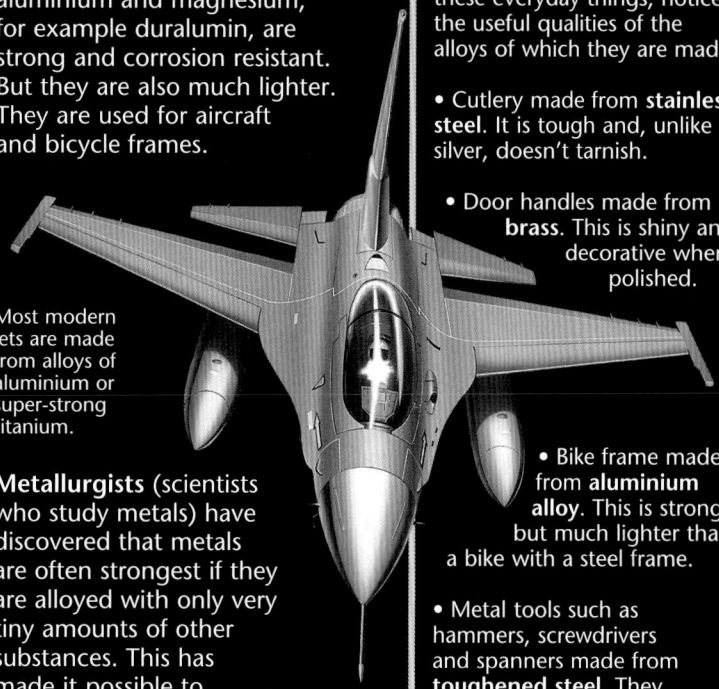

Most modern jets are made from alloys of aluminium or super-strong titanium.

Metallurgists (scientists who study metals) have discovered that metals are often strongest if they are alloyed with only very tiny amounts of other substances. This has made it possible to create alloys that are very strong but still light.

This plane's engines are constructed from superalloys.

SUPERALLOYS

The elements nickel, iron and cobalt have all been used as the main ingredient in what are called **superalloys**. These alloys are not only extremely strong, but also retain their strength even when exposed to great temperatures for long periods. They are used in jet and rocket engines.

Since the 1950s, the mining of titanium, a metal as strong as steel but with half its weight, has become affordable. Titanium is widely used in alloys that form the bodies of planes.

See for yourself

Next time you come across these everyday things, notice the useful qualities of the alloys of which they are made.

- Cutlery made from **stainless steel**. It is tough and, unlike silver, doesn't tarnish.
- Door handles made from **brass**. This is shiny and decorative when polished.
- Bike frame made from **aluminium alloy**. This is strong but much lighter than a bike with a steel frame.
- Metal tools such as hammers, screwdrivers and spanners made from **toughened steel**. They are practically unbreakable because the steel contains added quantities of vanadium or chromium. If they were not toughened, the tools would splinter or shatter dangerously when used.

Internet links

To find out more about alloys, go to **www.usborne-quicklinks.com** and type in the keyword "science".

There you'll find links to websites where you can:

- Watch an alloy presentation
- Investigate the uses for alloys
- Discover more with online activities

Go to Usborne Quicklinks for links to hand-picked websites on hundreds of subjects.

The links at Usbonre Quicklinks are regularly reviewed and updated, so you might find a slightly different selection of websites from the ones shown here.

IRON AND STEEL

Nearly all iron mined from the Earth is found as an **ore** (that is, combined with another substance). Most of it is made into steel, which is used to make many useful things, ranging from paper clips and tools to frames for giant buildings.

ELEMENT OR ALLOY?

Iron is an element which is extracted mostly from an ore called haematite, a compound of iron and oxygen. **Steel** is an alloy (that is, a mixture) of iron, carbon and traces of other metals.

Magnetite and haematite are the two most common iron ores.

MAKING IRON

Iron is extracted from iron ore in a **blast furnace**. In the furnace, iron ore, limestone and **coke** (coal heated to burn off oils and leave carbon) are blasted with very hot air. This process is called **smelting**. The carbon combines with oxygen to form carbon monoxide. The carbon monoxide then becomes carbon dioxide by pulling the oxygen away from the iron ore. This is an example of a reduction* reaction.

The iron extracted from iron ore contains some left-over carbon (about 4%) from the smelting process, plus other impurities such as sulphur. Called **pig iron**, it is used to make cast iron, or refined further to make steel.

The smelting process

1. Iron ore, coke and limestone are fed into the blast furnace. The limestone reacts with the impurities in the ore to produce waste that is called **slag**.

2. Hot air is blasted into the furnace. It reacts with the carbon to form carbon monoxide. This reaction raises the temperature to about 2,000°C. Then the carbon monoxide reacts with the oxygen in the ore leaving the metal free.

3. Molten iron is tapped off here.

4. Molten slag runs out near the bottom of the furnace. This is used in road making.

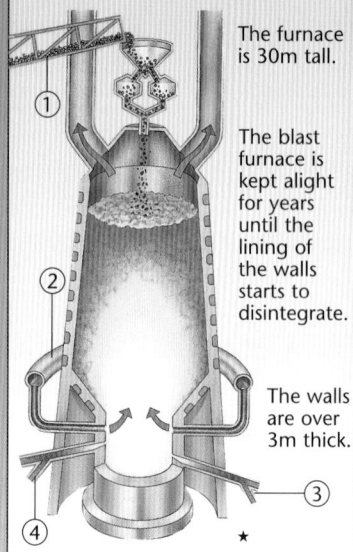

The steel frame of this unfinished building will eventually be covered with concrete panels, to create a huge office block like those in the background.

* Reduction, 81.

MAKING STEEL

Steel is made of iron that has been through a blast furnace, with other elements added to make it stronger. To make steel, molten iron is blasted with oxygen, removing more carbon. The oxygen combines with carbon in the iron to form the gas carbon monoxide, which is collected and used as fuel. At the end, the steel may contain as little as 0.04% carbon, although different grades of steel contain different amounts.

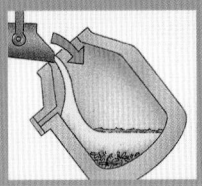

To convert iron to steel, molten iron is poured into a furnace called a **converter**.

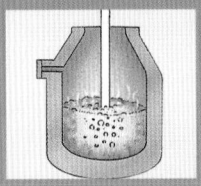

A high-pressure jet of almost pure oxygen is blasted into the converter. The oxygen combines with the carbon, forming carbon monoxide.

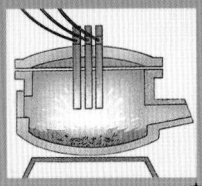

Steel is also made by melting down scrap steel in an **electric arc furnace**. The metal is melted by a powerful current of electricity.

See for yourself

Look out for iron and steel objects around your home. You can test to see if an object really is made of iron or steel (and not some other metal) by holding a magnet near it. If the object contains iron or steel, it will be attracted to the magnet.

Here are a few examples of things that you may have around your home, which you could test for their iron content.

Metal door handles
Hinges
Knives and forks
Garden gate
Washing machine
Bath
Bike parts
Food mixer
Spectacles
Belt buckles
Taps
Radiators

CAUTION
Do not put a magnet near to computers, television sets or watches. You could damage them.

The type of steel used for tools contains up to 1% carbon. This steel is very rigid but brittle. Chromium and vanadium are added to make the tools strong.

Steel that is used in construction, like the frame shown here, is painted to protect it from rusting before it is covered over by the rest of the building. A rusting frame would be dangerously weak.

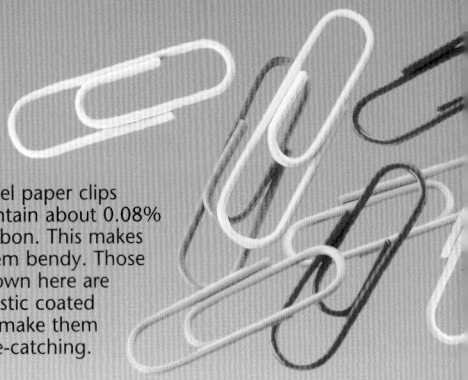

Steel paper clips contain about 0.08% carbon. This makes them bendy. Those shown here are plastic coated to make them eye-catching.

Internet links

Go to **www.usborne-quicklinks.com** and type in the keyword "science" to find out more about iron and steel.

There you'll find links to websites where you can:

- Find out how the blast furnace fuelled the industrial revolution
- Take an interactive look at the steel-making process

Go to Usborne Quicklinks for links to hand-picked websites on hundreds of subjects.

MAIN METALS AND ALLOYS

There are 65 metals that naturally exist on Earth. Of these, just 20 are used, on their own or as part of an alloy, to produce nearly all manufactured, metal-based things. You can find out about those metals here, plus the five most common alloys, and see examples of how some of them are used.

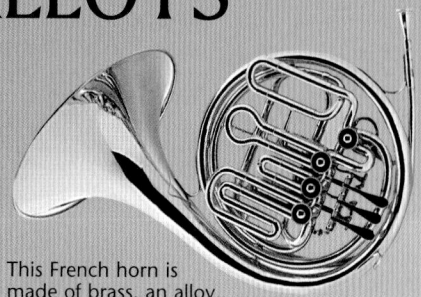

This French horn is made of brass, an alloy.

Aluminium
A very light, silvery-white metal that is resistant to corrosion. It is extracted from its ore, bauxite, by electrolysis*. Aluminium is used in overhead electric cables, aircraft, ships, cars, drinks cans and kitchen foil.

Brass
An alloy of copper and zinc. It is easy to shape and is used for decorative ornaments, musical instruments, screws and tacks.

Bronze
An alloy of copper and tin known since ancient times. It resists corrosion and is easy to shape. Coins made of bronze are used as low-value currency in many countries.

Calcium
A malleable, silvery-white metal found in limestone and chalk. It also occurs in animal bones and teeth. It is used to make cement and high-grade steel.

Chromium
A hard, grey metal used to make stainless steel and for plating other metals to protect them or give them a shiny, reflective finish.

Copper
A malleable, reddish metal used to make electrical wires, hot water tanks and the alloys brass, bronze and cupronickel.

Cupronickel
An alloy made from copper and nickel from which most silver-coloured coins are made.

Gold
A soft, unreactive, bright yellow element that is used for jewellery and in electronics.

Iron
A malleable, grey-white magnetic metal extracted mainly from the ore haematite by smelting in a blast furnace. It is used in building and engineering, and to make the alloy steel.

Lead
A heavy, malleable, poisonous blue-white metal extracted from the mineral galena and used in batteries, roofing and as a shield against radiation from X-rays.

Magnesium
A light, silvery-white metal that burns with a bright white flame. It is used in rescue flares and fireworks and in lightweight alloys.

Mercury
A heavy, silvery-white, poisonous liquid metal used in thermometers, dental amalgam for filling teeth, and in some explosives.

Platinum
A malleable, silvery-white unreactive metal used for making jewellery, in electronics and as a catalyst*.

Plutonium
A radioactive metal produced by bombarding uranium (see opposite) in nuclear reactors and used in nuclear weapons.

Potassium
A light, silvery, highly reactive metal. Potassium compounds are used in chemical fertilizers and to make glass.

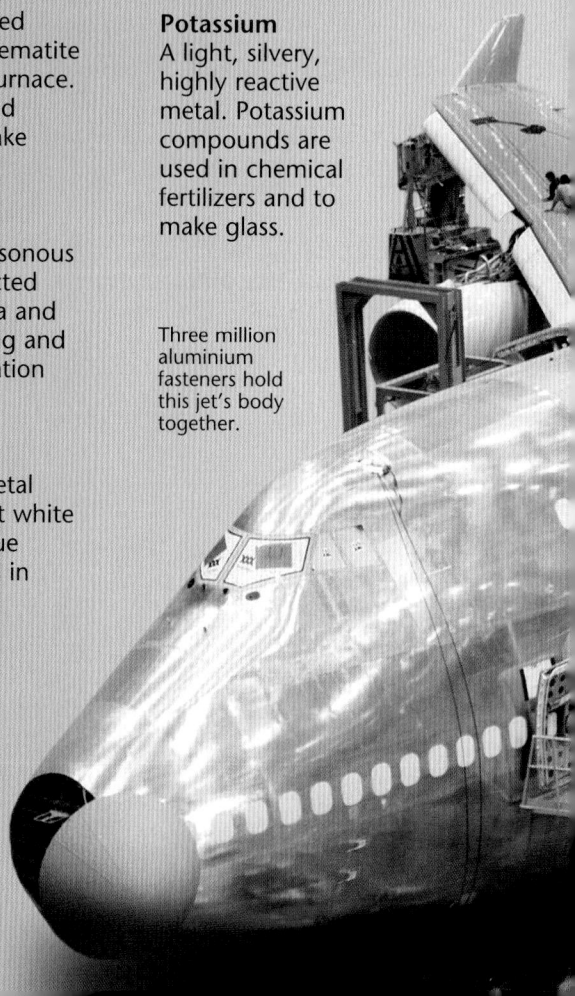

Three million aluminium fasteners hold this jet's body together.

* *Catalysts, 79; Electrolysis, 82.*

Silver
A malleable, grey-white metal that is a very good conductor of heat and electricity. It is used for making jewellery, silverware and photographic film.

Sodium
A very reactive, soft, silvery-white metal that occurs in common salt and is used in street lamps and in the chemical industry.

Solder
An alloy of tin and lead that has a low melting point and is used for joining wires in electronics.

Steel
An alloy of iron and carbon that is one of the most important materials in industry. Stainless steel, an alloy of steel and chromium, resists corrosion and is used in aerospace industries.

Tin
A soft, malleable, silvery-white metal. It is used for tin-plating steel to stop it corroding, and in the alloys bronze, pewter and solder.

Titanium
A strong, white, malleable metal. It is very resistant to corrosion and is used in alloys for spacecraft, aircraft and bicycle frames.

Tungsten
A hard, grey-white metal. It is used for lamp filaments, in electronics, and in steel alloys for making sharp-edged cutting tools.

Uranium
A silvery-white, radioactive metal used as a source of nuclear energy and also in nuclear weapons.

Vanadium
A hard, white, poisonous metal used to increase the strength and hardness of steel alloys. A vanadium compound is used as a catalyst* for making sulphuric acid.

Zinc
A blue-white metal extracted from the mineral zinc blende (sphalerite). It is used as a coating on iron to prevent rusting (called galvanizing). It is also used in certain electric batteries and in alloys such as brass.

This Boeing 747 is built using a high-strength alloy that contains mostly aluminium – a very light metal. The jet engines are made of titanium, which is also light, but can easily withstand the enormous temperatures that are generated in the engines.

Internet links

Go to **www.usborne-quicklinks.com** and type in the keyword "science" to find more about metals and alloys.

There you'll find links to websites where you can:

- Explore the aluminium industry
- Investigate how metals are extracted

Go to Usborne Quicklinks for links to hand-picked websites on hundreds of subjects.

* *Catalysts, 79. Galvanizing, 41.*

CORROSION

Corrosion is the chemical reaction that takes place when a metal is in contact with oxygen. The metal reacts with the oxygen to form a compound called an **oxide** on the surface of the metal. The metal becomes tarnished – that is, it loses its shine. Metals high in the reactivity series* corrode more quickly than less reactive metals.

Steel armour used to be rubbed with oil or beeswax to stop it from rusting.

USING METALS THAT CORRODE

Iron (from which steel is made) corrodes easily, but it is very strong and fairly easy to form into different shapes. It is ideal for building giant structures, such as bridges, but it has to be protected from corrosion, normally by painting it.

This bridge is protected from corrosion by painting it with phosphoric acid. The acid bonds to the metal and forms a protective coating, preventing rusting of the metal beneath. It is further protected by a layer of paint.

See for yourself

To remove the oxidized layer from a tarnished copper coin, leave it overnight in a glass containing a little vinegar. The acidic vinegar will react with the tarnish, removing it from the coin and exposing the copper alloy underneath. The coin will be left looking bright and shiny. Once it is back in the air though, it will corrode again, leaving a dull oxide layer on the surface.

* *Reactivity series, 30.*

EFFECTS OF CORROSION

When a metal corrodes, the surface becomes coated with a layer of oxide. On some, such as aluminium, this layer clings to the metal and protects it from further corrosion. On others this protective layer does not form. On iron and steel, for example, a flaky layer of **rust** (iron oxide) forms. This lifts away, allowing the metal beneath to corrode.

Aluminium immediately forms a layer of oxide on its surface. It is an ideal material for food trays, because it will not corrode further.

These steel drums were painted to protect them from rusting, but even a small scratch can let moisture under the paint, and rusting begins.

Moving parts, such as these gears, are coated with a layer of grease to stop them from rusting.

GALVANIZING

Galvanizing is a method of protecting steel by coating it with zinc. Zinc is more reactive than steel so oxygen reacts with it rather than the steel. Even if the layer of zinc is scratched, the oxygen in the air continues to react with the zinc rather than the steel.

Ships and oil rigs are protected by attaching a block of zinc or magnesium to them. This metal corrodes before the iron and is called the **sacrificial metal**.

Most modern cars are made from steel that has been galvanized. This stops them from rusting.

Internet links

To find out more about corrosion, go to **www.usborne-quicklinks.com** and type in the keyword "science".

There you'll find links to websites where you can:

- Find out what causes rust, and how to stop it
- Investigate the properties of other metals that corrode

Go to Usborne Quicklinks for links to hand-picked websites on hundreds of subjects.

The links at Usborne Quicklinks are regularly reviewed and updated, so you might find a slightly different selection of websites from the ones described here.

THE DISCOVERY OF METALS

People probably discovered how to extract metals from their ores by accident, when rocks containing a metal were heated with charcoal in fireplaces. A chemical reaction called reduction would have taken place which freed the metal from its ore. The same reaction is still used in blast furnaces (see page 36) to extract iron.

This decorated cauldron was made from bronze (a mixture of copper and tin) by the ancient Chinese, in around 1500BC.

THE FIRST METALS

The first metals worked by people were copper, gold and silver, probably because these are found as pure metals (see Noble Metals, page 32).

Later, in about 3500BC, the Sumerians learned how to make bronze by combining copper and tin. Bronze is stronger than the pure metals.

Iron was not used until about 1350BC, probably because it needs much higher temperatures to separate it from its compounds.

This golden cup was made in Northern Europe in about 3000BC.

Sumerian bronze bowl, made around 3000BC

Bronze axe-head made in 500BC

Sumerian people in the Middle East made this golden dagger and sheath in about 4000BC.

Here, molten iron is being poured into a furnace which will produce steel.

NEW METALS

Until 1735, the only known metals were copper, silver, gold, iron, mercury, tin, zinc, bismuth, antimony and lead. Aluminium was discovered in 1825.

Nowadays scientists can create new metal elements, such as mendelevium, by bombarding atoms with electrons in a type of nuclear reactor called a **particle accelerator**. The atoms break apart under the bombardment, enabling scientists to get a glimpse of their structure.

This is part of a huge particle accelerator. It can be used to create new metals. These metals are unstable and break down in a very short time.

In this furnace, oxygen is blasted through the molten iron. The oxygen removes carbon from the iron, leaving steel. This photograph was taken in 1958, but the steel-making process has changed little since then.

Internet links

To find out more about metals, go to **www.usborne-quicklinks.com** and type in the keyword "science".

There you'll find links to websites where you can:

- Take a look at the history of metals
- Discover which metals are used to make coins
- Learn more about common metals

Go to Usborne Quicklinks for links to hand-picked websites on hundreds of subjects.

RECYCLING METALS

Mining and extracting metals from ores is an expensive process. Fortunately, though, metals can be used again. The process of making them re-usable is called **recycling**, and it is much cheaper than extracting metals from ores. Recycling is done by melting down used metal, to produce a metal that is almost as good as new. It can be done over and over again.

THE RECYCLING PROCESS

Before a metal can be recycled it needs to be collected and separated from any other types of metal. This ensures that the recycled metal is as pure as possible. It is then melted down and poured into moulds. The metal cools into a solid block, ready to be made into a new, finished product.

WHICH METALS?

The most commonly recycled metals are steel and aluminium. However, other metals, such as copper, tin and lead and even precious metals, including gold, silver and platinum, are recycled too.

STEEL

Most steel for recycling comes from scrapped vehicles, such as cars and ships. Old industrial machinery is a good source too. Factories that use steel save offcuts and return them to steelworks to be melted and re-used.

Some of the things that people throw out from their homes, such as old washing machines, also contain steel. Much of this can be recycled.

Here, red-hot recycled steel is being poured into a mould.

This giant electromagnet* is picking up vast quantities of junk iron and steel. The metal will be dumped in a blast furnace to be melted down.

* *Electromagnets, 233, 234.*

ALUMINIUM

Recycled aluminium accounts for about 30% of all aluminium in use. It takes only 5% as much energy to recycle aluminium as it does to extract it from its ore, **bauxite**.

The biggest source of aluminium for recycling is old drinks cans. In North America, over 64 billion aluminium drinks cans are recycled every year. More than half of the aluminium in a drinks can has been recycled.

Crushed aluminium drinks cans, ready to be melted down.

The materials being picked up by this giant magnet all contain iron.

PRECIOUS METALS

Some industries use precious metals. The photographic industry, for example, uses lots of silver, which it recycles to cut costs and preserve resources. A great deal of recycled gold, silver and platinum comes from old jewellery and other ornaments.

When South America was invaded by Spaniards in the sixteenth century, thousands of golden treasures such as this were stolen, melted down and made into new ornaments.

See for yourself

Most drinks cans have information printed on them stating what they are made of. Take a look the next time you have a can of drink. Most likely, the can will be made of aluminium, and it will also have a symbol on it, signifying that it is recyclable.

Internet links

To find out more about metals, go to **www.usborne-quicklinks.com** and type in the keyword "science".

There you'll find links to websites where you can:

- Find fun games and puzzles and facts about recycling
- Investigate how aluminium drinks cans are recycled

Go to Usborne Quicklinks for links to hand-picked websites on hundreds of subjects.

HYDROGEN

Hydrogen is the lightest and most abundant element in the entire universe. The Sun and the stars are made of hydrogen gas, but on Earth, hydrogen is found only in compounds and does not occur naturally as a free element (that is, on its own).

Stars are globes of extremely hot hydrogen and other gases.

REACTIVE HYDROGEN

Hydrogen is very reactive. It burns easily and combines with many other elements. For example, water, the most plentiful compound on Earth, is made of hydrogen and oxygen. Fossil fuels, such as coal and oil, are compounds of hydrogen and carbon, and sugars and starch also contain hydrogen.

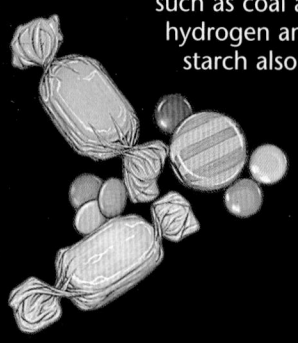

Sucrose ($C_{12}H_{22}O_{11}$) the sugar in sweets, is a compound of carbon, hydrogen and oxygen.

See for yourself

If you pour yourself a glass of water, try to imagine what it is made of. Water (H_2O) is a compound of hydrogen (H) and oxygen (O). It contains twice as many hydrogen atoms as oxygen atoms. However, although there are more of them, the hydrogen atoms have such a small mass that they make up only 12.5% of the water's total mass.

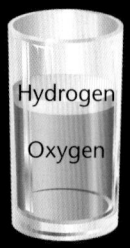

The Sun is a massive ball of constantly exploding gases. It consists mostly of hydrogen and helium.

Occasionally, vast streams of burning hydrogen flare out from the Sun. These are **solar prominences**.

MAKING HYDROGEN

Hydrogen (H_2) can be made by reacting methane gas (CH_4) with steam (H_2O) as shown by the following chemical equation:

$$CH_4 + 2H_2O \longrightarrow 4H_2 + CO_2$$

Most hydrogen made in this way is used to make ammonia (NH_3) for fertilizers. To make ammonia, hydrogen is combined with nitrogen using the **Haber process**, discovered by Fritz Haber in 1909.

THE HABER PROCESS

In the Haber process, nitrogen gas from the air and hydrogen extracted from methane (CH_4) are passed over a catalyst* of iron. Under very high pressure and at a high temperature, the gases react to produce ammonia gas (NH_3). This is cooled to form liquid ammonia.

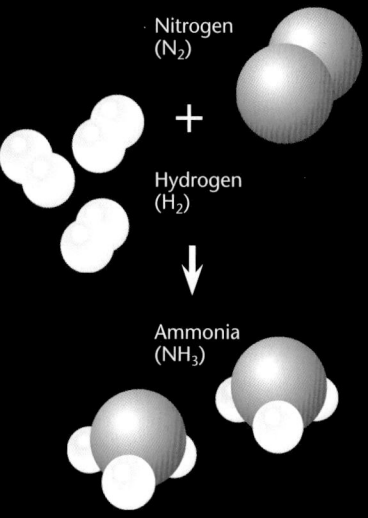

$$3H_2 + N_2 \rightleftharpoons 2NH_3$$

$\rightleftharpoons$ This symbol signifies that the reaction is reversible.

BURNING HYDROGEN

If hydrogen is mixed with air and then lit, it explodes. This can be used in the laboratory as a test for small amounts of gas. If the gas is hydrogen, it makes a little pop.

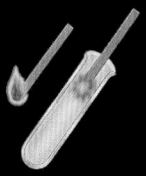

Hydrogen gas makes a small pop when tested with a burning splint.

If pure hydrogen (H_2) is burned in air or oxygen (O_2), it burns quietly with a blue flame and forms steam, as shown in this equation:

$$2H_2 + O_2 \longrightarrow 2H_2O$$

In theory, hydrogen is an ideal fuel as it produces a lot of energy when it burns and the only product is water, which is not a pollutant. But at present it is not suitable as an everyday fuel because it is difficult to store and transport safely.

In 1937, the Hindenburg airship caught fire. It was filled with hydrogen, which exploded, killing 36 people.

ROCKET FUEL

Liquid hydrogen is used as a fuel for rockets. In order for the fuel to burn in space, where there is no oxygen, rockets also carry separate tanks of oxygen. The liquid hydrogen and oxygen are fed into a combustion chamber where they burn safely.

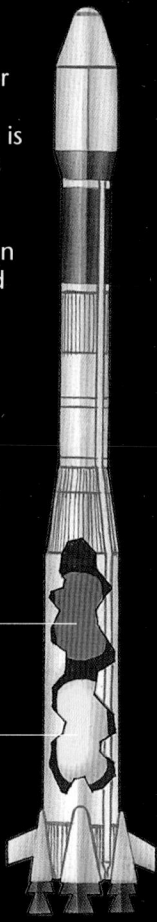

Internet links

To find out more about hydrogen, go to **www.usborne-quicklinks.com** and type in the keyword "science".

There you'll find links to websites where you can:

- Discover how hydrogen might be used in place of fossil fuels
- Uncover lots of fascinating hydrogen facts

Go to Usborne Quicklinks for links to hand-picked websites on hundreds of subjects.

The links at Usborne Quicklinks are regularly reviewed and updated, so you might find a slightly different selection of websites from the ones described here.

THE HALOGENS

The **halogens** are a group of five elements. They are fluorine, chlorine, bromine, iodine and astatine. They are all very reactive and poisonous and together form group VII of the periodic table.

Halogen lamps contain compounds of bromine that make them shine really brightly.

FLUORINE

Fluorine is a poisonous gas. It is extracted from the mineral fluorite. **Fluorides** (non-poisonous compounds of fluorine) are added to toothpaste and drinking water to reduce tooth decay.

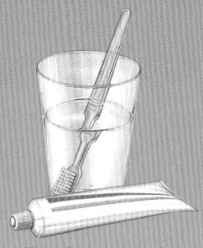

Toothpaste and water containing fluoride

Fluorine is also combined with carbon to make useful compounds called **fluorocarbons**. An example is PTFE (polytetrafluoroethene), which is used as a non-stick coating on frying pans and skis.

These skis have a coating of PTFE on their undersides. This non-stick layer helps them to slide freely over snow and ice.

CHLORINE

On its own, **chlorine** is a poisonous gas. It is very reactive and only occurs naturally in compounds, such as sodium chloride (common salt). Chlorine is used as a disinfectant and to make hydrochloric acid and PVC (polyvinylchloride) plastic.

Compounds of chlorine have many uses. **Sodium hypochlorite**, for example, is used to make household bleach, and to bleach paper pulp so that it turns white.

This juggling equipment is made from PVC.

Writing paper is bleached using sodium hypochlorite, a compound of chlorine.

This huge salt flat in South America contains sodium iodate. This is collected and used to produce the halogen iodine.

BROMINE

Bromine is a foul-smelling brown liquid. Traces of bromine are found in sea water and mineral springs. Compounds of bromine and one other element are called **bromides**. Silver bromide is used in photographic film.

When light hits silver bromide on photographic film, a reaction takes place in different layers of the film, creating various-coloured patches.

Bromine compounds are used to make rat poisons and products that treat wood for termite infestation.

IODINE

Iodine is a purple-black solid. It is used in medicine, photography and dyes, and is produced in large quantities from sodium iodate.

Traces of iodine are found in foods, and without it the cells in our bodies would not be able to convert food into energy. However, large quantities of iodine are harmful.

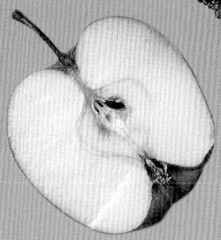

Iodine is found in seaweed, and in vegetables and fruit.

ASTATINE

Astatine is an unstable, radioactive element. It is the heaviest of all halogens, but hardly any of it is found in nature. Scientists estimate that only about 30g of astatine exists in the entire Earth's crust. They have been able to create more than 20 different astatine isotopes* during experiments, though.

See for yourself

You can buy iodine solution from a pharmacy and use it to test for the presence of starch. Drip some drops onto slices of food, such as raw potato, apple and a piece of bread. If starch is present, the food will turn blue-black very quickly.

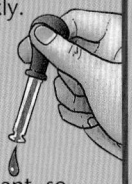

This type of dropper is called a pipette.

Iodine tastes unpleasant, so make sure that you don't get any in your mouth.

Internet links

To find out more about halogens, go to **www.usborne-quicklinks.com** and type in the keyword "science".

There you'll find links to websites where you can:

- Test your halogen knowledge
- Find detailed information about each halogen
- Take your pick from online activities

Go to Usborne Quicklinks for links to hand-picked websites on hundreds of subjects.

* *Isotopes, 13.*

CARBON

Carbon is a solid non-metallic element found in all living things. It occurs as a **free element** (on its own) mainly in the forms of hard, colourless diamond and crumbly black graphite.

FORMS OF CARBON

Carbon atoms can bond* together in different ways. These different forms are called **allotropes**. Carbon has three main allotropes – diamond, graphite and buckminsterfullerene.

DIAMOND

In **diamond**, each carbon atom is bonded to four other atoms. This makes diamond very hard – it is the hardest substance found in nature. Diamond forms naturally as tetrahedral (four-sided) crystals.

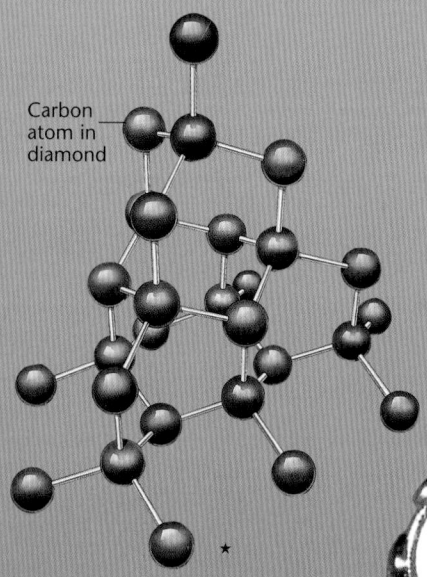

Cut diamonds sparkle with an intensity that is unmatched in the natural world. They can be several different colours, and are used to make expensive jewellery. The purest ones are transparent.

Diamonds are cut in such a way that their surfaces split up light into the colours of the rainbow.

The large diamond in this sceptre is the Star of Africa. It is about 6cm long and is the largest cut diamond in the world. The sceptre belongs to the British monarch.

* *Bonding, 68-69.*

DIAMOND VARIETIES

Impure varieties of diamond, such as **carbonado** (also called **black diamond**) are valued in industry for their hardness. They are used in cutting and drilling equipment, as well as in some very accurate watches.

Naturally occuring varieties of diamonds are mined from the Earth, but diamonds can also be manufactured. These synthetic diamonds are created by mixing graphite with a catalyst* and subjecting it to great heat and pressure.

GRAPHITE

In **graphite** (sometimes called **plumbago**), each atom of carbon is bonded to three other atoms, arranged in a honeycomb-like network of plates that easily slide over each other. This makes graphite soft and flaky. The plate network is held together by weak forces.

Carbon atom in graphite

The weak forces between the plates give graphite a very slippery structure. This makes graphite a very good lubricant, and it is used to reduce friction between the moving parts of machines. The weak forces also mean it is a good conductor of electricity so it is often used to make electrodes*.

Pencil "leads" are in fact made from powdered graphite mixed with clay. Soft pencils contain more graphite than hard ones.

BUCKMINSTERFULLERENE

Buckminsterfullerene is an allotrope of carbon discovered in 1985. Each molecule contains 60 carbon atoms linked in the shape of a hollow ball. It is formed by heating graphite in helium until it vaporizes, and then letting it cool and condense.

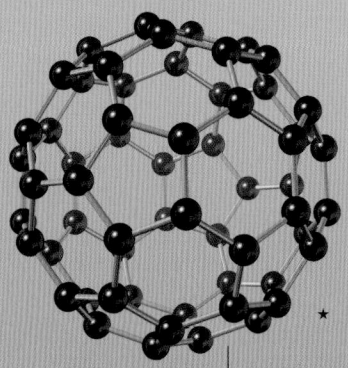

A buckminsterfullerene molecule

Buckminsterfullerene molecules are sometimes called **buckyballs**. Their atoms are arranged in a pattern of hexagons and pentagons similar to that on footballs.

Due to their robust spherical structure, buckyballs are really strong – a hundred times stronger than steel, but only a sixth of its weight.

Using a method similar to that for making buckyballs, scientists can also make tiny **nanotubes**. They hope to use them to build super-strong materials.

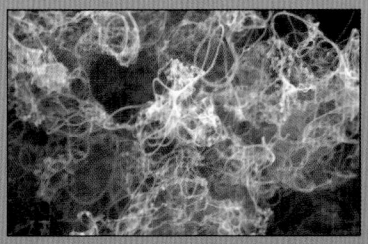

Nanotubes – made by vaporizing graphite with a laser and adding a metal catalyst*.

See for yourself

Take a look at your pencils, and compare the darkness of the lines that they make. A pencil containing more graphite than clay gives a darker, smudgier line than one that has more clay than graphite.

Letters and numbers printed on the side of a pencil indicate its graphite/clay content. A number followed by a B (for black) means that it has more graphite than clay. A number followed by an H (for hard) means it has more clay than graphite.

A medium pencil, one that gives lines that are neither dark nor light, has HB written on it.

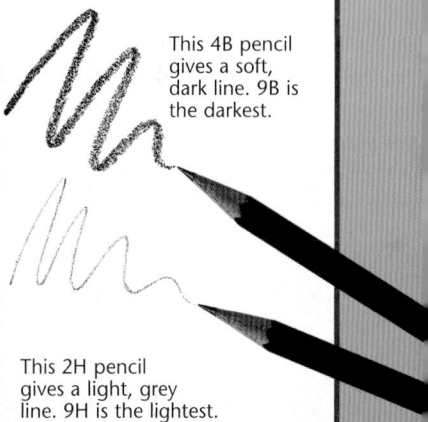

This 4B pencil gives a soft, dark line. 9B is the darkest.

This 2H pencil gives a light, grey line. 9H is the lightest.

Internet links

To find out more about carbon, go to **www.usborne-quicklinks.com** and type in the keyword "science".

There you'll find links to websites where you can:

- Discover fascinating diamond facts and photos
- View 3-D models and learn more of carbon's many different forms

Go to Usborne Quicklinks for links to hand-picked websites on hundreds of subjects.

** Catalysts, 79; Electrodes, 82.*

THE CARBON CYCLE

Most carbon atoms have existed since the world began. They circulate through animals, plants and the air in a process called the **carbon cycle**.

Plants use carbon dioxide to make carbon compounds by photosynthesis*. Animals eat plants (or other animals) and use the carbon compounds in their bodies. Carbon dioxide returns to the air when fuels burn and living things decay, and as a result of internal respiration, which is the way plants and animals break down sugars to release energy.

The carbon cycle

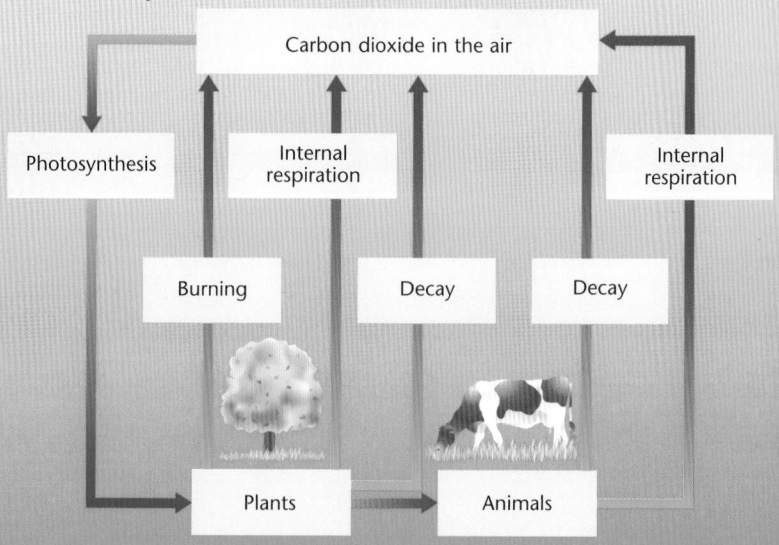

CARBON COMPOUNDS

Carbon atoms can bond with up to four other atoms, including other carbon atoms. This allows carbon to combine to form a vast number of different compounds. There are many more compounds of carbon than of any other element. All those compounds of carbon that are found in living things are called **organic compounds**.

Like all living things, both this kingfisher and the branch it is sitting on are made from compounds of carbon.

CARBON FIBRES

Silky threads of pure carbon, called **carbon fibres**, are used to reinforce plastics. This material is used to make lightweight boats and tennis racquets. A racing bike made of carbon fibre is eight times stronger than a steel one, but many times lighter.

This bike's frame is made from carbon fibre.

CARBON MIXTURES

Carbon can be found mixed with other elements and compounds. **Coal**, for example, is mainly carbon, but contains hydrogen, oxygen, nitrogen and sulphur. It is a **fossil fuel**, that is, a fuel formed over millions of years from the remains of plants.

There are three types of coal, containing varying amounts of carbon. **Lignite**, also called brown coal, only has 60-70% carbon. **Bituminous coal**, which is shiny and black, has more than 80%. **Anthracite** has more than 90% carbon.

Charcoal is another impure form of carbon. To make it, wood is heated in an airtight space. This removes the chemicals that produce wood smoke, leaving flaky black chunks of charcoal, which burn cleanly when ignited.

Unlike diamond and graphite, neither coal nor charcoal have a regular structure.

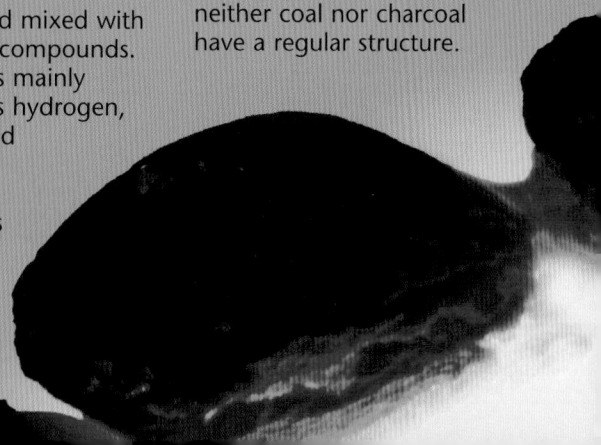

* *Photosynthesis, 264.*

USING COAL AND CHARCOAL

Coal is an important fuel. Over a third of the world's electricity is produced by power stations that burn coal. Lignite is cheap and plentiful, but produces a lot of pollution. Bituminous coal and anthracite are better since they cause less air pollution.

Power stations fuelled by coal can produce an average of 600 megawatts of electrical energy in an hour.

A form of charcoal called **activated charcoal** is used in filters and gas masks to remove poisonous fumes. It has countless tiny holes in its surface, which are ideal for trapping fumes. It is made by allowing charcoal to burn briefly in oxygen at the end of the charcoal-making process.

Charcoal is often used as a fuel on barbecues, and can be shaped into sticks to be used as an artists' drawing material.

Charcoal burns without smoke. This makes it an ideal heat source for barbecues, because it cooks things without coating them in soot.

See for yourself

The next time you see coal burning, try to imagine what is happening to the molecules that it is made of.

The heat gives the molecules enough energy to break apart. This gives off heat energy. As the bonds break, atoms, such as hydrogen, are freed from the molecules. These liberated atoms burn too, giving off additional heat.

Internet links

To find out more about carbon, go to **www.usborne-quicklinks.com** and type in the keyword "science".

There you'll find links to websites where you can:

- Discover how coal is formed and how it's used to produce electricity
- Watch animations about carbon and the carbon cycle

Go to Usborne Quicklinks for links to hand-picked websites on hundreds of subjects.

SULPHUR

The element **sulphur** is a bright yellow, crumbly solid. It is found in underground deposits in volcanic areas. It is also found in minerals such as iron pyrites and copper pyrites.

Pure sulphur

Iron pyrites, a compound of iron and sulphur

FORMS OF SULPHUR

Sulphur molecules form in crooked rings of eight atoms, sometimes referred to as crowns. The rings can combine together in different ways to make two distinct crystal forms, known as allotropes.

Sulphur becomes a gas at 444°C. The molecules split apart and float freely, as shown here.

Most sulphur is found in the form of **rhombic sulphur**.

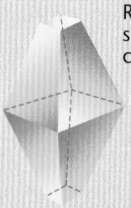

Rhombic sulphur crystal

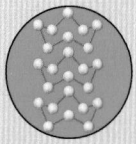

The molecules fit together closely in rhombic sulphur.

Above 96°C, **monoclinic sulphur** forms. Monoclinic sulphur crystals are long, thin and angular. They look a little like needles.

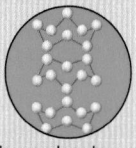

Monoclinic sulphur crystal

The molecules are less closely packed than in rhombic sulphur, so it is less dense.

PRODUCING SULPHUR

Most sulphur is obtained from fossil fuels*. It is also extracted from underground deposits by melting it with pressurized steam. This is called the **Frasch process**.

USES OF SULPHUR

One of the most important uses of sulphur is in the manufacture of **sulphuric acid**, which is used to make fertilizers, plastics and batteries. It is also used to **vulcanize** rubber (harden it), in black gunpowder and in medicines.

SULPHUR DIOXIDE

Sulphur burns with a blue flame to form **sulphur dioxide**, a poisonous gas made of sulphur and oxygen. This gas is used to kill insects and fungi, and as a preservative for fruit.

Sulphur dioxide can be used to preserve the colour of dried apricots.

Internet links

To find out more about sulphur, go to **www.usborne-quicklinks.com** and type in the keyword "science".

There you'll find links to websites where you can:

- See sulphur forming on volcanoes

** Fossil fuels, 108.*

PHOSPHORUS

Phosphorus is a non-metallic element. It occurs naturally in bones, teeth and the chemicals in the body that store energy. It is also found in the Earth, for example in the mineral apatite. Its most reactive form, white phosphorus, glows in the dark.

The minerals apatite (left) and turquoise (right) contain phosphorus.

FORMS OF PHOSPHORUS

Phosphorus occurs in three crystal forms, or allotropes.

White phosphorus is a poisonous, waxy, white solid that ignites easily when it is exposed to air.

Red phosphorus is a non-poisonous, dark red powder. It is made by heating white phosphorus without air. It is less reactive than white phosphorus.

Black phosphorus is made by heating white phosphorus under pressure using mercury as a catalyst*. Its name comes from its appearance, which is much like graphite. It is the least reactive form of phosphorus.

USES OF PHOSPHORUS

One of the main uses of phosphorus is in the production of **phosphoric acid** (H_3PO_4). This is used to make iron and steel rust-proof, and also in the manufacture of fizzy drinks.

Phosphoric acid is used to add fizz and flavour to cola drinks.

Red phosphorus is used in matches, pesticides, alloys and distress flares.

White phosphorus is used in rat poison.

When a match is struck, the red phosphorus becomes white phosphorus, burning fiercely in the air.

Compounds of phosphorus and oxygen are called **phosphates**. Phosphates are important in animal and plant growth. They are added to animal feed and used to make fertilizers.

Farm crops, like this cabbage, are fed with large amounts of phosphate-rich fertilizers.

See for yourself

Take a look at the list of ingredients on a tube of toothpaste.

The list will probably include certain phosphates, such as sodium phosphate and trisodium phosphate. These are compounds that contain phosphorus.

These phosphates are used in toothpastes because they help to loosen stain-forming chemicals from your teeth, helping to keep them white.

Internet links

For more about phosphorus, go to **www.usborne-quicklinks.com** and type in the keyword "science".

There you'll find links to websites where you can:

- Discover some of the many everyday uses of phosphorus

* *Catalysts, 79.*

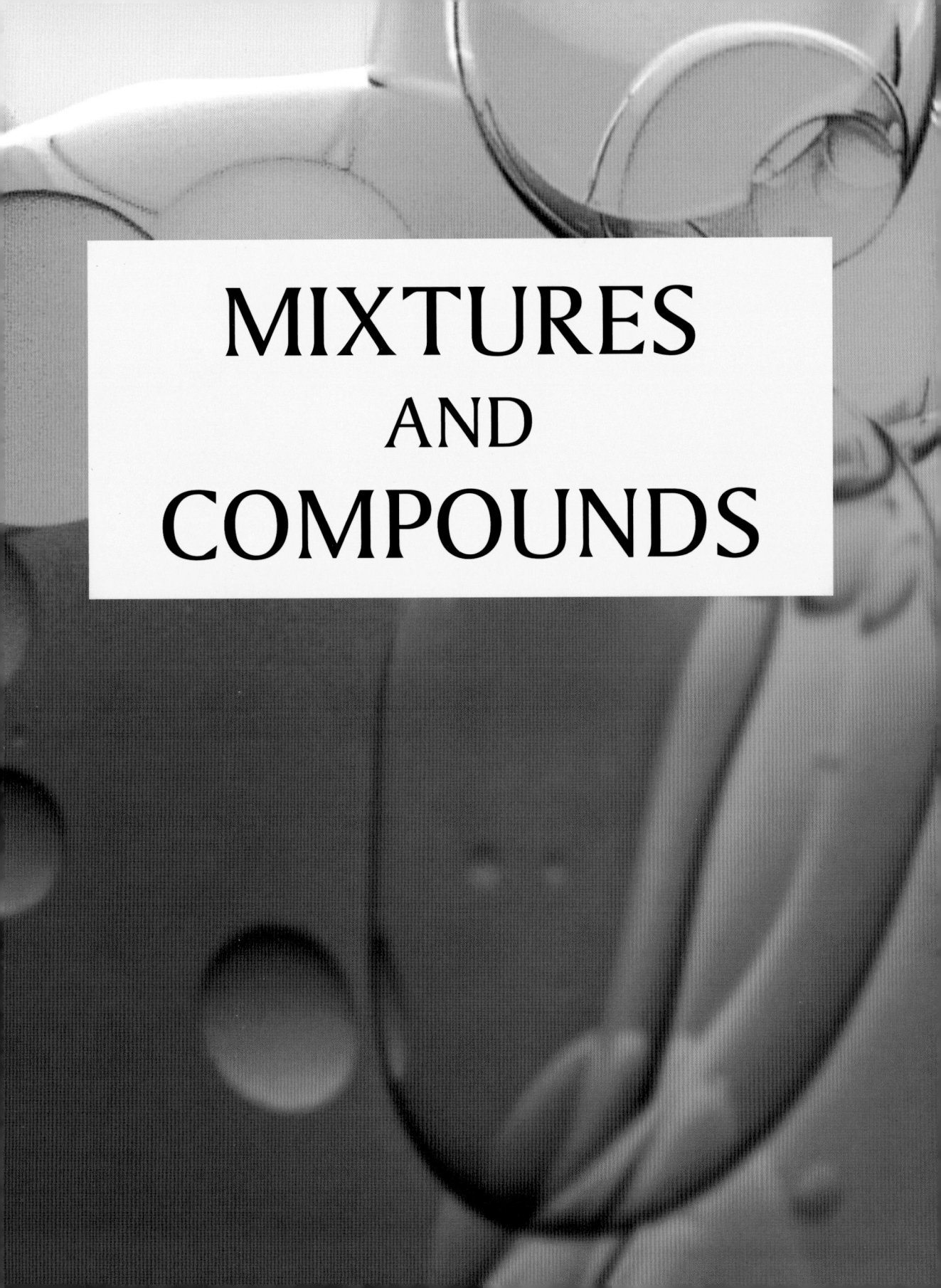

MIXTURES AND COMPOUNDS

MIXTURES

Most of the natural substances around us, such as sea water and the air, are mixtures. A **mixture** is a combination of different substances that can be separated because they have different physical properties – such as different boiling points.

Ice cream is a mixture of ice, milk fat, flavourings and air.

WHAT IS A MIXTURE?

The ingredients in a mixture are not chemically bonded*, so they can usually be separated easily. For example, iron can be removed from a mixture of iron filings and sulphur using a magnet. Other methods of separating mixtures are shown on pages 60-61.

This magnet is covered with iron filings. When held in a mixture of sulphur and iron filings, the filings cling to the magnet, leaving sulphur behind.

A mixture may contain any proportion of the substances of which it is made.

The substances keep their own properties, and the mixture has all the properties of the substances, except, for example, in a solution. In this case, the boiling and freezing points may change depending on the mixture.

WHAT'S IN A MIXTURE?

Some mixtures contain two or more elements (substances made up of only one type of atom), as shown in the diagram below.

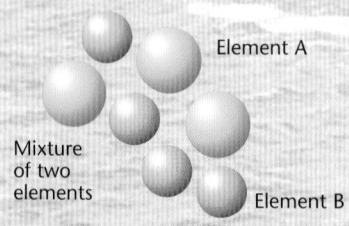

Some mixtures contain two or more different compounds (substances made up of different atoms bonded together).

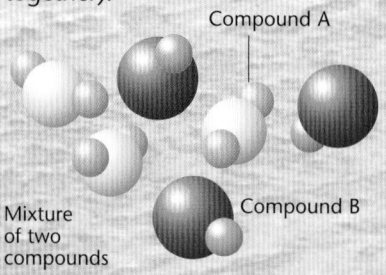

Other mixtures contain elements and compounds. Air is a mixture of elements such as oxygen, and compounds such as carbon dioxide and soot.

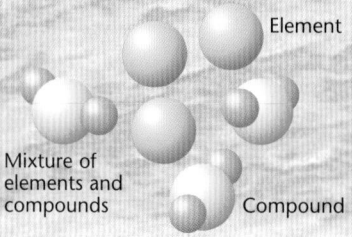

TYPES OF MIXTURE

A mixture can be any combination of solids, liquids and gases. For example, air is a mixture of gases, and sea water is a mixture of salt (a solid) and water (a liquid).

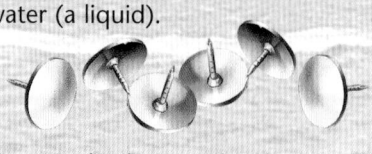

These metal tacks are made of brass, a mixture of copper and zinc. Mixtures of metals are called **alloys**.

A mixture of a solid dissolved in a liquid, such as salt in water, is called a **solution**. The liquid is called the **solvent** and the solid is called the **solute**. A solid that dissolves easily is said to be **soluble**, while a solid that won't dissolve is **insoluble**.

A mixture of solid particles floating in a liquid or a gas is called a **suspension**. Blood, milk and smoke are suspensions.

Milk is a suspension of fat particles in water.

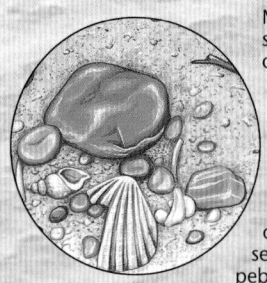

A beach is a mixture of sand, seashells and pebbles.

* *Bonding, 68-71.*

MIXING LIQUIDS

Liquids that mix easily, such as ink and water, are called **miscible** liquids. Liquids that don't mix easily, such as oil and water, are said to be **immiscible**.

They can be made to mix by adding an emulsifier. An **emulsifier** makes one liquid, such as oil, break up into minute droplets in another, such as water. The resulting liquid is called an **emulsion**.

Sea water is mainly a solution of salt (sodium chloride) and water.

Blobs of oil in water. If an emulsifier is added to this mixture, the oil breaks down into tiny beads, forming an emulsion with the water.

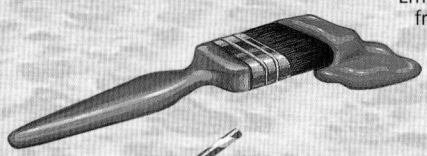

Emulsion paint is made from water, droplets of oil, coloured pigment and chemical emulsifiers.

Fizzy drinks are a mixture of two liquids (water and flavouring) and a gas (carbon dioxide). The gas makes the fizzy bubbles.

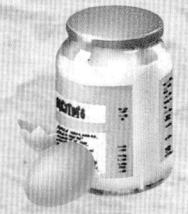

Mayonnaise is an emulsion of oil and vinegar. The emulsifier is egg yolk.

See for yourself

You can compare a solution with a mixture that contains non-soluble substances. Stir some sand into a jar of water. Then stir a spoonful of salt into a different jar of water.

The sand won't dissolve, no matter how hard you stir it. You are left with a simple mixture of water and sand.

As you stir the salt into the water, it dissolves and forms a solution. It breaks down into tiny parts and can't be seen. Both jars, though, contain mixtures.

Internet links

Go to **www.usborne-quicklinks.com** and type in the keyword "science" to find out more about mixtures.

There you'll find links to websites where you can:

- Test your knowledge of mixtures with online quizzes
- Get instructions for simple experiments with liquids that don't mix easily

Go to Usborne Quicklinks for links to hand-picked websites on hundreds of subjects.

SEPARATING MIXTURES

There are a number of different ways to separate the substances in a mixture. The method that you choose depends on the physical properties of the substances that the mixture contains.

In this coffee pot, the wire mesh separates the ground coffee from the hot drink.

DECANTATION

Decantation is a simple method of separating solid, insoluble particles from a liquid by leaving the particles to settle and pouring off the liquid.

Sand, soil and other matter settle in layers in a jar of muddy water.

Mud particles dispersed in water

Mud settled into layers

FILTRATION

Filtration is another method of separating insoluble, solid particles from a liquid. The mixture is poured through a filter which traps the particles and only allows the molecules of liquid to pass through. This method is used in waterworks* as part of the process of producing clean drinking water.

The liquid that passes through the filter is called the **filtrate**. The solid that remains behind is the **residue**.

CHROMATOGRAPHY

Chromatography is used to analyse the substances in a mixture. The mixture is dissolved and some of the solution is put on a piece of filter paper. The substances in the solution which dissolve most easily travel farthest, and form bands of colour called a **chromatogram**.

Scientists can identify the substances in a solution by comparing their chromatograms with those of known substances. This method can be used, for example, to identify the colourings used in foods.

This chemist is studying paper chromatograms to identify the chemicals used in various clothes dyes.

See for yourself

You can use chromatography (see above right) to separate the different coloured chemicals that make up inks. You need a piece of filter paper or kitchen towel, a bowl of water and some felt-tip pens.

1. Put some spots of ink about 3cm from the bottom of the paper.

2. Hang the paper over a bowl of water so that the water touches the paper but not the ink spots.

3. The paper absorbs the water. As the water reaches the blobs of ink, the dyes in the inks dissolve and are carried upwards. The dyes that dissolve most easily travel farthest.

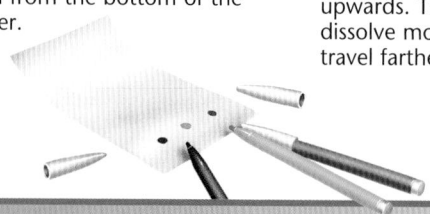

* *Waterworks, 74.*

EVAPORATION

Evaporation is a method of separating a soluble solid from the solvent* in which it is dissolved. The solution is heated until all the liquid turns to vapour (evaporates), leaving the solid behind.

Lemon juice, which is a solution of citric acid in water, separates by evaporation.

Water evaporates from boiling lemon juice. Eventually, only solid crystals of citric acid are left behind.

DISTILLATION

Distillation is a way of obtaining pure solvent, such as water, from a solution. First, the liquid is boiled. As it boils, the water evaporates into steam. This is cooled and condenses into pure water. The pure water is collected in another vessel. The other part of the solution is left behind.

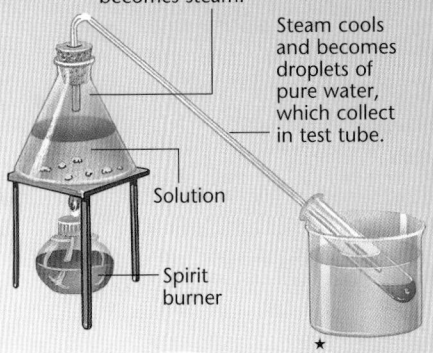

CENTRIFUGING

Centrifuging separates solid particles from a suspension*. The liquid is spun around very quickly in a machine called a **centrifuge**.

This forces the solid particles to the sides of the container and the liquid can be poured or filtered off.

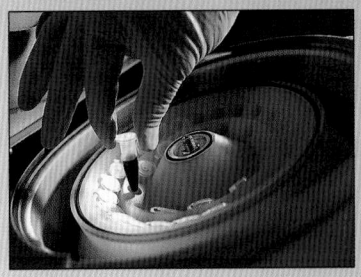

This is a centrifuge being used in a hospital to separate the components of human blood.

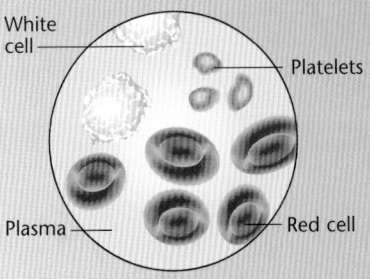

Blood can be separated in a centrifuge because it is a suspension of cells and platelets in a clear fluid called plasma.

Internet links

To find out more about mixtures, go to **www.usborne-quicklinks.com** and type in the keyword "science".

There you'll find links to websites where you can:

- Investigate some of the ways that mixtures can be separated
- Watch animations showing different methods for separating mixtures

Go to Usborne Quicklinks for links to hand-picked websites on hundreds of subjects.

** Solvent, Suspension, 58.*

THE AIR

The **air** is a mixture of gases that form a protective layer called the **atmosphere** around the Earth. Air is essential for life on Earth – for animals to breathe and for plants to make their food – and it also helps to protect the Earth from the Sun's dangerous ultraviolet rays*. The main gases in air are nitrogen and oxygen. There are also traces of the noble gases and of carbon dioxide, plus solid particles such as soot and pollen.

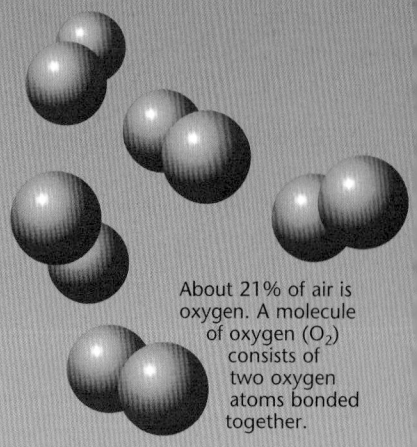

About 21% of air is oxygen. A molecule of oxygen (O_2) consists of two oxygen atoms bonded together.

GASES IN THE AIR

The amounts of the different gases in the air vary slightly from place to place, season to season and day to night. The pie chart below shows the average volumes of the gases as percentages.

Composition of the air

Nitrogen and oxygen are the main gases. The remaining 1% is noble gases, carbon dioxide, water vapour and pollutants such as nitrogen dioxide.

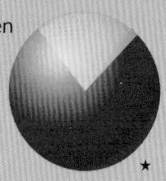

- Nitrogen 78%
- Oxygen 21%
- Other gases 1%

This diver is carrying a cylinder of compressed air on his back, which contains oxygen, to breathe under water.

SEPARATING GASES

The gases in air can be separated by a process called **fractional distillation**. The air is cooled and compressed until the gases become liquids. This mixture is heated. Each liquid boils at a different temperature and is collected separately as it boils.

Oxygen, nitrogen and carbon dioxide are continually removed and returned to the air by living things as part of natural cycles.

OXYGEN

Oxygen (O_2) is vital for life. Animals take oxygen into their bodies and use it to break down food and release energy. Plants also use oxygen to release energy from their food.

Oxygen is essential for **combustion** (burning). If there is lots of oxygen, things will burn very quickly. If there is no oxygen, nothing can burn.

All animals need oxygen. They take in oxygen when they breathe in, and release carbon dioxide when they breathe out.

Gills are under here.

When water is gulped in by a fish, it passes over its gills. The gills take oxygen that is dissolved in the water so that it can be used in the body.

* Ultraviolet rays, 213.

CARBON DIOXIDE

Carbon dioxide (CO_2) is a compound made of the elements carbon and oxygen. The air contains about 0.03% carbon dioxide.

A carbon dioxide (CO_2) molecule has a carbon atom and two oxygen atoms.

Carbon dioxide is slightly soluble in water, dissolving to form a weak solution of carbonic acid. Carbon dioxide is part of the carbon cycle*. Animals breathe it out. Plants release it, and use it in photosynthesis*.

Most substances cannot burn in carbon dioxide. That is why it is used in fire extinguishers.

Carbon dioxide is denser than air so it flows over a fire, suffocating it by preventing oxygen from reaching it.

Fuels containing carbon, such as wood, coal and petrol, produce carbon dioxide when they burn. Because we now burn so much fuel, the amount of carbon dioxide in the air is increasing. This has led to problems of global warming (see *Greenhouse Effect*, page 65).

See for yourself

Try this test to see how carbon dioxide gas puts out fire.

Light a small candle. Put five tablespoons of vinegar into a bottle. Add half a tablespoon of bicarbonate of soda. As the mixture fizzes, hold the mouth of the bottle near the candle, making sure none of the liquid escapes.

Small candle

The candle goes out as carbon dioxide from the reaction prevents oxygen from reaching the flame.

AIR QUALITY

Many polluting substances are released into the air from industrial chimneys. Inside many chimneys are filters and neutralizing substances which make waste gases safer. Samples of the gases released are frequently taken and levels of pollution checked.

The cooling tower below releases harmless water vapour into the air. Waste gases from the tall chimney on the right need to be filtered or neutralized before they are released, to reduce pollution.

THE NOBLE GASES

The six **noble gases** found in the air are the only elements that exist as single atoms. They are all very unreactive and they rarely form molecules.

Argon (Ar) is often used to fill the space inside household light bulbs. It is so unreactive that the glowing filament does not react with it and burn out. **Krypton (Kr)** is used inside fluorescent tubes. **Neon (Ne)** glows orange-red when electricity passes through it, so it is used in neon lights and, with sodium, in street lamps.

Xenon (Xe) is used in flash photography. **Radon (Rn)** is radioactive and occurs as a result of the radioactive decay* of radium, a metal element. **Helium (He)** is not known to form any compounds and it is thought to be completely unreactive. It is seven times less dense than air, so it is used in airships.

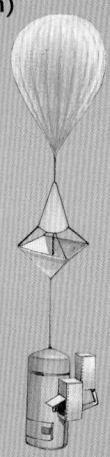

A helium-filled balloon carries these scientific instruments into the upper atmosphere.

Internet links

To find out more about the air, go to **www.usborne-quicklinks.com** and type in the keyword "science".

There you'll find links to websites where you can:

- Learn about all the different gases in the air we breathe
- Explore how these gases are used
- Discover more with online activities

Go to Usborne Quicklinks for links to hand-picked websites on hundreds of subjects.

** Carbon cycle, 52; Photosynthesis, 81; Radioactive decay, 115.*

NITROGEN

Most of the air (about 78%) is **nitrogen** (N_2). Nitrogen is continually being recycled between the air and living things. This is called the **nitrogen cycle**.

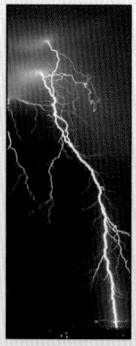

Nitrogen molecules in the air are split up by lightning, and the freed atoms bond with oxygen to form nitrogen oxide gases. Pollution from power stations also contains these gases.

The gases react with water to become nitric acid in rainwater. This forms nitrogen salts* called **nitrates** in the soil.

Fertilizers* also have a high nitrate content, so they add to the nitrates in the soil. Certain bacteria, in the roots of some plants, also add to the nitrates by taking nitrogen directly from the air and converting it into nitrates.

Plants absorb the nitrates and use them to make proteins. Animals eat plants and use the proteins in their own bodies. Ammonia and other nitrogen compounds are returned to the soil in animal waste, and when animals and plants decay after death.

The compounds are turned back into nitrates by the action of one type of bacteria in the soil. Another type takes in nitrates, breaks them down, and releases nitrogen back into the air.

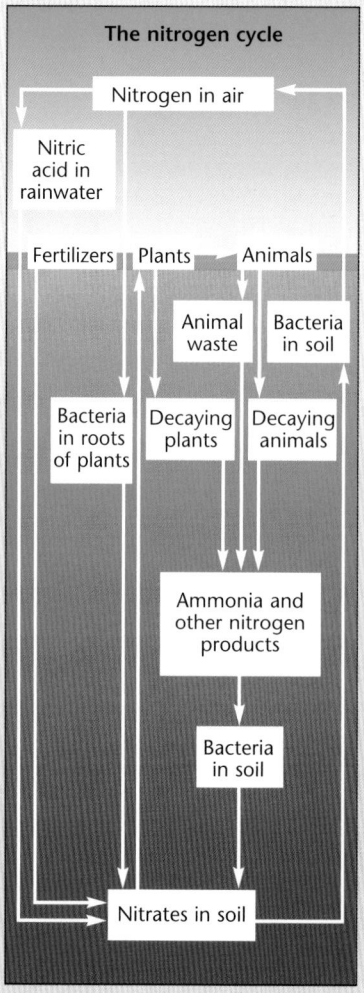

USES OF NITROGEN

The main use of nitrogen is in the production of ammonia for making fertilizers*. To do this, nitrogen is combined with hydrogen. Nitrogen is also used in packaging food such as bacon and crisps, because ordinary air would cause the food to oxidize* and go bad.

Liquid nitrogen is so cold and unreactive that it is used to preserve human organs for transplants.

GASES THAT POLLUTE

Carbon monoxide (**CO**) is formed when fuels burn in a limited air supply, such as in a car's engine. Most fuels burn so quickly it is difficult for them to get enough oxygen, and carbon monoxide is produced instead of carbon dioxide. Carbon monoxide is a very toxic gas that stops the red cells in animals' blood from carrying oxygen.

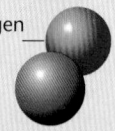

Carbon monoxide molecules have only one atom of oxygen.

Sulphur dioxide (SO_2) is produced by burning fossil fuels*, especially coal. Sulphur dioxide is poisonous and causes breathing problems. It reacts with rainwater to produce acid rain (see opposite page).

Sulphur dioxide molecules

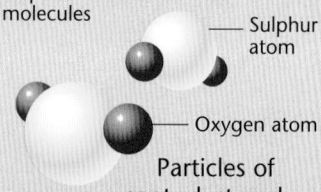

Particles of soot, dust and lead compounds produced by industry are other forms of pollution that can be breathed in and which settle on plants. Lead compounds are poisons that build up in the body and can cause brain damage in young children.

The pollution shrouding this city is made up of **smog**, a mixture of fog, smoke particles and sulphur dioxide. It can be very harmful to living things.

* Fertilizers, 89; Fossil fuels, 109; Oxidation, 80; Salts, 88.

THE OZONE LAYER

In the upper atmosphere, oxygen atoms combine in threes, forming molecules of **ozone** (O_3). This is an allotrope* (an alternative form) of oxygen. It is a poisonous gas, but it forms a layer in the upper atmosphere that absorbs most of the Sun's harmful ultraviolet rays* and protects the Earth.

Without the protective ozone layer around it, the Earth could not sustain life.

Carbon dioxide in the air prevents heat escaping from the Earth in the same way that glass prevents heat escaping from a greenhouse.

GREENHOUSE EFFECT

This term is used to describe the way that increasing levels of carbon dioxide in the air are causing **global warming** – a rise in average temperatures around the world.

As the level of carbon dioxide increases, more heat is trapped in the Earth's atmosphere (see picture above). Even a slight rise in temperature causes the sea level to rise as the water expands, affecting winds and weather and causing some of the ice at the polar ice caps to melt. Scientists say that if the carbon dioxide level continues to increase at its present rate, average temperatures will rise by between 1.5°C and 4°C in the next fifty years.

ACID RAIN

Rain is always slightly acidic from dissolved carbon dioxide, but pollutants such as sulphur dioxide and nitrogen dioxide make it more acidic. Rain containing dangerous levels of acid is called **acid rain**. It corrodes metals and damages stone buildings, and also makes the water in rivers and lakes more acidic.

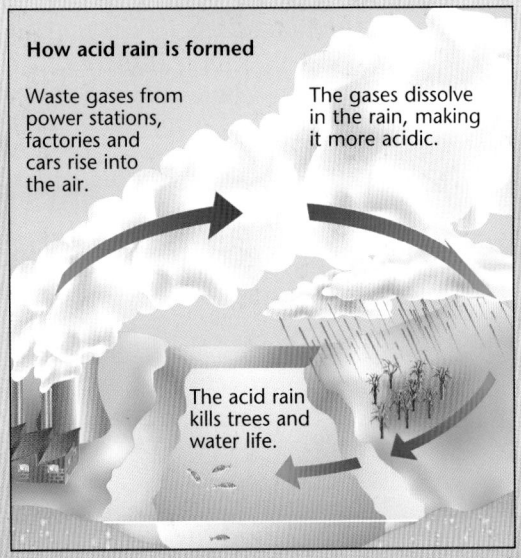

★

See for yourself

Try this test to see how acids affect building materials.

Put a small lump of dried cement into a glass and pour in enough vinegar to cover it. Leave the experiment for two to three days.

Ethanoic acid in the vinegar reacts with the cement, which is gradually dissolved by the acid.

Internet links

To find out more about the air, go to **www.usborne-quicklinks.com** and type in the keyword "science".

There you'll find links to websites where you can:

- Learn more about the science behind global warming
- Explore how humans are polluting the Earth's atmosphere

Go to Usborne Quicklinks for links to hand-picked websites on hundreds of subjects.

* *Allotropes, 71; Ultraviolet rays, 205.*

COMPOUNDS

There are just over a hundred different chemical elements, but they combine together in many different ways to make at least two million different compound substances. A **compound** contains atoms from two or more elements chemically bonded to form a new and different substance.

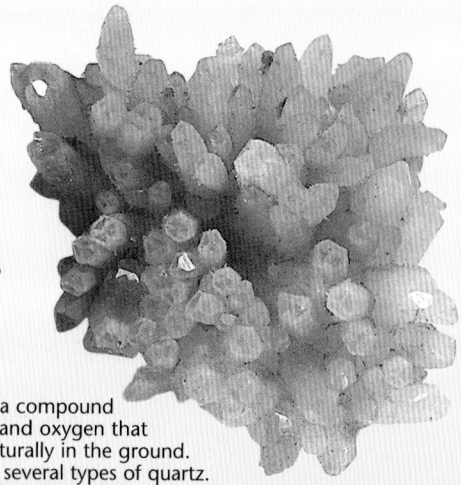

Quartz is a compound of silicon and oxygen that occurs naturally in the ground. There are several types of quartz. This type is called milky quartz.

CHEMICAL FORMULAE

Every sample of a compound contains the same proportions of the elements that make it up. These can be written as a **chemical formula**, which shows the proportions of the elements in the compound.

For example, the formula for water (hydrogen oxide) is H_2O, because every two atoms of hydrogen are bonded with one atom of oxygen.

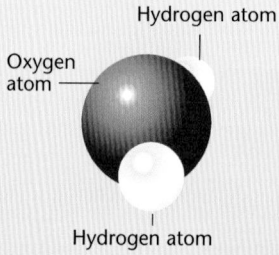

GROUPS OF COMPOUNDS

Compounds can be organized into separate groups, such as acids and bases, according to their chemical properties.

Compounds can also be classified according to the atoms they contain. For example, chloride compounds all contain chlorine, and oxides contain oxygen.

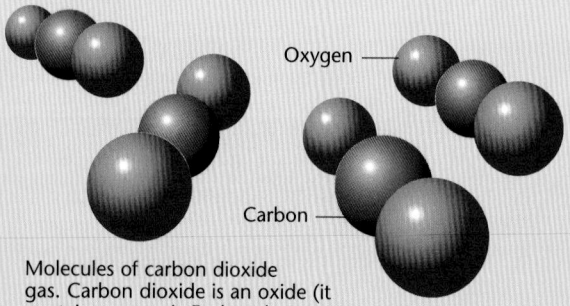

Molecules of carbon dioxide gas. Carbon dioxide is an oxide (it contains oxygen). Each carbon atom is bonded to two oxygen atoms.

CHARACTERISTICS OF COMPOUNDS

Compounds have two main characteristics:
- they cannot be separated by physical means, such as filtration or evaporation, because they are chemically bonded.
- they have different properties from the elements of which they are made.

Sodium chloride (**NaCl**), or **common salt**, for example, is a compound made from chlorine, a poisonous gas, and sodium, a very reactive metal. When they join together, they lose their dangerous properties.

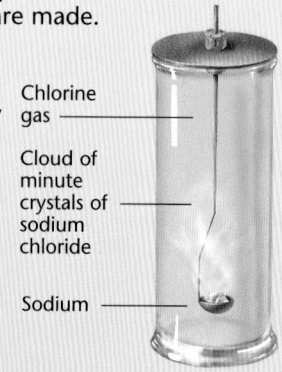

When iron and sulphur are heated together, the compound formed (iron sulphide) has different properties from the original elements.

Unlike iron, iron sulphide is not magnetic and unlike powdered sulphur, it sinks in water, as shown in the picture on the right.

After the reaction, the iron and sulphur can no longer be separated.

EVERYDAY COMPOUNDS

Many common substances are compounds. Bicarbonate of soda, used in cakes, combines sodium, hydrogen, carbon and oxygen. Its chemical name is **sodium hydrogencarbonate** (**NaHCO3**).

Butter is a mixture of compounds of carbon, hydrogen and oxygen.

Lemon juice contains citric acid, a compound of carbon, hydrogen and oxygen, mixed with water.

Glass contains compounds of silicon, oxygen, sodium and calcium.

Eggshells are made of a compound called calcium carbonate, which is also found in nature as limestone and chalk.

Eggs contain compounds of carbon, nitrogen, phosphorus, hydrogen, oxygen and sulphur.

See for yourself

Before a cake is cooked, its ingredients are a gooey mixture of different elements, compounds and other mixtures.

When the cake mixture is cooked, however, the heat causes chemical reactions* to occur, bonding the different substances into new compounds.

When a cake cooks, chemical reactions take place and new compounds are formed.

ORGANIC COMPOUNDS

Organic compounds all contain the element carbon. All living things are made of organic compounds. They are also used in the manufacture of plastics, detergents, paints and medicines. For more about organic compounds, see pages 92-95.

Many cosmetics contain organic compounds such as oils to give them their texture. Many of the compounds which give them colour, called pigments, are inorganic.

Internet links

To find out more about compounds, go to **www.usborne-quicklinks.com** and type in the keyword "science".

There you'll find links to websites where you can:

- Take a compound quiz
- Discover the importance of many different compounds
- Learn more with online activities

Go to Usborne Quicklinks for links to hand-picked websites on hundreds of subjects.

** Chemical reactions, 76-79.*

BONDING

The beautiful, symmetrical shapes of ice crystals and the hard, glittery surfaces of a diamond result from the way their atoms are joined together, or **bonded**. The properties of a substance, and the way it reacts with other substances, depend on those bonds.

Crystals of ice

ELECTRON SHELLS

A **stable atom** does not need to lose or gain electrons* from the outer electron shell around its nucleus (see *Atomic Structure*, pages 10-11). **Unstable atoms** attempt to bond with other atoms to become stable.

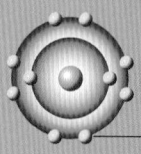

Neon has a full outer shell of electrons. It is stable and is not known to bond with any other atoms.

Most atoms have several shells of electrons. The first shell can hold up to two electrons and the second and third shells up to eight, although some atoms in compounds can have up to 18 electrons in their third shells. When a shell is full, the electrons begin a new shell.

The arrangement of electrons around the nucleus is called the **electron configuration**. This can be written as numbers after an atom's name.

Hydrogen (1)

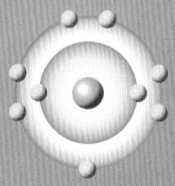

Fluorine (2,7)

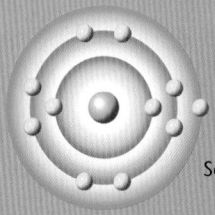

Sodium (2,8,1)

To achieve a stable outer shell, an atom may share electrons with other atoms or give or take electrons from another atom (see *Covalent*, *Ionic* and *Metallic Bonding* on pages 69-70).

See for yourself

The atomic number of an atom shows how many protons* it has. An atom has the same number of protons as electrons. Try calculating the electron configurations of the atoms below. Remember that they can have two electrons in the first shell, and up to eight in the second shell.

Magnesium (atomic number 12)
Argon (atomic number 18)
Nitrogen (atomic number 7)
Potassium (atomic number 19)
Silicon (atomic number 14)

(Answers on page 447.)

SHELL MODELS

Shell models, like the one on the left, are useful for understanding the make-up of an atom, but atoms don't actually look like this and the positions of electrons cannot be pinpointed with accuracy.

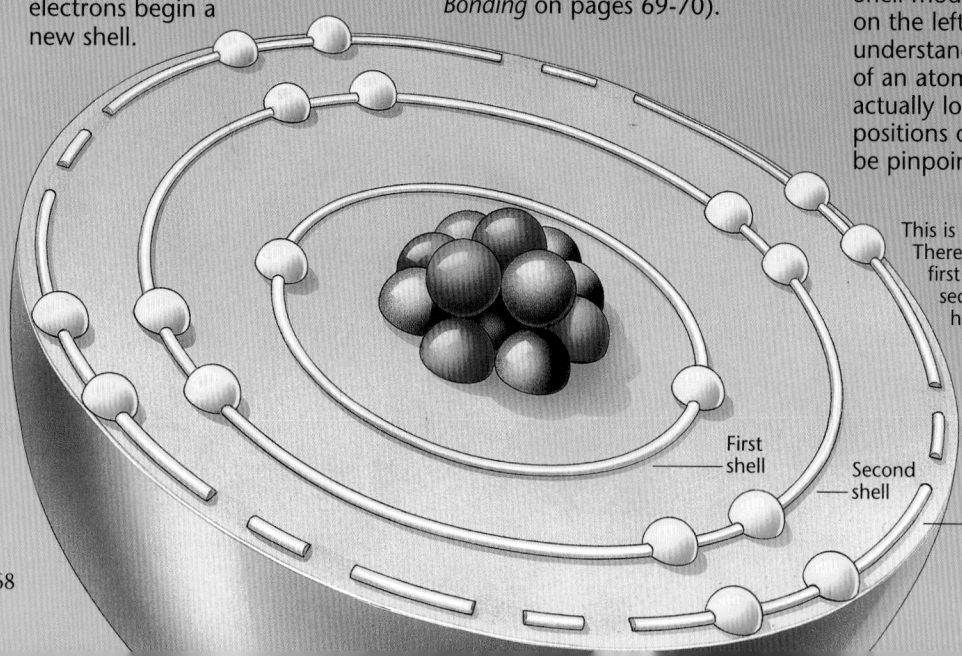

This is a shell model of an atom. There are two electrons in the first shell and eight in the second. The third shell can have up to 18 electrons.

The gaps in the third shell show where extra electrons could go if this atom were to bond with another.

* *Electrons, Protons, 10.*

COVALENT BONDING

A **covalent bond** is formed when atoms share electrons. In most covalent elements and compounds, the atoms bond to form molecules. For example, hydrogen atoms have one electron, and a molecule of hydrogen is formed when two atoms share their electrons. This gives both atoms a full outer shell.

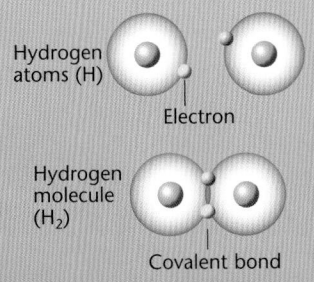

The atoms in carbon dioxide are also held together by covalent bonds. In this case, each of the atoms shares two electrons with its partner. This is called a **double bond**. For more about covalent bonds, see pages 92-93.

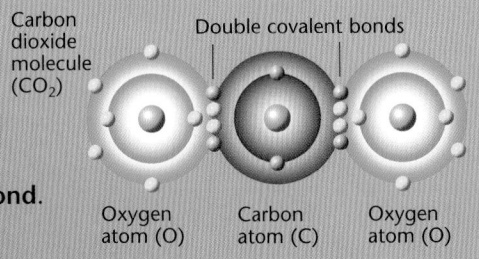

COVALENT SUBSTANCES

Non-metal elements, and compounds made only of non-metals, tend to form covalent bonds.

Covalent bonds between atoms in a molecule are strong, but the attraction between two molecules is not very strong. The molecules tend to break apart from each other when heated, so these substances have quite low melting and boiling points. Many are liquids or gases at room temperature.

Water molecules (H_2O)

The atoms in a molecule of water are held together by covalent bonds.

Oxygen atom

Hydrogen atom

Water, for example, is liquid at room temperature and evaporates easily. This is because the attraction between water molecules is not very strong.

Many covalent substances, such as oil, don't dissolve in water and don't conduct electricity.

Heat weakens the attraction between the water molecules in ice, and makes the ice melt.

GIANT MOLECULES

Some covalent elements, such as carbon, and many covalent compounds form giant molecules. Each atom is covalently bonded to the next atom, forming a huge, single covalent molecule that is very strong. These substances have very high melting and boiling points.

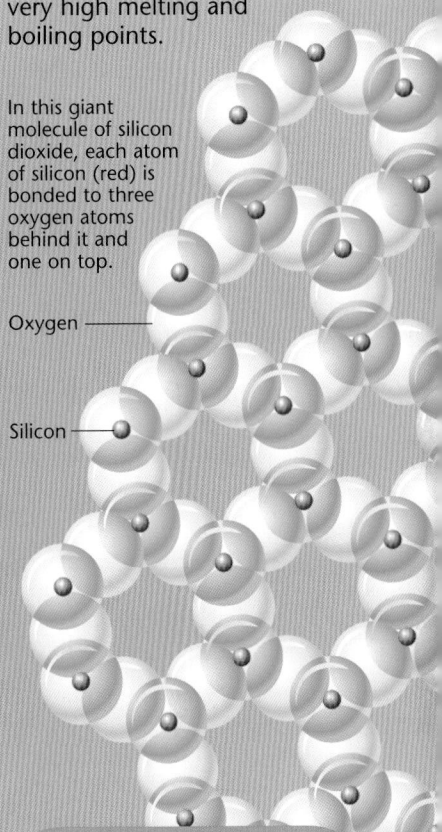

In this giant molecule of silicon dioxide, each atom of silicon (red) is bonded to three oxygen atoms behind it and one on top.

Internet links

To find out more about bonding, go to **www.usborne-quicklinks.com** and type in the keyword "science".

There you'll find links to websites where you can:

- Take part in an interactive lesson
- Test your knowledge with an online quiz
- Learn how to draw covalent bonds

Go to Usborne Quicklinks for links to hand-picked websites on hundreds of subjects.

An atom that has gained or lost electrons becomes an **ion**. Ions have electrical charges as they do not have an equal number of positively charged protons* and negatively charged electrons.

An atom that has lost electrons becomes a **cation**. It has a positive charge. An atom that has gained electrons becomes an **anion**. An anion has a negative charge as it has more electrons than protons.

Ionic bonds are created by ions that combine in order to share electrons and therefore become electrically stable. Compounds made of a metal and a non-metal bond in this way. Electrons from the outer shell of the metal ions become part of the outer shell of the non-metal ions. The compound is an **ionic compound**.

Here, an electron from a sodium atom is shared by a chlorine atom. Effectively, sodium becomes a cation with 11 protons and only 10 electrons.

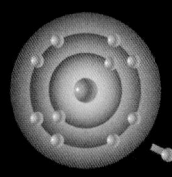

Sodium cation

Sodium and chlorine ions become bonded together ionically.

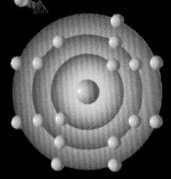

The chlorine becomes an anion with 17 protons and 18 electrons. (This is called a chloride ion.)

Chlorine anion

The type and strength of the charge is written after the ion's name. For example, Na^+ shows that sodium has lost one electron and Cl^- shows that chlorine has gained one electron. O^{2-} shows oxygen has gained two electrons.

Ions with opposite charges are attracted to each other. This creates the ionic bond that holds them together. Ionic compounds are not made of separate molecules. Instead, the ions gather in a regular arrangement called an **ionic lattice**. The bonds are strong. It takes a lot of heat to break them, so ionic compounds have high melting and boiling points.

Ionic lattice of sodium chloride (common salt)

Molecular lattices are a different type of lattice. They are made of molecules that are held together by weak forces, which tend to break apart when heated. Crystals with low melting and boiling points tend to have molecules formed in this way.

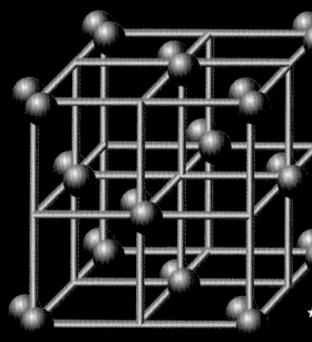

Molecular lattice of solid iodine. The molecules come apart easily.

METALLIC BONDING

Metallic bonding is the type of bonding found in metal elements. The atoms cling together to form a **metallic lattice** which is a regular arrangement of metal cations with free electrons travelling between them. Free electrons allow the atoms to cling together.

The forces between the electrons and the cations are strong. Most metals have high melting and boiling points, and because the electrons can move, metals can conduct heat and electricity. (See *Conduction*, page 113 and *Electric Current*, page 230.)

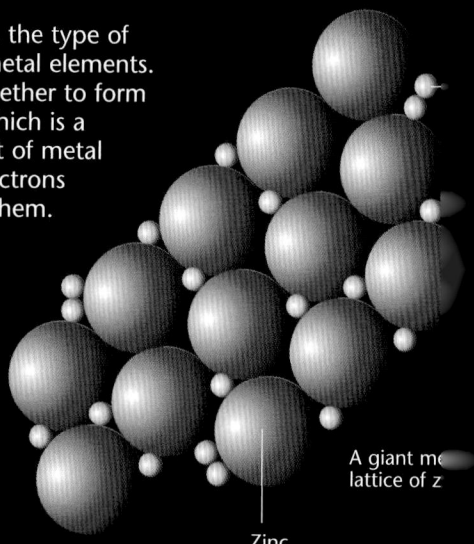

A giant me lattice of z

Zinc cation

VALENCY

The number of electrons an atom needs to gain or lose to form a stable outer shell of electrons is called its **valency**, or **combining power**.

A sodium atom needs to lose one electron. Its valency is 1.

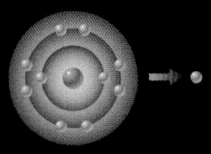

A sulphur atom needs to gain two electrons. Its valency is 2.

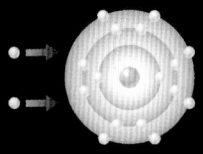

An atom with a stable outer shell of electrons has a valency of 0. If an atom needs to gain or lose just one electron it has a valency of 1. Valencies of 2, 3 or 4 indicate that atoms have two, three or four electrons more or less than a stable structure.

Fluorine has seven electrons in its outer shell. It needs to gain one electron to have a full shell so its valency is 1.

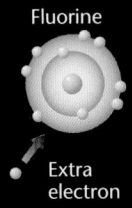

Phosphorus has five electrons in its outer shell and needs to gain three to form a full shell, so its valency is 3.

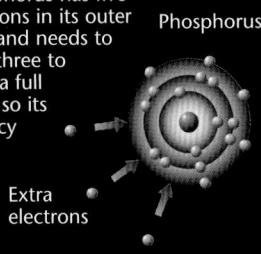

The valency of an ion is the same as the size of its charge. For instance, the oxide ion (O^{2-}) has a negative charge of 2 and its valency is 2. Some elements can form different ions so can have more than one valency. Iron, for example, forms Fe^{2+} and Fe^{3+} ions. Roman numerals after the name, for example iron(II) and iron(III), indicate the valency.

ALLOTROPES

Some elements can exist in different physical forms because their atoms can bond together in different ways. The different forms are called **allotropes**. Diamond and graphite are both allotropes of the element carbon.

In **diamond**, each carbon atom is linked to four other carbon atoms and the atoms are packed tightly together. Because of this, diamond is very strong.

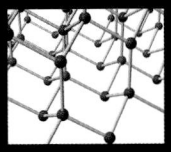

Diamond molecule

In **graphite**, each carbon atom bonds to just three other carbon atoms. The atoms form layers and the forces between the layers are quite weak, making graphite flaky.

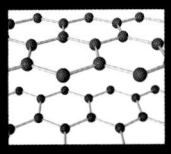

Graphite molecule

Carbon has a third allotrope, called **buckminsterfullerene**, in which 60 carbon atoms are bonded together to make a hollow sphere. Many other elements, such as phosphorus, tin and sulphur, also have allotropes.

A model of a buckminsterfullerene molecule. These are usually hollow, but one in a million, like this one, traps an atom of helium during its formation.

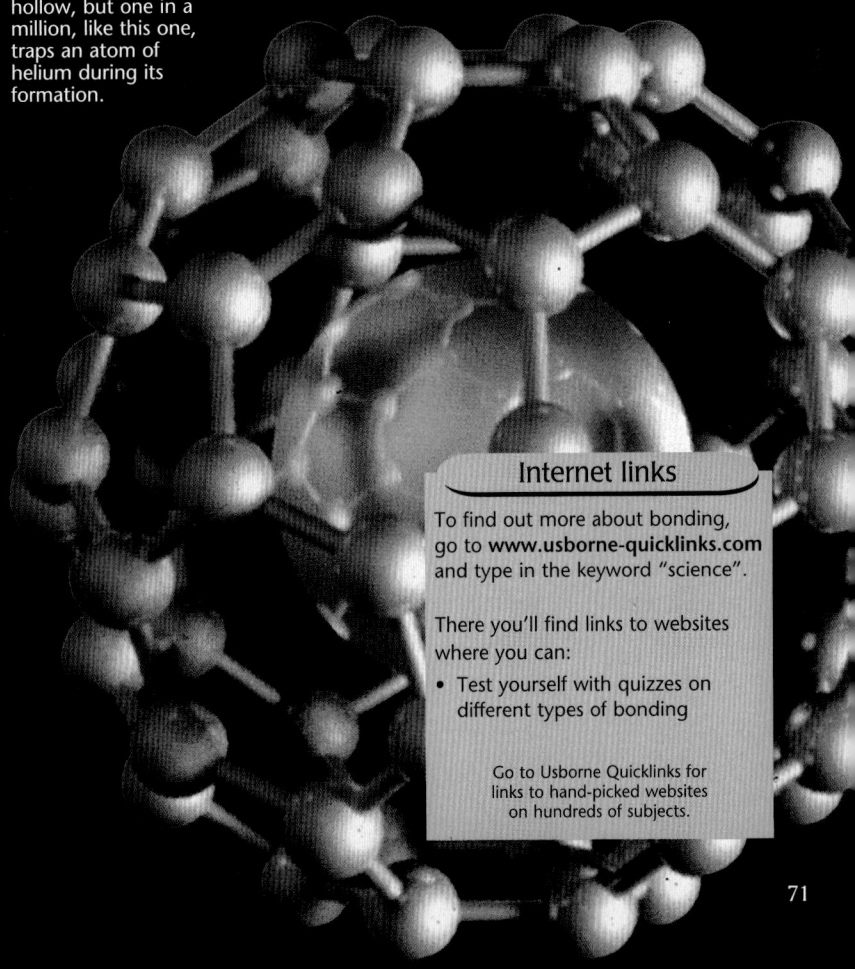

Internet links

To find out more about bonding, go to **www.usborne-quicklinks.com** and type in the keyword "science".

There you'll find links to websites where you can:

- Test yourself with quizzes on different types of bonding

Go to Usborne Quicklinks for links to hand-picked websites on hundreds of subjects.

WATER

Water is one of the most common compounds on Earth. As well as the water in rivers and seas, all living things contain water and cannot survive without it. Blood and plant sap are mainly water. Water is a very good solvent – other substances dissolve easily in it.

About 70% of the surface of the Earth is covered with water.

WHAT IS WATER?

Water is a compound. Each molecule of water contains two atoms of hydrogen bonded to an atom of oxygen. The chemical formula for water is **H_2O**. The chemical name for water is **hydrogen oxide**. Water is formed when hydrogen burns in air.

Pure water, that is, water that does not contain any dissolved substances, boils at 100°C and freezes at 0°C. If water contains any dissolved substances, the boiling point is raised and the freezing point is lowered. This fact can be used to test whether a liquid is pure water.

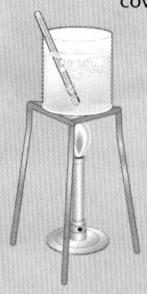

If it is pure, the water in this beaker will boil at 100°C.

Model of a molecule of water

Ice is the solid form of water. Icebergs float because ice is less dense than water. This huge iceberg in Antarctica rises 100m above the sea.

When water evaporates*, it forms a gas called **water vapour**. When it freezes, it forms a solid called **ice**. Unlike most other substances, water expands when it freezes, so ice is less dense* than water and it floats on water. Because of this, fish and other creatures can live in the water under the ice at the Poles.

** Density, 17, 138; Evaporation, 20.*

WATER AS A SOLVENT

Water is a very good **solvent**, that is, many substances dissolve easily in water to form a solution*. This is why water is rarely found in a pure state.

Many substances, like these paints, dissolve easily in water.

Water molecules have a slight electrical charge because their hydrogen atoms are grouped on one side. Because of this, ionic compounds* dissolve easily in water. Their ions* have an electrical charge and they are attracted to the charges on the water molecules.

The electrons (yellow) give this side of the molecule a slight negative charge.

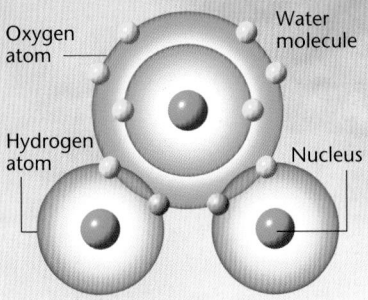

Protons in the hydrogen nuclei give this side a slight positive charge.

A solvent, such as water, will only accept a certain amount of a substance dissolved in it. When no more will dissolve, the solution is **saturated**. The amount of solid that will dissolve usually increases if the liquid is heated.

It is easier to dissolve sugar in a hot drink than in a cold one.

FIZZY DRINKS

The fizz in fizzy drinks is made by dissolving carbon dioxide gas in water, under pressure. The amount of gas that can be dissolved in a solution decreases when the pressure of the solution is decreased. This is why carbon dioxide bubbles out when you open a fizzy drink and release (lower) the pressure.

HARD WATER

Hard water contains dissolved minerals from rocks it has flowed over. Soap does not lather well in hard water – the minerals react with the soap to form scum. There are two types of hard water, depending on which minerals it contains.

Temporary hard water is caused by a chemical reaction between limestone and rainwater. Limestone is made of calcium carbonate, which is insoluble, and rainwater is a weak solution of carbonic acid. The acid reacts with the calcium carbonate to form calcium hydrogencarbonate which then dissolves in the water, making it hard.

Permanent hard water contains calcium and magnesium compounds from rocks such as gypsum. These cannot be removed by boiling.

Water contains dissolved oxygen. This is why plants and animals can live in it.

SOFTENING WATER

The minerals that make water hard can be removed by adding washing soda, or by ion exchange.

Ion exchange tank

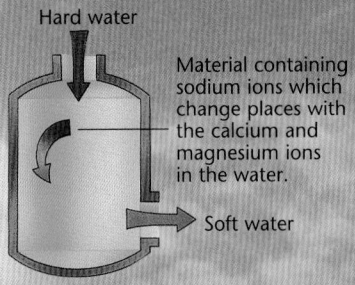

In an **ion exchange tank**, hard water containing calcium and magnesium compounds is passed through a material such as zeolite (sodium aluminium silicate). The calcium and magnesium ions are swapped for sodium ions which do not make the water hard.

Washing soda is sodium carbonate. When added to hard water, it reacts with the calcium and magnesium compounds and changes them into insoluble compounds that do not make scum.

Internet links

To find out more about water, go to **www.usborne-quicklinks.com** and type in the keyword "science".

There you'll find links to websites where you can:

- Watch the changes that take place when water freezes, and when it evaporates

Go to Usborne Quicklinks for links to hand-picked websites on hundreds of subjects.

* *Ionic compounds, Ions, 70; Solution, 58.*

THE WATER CYCLE

All the Earth's water is continually being recycled between the Earth, the atmosphere and living things. This is called the **water cycle**.

The water in rivers, lakes and seas is continually evaporating* and becoming tiny droplets of water vapour in the air. The droplets form clouds and fall again as rain, hail or snow.

The water cycle

When vapour in clouds cools, it falls as rain, hail or snow.

Rainwater drains into rivers.

Water vapour forms clouds.

Water for use is stored in reservoirs.

Plants give off water vapour.

Waterworks purify water before use.

Sewage works

Water evaporates

Houses and factories use water.

Rivers flow into the sea.

CLEANING WATER

Water that has flowed over land and through rocks contains impurities. These impurities can be removed at a **waterworks**. The water is stored in reservoirs to allow solid matter to settle and then, in the waterworks, the water is filtered to remove smaller particles of mud and solids.

A waterworks

Water trickles through beds of clean gravel and sand, or carbon, to remove particles of mud and other solids. After filtering, the water is treated with chlorine to kill harmful bacteria and then pumped to storage tanks and piped to houses and factories.

SEWAGE TREATMENT

Sewage (waste water) should be cleaned before it is pumped into the sea. In a **sewage works**, the water is filtered to remove rubbish, and then left in **sedimentation tanks** for the solid particles to settle. Bacteria decompose any remaining organic matter and break it down into harmless substances.

Here you can see part of the water cycle in action. Water vapour is rising from a rainforest and forming clouds.

* *Evaporation, 20.*

PURIFYING WATER

Water is a good solvent*, so it usually contains dissolved substances. Pure water can be obtained by distillation*, but a more efficient method is by **deionization**. Ions are atoms or molecules that have lost or gained an electron and so have a positive or negative electrical charge (see also page 70).

Deionization

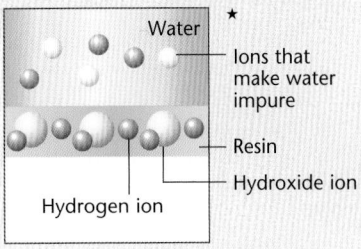

Ion exchange resin has hydrogen ions (H^+) and hydroxide ions (OH^-) clinging to it. The water contains different ions which make it impure. The water is passed through the ion exchange resin.

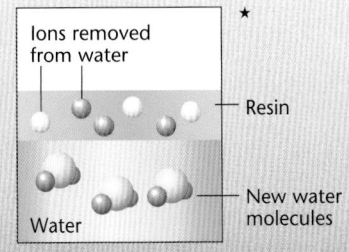

As the water goes through the resin, the ions in the water are more strongly attracted to the resin than to the water. The ions from the resin are displaced. They pass into the water, and combine to create extra molecules of water (H_2O).

WATER POLLUTION

Water pollution is caused by untreated water from houses and factories flowing into rivers and the sea.

When water contains a lot of waste, bacteria that break down organic waste matter become very numerous and use up most of the oxygen. The water becomes lifeless, except for other, harmful bacteria that can survive in water without oxygen.

Oxygen in water can also be used up by too much plant growth caused when fertilizers from farmland, and detergents that contain phosphates, drain into rivers. The oxygen in the water is used up by the plants and by bacteria that feed on the plants when they die.

POISONOUS POLLUTION

Pollution is also caused by litter, pesticides and by poisonous substances such as lead and mercury. Poisonous substances build up in the bodies of fish and may be passed on to other animals and to people. Pesticides kill tiny creatures and larger animals and disturb the balance between living things.

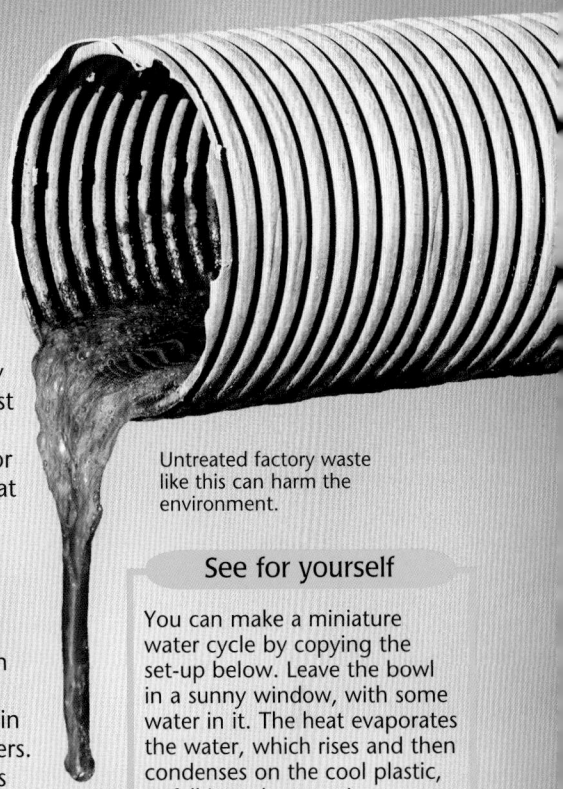

Untreated factory waste like this can harm the environment.

See for yourself

You can make a miniature water cycle by copying the set-up below. Leave the bowl in a sunny window, with some water in it. The heat evaporates the water, which rises and then condenses on the cool plastic, to fall into the container.

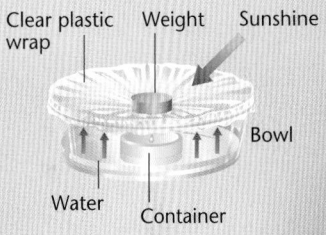

Internet links

To find out more about water, go to **www.usborne-quicklinks.com** and type in the keyword "science".

There you'll find links to websites where you can:

- Follow the water cycle step by step
- Discover how waste water is cleaned and treated
- Learn more about water pollution

Go to Usborne Quicklinks for links to hand-picked websites on hundreds of subjects.

The links at Usborne Quicklinks are regularly reviewed and updated, so you might find a slightly different selection of websites from the ones shown here.

** Distillation, 61; Solvent, 58.*

CHEMICAL REACTIONS

Chemical reactions are happening around us all the time – in our digestive system when we eat, in a baking cake or in a car's engine when it's being driven. During a chemical reaction, the atoms in the substances, called the **reactants**, are rearranged to form new substances, called the **products**.

Striking a match activates the chemical reaction that takes place when the match burns.

WHAT HAPPENS IN A REACTION

During a chemical reaction, the bonds between the atoms of substances are broken. The atoms rearrange themselves and form bonds with new partners. The diagrams on the right show what happens when water and sulphur trioxide react together to form sulphuric acid.

During a chemical reaction energy is always either taken in or given out. Breaking bonds requires energy and creating new bonds releases energy. This is usually heat energy, although some reactions give off or take in light. A reaction that produces heat is called an **exothermic reaction**. If heat is taken in, it is an **endothermic reaction**. For more about these, see page 78.

Most chemical reactions also need a certain amount of energy, usually in the form of heat, to start them off. This makes the molecules in the substances move around so they collide and can react together. The minimum amount of energy needed to start off a reaction is called the **activation energy**.

Each molecule of water (H_2O) is made of two atoms of hydrogen and one atom of oxygen. Sulphur trioxide (SO_3) is made of three atoms of oxygen bonded to one atom of sulphur.

Molecule of sulphur trioxide

Water molecule

The atoms in the substances separate and combine with each other to form a molecule of sulphuric acid (H_2SO_4).

Molecule of sulphuric acid

These unusual formations at Mono Lake in California, USA, are called tufa towers. They are formed when a chemical reaction takes place between carbonates in the lake water and calcium from spring water (the reactants). The product is calcium carbonate, or limestone.

LAW OF CONSERVATION OF MASS

Matter cannot be created or destroyed during a chemical reaction. This is the **law of conservation of mass**. (Mass is the amount of matter a substance contains.)

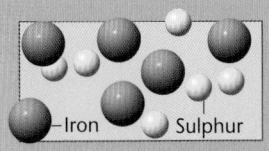

During a reaction between iron and sulphur, the atoms in the substances rearrange themselves.

Iron sulphide

After the reaction there is the same number of atoms and there is therefore the same amount of matter.

CHEMICAL EQUATIONS

Chemical reactions can be written as **equations** using the chemical formulae of the substances. In an equation, the reactants are written on the left and the products are written on the right. They are separated by an arrow. Because of the law of conservation of mass, both sides of an equation balance: the reactants and the products contain the same number of atoms.

This equation shows how hydrogen and oxygen react to form water. Both sides of the equation have the same number of atoms.

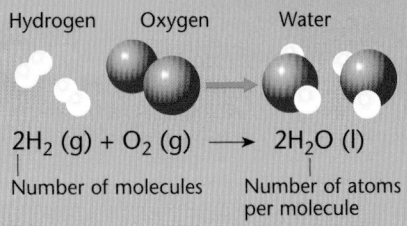

Equations may also show the physical states of the substances involved in the reaction (**g** for gas, **l** for liquid, **s** for solid and **aq** for aqueous, that is, dissolved in water). If a catalyst* is used, it is shown above the arrow.

MOLES

Chemists measure chemical substances in **moles**. One mole is 602,300 billion, billion molecules or atoms. This can be written as 6.023×10^{23} and is called the **Avogadro number**. It is the number of atoms found in a mass of 12g of carbon-12. A mole of a different element will have a different mass, but the same number of particles. A mole of magnesium has a mass of 24g because magnesium atoms weigh twice as much as carbon atoms.

A mole of magnesium has a mass of 24g.

A mole of carbon has a mass of 12g.

See for yourself

To produce an exothermic reaction, mix plaster of Paris with water. You will notice that the mixture becomes warm.

This is because plaster of Paris is made by heating gypsum (hydrated* calcium sulphate) until it loses some of its water and becomes a powder. When water is added, it bonds again with the plaster to produce solid gypsum and heat.

Internet links

To find out more about reactions, go to **www.usborne-quicklinks.com** and type in the keyword "science".

There you'll find links to websites where you can:

- Watch film clips of chemical reactions taking place

Go to Usborne Quicklinks for links to hand-picked websites on hundreds of subjects.

* *Catalysts, 79; Hydration, 91.*

TYPES OF REACTION

All chemical reactions either give off or take in energy. In **endothermic reactions**, energy is absorbed in the form of heat. For instance, when sherbet reacts with moisture on your tongue, heat is taken from your tongue, making it feel cool.

Any reactions that give off heat energy are **exothermic reactions**. (Combustion, also called burning, is one example of an exothermic reaction.) Your body feels warm because of exothermic reactions which are happening inside you all the time.

Some reactions take in or give off energy in the form of light rather than heat. These are called **photochemical reactions**. Plants take in light energy from sunlight. This enables them to make food, as part of a process called photosynthesis*.

These plants are taking energy from sunlight and making food in a photochemical reaction.

Synthesis reactions (also called **combination reactions**) involve substances combining to make a single new substance. For example, when magnesium is heated, it combines with oxygen in the air to produce a white ash called magnesium oxide.

Neutralization reactions take place when one substance reacts with another and each cancels out the other's properties. This is what happens when acids and alkalis are mixed. (See *Bases and Alkalis*, page 85.)

Reactions where a single substance breaks down into simpler substances are called **decomposition reactions**. When food rots, many of these reactions take place.

When heat is needed to break down a compound, the reaction is called a **thermal decomposition reaction**. For example, when limestone (calcium carbonate) is heated, it breaks down to form quicklime (calcium oxide) and carbon dioxide.

Heating limestone causes it to break down into different substances.

Reversible reactions are reactions in which the products, given the right conditions, react together to form the original reactants once again. Reactions of this type can be written as an equation. A symbol indicates that the reaction is reversible:

$$2NO_2 \rightleftharpoons 2NO + O_2$$

Nitrogen dioxide (NO_2) splits to produce nitrogen monoxide (NO) and oxygen (O_2). As they cool, they recombine to give nitrogen dioxide.

The first part of the reaction is called the **forward reaction**. The second part is called the **backward reaction**.

Displacement reactions occur when a more reactive substance displaces a less reactive one. For example, when an iron nail is placed in copper(II) sulphate solution, the iron "pulls" the copper out of the solution and takes its place in the solution. The copper collects around the nail. The more reactive element (iron) displaces the less reactive copper.

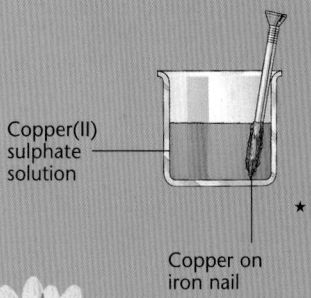

* *Photosynthesis, 81*

RATES OF REACTION

Some chemical reactions, such as rusting, take place slowly over a long period of time. Others, such as the chemical reaction that takes place when gunpowder explodes, are almost instantaneous.

The rate of a reaction is affected by the **reactivity** of the substances. Very reactive elements react more quickly than less reactive elements.

During a chemical reaction, the atoms of the different substances must come into contact with each other in order to form new bonds. This happens more easily in gases and liquids, in which molecules are free to move around, so they tend to be more reactive than solid substances.

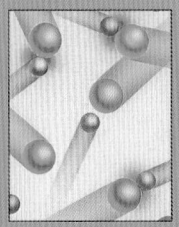

Heating substances increases the rate of a reaction. The heat makes more of the particles move fast enough to collide and react.

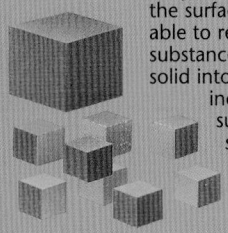

Only the molecules on the surface of a solid are able to react with another substance. Breaking the solid into smaller particles increases the surface area and so increases the rate of reaction.

When rainwater hits limestone, a chemical reaction occurs. The rainwater slowly dissolves the limestone to form carbonic acid. This eats away the limestone further.

CATALYSTS

Catalysts are substances that can change the rate of a chemical reaction, but are themselves left unchanged. Some catalysts speed up reactions while others, called **inhibitors**, slow them down.

Catalysts work by lowering the activation energy* of a reaction. They make it easier for the reaction to take place.

Metals are often used as catalysts. For example, **catalytic converters**, which remove toxic gases from car exhaust fumes, use metal catalysts, as shown below.

How a catalytic converter works

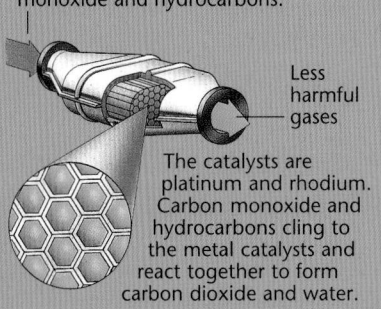

See for yourself

Here you can see how to make use of an exothermic reaction to reveal something written in invisible ink.

Dip a fine paintbrush in lemon juice and write a message on a piece of paper. Leave it to dry until it is invisible. To reveal the message, place the paper face down on a shelf in the oven and leave it there for ten minutes at 175°C.

The heat of the oven causes the lemon juice to burn – an exothermic reaction which makes the writing go brown. The heat is not enough, though, to burn the paper.

ENZYMES

Many chemical reactions that take place in living things are speeded up by catalysts called **enzymes**.

Enzymes, and many other catalysts, are **action specific**, that is, each speeds up only one type of reaction. Many different enzymes in the digestive systems of animals, including humans, help speed up the chemical reactions that break complex foods into simpler substances.

The picture shows the three main areas of your digestive system where enzymes work on your food.

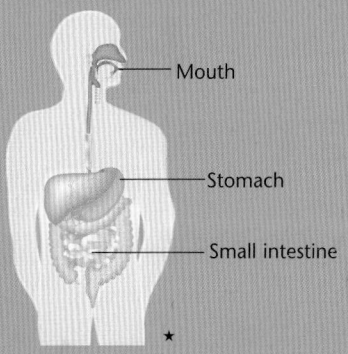

Internet links

To find out more about reactions, go to **www.usborne-quicklinks.com** and type in the keyword "science".

There you'll find links to websites where you can:

- Explore the chemical changes that happen when food is cooked
- Create chemical reactions with interactive experiments

Go to Usborne Quicklinks for links to hand-picked websites on hundreds of subjects.

The links at Usborne Quicklinks are regularly reviewed and updated, so you might find a slightly different selection of websites from the ones shown here.

** Activation energy, 76.*

OXIDATION AND REDUCTION

Oxidation and reduction are terms which describe two types of chemical reaction. Unless specific conditions prevent it, these two reactions always occur together, in what are described as **redox reactions**. In a redox reaction, when one substance is oxidized, the other is reduced. For example, when wood burns, it is oxidized, while the air around it is reduced.

OXIDATION

The term **oxidation** describes reactions in which a substance combines with oxygen. This comes from another substance, called the **oxidizing agent** (which itself is reduced). For example, when iron is exposed to damp air, it slowly combines with oxygen in the air, forming hydrated iron oxide (rust).

Rusting (the corrosion of iron) is an oxidation reaction.

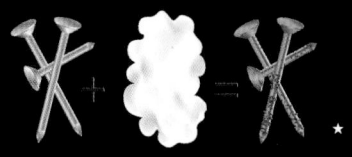

Iron Damp air Rust

Oxidation also describes reactions in which a substance loses hydrogen or electrons to another substance (the oxidizing agent). For example, when magnesium and chlorine combine to form magnesium chloride, magnesium loses two electrons (see Ionic Bonding, page 70). It is oxidized.

The magnesium atom loses two electrons to the chlorine atoms, and is oxidized.

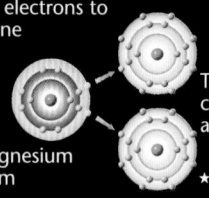

INTERNAL RESPIRATION

Internal respiration, the process by which animals and plants break down glucose to release energy, is an oxidation reaction. In fact, it is a slow form of combustion (see below). This is the equation for internal respiration:

$$C_6H_{12}O_6 + 6O_2 \rightarrow 6CO_2 + 6H_2O$$

Glucose + Oxygen → Carbon dioxide + Water

COMBUSTION

Combustion (burning) is an oxidation reaction that gives off energy in the form of heat. When a substance burns, it combines with oxygen to form an oxide. Most fuels, for example, wood, gas and petrol, contain hydrogen and carbon. Both these substances oxidize to produce water and carbon dioxide when they burn.

We now burn so much fuel for energy that the level of carbon dioxide in the air is increasing. Scientists think that the amount of combustion may be causing changes in the weather (see *Greenhouse Effect*, page 65).

The colours in fireworks come from the combustion of different elements. Strontium burns to give red sparks, copper gives blue and magnesium brilliant white.

Petrol burning inside a motorbike's engine is an example of combustion.

REDUCTION

During **reduction**, a substance loses oxygen to, or gains hydrogen or electrons from, another substance (the **reducing agent**, which is oxidized). For example, when copper oxide reacts with carbon, the copper oxide loses oxygen to the carbon, as shown below.

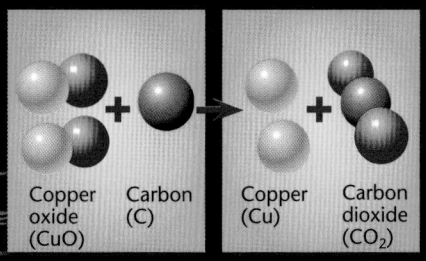

In this reaction, the copper oxide is reduced to pure copper by carbon, and the carbon is oxidized to form carbon dioxide.

$$2CuO + C \rightarrow CO_2 + 2Cu$$

Copper oxide + Carbon ⟶ Carbon dioxide + Copper

IRON SMELTING

The iron production process, called **smelting**, produces pure iron from iron ore. It is an example of a useful redox reaction.

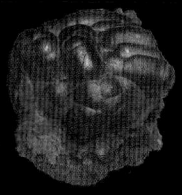

Iron ore

Inside a blast furnace, carbon is used to reduce iron ore (iron oxide) to pure iron. The carbon pulls oxygen away from (reduces) the ore. The carbon itself oxidizes to become carbon dioxide.

See for yourself

When a chunk of apple is left for a few minutes, it begins to turn brown. This is because chemicals on the apple's flesh take part in an oxidation reaction, using oxygen from the surrounding air. If you cover the apple with plastic food wrap, you stop the air from reacting with the apple, so it doesn't go brown.

PHOTOSYNTHESIS

Photosynthesis, the process by which plants make their food, is a reduction reaction. In photosynthesis, plants build glucose ($C_6H_{12}O_6$) from carbon dioxide and water, using energy from sunlight. Photosynthesis is the opposite of internal respiration (see opposite page). This is the equation for photosynthesis:

$$6CO_2 + 6H_2O \rightarrow C_6H_{12}O_6 + 6O_2$$

Carbon dioxide + Water ⟶ Glucose + Oxygen

This tulip plant feeds itself with the glucose it makes during photosynthesis.

Plants produce oxygen when they are photosynthesizing. They use some of it for internal respiration and the rest goes back into the air.

Internet links

Go to **www.usborne-quicklinks.com** and type in the keyword "science" to find out more about oxidization and reduction.

There you'll find links to websites where you can:

- Discover the science behind fireworks and matches
- Learn the basics of redox reactions

Go to Usborne Quicklinks for links to hand-picked websites on hundreds of subjects.

ELECTROLYSIS

Electrolysis is a method of separating the elements in a compound by passing an electric current through the compound when it is molten or in a solution. The process is used to separate very reactive metals from their ores and to purify metals. It is also used to coat objects with a thin layer of metal in a process called electroplating.

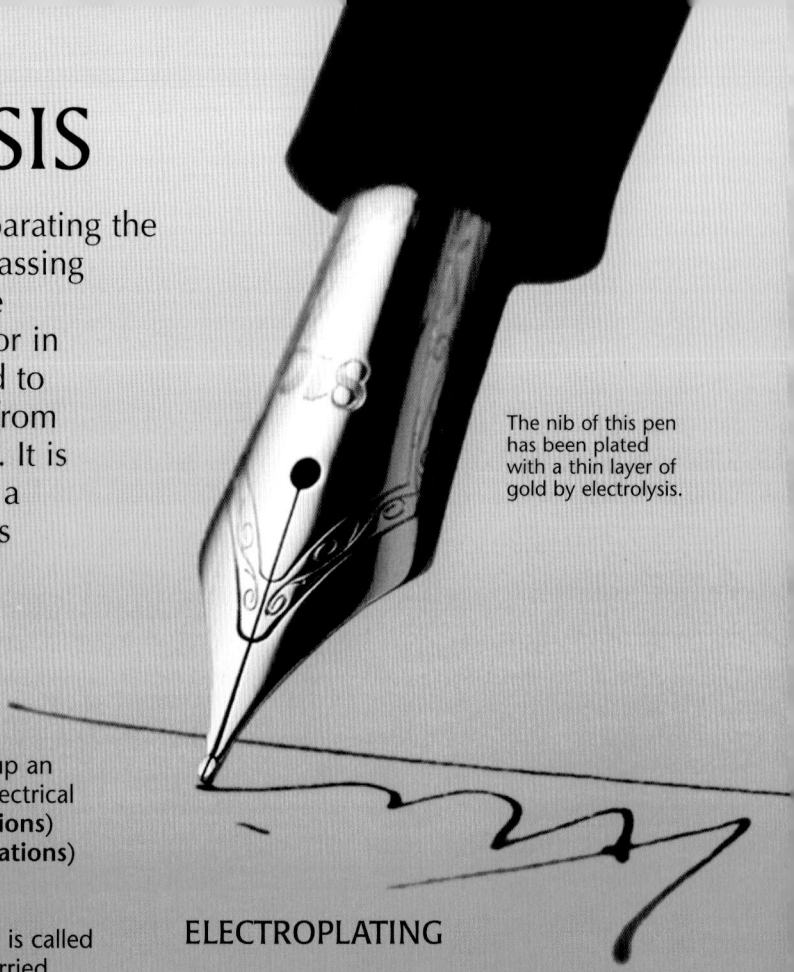

The nib of this pen has been plated with a thin layer of gold by electrolysis.

HOW ELECTROLYSIS WORKS

Only ionic compounds* can conduct electricity during electrolysis. This is because the particles that make up an ionic compound, called ions, have an electrical charge. Some of the particles (called **anions**) are negatively charged. Others (called **cations**) are positively charged.

During electrolysis, the ionic compound is called the **electrolyte**. An electric current is carried to it by two **electrodes**. One electrode (the **anode**) carries a positive charge. The other (the **cathode**) carries a negative charge.

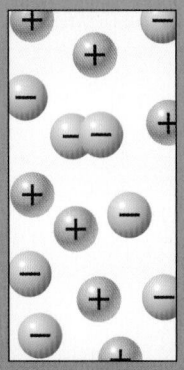

Copper(II) chloride solution can be used as an electrolyte. It is made up of positively charged copper cations and negatively charged chloride anions.

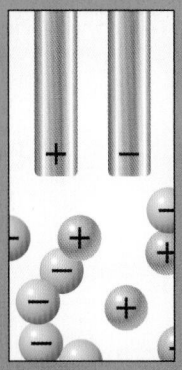

To carry the current, two electrodes, attached to an electric source, are placed in the compound. Nothing happens until the electric current flows.

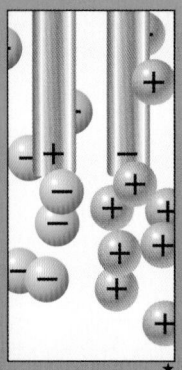

As the electric current flows, the cations flow to the negative electrode where they gain electrons. The anions rush to the positive electrode and lose electrons.

ELECTROPLATING

Electroplating uses electrolysis to cover objects with a thin layer of metal. The object that is to be plated is used as a cathode and during electrolysis it becomes coated with metal from the electrolyte.

In industry, electroplating is used to protect cheap but reactive metals with a layer of less reactive metal. For example, steel is plated with tin or chromium to stop it rusting.

These steel food cans have been plated with a very fine layer of tin to prevent rust.

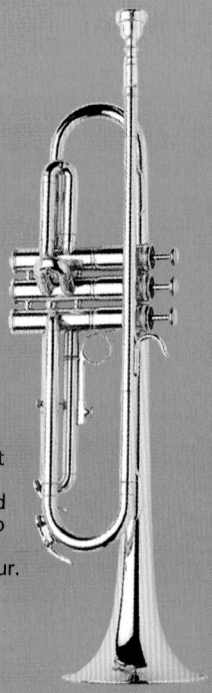

This trumpet has been electroplated with brass to give a rich golden colour.

* *Ionic compounds, 70.*

ELECTROREFINING

Electrorefining purifies metals by electrolysis. To purify copper, impure copper is used as an anode and pure copper as a cathode. A solution of copper(II) sulphate is used as an electrolyte.

Copper ions in the solution are attracted to the cathode. They are replaced in the solution by copper ions which split off from the anode, leaving the impurities behind.

Electrorefining copper

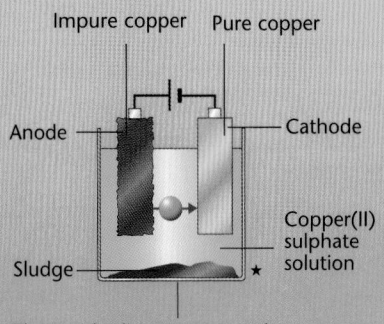

The anode disintegrates as the copper ions split off. Its impurities fall off, forming a sludge.

METAL EXTRACTION

Very reactive metals, such as aluminium, are extracted from impure forms by electrolysis.

Aluminium is mined as **bauxite**, which is mainly aluminium oxide. For electrolysis, aluminium oxide is dissolved in cryolite to allow the ions to move. A graphite-lined tank forms the cathode. Aluminium ions are attracted to the cathode and become atoms of molten aluminium.

Extracting aluminium

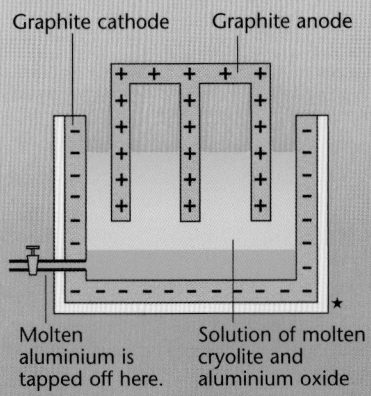

ANODIZING

Electrolysis can be used to coat some metals, such as aluminium, with a thin layer of their oxide (the compound it forms when it reacts with oxygen). This is called **anodizing**. The oxide forms a protective layer that prevents corrosion of the metal.

When anodizing aluminium, the object is used as the anode and placed in a solution of sulphuric acid, which is the electrolyte.

Oxide ions from the electrolyte collect at the anode and they react with the aluminium to form a layer of aluminium oxide.

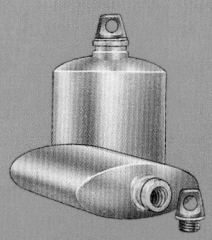

Anodized aluminium water flasks

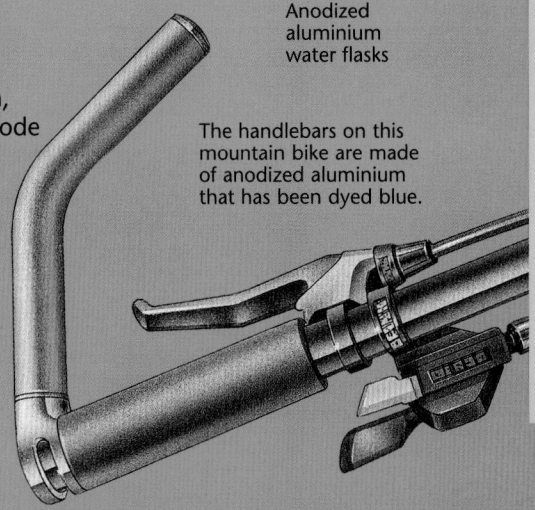

The handlebars on this mountain bike are made of anodized aluminium that has been dyed blue.

See for yourself

You can use electrolysis to split water, which is a compound of hydrogen and oxygen, into bubbles of hydrogen and oxygen gas. Set up the equipment as shown below.

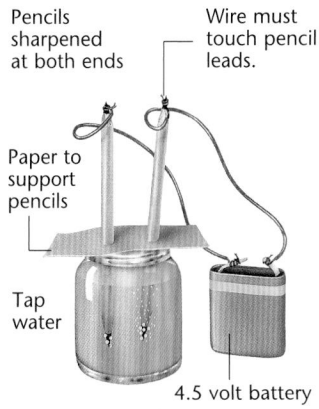

When you attach the wires to the battery, bubbles of hydrogen rush to the pencil attached to the negative battery terminal (cathode) because hydrogen forms positive ions. The bubbles on the other pencil, attached to the positive terminal, or anode, are oxygen. There are more hydrogen bubbles because each molecule of water (H_2O) contains two atoms of hydrogen but only one of oxygen.

Internet links

To find out more about electrolysis, go to **www.usborne-quicklinks.com** and type in the keyword "science".

There you'll find links to websites where you can:

- Try out some interactive electrolysis experiments
- Watch animated presentations
- Find practical uses for electrolysis

Go to Usborne Quicklinks for links to hand-picked websites on hundreds of subjects.

ACIDS AND BASES

The word acid comes from the Latin word *acer*, which means "sour". Acids contained in some foods make the food taste sour. For example, citrus fruits such as lemons, limes, oranges and grapefruits contain citric acid and ascorbic acid. The chemical opposite of an acid is a base. (A substance that is neither an acid nor a base is neutral.)

A bee's sting contains an acid. It can be neutralized with soap, which is an alkali.

ACIDS

Acids are compounds that contain hydrogen and which dissolve in water to produce hydrogen ions (H^+). Ions are particles that have an electrical charge. The hydrogen ions give acids their special properties, but they only exist in solution, so an acid only displays its properties when it is dissolved.

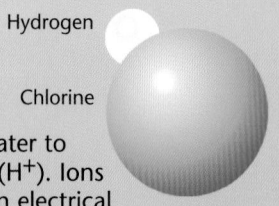

Hydrochloric acid (HCl) is made from hydrogen and chlorine.

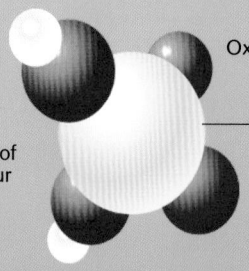

A molecule of sulphuric acid (H_2SO_4) is made of hydrogen, sulphur and oxygen.

A **strong acid** is one in which most of the molecules separate to form a large number of hydrogen ions when it is in solution. Hydrochloric, sulphuric and nitric acid are all strong acids.

Strong acids are very **corrosive**. This means that they will burn your skin or the surface of an object.

The containers of strong acids are marked with the international warning symbols shown below, which mean corrosive (left) and harmful (right).

Corrosive

Harmful

ORGANIC ACIDS

Acids that are produced by living things, such as citric acid and ethanoic acid, are called **organic acids**. These are examples of **weak acids** (they contain few hydrogen ions). There is more about organic acids on page 94.

The colourful markings on the skin of sea slugs contain acids that taste horrible. This discourages predators from eating them.

Vinegar, which can be made from grapes, contains a weak acid called ethanoic acid.

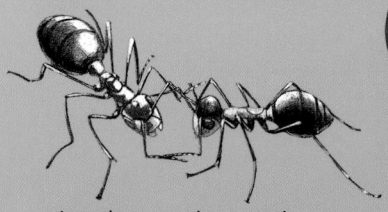

Ants that can sting contain an acid called methanoic (or formic) acid.

Tomatoes contain an organic acid called salicylic acid.

HOW ACIDS BEHAVE

Acids react in certain ways with other substances. For example, they react with most metals to form salts and hydrogen gas. They also react with carbonates to give a salt, carbon dioxide gas and water.

BASES AND ALKALIS

A **base** is the chemical opposite of an acid. A base that can dissolve in water is called an **alkali**. When a base is mixed with an acid, it **neutralizes** (cancels out) the properties of the acid and the reaction produces a salt plus water.

Toothpaste is a base that neutralizes the acids made in your mouth.

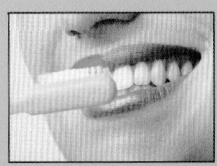

Indigestion tablets contain alkalis that neutralize the acids produced by the stomach.

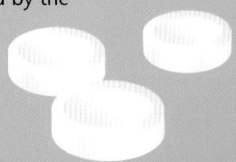

Bases neutralize acids because they contain negative ions, which cancel out the positive hydrogen ions. The oxide ion (O^{2-}) and the hydroxide ion (OH^{-}) are both negative, so metal oxides, such as magnesium oxide, and metal hydroxides, such as sodium hydroxide (caustic soda), are bases.

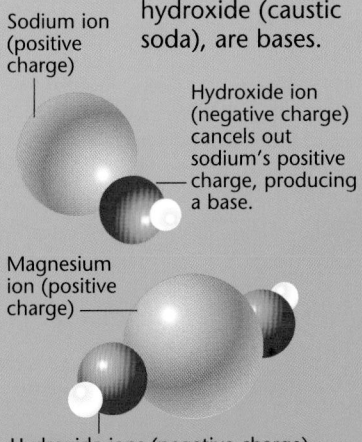

When this wasp stings, it injects an alkali into its victim. If you get stung, you can neutralize the sting with vinegar (an acid).

USING BASES

Many bases and alkalis can be very dangerous as they are **caustic** (dissolve the flesh). Liquid floor cleaners contain alkalis, such as ammonium hydroxide, that dissolve dirt. Sodium hydroxide is used in paper-making to dissolve the resin in wood, leaving the natural fibres of cellulose that are used to make paper.

Sodium hydroxide is also used to make oven cleaners, and mixed with potassium hydroxide to make soap.

See for yourself

To see how an acid and a base react together, pour some vinegar into a glass and add some bicarbonate of soda.

Bicarbonate of soda is a base. It reacts with ethanoic acid in the vinegar to produce sodium ethanoate (a salt), water and carbon dioxide.

As the substances mix, carbon dioxide bubbles out.

Internet links

Go to **www.usborne-quicklinks.com** and type the keyword "science" to find out more about acids and bases.

There you'll find links to websites where you can:

- Test yourself with simple quizzes on acids and alkalis
- Stretch your knowledge with interactive experiments

Go to Usborne Quicklinks for links to hand-picked websites on hundreds of subjects.

pH NUMBERS

The strength of an acid or base can be expressed as a **pH number**. pH stands for "power of hydrogen" and is a measure of the concentration of hydrogen ions in a solution. pH values generally range between 0 and 14. The lower the pH number, the greater the concentration of hydrogen ions. A solution with a pH value of less than 7 is an acid. Substances with a pH value of 7 are neutral and those with pH values higher than 7 are bases or alkalis.

Orange juice has a pH value of 4, so it is a weak acid.

This wasp's sting is a weak alkali with a pH of 9.

INDICATORS

An **indicator** can show whether something is an acid or an alkali. An indicator is a substance that changes colour when it is placed in an acid or an alkali. One indicator, called **litmus**, turns red in an acid and blue in an alkali.

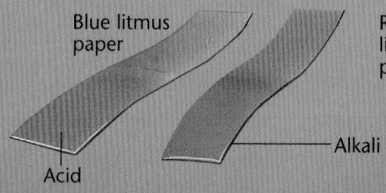

Acids turn blue litmus paper red. Alkalis turn red litmus paper blue.

Litmus is an extract from plant-like organisms called lichens. Some plants, for example hydrangeas and red cabbage, are also natural indicators. Another indicator, called **universal indicator**, is a mixture of several dyes that change colour according to the pH scale, as shown in the picture below.

Pure water is neutral. It has a pH of 7.

Sodium hydroxide, used in household cleaners, is a strong alkali with a pH of 13.

Paper strips containing universal indicator change colour when they touch an acid or alkali. The numbers beside each colour show the pH value.

ACIDS IN THE SOIL

The acidity of the soil depends on the type of rocks from which it is formed and the plants that grow in it. In chalk or limestone areas, the soil is usually alkaline, but in moorlands, sandstone and forested areas, it is more acidic. Acid rain* also adds to the acidity of the soil. Neutral or slightly acid soils with pH values of 6.5 to 7 are the best for farming.

In areas where the soil is too acidic, it can be improved by adding limestone (calcium carbonate) or slaked lime (calcium hydroxide). These are bases that neutralize the acidity.

Some plants, such as azaleas and rhododendrons, grow well in acid soil. Plants such as hydrangeas have blue flowers in acid soils and pink ones in alkaline soils.

Hydrangeas are natural indicators, producing different coloured flowers in acid and alkaline soils.

When leaves die and decompose, they form an acid called humic acid, which adds to the acidity of the soil.

* Acid rain, 65.

SULPHURIC ACID

Sulphuric acid (H_2SO_4) is a chemical used in many different industries. Its main use is in the production of superphosphates and ammonium sulphate for fertilizers. Sulphuric acid is also used in car batteries, and in the manufacture of some synthetic fibres (such as rayon), dyes, plastics, drugs, explosives and detergents.

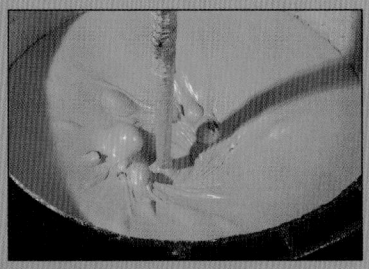

Sulphuric acid is used in the production of titanium oxide, a pigment used to make coloured paint such as this.

Sulphuric acid is a type of **mineral acid**. Mineral acids are made from elements (in this case, sulphur) found as minerals in the Earth's crust.

Here you can see yellow crystals of sulphur produced by a volcano. Sulphur can be collected from volcanic areas and used in the manufacture of sulphuric acid.

Concentrated sulphuric acid is very reactive and highly corrosive. It produces lots of heat when dissolved in water and must always be added to the water, not the other way around. That way, the acid is rapidly diluted and the heat is absorbed by the water.

Concentrated sulphuric acid is a powerful oxidizing agent (it gives oxygen to other substances during oxidation*). It is also a **dehydrating agent** (it removes water that is chemically combined in another substance).

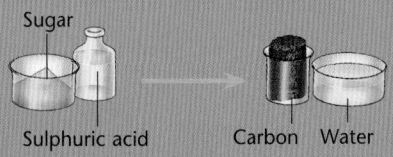

When sugar is warmed with concentrated sulphuric acid, the acid removes water from the sugar, leaving a foamy mass of black carbon and water.

See for yourself

You can do your own tests to see whether something is acidic or alkaline.

First, make an indicator from red cabbage. Chop three large cabbage leaves and boil them in half a litre of water for ten minutes. Cool, strain and pour a little of this indicator into three jars. Add half a teaspoon of bicarbonate of soda to one jar, some vinegar to the second jar and some rainwater to the third jar.

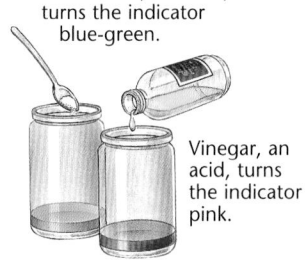

Compare the colour of the rainwater jar to the other two jars.

If the rainwater is acidic, the cabbage water will turn pink when it is added.

Internet links

Go to **www.usborne-quicklinks.com** and type the keyword "science" to find out more about acids and bases.

There you'll find links to websites where you can:

- Discover useful pH information and try some simple experiments
- Use your knowledge to complete online games

Go to Usborne Quicklinks for links to hand-picked websites on hundreds of subjects.

* *Oxidation, 80.*

SALTS

In chemical terms, compounds made of a metal and a non-metal bonded together are **salts**. Many salts occur naturally in the Earth's crust and under the right conditions they form beautiful crystals. Salts have many different uses. For example, anhydrous calcium sulphate, also called **plaster of Paris**, is a salt used in decorative mouldings, model-making and to make protective casts for broken limbs.

Here, plaster of Paris, a salt that sets hard when it is mixed with water, is being used to make a cast of an animal track.

WHAT IS A SALT?

Salts are ionic compounds*, that is, they are made up of ions (particles with an electric charge). Most salts form into regular crystal structures.

Salts are made when the hydrogen ions in an acid are replaced by a metal. For example, when hydrochloric acid and sodium hydroxide (an alkali) react together, sodium replaces the acid's hydrogen ions, creating sodium chloride (a salt) and water. (See picture, above right.)

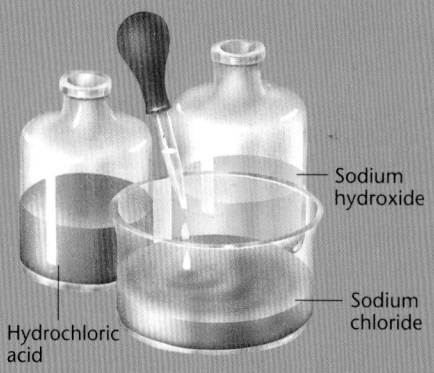

In the picture above, each ingredient of the experiment has had litmus added to it to show whether it is an acid or a base.

SALT FAMILIES

There are several families of salts made with different acids. **Sulphates** are made with sulphuric acid, **chlorides** are made with hydrochloric acid, **nitrates** are made with nitric acid and **carbonates** with carbonic acid.

Bath salts and washing soda are sodium carbonate. They react with magnesium and calcium salts in hard water* to form insoluble particles of calcium carbonate.

Soluble salts are those, such as washing soda, that dissolve in water to form a solution. **Insoluble salts** are ones that do not dissolve in water. Limestone and chalk are made of calcium carbonate, which is an insoluble salt.

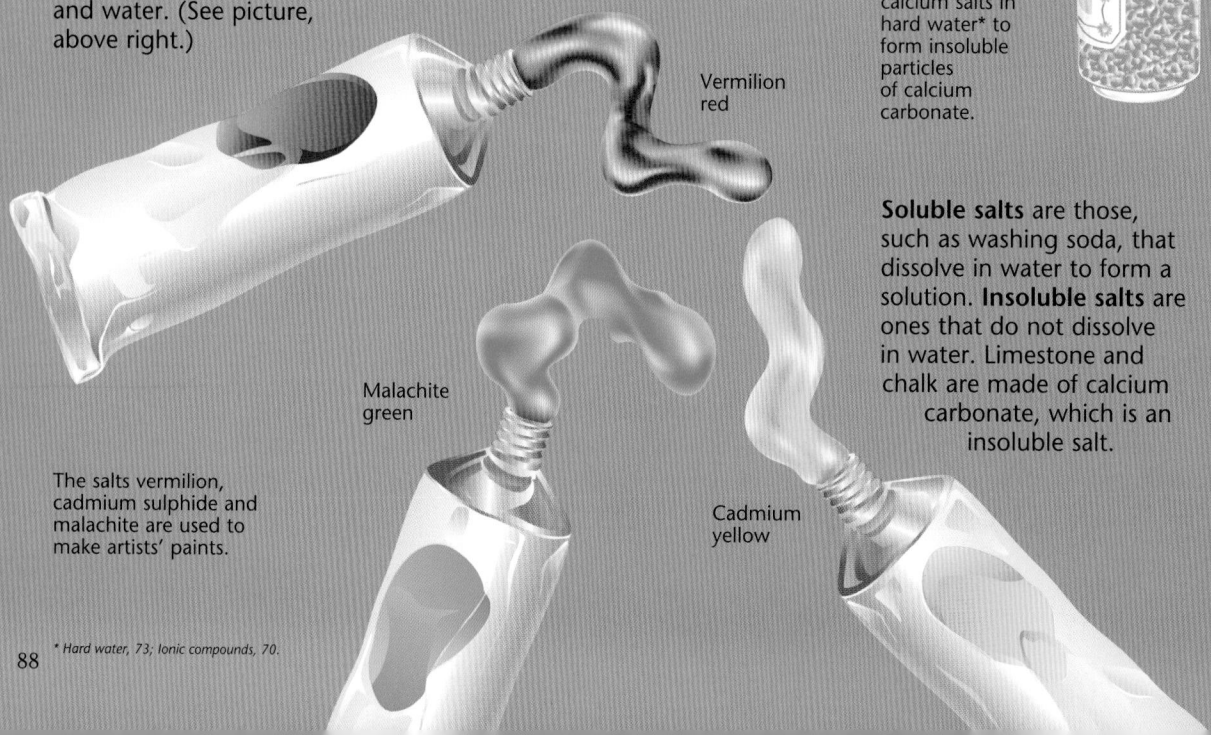

The salts vermilion, cadmium sulphide and malachite are used to make artists' paints.

** Hard water, 73; Ionic compounds, 70.*

SODIUM CHLORIDE

Sodium chloride (NaCl) is the chemical name for common salt. It is a soluble salt. A concentrated solution of sodium chloride in water is called **brine**.

Sodium chloride can be extracted from sea water by evaporation, and it is also found in solid form as **rock salt**, or **halite**. It is used to flavour and preserve food and is essential to animal life.

Sodium chloride is an important raw material and it is used in the manufacture of hydrochloric acid, chlorine, sodium hydroxide (caustic soda) and sodium carbonate (washing soda). It is sprinkled on roads in winter because it lowers the freezing point of water and stops ice from forming.

This picture shows crystals of sea salt, enlarged to hundreds of times their real size.

MAKING SALTS

There are several ways to make salts in the laboratory. Soluble salts can be made by reacting an acid and a metal, or metal oxide (a base).

Copper(II) sulphate is made by adding copper oxide to dilute sulphuric acid.

The mixture is then filtered. The filtrate is a solution of copper(II) sulphate. Unused copper oxide is left in the filter paper.

The solution is heated to remove water, then left to form crystals of copper(II) sulphate.

Insoluble salts are made from two soluble salts that react together to form a **precipitate** (insoluble solid particles) of salt in a solution. The solution is then filtered to remove the precipitate. Salts can also be made by combining two elements. For example, iron sulphide is made by heating iron with sulphur (see page 66).

FERTILIZERS

Fertilizers are nutrients that help plants to grow. Many fertilizers contain salts, such as nitrates, phosphates and potash, that are soluble in water and can be absorbed by plants' roots. Nitrates contain nitrogen, phosphates contain phosphorus, and potash contains potassium salts. All of these are needed for healthy plant growth.

The smaller plant shown here was grown in poor soil. The larger one was grown in fertilized soil.

See for yourself

Crystals of common salt contain water (see Hydration, page 91), but you can turn them powdery just by leaving them on a plate for a few days.

When you leave the crystals in the air the water escapes, leaving a dry powder. Similarly, if you leave the lid off a bottle of bath crystals, these also lose their shape and turn powdery.

Internet links

To find out more about salts, go to **www.usborne-quicklinks.com** and type in the keyword "science".

There you'll find links to websites where you can:

- Discover the practical uses for salts throughout history
- Test your knowledge of salts with an online quiz

Go to Usborne Quicklinks for links to hand-picked websites on hundreds of subjects.

CRYSTALS

When allowed to form slowly, salts and many other substances form crystals. A **crystal** is a solid that has a definite geometrical shape with straight edges and flat surfaces. Most solids, even metals, are made up of crystals but they are so small that you cannot see them. Some of the minerals in the Earth's crust form beautiful crystals, such as diamonds and emeralds.

Pyrite (also called iron pyrites or fools' gold) is a common mineral made of iron and sulphur. Its crystals are often cubic in shape.

HOW CRYSTALS FORM

Some substances form crystals as they cool and solidify. Others crystallize when the water in which they were dissolved evaporates. The shape of the crystals depends on the regular arrangement and bonding of the particles in the substance. Different substances form different shaped crystals. The main crystal shapes are shown in the picture below.

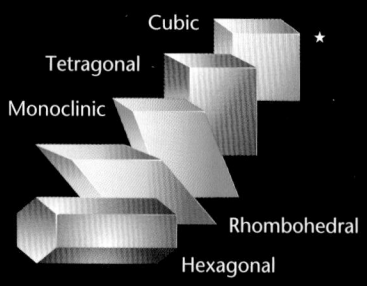

SPLITTING CRYSTALS

The boundaries between the particles in a crystal are called **cleavage planes**. Crystals split along these planes, leaving the flat surfaces of the crystal exposed. If a crystal is not split along a cleavage plane, it will shatter.

Natural emerald embedded in limestone

The emerald set in this ring has been split along its cleavage planes to make a beautiful gem.

LIQUID CRYSTALS

Liquid crystals are crystals that become cloudy when heated. They are used in **liquid crystal displays** (**LCDs**) in watches, calculators and televisions.

When an electric current is passed through the crystals, their molecules line up and block the light, creating the pattern of the display. LCD TV screens contain many thousands of tiny crystal units. They build up the moving pictures that you see by flashing on and off very quickly.

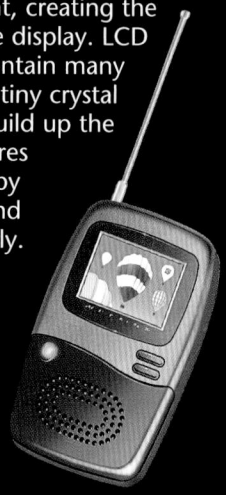

This handheld digital television has a liquid crystal display.

Calcite crystals can be ground up to make cement.

Amethyst crystals form from the mineral quartz.

Crystals of apatite. This substance is also found in teeth.

HYDRATION

Hydration occurs when a substance combines with water. The substance is said to be **hydrated**. Many salts combine and chemically bond with water to form crystals. The water is then known as **water of crystallization**.

Hydrated copper(II) sulphate crystals ($CuSO_4.5H_2O$) form when copper(II) sulphate ($CuSO_4$) bonds with water (H_2O).

This crystal is halite. It was formed by the evaporation of sea water thousands of years ago.

In a crystal, the water is chemically bonded with the atoms of the substance, unlike in a solution where the atoms of the substance are mixed but not bonded with the molecules of water. Water can be made to separate from a hydrated solid by heating the solid. This is called **dehydration**.

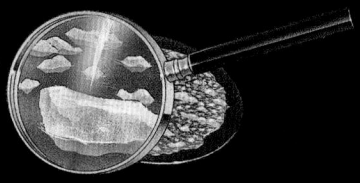

If you heat washing soda ($Na_2CO_3.10H_2O$) crystals, the water of crystallization separates off, and a solution of washing soda is formed.

Dehydration can also be carried out using a **dehydrating agent**, such as sulphuric acid.

White, anhydrous copper(II) sulphate powder goes blue when water is added. It can be used to test for the presence of water.

The dry solid which results from dehydration is said to be **anhydrous**.

See for yourself

You can grow a crystal using **alum** (a sulphate of potassium and aluminium). It will take about three weeks to grow. You can buy alum from a pharmacist. Alum can be harmful if eaten, so remember to wash your hands after touching it.

1. Gently warm 100g of alum in 500ml of water over a low heat until it dissolves, then add more alum until no more will dissolve.

2. Pour a little of this saturated solution into a saucer and leave it for three days. Keep the rest of the solution in a clean, covered jar.

3. When crystals appear on the saucer, tie a thread around one and suspend it in the solution in the jar. This crystal is called the **seed crystal**. The solution will slowly crystallize around it.

Seed crystal on saucer

QUARTZ CRYSTALS

Quartz crystals are crystals of the mineral quartz that form in the Earth's crust. When a current of electricity is passed through a quartz crystal, it vibrates 32,768 times a second. This is called the **piezoelectric effect**. The vibrations can be used to measure time in clocks and watches.

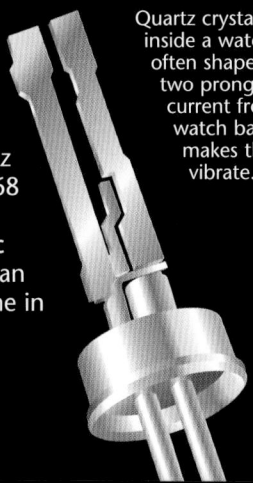

Quartz crystals inside a watch are often shaped into two prongs. The current from the watch battery makes them vibrate.

Internet links

Go to **www.usborne-quicklinks.com** and type in the keyword "science" to find out more about crystals.

There you'll find links to websites where you can:

- Discover how to grow your own crystals
- See beautiful photos of crystals
- Find out how to identify minerals

Go to Usborne Quicklinks for links to hand-picked websites on hundreds of subjects.

ORGANIC CHEMISTRY

Organic chemistry is the study of compounds of carbon, called **organic compounds**. All living things contain organic compounds, and many can be made artificially. They are used to create fabrics, medicines, plastics, paints, cosmetics and many other products.

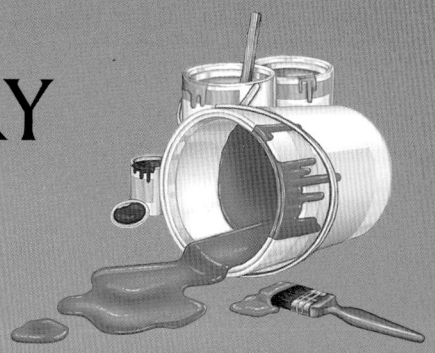

Paints contain organic compounds.

ORGANIC COMPOUNDS

Organic compounds are made up of carbon atoms bonded to atoms of other elements such as hydrogen and oxygen. The atoms are held together by strong covalent bonds (see right). Compounds that contain only carbon and hydrogen atoms are called **hydrocarbons**.

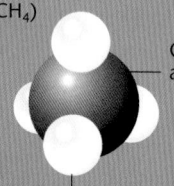

Organic compounds are grouped in families called **homologous series**. For example, alkanes and alkenes (see pages 96-97) are two homologous series. Each series contains hundreds of compounds, with increasing numbers of carbon and hydrogen atoms in their molecules.

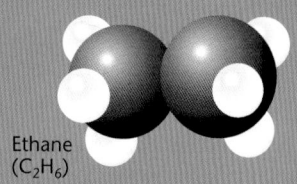

Here are models of molecules of the first three compounds in the alkane series. **Methane** has one carbon atom, **ethane** has two and **propane** has three.

The names of compounds with molecules containing one carbon atom start with "meth". Those with molecules containing two carbon atoms start with "eth" and those with three carbon atoms begin with "prop". The compounds in each homologous series have the same chemical properties, but their physical properties change from gas to liquid to solid as the molecules increase in size.

The dyes used on these ballet shoes are made from an organic compound called **aniline**, which is found in coal tar.

COVALENT BONDS

Covalent bonds (see page 69) are the strong links between atoms that share electrons in their outer shells.

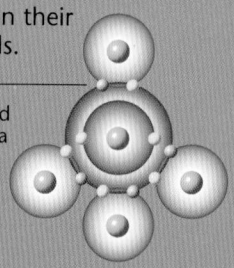

Each carbon atom can form single bonds with four other atoms, or it can form double, or even triple bonds. In **single bonds**, each pair of atoms shares one pair of electrons, in **double bonds** they share two and in **triple bonds** they share three pairs of electrons. In diagrams of organic molecules, the bonds are usually shown as sticks between the atoms.

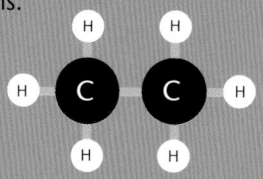

Single covalent bond in ethane, an alkane

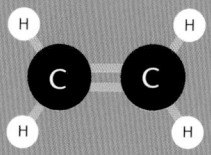

Double covalent bond in ethene, an alkene

Carbon atoms can join together to form long chains or rings which makes a huge number of organic compounds possible.

UNSATURATED

Organic compounds with double or triple bonds are described as **unsaturated**. They have bonds that can open up and join with other atoms without the original molecules breaking up. When this happens, the type of reaction that takes place is called an **addition reaction**.

Unsaturated compounds are more reactive than saturated compounds (see right).

An addition reaction

When ethene reacts with bromine, its double bonds open up, making space for bromine atoms.

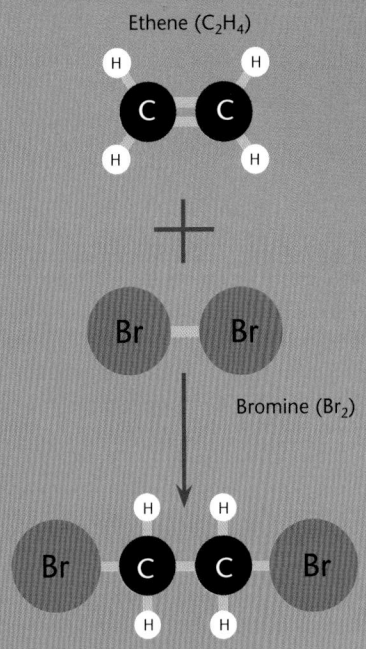

1,2-dibromoethane (CH_2BrCH_2Br)

$$C_2H_4 + Br_2 \longrightarrow CH_2BrCH_2Br$$

Ethene and bromine react to form 1,2-dibromoethane, which is used in insecticides and rat poisons.

SATURATED

Organic compounds with single bonds are said to be **saturated**, or "full up", as they have no free bonds to join with other atoms.

When saturated organic compounds react with other compounds, the bonds in their molecules break open and some of their atoms are replaced by different atoms. This is called a **substitution reaction**. For example, dichlorodifluoromethane (CCl_2F_2) is made by replacing the hydrogen atoms in methane (CH_4) with chlorine (Cl) and fluorine (F).

$$CH_4 + 2Cl_2 + 2F_2 \longrightarrow CCl_2F_2 + 2HF + 2HCl$$

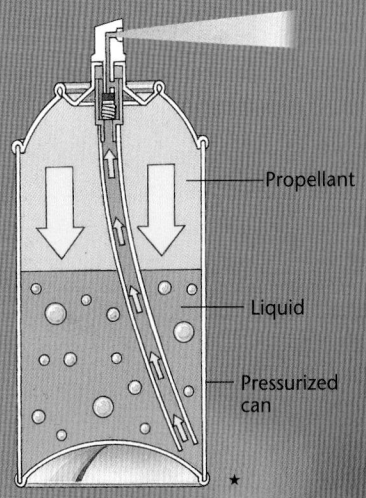

Cutaway drawing of an aerosol spray-can.

Aerosol propellants used to be made of dichlorodifluoromethane, but this is a chlorofluorocarbon (a chlorine-fluorine-carbon compound) and damages the atmosphere. Other propellants are now used in aerosols.

SYNTHETIC COMPOUNDS

By studying the way different organic compounds react, chemists have been able to synthesize (copy) substances that occur naturally, and make them in laboratories. Chemists have also created completely new, artificial organic compounds.

Chemists make vitamin tablets by synthesizing (copying) the structure of vitamins, which are naturally occurring organic compounds.

Tablet containers like these are called blister packs. They are made from artificial organic compounds such as PVC (polyvinylchloride).

Internet links

Go to **www.usborne-quicklinks.com** and type in the keyword "science" to find out more about organic chemistry and compounds.

There you'll find links to websites where you can:

- Find a simple introduction to organic chemistry
- Examine 3-D molecular models

Go to Usborne Quicklinks for links to hand-picked websites on hundreds of subjects.

ALCOHOLS

Alcohols are organic compounds that contain carbon, oxygen and hydrogen. They are a **homologous series**, that is, a group of compounds with the same chemical properties.

The oxygen and hydrogen atoms in an alcohol molecule form a **hydroxyl group** that gives the alcohols their special properties.

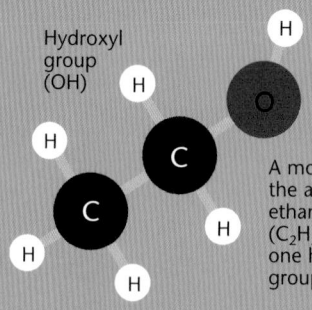

A molecule of the alcohol ethanol (C_2H_5OH) has one hydroxyl group.

In industry, an alcohol called **ethanol** (C_2H_5OH) is made by fermentation (see below), or by reacting ethene (C_2H_4) with steam:

$$C_2H_4 + H_2O \longrightarrow C_2H_5OH$$

Ethanol is used as a solvent* for paints, varnishes and perfumes. Drinks such as wine and beer contain ethanol.

FERMENTATION

Fermentation is a chemical reaction that has been used for thousands of years to produce alcoholic drinks. It is now an important industrial process for producing the alcohol ethanol.

Yeast, a fungus, causes fermentation. It produces **enzymes** – catalysts that speed up chemical reactions in living things. These convert the sugars in fruit or grain into ethanol and carbon dioxide.

ORGANIC ACIDS

Organic compounds that are acidic are called **organic acids**. They behave like typical acids, turning litmus paper red and forming salts when they react with bases.

Organic acids can be made by oxidizing (adding oxygen to) alcohols. Vinegar has been made for thousands of years by allowing wine, which contains the alcohol ethanol, to oxidize and form ethanoic acid.

TYPES OF ORGANIC ACID

Ethanoic acid, which gives vinegar its sour taste, and **methanoic acid**, the poison in the sting of some ants, are organic acids. They belong to a group called **carboxylic acids**.

Carboxylic acids contained in natural oils and fats are called **fatty acids**.

Coconut oil contains a fatty acid called lauric acid or dodecanoic acid.

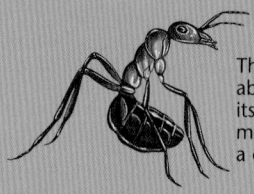

This ant is about to squirt its poison of methanoic acid, a carboxylic acid.

Ethanoic acid is used in the manufacture of polyester. This can be spun very fine and dyed to make sewing threads.

DETERGENT

A **detergent** is a substance that enables water to remove dirt. Detergents reduce the attraction between the water molecules so the water spreads easily over the washing. It is this loss of attraction between the molecules that allows stretchy bubbles to form on the water.

Without detergent, water molecules will not stretch apart very well. Any bubbles that form will pop within seconds.

Soap is a type of detergent made from vegetable oils, which contain fatty acids. When the oils are boiled with sodium hydroxide, an alkali, the acids react with the alkali to produce a salt, which is soap.

How detergents work

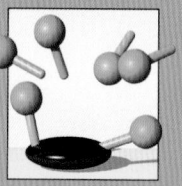

Detergents are made of ions* that have a charge at one end. This end is attracted to water. The other end (the tail) is attracted to grease.

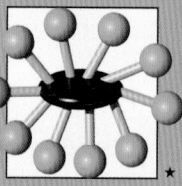

The tails attach themselves to grease and form a bridge between the water and the grease. Their attraction to water pulls the grease away from the washing.

Soapless detergents work in the same way as soap. However, they are unaffected by the minerals in hard water*, which react with the soap to form a scum.

* *Solvent, 58.*

See for yourself

To see a detergent at work, sprinkle some talcum powder over the surface of a bowl of water. The talc will settle on the water's surface.

Now drip a drop of washing-up liquid (a detergent) into the middle of the bowl and watch.

The detergent reduces the water's pulling power near where it lands, but not further away. As a result, the talc is pulled outwards by the water with the greater pulling power.

ESTERS

When carboxylic acids react with alcohols, they produce compounds called **esters**, and water. Esters give fruit and flowers their flavours and smells. **Fats** and **oils** are esters made from propan-1,2,3-triol (an alcohol known as **glycerol**) combined with fatty acids.

This picture shows how esters from a rose are dispersed into the air. The metal devices are used to measure the strength of the scent. The areas containing most esters are shown in pink.

Internet links

Go to **www.usborne-quicklinks.com** and type in the keyword "science" to find out more about organic chemistry.

There you'll find links to websites where you can:

- Try out some soapy activities
- Find out how organic chemicals are used in everyday life

Go to Usborne Quicklinks for links to hand-picked websites on hundreds of subjects.

** Hard water, 73; Ions, 70.*

ALKANES AND ALKENES

Alkanes are found in the Earth's crust in crude oil and natural gas, and many are used as fuels. Alkenes are not found naturally in great quantities and are obtained by breaking up large alkane molecules. They are both homologous series of hydrocarbons (see *Organic Compounds*, page 92).

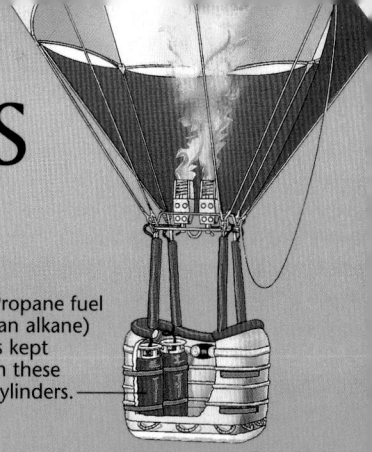

The alkane propane is used as a fuel to heat the air in hot-air balloons.

ALKANES

Alkanes are a homologous series of saturated compounds. This means that their carbon atoms are held together by single covalent bonds*.

All alkane names end in "ane". Those with small molecules, such as methane, are gases, but those with larger ones are liquids. Alkanes with more than 16 carbon atoms are solids.

USES OF ALKANES

Alkanes burn easily and many are used as fuels. Petrol is a mixture of alkanes, and propane and butane are used in caravans and camping stoves, stored under pressure as liquids in portable cylinders.

Alkanes are used to make many other organic chemicals. For example, the hydrogen atoms in methane can be replaced with chlorine and fluorine to make compounds called **chlorofluorocarbons** (**CFCs**). Many chlorofluorocarbons are no longer used, though, as they are thought to harm the atmosphere.

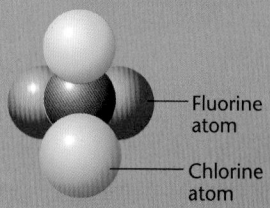

The molecule above is dichlorodifluoromethane, a CFC. It was once widely used as a coolant in refrigerators and in car air conditioning systems.

Methane, the main compound in natural gas, is used as a fuel for cooking and heating.

Aircraft use kerosene, a mixture of alkanes, for fuel. It is produced by the purification of petroleum.

Enormous amounts of fuel are used by jet planes. A Boeing 747 can carry over 215,000 litres. It uses the fuel at a rate of about 11 litres per kilometre.

Kerosene is an ideal fuel for a jet engine because, unlike some other fuels, it burns well in the freezing temperatures of high altitudes.

* *Covalent bonds, 92.*

ALKENES

Alkenes are a homologous series of hydrocarbons whose molecules contain some double covalent bonds (see page 93). The names of the compounds in this series end in "ene". Ethene (C_2H_4) is the first alkene. There is no alkene beginning with "meth" (see page 92) as all alkenes must have at least two carbon atoms to form a double bond.

The diagrams below show molecules of the first two compounds in the alkene series.

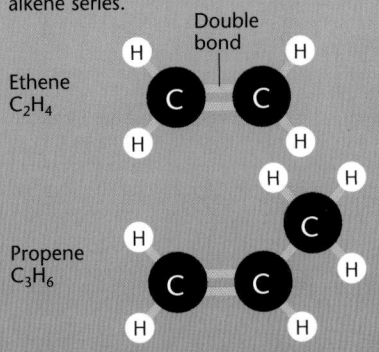

Alkenes are unsaturated* compounds and are more reactive than alkanes. Each carbon atom can give up one of its double bonds to other atoms in an addition reaction* without the molecules breaking open. Alkenes are used in industry to make plastics, such as polythene, by joining many molecules together.

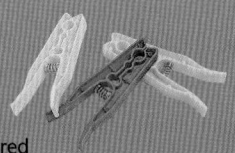

Plastic clothes pegs. Plastics are manufactured by addition reactions, using molecules of compounds such as ethene.

Racing cars are made of a very strong, rigid material called Kevlar®, which is plastic reinforced with synthetic fibres. It is much lighter than metal.

HYDROGENATION

Hydrogenation is an addition reaction* in which atoms of hydrogen are added to unsaturated* molecules, such as those of alkenes, to fill up the double covalent bonds. The new compounds are saturated* as they contain only single covalent bonds.

Ethene and hydrogen react together to form ethane. The hydrogen fills up the spare bonds in the double covalent bond.

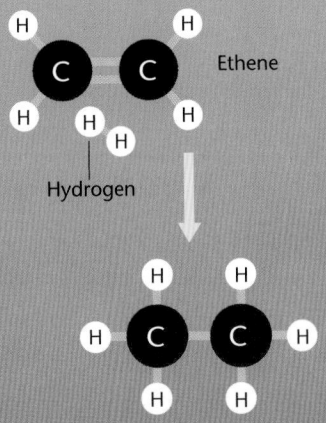

Ethane is an alkane and it is a saturated compound.

Food scientists use hydrogenation to make margarines from certain vegetable oils, such as olive oil. These oils contain alkenes.

To create the margarine, hydrogen is forced through the oil while it is hot and pressurized. Some bonds break open and the hydrogen atoms attach to the newly available bonds. This causes the runny oil to become more solid.

Peanut oils consist of alkanes. They are used to make margarines.

The more hydrogenated vegetable oil becomes, the harder it is to spread.

See for yourself

Watch out for advertisements for margarines. There is a strong chance that the manufacturers will claim that their product is the "healthy" alternative to butter.

This is because margarines contain more unsaturated compounds than butter (which consists mostly of saturated compounds).

Scientists think that saturated compounds are bad for you, since your body converts them into a type of cholesterol that can clog up your blood vessels. The unsaturated compounds in many margarines don't do this.

Internet links

Go to **www.usborne-quicklinks.com** and type "science" to find out about alkanes, alkenes and hydrogenation.

There you'll find links to websites where you can:

- See how CFCs harm the atmosphere
- Discover some of the uses for hydrocarbons

Go to Usborne Quicklinks for links to hand-picked websites on hundreds of subjects.

The links at Usborne Quicklinks are regularly reviewed and updated, so you might find a slightly different selection of websites from the ones shown here.

** Addition reactions, Saturated, Unsaturated, 93.*

CRUDE OIL

Crude oil is the raw material from which fuels such as heating oil, petrol and gas are obtained, as well as many different chemicals for industry. It is a mixture of hydrocarbons, which are organic compounds made only of carbon and hydrogen. The different compounds in the mixture are separated in oil refineries by a process called fractional distillation.

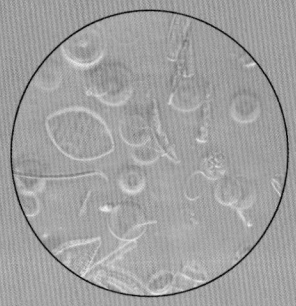

The microscopic organisms from which oil formed were similar to these plankton that live in the sea today.

HOW OIL AND GAS FORMED

Crude oil and natural gas are **fossil fuels**. They formed from the bodies of microscopic organisms that lived in the sea millions of years ago. When the organisms died, their bodies sank to the bottom of the sea and became buried in sand and mud. As the layers of sand and mud built up and became rock, the minute organisms rotted and formed oil and gas.

Oil platforms like this one are used to drill for deposits under the seabed.

OIL FROM UNDER THE SEA

Nearly a third of all oil supplies are found under the seabed. The oil and gas are contained in pockets, called **reservoirs**, which are found in porous layers of rock. These reservoirs can be hundreds of metres below the seabed.

To extract the oil, giant oil platforms, like the one on the left, are built out at sea. Wells are drilled down from the seabed into the reservoirs. Oil is piped up to the platform from the reservoirs.

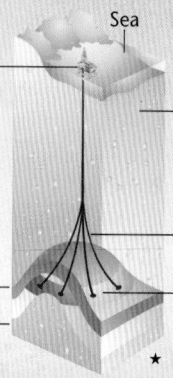

This picture shows four separate wells which have been drilled down from one platform.

Drill pipes

FRACTIONAL DISTILLATION

Fractional distillation is a process by which substances in a mixture can be separated by boiling. In an oil refinery, crude oil is heated until the compounds become gases at about 340°C. The gases are piped into a tower called a **fractionating column**. As they rise up the tower, they cool, condense (become liquids again) and are collected.

Fractionating columns at an oil refinery

The compounds with the largest, heaviest molecules condense first and are collected near the bottom of the tower. Compounds with smaller, lighter molecules have lower boiling points, so they rise higher up the tower before they condense. The mixture of compounds that condense at each level is called a **fraction**.

Fractionating column

Below 0°C

Refinery gases
1-4 carbon atoms per molecule. Used as fuels for heating and cooking.

110°C

Gasoline compounds
5-12 carbon atoms per molecule. Used for petrol and for making medicines, plastics, paints and chemicals.

180°C

Kerosene compounds
9-15 carbon atoms per molecule. Used for heating, lighting and jet fuels.

260°C

Diesel oils
12-25 carbon atoms per molecule. Used as fuels for trucks and trains.

500°C

Residue compounds
20-40 carbon atoms per molecule. Used for heating oil, candle waxes, polishes, lubricants and bitumen for surfacing roads.

Furnace where crude oil is heated until it boils and the compounds become gases.

CRACKING

Cracking is a method by which compounds with large molecules, such as decane, an alkane*, are converted to compounds with smaller molecules that are more useful and can be used as fuels or in the chemicals industry.

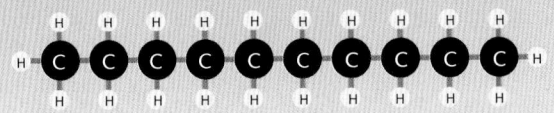

Decane ($C_{10}H_{22}$)

When heated and mixed with steam and a catalyst*, the large molecules break up to make smaller, lighter molecules.

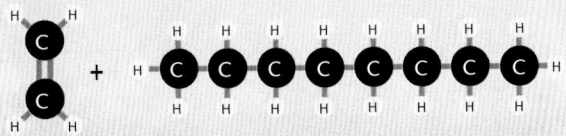

Ethene (C_2H_4) + Octane (C_8H_{18})

Internet links

To find out more about crude oil, go to **www.usborne-quicklinks.com** and type in the keyword "science".

There you'll find links to websites where you can:

- Find out where oil comes from
- Explore an oil rig
- See an oil refinery in action

Go to Usborne Quicklinks for links to hand-picked websites on hundreds of subjects.

** Alkanes, 96; Catalyst, 79.*

POLYMERS AND PLASTICS

Polymers are substances made of many small molecules joined together to make long chains. Plastics and synthetic fibres, such as **nylon**, are polymers made from chemicals found in crude oil. As well as these synthetic polymers, there are natural polymers, such as rubber, starch, wool and silk – and the hair on your head.

Plastic balls are made by pouring molten polymers into a mould. As they cool, the shape solidifies.

MAKING PLASTICS

Plastics are easily-moulded synthetic polymers made from the organic compounds found in crude oil. Many plastics, such as polythene, PVC and polystyrene, are made using ethene, which belongs to the group of organic compounds called alkenes*.

PVC drinks bottles are light and shatterproof.

Polythene can be made into thin sheets for wrapping food.

Polythene and polystyrene can be moulded to make things such as cups.

See for yourself

To make your own polymer, put a tablespoon of water in a cup with a teaspoon of egg white and a teaspoon of baking soda, and mix well. Then sprinkle a teaspoon of citric acid into the mixture and swirl it around.

The baking soda reacts with the citric acid, producing bubbles of carbon dioxide gas, turning the mixture into a foam. As this happens, monomers in the egg white bond together to form a polymer.

Don't eat the polymer – it may upset your stomach.

POLYMERIZATION

Joining molecules together to make polymers is called **polymerization**. The small molecules that make up polymers are called **monomers**.

For example, using heat, pressure and catalysts*, monomers of ethene are made to react together. Ethene has double bonds which open up and the carbon atoms join together to form long chains that are giant molecules of **polythene**.

Different plastics can be made by changing some of the atoms in the monomers. For example, by replacing a hydrogen atom in ethene with an atom of chlorine, chloroethene monomers are made. Long chains of these form **PVC** (polyvinylchloride).

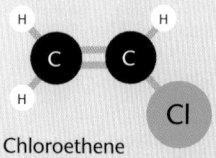

Chloroethene

Making polythene

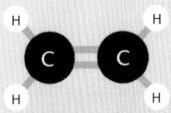

Each monomer of ethene (C_2H_4) contains two atoms of carbon joined by a double bond.

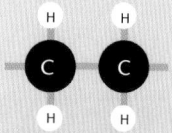

The double bond opens up to form bonds with other monomers to build the polymer.

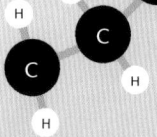

A giant molecule of polythene contains up to 20,000 atoms of carbon.

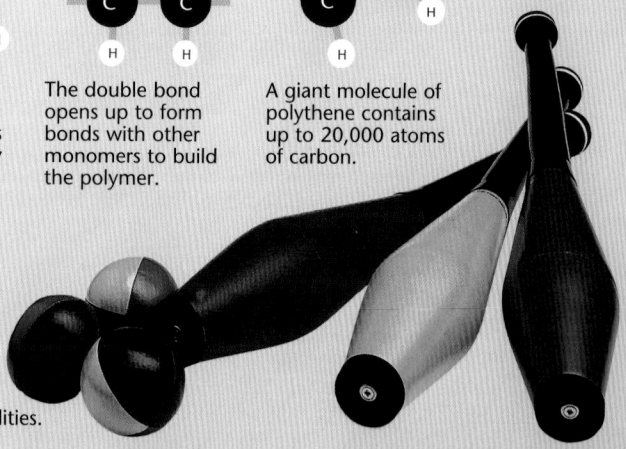

PVC is light, hardwearing and can be dyed easily. This juggling equipment makes use of all these qualities.

* *Alkenes, 97; Catalysts, 79.*

TYPES OF PLASTIC

Plastics can be divided into two groups. **Thermoplastics** can be melted and used again, while **thermosetting plastics** can be moulded only once.

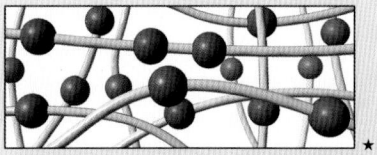

In thermoplastics, the polymer chains are not linked together.

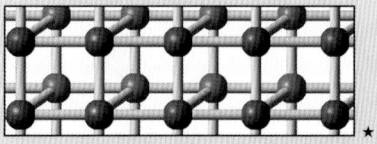

In thermosetting plastics the polymers are linked firmly together.

Thermoplastics are flexible but they are not heat resistant. Polythene, polystyrene, nylon and polyester fabrics are thermoplastics. These types of plastic are widely recycled.

Fibres for clothing can be made from recycled thermoplastics.

Thermosetting plastics have a rigid structure and are hard and heat resistant. Melamine, from which mugs, plates and kitchen work surfaces are made, is a thermosetting plastic.

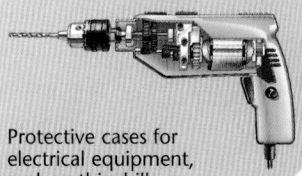

Protective cases for electrical equipment, such as this drill, are often made from thermoplastics reinforced with glass fibre. They are strong, light and do not conduct electricity.

SYNTHETIC FIBRES

Some plastics can be drawn out to make fibres. Nylon, polyester and acrylic are three different types of plastic used to make fibres. They can be spun and woven, often together with natural fibres such as wool and cotton, to make clothes, carpets, ropes and strong fabrics for sails and parachutes.

This swimmer's costume is made from a strong, lightweight, flexible synthetic fibre. The material doesn't hold water, so it won't become heavy when wet.

Synthetic fibres are stronger and lighter than natural fibres such as wool and cotton. They can also be drawn out to make very long threads, unlike most natural fibres that have to be spun to make long lengths.

This picture shows a microscopic view of nylon fibres in a stocking. Nylon is a plastic made by reacting carboxylic acids and amine.

NATURAL POLYMERS

Not all polymers are synthetic. Before the invention of plastics, natural polymers such as wool and plant fibres (such as cotton and jute) were used for weaving. Like plastics, natural polymers are chains of simple molecules. The proteins in your body are also natural polymers.

Rubber is made from a natural polymer called **latex**, a milky fluid that seeps out of the bark of rubber trees. Rubber is strengthened by heating it with sulphur. This is called **vulcanized rubber** and is used mainly for making tyres.

Latex is a natural polymer produced by rubber trees. It is collected in pots that are nailed to the sides of the trees. It is used to make tough, waterproof items such as wellington boots.

Internet links

To find out more about plastics, go to **www.usborne-quicklinks.com** and type in the keyword "science".

There you'll find links to websites where you can:

- Find out all about plastics
- Discover fascinating polymer facts
- Try out experiments with plastics

Go to Usborne Quicklinks for links to hand-picked websites on hundreds of subjects.

The links at Usborne Quicklinks are regularly reviewed and updated, so you might find a slightly different selection of websites from the ones shown here.

USING PLASTICS

Plastics are extremely versatile. They have been developed to the point where they are now used to make all sorts of different appliances, toys, tools and gadgets. Here are some examples of common plastics, along with examples of how they are used.

Plastics don't conduct electricity, so they are used as a protective covering for things that do, such as computer cables.

THE FIRST PLASTICS

The first plastics were made over 150 years ago. After early experiments, celluloid and then Bakelite were developed. Early in the twentieth century, Bakelite was used to make equipment such as radios and telephones.

Bakelite is heavy, so lighter plastics were developed to take its place.

This mobile phone has a lightweight case made from polypropene.

A 1930s telephone made from Bakelite

POLYTHENE

Polythene was first made in the 1930s. It can be made into thick, chunky shapes, or drawn out into very thin sheets.

Polythene is used to make many different things, from tough buckets to lightweight carrier bags.

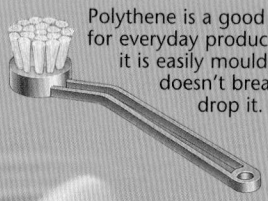

Polythene is a good material for everyday products because it is easily moulded and doesn't break if you drop it.

Polythene is waterproof so it is good for moulding into bath toys such as these ducks.

These polythene ducks are safe for children. Some plastics, though, are never used for toys because they can give off poisonous chemicals if chewed.

See for yourself

Most products have some plastic parts, or plastic in the packaging. Look around you now. You will probably see many different types of plastics.

POLYSTYRENE

Polystyrene is a plastic which sets firm. It can be made into lightweight foam which is a very good insulator. It is used for packaging food and fragile equipment.

COMPOSITES

Many modern plastics can be combined to make even stronger materials called **composites**. These are used in spacecraft, aircraft, car components and sports goods as they are much stronger and lighter than more traditional materials.

Windsurfing boards are made of plastics reinforced with carbon or synthetic fibres.

Sails made of plastic fibre called Mylar® are extremely strong and light.

This remotely operated vehicle is used for underwater filming and gathering samples. It is made from plastics, which do not corrode.

Transparent, shatterproof PVC covering for video camera.

PLASTICS IN SPACE

Since space exploration began in the 1950s, lots of research has been done into finding new, lightweight, tough fabrics to protect astronauts. This has resulted in the invention of new plastics, such as those mentioned below.

Space suits contain eight or nine layers of plastic fabrics that can resist extremes of cold and heat.

Outer surface of the suit, made of super-strong plastic fibre called Kevlar®.

Inner suit of polyurethane-coated nylon mixed with polyester fibre.

Layers of a plastic fabric called Mylar® insulate against the cold.

PLASTIC PROTECTION

Plastics can be both strong enough to resist impact and light enough to wear, making them ideal for protective headgear.

American Football helmets are made of polycarbonate.

The steel face mask is coated with polyvinyl.

Helmets for racing drivers are made of thermosetting plastic reinforced with Kevlar®. The gloves are made of a fire-resistant plastic called Nomex®.

Internet links

To find out more about plastics, go to **www.usborne-quicklinks.com** and type in the keyword "science".

There you'll find links to websites where you can:

- Explore a museum of plastics
- Make your own virtual plastic

ENERGY, FORCES AND MOTION

ENERGY

Without energy, nothing could live or grow, and there would be no movement, light, heat or noise. Energy can take many different forms: heat, light and sound are all different forms of energy. For anything to happen, energy is needed, and whenever anything happens, energy is converted from one form to another.

The energy from the Sun is about equal to that supplied by one million million million large power stations.

FORMS OF ENERGY

Energy can exist in many forms and the different forms make different things happen. As well as heat, light and sound, there are other forms such as chemical energy, kinetic energy and potential energy.

Chemical energy is energy that is released during chemical reactions. Batteries, food, and fuels such as coal, oil and petrol, are stores of chemical energy.

The energy used to move this hammer comes from food eaten and stored in the body of the person using the hammer. Chemical energy is released from the food by reactions in the body cells.

Potential energy is the energy an object has because it is in a position where it is affected by a force, such as magnetism* or gravity*. Objects that can be stretched or squashed, such as elastic bands and springs, have **elastic potential energy** or **strain energy**.

The higher the hammer, the greater its potential energy.

Moving objects have **kinetic energy**, the energy of movement. The faster something moves, the more kinetic energy it has. As it slows down, it loses kinetic energy.

The moving hammer transfers kinetic energy to the nail, which moves into the wood.

* *Gravity, 130; Magnetism, 232.*

ENERGY CONVERSION

The **law of conservation of energy** states that energy can never be created or destroyed. Whenever anything happens, energy is converted into a different form. This is what happens, for example, when plants use energy from sunlight to make food, and when animals eat them in turn.

Example of energy conversion

1. Plant uses energy from sunlight to make food.

2. Plant stores food as chemical energy.

3. Hummingbird feeds on plant. Chemical energy is converted to kinetic energy and some heat energy when bird moves.

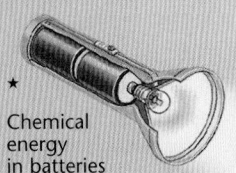

★ Chemical energy in batteries is changed to electrical energy in a flashlight.

Electrical energy is changed to light and heat energy in the bulb.

ENERGY CHAINS

An **energy chain** is a way of showing how energy is converted from one form to another. The pictures on the right show the energy changes that take place in a power station, where the chemical energy in coal is converted into electrical energy.

A coal-fired power station

The final forms in most energy chains are heat and light. Even this energy is not lost, but it spreads out into the environment and is very difficult to harness for any useful purpose.

Energy conversion in a power station

Coal is the fossilized remains of plants that grew long ago. It is a chemical store of energy that came originally from the Sun.

When the coal is burned, the chemical energy is converted to heat energy, which is used to heat water to make steam.

The steam turns turbines*. This produces kinetic energy – the energy of movement.

The kinetic energy is converted to electrical energy in a device called a **generator**.

Appliances such as lamps, televisions, heaters and audio equipment convert electrical energy into light, heat and sound. ★

See for yourself

In this matchbox paddle-boat, the elastic potential energy stored by a twisted elastic band is changed into kinetic energy that moves the boat forwards.

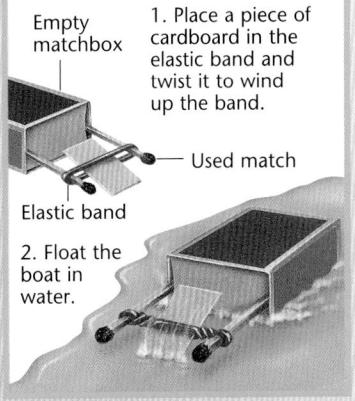

Internet links

To find out more about energy, go to **www.usborne-quicklinks.com** and type in the keyword "science".

There you'll find links to websites where you can:

- Learn about types of energy
- Explore a virtual power plant
- Play energy games

Go to Usborne Quicklinks for links to hand-picked websites on hundreds of subjects.

* *Turbines, 147.*

ENERGY RESOURCES

Energy is used to heat and light houses, to cook food and provide the power for factories and cars. This energy can be obtained by burning fuels, or by harnessing the power of, say, the wind, the Sun, or moving water.

This wind turbine uses the power of the wind to provide energy. The turning motion of the massive blades is transformed into electricity in a generator, which is in a box just behind the blades.

About half the people of the world burn wood, dung or charcoal to provide the energy that they need for cooking and heating.

Oil, coal, wood and natural gas are called **non-renewable fuels** because they can be used only once. Other sources of energy, such as the Sun, wind and water, are called **renewable energy resources** because they generate power without being used up themselves.

ENERGY USAGE

The pie chart below shows the percentages of the different power resources that are used to provide energy for homes and industry.

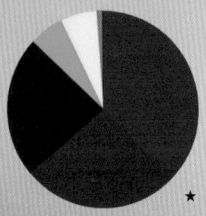

- Oil 37%
- Coal 27%
- Gas 23%
- Nuclear energy 6%
- Hydroelectric power 6%
- Other renewables 1%

FOSSIL FUELS

Here you can see the fossilized remains of a prehistoric plant in a lump of coal.

Coal, oil and natural gas are called **fossil fuels** because they formed from the fossilized remains of plants or animals. Over 25% of the world's energy comes from coal. When fossil fuels burn, they release carbon dioxide and other gases into the air and they are partly to blame for problems such as acid rain* and the greenhouse effect*.

RENEWABLE ENERGY

Only about 7% of the world's energy comes from renewable energy resources, and yet the world's oil supplies are running out. Renewable energy also produces far less carbon dioxide than fossil fuels.

Hydroelectric power

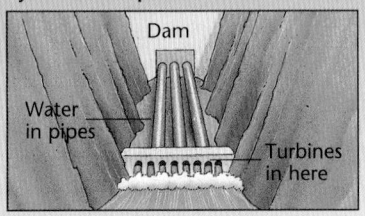

Water stored behind a dam is released through pipes. As it gushes down, it turns turbines, which generate electricity. This is hydroelectric power.

Biofuel

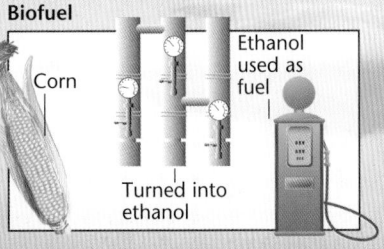

Biofuel is fuel that can be made from fermented* corn or sugar cane. But the process of land clearing, farming and transporting produces carbon dioxide.

* Acid rain, Greenhouse effect, 65; Nuclear energy, 116, Fermentation, 94.

SOLAR ENERGY

Energy from the Sun is called **solar energy**. It consists of heat and light energy, both of which move in the form of electromagnetic waves*. It can be used to produce electricity with a device called a **solar cell**, or to heat water using **solar collectors**.

In a solar collector, heat from the Sun is absorbed by the black absorber panel, which heats the water in the pipes.

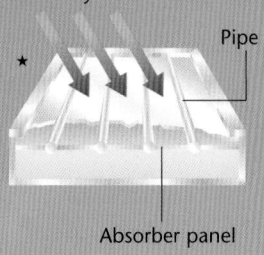

Cutaway diagram of a roof with a solar heating system. The hot water is for domestic use, such as washing, and also for the central heating system.

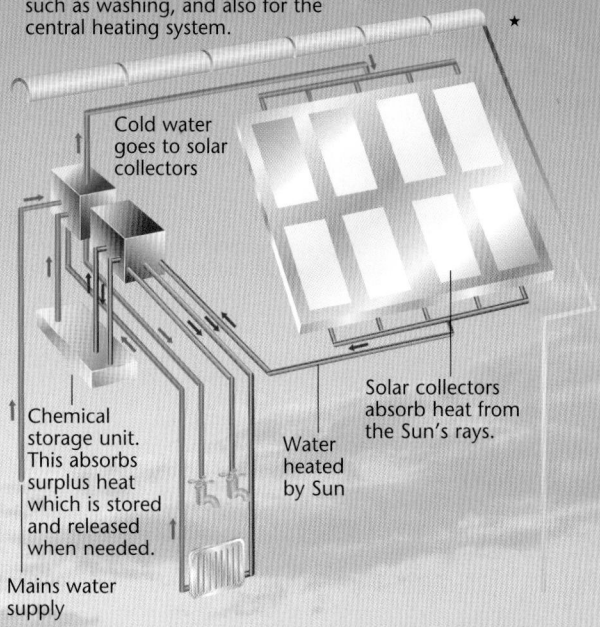

See for yourself

On a hot day you can see how the Sun's energy heats things up. Coil a garden hose so that as much of it as possible is in sunlight. Attach it to a water supply and turn it on so that water comes out. Then turn off the water and block up the end of the pipe using, say, a cork. Leave it in the sun for an hour.

When you go back to the hose, unblock the pipe and feel the warmth of the water that runs out. The hose will have soaked up the Sun's energy, heating up the water inside.

ENERGY EFFICIENCY

Machines take one form of energy, for example, electricity, and change it into another form of energy. Machines are described as efficient if they change most of the energy that is used to power them, into the useful form of energy that is needed.

Energy-saving fluorescent tube lights are more efficient than normal light bulbs because they turn more electrical energy into light and waste less as heat.

MEASURING ENERGY

Energy is measured using units called **joules** (J). One thousand joules is a **kilojoule** (kJ). The foods that you eat give you varying amounts of energy.

An ordinary sized apple (100g) contains 150kJ of chemical energy. The same mass of chocolate contains 2,335kJ.

Power is the energy used in a certain time and it is measured in units called **watts (W)**. One watt is equal to one joule per second. The more energy a machine produces in a certain period of time, the more powerful it is.

A 60 watt light bulb uses 60 joules of energy each second. A 100 watt bulb uses 100 joules per second and produces more heat and light energy.

60 watt light bulb

100 watt light bulb

Internet links

Go to **www.usborne-quicklinks.com** and type in the keyword "science" to find out more about energy.

There you'll find links to websites where you can:

- Test your knowledge with energy quizzes
- Learn about fossil fuels and renewable energy with online activities

Go to Usborne Quicklinks for links to hand-picked websites on hundreds of subjects.

* *Electromagnetic waves, 212.*

HEAT

Heat is a form of energy that flows from one place to another because of a difference in temperature. **Temperature** is a measure of how hot something is.

HEAT ENERGY

When a substance absorbs heat, its **internal energy** increases. Internal energy is made up of two types of energy. Firstly, there is the kinetic energy* of the particles as they move about in the substance. Secondly, there is the potential energy* of the particles, ready to be used.

This red-hot river of liquid rock was formed when rocks inside the Earth absorbed so much heat that they melted.

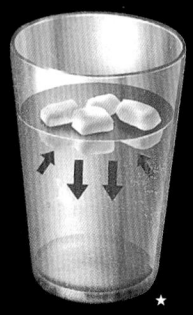

Ice in water

Heat energy flows from hot objects to cooler ones and continues to flow until they reach the same temperature. For example, water that has ice in it loses heat energy to the ice, which gains heat energy. Eventually, all the water molecules (from the water and the ice) reach the same temperature.

MEASURING HEAT ENERGY

Like all forms of energy, heat is measured in **joules (J)**, named after the English scientist James Joule (1818-89). He was the first to recognize that heat is a form of energy. Using a contraption like the one below, Joule showed how potential energy lost by the falling weights was gained by the water in the form of heat energy, as its temperature rose.

Joule's experiment

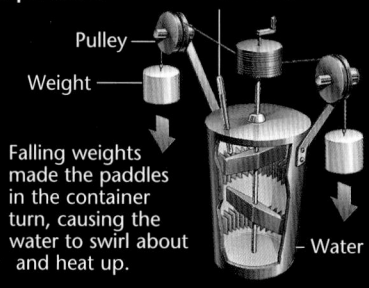

It takes 4,200J to raise the temperature of 1kg of pure water by just 1°C.

** Kinetic energy, Potential energy, 106.*

HEAT AND EXPANSION

Most substances expand when they are heated because, as their particles vibrate more vigorously, they push each other further apart. Gases and most liquids expand more than solids because their molecules have more energy to break free of the forces that hold them together (see *The Kinetic Theory*, page 16).

Different solids expand at different rates. This can be seen in a **bimetallic strip**, a strip of copper and iron fixed firmly together. When heated, the copper expands more than the iron, so the strip bends.

Bimetallic strips are used in **thermostats** – devices that switch an electrical circuit on and off in response to a change in temperature.

Bimetallic strip in a thermostat

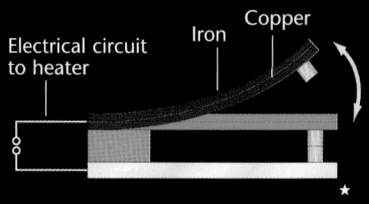

See for yourself

Take a jar of dried peas or beans and shake it gently. The contents vibrate but stay in roughly the same places. This is what happens to the particles in a solid when they are heated a little.

f you put the same amount of heat into two different substances, their temperatures change by different amounts. The substances are said to have different **thermal** (or **specific heat**) **capacities**.

Oil and water, for example, have different specific heat capacities.

The same amount of heat makes oil hotter than water.

The different thermal capacities of the land and the sea cause sea breezes. In the day, the land heats up faster than the sea. Warm air over the land rises and cooler air blows in from the sea.

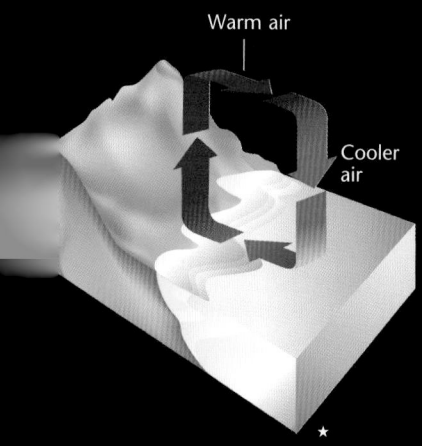

Coastal wind patterns like this one develop mostly during spells of warm weather.

Temperature can be measured in degrees Celsius (°C) or Fahrenheit (°F), or on the absolute temperature scale.

The **Celsius scale** has two fixed points: ice point (0°C) and steam point (100°C). Each Celsius degree is one hundredth of the difference between these two points.

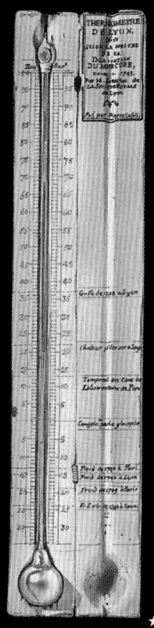

An early Celsius thermometer

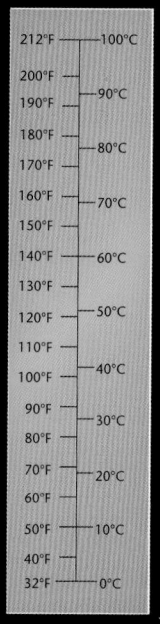

The Celsius and Fahrenheit scales

In the **Fahrenheit scale**, the values 32°F and 212°F are given to the ice and steam points. There are 180 degrees between them.

The **absolute temperature scale** is measured in units called **kelvins (K)**, which are the same size as degrees Celsius. The scale starts at a point called **absolute zero** (zero K) which is the same as -273°C. This is the temperature at which no more energy can be removed from a substance.

A **thermometer** is an instrument for measuring temperature. It may contain a liquid that expands when heated, or a wire whose resistance* to electric current changes if the temperature changes.

Liquid in glass thermometers contain mercury or, for measuring very low temperatures, alcohol.

Constriction stops liquid returning to the bulb before a reading is taken.

Maximum and **minimum thermometers** contain pointers that record the highest or lowest temperature reached.

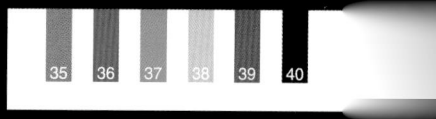

Liquid crystal thermometers contain liquid crystals that change colour when heated.

Digital thermometers contain an electronic component that is sensitive to heat. It shows the temperature on a digital display.

Internet links

To find out more about heat, go to **www.usborne-quicklinks.com** and type in the keyword "science".

There you'll find links to websites where you can:

- Watch and try out heat experiments
- Learn how to read a thermometer

HEAT TRANSFER

Heat can be transferred from one place to another by convection, conduction or radiation.

CONVECTION

Convection is the main way in which heat energy is transferred in liquids and gases. When a liquid or gas is heated, the part nearest the heat source expands and becomes less dense*, so it rises. The cooler, denser liquid sinks. Movements like this in liquids or gases are called **convection currents**.

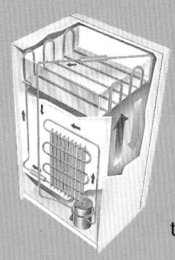

Fridges are kept cold by convection currents. Cool air near the top of the fridge sinks, while warmer air rises to be cooled.

Glider plane takes spiral path upwards.

Convection currents in the atmosphere lift the glider.

The pattern of winds around the Earth are caused by convection currents. These occur because more of the Sun's energy hits the surface near the equator. As the air is heated, it expands and rises and colder, denser air rushes in, creating a wind.

Warm air rises.

Air cools and sinks.

Convection currents are carrying clouds of ash from this volcano into the upper atmosphere.

See for yourself

Gently drop a small feather or piece of tissue paper above a warm radiator. See which way the feather or paper floats.

The radiator heats the air above it, causing the air to rise and form a convection current. If it is light enough, the feather or paper will be carried upwards on the convection current.

* *Density, 138.*

CONDUCTION

Conduction is the way in which heat energy in a solid is transferred. The energy of the particles nearest to the heat source increases. These particles vibrate and pass on some of their energy, spreading heat through the substance.

A desert fox has large ears which help it to keep cool. Excess heat is transferred from its ears to the air by conduction and spreads away by convection.

Metals are good **conductors** because, as well as their vibrating particles, they contain freely moving electrons*. These carry heat energy around more quickly than the vibrations alone. Substances that conduct heat slowly, such as wood and water, are called **insulators**. Air is a good insulator and so are materials that trap air, such as wool, fur and feathers.

Metal heats up quickly as it is a very good conductor of heat.

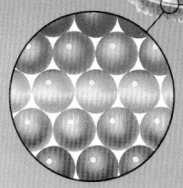

Heat spreads quickly through metal particles.

Fat and feathers insulate birds such as penguins, helping to keep them warm.

RADIATION

Heat transfer by **radiation** refers to energy that moves in the form of electromagnetic waves*.

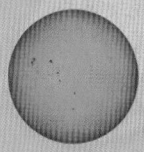

The Sun's radiation travels at 300 million metres per second. It takes about eight minutes to reach the Earth.

Radiation does not depend on particle movement, and is the only form of energy that can cross a **vacuum** (a space completely empty of matter). All types of radiation, for instance light rays, cause things to heat up, but **infrared radiation** is the type which causes the greatest temperature rise.

The Sun sends out infrared radiation, as do hot objects, such as fires and light bulbs. Dark-coloured objects absorb the radiation, while light ones reflect it, and stay cool.

In Antarctica, the snow reflects over 90% of the radiation from the Sun back into the atmosphere. The surface receives very little heat, so the air remains cold.

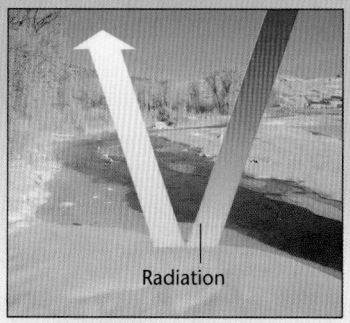

Snow reflects the Sun's radiation.

Sun's heat

VACUUM FLASKS

A **vacuum flask** is a container for keeping liquids at a constant temperature. It is made up of two glass containers, one inside the other, with a vacuum between them. The vacuum prevents the transfer of heat by conduction or convection (see left). Very shiny surfaces reduce the amount of heat transferred by radiation.

Vacuum flask

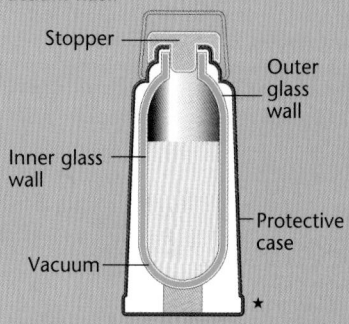

Internet links

To find out more about heat transfer, go to **www.usborne-quicklinks.com** and type in the keyword "science".

There you'll find links to websites where you can:

- Discover more about heat transfer with interactive experiments
- Take a closer look at refrigerators and vacuum flasks

Go to Usborne Quicklinks for links to hand-picked websites on hundreds of subjects.

** Electromagnetic waves, 212; Electrons, 10.*

RADIOACTIVITY

All matter is made of particles called **atoms**. Every atom contains a **nucleus** which is made up of **protons** and **neutrons**. Nuclei hold vast amounts of energy, called **nuclear energy**. Some substances are **radioactive**. This means that their atoms release some of this energy as radiation*. This can be dangerous to living things, but can be used in many ways.

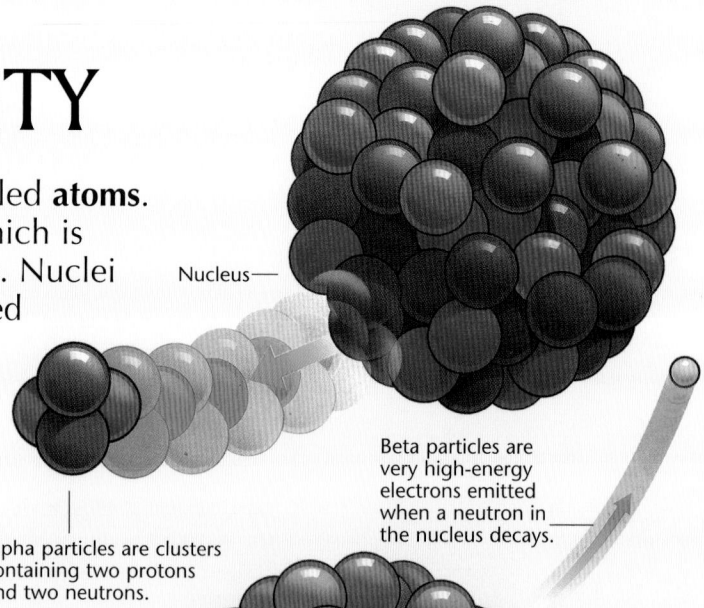

TYPES OF RADIATION

When a substance is radioactive, it is said to be **unstable**. The atoms become stable by losing some of their nuclear energy as radiation.

The type of radiation that the atoms give out is either **alpha**, **beta** or **gamma radiation**. The first two are streams of particles. The last takes the form of **gamma rays**, which are an extremely powerful form of electromagnetic waves*.

The Greek letters below are used to describe the different types of radiation.

Alpha Beta Gamma

A nucleus first throws off either alpha or beta particles, and then, if it has extra energy, gamma radiation.

The three nuclei shown on this page are all unstable. Each nucleus is emitting a different type of radiation.

Alpha particles move slowly and are stopped by any substance thicker than paper. They are identical to the nuclei of helium atoms and scientists think helium is created by natural radioactivity in the Earth. Beta particles are more penetrating than alpha particles and many move almost at the speed of light. Gamma rays are the most penetrating.

Range of radioactive particles

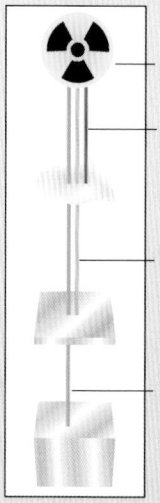

★

★ Gamma rays are very high-energy electromagnetic waves that move at the speed of light.

* *Electromagnetic waves, 212; Radiation, 113.*

USES OF RADIATION

In industry, radiation is used to check the thickness of sheets of paper and plastic. Tiny irregularities can be detected by measuring the amount of beta radiation that passes through the sheets. Food, such as fruit and meat, can be irradiated with gamma rays, and this keeps it fresh.

After two weeks, these irradiated strawberries are still fresh.

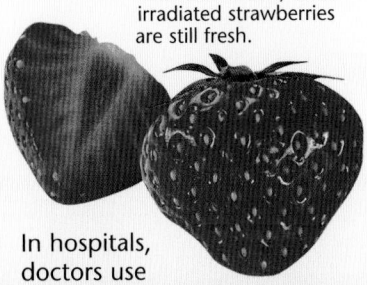

In hospitals, doctors use **radioactive tracing** to follow a substance through a patient's body. For example, to see how a patient's body deals with sugar, they can attach some radioactive carbon-14 to molecules of sugar and track the radiation given off by the carbon-14.

Radiotherapy uses carefully controlled doses of radiation to kill cancer cells, which are living cells that are growing in a disorderly way.

A patient being given radiotherapy

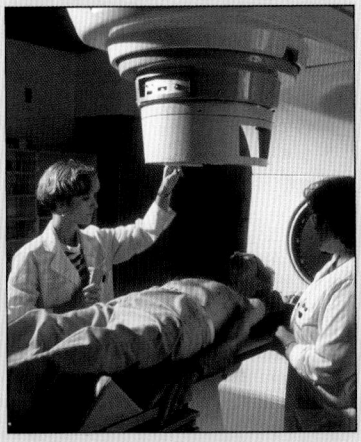

RADIOACTIVE DECAY

After ejecting particles, a nucleus becomes the nucleus of a different element. This is called **radioactive decay**. If the new element is also unstable, the process of decay will continue until there are atoms with stable nuclei.

For example, when the unstable radioactive substance plutonium-242 gives off an alpha particle (which consists of two protons and two neutrons), it becomes uranium-238. The diagram below shows how plutonium decays to become uranium and then thorium.

The numbers written in front of the symbol for the substance are the mass number (top) and atomic number (bottom). The **mass number** is the number of neutrons and protons in a nucleus. The **atomic number** is just the number of protons.

Radioactive decay of plutonium

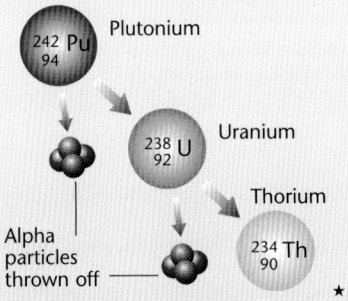

The length of time it takes for the nuclei of an element to decay is measured by its **half-life**. This is the time taken for half of the nuclei in a sample to decay. Every element has a different half-life. Radium-221 has a half-life of 30 seconds. Uranium-238 has a half-life of 4,500,000,000 years.

CARBON DATING

Carbon dating is a method of calculating the time that has passed since living matter died. All living things contain a small amount of carbon-14, which has a half-life of 5,700 years. When living things die, the carbon-14 decays. The age of the remains can be calculated by measuring how much radiation is still being given off.

Carbon dating showed that this insect was trapped in amber resin five thousand years ago.

DANGER!

Radioactive substances are transported in thick lead containers to prevent radiation from escaping. Exposure to radiation can cause burns, cataracts and cancer.

Robots are used to handle dangerous radioactive substances.

Internet links

To find out more about radioactivity, go to **www.usborne-quicklinks.com** and type in the keyword "science".

There you'll find links to websites where you can:

- Take a tour of the European Organization for Nuclear Research (CERN)
- Investigate the uses of radiation

Go to Usborne Quicklinks for links to hand-picked websites on hundreds of subjects.

NUCLEAR POWER

Nuclear energy can be harnessed, using controlled nuclear reactions, to produce power for industrial and home use. It can also be released, in an extremely violent way, when nuclear weapons explode.

NUCLEAR REACTIONS

There are two types of nuclear reactions: **nuclear fusion** and **nuclear fission**. Fusion means "joining" and during nuclear fusion, two small nuclei combine to form a larger one. Nuclear fusion only takes place at extremely high temperatures and releases huge amounts of energy.

Nuclear fusion

Two nuclei join to form one large one.

Fission means "splitting apart" and nuclear fission occurs when the nucleus of an atom is bombarded with neutrons*. The nucleus splits open, releasing neutrons and large amounts of energy. This process takes place inside nuclear reactors (see opposite page).

Nuclear fission

A nucleus splits open, forming two or more new nuclei.

The dust created by this nuclear explosion is highly radioactive*. It contaminates everything on which it falls.

NUCLEAR WEAPONS

Nuclear weapons produce uncontrolled nuclear reactions. The energy is released in massive explosions. **Atomic bombs** use nuclear fission reactions. **Hydrogen bombs** use nuclear fusion. In World War II, the USA dropped atomic bombs on the cities of Hiroshima and Nagasaki in Japan, killing many thousands of people.

World War II atomic bomb

Radioactive* plutonium in here

* *Neutrons, Radioactivity, 114.*

NUCLEAR REACTORS

The energy released by controlled fission reactions can be used to generate electricity, and to power submarines and aircraft carriers.

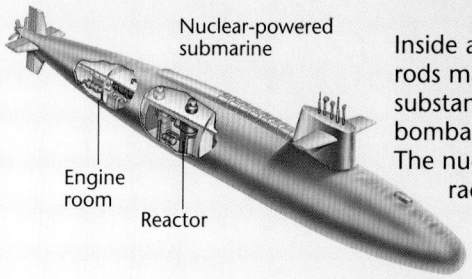

Such reactions take place in **nuclear reactors**, such as the pressurized water reactor shown in the diagram at the bottom of the page.

Inside a nuclear reactor, rods made of a radioactive substance such as uranium are bombarded with neutrons*. The nuclei split up, releasing radiation and more neutrons, which set up a chain reaction.

Nuclear power stations generate lots of electricity. However, the used fuel rods remain dangerously radioactive for thousands of years. Disposing of them safely is very difficult.

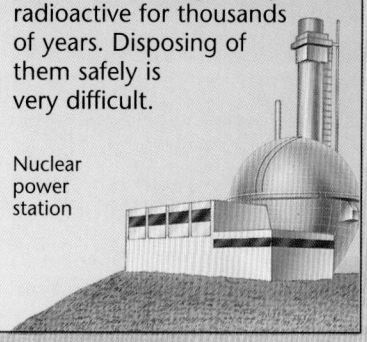

PRESSURIZED WATER REACTOR

A **pressurized water reactor** is one type of nuclear reactor found in power stations. The energy released in the core of the reactor is used to heat water to make steam. The steam turns turbines* that generate electricity.

Nuclear fission reactions take place in the core of the nuclear reactor (1).

The energy released heats pressurized water in the primary water circuit (2).

Heat from the primary water circuit heats the water in the secondary circuit to make steam (3).

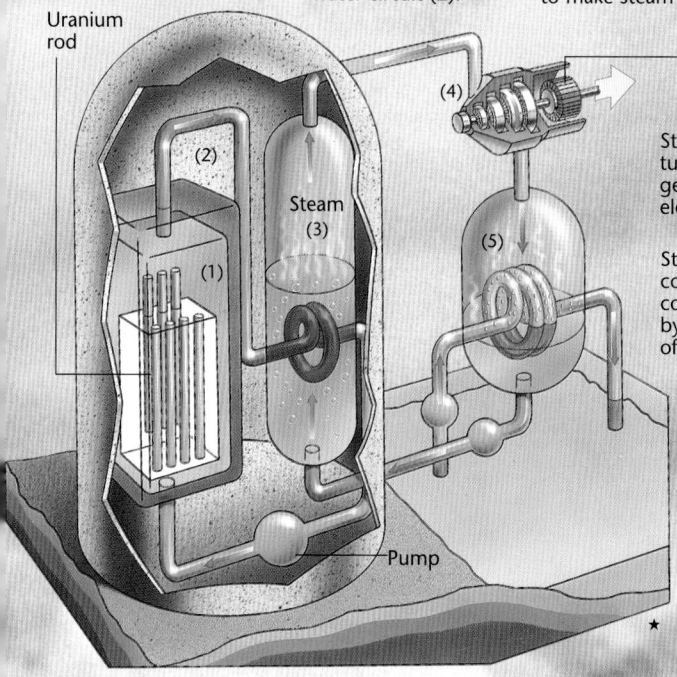

Steam-driven turbines (4) generate electricity.

Steam is cooled in the condenser (5) by a supply of water.

SAFETY FIRST

Nuclear reactions are dangerous to living things. To prevent accidents which would pollute land and air with radiation, the workings in power stations are monitored closely.

Dangerous processes inside a nuclear power station are carefully monitored.

Internet links

Go to **www.usborne-quicklinks.com** and type in the keyword "science" to find out more about nuclear power.

There you'll find links to websites where you can:

- Take a tour around a nuclear power station
- Investigate the pros and cons of nuclear technology

Go to Usborne Quicklinks for links to hand-picked websites on hundreds of subjects.

** Neutrons, 114; Turbines, 147.*

FORCES

A **force** is any push or pull on an object. When you pick up an object, you are exerting a force on it. If you leave it sitting where it is, there are still forces acting on it, but they cancel each other out. Forces can make things move faster or slower, stop, change direction, or change size or shape.

The force of gravity makes these dice fall downwards.

TYPES OF FORCES

Forces affect objects in many different ways. There are forces you can see, such as a foot kicking a ball, and invisible forces, such as magnetism* and gravity*.

The magnetic force which pulls these tacks to the magnet is an invisible force.

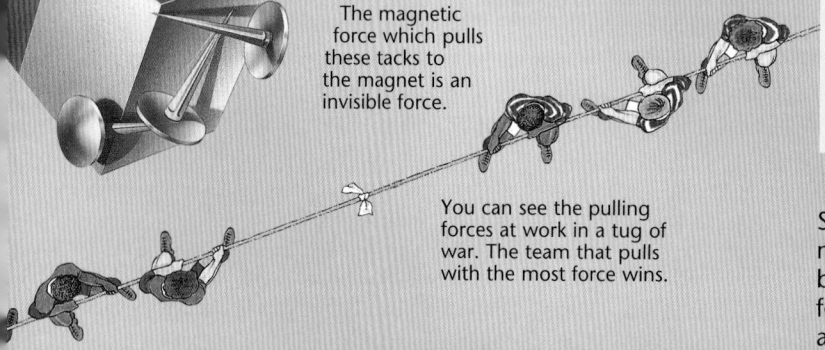

You can see the pulling forces at work in a tug of war. The team that pulls with the most force wins.

See for yourself

Try rolling one ball into another on a smooth surface. The force of your movement will set the ball rolling. The moving ball will exert a force on the stationary one, causing it to move too.

The surface will exert a force (friction*) on both balls, causing them both to slow down, and eventually stop.

A single force acting on an object will make it start to move, or move faster or slower. Two equal forces acting in opposite directions try to change the object's size or shape.

Forces that need two or more objects to be touching each other are called **contact forces**. You are using contact forces when you move an object with your hands.

When you kick a football, the single force of your kick makes the football start to move.

As you catch a ball, the pushing force of your hands makes the ball slow down and stop.

If you step on a ball, the equal forces of your foot pushing down and the ground pushing up squash it.

Some forces don't need objects to be touching. The forces that act at a distance include electric force*, magnetism and the force of gravity.

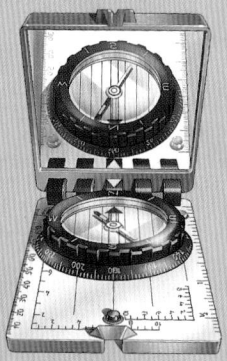

Compasses work because of the Earth's magnetism*.

The contact force of friction* enables pencils to make marks on paper.

* Electric force, 228; Friction, 124; Gravity, 130; Magnetism, 232.

A rollercoaster makes use of lots of different forces to gain speed, twist, turn upside down and race along without flying off the track.

When you are on a rollercoaster, you can feel the different forces acting on your body as you are thrown around.

MEASURING FORCES

The strength of a force is measured in **newtons (N)**, named after the English scientist, Isaac Newton (1642-1727). One newton of force causes a mass of 1kg to accelerate* by one metre per second per second ($1 m/s^2$). This is about the force you would need to lift an empty glass.

A **spring balance** (see right) measures how many newtons a force is exerting. The spring, fixed at one end, is extended (stretched) by the force. **Hooke's law** states that the extension of a material is proportional to the force stretching it. The more the spring stretches, the more newtons the force is applying.

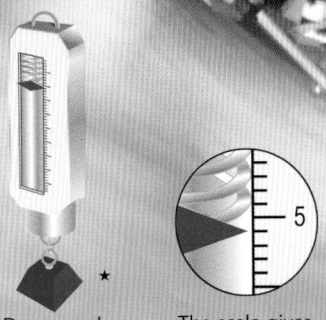

Downward force of weight stretches spring.

The scale gives the strength of the force in newtons.

VECTOR AND SCALAR QUANTITIES

Forces have magnitude (size) and direction. In physics, things that have both these quantities are called **vector quantities**. Acceleration* and velocity* are also vector quantities. A quantity that has magnitude but no direction is called a **scalar quantity**. Temperature, time and mass are examples of scalar quantities. These quantities can be low or high, but they don't have a direction.

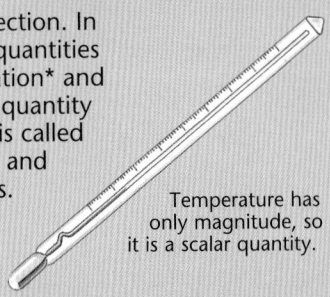

Temperature has only magnitude, so it is a scalar quantity.

Internet links

To find out more about forces, go to **www.usborne-quicklinks.com** and type in the keyword "science".

There you'll find links to websites where you can:

- Uncover the forces you experience on a rollercoaster
- Take a forces quiz
- Find out more with online activities

Go to Usborne Quicklinks for links to hand-picked websites on hundreds of subjects.

** Acceleration, Velocity, 127.*

COMBINING FORCES

There is usually more than one force acting on an object. For example, a sailboard can experience the forces of gravity, the wind, upthrust and waves. The combined effect is a single force called the **resultant force**. If the strength and direction of all forces is known, you can calculate the resultant force and predict what will happen to the object.

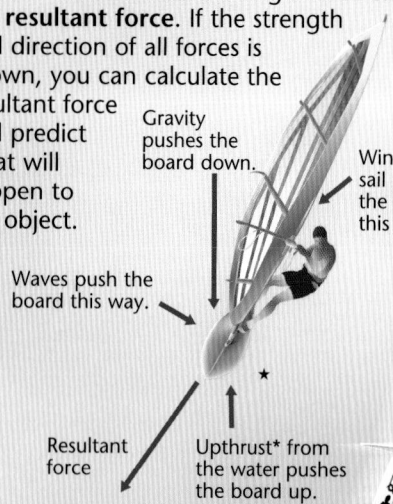

EQUILIBRIUM

There are forces acting on an object even when it is not moving. The forces are all balanced, so they cancel each other out and the object is said to be in **equilibrium**. For example, the force of gravity* pulls down on a tower of cards, while the surface it stands on pushes up with an equal force. The resultant force is zero, so the tower stays in place.

See for yourself

To see forces of equilibrium in action, try building a tower of cards for yourself.

If you knock a card, the forces acting on the structure will no longer be in equilibrium and the tower will collapse.

Making sure that the forces balance is tricky, because each card depends on others to keep it in place. Cards are so flimsy that a slight knock will unbalance them.

* *Gravity, 130; Upthrust, 138.*

TURNING FORCES

To turn something around a fixed point, for example a door around its hinges, a force with a turning effect is needed. The fixed point is known as a **fulcrum** or **pivot**. It is much easier to turn something around a fulcrum if the force is applied at a distance. This is why a long spanner is more efficient than a shorter one.

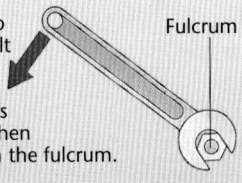

It is easiest to undo this bolt by holding the spanner at the end, as the force is then furthest from the fulcrum.

The force of a turning effect is called a **moment**. The moment around a fulcrum is found by multiplying the strength of the force by its distance from the fulcrum. Moment is measured in **newton metres (Nm)** and can be either clockwise or anticlockwise in direction.

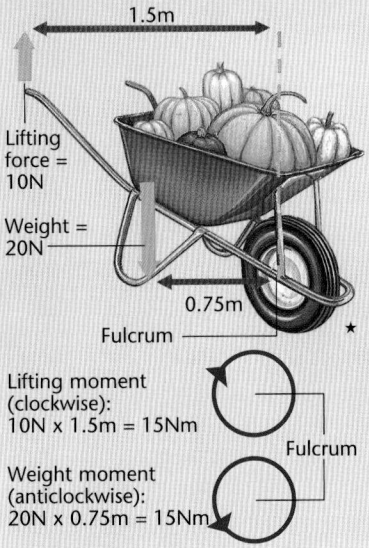

The picture of the wheelbarrow above shows how turning forces can be in equilibrium just like any other forces. The clockwise moment can cancel out the anticlockwise moment.

ELASTICITY

When forces act on an object that cannot move, they may change its size or shape. Some substances, like rubber, return to their original form when the force is removed. These are called **elastic** substances.

A trampoline is elastic. When the forces stretching it are removed, it goes back to its original shape.

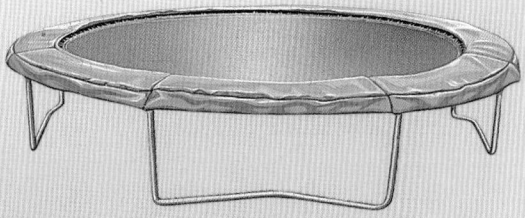

The amount that an elastic substance will stretch obeys Hooke's law*, which states that if the force increases in equal steps, so does the stretch.

If something is stretched beyond its elastic limit, though, Hooke's law no longer works. The **elastic limit** is the point at which a substance alters permanently when it is stretched.

A rubber band is elastic, but will snap if you stretch it too far (that is, beyond its elastic limit).

Some materials do not return to their original form after being stretched and they can hold a new shape. This is called **plastic** behaviour.

Modelling clay behaves in a plastic way.

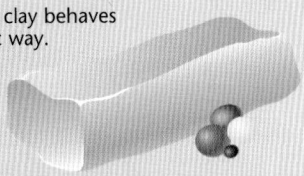

After it has been modelled, the clay keeps the shape that it has been given. This is an example of plastic behaviour.

Internet links

Go to **www.usborne-quicklinks.com** and type in the keyword "science", to find out more about different forces.

There you'll find links to websites where you can:

- Follow interactive demonstrations of forces
- Carry out online experiments
- Use your knowledge of forces to play online activities
- Explore more with forces investigations

** Hooke's law, 119.*

DYNAMICS

The study of how forces affect movement is called **dynamics**. The terms inertia and momentum are used to describe how easily objects both start and stop moving. There are three laws of motion which explain the principles governing the movement of all objects. These laws were formulated by the English scientist, Isaac Newton, in 1687.

Isaac Newton, English scientist (1642-1727)

NEWTON'S LAWS OF MOTION

Isaac Newton made important discoveries about many subjects, including motion, gravity and light. His three **laws of motion** have had a major influence on scientific thinking.

Newton's first law states that if an object is not being acted on by a force, it will either stay still or continue moving at a constant speed in a straight line. This is the principle of inertia (see right).

To start this truck moving, it will take a force to overcome its inertia. (See Newton's first law.)

Newton's second law states that any force acting on an object will change its motion. How much change there is depends on the object's mass and the size of the resultant force.

The same force of wind will move a pine cone less than a leaf because the cone's mass is greater. (See Newton's second law.)

Newton's third law states that when a force acts on an object, the object exerts an equal force in the opposite direction. The first force is called the **action** and the second is the **reaction**.

The ball exerts a force on a bat, felt as the slowing down of the bat, that is equal and opposite to the force the bat exerts on the ball. (See Newton's third law.)

INERTIA

Objects resist change in their movement. This tendency, called **inertia**, applies to stationary and moving objects. The inertia of a stationary object makes it hard to get moving. If moving, inertia makes the object want to continue moving in a straight line. It takes a force to overcome inertia.

Without the restraining force of a seatbelt or airbag, the inertia of this crash test dummy would send it through the windscreen.

The larger an object's mass, the more inertia it has. A big animal has to exert more force to change its movement than a small one. Twice the mass means twice the inertia.

This adult elephant has five times as much mass as the baby. Its inertia is five times as great.

MOMENTUM

Momentum is a measure of an object's tendency to carry on moving. It is found by multiplying the object's mass by its velocity. The greater the mass and the velocity, the greater the momentum. Like velocity, momentum is a vector quantity, which means it has both size and direction.

Buzzard

Seagull

If a buzzard and seagull are flying at the same speed, the bird with the greater mass (the buzzard) has greater momentum.

This full trolley's mass is 10kg and its velocity is 1m/s east. Its momentum is 10kg m/s east.

This almost empty trolley has a mass of 2kg and a velocity of 5m/s east. Its momentum is also 10kg m/s east.

An object with a small mass can have the same momentum as an object with a large mass, providing it is moving faster.

See for yourself

Contraptions called Newton's cradles are sometimes sold as interesting, grown-up "toys" which show conservation of momentum. See if you can find one. As the first ball hits the other balls, its momentum is transferred through to the last ball, making it move.

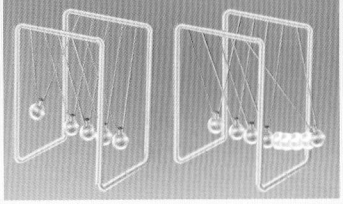

CONSERVATION OF MOMENTUM

When two objects collide, such as the pink ball and the blue ball shown here, their total momentum stays the same as it was just before the collision. This is called the **law of conservation of momentum**. So when one object loses momentum in a collision, the other gains the same amount.

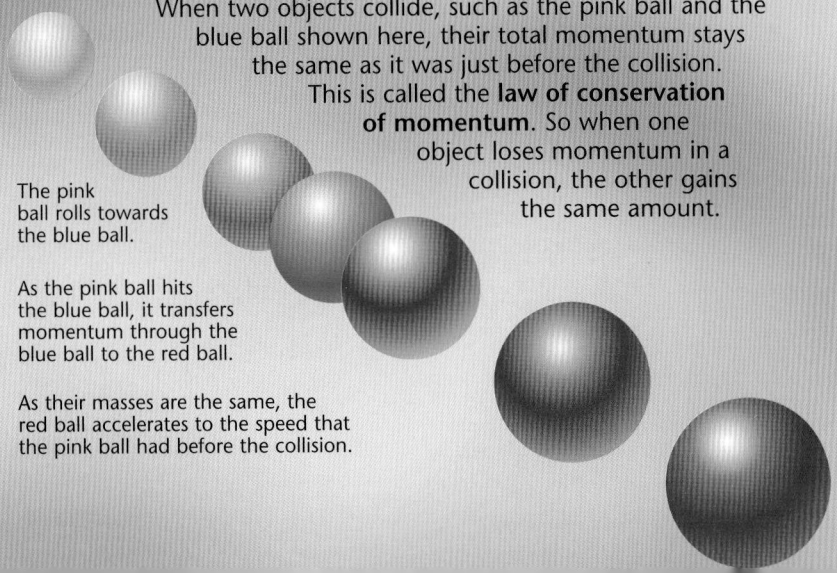

The pink ball rolls towards the blue ball.

As the pink ball hits the blue ball, it transfers momentum through the blue ball to the red ball.

As their masses are the same, the red ball accelerates to the speed that the pink ball had before the collision.

Internet links

To find out more about dynamics, go to **www.usborne-quicklinks.com** and type in the keyword "science".

There you'll find links to websites where you can:

- Get instructions for experiments that demonstrate dynamics
- Learn more about Newton
- Watch online demonstrations

Go to Usborne Quicklinks for links to hand-picked websites on hundreds of subjects.

FRICTION

When a moving object is touching another object, like a coin sliding across a table, the moving object slows down. The force that causes this is called **friction**. The rougher the surfaces are, and the harder they press together, the more friction there will be. Friction occurs in liquids and gases as well as between solids. Anything that experiences friction warms up.

New shoe

Old shoe

Constant friction with the floor means a ballet dancer's shoes wear out after a few weeks.

USING FRICTION

Friction is useful in some situations and a nuisance in others. If there were no friction between surfaces, it would be impossible to grip anything.

Many kinds of machines make use of friction. With too little friction between tyres and the surface of a road, for example, drivers wouldn't be able to stop their vehicles from sliding around.

The skis' smooth undersides minimize friction with the snow, allowing them to slide very easily. However, their sharp edges create friction when the skier turns, enabling him to control his speed and direction.

Water and mud on the road reduce friction because they act as lubricants (see opposite page). The grooves on a tyre channel water or mud through them, so that the raised rubber pieces (the **tread**) can grip the surface of the road.

Some devices need friction to be able to work at all. For example, friction between a match and a matchbox generates enough heat for chemicals in the match head to burn. All brakes work by using friction to slow down a vehicle's wheels.

Disc brake

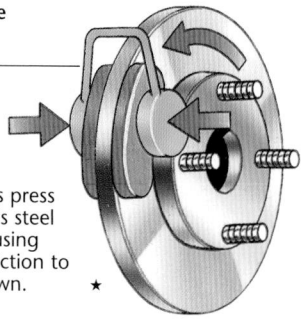

Brake pads press against this steel wheel, causing enough friction to slow it down.

The soles of sports shoes are made from materials, such as rubber, which provide a lot of friction.

REDUCING FRICTION

Lots of friction between machine parts is damaging. It causes wear and tear, and some of the energy needed to run the machine is wasted on heat instead of movement. Oil is used to reduce friction because it is smoother than any solid surface, so it allows objects to slide across each other more easily. A liquid used like this is called a **lubricant**.

Magnification shows how a smooth-seeming metal surface is actually fairly rough. A layer of oil between moving metal surfaces reduces friction.

A layer of **ball bearings** between two surfaces in a machine reduces the amount of contact between the surfaces. This reduces the friction between them, and the amount of wear.

Ball bearings lie around the axle of this wheel. They rotate as the wheel turns. ★

FRICTION IN AIR AND SPACE

Drag, or **air resistance**, is the friction that occurs between air and any object moving through it (see also page 142). In space, there is no air, so there is no friction. The Space Shuttle, for instance, experiences no friction as it moves through space, until it re-enters the Earth's atmosphere.

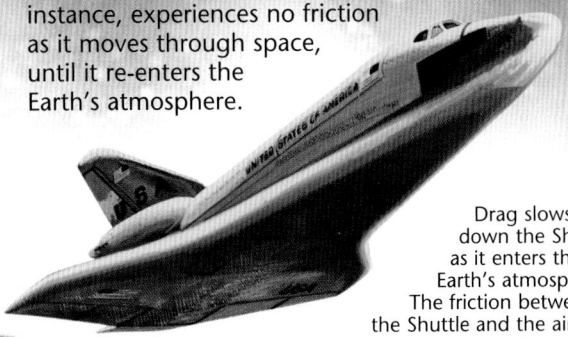

Drag slows down the Shuttle as it enters the Earth's atmosphere. The friction between the Shuttle and the air makes it glow red hot.

See for yourself

You can see how ball bearings reduce friction using some marbles and a big book. First, push the book along on its own. Notice the friction. Now put marbles under the book and push again. The marbles roll between the book and the surface, reducing friction.

STREAMLINING

To reduce drag, vehicles are designed so that they are **streamlined**. Streamlining lets the air flow over a vehicle in smooth lines, so that it can move forwards with less effort.

Car manufacturers use jets of smoke to test the streamlining of new cars. Here, the Ford Ka is being tested.

FRICTION IN WATER

Water is denser* than air, so more friction acts on objects moving through water. Fish, and sea mammals such as whales, have naturally streamlined bodies that reduce the friction between themselves and the water.

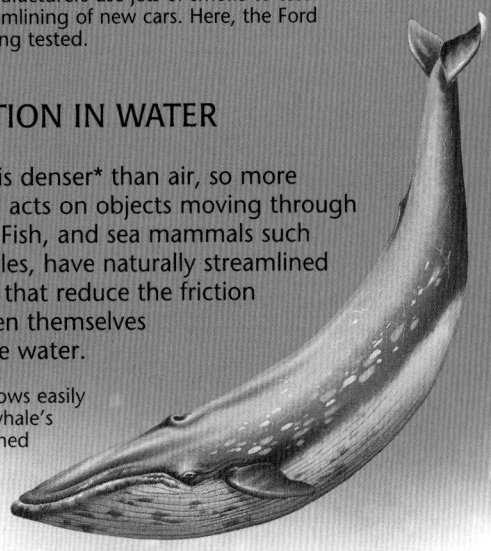

Water flows easily over a whale's streamlined body.

Internet links

Go to **www.usborne-quicklinks.com** and type in the keyword "science" to find out more about friction.

There you'll find links to websites where you can:

- Discover how friction affects your everyday life
- Have a go at experiments that show friction in action

Go to Usborne Quicklinks for links to hand-picked websites on hundreds of subjects.

** Density, 138.*

MOTION

In physics, **motion** is the study of how something moves, whether it is a planet moving around the Sun or a snowboarder flying through the air. An object's motion is usually described in terms of its velocity and acceleration, and its motion only changes if a force, or several forces, act on it.

Snowboarders can reach speeds of 22m/s, which is the same as 80km/h.

SPEED

Speed is a measure of how fast an object is moving. The average speed of a moving object can be calculated by dividing the distance it has travelled by the time it has taken to do so.

Speed calculation

This cyclist has gone 500m in 40 seconds. The calculation below gives her average speed.

$$\text{Average speed} = \frac{\text{Distance (metres)}}{\text{Time (seconds)}}$$

$$= \frac{500}{40} = 12.5\text{m/s}$$

Speed is a scalar quantity. This means that it measures the amount of speed a moving object has, but not the direction in which it is moving. In physics, the unit of measurement most often used is metres per second (m/s). However, you will often see kilometres per hour (km/h) as well. This measures how far something will go in an hour.

CHANGING SPEED

The speed of a moving object can change from moment to moment. A sprinter, for instance, runs slowest when setting off at the start of a race. He is likely to be running fastest as he approaches the finishing line. The speed of something at any particular moment is called its **instantaneous speed**.

For example, in 2008 the men's world record for the 100m race was 9.69 seconds. This is an average speed of 10.32m/s. After running 1m of the race, though, the winner's instantaneous speed might have been 3m/s. After a few more metres, it could have been as high as 11m/s.

A 100m sprinter doesn't reach top speed until 60m.

VELOCITY

Velocity measures the direction in which an object is travelling as well as its speed. This makes velocity a vector quantity. The velocity of a moving object can change even if its speed remains exactly the same because a change in direction changes the velocity.

When they first leave the plane, the Earth's gravity causes skydivers to accelerate at a rate of 9.8m/s².

Although this car is travelling at a steady speed of 10km/h, (6mph) its velocity is changing all the time because it is constantly changing direction.

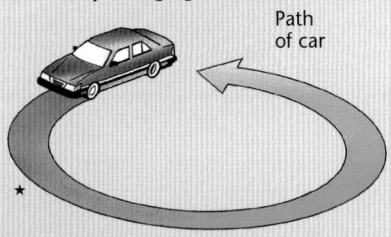

Velocity is measured in metres per second (m/s) in a particular direction. For instance, someone walking north at 1.5m/s has a velocity of 1.5m/s north. **Relative velocity** is the velocity a moving object appears to have when viewed from another moving object.

These stunt jets are both flying at a velocity of 83m/s in the same direction.

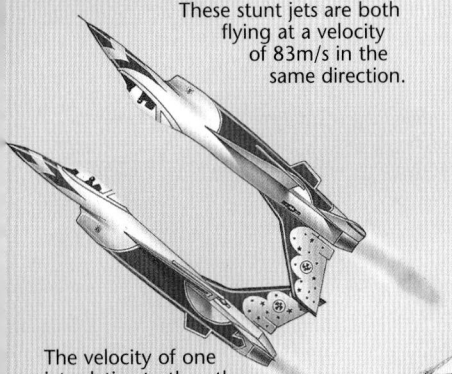

The velocity of one jet relative to the other (from the point of view of either) is zero.

ACCELERATION

Acceleration is a change in the velocity of an object, that is, a change in its speed or direction in a given time. In physics, acceleration is measured in metres per second per second, or m/s². This is not as confusing as it looks. If something accelerates at 1m/s² (1 metre per second per second), it gets faster by one metre a second, every second.

A decrease in velocity is called **negative acceleration**, or **deceleration**. Any change in speed or direction means that an object accelerates, or decelerates, as both affect velocity. Car manufacturers usually consider acceleration in kilometres (or miles) per hour per second. This is simply using different units to measure the same thing.

If a car is travelling at a steady 50km/h (30 mph) in one direction, its acceleration is zero. This is because neither its speed nor its direction are changing.

This Porsche 911 Turbo accelerates from 0-100km/h (0-60mph) in 4.5 seconds. This works out at an average acceleration of 6.2m/s².

When skydivers open their parachutes, they suddenly decelerate.

See for yourself

Make three small balls using modelling clay. Drop each one from a different height. The greater the drop, the bigger the dent in the ball when it hits the floor. This is because the further things fall, the faster they go.

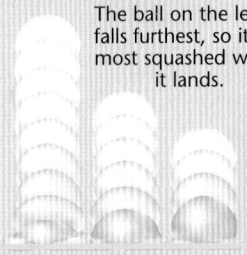

The ball on the left falls furthest, so it is most squashed when it lands.

Internet links

To find out more about motion, go to **www.usborne-quicklinks.com** and type in the keyword "science".

There you'll find links to websites where you can:

- Follow online tutorials on speed
- Learn about intantaneous speed
- Investigate speed with an online game

Go to Usborne Quicklinks for links to hand-picked websites on hundreds of subjects.

TERMINAL VELOCITY

When something falls through a gas or liquid it accelerates, at a decreasing rate, until it reaches its maximum constant velocity. This is called its **terminal velocity**.

As an example, imagine skydivers jumping from a plane. They start to accelerate the moment they jump from the plane.

They continue accelerating, but at a slower and slower rate, until they reach a speed of about 200km/h. At this point they stop accelerating.

When the acceleration has dropped to zero, they have reached their terminal velocity.

When something begins to fall, it accelerates quickly.

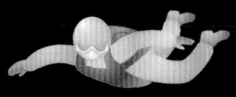

The longer it falls, the less quickly it accelerates.

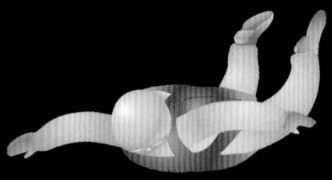

When it stops accelerating. It has reached its terminal velocity.

RESISTANCE

The pull of **gravity** is the force that makes an object accelerate downwards. But as the object starts to move, it experiences **resistance**, an upward force, from the gas or liquid it is falling through. The faster the object falls, the stronger the resistance becomes, until it equals the downward force of the weight of the object. The object stops accelerating at this point and has reached its terminal velocity.

The terminal velocity of an object is slower in a liquid than it is in a gas. This is because a liquid provides more resistance than a gas. As a result, the forces become balanced earlier and the object stops accelerating sooner.

A falling coin takes longer to reach its terminal velocity in air than in water.

MOTION IN A CIRCLE

All moving objects try to travel in a straight line (see Newton's first law, page 122). The force which makes something turn in a circle instead is called a **centripetal** force. This is any force that constantly pulls towards the centre of a circle.

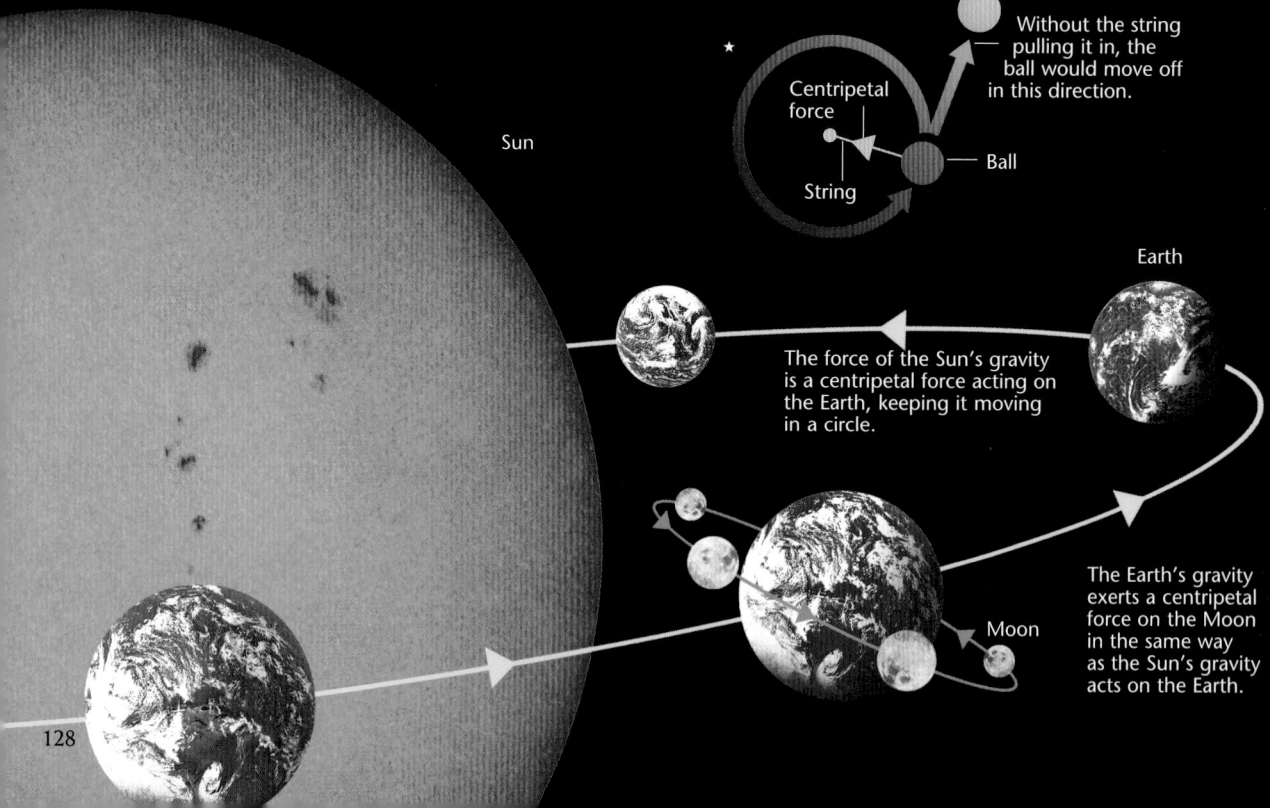

CENTRIPETAL FORCE - AN EXAMPLE

f you tie a small object to a piece of string and whirl it around your head, the pull of the string on the object is a centripetal force. As long as you whirl fast enough, the object will not fall in on you. If you let go of the string, you remove the centripetal force and the object will fly off at a tangent, as when an athlete throws the "hammer".

. The athlete pulls on the wire to make the hammer move.

2. His pull is a centripetal force on the hammer as it moves.

3. The faster the hammer moves, the more centripetal force is needed.

4. The hammer flies off when the centripetal force is removed.

GYROSCOPES

Gyroscopes are wheels that can spin very fast within a frame. The centripetal force created means that the frame can resist the force of gravity. It can even tilt steeply without toppling over. However, when the wheel slows, the gyroscope will fall. (You can buy gyroscopes in some toy shops.)

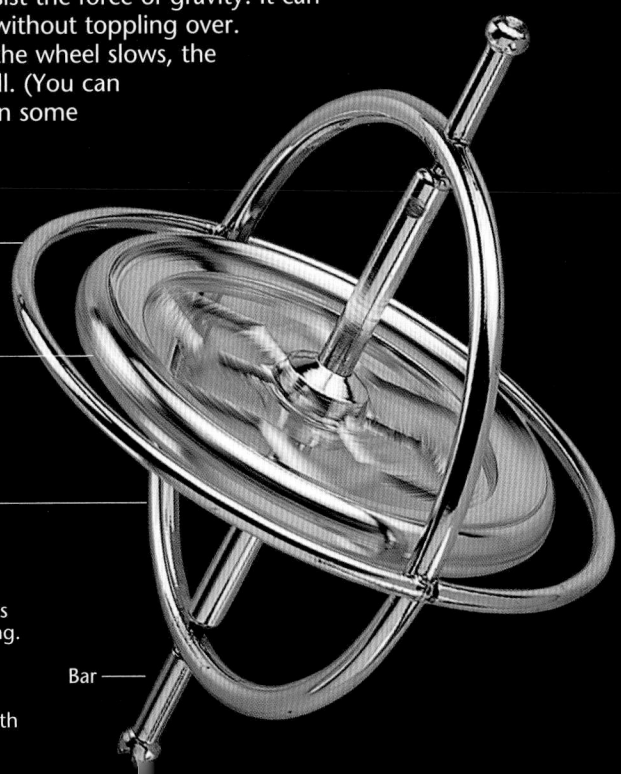

This gyroscope resists gravity when spinning. It can stand on the end of a bar, which is attached to the frame directly beneath the middle of the spinning wheel.

See for yourself

You can see the effect of centripetal force for yourself.

Put a marble in a plastic bowl and move the bowl so that the marble moves in a circle. You have created a centripetal force on the marble.

However, the marble will fly out of the bowl when it reaches a certain speed. The centripetal force is not strong enough to keep it moving in such a tight circle.

Notice that the marble flies off in a straight line.

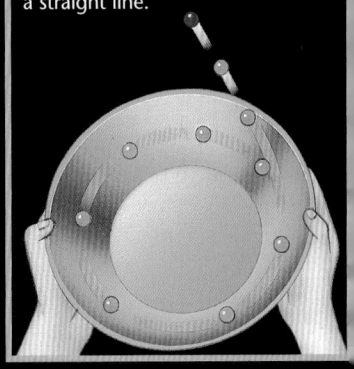

Internet links

To find out more about motion, go to **www.usborne-quicklinks.com** and type in the keyword "science".

There you'll find links to websites where you can:

- Experiment with centripetal force
- See if you can get a cannon ball to hit a target by controlling different forces
- Investigate forces with online experiments and activities

Go to Usborne Quicklinks for links to hand-picked websites on hundreds of subjects.

Always follow the internet safety guidelines on the Usborne Quicklinks Website.

GRAVITY

The force of **gravity** attracts objects to each other. This attraction is not noticeable unless one of the objects is very large, such as a planet. The area within which gravity has an effect is called a **gravitational field**. The Earth and Moon both have gravitational fields, although the Earth's is a lot stronger than the Moon's because it is a much bigger object.

The force of the Sun's gravity keeps a belt of rocks, called asteroids, orbiting around it.

GRAVITY AND MASS

The strength of the pull of gravity between two objects depends on how far apart they are and their masses. **Mass** is the amount of matter that an object contains and this never varies. Any two objects, such as two tomatoes, are attracted to each other, but as their masses are small, the force of gravity between them is tiny and there is no visible effect.

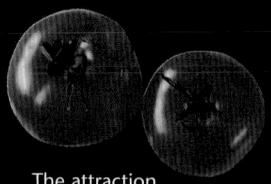

The attraction between these small objects is so tiny that it cannot be felt.

EARTH'S GRAVITY

The force of gravity between the Earth and anything on it is extremely noticeable because the mass of the Earth is so large.

The pull of the Earth's gravity makes any object, such as this conker, fall to the ground.

GRAVITY AND WEIGHT

Weight is a measure of the pull of gravity on an object's mass. The further away an object is from the centre of the Earth, the less the pull of gravity on it. Because of this, you weigh slightly less at a high altitude (for example, at the top of a high mountain) than at the bottom, even though your mass stays the same.

When they are space walking, astronauts weigh far less than they do on Earth. They are so far from the Earth's centre that the planet's gravity has little effect on them.

CENTRE OF GRAVITY

Gravity affects every part of an object, but there is one point where the object's whole weight seems to act. This is its **centre of gravity**. An object can often be balanced at its centre of gravity.

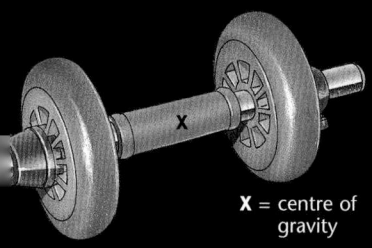

X = centre of gravity

Regularly shaped and symmetrical objects, like this handweight, have their centre of gravity exactly in the middle.

A **stable object** returns to its original position when tilted. Centre of gravity is the key to stability. If an object tilts, but its centre of gravity remains above its base, it won't fall over.

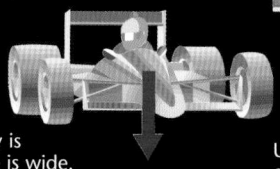

A racing car is very stable. Its centre of gravity is low and its base is wide.

An **unstable object** has its centre of gravity high up, and has a relatively narrow base. If an unstable object is tilted, its centre of gravity soon stops being above its base.

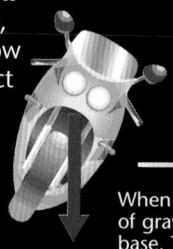

A stationary motorbike is a good example of an unstable object. It will soon fall over when it is tilted.

Tall, narrow things aren't necessarily unstable. For example, a double-decker bus is built so that its centre of gravity is low, making it stable.

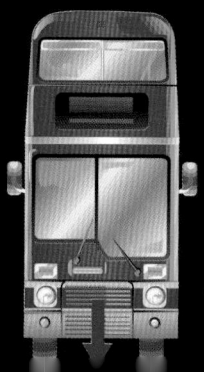

The bottom part of the bus is heavy, containing the engine, wheels and chassis. The top part of the bus is light. As a result, the

See for yourself

Follow these steps to find the centre of gravity of a piece of paper.

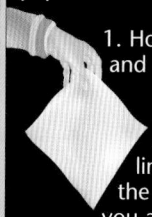

1. Hold up the paper and let it dangle.

2. Hold it against a wall and draw a line straight down the paper from where you are holding it.

3. Hold the paper at a different point and repeat step 2. The centre of gravity will be where the lines cross. If you carry on repeating this, the lines should cross in the same place.

Stable object

X = centre of gravity

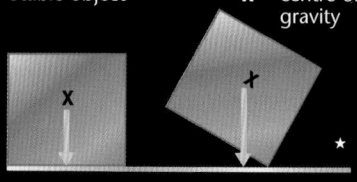

Unless a stable object is tilted a very long way, its centre of gravity stays above its base. As a result, it tends to fall back onto its base.

Unstable object

X = centre of gravity

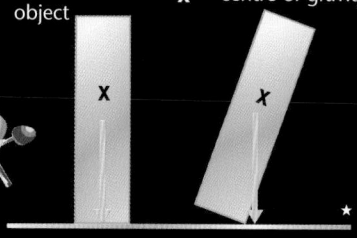

When an unstable object is tilted, its centre of gravity quickly stops being above its base. This causes the object to topple over.

Tall, stable object

X = centre of gravity

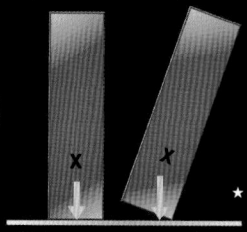

With a low centre of gravity, the tall object must tilt a long way befo

EARTH AND MOON

As the Moon goes around the Earth, its gravity pulls at the planet. This has an effect on the seas of the Earth, which rise and fall. Areas where the water has risen are having a **high tide**. Areas that are not having a high tide are having a **low tide**.

The Moon's effect on the tides

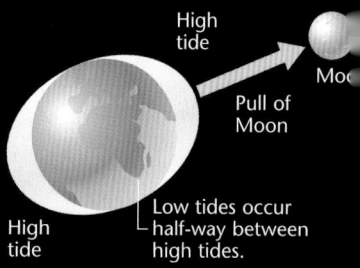

Similarly, the Earth's gravity also pulls at the Moon. It is providing the force, called centripetal force, which is needed to keep the Moon locked in orbit around the Earth itself.

For more information on centripetal force, see *Motion in a Circle*, on page 128.

Internet links

To find out more about gravity, go to **www.usborne-quicklinks.com** and type in the keyword "science".

There you'll find links to websites where you can:

- Play a game about the effects of gravity on different planets
- Find out more with experiments and online activities

Go to Usborne Quicklinks for links to hand-picked websites on hundreds of subjects.

PRESSURE

A needle will go through a piece of cloth, but with the same amount of force, a pencil will not. The differently shaped points of the needle and pencil exert different amounts of pressure. Pressure is everywhere. It operates many machines and affects our weather. Solids, liquids and gases all apply pressure to the surfaces they touch.

Sharp scissors cut well because the blades exert pressure over a tiny area.

WHAT IS PRESSURE?

When a force acts on an object it exerts **pressure**. The pressure acts at a right-angle to the object itself, and its strength depends on the amount of force and the area over which it is applied. For example, someone walking on soft snow will sink into it in normal shoes but not if they wear snowshoes. The person's weight is the same but snowshoes spread the weight over a larger area. This reduces the pressure.

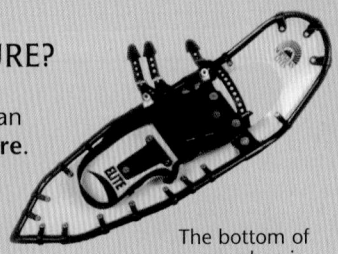

The bottom of a snowshoe is about six times bigger than the sole of a foot.

ATMOSPHERIC PRESSURE

Atmospheric pressure is the weight of air pressing down on the Earth's surface. Over one square metre, the weight of air pressing down is heavier than a large elephant. Air pressure is greatest near the ground, and reduces with height. At 10,000m above the ground, where jets fly, air pressure is very low as there is less air pressing down on anything up there. Less air means less oxygen, and aircraft have pressurized cabins so that people can breathe. The air pressure inside the plane is kept roughly the same as it would be at ground level.

Pressure is measured in **pascals (Pa)**, which are named after the French scientist Blaise Pascal (1623-1662), who made many discoveries about air pressure.

CHANGING WEATHER

Atmospheric pressure is measured in **millibars (mb)**. Weather changes as the pressure changes, with low pressure signalling bad weather and high pressure bringing a settled, fine spell. For example, usual atmospheric pressure at sea level is 1,013mb. However, this can fall to 910mb in a hurricane.

Heavy rains and strong winds are brought by low atmospheric pressure.

PRESSURE IN FLUIDS

Fluids (liquids and gases) change shape according to the container that they are in. The pressure inside them acts outwards in all directions.

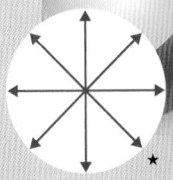

Air inside a beach ball pushes out in all directions, keeping it blown up.

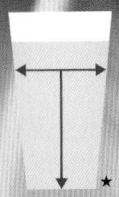

Liquid in a glass exerts pressure against the sides as well as the bottom.

HYDRAULIC MACHINES

Hydraulic machines are machines powered by liquid pressure. A liquid cannot be squashed, so if you press one part of the liquid, pressure increases throughout and the liquid has to move somewhere.

This robot arm works using hydraulic pressure.

Car brakes are hydraulic. Brake fluid is pushed through the brake system, forcing the wheels to slow down.

How a car's footbrake works

Driver presses pedal, pushing piston (1) which forces fluid through cylinder (2). Fluid goes down pipe into two more cylinders (red arrows). These press brake pads (3) against disc in wheel. Friction* slows down wheel (4).

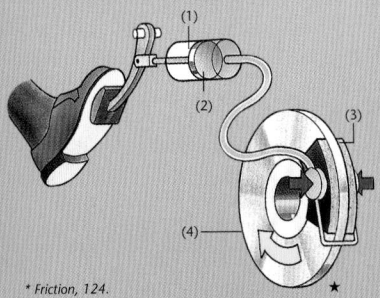

* Friction, 124.

PNEUMATIC MACHINES

Pneumatic machines are driven by the pressure of gases, usually air. Unlike liquid, air can be compressed into a smaller space, and this increases its pressure.

A pneumatic drill, for example, is powered by a piston which squashes air inside the drill to a very high pressure. The compressed air pushes out with enough force to power the drill to crack rock.

Pneumatic drill

A foam and water fire extinguisher is a pneumatic machine which uses compressed carbon dioxide gas.

How a fire extinguisher works

Squeezing handle (1) releases carbon dioxide gas from canister (2). Gas pushes down on a mixture of water and detergent (3), forcing it up a tube (4) and through a hose (5). It shoots out as a jet of foam and water.

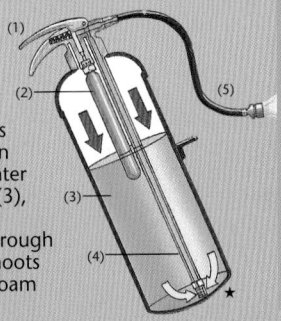

See for yourself

This experiment shows how air pushes out in all directions. You need a lightweight book and a plastic bag.

Put the book on the bag and blow into the bag.

Air pressure increases inside the bag and lifts the book.

Internet links

To find out more about pressure, go to **www.usborne-quicklinks.com** and type in the keyword "science".

There you'll find links to websites where you can:

- Discover interesting facts about air pressure
- Review forces and pressure in solids, liquids and gases

Go to Usborne Quicklinks for links to hand-picked websites on hundreds of subjects.

SIMPLE MACHINES

All machines make physical work easier to do by taking the effort needed to operate them and using it in a more efficient way. Simple machines are devices such as levers and screws. Complex machines, such as drills and cranes, are made up of combinations of simple machines.

The wheel, one of the most important devices ever invented, forms the basis of many machines.

OVERCOMING LOAD

To move any object, you need to overcome a force called the **load**, which is often the weight of the object. A simple machine helps you to do this by taking the force of your **effort** and applying it more efficiently.

It is possible to find out how much more force a simple machine provides compared with the amount of effort that is put in. This is done by dividing the load by the amount of effort used, and is called the **force ratio**.

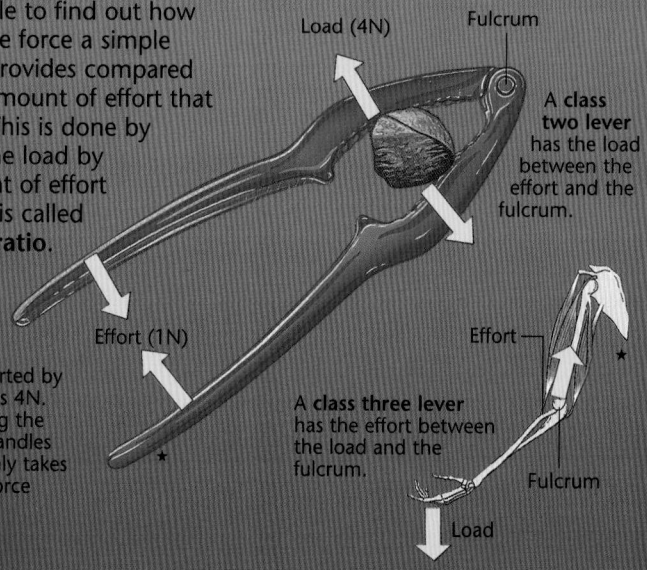

The load exerted by the nutshell is 4N. But squeezing the nutcracker handles to crack it only takes 1N. So the force ratio is 4:1.

If a force ratio is 4:1, the load which the machine overcomes is four times greater than the effort used. Machines like this are called **force magnifiers**.

LEVERS

A **lever** is a rod that turns at a fixed point, called a **fulcrum**, making it easier to perform a task. There are three classes of lever, each with a different arrangement of the fulcrum, effort and load.

The further the effort is from the fulcrum, the easier a lever is to use, so longer levers are generally more useful. (See *Turning Forces* on page 121.)

WHEELS

When a **wheel** turns a rod (such as a steering wheel turning a steering column in a car) the force applied on the wheel is turned into a bigger force by the rod. The bigger the wheel is, the more easily the rod turns.

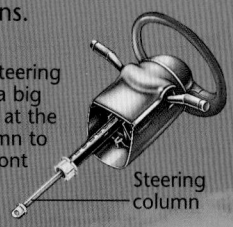

When an axle is turned, a wheel connected to it will convert the axle's circular motion into a straight line motion that can move loads across the ground. A car's wheels are an example of this. The wheel turns further than the axle because it is bigger.

See for yourself

To see how a class one lever works, put a pencil under the middle of a rigid ruler. Put a lightweight book on one end.

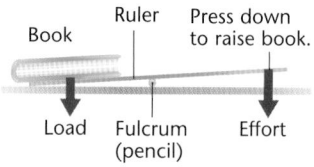

Try changing the position of the pencil under the ruler. The further the effort is from the fulcrum, the easier it is to lift the load.

PULLEYS

Pulleys help to lift heavy loads and are often used in lifts and cranes. The load is attached to a rope which passes around one or more grooved wheels. When the other end of the rope is pulled, the load is lifted.

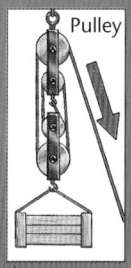

Pulleys let you pull down instead of up, so you can use your weight to help.

The more wheels a pulley has, the easier it is to lift a load, as the weight of the load is spread out over more rope.

This crane works like a giant pulley. The rope is made of strong steel cable. The pulling strength is provided by the crane's engine.

The strong steel cable passes over grooved wheels.

The cable can lift very heavy objects, such as steel and concrete building materials.

The crane's engine is housed here.

SCREWS

A **screw** has an axle and a thread which work together like an inclined plane (see below) wrapped around a cylinder. The axle is the cylinder and the thread the inclined plane.

The turning screw converts the force applied into a much greater straight line force. As a result, the axle easily drives straight into the object.

A corkscrew converts a turning motion into a straight line force.

GEARS

Gears are used to change speed in many different kinds of complex machines, from cars to clocks. They do this by changing the size of a turning force.

Gears consist of two or more toothed wheels, or **cogs**, that fit into each other, so that turning one cog turns the other. A large cog makes a smaller one turn faster.

This gear changes the size and direction of the turning force.

This clock works using a complicated system of geared wheels.

INCLINED PLANES

An **inclined plane** is just a slope, like a ramp. It is easier to move an object up an inclined plane than vertically upwards, because you travel further, so less force is needed for the same amount of work.

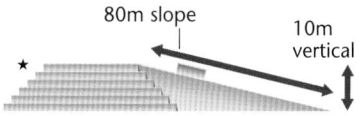

If you push an object eight times as far up an inclined plane as lifting it straight up, you only need one eighth of the force.

Internet links

To find out more about machines, go to **www.usborne-quicklinks.com** and type in the keyword "science".

There you'll find links to websites where you can:

- Play games to find out more about simple machines
- View animations of simple machines in action

Go to Usborne Quicklinks for links to hand-picked websites on hundreds of subjects.

USING SIMPLE MACHINES

Simple machines can be used to make up more complex machines. Here are some examples. Even animals, such as the lobster on the right, can have body parts which work in the same way as a machine.

Propellers are a simple form of screw. They are used to push ships through water – and to pull aircraft through the air.

Archimedes' screw was an early device for pumping water from rivers or lakes.

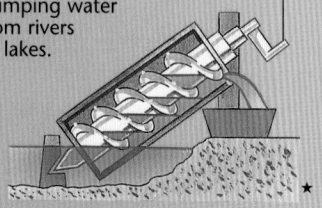

Water was drawn up on the inclined planes of a turning screw.

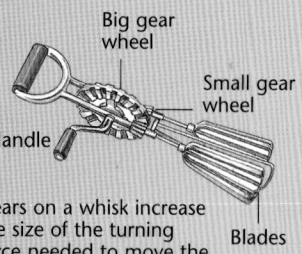

Gears on a whisk increase the size of the turning force needed to move the handle, so that the blades can be turned very fast.

A lobster's claws, or pincers, are third class levers.

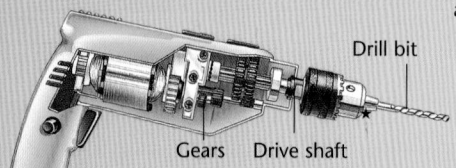

An electric drill combines gears and a screw at the tip, called a **bit**. The gears change the speed at which the bit rotates, so that it can drill a hole quickly or slowly.

An axe turns a downward force into a sideways cutting force. The blade is a **wedge** that pushes apart as it cuts down.

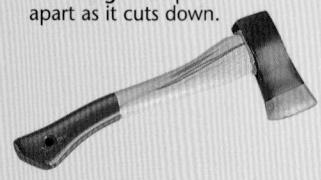

A motor provides power to a system of gears and wheels which move the stairs and handrails on an escalator.

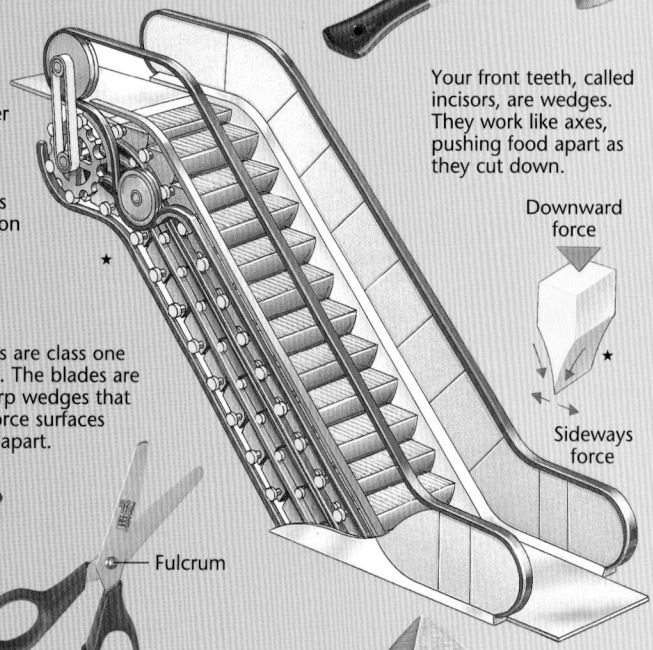

Your front teeth, called incisors, are wedges. They work like axes, pushing food apart as they cut down.

Scissors are class one levers. The blades are sharp wedges that force surfaces apart.

A fan is a third class lever. When you wave it, your wrist acts as the fulcrum.

The Ancient Egyptians, who built the pyramids, may have used inclined planes, in the form of spiral slopes, to push enormous blocks of stone up into place. The tallest pyramids were about 146m high.

WORK AND POWER

In science, the word "work" has a particular meaning. **Work** is done when a force makes an object move. Work is only done when the object moves.

MEASURING WORK

Work transfers energy from one object to another and, like energy, is measured in **joules (J)**. One joule equals the work done (and energy transferred) when a force of 1 newton (N) moves an object 1 metre in the direction of the force.

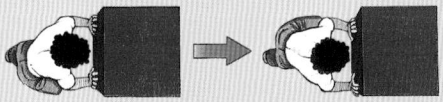

If this man pushes the box with a force of 100 newtons for 3 metres, he performs 300 joules of work.

POWER

Power is the rate at which work is done, or energy is transferred. It is measured in **watts (W)**, named after James Watt, and is worked out by dividing the work done by the time taken to do it.

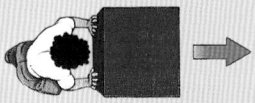

It takes twice as much power to move the box 3 metres in one minute as to move it 3 metres in two minutes.

AN EXAMPLE OF WORK

In the picture, the male dancer's lifting force is overcoming the force of gravity, and work is being done as he raises the ballerina in the air.

The male dancer is using his energy to lift the ballerina. Most of this energy is being converted to potential energy* in the dancer in the air. Also, some heat energy is being released by the male dancer's body.

The ballerina has to do work as she moves her body into the correct pose.

See for yourself

You can measure how much work you do (in joules) when you go upstairs by measuring the height of the stairs and multiplying it by your weight in newtons (your weight in kilograms x 10). Divide the work you do by the time it takes to do it to find out how much power you exert (in watts). The quicker you go, the more power you exert.

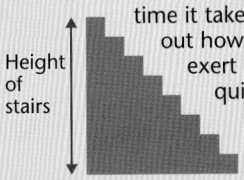

Internet links

To find out more about work and power, go to **www.usborne-quicklinks.com** and type in the keyword "science".

There you'll find links to websites where you can:

- Read an entertaining article about work, joules, power and watts
- Take part in an animated lesson with short quizzes on work and power

** Potential energy, 106.*

FLOATING

Why do some substances float in water, but not others? And why are there so few substances that are able to float in air? By understanding the principles of floating (and sinking), engineers can build ships out of metals that are heavier than the water they float in, and design airships and hot-air balloons that can float in the air.

Hot-air balloons are filled with air that is lighter than the cool air outside them. They rise up because hot air floats.

WHY THINGS FLOAT

When an object is put into water, it pushes aside, or **displaces**, some of the water. It takes up the space where the water was, and the level of the water rises.

According to legend, the Ancient Greek scientist Archimedes (287-212BC) first realized how objects displace water when he got into his bath.

This is a medieval picture of Archimedes making his discovery.

Water pushes back against an object placed in it with a force called **upthrust**. If this is the same as the weight of the object, the object floats. The weight of the object and the weight of the water it displaces are equal.

ARCHIMEDES' PRINCIPLE

Archimedes' principle states that the upthrust acting on an object is equal to the weight of the fluid that the object displaces. An object will sink into a fluid, such as water, and keep on sinking unless the force of the upthrust from the fluid becomes equal to the weight of the object.

Water is displaced (yellow arrows) as boat is lowered. Upthrust (red arrow) pushes back on boat.

When upthrust of water equals weight of boat, boat settles on water and floats steadily.

DENSITY

One object may float while another of the same size may sink. Same-sized objects have different weights if their density is different. **Density** is a measure of the amount of matter in an object (its **mass**) compared to its volume (size).

A steel ball is heavier than an apple of the same size because it is denser. Its matter is packed more tightly together. The apple floats (just) in water but the steel ball sinks.

FLOATING IN THE AIR

Air, like water, pushes back at an object with a force called upthrust. This equals the weight of air pushed aside by the object. If the upthrust equals the weight of the object, the object floats. But air is so light that few things float in it. Hot-air balloons and helium-filled airships can both float in air, though, because hot air and helium are both lighter than cold air.

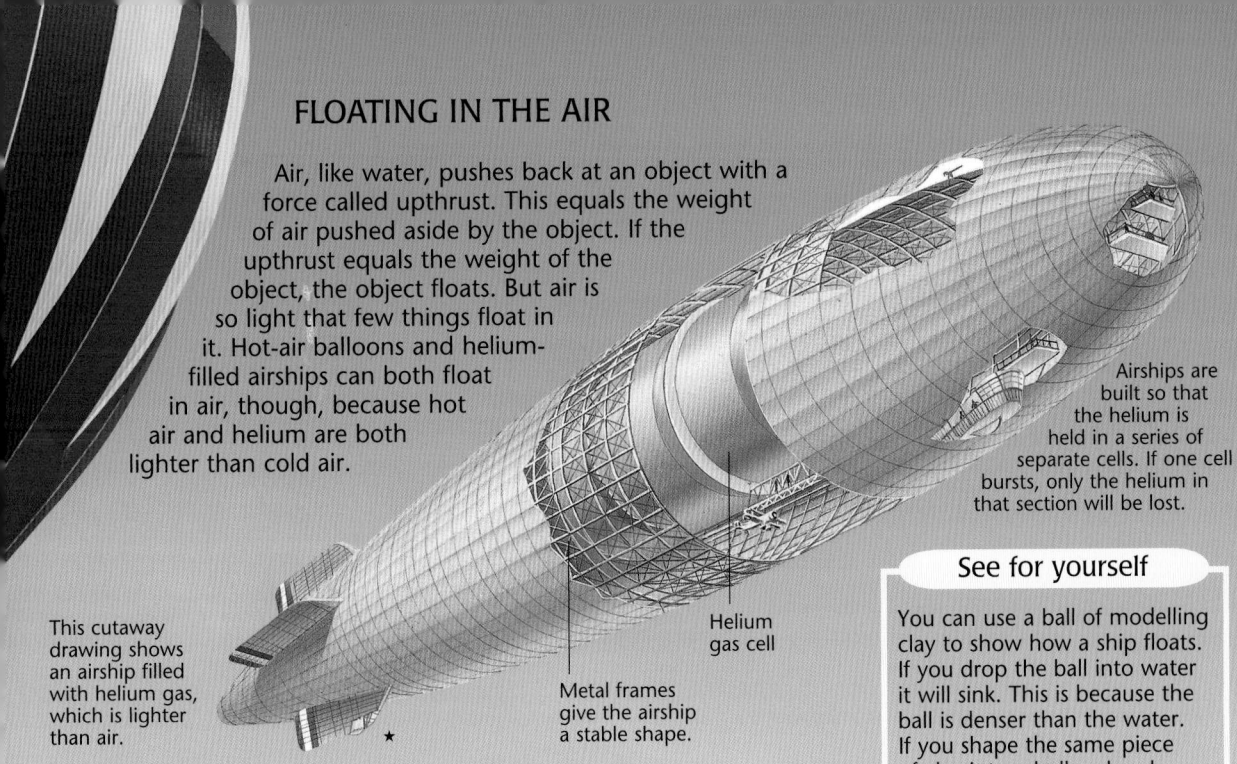

This cutaway drawing shows an airship filled with helium gas, which is lighter than air.

HOW SHIPS FLOAT

Modern ships are made of steel, which is eight times denser than water. But they don't sink because their overall density is lower than water. This is because ships are hollow. All the space inside them makes them less dense than water. Their huge volume pushes aside (or displaces) a large amount of water and so creates a lot of upthrust on the ship.

Even when fully laden, a container ship still displaces so much water that it floats. The displaced water creates a massive upthrust on the huge ship.

RELATIVE DENSITIES

For an object to float in water, its density needs to be less than, or the same as, the density of water. If not, the water cannot provide enough upthrust to support it.

The **relative density** of an object is its density when compared to the density of water. The relative density of water is 1, so an object will sink if its relative density is more than 1, but float if it is 1 or less.

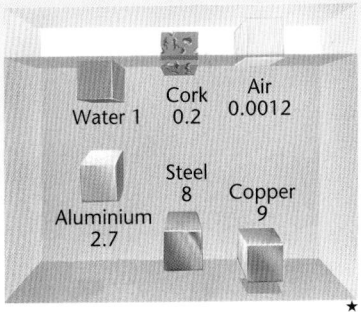

This picture shows the relative densities of different substances. Nearly all metals are denser than water.

See for yourself

You can use a ball of modelling clay to show how a ship floats. If you drop the ball into water it will sink. This is because the ball is denser than the water. If you shape the same piece of clay into a hollow bowl, though, it should float.

Although it is the same weight as the ball, the bowl floats because it pushes aside more water. The force of the upthrust equals its weight.

Internet links

To find out more about floating, go to **www.usborne-quicklinks.com** and type in the keyword "science".

There you'll find links to websites where you can:

- Find density and buoyancy facts and diagrams, with puzzles to solve about floating
- Test objects in online experiments

Go to Usborne Quicklinks for links to hand-picked websites on hundreds of subjects.

SHIPS AND BOATS

Ships and boats once relied on the wind or human strength for their power. The invention of engines meant that propellers* could be used to drive ships through the water. More recent boat designs include hydrofoils and hovercraft.

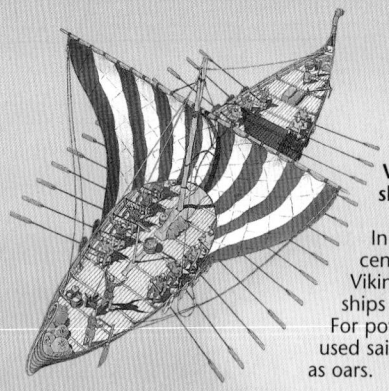

Viking ship

In the ninth century, the Vikings used ships like this. For power, they used sails as well as oars.

Tankers

Tankers carry oil or other liquid cargo in tanks. Big tankers, called supertankers, are the largest ships in the world.

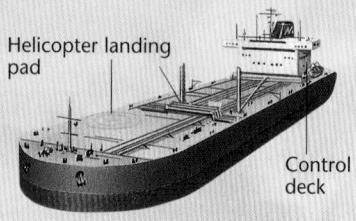

Hovercraft

A hovercraft (also called an Air-Cushion Vehicle, or ACV) skims over the water on a cushion of air inside a rubber skirt.

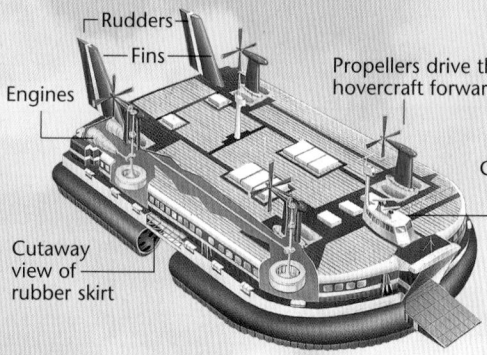

Hydrofoils

Hydrofoils have stilts attached to underwater "wings" called foils. When a hydrofoil speeds up, its hull lifts out of the water, reducing water resistance. Two designs of foil are surface-piercing foils and ladder foils.

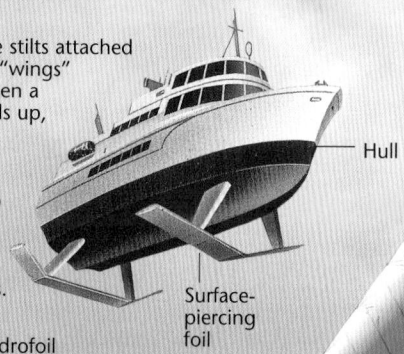

Hydrofoil with surface-piercing foils

Hydrofoil with ladder foils

Cruise ships

Large, luxurious cruise ships are designed to carry hundreds of people on holidays.

Container ships

Container ships carry goods in large metal boxes. These can be unloaded or loaded quickly by cranes. One ship can carry hundreds of containers.

Racing yacht

This racing yacht was built using heavy wood, and has weighty canvas sails. Modern versions use more lightweight materials, so they are faster and easier to steer.

* Propellers, 136.

Iron ship

This nineteenth century boat had sails and a steam engine that drove a propeller (shown with the rudder in the circle). It had an iron hull.

Clipper

Clippers were used in the nineteenth century to carry goods around the world. They had so many sails that they could reach speeds of nearly 40km/h (25mph).

SUBMARINES

Submarines can dive and surface by altering their relative density*. They carry large containers called **ballast tanks**. When air is expelled from these tanks and replaced with water, the submarine's density increases and it dives. When it needs to surface, air is pumped back into the tanks and water is forced back out. This makes the submarine less dense, and it rises to the surface.

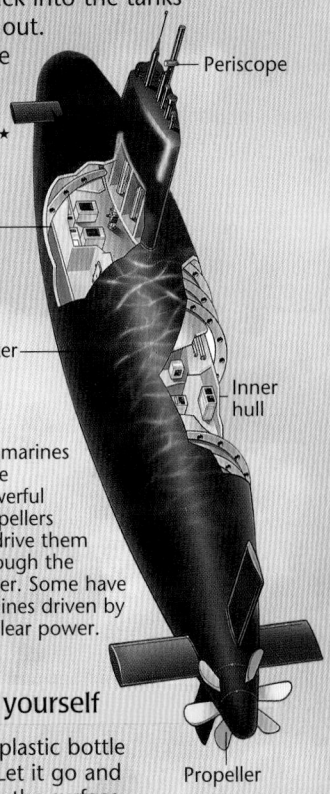

A submarine dives as its ballast tanks are filled with water.

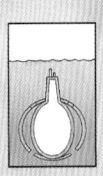

A submarine rises as air is pumped back into the tanks and water is forced out.

Submarines have powerful propellers to drive them through the water. Some have engines driven by nuclear power.

See for yourself

Put the top on an empty plastic bottle and hold it under water. Let it go and the bottle will shoot up to the surface.

Now fill the bottle with water. You are making the bottle denser, so it will now remain underwater, just like a submarine with water in its ballast tanks.

Internet links

Go to **www.usborne-quicklinks.com** and type in the keyword "science" to find out more about ships and boats.

There you'll find links to websites where you can:

- Find out how submarines work, with experiments, animations and video clips.
- Take a virtual tour of a warship and find out more about oil tankers

Go to Usborne Quicklinks for links to hand-picked websites on hundreds of subjects.

* *Relative density, 139.*

FLIGHT

The first powered flight took place a century ago and lasted only twelve seconds. Now planes can travel faster than the speed of sound, and helicopters can hover in the air without moving. The wings of planes and the blades of helicopters have a special shape which helps them to fly.

Kites were the first things that people managed to fly.

HOW PLANES FLY

Planes can fly because of the shape of their wings. The wings are curved on top and flatter underneath. A bird's wings have the same shape. It is called an **aerofoil**.

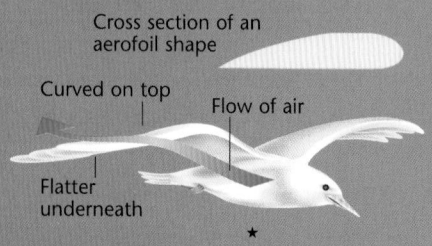

The air above an aerofoil wing has further to travel than the air under it. When the flow of a gas such as air gets faster, its pressure is reduced. This is called **Bernoulli's principle**. Because of this, the slower air flowing under the wing has a higher pressure and pushes up on it. This force is called **lift**, and it causes the wing to rise up into the air.

Cross section of an aircraft wing

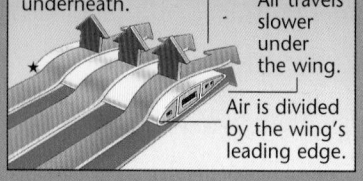

Gliders are very light and the lift from their wings is strong enough to overcome the downward pull of gravity. Heavier aircraft need a force called **thrust** to stay in the air. Thrust, the force that moves a plane forwards, is provided by a plane's engines.

The more thrust an engine provides, the faster the plane goes. This greater speed improves the lift on the aircraft. The faster the wings are moving through the air, the greater the difference in air pressure above and below them.

Propellers provide thrust by pulling a plane through the air.

Jet engines provide thrust by pushing a plane through the air.

The four forces of flight

The arrows on this picture show the four forces of flight: lift, gravity, drag and thrust.

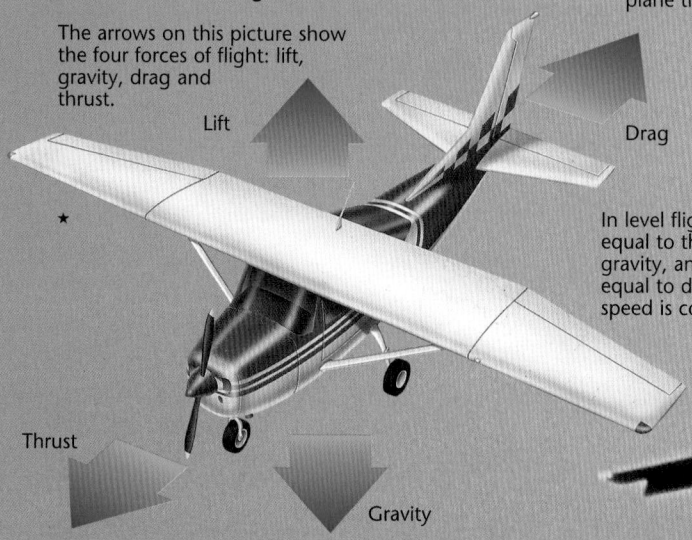

In level flight, lift is equal to the pull of gravity, and thrust is equal to drag if the speed is constant.

Drag, or **air resistance**, is another force acting on a plane. It is the force of friction* that occurs when something moves in air.

Drag increases as speed increases, so very fast aircraft are streamlined to reduce drag. A streamlined plane is designed so that air moves around it more smoothly.

* Friction, 124.

HOW PLANES ARE CONTROLLED

A plane needs to be able to move up and down, and to turn and bank (tip) to each side. To do this, the wings and tail are fitted with hinged flaps. These are known as **control surfaces**. They are made up of **ailerons** on the wings, and **elevators** and a **rudder** on the tail. By using a particular control surface, a pilot increases the drag on that part of the plane. This pushes it into a new position, as shown in the diagrams below.

How control surfaces work

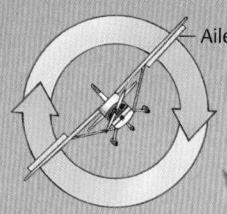

When turning, a plane also banks. This is called **rolling**. It is controlled by the ailerons on the wings.

Turning to the left or right is called **yawing**, and is controlled by the rudder on the tail fin.

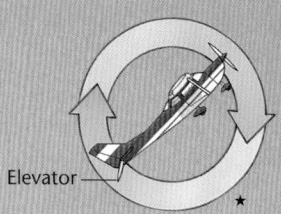

Moving up and down is called **pitching**. Elevators on the tailplane control this.

See for yourself

You can create an aerofoil wing with a strip of paper 15cm x 5cm and a pencil.

Fold the strip in half with the short edges together. Then move one edge back so that it is about 1.5cm from the other edge and tape it down. This will make an aerofoil. Slide it onto a pencil, as shown.

Put the edge that hangs over the pencil close to your lips. Blow steadily over the top of the fold. The difference in air flow above and below the wing makes it rise.

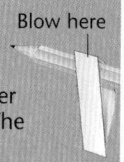

This DC-10 is just about to land. As the pilot controls the jet's descent, its ailerons, elevators and rudder are constantly twitching up and down or back and forth.

Big passenger jets have three or four engines.

The engine's thrust is reduced little by little so that the plane loses lift. Gradually, it comes down to the ground.

Big jets like this have their wheels, or undercarriage, tucked away during flights. This reduces the drag on the plane.

Aileron. The next time you fly, look out for these moving on the backs of the wings.

Internet links

To find out more about flight, go to **www.usborne-quicklinks.com** and type in the keyword "science".

There you'll find links to websites where you can:

- Discover the principles of flight
- Fly a plane in an online game
- Learn more with online activities

Go to Usborne Quicklinks for links to hand-picked websites on hundreds of subjects.

AIRCRAFT DESIGN

The design of an aircraft depends on its function. Some planes need to be able to land on water, and some helicopters are used to lift huge weights. Here you can see some examples of different aircraft designs.

Tail fin

Tailplane

Rudder

Body of plane, called **fuselage**

Elevator

Passenger jet

This Boeing 747 is called a jumbo jet because of its size. It can carry up to 500 passengers.

Seating for passengers

Flight deck

Fuel tanks

Aileron

Undercarriage (main landing gear)

Jet engines

Radar equipment

Swing-wing plane

This Panavia Tornado is a swing-wing jet fighter. Its moveable wings can be straight (better for flying at slow speeds and landing) or swept-back (better for high-speed flying).

Wings sweep through this angle.

Sea plane

This Canadair CL-415 is a sea plane. It can take off and land on water. It floats because its body is shaped like a boat.

This plane also has wheels so it can move on land. Planes like this are called amphibians.

Supersonic passenger plane

Supersonic planes fly faster than the speed of sound*. The Concorde was the only supersonic passenger plane.

Concorde's delta-shaped wings (see page 145) helped it to fly at speeds of up to 2,333km/h (1,450mph).

"Invisible" plane

The Northrop B2 Stealth bomber's strange "flying wing" shape helps it to avoid radar detection. It has a wingspan of over 52m.

The Stealth bomber is made of radar-absorbent materials.

Load-carrying helicopter

The Sikorsky Skycrane carries heavy loads to hard-to-reach places.

The Skycrane can carry the weight of over 150 people. Here, it is unloading a ready-made cabin to a building site.

* *Speed of sound. 207.*

FIRST FLIGHT

The first successful powered flight was made in 1903 by Flyer I. It was designed and built by the Wright brothers in the USA. The plane flew for about twelve seconds and lifted only a little way off the ground.

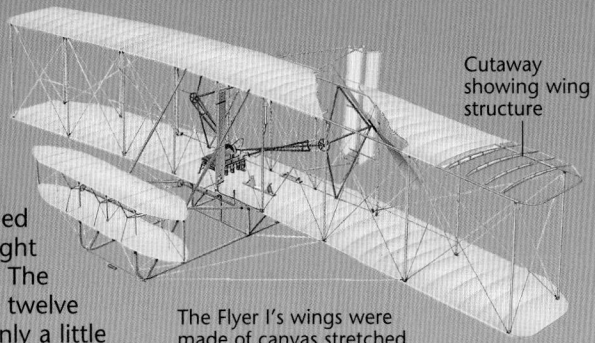

The Flyer I's wings were made of canvas stretched over a wooden frame.

HELICOPTERS

Helicopters can travel in any direction, or just hover in the air without moving. Their rotor blades are aerofoils*, which provide lift as they spin around rapidly. To provide thrust*, the blades are tilted forwards. They push the air behind them and this moves the helicopter forwards.

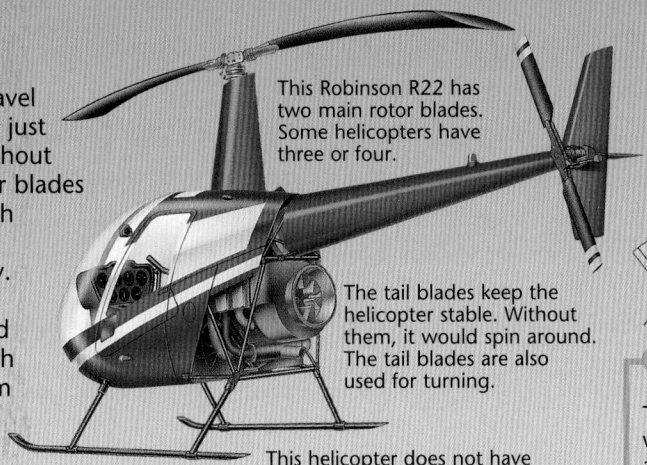

This Robinson R22 has two main rotor blades. Some helicopters have three or four.

The tail blades keep the helicopter stable. Without them, it would spin around. The tail blades are also used for turning.

This helicopter does not have wheels, but rests on the ground on flat blades called **skids**.

JUMP JETS

The Harrier is a **Vertical Take Off and Landing (VTOL)** plane, or **jump jet**. It does not need a runway to take off.

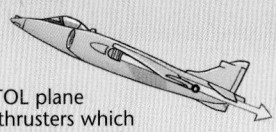

A VTOL plane has thrusters which direct the power from its jet engines. In normal flight, the thrusters point to the back. This pushes the plane forwards.

This Harrier is taking off. Its thrusters point down at the ground, pushing the plane upwards.

WING SHAPE

How fast a plane can go depends on the shape of its wings, as well as the size of its engines.

Straight wings give enough lift* for low-speed flying, with not much drag*.

Swept-back wings reduce drag at greater speeds, and are needed for larger-sized planes, such as passenger jets.

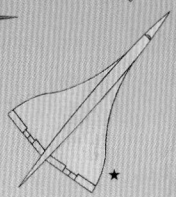

Delta-shaped wings enable an aircraft to fly at supersonic speeds. The fastest planes use this wing shape.

See for yourself

The wings on a model plane work in the same way as on a real plane.

You can make a paper plane of your own that can do turns and stunts. For a template, plus a step-by-step guide and flying tips, go to the website **www.usborne-quicklinks.com** and follow the instructions.

Internet links

Go to **www.usborne-quicklinks.com** and type the keyword "science" to find out more about aircraft design.

There you'll find links to websites where you can:

- Explore how planes are designed
- See inside a passenger jet
- Learn more about the Wright brothers and their aircraft

Go to Usborne Quicklinks for links to hand-picked websites on hundreds of subjects.

** Aerofoil, Drag, Lift, Thrust, 142.*

Engines are machines that convert the energy stored in fuel into movement. They release the energy in fuel by **combustion**, that is, by burning it. This can take place outside the engine (**external combustion**) or inside the engine (**internal combustion**).

STEAM ENGINES

The first engines were **steam engines**. They were invented about 300 years ago, and used external combustion.

In a chamber outside the engine called the **furnace**, wood or coal was burned to boil water. This produced steam. Because steam expands to take up to 2,000 times more space than water, it could be used to move a piston.

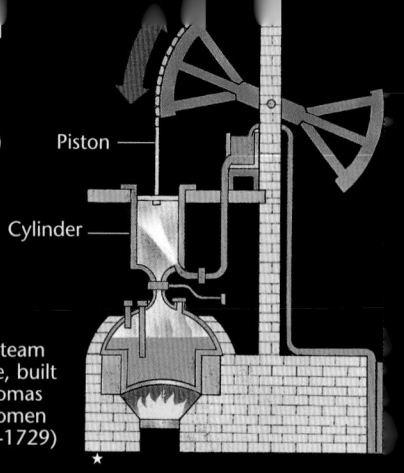

Early steam engine, built by Thomas Newcomen (1663-1729)

BETTER ENGINES

The earliest steam engines were not very reliable or efficient, but by the nineteenth century the technology had been improved and steam engines were being used to drive trains and power machinery in factories. James Watt (1736-1819) designed the widely-used steam engine shown here.

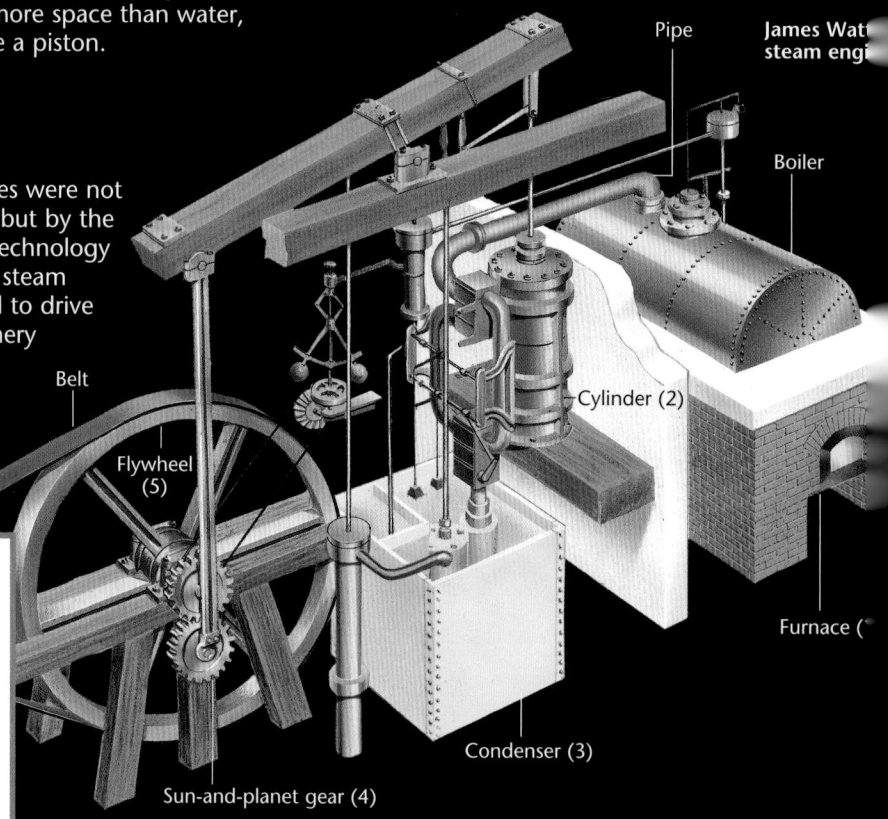

1. To make this steam engine work, coal was burned in a furnace to heat water in the boiler.

2. A pipe carried steam from the boiler to the cylinder. The steam pushed a piston up inside the cylinder.

3. The condenser took used steam from the cylinder and the piston went down. The steam turned back into water.

4. A gear called a sun-and-planet gear converted the up-and-down movement of the piston into a rotating motion.

5. The flywh rotated to power indu machinery, which it wa connected by a belt.

See for yourself

You can see the power of steam when a covered pan of water boils on a stove.

As the water boils, notice that the lid starts to bounce up and down. This is the expanding steam pushing against the lid.

Steam engines make use of this power to make things move.

TURBINES

Many modern power stations still use steam. Pressurized steam turns huge **turbines** – devices with rotating blades. This rotation generates electricity.

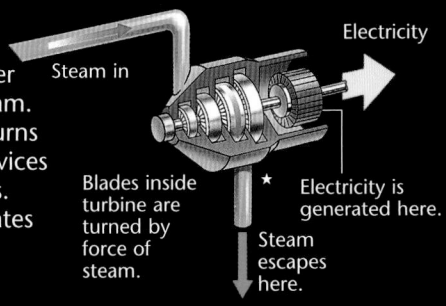

This is part of a huge steam turbine in a power station. The simplified diagram on the left shows how it works.

INTERNAL COMBUSTION

Internal combustion is more efficient than external combustion. **Internal combustion engines** burn a mixture of fuel and air inside the engine itself. This produces hot gases. These take up more space than the fuel and air they come from, and are used to create movement.

Modern cars have efficient internal combustion engines. In most cars, the engine drives the front wheels.

EXHAUST FUMES

Some of the gases produced by combustion are poisonous. They leave the engine as **exhaust fumes**.

To reduce pollution, new car engines are fitted with **catalytic converters**. These contain **catalysts**, substances that can alter the speed of chemical reactions. The converter changes the poisonous exhaust fumes into less poisonous gases.

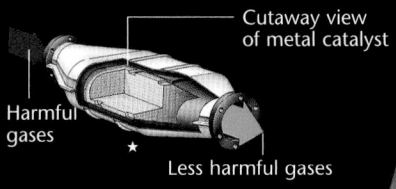

In a catalytic converter, carbon monoxide is converted into carbon dioxide and water, and nitrogen oxide into nitrogen and oxygen.

Internet links

To find out more about engines, go to **www.usborne-quicklinks.com** and type in the keyword "science".

There you'll find links to websites where you can:

- Investigate "The Rocket", an early steam engine
- Find out how wind turbines work
- Meet the inventor, James Watt

Go to Usborne Quicklinks for links to hand-picked websites on hundreds of subjects.

PETROL ENGINES

Most car engines burn petrol. **Petrol engines** use internal combustion* to drive pistons up and down in hollow cylinders.

Each piston works in four stages called a **four-stroke combustion cycle**, as shown in the pictures on the right.

How a four-stroke engine works

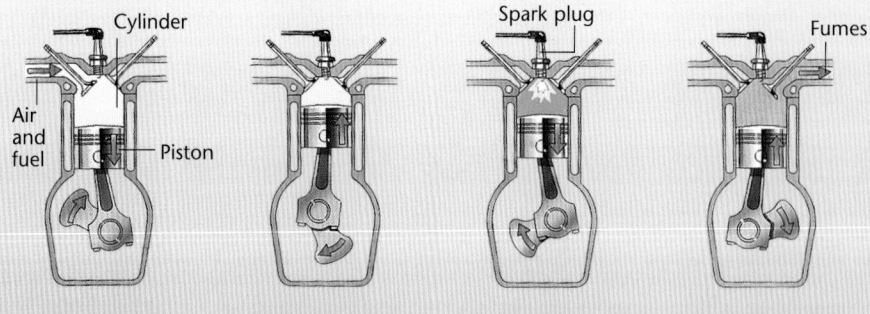

1. Piston goes down, sucking a mixture of air and fuel into cylinder.

2. Piston goes up, compressing fuel and air mixture. This heats mixture.

3. Spark from spark plug ignites mixture. Gases expand and force piston down.

4. Piston rises again, pushing out remains of burned gases as exhaust fumes.

This is a four cylinder internal combustion car engine. It is built by Ford and called the Zetec.

Spark plug

A small spark is set off at this end of the plug.

This is the end of the crankshaft (see below).

One of the cylinders

One of the pistons

DIESEL ENGINES

Diesel fuel is used mainly by larger vehicles and some trains. **Diesel engines** work in a similar way to petrol engines, but at stroke one, only air is taken into the cylinder. This is compressed and heated to a very high temperature at stroke two. Diesel fuel is forced into the cylinder at stroke three, where it is so hot that the fuel burns without a spark.

TRANSMISSION

The four-stroke combustion cycle takes place in each of a car's cylinders. A series of shafts and gears, called the transmission, converts the up-and-down motion of the pistons into a rotating motion used to turn the wheels of the car. The system works in a similar way whether it drives the front or rear wheels of the car. (See also *Transmission* on page 151.)

Transmission system of a rear-wheel drive car

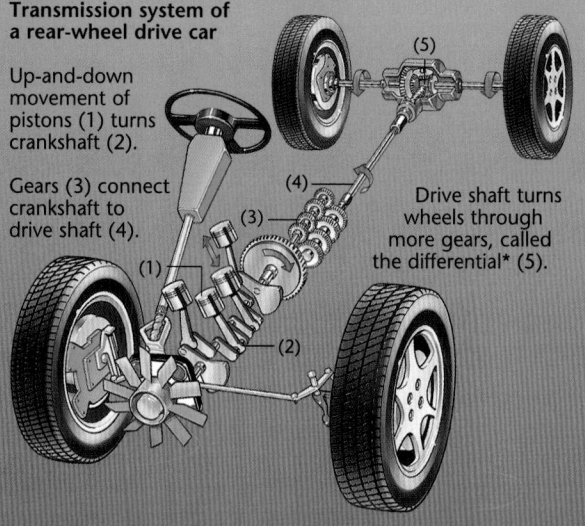

** Differential, 151; Internal combustion, 146.*

JET ENGINES

Jet engines are very powerful internal combustion engines* used by aircraft. The hot gases they produce are forced out of the back of the engine at high speed. This pushes the plane through the air.

Jet engines are also known as **gas turbine engines** because the hot gases turn blades called turbines in the engine. The turbines suck air into the engine and compress it before it is mixed with fuel and burned.

TURBOJET ENGINES

The **turbojet engine** below is the simplest and fastest type of jet engine. It is noisy and less efficient with fuel than a turbofan engine (see right). Turbojet engines are only used for high-speed jet planes.

Cutaway of a turbojet engine

Air enters front of engine (1). Turbines in compression chamber (2) compress air. Compressed air is channelled into combustion chamber (3) and mixed with kerosene fuel. Mixture burns and produces hot, expanding gases.

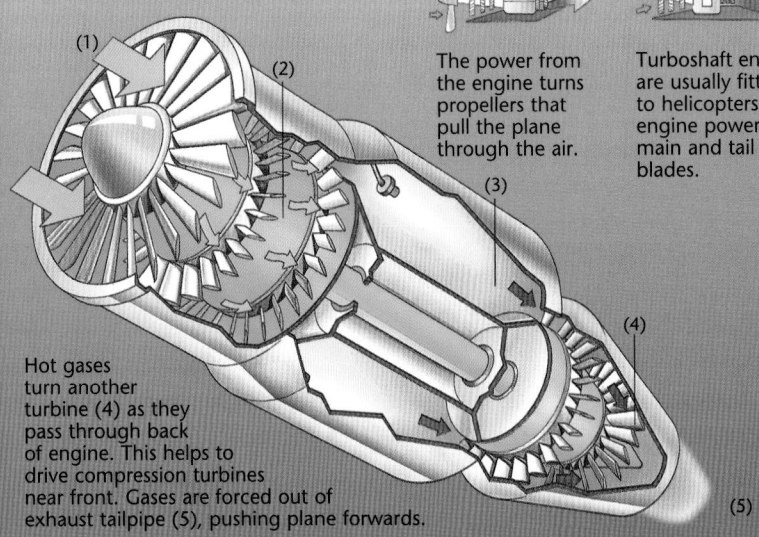

Hot gases turn another turbine (4) as they pass through back of engine. This helps to drive compression turbines near front. Gases are forced out of exhaust tailpipe (5), pushing plane forwards.

TURBOFAN ENGINES

Turbofan engines are not as fast as turbojets, but they are quieter and use less fuel. They are fitted to passenger jets.

Cutaway of a turbofan engine

Extra large fan at front (1) sucks in huge amounts of air. Some air goes through compression and combustion chambers (2), as in turbojet, producing hot expanding gases which are forced out of back (3).

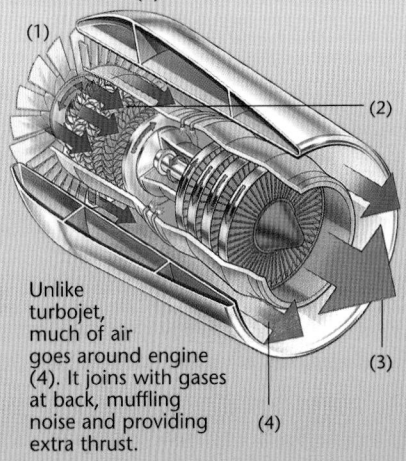

Unlike turbojet, much of air goes around engine (4). It joins with gases at back, muffling noise and providing extra thrust.

There are two other kinds of gas turbine engine:

Turboprop

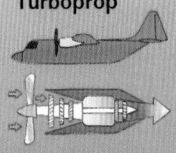

The power from the engine turns propellers that pull the plane through the air.

Turboshaft

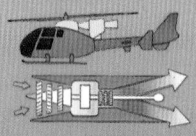

Turboshaft engines are usually fitted to helicopters. The engine powers the main and tail rotor blades.

ROCKET ENGINES

Like jet engines, **rocket engines** produce hot gases which are forced out at speed. Instead of sucking in air for combustion, rocket engines carry liquid oxygen. This means that they can travel in space where there is no air.

Space rockets were developed from rocket missiles, such as this V-2 made in 1942.

See for yourself

Try this to give you an idea of how jet engines work. Thread some string through a straw and tie it tightly between two pieces of furniture. Blow up a balloon and hold the end so that it doesn't deflate. Ask a friend to tape the balloon to the straw.

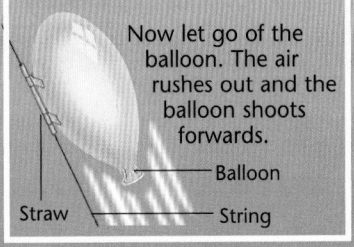

Now let go of the balloon. The air rushes out and the balloon shoots forwards.

Internet links

To find out more about engines, go to **www.usborne-quicklinks.com** and type in the keyword "science".

There you'll find links to websites where you can:

- Watch an animation of how an engine works
- Find online rocket activities

** Internal combustion engines, 147.*

CARS AND MOTORBIKES

Cars, motorbikes and other road vehicles have transformed the way we live. They allow us to move from one place to another quickly and whenever we want to. But their popularity has led to problems of pollution and traffic jams. Car makers are constantly trying to develop cars that are less damaging to the environment.

This is one of the very first cars. It was built in Germany in 1885.

CAR TECHNOLOGY

The first cars were invented about 120 years ago. At first, they were slow, noisy, unreliable and dangerous. Since then, engineers and designers have refined all aspects of how cars work. These include making improvements to vital parts such as the engine, brakes, transmission and suspension. The vehicle below shows a good example of modern car design.

This cutaway car is a Ford Puma. It was first made in 1997 and has a top speed of around 200km/h (125mph).

Laminated, shatterproof glass

Suspension

The hydraulic reservoir contains brake fluid.

Battery. This powers the electrical system.

Exhaust pipe under car takes fumes from engine.

Radiator fan. This keeps the engine cool.

Engine block

Disc brake

Drive shaft. This takes the power from the engine to the wheels.

ENGINE POWER

Internal combustion engines burn petrol or diesel, creating gases that push pistons up and down in a cylinder. This motion creates the engine's power. The power is transferred from the engine to the drive shaft to the wheels, via the gear box, enabling the car to move. An engine's cylinders are measured in litres. A 1.4 litre car has cylinders that measure 1.4 litres in total.

* *Internal combustion engines, 147.*

MOTORBIKES

Motorbikes and cars share many features, although motorbikes don't need a differential (see below). Because they are relatively light, motorbikes can have engines with small cylinder capacities, down to about 50cm³ (50 cubic centimetres) in total. Bikes with large engines are powerful, and can accelerate faster than cars.

TRANSMISSION

The **transmission** (see also page 148) is a system of **gears** that transmits an engine's power to the wheels. Gears are made of cogs (metal wheels with serrated edges called teeth). Engine power turns a rod called the input shaft, which is attached to one set of cogs. These turn another set of cogs which are attached to another rod – the output shaft. The output shaft turns drive shafts, which are attached to the wheels.

DIFFERENTIAL

The **differential** is a vital part of a car's transmission. It is a system of gears on the axles which allows the wheels to spin at different speeds. This is necessary for corners, when the outer wheels turn further and faster than the inner ones.

The inner wheel travels a shorter distance than the outer one.

SUSPENSION

Suspension is made up of two parts, a spring and a damper. The spring compresses and expands as the wheel goes over a bump. The damper delays the spring's action, so that the ride is not too bouncy.

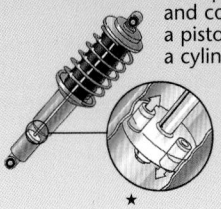

The spring expands and contracts, moving a piston up and down a cylinder.

In the damper, oil is forced through valves, slowing down the piston.

BRAKES

Cars and motorbikes use **disc brakes**. When the brake pedal or lever is pressed, brake fluid is pushed down tubes, forcing brake pads to press against a disc in the wheel. The friction* causes the wheel to slow down.

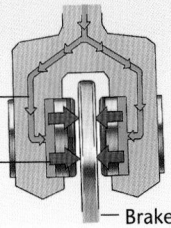

Brake fluid is forced down pipes.

Fluid pushes brake pads against the disc.

Brake disc

See for yourself

To see how a differential works, use two pencils, two cotton reels, a strip of paper and some tape. Roll the paper around one pencil and secure it with tape. Slide it to the blunt end and insert the other pencil. Jam the sharp end of each pencil into a cotton reel. Paint a bright spot on each pencil.

As the "wheels" turn a corner, count how many times each pencil turns.

Internet links

Go to **www.usborne-quicklinks.com** and type in "science" to find out more about cars and motorbikes.

There you'll find links to websites where you can:

- Find explanations of how various parts of a car work
- Explore an online museum of classic cars and motorbikes

Go to Usborne Quicklinks for links to hand-picked websites on hundreds of subjects.

** Centre of gravity, 131; Drag, 142; Friction, 124.*

EARTH AND SPACE

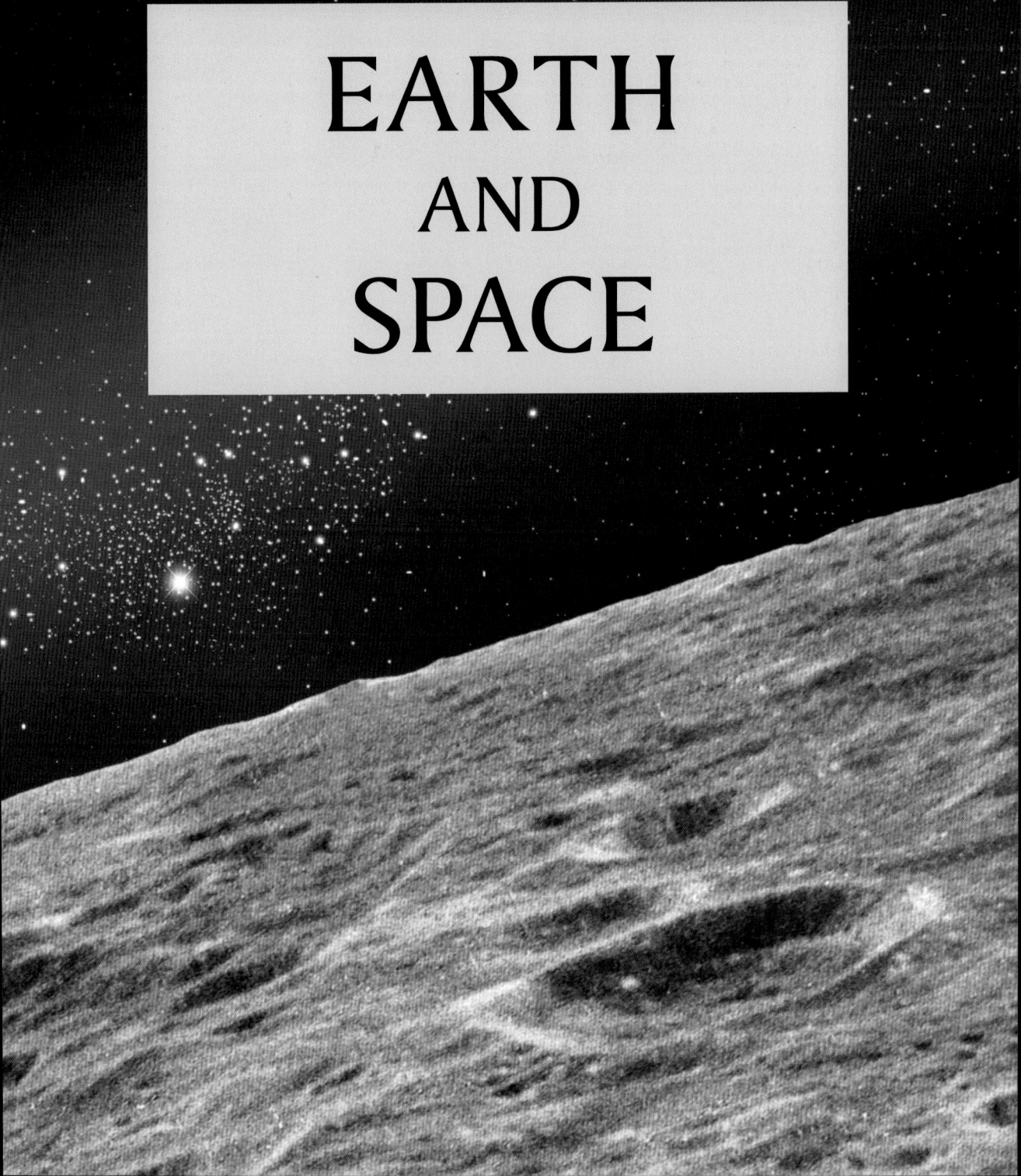

THE UNIVERSE

The **universe** or **cosmos** is the name used to describe the collection of all matter, energy and space that exists. How the universe was created is not fully understood. Most scientists believe that it began about 15,000 million years ago with an unimaginably violent explosion known as the **Big Bang**. This idea is called the **Big Bang theory**.

SIZE AND DISTANCE

The universe is so enormous, it is impossible to imagine. Distances across it are colossal and are usually measured in **light years**. One light year is the distance light travels in one year – that is about 9.46 million million kilometres. Light travels 300,000 kilometres in a second.

The nearest star to the Earth is the Sun. It is about 150 million kilometres away.

A ray of light takes eight minutes to travel from the Sun to the Earth.

The universe contains billions of stars gathered together in huge collections called **galaxies**. So far, astronomers have spotted galaxies that are up to 15,000 million light years away, which gives an idea of just how vast the universe must be.

This cluster of galaxies, called Abell 2218, is about 2,000 million light years away from the Earth.

THE BIG BANG THEORY

The Big Bang created a huge fireball, which cooled and formed into tiny particles. Everything in the universe is made up of these tiny particles, called **matter**.

The particles spread out and the universe began to expand. Over time, thick clouds of hydrogen and helium gases formed. These clouds then gathered together in dense clumps.

To begin with, the universe was so dense that light could not travel far within it, so it was very dark. After a few thousand years, the temperature fell to a few thousand degrees.

Very gradually, the fog cleared. This meant that light could travel further, and the universe became as transparent as it is today. The first galaxies began to form from the dense clumps of gases.

About 10,000 million years after the Big Bang, the Sun and planets of our Solar System formed near the edge of a galaxy that would later be named the Milky Way.

The modern universe contains countless millions of stars and planets, and huge clouds of dust and gas, separated by vast areas of empty space. Even today, parts of the universe are still forming.

Events after the Big Bang

After the Big Bang, the fireball spread out and the universe started to expand.

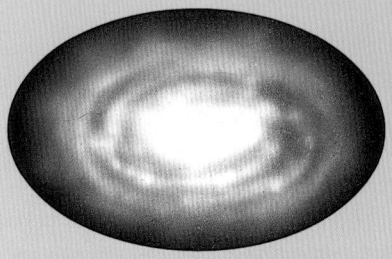

Thick clouds of gases collected into vast clumps of dense matter.

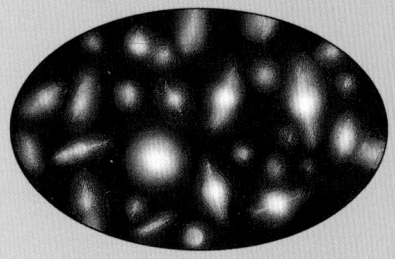

Stars and galaxies began to form. The universe became transparent as light was now able to travel through it.

Almost 10,000 million years after the Big Bang, the Solar System formed.

When you look at the night sky, you are looking out upon millions and millions of stars.

BIG BANG EVIDENCE

One reason why most scientists think that the Big Bang theory is correct is that a weak signal, like an echo, has been detected from space by powerful radio telescopes. It could be that this echo is from the energy in the early fireball, which spread out into space after the Big Bang.

The energy from the Big Bang explosion spread out into space.

Astronomers have calculated that if the universe contains only the matter that they know about, it would have expanded too quickly after the Big Bang for galaxies to form. This means that for the Big Bang theory to be true, the universe must contain a lot more matter than scientists currently know about.

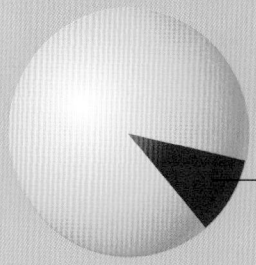

Scientists think that they only know about 10% of the universe. The rest is still to be found.

THE FUTURE

At the moment there are three main theories about the future of the universe.

The **Slowing Down theory** states that the universe could go on expanding continuously, and everything would gradually fade away. Eventually the whole universe would become just a mist of cold particles.

The universe could slow down and then simply fade away.

If more matter exists than is known about, a pulling force, called **gravity**, may eventually slow down the expansion of the universe. It will pull everything back until the galaxies crash. There could then be a Big Crunch, like the Big Bang in reverse. This idea is known as the **Big Crunch theory**.

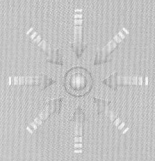

The galaxies could collide in a Big Crunch.

Some scientists think that the universe works like a heart, beating in rhythm. They believe that it expands, then shrinks, then expands again, and so on. So a Big Bang is followed by a Big Crunch, in a repeating cycle. This idea is called the **Oscillating Universe theory**.

Big Bang Big Crunch Big Bang

Internet links

To find out more about the universe, go to **www.usborne-quicklinks.com** and type in the keyword "science".

There you'll find links to websites where you can:

- Explore an interactive guide to the universe
- Travel back in time to the Big Bang or take a trip to a star

Go to Usborne Quicklinks for links to hand-picked websites on hundreds of subjects.

GALAXIES

Stars are grouped together in vast collections called **galaxies**. Each galaxy contains billions of stars. Galaxies are themselves generally grouped together. Our Solar System forms a tiny part of a galaxy called the **Milky Way** in a group called the **Local Group**. This contains about 30 galaxies and stretches across five million light years*.

The Cartwheel galaxy is 500 million light years away.

STAR CLUSTERS

Inside galaxies, stars often group together in clusters. Stars within a cluster move at the same speed and in the same direction. There are two types of star clusters.

Open clusters are found in areas of space that are rich in gas and dust. They contain from a few dozen to a thousand bright young stars which are scattered loosely in the cluster.

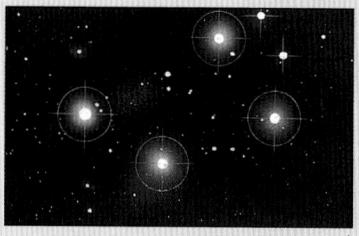

This is an open cluster of stars called the Pleiades. ★

Globular clusters are much larger than open clusters. They contain up to a million stars, densely packed together in sphere-shaped clumps.

Globular clusters like this one appear like very faint stars to the naked eye. ★

TYPES OF GALAXIES

Galaxies form in different shapes. The four most common shapes are spiral, barred spiral, elliptical and irregular.

A **spiral galaxy** has a bright middle and two or more curved arms of stars.

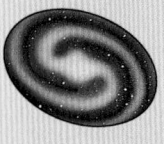

A **barred spiral galaxy** has a central bar of stars with an arm at each end.

Elliptical galaxies vary in shape from round to oval. They contain many old, red stars.

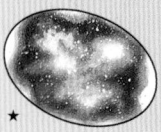

An **irregular galaxy** is a cloud of stars with no definite shape. ★

One third of all known galaxies are spiral shaped. Using sophisticated telescopes, astronomers have recently found new galaxies which are bigger and less tightly packed with stars than any they have seen before. These galaxies do not give off much light, so they are known as **low surface brightness galaxies**.

CARTWHEEL GALAXY

The Cartwheel galaxy (shown above) is an enormous galaxy, 150,000 light years across. Its rare shape was formed when a smaller galaxy smashed into it.

The outer ring is an immense circle of billions of new stars. These formed from the gas and dust which expanded from the core after the collision. Its original spiral shape is now starting to re-form.

NEAREST GALAXIES

The galaxies closest to our Milky Way are the Large and Small Magellanic Clouds. These are small, irregular galaxies. The nearest large galaxy is the spiral Andromeda galaxy. It is over 2.5 million light years away, and is the most distant object that can be seen with the eye on its own.

The Large Magellanic Cloud is one of the closest galaxies to the Milky Way.

** Light years, 154.*

THE MILKY WAY

Compared with other galaxies, the Milky Way is relatively large, measuring about 100,000 light years across. The Earth and the rest of our Solar System lie about 32,000 light years from the middle of the Milky Way.

Most astronomers believe that the Milky Way is a spiral galaxy, although some describe it as a barred spiral galaxy. It gets its name because in ancient times, people thought that it looked like a trail of spilled milk in the night sky.

The Milky Way

See for yourself

On a clear night you could look for the Milky Way. In the northern hemisphere, the best time to see it is between July and September, although it also looks impressive on dark midwinter nights.

In the southern hemisphere, the Milky Way is at its most spectacular between October and December. It looks like a band of glowing light.

Like all spiral galaxies, the Milky Way rotates slowly. Closer to the middle it spins faster than at its edges. Our Solar System is thought to revolve around the middle of the galaxy about once every 225 million years. According to this theory, the Milky Way has rotated only once since the dinosaurs were living on the Earth.

This side view of the Milky Way shows that it has a bulge in the middle, like two fried eggs placed back to back.

Internet links

To find out more about galaxies, go to **www.usborne-quicklinks.com** and type in the keyword "science".

There you'll find links to websites where you can:

- Take a virtual voyage through the Milky Way
- See amazing deep space images of galaxies

Go to Usborne Quicklinks for links to hand-picked websites on hundreds of subjects.

STARS

Every galaxy in the universe contains millions and millions of stars. A **star** is a ball of tremendously hot gas, which produces heat and light from nuclear reactions within its core. The nearest star to the Earth is the Sun, which is 150 million kilometres away. The second closest star is Proxima Centauri, 4.5 light years* away.

NEBULAE

Stars are formed in huge clouds of dust and gas called **nebulae**. Some nebulae are bright and some are dark. **Dark nebulae** look like dark patches in the sky. They are made mostly of dust, which blots out the light of stars behind them. The gases in **bright nebulae** are so hot that they glow in beautiful colours.

The Horse's Head Nebula is a dark nebula. It is silhouetted against a bright nebula.

The colours in a bright nebula depend on the types of gases it contains. For example, hydrogen glows pink, while oxygen glows green-blue.

The Trifid Nebula is a bright nebula. Its colours are caused by hot, glowing gases.

These columns of gas and dust, known as the Pillars of Creation, are part of the Eagle Nebula. The taller column measures about a light year from base to tip.

THE BIRTH OF A STAR

The clouds of gases and dust in some nebulae swirl around and form into clumps which grow larger and larger. Eventually, something causes these new clouds to collapse. Astronomers think this might happen when they pass through the arms of a spiral galaxy, or that the collapse is caused by a shock wave from an exploding star.

As each cloud collapses, the temperature inside it rises. After tens of thousands of years of collapse, a hot core forms. The core gets hotter and hotter until nuclear reactions begin inside, making the cloud of gases, now a star, start to shine.

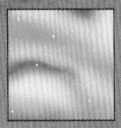

Gases and dust in the nebula swirl around.

The clouds collapse.

A hot core forms.

A new star is born.

* Light years, 154.

VARIABLE STARS

Some stars appear to change occasionally in brilliance. These are called **variable stars** and they fall into three main types – pulsating, eclipsing and cataclysmic variables.

Pulsating variables are usually larger than the Sun. They change in size and temperature, giving off more light when large and less light when small. Some variable stars shrink and grow in a regular cycle, but others are more erratic. The series of pictures below shows Mira, a pulsating variable star with a regular cycle.

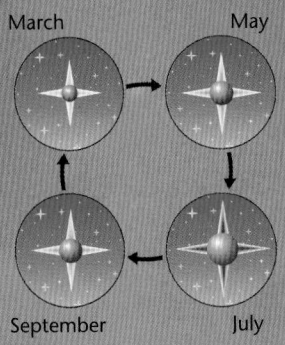

An **eclipsing variable (EcV)** is a type of **binary star**. A binary is actually two stars which orbit around each other, held in place by gravity. In an EcV, one star passes behind the other, as seen from Earth, so the brightness changes. The diagram below shows an EcV with a small, bright star and a larger, dimmer one.

An eclipsing variable

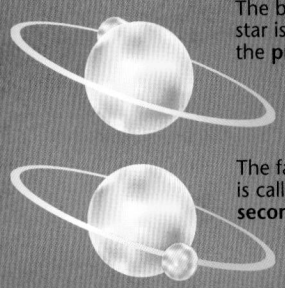

Cataclysmic variables are binary stars that are very close together. When the gravity of one of them (usually a white dwarf*) pulls material away from the other (usually a red giant*), a huge and sudden increase in brightness occurs between and around them. This is caused by violent nuclear reactions.

One type of cataclysmic variable, called a **nova**, flares suddenly, then fades back to its original brightness. It does this over several months or even years.

THE LIFE OF A STAR

At first, most new stars burn very brightly, appearing either blue or white. They exist in this state for millions of years. As a star gets older, it shines less brightly but more steadily.

The lifespan of a star varies. Stars such as our Sun have a lifespan of about 10,000 million years. Stars smaller than the Sun, called **dwarf stars**, live longer. Stars that are larger than our Sun are **giant stars**. The biggest stars of all are **supergiant stars**. They have short lives of only a few million years.

Four bright stars

Here is a comparison of the sizes and colours of some stars. You can find out more about star colours over the page.

Arcturus is an orange giant star.

Rigel is a blue supergiant star.

See for yourself

If you look up at the sky on a clear night, you will notice that some stars seem to twinkle.

This happens because starlight passing through the Earth's atmosphere is bent and broken up. The angle at which it bends depends on the temperature of the air. The light passes through both warm and cold air, so the starlight shines at you from different directions at once, making it appear to flicker.

Barnard's Star is a red dwarf star, cooler than our Sun.

The Sun is a yellow star.

Internet links

To find out more about stars, go to **www.usborne-quicklinks.com** and type in the keyword "science".

There you'll find links to websites where you can:

- Explore the night sky
- Discover the life of a star
- See amazing images of stars and nebulae

Go to Usborne Quicklinks for links to hand-picked websites on hundreds of subjects.

** Red giant, White dwarf, 161.*

tars burn with different amounts f brightness. Star brightness measured on a scale called **agnitude**. The actual rilliance of a star in space is its **bsolute magnitude**. A star's rightness seen from the Earth its **apparent magnitude**. The rightest stars are classed as 0 r even minus magnitude.

agnitude scale

0 1 2 3 4 5 6 7 8 9

ightest stars — Dimmest stars

tars are classified by their colour. he youngest, hottest stars are sually blue or white, and the ldest, coolest ones are red. A ass of star is called a **spectral ype**. The main spectral types re shown in the chart below.

Since earliest times, people have noticed patterns of bright stars in the sky. These patterns are called constellations. There are 88 **constellations** visible from the Earth. Many of them are named after characters or objects taken from ancient Greek myths.

Within constellations, there are smaller patterns called **asterisms**. The Plough, or Big Dipper, is a famous asterism. It is part of the constellation Ursa Major.

The constellation of Ursa Major, or the Great Bear. Here, the imaginary shape of a bear is drawn around it.

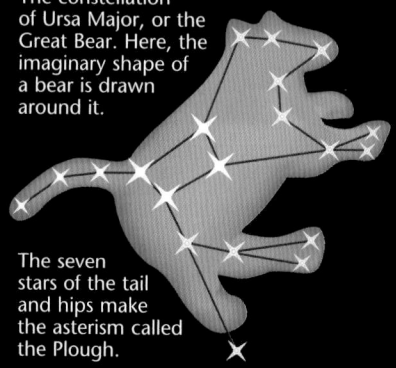

The seven stars of the tail and hips make the asterism called the Plough.

The constellations are made up of the most prominent stars in the sky. From the Earth, the sta in a constellation may look quit close to one another. In reality, they are extremely far apart. Th stars in the constellation Orion, for example, vary between less than 500 light years* and over 2,000 light years away. Viewed from the Earth, the stars look lik a connected group, as they lie ir the same direction.

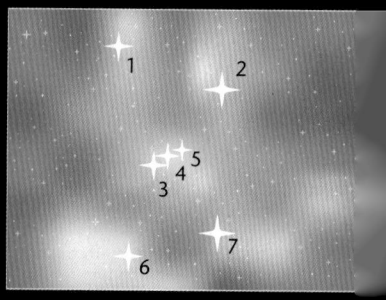

The stars in Orion look close together and the same distance from the Earth.

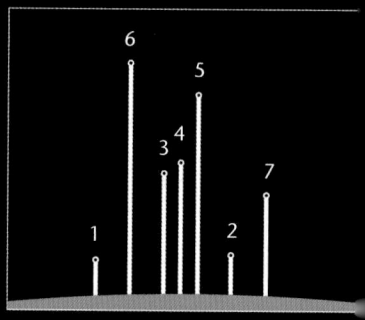

Here you can see that Orion's stars lie a very different distances from the Earth.

See for yourself

All constellations and asterisms can be seen with the naked eye, though what you can see depends on the time of year and your geographical position. Next time you are outside on a clear, starry night, see if you can spot the Plough in the northern hemisphere, or the four stars that make the Southern Cross in the southern hemisphere.

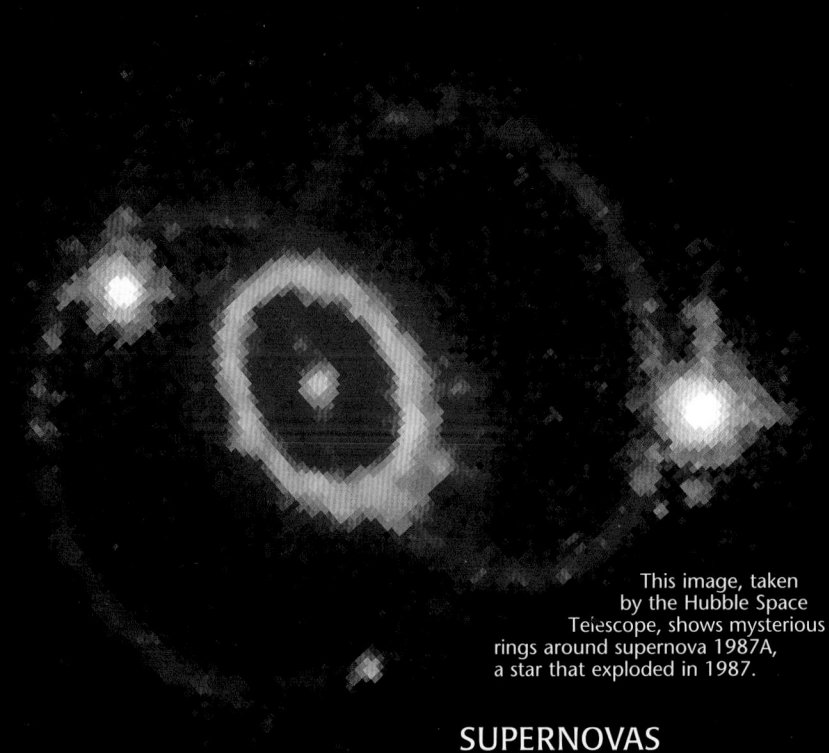

This image, taken by the Hubble Space Telescope, shows mysterious rings around supernova 1987A, a star that exploded in 1987.

THE DEATH OF A STAR

Eventually a star's supply of gas runs out and it dies. As it dies, a star the size of the Sun swells up and turns red. At this stage it is called a **red giant**.

Slowly it puffs its outer layers of gas into space, leaving behind a small, almost dead star called a **white dwarf**. This is about the size of a planet and is extremely dense and heavy for its size. (Imagine a golf ball that weighs as much as a truck.) The white dwarf gradually cools and fades.

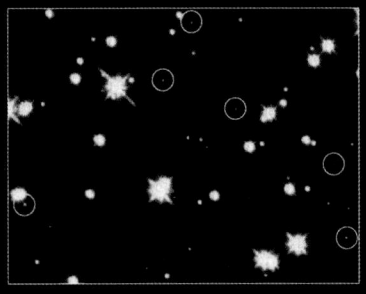

This Hubble Space Telescope* image shows six white dwarf stars (shown in circles) surrounded by yellow, Sun-like stars and cooler, red dwarf stars*.

SUPERNOVAS

Giant stars* have a really spectacular death. First they swell into vast red stars, called **red supergiants**. Then they blow up with a colossal explosion, called a **supernova**.

The supernova leaves a rapidly expanding layer of gases and dust with a small, spinning star in the middle. This is a **neutron star**. It is even denser and heavier than a white dwarf (see left). (Imagine a golf ball that weighs as much as a skyscraper.)

Some neutron stars send out beams of radiation that swing around as the star spins. These stars are called **pulsars**.

When a star dies in a huge supernova explosion, only its dense core may survive.

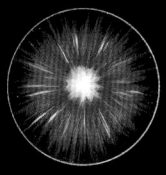

Pulsars are neutron stars which spin rapidly and flash like lighthouses.

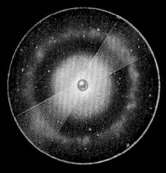

BLACK HOLES

When the very biggest stars die, they form red supergiants, then explode into a supernova. However, when they collapse, they shrink so much that they virtually vanish from the universe. They may become what are called **black holes** – bottomless pits from which nothing escapes.

A black hole is so heavy and dense that its gravity sucks everything inside it, even light. This means that it cannot be seen. Anything that goes into a black hole is likely to be crushed. Some scientists think that in the middle of our galaxy lies an enormous black hole, surrounded by a mass of ancient red stars.

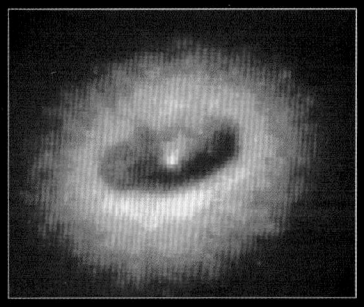

A ring of cool gas around a suspected black hole, as pictured by the Hubble Space Telescope*.

Internet links

To find out more about the stars, go to **www.usborne-quicklinks.com** and type in the keyword "science".

There you'll find links to websites where you can:

- Find out what's in the sky tonight
- Learn how to spot constellations
- FInd out more about black holes

Go to Usborne Quicklinks for links to hand-picked websites on hundreds of subjects.

** Dwarf stars, Giant stars, 159; Hubble Space Telescope, 175.*

THE SUN

Like all stars, the **Sun** is a massive ball of exploding gas. Although it is only a medium-sized star, life on Earth could not exist without the heat and light it provides. It also applies a pulling force called **gravity** to everything within billions of kilometres. This is why planets, moons and other objects travel around or **orbit** the Sun.

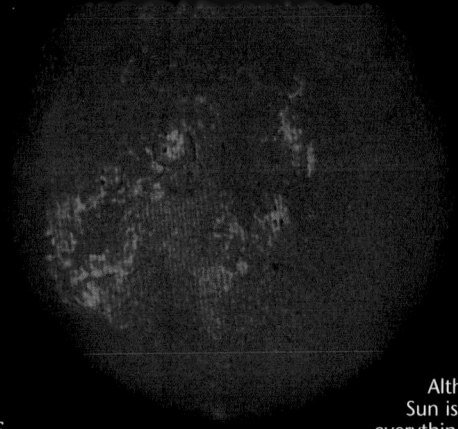

Although the Sun is larger than everything else in the Solar System put together, it is only a medium-sized star.

INSIDE THE SUN

Within the Sun, atoms of hydrogen are continually split apart. The pieces fuse together in a different structure to make a light gas called helium. This process, called a **nuclear fusion reaction**, gives out massive amounts of energy.

Structure of the Sun

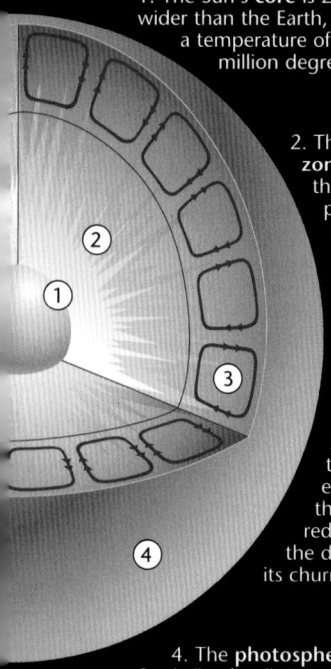

1. The Sun's **core** is 27 times wider than the Earth, and has a temperature of over 15 million degrees Celsius.

2. The **radiative zone** surrounds the core. Heat produced in the core spreads through this part in waves.

3. The **convective zone** carries the Sun's energy up to the surface. The red arrows on the diagram show its churning motion.

4. The **photosphere** is the Sun's "surface". It is made of churning gases.

SURFACE OF THE SUN

Sunspots are small, dark patches on the Sun's surface which are slightly cooler than their surroundings. Clouds of glowing gas called **faculae** often surround sunspots. Huge loops of gas, called **prominences**, leap from the surface at up to 600 kilometres per second. Explosions called **solar flares** are even more violent and spectacular.

ECLIPSES

The Moon occasionally passes between the Earth and the Sun, blocking its light. This is called a **total solar eclipse**. The Moon can cover the Sun because although it is much smaller, it is also closer to us. If you close one eye and hold up a coin between your face and a ceiling light, you can see how this works.

During a total solar eclipse, a thin layer of gas around the Sun, called the **corona**, can be seen.

AURORAS

The Sun blows a constant stream of invisible particles out into space, in all directions. This is called the **solar wind**. When particles become trapped near the Earth's Poles, they create a dazzling light display called an **aurora**. In the north, this is called the **aurora borealis**, or **northern lights**. In the south, it is called the **aurora australis**, or **southern lights**.

See for yourself

You should never look directly at the Sun, as even glimpsing it could blind you. But there is a simple way in which you can see it indirectly.

Point a pair of binoculars at the Sun with a piece of white cardboard behind them. Move the binoculars around until a white circle appears on the cardboard, then focus them until the image is sharp. You may see dark smudges on the image. These are sunspots.

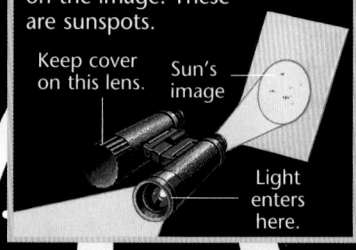

ogether, the Sun and everything that orbits it is called the **Solar System**. It includes planets, moons, chunks of rock, metal and icy debris, and huge amounts of dust.

After the Sun, the most important members of the Solar System are its planets – Mercury, Venus, Earth, Mars, Jupiter, Saturn, Uranus, Neptune and Pluto. They all orbit the Sun at different distances and speeds, spinning as they do so.

A planet's **day** is the length of time it takes to make a complete 360° turn. An Earth day, for example, lasts 24 hours. A planet's **year** is the length of time it takes to orbit the Sun. The Earth's year is 365.3 days long.

Many of the planets in the Solar System have smaller companions, called **moons,** orbiting them. Moons vary greatly in size, shape and number. For instance, Earth has only one, but Saturn has at least 60. You can find out more about Earth's moon on page 167.

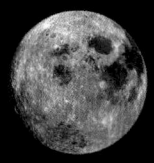

Earth's moon is a rocky, dusty ball.

Dwarf planets are round, like a planet, but aren't large enough to have cleared their orbit of other objects. There's more about dwarf planets on page 171. Large lumps of rock and metal called **asteroids**, and chunks of frozen gas and dirt called **comets**, also orbit the Sun. Most asteroids are found between Mars and Jupiter but a comet's orbit may be in any part of the Solar System. Find out about asteroids and comets on pages 172-173.

The Solar System

Below are the planets of the Solar System, and Pluto. The distances between them are not shown to scale because they are too vast.

Pluto (dwarf planet)

Neptune

Uranus

Sun

Mercury

Venus

Mars

Earth

Most asteroids are found in this area, called the **Asteroid Belt**.

Jupiter

Saturn

Internet links

To find out more about the Sun, go to **www.usborne-quicklinks.com** and type in the keyword "science".

There you'll find links to websites where you can:

- Watch an animated guide to the Solar System
- Discover more about the Sun
- Find out about eclipses

Go to Usborne Quicklinks for links to hand-picked websites on hundreds of subjects.

THE INNER PLANETS

Mercury, Venus, Earth and Mars are known as the **inner planets**. This is because they are the closest planets to the Sun. Although they all have a similar small size and rocky structure, only Earth is the right distance from the Sun for life to exist on its surface. You can find out more about Earth on pages 166-167.

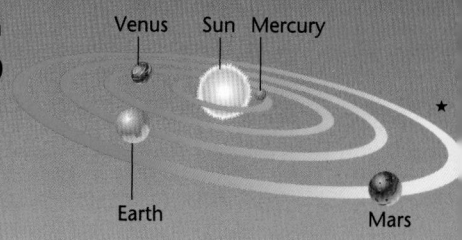

The diagram above shows the four inner planets and their orbits around the Sun.

MERCURY

Mercury is a very small planet, with a diameter of only 4,880km. It is the nearest planet to the Sun, orbiting it at a distance of about 58 million kilometres. This closeness means that Mercury is blasted by the Sun's rays. Its daytime temperature can reach 427°C, which is over four times hotter than boiling water.

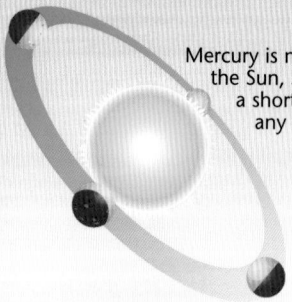

Mercury is nearest to the Sun, so orbits it in a shorter time than any other planet.

It takes Mercury 88 Earth days to orbit the Sun. As it travels, it spins slowly. In fact, each day on Mercury is equal to 58.7 Earth days. This means that there are fewer than two days in one Mercury year. So during its long night, when half of the planet faces away from the Sun, the temperature can plummet as low as -183°C.

VENUS

Venus, the second planet from the Sun, is a similar size to the Earth. It orbits the Sun at a distance of about 108 million kilometres. The planet's surface is mainly flat, but it has raised areas which look like Earth's continents.

Venus has an atmosphere that is mostly made up of carbon dioxide gas. It presses down on the planet's surface like a great weight. Dense clouds of sulphuric acid reflect the Sun's rays, making Venus shine like a very bright star. Any rays which are not reflected become trapped around the planet, raising its temperature to around 480°C.

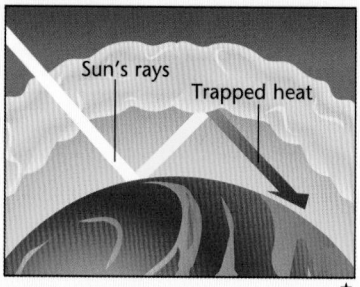

Venus's thick atmosphere acts like the glass in a greenhouse. Any rays that travel through it become trapped.

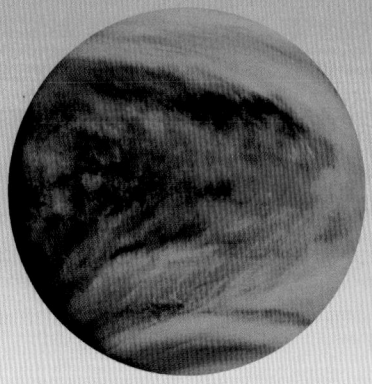

This computer-coloured image shows dense clouds swirling around Venus.

See for yourself

You can try spotting the inner planets yourself. Mercury and Venus can sometimes be seen just before sunrise and just after sunset. After the Sun and Moon, Venus is the brightest object in the sky. It is often called the **Morning Star** or the **Evening Star**, depending on what time of day it appears. Mercury looks like a bright star close to the horizon.

CAUTION
When you are planet spotting, always make sure that the Sun has not begun to rise in the morning or has fully set in the evening. Glimpsing the Sun's rays might damage your eyes.

STUDYING VENUS

Nobody knew what the surface of Venus looked like until 1975, when two space probes named Venera were sent by the Soviet Union. Smaller probes were dropped from them. Their cameras revealed that the surface of Venus was covered with sharp rocks and looked like a gloomy, orange-brown desert.

Venus's surface has shallow craters. Objects cannot strike with enough force to make deep craters because the atmosphere slows them down.

In the late 1980s and early 1990s, an American space probe named Magellan used radar to map the planet's surface in greater detail. It was found to be covered mostly by areas of solidified lava, which had flowed out of Venus's many volcanoes.

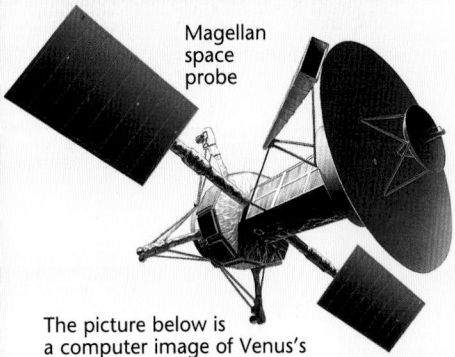

Magellan space probe

The picture below is a computer image of Venus's surface. It was created using information collected by the Magellan probe.

MARS

Mars is the fourth planet from the Sun. It is just half the size of the Earth and orbits the Sun at a distance of about 228 million kilometres, taking just under 687 days to do so.

Mars is sometimes called the **Red Planet**, because of the reddish dust covering its surface.

Mars has two moons, called **Phobos** and **Deimos**, which are dark and dusty. Many scientists think that these odd-shaped moons are really asteroids that became trapped in orbit around Mars millions of years ago.

Deimos, Mars's smaller moon, is about 15km across at its widest.

Phobos is 28km across at its widest. It has a large crater named Stickney on its surface which is about 5km across.

STUDYING THE SURFACE

In the 1960s and 1970s, the Mariner and Viking space probes sent back detailed pictures of the surface of Mars. It was shown to be covered in reddish-orange dust, with many rocky canyons and craters. Huge dust storms, which may last for weeks, often rage across the landscape.

The most recent successful missions to Mars were in 2004, when the two rovers Spirit and Opportunity landed on opposite sides of the planet. They have driven great distances across its surface, and photographed many mountains, craters and rocks along the way.

The twin Spirit and Opportunity rovers have provided scientists with their clearest photos yet of Mars's surface.

Internet links

Go to **www.usborne-quicklinks.com** and type in "science" to find out more about the inner planets.

There you'll find links to websites where you can:

- Drive a robot rover on Mars
- Discover more about Mercury, Venus and Mars
- Learn more with online activities

Go to Usborne Quicklinks for links to hand-picked websites on hundreds of subjects.

THE EARTH AND MOON

The **Earth** orbits the Sun at a distance of 149.6 million kilometres. This distance makes it just the right temperature for water to exist as a liquid, rather than just ice or vapour. The Earth also has a breathable atmosphere. All these things create the right conditions for life to exist.

The Earth as seen from spac
Early astronauts described it
as a beautiful blue jewel.

EARTH'S ATMOSPHERE

From space, the Earth's atmosphere looks like a very thin blue layer surrounding the planet. It is a mixture of nitrogen and oxygen, with traces of other gases. It contains more oxygen than the atmosphere of any other planet. This gas is vital to life.

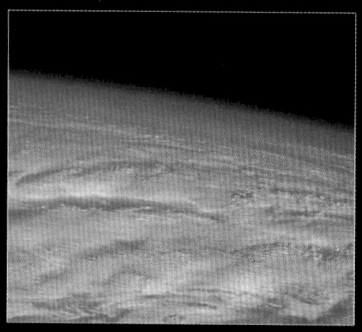

From space, the Earth's atmosphere looks like a thin haze. It appears blue because of the way sunlight is filtered through atmospheric gases.

EARTH'S SURFACE

Beneath the atmosphere is the planet's surface, called the **crust**. This is split into a number of enormous slabs called plates*, which have pushed and pulled against each other for millions of years, creating mountains, valleys and other features.

Mountain ranges like the Himalayas formed when the Earth's vast plates crushed together.

Two-thirds of the Earth's surface is covered in vast oceans of water. These are believed to be the birthplace of Earth's first life-forms, around 3,500 million years ago. Scientists study other planets and moons for signs of water or ice on their surface. This could show that they are or were once home to primitive life.

THE EARTH FROM SPAC

Today, people are learning more and more about the Earth from information sent back by satellites and space stations. For instance, weather forecasters use data collected by satellites to predict weather patterns. They can use this information tc warn people of severe weather anywhere in the world.

Information from satellites is also used to find out more about the Earth's surface. Even areas that are normally hard to see, such as the ocean floor, can now be seen in detail using sophisticated satellites.

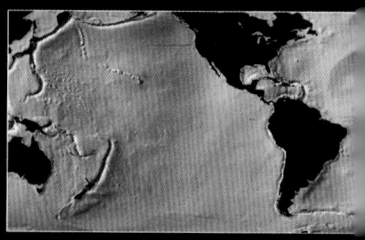

This map of the ocean floor was produced by a satellite named Seasat. The dark shapes are continents.

The Earth is the only planet in the Solar System which is definitely known to support life. This is because it is mostly covere in water, which has ye to be found on an other planet's surface.

* Plates, 18

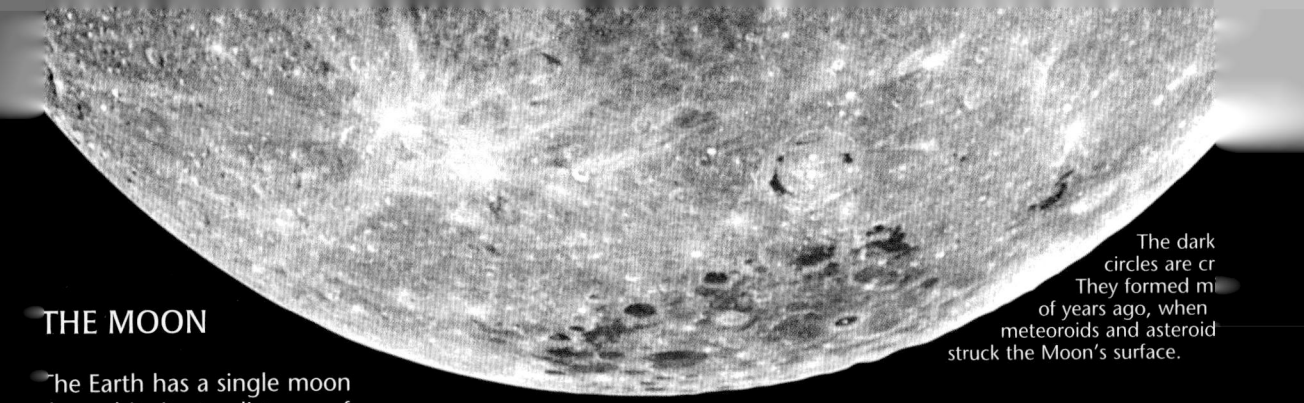

The dark circles are cr They formed m of years ago, when meteoroids and asteroid struck the Moon's surface.

THE MOON

The Earth has a single moon that orbits it at a distance of about 384,400km. Most moons are tiny compared to the objects they orbit, but our **Moon** is a quarter of the Earth's size.

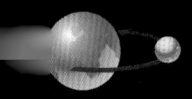

The Moon is kept in orbit by the pull of the Earth's gravity.

Because of the Earth's gravity, the same side of the Moon always faces Earth as it orbits. The other side of the Moon, known as the **far** or **dark side**, has only ever been seen by space probes and astronauts.

Unlike the Earth, the Moon has no atmosphere to prevent it from becoming too hot or too cold. This means that the Sun's rays can make its temperature rise to 123°C. When the Sun is not shining on the Moon, the temperature can fall to -163°C.

See for yourself

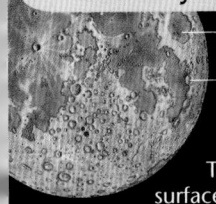

The Moon's surface is marked with many craters. You can see some of them with the naked eye, but binoculars will give a much better view. The dark patches you can see on the Moon's surface are known as seas. They formed millions of years ago from solidified lava.

PHASES OF THE MOON

The Moon does not make its own light, but it reflects the Sun's rays. This can make it look very bright in the night sky. Different amounts of the Moon's sunlit side can be seen as it orbits the Earth. This makes the Moon appear to change shape each night. The different shapes are called the **phases** of the Moon.

It takes 28 days for the Moon to orbit the Earth once. The diagram below shows the Moon's phases during this time.

The phases of the Moon

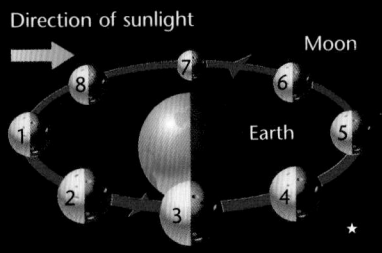

The pictures below show what the Moon looks like from the Earth when it is in each of the numbered positions shown above.

1. New moon
2. Crescent
3. Half moon
4. Waxing (becoming larger)
5. Full moon
6. Waning (becoming smaller)
7. Half moon
8. Crescent

THE MOON'S FORMATIC

Scientists are still not completely sure where the Moon came fror They used to think it was forme at the same time as the Earth, but studies of Moon rocks seem to show that this is not the case

Most astronomers now think th the Moon was formed when a massive object, the size of a sm planet, collided with the Earth. This threw out an enormous amount of rocky debris, which joined together in a single mas to form the Moon.

The Moon may have formed from rocky debris thrown out after a huge object smashed into the Earth.

Internet links

Go to **www.usborne-quicklinks.com** and type in "science" to find out more about the Earth and Moon.

There you'll find links to websites where you can:

- See satellite images of Earth and animations of the Moon's phases

Go to Usborne Quicklinks for links to hand-picked websites on hundreds of subjects.

THE OUTER PLANETS

Jupiter, Saturn, Uranus, Neptune and Pluto are known as the **outer planets**. They lie in the outer regions of the Solar System. Except for tiny, rocky Pluto, all of these planets are huge balls made almost entirely of gas, so they are sometimes called the **gas giants**.

The New Horizons space probe studied Jupiter in 2007, on its way to Pluto.

JUPITER

Jupiter is the largest planet in the Solar System, measuring 142,984km at its equator. It takes about 11.9 Earth years to orbit the Sun once. Despite its distance from the Sun, Jupiter is not a frozen planet. Pressurized hydrogen at its heart breaks down to create huge amounts of heat.

Several space probes have been sent to Jupiter. In 1979 the Voyager probes discovered that Jupiter has faint rings, which cannot be seen from the Earth.

In 1995, the Galileo space probe took a new series of photos, and sent a mini-probe down into Jupiter's atmosphere. The probe discovered Jupiter's winds blew harder than any on Earth, and Galileo gathered information on the planet's rings and moons.

Structure of Jupiter

Scientists base this idea of Jupiter's structure on information from space probes.

1. The atmosphere's top layer is broken into vast clouds by high winds. Violent storms rage around the planet.

2. The dark bands are gaps in the clouds. Deeper, hotter layers of the planet's churning atmosphere can be seen beneath.

3. This layer is 17,000km thick. It is made of hydrogen gas which is so compressed that it acts like a liquid.

4. This layer is also made of hydrogen, but it is so compressed that it behaves like a solid.

5. The core, which is slightly larger than the Earth, is thought to be solid and rocky.

Ganymede

Io

Callisto

Europa

Great Red Spot

JUPITER'S MOONS

So far, astronomers have discovered at least 63 moons around Jupiter. The four largest are called the **Galilean Moons**, after the Italian scientist Galileo, who discovered them in 1610. Jupiter's other moons are much smaller. Some may be just asteroids, captured by the planet's gravity.

The Galilean Moons (not shown to scale above)

Ganymede is the largest moon in the Solar System. It is even bigger than the planet Mercury.

Io is covered with volcanoes that pour sulphur onto its surface.

Callisto is a ball of dusty ice. Its surface is scarred with hundreds of craters.

Europa may have a deep ocean beneath its fractured, icy crust. Some scientists believe that this ocean may contain simple life.

See for yourself

After the Sun, Moon and Venus, Jupiter is the brightest object in the sky. With the naked eye it looks like a very bright star. If you have a telescope, you may be able to see its tinted cloud bands and the **Great Red Spot**, a vast storm which rages through the planet's atmosphere.

SATURN

Saturn is the second largest planet in the Solar System. It measures about 120,536km around its equator – nine times wider than the Earth. Saturn orbits the Sun once every 29.5 Earth years, at a distance of about 1,429 million kilometres.

The planet is made up mostly of hydrogen and helium, which are very light gases. This makes Saturn very light compared to the other planets. Astronomers believe that Saturn may be similar to Jupiter on the inside, because it also generates its own fierce heat.

SATURN'S MOONS

Saturn has at least 60 moons, some of which are shown on the right. Scientists think that Saturn's and Jupiter's moons are among the places in the Solar System where evidence of simple life is most likely to be found.

Saturn's biggest moon, **Titan**, is surrounded by dense orange clouds.

Mimas is 398km wide and covered in craters. The impact that created its largest crater almost destroyed it completely.

Enceladus is slightly larger than Mimas. Giant jets of water vapour erupt through its smooth, icy surface.

Tethys has huge craters and long valleys. The longest valley, Ithaca, is 2,000km. The largest crater, Odysseus, is 400km wide.

Saturn is the second largest planet in the Solar System. It is about nine times the size of the Earth.

Saturn's rings are made of dust and rocks.

Saturn spins so fast that it appears to bulge slightly in the middle and to be squashed at the poles.

SATURN'S RINGS

Saturn is often called the **Ringed Planet**, because it is surrounded by rings of rock and dust. These were identified in the seventeenth century by Galileo. Space probes such as Cassini and the Voyagers have sent back thousands of incredible pictures of Saturn's rings, and astronomers have discovered rings around other planets too.

Saturn's rings are about one kilometre thick and are made up of dust, rocks and icy boulders. The rings that can be seen from the Earth are actually made up of thousands of smaller **ringlets**. The outer ring particles are kept in place by the gravity of two small moons, known as the **Shepherd Moons**.

Internet links

Go to **www.usborne-quicklinks.com** and type in the word "science" to find out more about the outer planets.

There you'll find links to websites where you can:

- Discover the latest images of Saturn and Jupiter

Go to Usborne Quicklinks for links to hand-picked websites on hundreds of subjects.

URANUS

Uranus was discovered by British astronomer William Herschel in 1781. It takes just over 84 Earth years to orbit the Sun, at a distance of around 2,870 million kilometres. It travels slowly, moving at about 7 kilometres per second. By comparison, the Earth moves at nearly 30 kilometres per second.

Most planets spin around like tops, but Uranus rolls around the Sun on its side, like a barrel. It may have been tipped onto its side millions of years ago by a collision with a planet-sized comet. Uranus spins quickly, making one turn in 17.9 hours.

Like Saturn, Uranus has a system of rings, which were discovered in 1977. In 1986, the Voyager 2 space probe photographed and measured them. The rings were found to be made up mostly of dark dust.

MOONS OF URANUS

For many years, Uranus was thought to have 15 moons. By 2003, astronomers had officially identified 27, and there may be more awaiting discovery.

The five largest moons are shown below. **Ariel** and **Umbriel** are both dark and cratered, while **Titania** has deep, long valleys. **Oberon** is heavily cratered, but little else is known about it. **Miranda** is a small ball of ice, about 472km across. It is thought that it may once have been broken apart by a comet.

This picture of Uranus and its rings was created using information taken with the HST's* Near Infrared Camera. The red patches are high clouds.

A photo of Neptune, taken by the Voyager 2 space probe in 1989.

NEPTUNE

Neptune was first discovered by astronomers John Couch Adams and Urbain Jean LeVerrier. It is slightly smaller than Uranus, and spins once every 19.2 hours. Neptune is about 4,504 million kilometres from the Sun. It takes about 165 Earth years to complete a single orbit.

You cannot see Neptune with the naked eye, and even through a telescope it only looks like a small, bluish circle.

NEPTUNE'S ATMOSPHER

Methane gas in the atmosphere gives Neptune its blue appearanc Neptune's atmosphere also contains ammonia and helium. Beneath its dense blanket of gases the planet is thought to have an outer layer of liquid hydrogen.

Voyager 2 observed long, wispy clouds swirling around Neptune, blown by winds of up to 2,000 kilometres per hour. It also saw dark spots. The largest, named the **Great Dark Spot**, was a vast storm the size of the Earth.

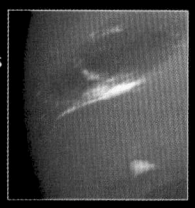

Neptune's Great Dark Spot. Voyager 2 scientists named the little cloud below it the Scooter, because it raced around the planet every 16 hours.

** HST (Hubble Space Telescope), 175.*

NEPTUNE'S MOONS

Neptune has 13 moons. The largest of them are **Triton** and **Nereid**. Triton is bigger than the planet Pluto. Most moons orbit their planet in the same direction as the planet spins. Triton, however, travels in the opposite direction.

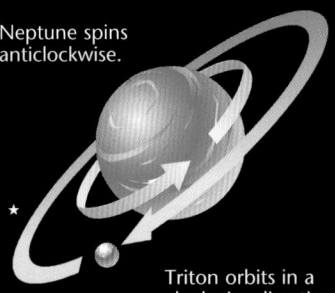

Most of Triton's surface is bright and smooth. It has some dark streaks over it and pink ice around its south pole. Triton has a thin atmosphere of nitrogen and methane.

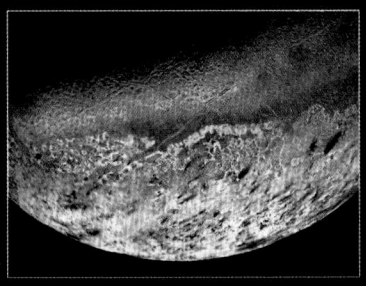

This photograph of Triton shows the polar cap. Its pink tinge may be due to the evaporation of frozen nitrogen gas.

PLUTO

Pluto was first discovered in 1930 by American astronomer Clyde Tombaugh. For a long time it was known as the Solar System's smallest planet (measuring just 2,274km across), but the discovery of many other nearby objects of a similar size led to scientists reclassifying Pluto as a dwarf planet*. It is the second largest dwarf planet in the Solar System. The largest is Eris, which was discovered in 2005. Dwarf planets, like Pluto, that orbit the Sun beyond Neptune are called plutoids.

Pluto has an oval orbit, so its distance from the Sun varies a great deal. For twenty years of its 248-year orbit, Pluto is actually closer to the Sun than Neptune. Pluto has three moons. The largest is called **Charon**, which was discovered in 1978. It is nearly half Pluto's size, making it unusually large for a moon.

An artist's impression of Pluto and its moon Charon. They're very close to each other, only about 20,000km apart.

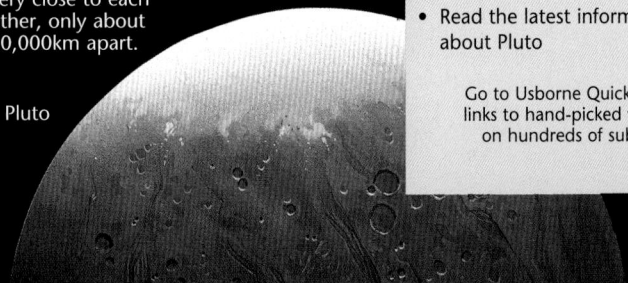

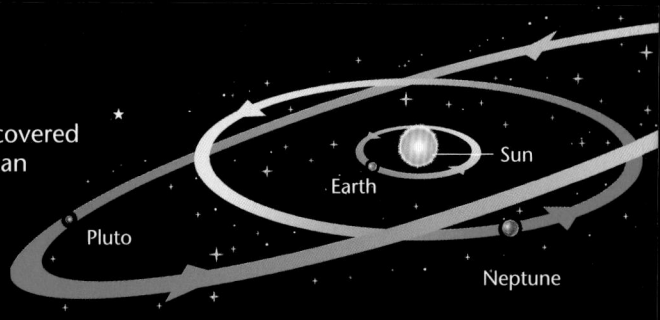

Pluto's orbit is tilted at an angle compared with the other planets. It cuts across Neptune's orbit.

STUDYING PLUTO

Pluto is very hard to see, because it is so far away. Even powerful telescopes on Earth show Pluto as just a tiny circle with no surface markings. But images from the Hubble Space Telescope* suggest that it may be an icy, rocky ball like Neptune's moon, Triton, with an atmosphere of frozen methane and nitrogen.

NASA's New Horizons space probe was launched in 2006 to study Pluto in more detail. When it flies past the dwarf planet in 2015 it will provide astronomers with their first detailed pictures of its surface, and will assess the atmosphere to confirm what it's made from. The probe will also examine Charon, and will then continue on into the outer regions of the Solar System, where it will explore small objects that orbit the Sun even further out.

Internet links

Go to **www.usborne-quicklinks.com** and type "science" to find out more about the outer planets.

There you'll find links to websites where you can:

- See amazing images of Uranus, Neptune and Pluto
- Read the latest information about Pluto

Go to Usborne Quicklinks for links to hand-picked websites on hundreds of subjects.

** Hubble Space Telescope (HST), NASA (National Aeronautics Space Administration), 175; Dwarf planet, 163.*

SPACE DEBRIS

As well as many planets and moons, the Solar System also contains millions of smaller objects, called asteroids, comets and meteoroids. They are believed to be pieces of debris left over from the birth of the universe.

Hale-Bopp, the clearest comet to be seen for 100 years, came into view between 1995 and 1997.

ASTEROIDS

Asteroids are large pieces of rock, or rock and metal. The first was spotted in 1801, by an Italian astronomer named Piazzi. He found an object in space which he believed was a tiny planet. Piazzi named his discovery **Ceres**.

Soon, other astronomers noticed similar objects, which they called asteroids. This means "like stars". Most orbit the Sun between Mars and Jupiter, in an area called the **Asteroid Belt**.

The first close-up pictures of an asteroid were taken in 1991, by the space probe Galileo. It photographed the asteroid **Gaspra**. The images showed Gaspra to be about 19km across with an irregular shape. Its surface is grooved and pitted with craters.

Gaspra is one of the largest asteroids in the Asteroid Belt. It is dark reddish-brown, with patches of grey and blue.

NUMBERS AND TYPES

Several hundred thousand asteroids have already been discovered and many more are discovered every year. Most asteroids fall into one of three main groups, depending on what they are made of. These groups are carbonaceous (like Ceres), silicaceous (like Gaspra) and metallic.

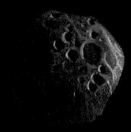

Carbonaceous (or **C-type**) asteroids are the most common. They are stony and darker than coal.

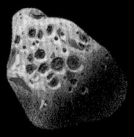

Silicaceous (or **S-type**) asteroids are bright and shiny. They contain metal.

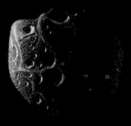

Metallic (or **M-type**) asteroids may be the exposed, metal cores of originally much larger objects.

Asteroids are often scarred with craters, made by smaller pieces of space debris colliding with them.

TROJANS AND APOLLOS

There are several other groups of asteroids besides the ones in the main Asteroid Belt. For instance, Jupiter holds clusters of asteroids in its gravity. These asteroids are called the **Trojans**. Some orbit in front of Jupiter, and others orbit behind it.

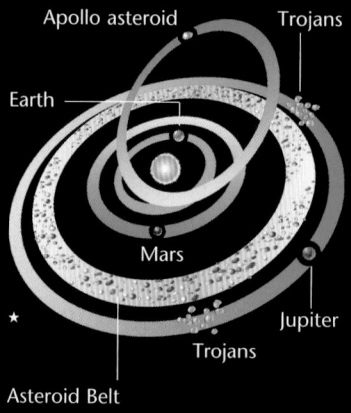

Other asteroids, known as the **Apollo asteroids**, sometimes cross the Earth's path. Their usual orbit, however, is further away from the Sun.

Although they are shown close together here, the distances between these asteroids are so huge that spacecraft can pass through without hitting any of them.

NEAR ENCOUNTER

Asteroids which closely approach the Earth are called **near-Earth asteroids**. The NEAR project, which stands for **Near Earth Asteroid Rendezvous**, was created to study one of these asteroids, called **Eros**. The NEAR spacecraft was launched in February 1996, and reached Eros in February 2000, to complete a one-year orbit.

Before it landed, NEAR took thousands of pictures of Eros' rocky, cratered surface. These taught astronomers much about the structure of asteroids. NEAR ended its mission by landing on Eros, where it may be picked up by future space explorers.

The NEAR spacecraft. Pictures from it have revealed lots of new information about near-Earth asteroids.

COMETS

Comets are balls of dirty ice. They travel around the Sun in huge, oval orbits. This means that they spend most of their time far away from the Sun. Some comets have such wide orbits that they may travel far above or below the Solar System for thousands of years. The diagram on the right shows some comets' orbits.

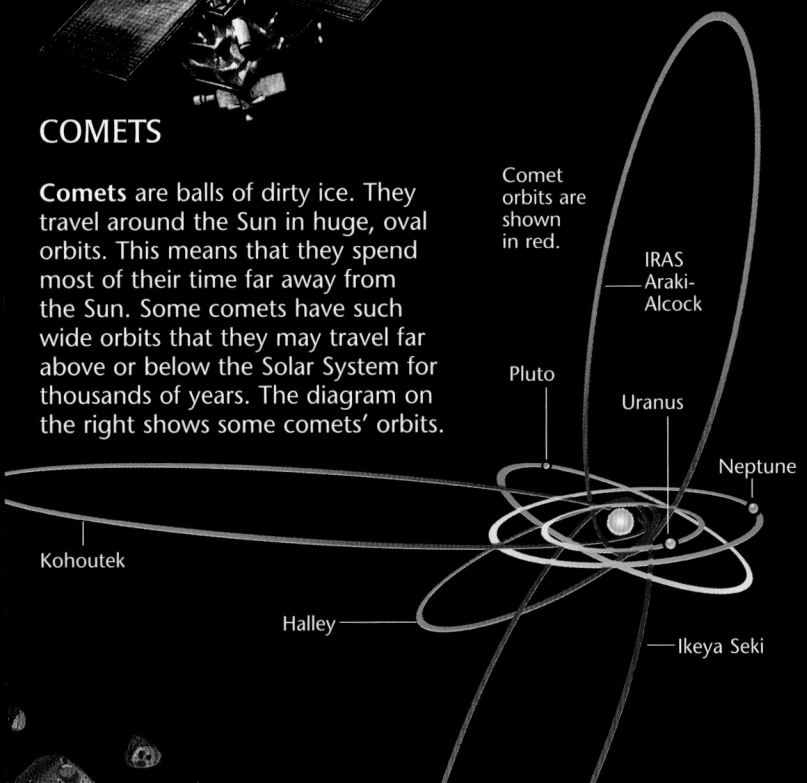

A COMET'S TAIL

The central, solid part of a comet is called the **nucleus**. This is made up of frozen gases, ice, grit and rock. When a comet is near to the Sun, its nucleus becomes warmer. As the comet begins to melt, a tail is formed. Some comets have more than one tail.

How a comet tail forms

This is a comet flying through space, far from the Sun. At this stage it has no tail.

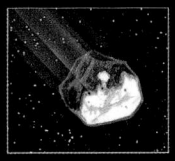

As the comet approaches the Sun, it melts. Gas and dust stream out into space, forming a cloud called a **coma**.

A constant stream of particles from the Sun, called the **solar wind**, blows the coma out behind. This creates the comet's tail.

METEOROIDS

Meteoroids are very small pieces of space debris. They may be grains of dust from comets, chunks of rock, or even bits of shattered asteroids.

Occasionally, the Earth crosses the path of these meteoroids. As they plummet through the atmosphere, they burn up in a streak of light. At this stage, they are called **meteors**, or **shooting stars**. Meteoroids that survive their fiery passage through the atmosphere to land on the Earth are called **meteorites**.

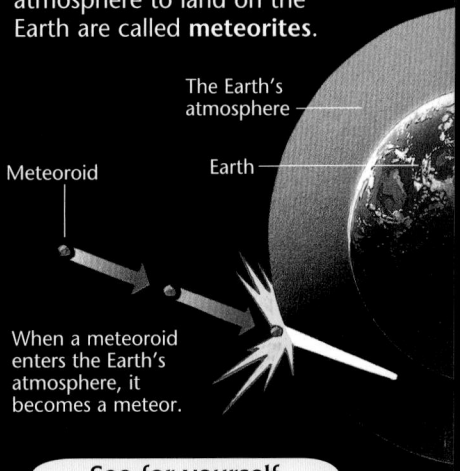

When a meteoroid enters the Earth's atmosphere, it becomes a meteor.

See for yourself

A **meteor storm** is a short but spectacular display of meteors caused by the Earth crossing a comet's path. Astronomy magazines and the internet can tell you the best dates to look for storms in your hemisphere.

Internet links

To find out more about space debris, go to **www.usborne-quicklinks.com** and type in the keyword "science".

There you'll find links to websites where you can:

- Watch animated presentations on comets and asteroids
- Study comets and asteroids in more detail

SPACE EXPLORATION

Studying space in detail only became possible after the invention of the telescope in the seventeenth century. Since then, astronomers have used many more sophisticated devices to look further and further into space. In the twentieth century, scientists worked out how to send man-made satellites, and then people, into space to study it in even greater detail.

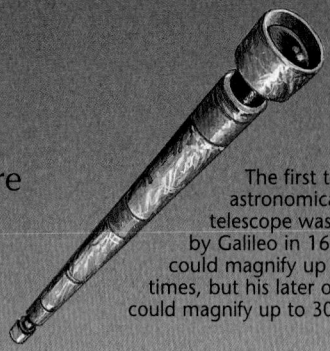

The first true astronomical telescope was built by Galileo in 1610. It could magnify up to nine times, but his later ones could magnify up to 30 times.

OPTICAL TELESCOPES

Optical telescopes create images using light. Some optical telescopes, called **refractors**, collect light through lenses. **Reflectors** use mirrors to collect light and reflect it back to the observer. Astronomers use vast reflector telescopes, housed in buildings called **observatories**, to look far into space.

The Keck observatories in Hawaii house the world's most powerful optical telescopes. Like many observatories, they are built on mountaintops, which are above most of the haze and pollution in the atmosphere.

This reflector telescope, Keck 1, is over 10m wide. Its mirror is made up of 36 segments which act like a single, giant mirror.

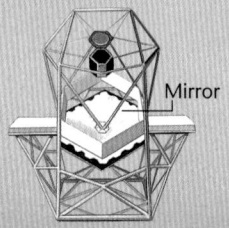

RADIO TELESCOPES

Radio telescopes have very large dishes with moveable antennas, that collect the faint signals given out by objects in space. They allow astronomers to detect things that are too dark or too far away to see, even through the most powerful optical telescope.

The largest radio telescope is the Arecibo dish in Puerto Rico. Its 305m wide dish is built into a natural valley. It is sensitive enough to detect faint signals from galaxies in distant areas of the universe. These signals are 100 million years old when they reach the Earth.

A radio telescope. It can be steered to face a particular target in space.

SPACE TELESCOPES

Telescopes that are placed out in space can see much further than telescopes on Earth, because the planet's atmosphere does not block their view. The largest telescope to have been placed in space so far is the Hubble Space Telescope (HST), an optical telescope launched by NASA (the National Aeronautics Space Administration) in 1990.

The HST's main mirror measures 2.4m across.

When the HST was launched, astronomers hoped it would provide the answers to many questions about the nature and size of the universe. After its main mirror was repaired in 1993, it sent back some of the most astonishing pictures of the universe ever seen.

Galaxy M100 is tens of millions of light years away. This image was taken by the HST after its mirror was repaired.

SATELLITES

There are many man-made devices orbiting the Earth. These are known as **satellites** – the same word that is used for any object, such as a moon, which orbits a planet or star. Some man-made satellites gather and transmit information about space directly to scientists on Earth. Others pick up radio, TV or telephone signals, and send them back down to other places on Earth.

The first man-made object ever to go into space was a satellite named Sputnik 1, which was launched in 1957 by the Soviet Union. It could not take pictures or record information, but it proved that man-made structures could be launched successfully into space.

In 1989, the satellite Hipparcos was launched by the European Space Agency. For three and a half years, it mapped the night sky in the greatest detail ever. Results were published in 1997 and this new information has since allowed astronomers to calculate, with greater accuracy than ever before, how far away thousands of stars and other objects are.

This satellite orbits at the same speed as the Earth spins. This is known as a **geostationary** orbit.

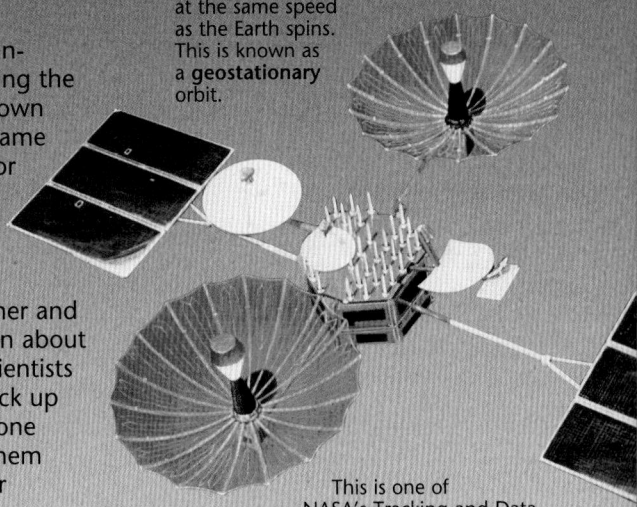

This is one of NASA's Tracking and Data Relay Satellites (TDRS). They communicate with spacecraft orbiting close to the Earth.

See for yourself

If you would like to look at the stars and planets yourself, you will need a map of the night sky. Star maps in astronomy books will help you to identify the constellations, but the sky looks different from the northern and southern hemispheres, so you need to have the right map for your part of the world. If you want to spot planets, charts in the monthly astronomy magazines show which planets can be seen at a particular time.

Internet links

Go to **www.usborne-quicklinks.com** and type "science" to find out more about space exploration.

There you'll find links to websites where you can:

- Take online tours of famous observatories
- Discover how scientists receive signals from space telescopes

Go to Usborne Quicklinks for links to hand-picked websites on hundreds of subjects.

These astronauts have been sent into space to repair a damaged satellite.

SPACE PROBES

Since the 1960s, unmanned spacecraft called **space probes** have been sent to explore the Solar System. Many carry cameras, which take detailed photographs of distant planets. They beam the pictures back to Earth, where they are studied by astronomers.

One such project was NASA's Cassini mission to Saturn, launched in 1997. It entered into orbit around Saturn in 2004, and began sending back detailed images of the planet's surface, its famous rings, and its moons. Cassini also carried a small probe called Huygens, which split from its mother ship and landed on Saturn's largest moon, Titan.

So far, Pioneer 10 (which studied Jupiter and Saturn) and Pioneer 11 (which studied Saturn) have journeyed further than any other probes. After completing their missions, they drifted out

FIRST MAN IN SPACE

For many years, space travel was thought to be too dangerous for humans. But advances in technology throughout the 1950s led to Russian astronaut Yuri Gagarin becoming the first man in space, in 1961. His flight lasted for one and a half hours.

MEN ON THE MOON

In 1959, a Soviet space probe, Luna 9, was the first man-made object to land on the Moon. Ten years later, American astronauts Neil Armstrong and Edwin "Buzz" Aldrin travelled to the Moon in the Apollo 11 spacecraft and became the first people to walk on its surface.

During the 1960s and 1970s there were six Moon landings. Each crew collected information and rock samples. Scientists are still studying these rocks in order to understand more about how the Moon formed and evolved billions

This is the Space Shuttle's Remote Manipulator System, a moveable "arm" which can retrieve objects and bring them into the Shuttle.

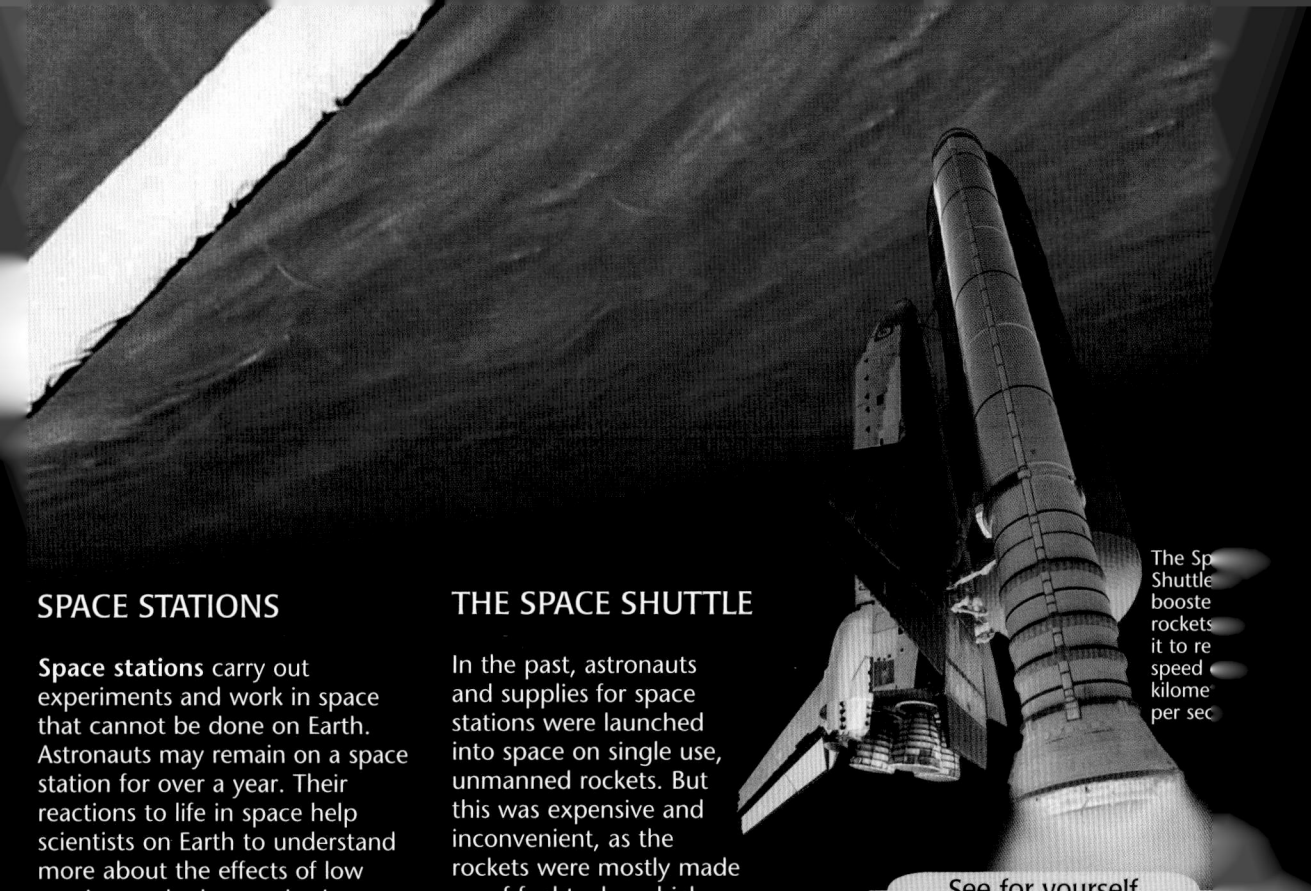

The Sp
Shuttle
booste
rockets
it to re
speed
kilome
per sec

SPACE STATIONS

Space stations carry out experiments and work in space that cannot be done on Earth. Astronauts may remain on a space station for over a year. Their reactions to life in space help scientists on Earth to understand more about the effects of low gravity on the human body.

The first space station was the USA's Skylab. It was launched in 1973 and retired in 1979, by which time Russia's more modern station, Mir, was in orbit. Mir was made of modules that are connected together in space. This allows space stations to develop over time and to house larger crews. Mir was retired in 2001.

Huge solar cell panels on the International Space Station provide it with power.

When it is completed, a joint project between 17 nations called the **International Space Station (ISS)** will provide six laboratories for space research and help astronauts train for flights to the Moon and Mars.

THE SPACE SHUTTLE

In the past, astronauts and supplies for space stations were launched into space on single use, unmanned rockets. But this was expensive and inconvenient, as the rockets were mostly made up of fuel tanks, which were jettisoned when empty and could not be re-used.

Since 1981, a fleet of US **Space Shuttles** have carried astronauts and pieces of space hardware into orbit. Shuttles are launched into space by two huge booster rockets. After launch these fall into the sea on parachutes, to be retrieved and used again. At the end of a mission the Shuttle glides back to Earth, landing on a runway like an aeroplane.

The Shuttle's missions usually last about a week. They have included taking astronauts to repair the Hubble Space Telescope*.

Around 2014, the Shuttle will be replaced by a cone-shaped capsule called Orion. This is to take astronauts back to the Moon and, in the future, to Mars.

See for yourself

At certain times, you can see the ISS, Shuttles and satellites drifting across the sky like moving stars. For links to a site that tells you how to spot the ISS in the night sky, go to **www.usborne-quicklinks.com**, type in the keyword "science" then enter page number 177.

Internet links

Go to **www.usborne-quicklinks.com** and type "science" to find out more about space exploration.

There you'll find links to websites where you can:

- Take an online tour of the International Space Station
- Find out what it's like to live on a space station

Go to Usborne Quicklinks for links to hand-picked websites on hundreds of subjects.

THE EARLY EARTH

The Earth is a tiny planet in a vast universe, which contains billions of stars, planets and moons, as well as huge areas of space containing other, smaller particles. There is no definite proof of how ancient events such as the Earth's formation took place. Many scientists, however, believe that patterns of radiation in space show that the universe was created in a huge explosion about 15 billion (15,000 million) years ago. This idea is called the **Big Bang theory**.

Icy comets and rocky asteroids rained down on the Earth's early surface.

BIRTH OF THE EARTH

The Earth is thought to have formed about 4,600 million years ago, and it has been constantly changing and developing ever since. It probably started as a huge, swirling cloud of dust and gases. Over time, this cloud began to shrink and become solid. Heavy iron-rich minerals collected at the middle of the growing planet, eventually creating a core of iron.

As the Earth formed, gases such as methane, hydrogen and ammonia rose from volcanoes on its surface. Over time, ultraviolet radiation from the Sun broke down these poisonous gases, leaving a thick blanket of nitrogen and carbon dioxide. At the same time, steam from volcanoes, and huge chunks of ice which rained down from space, formed early oceans.

EARLY LIFE

Around 3,500 million years ago, simple life-forms developed from the churning chemical soup of the Earth's early oceans. Like modern green plants, they made food using water, carbon dioxide and energy from sunlight. This released oxygen into the early atmosphere.

For many millions of years, these tiny organisms continued to make oxygen from the carbon dioxide surrounding the Earth. This formed a barrier, preventing most of the Sun's harmful ultraviolet rays from reaching the planet. Eventually, conditions were right for complex life-forms to begin their development. For more about life on Earth, see pages 186-187.

This cluster of stars formed many billions of years before the Earth and Sun. Scientists study these ancient stars to try to learn more about the early universe.

ANCIENT HISTORY

The amount of time it has taken the Earth to develop is so vast that it can barely be imagined. For some idea of how ancient the Earth is, try to picture its entire history taking place in one hour. On this scale, each minute would equal about 76.7 million years. Because the history of the Earth goes back so far, scientists must measure its development in periods of millions and billions of years. They use the terms **deep time** or **geological time** to refer to such a vast timescale.

CHANGING CLIMATE

Ever since the Earth began to form, its climate has been changing. For instance, at certain times it was much warmer than it is now. At other times, huge areas were covered with ice.

A glacier forms as snow builds up over many years and becomes a mass of ice. Its huge weight causes it to move slowly downhill.

Ice ages are periods of time lasting for thousands of years, when huge, moving layers of ice called **glaciers** cover much of the Earth. Many scientists think that past ice ages were caused by the Earth's orbit around the Sun changing shape. This would have reduced the amount of sunlight the planet received, leading to an ice age as its climate cooled.

Diagram showing change in Earth's orbit

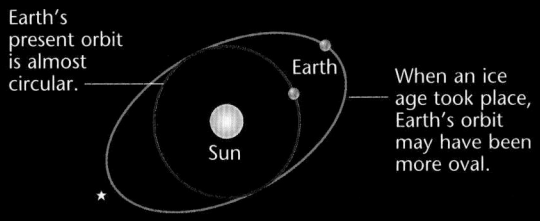

During an ice age, glaciers travel slowly across the land. In the past, these have helped to shape the landscape in many parts of the world, by carving vast valleys out of rock as they moved. Most of the ice at the North and South Poles may also have been formed during the last ice age.

THE SHAPE OF THE LAND

Soon after the Earth was formed, the first landmasses appeared. They moved around, joined together and split up again many times. About 250 million years ago there was just one giant landmass, called **Pangaea**. It began to split up about 225 million years ago, and the continents which exist today were slowly formed.

Development of modern continents

Pangaea

The spreading sea floor (pink area) caused the land to break up.

STUDYING THE PAST

Most of the information scientists have about the Earth's past comes from rocks. Most rocks form in layers over many thousands and millions of years. By studying these layers, scientists called **geologists** can work out what conditions may have been like as each one was formed.

Rocks formed in warm climates contain more fossils than those formed in cooler climates.

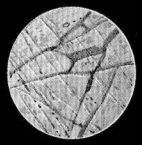

Rocks which were on the Earth's surface during ice ages show signs of being worn away by glaciers.

Internet links

Go to **www.usborne-quicklinks.com** and type in the keyword "science" to find out more about the early Earth.

There you'll find links to websites where you can:

- Discover how the Earth's climate has changed over billions of years
- Follow an interactive lesson about the Earth's history

Go to Usborne Quicklinks for links to hand-picked websites on hundreds of subjects.

EARTH'S STRUCTURE

The Earth has a solid surface, but is not solid all the way through. Inside, it is made up of layers, some of which are partly **molten**. This means that they are partly made up of hot liquid. The Earth's middle is an incredibly hot ball of iron and nickel. All the layers are pulled together by the enormous force of gravity from the centre.

Diamonds are formed by the tremendous heat and pressure within the Earth's crust.

Cutaway showing the Earth's layers

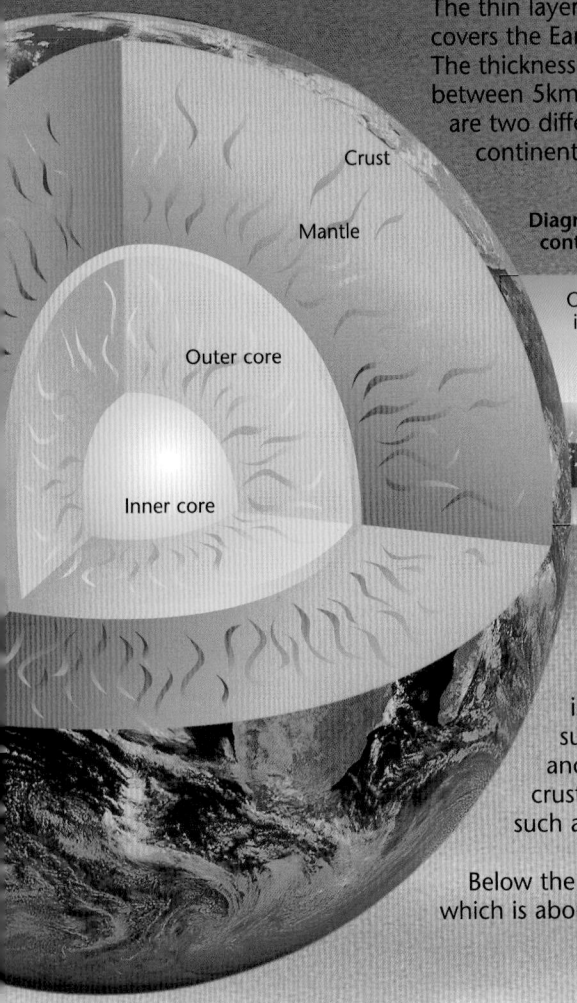

LAYERS OF THE EARTH

The thin layer of solid rock which covers the Earth is called the **crust**. The thickness of the crust varies between 5km and 70km. There are two different kinds of crust: continental and oceanic.

Diagram showing oceanic and continental crust

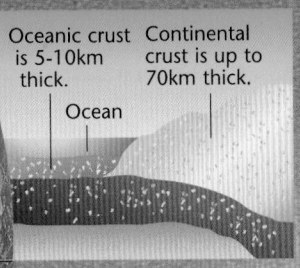

Thick **continental crust** forms land, and much thinner **oceanic crust** makes up ocean floors. Continental crust is made of light rocks such as granite, sandstone and limestone. Oceanic crust is made of heavier rock such as basalt and dolerite.

Below the crust is the **mantle**, which is about 3,000km thick.

Within the mantle is a thin layer called the **asthenosphere**. This is mostly solid rock, but a small amount is molten rock, called **magma**. This makes the whole layer weak. The upper mantle and crust, together called the **lithosphere**, move about on this weak layer.

The Earth's **core** has two parts. The **outer core**, which is about 2,200km thick, is molten. The **inner core** is solid. It is about 1,250km thick, extremely hot (about 5,000°C), and is about the same size as the Moon.

See for yourself

The movement of the liquid outer core is believed to create the Earth's magnetic field. This field creates two poles, called magnetic north and magnetic south. You can see their effects using an ordinary compass. Whichever way you hold the compass, its needle always points to magnetic north.

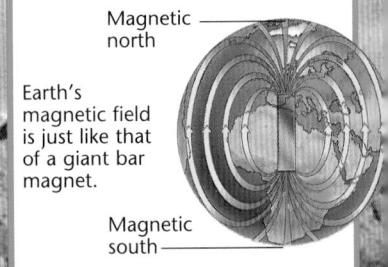

PLATES

The lithosphere is divided into large areas called **plates**, which are constantly moving. There are about seven main plates and many smaller ones. Each one is made of continental or oceanic lithosphere, or both. The areas where the plates' edges meet are called **plate boundaries**.

All the Earth's plates fit together like the pieces of a jigsaw puzzle.

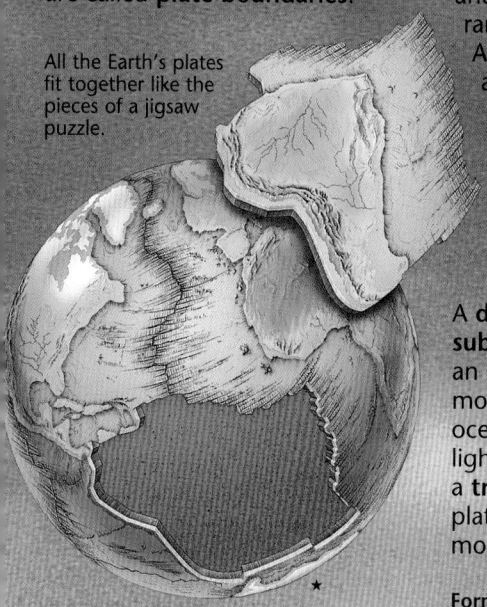

The plates move very slowly over the asthenosphere, typically at about 3cm per year. They can move towards each other, move apart or shift sideways.

Because all the plates fit together, movement of one plate affects the others around it. The study of plate movement and its effects is called **plate tectonics**.

NEW FEATURES

Plate movement is constantly causing the formation of new features on the Earth's surface.

For example, where plates move apart below the ocean, magma from the mantle wells up all along the boundary. It cools and hardens to form a mountain range, or **ridge**, of new crust. As the movement continues and more magma wells up along the centre, the ridge spreads out sideways, becoming a **spreading ridge**. Boundaries where new crust is formed are called **constructive boundaries**.

A **destructive boundary**, or **subduction zone**, occurs where an oceanic and continental plate move together. The heavier oceanic plate moves beneath the lighter continental plate, forming a **trench** where they meet. As the plate sinks, some of it becomes molten, forming new magma.

Formation of ridges and trenches

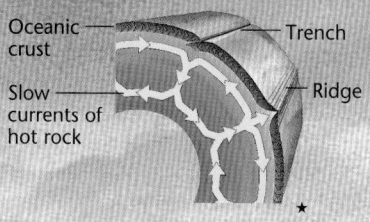

Where two plates push together above ground, the crust buckles and folds upwards to form high mountain ranges, called **fold mountains**. The Earth's crust is thickest at these points.

This mountain range was formed by two plates crushing together.

TYPES OF ROCK

The rock that makes up the Earth's surface is constantly being added to. It can be divided into three basic types: igneous, sedimentary and metamorphic.

Igneous rock is formed when molten rock cools and becomes solid. **Sedimentary rock** is formed when sediments, such as rock particles, are deposited by water or weather, buried and then squashed into layers called **strata**. When any type of rock is changed by intense heat or pressure, **metamorphic rock** is formed.

Granite is a type of igneous rock.

Limestone is a type of sedimentary rock.

Marble is a type of metamorphic rock.

Internet links

Go to **www.usborne-quicklinks.com** and type "science" to find out more about the Earth's structure.

There you'll find links to websites where you can:

- Find out more about plates, and how they shape our world
- Explore an interactive exhibit of rocks and minerals

Go to Usborne Quicklinks for links to hand-picked websites on hundreds of subjects.

FAULTS

As plates move, the strain sometimes causes brittle rock to crack. These cracks, called **faults**, are often weak zones where more movement or cracking may occur. For example, **rift valleys** may form when land containing faults is forced in opposite directions. All plate boundaries are major faults which began as minor ones.

Formation of a rift valley

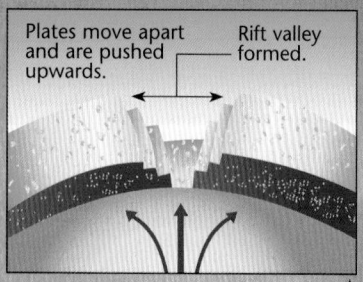

Rock is pushed upwards from underneath and pulled apart at faults.

EARTHQUAKES

The constant movement of plates causes pressure to build up at faults, and at the plate boundaries themselves. If there is a sudden slippage of rock, this pressure is released quickly, and an **earthquake** occurs. Most earthquakes are too weak to be felt by people, but some cause huge damage, as the ground shakes and buildings collapse.

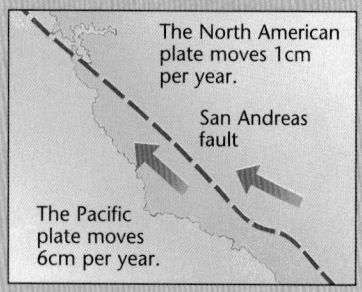

Earthquakes often occur on the San Andreas fault, on America's west coast. This is because the two plates either side of the fault slide in the same direction at different speeds.

FOCUS

The point where energy is suddenly released and an earthquake starts is called the **focus**. It is usually 5-15km under the ground. The point on the surface directly above the focus is called the **epicentre**. Vibrations called **seismic waves** travel from the focus in all directions.

An earthquake is caused when rock gives way at a fault, releasing vast amounts of built-up energy.

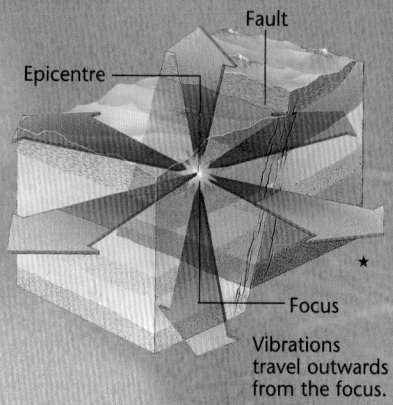

PREDICTION

Scientists who study earthquakes, called **seismologists**, use plate movement to predict when major earthquakes are going to happen. Horizontal movement along plates can be measured by bouncing a laser beam off a series of reflectors on the ground. A computer records the time it takes to travel between them. If this changes, it shows that ground movement has taken place. Animal behaviour may also be used to predict an earthquake.

Snakes came out of hibernation early before an earthquake in China in 1975. This may have been because they were disturbed by very slight vibrations in the ground.

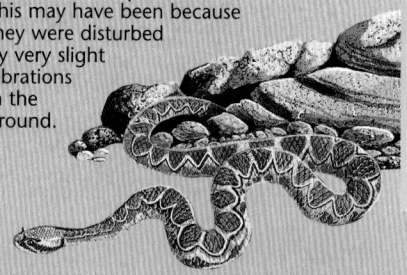

VOLCANOES

The magma within the largely solid mantle sometimes rises and collects in certain places. **Volcanoes** are formed when it rises to the Earth's surface and bursts out. At this stage magma becomes known as **lava**. This explosive effect is known as an **eruption**. Most volcanoes form along plate boundaries or under the sea.

Inside an erupting volcano

The volcano below, called a **composite volcano**, is made up of alternating layers of lava and ash. These have built up over long periods of time to form a steep-sided cone.

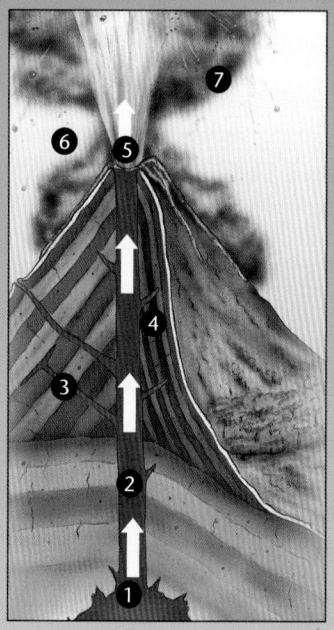

1. Place where magma gathers beneath Earth's crust, called **magma chamber**
2. **Vent** – the main pipe up the middle of a volcano
3. **Dyke** – a sheet of igneous rock which cuts across existing rocks
4. Layers of ash and lava
5. Hole at top of volcano, called a **crater**
6. Dust, ash and gases
7. Lumps of lava, called **volcanic bombs**

VOLCANO FORMATION

A row of volcanoes may form where plates are moving apart, particularly at spreading ridges*.

Spreading ridges form when plates move apart.

Volcanoes may also form above subduction zones*, where one plate is forced beneath the other.

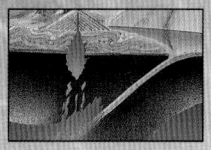

At subduction zones, one plate is forced below the other plate, where it starts to melt.

Some volcanoes form in the middle of plates, at hot patches on the Earth's surface called **hot spots**. Scientists think that these are formed when especially hot currents of magma called **plumes** shoot up and burn through the crust, bursting out of the surface.

DEAD OR ALIVE?

Volcanoes that erupt regularly are known as **active** volcanoes. If it is thought that a volcano will never erupt again, it is said to be **extinct**. Sometimes, people think a volcano has become extinct, but it is actually just inactive, or **dormant**.

SUPERVOLCANOES

Supervolcanoes are formed from huge collapsed craters, called **calderas**, with a magma chamber beneath. Only a few supervolcanoes exist, but they are so powerful and destructive that a single eruption could alter all life on Earth. This is because enormous pressure builds up in the magma chamber over thousands of years, then bursts in a devastating explosion.

Scientists think that the last supervolcano eruption was in Sumatra, 74,000 years ago. It is believed that this eruption blew out enough ash to block the Sun's light for around six months, causing the Earth to cool down. This would have caused environmental changes all over the world, killing huge numbers of living things.

Here, fountains of lava are shooting out of an erupting volcano. They may travel up to 600m into the air.

See for yourself

You can do a simple test to show how seismic waves travel from an earthquake focus. Place a handful of sand or grit on a table, then tap the table gently with a hammer. This point is the "focus", and the waves which travel outwards will make the sand jump. Try striking the table further from the sand, and see what happens. The waves lose strength as they travel further away from the focus.

Internet links

Go to **www.usborne-quicklinks.com** and type in "science" to find out more about the Earth's structure.

There you'll find links to websites where you can:

- Find animated guides to earthquakes and volcanoes
- Watch video clips of volcanic eruptions around the world

Go to Usborne Quicklinks for links to hand-picked websites on hundreds of subjects.

The links at Usborne Quicklinks are regularly reviewed and updated, so you might find a slightly different selection of websites from the ones shown here.

* *Spreading ridges, Subduction zones, 181.*

THE ATMOSPHERE

The Earth is surrounded by a blanket of different gases called the **atmosphere**. It is the presence of this atmosphere that allows life on Earth to exist, as it contains oxygen and other gases needed by living things. The atmosphere also acts as a shield against harmful ultraviolet rays from the Sun.

The atmosphere protects our planet from the Sun's powerful rays.

EARLY FORMATION

When the Earth was forming, it was first surrounded by hydrogen and helium. However, as the Sun heated these light gases, they escaped into space.

An atmosphere which could be held in place by the Earth's gravity was eventually formed from gases such as methane, ammonia and water vapour. These poured out of volcanoes on the surface, in a process known as **outgassing**. Over billions of years, these gases reacted to form an atmosphere of nitrogen and carbon dioxide.

Earth's early atmosphere would have been poisonous to living things. It took millions of years to become the way it is today.

The atmosphere as we know it did not start to form until plant-like organisms appeared in Earth's oceans, around 3,500 million years ago. These very simple living things used the Sun's light to make food from water and carbon dioxide, releasing oxygen as a by-product. This process continued for many millions of years, until there was enough oxygen in the atmosphere to support other forms of life.

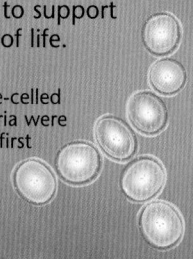

These single-celled cyanobacteria were among the first organisms on Earth.

OUR ATMOSPHERE

The atmosphere is a mixture of gases – around four-fifths nitrogen and one-fifth oxygen, with traces of others. Water also exists in the atmosphere as vapour, droplets in clouds, and as ice crystals.

Snowflakes are formed from ice crystals.

Percentage of gases in the atmosphere

Nitrogen	78%
Oxygen	21%
Argon	0.9%
Carbon dioxide	0.03%
Other gases (such as xenon, neon, krypton)	0.07%

ATMOSPHERIC LAYERS

The atmosphere is around 500km thick and is made up of several layers. These extend out from the Earth and fade into space. All the Earth's weather happens in the layer nearest the surface. Most of the higher atmosphere is a thin mix of calm, unchanging gases.

Layers in the atmosphere, showing number of kilometres from Earth

Exosphere (over 500km)

The atmosphere merges into space. This layer contains almost no gases.

Thermosphere (up to 500km)

Temperature in this layer is very high, because of a gas called atomic oxygen. This helps to absorb some radiation from the Sun.

The Space Shuttle orbits in the thermosphere.

Mesosphere (up to 80km)

This layer has no ozone and no clouds, so the temperature is low.

Meteors burn up here.

Stratosphere (up to 50km)

This layer contains about 19% of all the atmosphere's gases. Temperature is higher, because it contains the ozone layer (see right).

Jet planes fly in the stratosphere.

Troposphere (up to 10km)

Contains 80% of all gases in the atmosphere, as well as all weather. Temperature in this layer decreases with height.

CHANGING ATMOSPHERE

Greenhouse gases, such as carbon dioxide, trap heat around the Earth and keep it warm enough for life to exist. This is called the **greenhouse effect**. But fuel and forest burning are adding more gases, and making the greenhouse effect stronger. This leads to **global warming**, a rise in global temperatures.

Smoke from burning fuels adds carbon dioxide to the atmosphere.

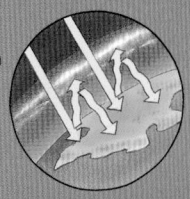

The Sun's rays, absorbed and given back out by the Earth, are trapped by the carbon dioxide and sent back down.

Governments and businesses are being urged to cut the amount of carbon dioxide released into the atmosphere as scientists predict this will reduce the effects of global warming. Energy sources such as wind or solar power release much less carbon dioxide.

This mountaineer has to carry a supply of oxygen, because the air in the troposphere contains less oxygen as he climbs higher.

Satellite images such as this are used to monitor the ozone layer. Orange areas show where ozone levels are highest.

THE OZONE LAYER

Within the stratosphere is a layer of **ozone** gas. This absorbs most of the Sun's harmful ultraviolet radiation, preventing it from reaching the Earth.

The ozone layer is being damaged by man-made gases called **chlorofluorocarbons (CFCs)**. These are released by some refrigerators and aerosols, and react with sunlight in the stratosphere. The products of this reaction break down the ozone. As the layer becomes thinner, more ultraviolet rays reach the Earth's surface.

Internet links

Go to **www.usborne-quicklinks.com** and type "science" to find out more about the atmosphere.

There you'll find links to websites where you can:

- Read a guide to global warming, with games and animations
- Find facts, experiments and quizzes about the atmosphere

Go to Usborne Quicklinks for links to hand-picked websites on hundreds of subjects.

LIFE ON EARTH

The Earth is the only planet on which life is known to exist. To survive, living things need the right amounts of light and heat from the Sun, along with food, water and oxygen. It has taken many millions of years for conditions on Earth to become suitable for the wide variety of plants and animals which exist today.

LOOKING AT THE PAST

Scientists measure the Earth's ancient past in **geological (deep) time**. This divides into four **eras**, which break down further into **periods** of several million years.

Evidence from rock formations suggests that five **mass extinction** events have taken place in the Earth's past. During each one, huge numbers of living things died out in a very short time. Only the organisms which were best suited to conditions on the Earth at that time survived and multiplied.

ANCIENT LIFE

The first single-celled organisms appeared on Earth around 3,500 million years ago, during the **Precambrian Era**. The earliest known fossils date back to this time. Around 545 million years ago, many-celled organisms began to increase rapidly in number. This was the start of the **Paleozoic Era**.

These worm-like creatures, called Spriggina, lived on the ocean floor at the end of the Precambrian Era.

Some of the earliest evidence of life comes from fossils known as **stromatolites**, which contain the remains of cyanobacteria. Some of them are 3,500 million years old.

4,600-545 mya
First single-celled organisms, then early many-celled, soft-bodied creatures

545-495 mya
Cambrian Period
First creatures with hard outer coverings

495-445 mya
Ordovician Period
First land plants, first fish

445-415 mya
Silurian Period
First small land animals

415-355 mya
Devonian Period
First amphibians

355-290 mya
Carboniferous Period
Large insects, first reptiles, first forests

290-250 mya
Permian Period
First swimming reptiles

250-205 mya
Triassic Period
First dinosaurs, bony fish

205-140 mya
Jurassic Period
Large dinosaurs, first mammals and birds

This timeline shows all the periods of the Earth's history, and which life-forms were present during each one. "Mya" stands for "millions of years ago", and the numbers given are approximate.

- **Precambrian Era** (dawn of life)
- **Paleozoic Era** (ancient life)
- **Mesozoic Era** (middle life)
- **Cenozoic Era** (recent life)
- Mass extinction

DEVELOPING LIFE

Fossil records suggest that in a part of the Paleozoic Era called the Cambrian Period, there was a huge increase in the number of different creatures on the Earth. Sea creatures began to develop hard body parts. These protective coverings would have made the creatures tougher, increasing their chances of living long enough to reproduce.

Many creatures with hard body coverings, like this trilobite, began to appear in seas during the Cambrian Period.

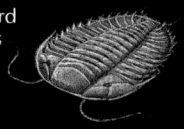

Some small arthropods (creatures with jointed bodies), such as millipedes and insects, were able to move onto the land. This was because the Earth's temperature had cooled enough for land plants to grow in large numbers, providing food. The earliest vertebrates (animals with backbones) also appeared.

During the **Devonian Period** (around 415-355 million years ago), the climate in many areas was hot and dry, and water levels dropped in rivers and lakes. One group of fish became able to breathe both in and out of water. These were the earliest amphibians.

This fossil shows that seed-carrying plants existed in the Devonian Period.

Around 355 million years ago, during the **Carboniferous Period**, many parts of the world became hot and humid. This allowed huge numbers of plants to grow, forming vast, steamy swamps. These became home to many types of bugs and amphibians.

Meganeura, a giant dragonfly, had wings that measured 60cm across.

THE AGE OF REPTILES

During the **Permian Period**, amphibians evolved into early reptiles. They were able to spread all over the world because all the land became joined together as one huge continent. At the same time, huge numbers of sea creatures died because the shallow seas around the continents disappeared.

Hylonomus was one of the earliest known reptiles.

The **Mesozoic Era** began 250 million years ago, with numbers of reptiles increasing rapidly. During this era, the dinosaurs appeared. They became the dominant vertebrate life-forms on the Earth until 65 million years ago, when they suddenly died out, probably as a result of a major climatic change.

THE AGE OF MAMMALS

The current age of mammals, called the **Cenozoic Era**, began after the dinosaurs died out. It is thought that mammals may have survived the change in climate which killed the dinosaurs because they can control their own body temperature. Dinosaurs probably could not do this.

MODERN EXTINCTION

Extinction has always happened naturally over time. However, the current extinction rate is thought to be about 10,000 times greater than it would be if humans did not exist. Modern extinctions are almost always caused by pollution or loss of habitats (natural living spaces), brought about by the growing human race, and its need for land, food and water.

The white rhino is one of many species threatened by habitat loss or hunting.

Unless we can make better use of the Earth's resources, it is possible that humans may be responsible for the next major extinction event.

140-65 mya

Cretaceous Period

Flowering plants

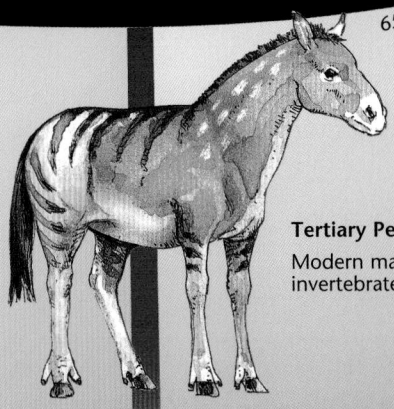

65-1.8 mya

Tertiary Period

Modern mammals, invertebrates, birds

1.8 mya to present day

Quaternary Period

Appearance of humans

Internet links

For links to websites where you can find out more about life on Earth, go to **www.usborne-quicklinks.com** and type in the keyword "science".

Always follow the internet safety guidelines on the Usborne Quicklinks Website.

SEAS AND OCEANS

Around 71% of the Earth's surface is covered in salty water, which makes up five vast oceans and several smaller seas. Oceans are very important to life on Earth, and are home to huge numbers of living things. The oceans also influence weather and climate conditions all over the world.

The largest of Earth's vast oceans, called the Pacific, covers around 30% of the planet's surface.

OCEAN CURRENTS

Ocean water constantly moves in huge, flowing bands called **currents**. These carry vast amounts of water around the Earth. There are two main types of ocean currents: surface and deep. **Surface currents** affect the top 350m or so of oceans. They are pushed along by **prevailing winds** (the most common types of wind in an area).

Deep currents are made up of very cold water coming from the North and South Poles. Cold water is heavier, so it sinks beneath the warmer surface currents which constantly arrive at the Poles. It then drifts towards the equator, where it warms up and rises to become a surface current itself. It then changes direction and starts to drift back towards the Poles.

How currents circulate

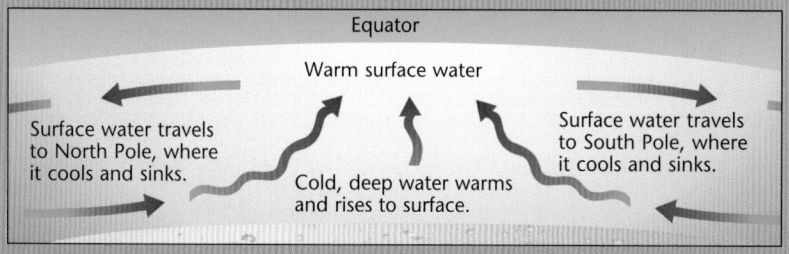

See for yourself

You can do a simple activity to show that cold water is heavier than warmer water. Half fill a large, clear bowl with warm water. Fill a jug with ice-cold water containing a little food colouring. Gently pour the water into the bowl. You should notice that it sinks, just as cold water does at the Poles.

Ice-cold water sinks to the bottom of the bowl.

Waves such as this are created by strong winds sweeping across the surface of the water.

CLIMATE CONTROL

Oceans and seas play an important role in controlling the world's climate. Their waters absorb heat from the Sun, especially in tropical regions, and spread it around the Earth in surface currents.

Warm ocean currents may cause **tropical cyclones** (called **hurricanes** in America and **typhoons** in the Far East). These are fierce storms, with strong winds which form waves up to 25m high.

How a tropical cyclone forms

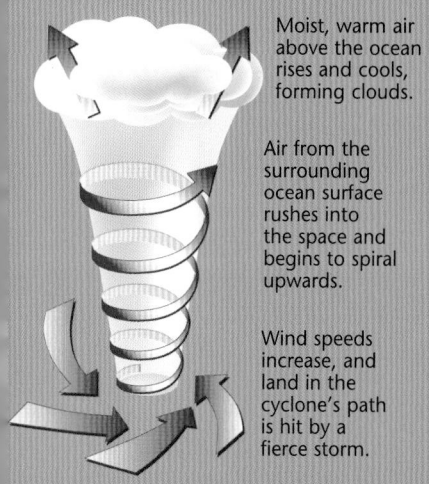

TIDAL MOVEMENT

Seas and oceans are constantly moved by the tides. Tidal movement is caused mainly by the Moon. As it travels around the Earth, the force of its gravity makes the water on either side of the Earth bulge out. In a 24-hour period, this causes two **high tides**, when sea levels are at their highest, and two **low tides**, when they are at their lowest.

Tides are also influenced by the Earth, Moon and Sun lining up in certain ways. At full moon and new moon, there are very high **spring tides**. At quarters, when the Moon and Sun are at right angles to each other, there are very low **neap tides**.

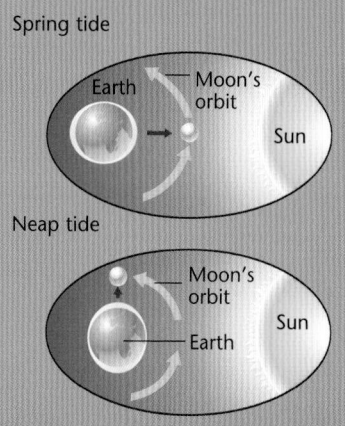

LIFE IN THE OCEANS

Seas and oceans contain a huge variety of plant and animal life, from the surface all the way down to the deepest trenches. Billions of microscopic plants called **phytoplankton** drift near the surface of the water. These are the main source of food for many creatures which live and feed at different ocean levels, called **zones**.

Ocean feeding zones

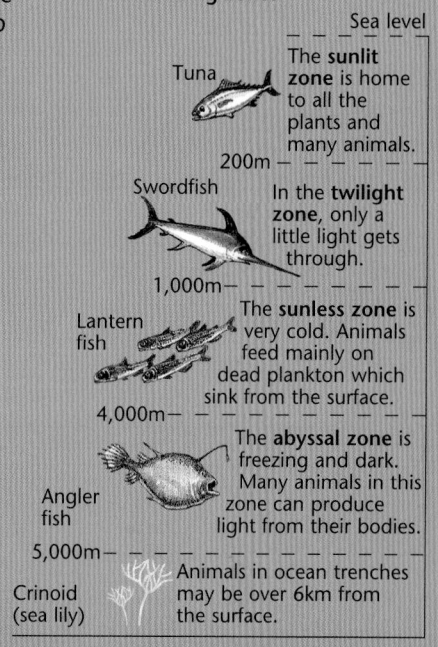

Internet links

Go to **www.usborne-quicklinks.com** and type in "science" to find out more about the seas and oceans.

There you'll find links to websites where you can:

- Find out how El Niño affects weather around the world
- Explore an interactive guide to ocean life

Go to Usborne Quicklinks for links to hand-picked websites on hundreds of subjects.

RIVERS

Rivers are formed when small streams join together and flow across the land, eventually flowing into a sea or lake. Rivers shape the Earth's surface by wearing away the rock they flow over and depositing rocks, pebbles, sand and silt as they do so.

A RIVER'S SOURCE

The beginning of a river is called its **source**. Many rivers have their source in mountain regions where water has run across the surface from various places and flowed into one channel. A river may also begin as a spring or a flow from a glacier.

How springs are formed

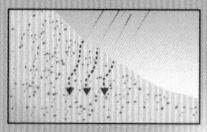

Rain or snow falls on **permeable** rock, which lets in water.

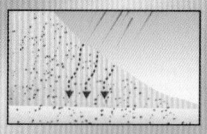

Water soaks into rock, building up from the lowest permeable level.

Springs begin to flow where the water-filled rock meets the surface.

A waterfall forms when a river flows from hard to soft rock. The water wears away the soft rock more quickly and forms a ledge.

STAGES OF A RIVER

A river's course can be divided into three stages. In its **upper** stage, the valley tends to be V-shaped with steep sides, formed as the turbulent water cuts down into the rock. The slope or **gradient** of the river's rocky bed is steep.

In the **middle** stage, the river's speed increases because the bed is smoother. The gradient is more gentle, and the valley becomes wider as the water wears away its sides. The river flows from side to side in wide loops. This is called **meandering**.

In the **lower** stage, the river's muddy or sandy bed is even smoother, so it flows faster. The river is large, because it has been joined by others, called **tributaries**. At its end it flows into the sea or a lake.

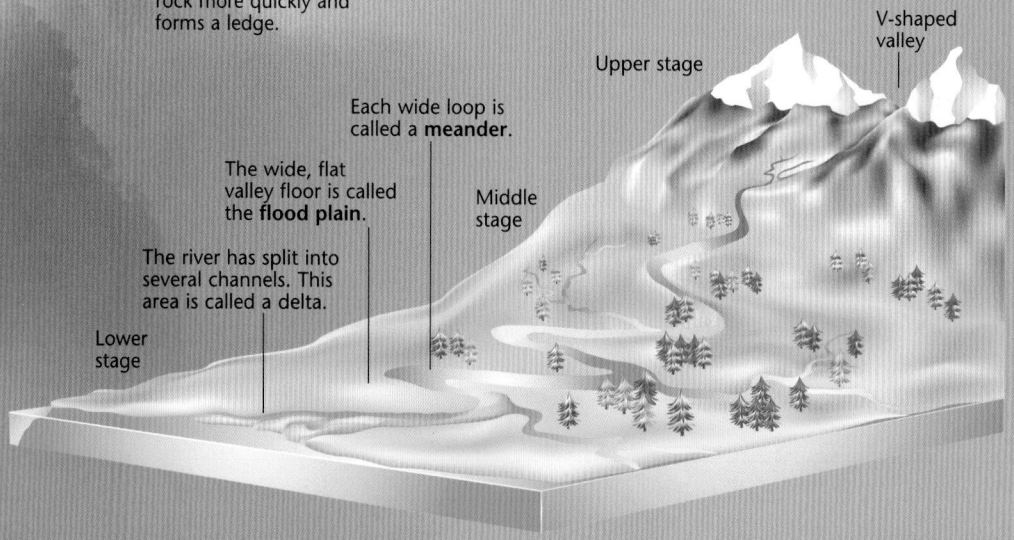

EROSION

Running water wears away or **erodes** rock by the constant movement of the pebbles and sand grains it carries. This is how a river bed forms. The amount of erosion depends on the speed and amount of water, how much material it carries and the rock it flows over. Softer rock, such as sandstone, is eroded faster than harder rock, such as granite.

The diagram below shows four types of erosion which take place at different stages of a river's course. The length of the river is not shown to scale.

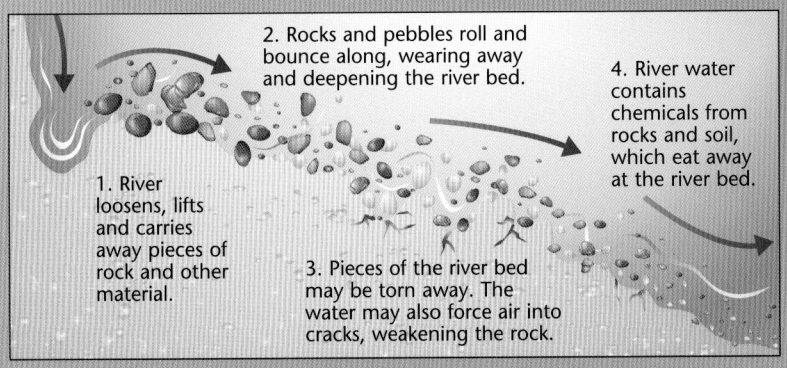

TRANSPORTATION

All the material **transported**, or carried along, by a river is called its **load**. Finer particles of clay and silt are carried along with heavier ones, such as pebbles and boulders. Wherever a river slows down, some of this material is deposited. The heaviest material is deposited first, followed by the smaller particles, creating a layering effect.

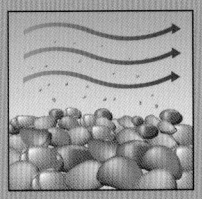

Large particles sink to the river bed before smaller ones.

DELTAS

As a river flows into the sea, any material it is still carrying is deposited. If this is deposited faster than it is washed away by the sea's currents and tides, it builds up in an area of flat land called a **delta**. The river splits into narrower channels as it crosses the delta and travels to the sea, creating a number of **sediment islands**. As the fresh river water and the salty sea water meet, chemical reactions take place and minerals that have been carried down, dissolved in the fresh water, come out of solution and are added to the sediment.

This is a delta in the Tenakee Inlet, Alaska. You can see how the sediment has built up in islands.

The mineral-rich sediment in delta areas makes the land fertile and ideal for farming. In Bangladesh, for example, millions of people live on islands formed in the delta of the River Ganges, despite the threat of flooding.

See for yourself

You can show how water deposits materials in layers. First, cut two 2cm slits in the bottom of a 1 litre plastic bottle. Cover each slit with sticky tape.

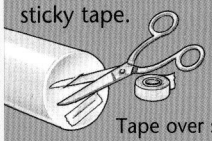

Tape over slits.

Next, use a funnel to half fill the bottle with soil. Then almost fill the bottle with water. Screw on the lid, shake vigorously, and leave for 24 hours.

Plastic tubing

Remove the lid and place one end of some plastic tubing in the water. Suck the water up, making sure not to swallow any, then put your thumb over the end. Bend the tube downwards into the sink or a container. Move your thumb, and the water will drain out.

Finally, pull the tape off the slits in the base, and leave to drain for 24 hours. You should see the soil has settled in layers.

Bottle cut away

Internet links

To find out more about rivers, go to **www.usborne-quicklinks.com** and type in the keyword "science".

There you'll find links to websites where you can:

- Explore the different stages of a river with pictures and diagrams
- Find animated diagrams of waterfalls and river erosion

Go to Usborne Quicklinks for links to hand-picked websites on hundreds of subjects.

WEATHER

The conditions in the atmosphere near to the Earth's surface are called the **weather**. These conditions include the temperature of the air, wind speed, air pressure, and the amount of water in the air, called **humidity**. Other factors include the amount of cloud and how much rain or snow falls, called **precipitation**.

THE SUN'S EFFECT

The Sun plays the most important part in causing the weather. Its heat, known as **solar radiation**, is absorbed by the Earth, which warms up as a result. In turn, the heat passes out from the Earth to the air above, which also becomes warmer.

The Sun's rays have the strongest effect where they hit the Earth's surface straight on, that is, around the middle of the Earth (the **equator**). Further away from the equator, the rays do not strike directly, so the heat is spread over a larger area. Its effect is therefore weaker.

How the Sun's rays strike the Earth

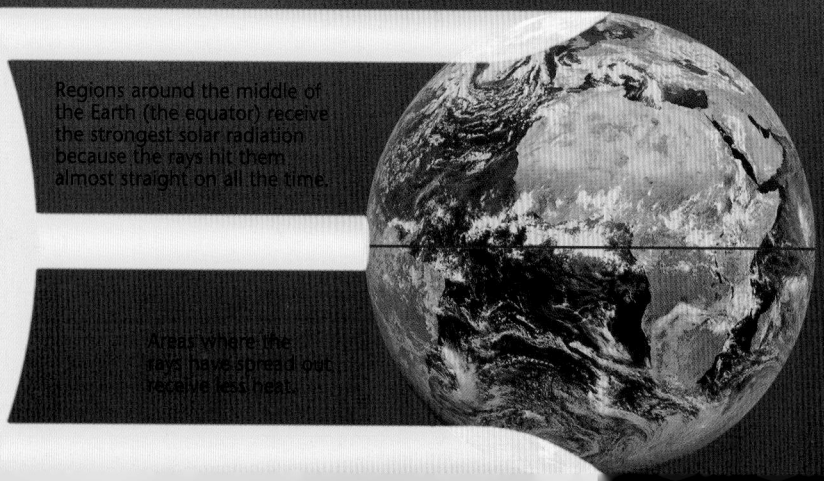

AIR PRESSURE

The atmosphere presses down on the Earth's surface, creating **atmospheric pressure**. When air is heated from below, it expands and begins to rise. As it does so it stops pressing down so hard on the surface. This creates an area of **low pressure**. At the surface, air flows in from surrounding areas to even up the pressure.

Low pressure

As warm air rises from the surface, more air moves in from higher pressure areas.

High pressure

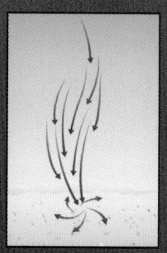

As cooler air pushes down, the surface air moves away to lower pressure areas.

Around the Earth there are areas of high and low pressure. These areas are called **belts**. Strong winds blow from high pressure belts to low pressure belts. However, the winds do not just blow straight from one belt to the other. They are deflected sideways (made to swerve) by the Earth's rotation. This is known as the **Coriolis effect**.

Red arrows show how winds are deflected around the Earth. Yellow arrow shows which way the Earth rotates.

HOT AND COLD AIR

As warm air rises, it cools and sinks back to Earth. There, it may be heated again if the surface is still warmer than the air above. The circulation of warm and cold currents of air is called **convection** and the currents are **convection currents**.

These dark clouds are full of water droplets, which may fall as rain, snow or hail.

CLOUDS

The Sun's heat causes water to evaporate from the seas. The water vapour rises and cools, condensing as it does so, to form tiny water droplets. These mass together as **clouds**. When clouds form slowly and steadily, they spread out across the sky in sheets. On hot days, they grow faster and puff up into heaps.

Common types of cloud

Cirrus clouds are high and wispy.

Cumulus clouds often form high in the sky in warm, sunny weather.

Stratus clouds form low, flat layers.

THE SEASONS

Weather conditions change throughout the year. These changes are called the **seasons**, and they occur because the Earth is tilted at an angle in relation to the Sun. As the planet makes its year-long journey around the Sun, the most direct sunlight falls on different areas.

In January, at the start of each orbit, the **southern hemisphere** (the half of the Earth below the equator), is tilted towards the Sun, causing temperatures to rise there. In June, the **northern hemisphere** is tilted towards the Sun. Temperatures rise in the north and fall in the south. In spring and autumn, neither hemisphere is tilted more towards the Sun.

Diagram showing how seasons change

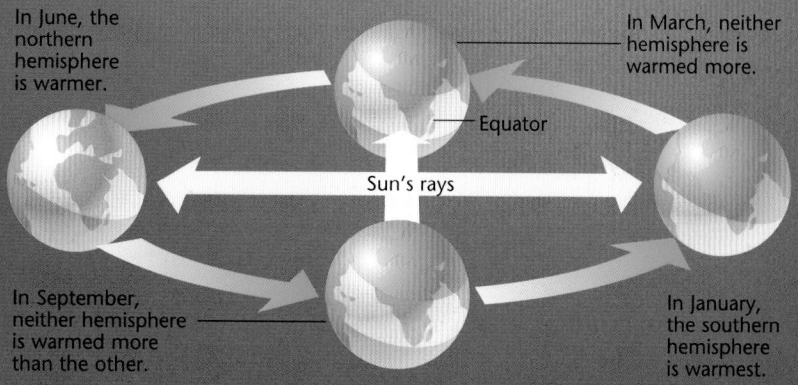

See for yourself

You can do this simple activity to create a miniature cloud. First, fill a large, clear plastic container about a third full with hot water. Next, place some ice cubes on a baking tray and put this on top of the container. As the air inside the container rises and is cooled by the ice, the water vapour it contains forms droplets, making a small "cloud".

Internet links

To find out more about the weather, go to **www.usborne-quicklinks.com** and type in the keyword "science".

There you'll find links to websites where you can:

- Investigate the causes of weather with online activities
- Find out more about the seasons

CLIMATE

An area's **climate** is its typical pattern of weather conditions and temperature over a long period of time. One type of climate may affect a large region, or a small, local area, where it is called a **microclimate**. Climates depend on latitude, distance from the sea, and height above sea level.

Banana trees such as this grow in equatorial areas.

CLIMATIC REGIONS

A **climatic region** is a large area on the Earth within which the climate is generally the same. The world's major climatic regions are described on this page.

Polar climates are harsh and change very little throughout the year. The temperature is extremely low and there is little rain or snowfall. Hardly any plant life can grow in these conditions.

Many polar animals, such as this polar bear, are kept warm by a thick layer of fur or fat.

Tundra regions have harsh winds and low winter temperatures, averaging from -30°C to -20°C. The temperature rises to around 17°C during the summer.

Tough, low-growing land plants such as lichens are examples of tundra vegetation.

In **temperate** regions, rain falls throughout the year, and the temperature varies with the seasons. It is generally between -6°C and 25°C. Day-to-day weather changes are a feature of temperate regions.

Deciduous trees, which lose their leaves in autumn, are found in temperate areas.

Tropical regions have a warm climate all year round. There are two seasons, dry and wet. Temperatures tend to be between 21°C and 30°C.

Grasslands in tropical regions are mostly made up of scattered trees and tall grasses, which die off in the dry season.

Mediterranean areas are warm and wet in winter but dry in summer. Their climate is heavily influenced by currents of air which move between the land and sea.

Citrus fruits grow well in Mediterranean climates. Their thick skins prevent them from drying up during the hot summer months.

Continental areas, such as the central parts of Asia and North America, have hot summers and cold winters.

North American prairies have very hot summers.

Equatorial regions have a constantly hot and wet climate, which supports rainforests in many areas. The temperature never drops below around 17°C, creating ideal growing conditions for huge numbers of plants.

Desert climates are generally very dry, with less than 250mm of rainfall per year. Daytime temperatures in the hottest deserts may be over 38°C, although some become much cooler in winter. Many living things in the desert can store water.

Cacti and many other desert plants store large amounts of water in their thick, fleshy leaves.

MOUNTAIN CLIMATES

In mountain areas, temperatures drop as height above sea level (**altitude**) increases, producing different climates and vegetation at different altitudes. Trees can't survive on high mountain slopes because there is little soil, and the ground may be frozen and blasted by harsh, icy winds.

The direction which a mountainside faces (called its **aspect**) also affects its climate. If one side of a mountain receives more sunlight than the other, more vegetation may grow there.

Plant life in a mountain climate

COASTAL CLIMATES

In coastal areas, the land and sea gain and lose heat at different rates during the day and night. The air above them constantly circulates, creating a mild, wet climate. This is known as a **coastal** or **maritime** climate.

During the day

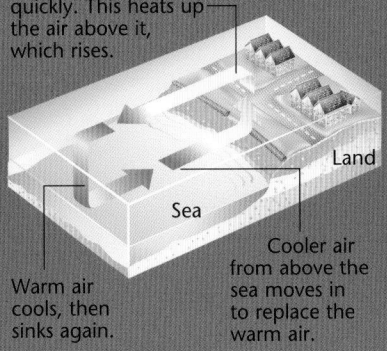

During the night

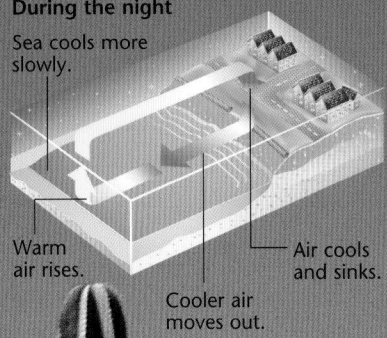

CITY CLIMATES

Cities tend to be warmer than the areas surrounding them. This is because concrete absorbs more heat than vegetation. It also holds on to heat for longer, making nights warmer in cities than in the countryside.

The ground beneath a city also tends to be drier, as roads and pavements prevent water from draining into the soil beneath.

CLIMATE CHANGE

Most scientists think that **global warming** is causing more extreme weather in many parts of the world. Areas in Africa that already get little rain are getting still less, making it even more difficult for people to grow crops to eat.

Many places, such as Bangladesh, London and New York, are at increased risk of flooding. Ocean water expands as it warms, and this, together with the melting of ice sheets and glaciers, means that sea levels are rising.

Large areas of China and India may suffer drought, because major rivers could dry up entirely for parts of the year, as the glaciers supplying them with water disappear.

Internet links

To find out more about climate, go to **www.usborne-quicklinks.com** and type in the keyword "science".

There you'll find links to websites where you can:

- Find an interactive guide to the Earth's climates
- Explore an online climate map

Go to Usborne Quicklinks for links to hand-picked websites on hundreds of subjects.

WORLD POPULATION

All the people living in a particular place are called its **population**. Today, the world's population is greater than ever before, and it is increasing all the time. People's need for food, shelter and fuel creates demands on the Earth and its resources. As a result, people have altered the natural environment to suit their needs.

In some places, where the land is crowded, some people live in houseboats on rivers or lakes.

SPREADING OUT

If all the Earth's surface were suitable to live on, there would be plenty of room for everyone. However, few people live where the climate is very hot or cold, or where the soil is unsuitable for farming. This means that the world's population is spread unevenly over the continents.

This satellite image shows Washington DC, USA. Over a third of the world's population lives in cities like this.

There are now over 6,000 million people in the world, compared to around 4,000 million in 1980. In countries with fast-growing populations, more people are being forced to live in overcrowded conditions or unsuitable places.

Graph showing world population since the year 1000

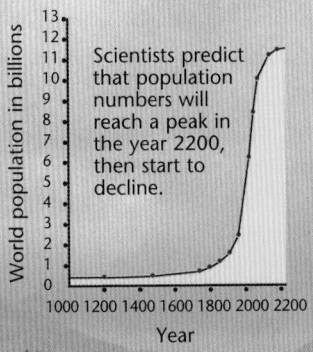

CITY PROBLEMS

All over the world, people move from the country into towns and cities, to find work. This is called **urban migration**. As city populations grow, some areas become crowded, and pollution increases.

In some countries, **shanty towns**, made up of makeshift buildings, build up on the edges of cities to house the extra people. Houses in shanty towns are usually built from waste materials and scrap. There is often no clean water supply, electricity or sewage system.

This is a shanty town on the outskirts of Cape Town, South Africa. People may be forced to build these when they can't afford housing in the city, or when there isn't enough available.

POPULATION CONTROL

Many countries are trying to prevent their population from growing too quickly. For example, in China, couples are discouraged from having more than one child. Health education projects also teach people **birth control** – how to avoid having too many children. However, many people object to birth control because of their religious or cultural beliefs.

PEOPLE AND THE LAND

Since early times, people's lives have been influenced by the natural features of their surroundings. People looked for areas where they could find water, food and safety from attack. When they discovered a suitable place, they formed permanent groups called **communities**.

Many communities began near rivers, springs or wells, or in areas that were not likely to flood. Fertile soils for farming and natural resources, such as coal, also encouraged people to settle in particular places.

EFFECTS ON THE LAND

People often change their surroundings to suit their needs. Over the centuries, more and more land has been cleared for building, transport systems and growing crops. Huge areas of forest have been destroyed and natural wetlands drained. Dry areas have been watered artificially or **irrigated**.

Here, a wooded area is being cleared to make way for a building site.

These methods help to provide more food, housing, and transport routes. But the natural world suffers as a result. In many areas of cleared land, fertile topsoil has been washed or blown away. This is called **soil erosion**. It leaves infertile soil, which cannot be used to grow crops. In some countries, soil erosion combined with drought has led to famine.

FARMING

As the world's population increases, so does the demand for food. Many international charities are helping to improve farming techniques in developing countries. They set up projects to teach farmers how to produce more crops from the same amount of land. This removes the need to clear more land.

Some new farmland has been created in desert border land. These areas once had trees and shrubs, but have been turned to desert through soil erosion. This is caused by overgrazing, tree felling and dry winds. But with the help of irrigation, this land may be used to grow crops.

In areas with very little water, drip irrigators deliver water drop by drop to each plant. Sometimes fertilizers are added to the water. This is known as **fertigation**.

Internet links

Go to **www.usborne-quicklinks.com** and type in "science" to find out more about world population.

There you'll find links to websites where you can:

- Find up-to-date population facts and figures
- Explore an interactive population atlas with graphs and animations

Go to Usborne Quicklinks for links to hand-picked websites on hundreds of subjects.

EARTH'S RESOURCES

Beneath the Earth's surface are many resources which are used by people all over the world. Some of these are precious stones, which can be sold or traded; others are metals, which are used for building and other purposes. Almost all the fuel currently used also comes from within the Earth.

This drinks can contains aluminium, one of several metals that can be melted down and re-used.

FOSSIL FUELS

Oil, coal and gas are known as **fossil fuels**. They are formed from the remains of plants and animals which have built up in rock for millions of years. The chemical energy trapped in these organisms is released when fossil fuels are burned.

Coal is formed from the remains of ancient plants.

People need fuel for cooking, heating, lighting, running motor vehicles, generating electricity, and many other things. But demand is great and supplies are limited, so all of the Earth's oil and gas may be used up within a few decades. This means that people need to find other fuel sources to meet their needs.

RENEWABLE ENERGY

Sources of energy which will not run out are described as **renewable**. These include the Sun's rays, which are captured by solar panels*; the wind, which turns wind turbines*; and moving water, used in hydroelectric power stations. **Geothermal energy** (heat energy from underground rocks) is used in volcanic areas. **Biofuel**, which is made from fermented corn or sugar cane, can also be used as fuel.

However, only 7% of the Earth's energy currently comes from renewable sources. This is mainly because they are often less reliable or less efficient than fossil fuels. For instance, many rely on certain climatic conditions, such as strong winds or constant, bright sunshine, which are not always available in some areas.

NUCLEAR POWER

Nuclear energy is produced from radioactive substances, such as uranium, when their tiny particles, called atoms, are broken apart. Many people believe it could be the most convenient energy source for the future, but it creates dangerous radioactive waste, which is difficult to dispose of safely.

Waste from nuclear power plants may remain dangerous for thousands of years. Radioactive material carries a warning symbol.

These rows of huge, reflective solar panels capture the Sun's rays and use the energy to generate electricity.

Solar power provides a clean, safe form of energy.

* Solar panels, 109; Wind turbines, 108.

MINERALS

For centuries, people have dug rocks out of the Earth because of the useful **minerals** they contain. Minerals are usually made up of a mixture of elements, for instance carbon, silicon and metals such as iron.

Gemstones, such as these garnets, are minerals which are mined for their beauty. They are usually cut and polished before being sold.

Rocks which contain a high level of minerals, particularly metals, are called **ores**. Metal ores taken from the Earth have to be processed to extract the pure metal. There are various ways of doing this, including smelting*, which involves heat, and electrolysis*, which uses electricity.

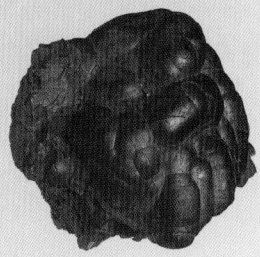

Iron is extracted from an ore called **haematite**.

MINING

Rocks which contain useful minerals are **mined**, or taken from the ground. The mining technique used depends on the depth, value and amount of the ore. If it is found in large amounts underground, tunnels are dug beneath the Earth's surface to reach it. Ore near the surface can be dug out from an open pit.

Here, coal is being extracted from a mine at the surface of the ground. This is called an **open cast** mine.

Although people rely heavily on mining to supply many substances that they need, it can be bad for the environment. Mining for a single tonne of ore may produce thousands of tonnes of waste rock, which may be spread over a wide area. Plant and animal life in the areas around a mine may be badly affected.

MANAGING RESOURCES

People have always depended on metals, fuels and the Earth's other natural resources. But mining and extracting different fuels and ores is an expensive and difficult process. Some substances, such as oil, are also becoming harder to find, as the best sources have already been used up.

At some time in the future, there will no longer be enough non-renewable resources to meet everyone's needs. Re-using and recycling materials, and using renewable fuel sources wherever possible, are the best ways to make the Earth's existing resources last as long as possible.

See for yourself

There are many materials which can be recycled. These include paper, glass, aluminium cans and steel. You could find out if there are any recycling points near to where you live. Your school might also organize recycling activities.

You can help to save energy by remembering to switch off lights when leaving a room, or by asking your parents to use energy-efficient light bulbs, like this one.

Internet links

Go to **www.usborne-quicklinks.com** and type in "science" to find out more about Earth's resources.

There you'll find links to websites where you can:

- Find more about renewable energy
- Read arguments for and against the use of nuclear power

Go to Usborne Quicklinks for links to hand-picked websites on hundreds of subjects.

* *Electrolysis, 82-83; Smelting, 36.*

LIGHT, SOUND AND ELECTRICITY

WAVES

All **waves** carry energy. There are two main types of wave – mechanical and electromagnetic. **Mechanical waves**, including water waves and sound waves, are vibrations in a solid, liquid or gas. Electromagnetic waves, such as light waves and radio waves, are vibrations of a different kind. For more about these waves see pages 212-213.

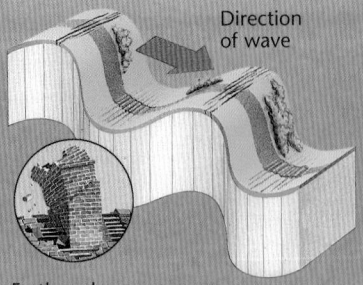

Earthquakes are waves that travel through rock. The vibrations can be strong enough to destroy buildings.

TRANSFERRING ENERGY

Any substance through which waves travel is called a **medium**. Water, glass and air are different types of medium. A mechanical wave carries energy through a medium by making its particles vibrate. Each vibrating particle makes its neighbour vibrate, so passing the energy through the substance.

Waves such as those shown in the pictures below are caused by the water's particles vibrating up and down. The particles don't travel onwards with the wave.

Like the water particles themselves, the bird isn't moved forwards by the passing wave.

A wave does not permanently disturb the medium it travels through. Each particle gradually stops vibrating and settles in its original position.

The particles in a wave vibrate less as they lose energy, and the water becomes still.

As these droplets fall into the water, waves spread out in a circle, carrying energy away from the disturbed area.

The ripples on this pond are water waves. As they move away from the source of the disturbance they lose energy, and so become smaller.

TYPES OF WAVE

All waves can be described as either transverse or longitudinal, depending on the direction of their vibrations.

Transverse waves are waves in which the particles vibrate at right angles to the direction the wave is travelling. Water waves are transverse waves.

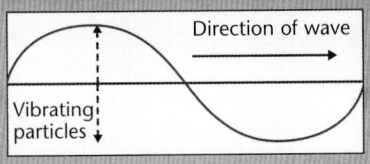

Particles in a transverse wave vibrate at right angles to the direction of the wave.

In **longitudinal waves**, the particles vibrate in the same direction as the wave is travelling. The particles of the medium vibrate forwards and backwards, acting like the coils in a spring as they are squeezed together and then spread out. Sound waves are longitudinal waves.

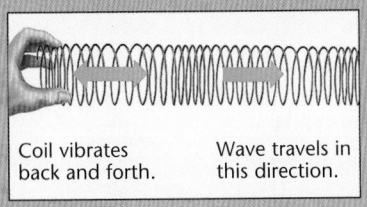

The coils in this moving spring show how longitudinal waves travel.

MEASURING WAVES

Transverse waves create a regular pattern of high points, called **peaks**, and low points, called **troughs**. A complete wave is known as a **cycle**. It has one peak and one trough.

The number of complete waves that pass a point in one second is called the **frequency**. This is measured in **hertz (Hz)**, named after the German scientist, Heinrich Hertz (1857-1894), who was the first person to discover and use radio waves.

The distance between a point on one wave and the same point on the next, for example, between two troughs, is called the **wavelength**.

The height from a particle's rest position to a peak is called **amplitude**. This becomes less as a wave moves away from its source and loses energy.

A wave is measured by its frequency, wavelength and amplitude.

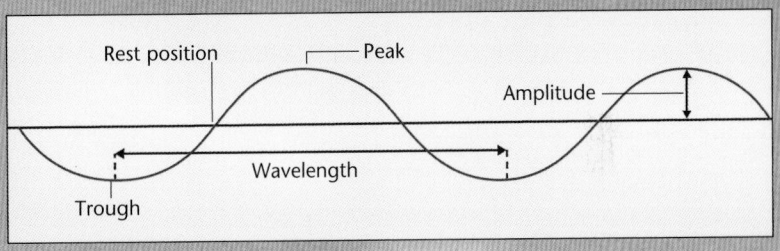

See for yourself

You can use this experiment to see the form of a transverse wave. Tie one end of a piece of string to a fixed point, such as a door knob, hold the other end and give it a sharp shake. You will see the form of the wave moving along the string. The string vibrates at right angles to the direction of the wave.

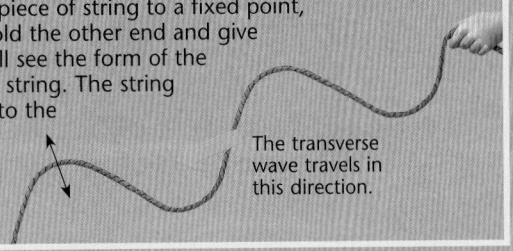

Internet links

To find out more about waves, go to **www.usborne-quicklinks.com** and type in the keyword "science".

There you'll find links to websites where you can:

- Watch animated explanations of different waveforms
- Find out more about earthquakes and how seismic waves are detected
- Follow an online lesson on waves, then try a test-yourself quiz
- Watch animations of ocean waves and learn how they behave

Go to Usborne Quicklinks for links to hand-picked websites on hundreds of subjects.

WAVE BEHAVIOUR

When a wave hits an obstacle, or passes from one substance (medium) to another, it can change in speed, direction or shape. Before the change, the wave is called the **incident wave**. The examples on these pages show water waves, but all waves behave in the same way.

Tsunami are giant waves that slow down and rapidly increase in height as they enter shallow water.

REFLECTION

When an incident wave hits an obstacle, for example when a water wave hits a sea wall, it bounces back. This is called **reflection**. The wave is reflected back at an angle equal to its angle of approach. It is then called a **reflected wave**.

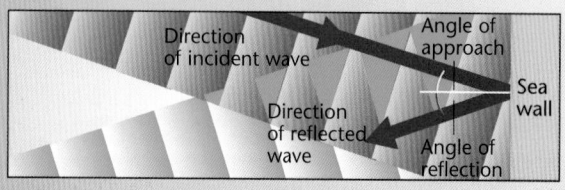

The angle of reflection of a wave is the same as the angle of approach of the incident wave.

The shape of a reflected wave depends both on the shape of the incident wave and the shape of the obstacle it hits. The diagrams below show what happens when straight and curved incident waves hit differently shaped obstacles.

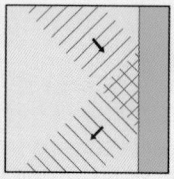

Straight waves hitting a straight barrier produce straight reflected waves.

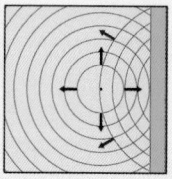

Circular waves hitting a straight barrier produce circular reflected waves.

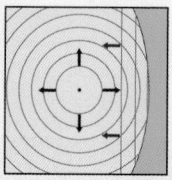

Circular waves hitting an inward-curving barrier produce straight reflected waves.

Waves at sea are relatively straight. As they approach the shallow waters of a beach, they bend until they match the curves of its shoreline. This is an example of refraction.

REFRACTION

When an incident wave enters a new medium it changes speed. Its wavelength* changes, but its frequency* doesn't. In the diagram below, the waves slow down in the new medium. Their wavelength gets shorter, but the number of peaks passing in a second (the frequency) stays the same.

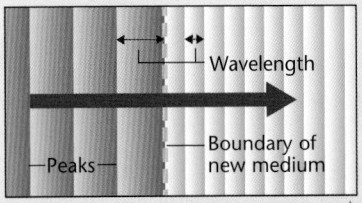

Waves change speed as they enter a new medium.

If a wave enters a new medium at an angle, it changes both speed and direction. This is called **refraction**. A wave that has undergone refraction is called a **refracted wave**.

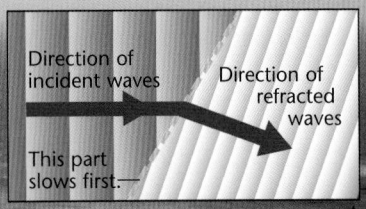

Waves change speed and direction as they enter a new medium at an angle.

Deep and shallow water act as different substances. The first part of the wave to enter the shallows slows down before the rest of the wave. This changes the wave's direction.

INTERFERENCE

If two or more waves meet, they have an effect on each other. This effect is called **interference**. The kind of interference depends on which parts of the waves coincide.

If two peaks of the same amplitude* arrive in the same place at the same time, they combine to form a peak twice as large. This is an example of **constructive interference**.

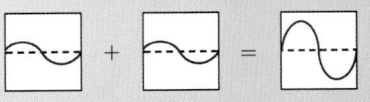

If a peak meets a trough of the same size, they cancel each other out and the wave disappears. This is an example of **destructive interference**.

See for yourself

To see wave interference, hold a small pebble in each hand and drop them, at the same time, into a bath filled with water. The ripples made by the pebbles will move out in circles. Where they cross each other you might see, very briefly, both constructive and destructive interference.

Constructive interference

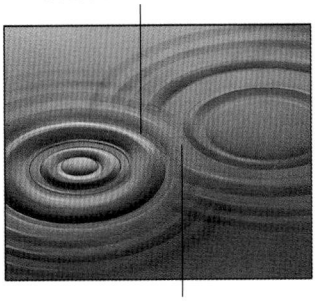

Destructive interference

DIFFRACTION

When an incident wave passes through a gap, it spreads out and bends. This is an example of **diffraction**. The smaller the gap compared to the wavelength of the wave, the more it is diffracted.

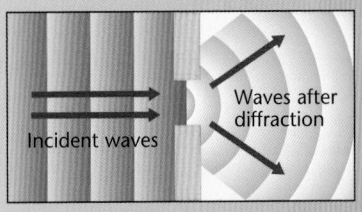

A wave passing through a gap smaller than its wavelength is diffracted a lot.

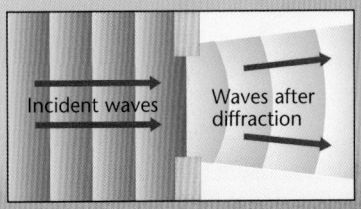

A wave passing through a gap larger than its wavelength is hardly diffracted at all.

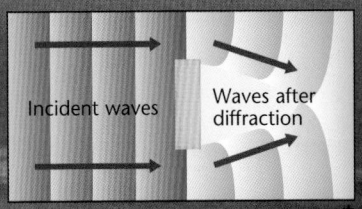

Waves can also be diffracted when striking the edge of an obstacle.

Internet links

Go to **www.usborne-quicklinks.com** and type in the keyword "science" to find out more about wave behaviour.

There you'll find links to websites where you can:

- Follow a lesson on wave behaviour
- Find out more with online activities

Go to Usborne Quicklinks for links to hand-picked websites on hundreds of subjects.

* Amplitude, Frequency, Wavelength, 203.

SOUND

Sound is a form of energy carried by waves of vibrating particles. These waves, called **sound waves**, can travel through solids, liquids and gases, but they cannot travel through a vacuum as there are no particles of any sort to vibrate. For this reason, sound cannot travel out in space.

The sound of falling leaves measures 10dB.

SOUND WAVES

Sound waves are longitudinal waves. This means that the particles vibrate in the same direction as the wave travels.

For instance, inside a loudspeaker a paper cone vibrates forwards and backwards, sending sound energy into the air. As the cone moves forwards, it presses together air particles in front of it. As it moves backwards, it leaves an area where the particles are more spaced out.

Cone of loudspeaker (not moving)

Air particles

Cone moves forwards.

Particles pressed together

Cone moves backwards.

Particles spread out

See for yourself

You can feel sound vibrations with a balloon and a radio. Turn on a radio and hold a balloon about 10cm away from the speaker. The vibrations of the sounds make the air in the balloon vibrate.

Sound waves can be shown as a wavy line. The peaks show where particles have been squashed. The troughs show where particles are spread out. Wave diagrams show the number of waves per second (frequency) and their strength (amplitude).

Diagram showing sound waves

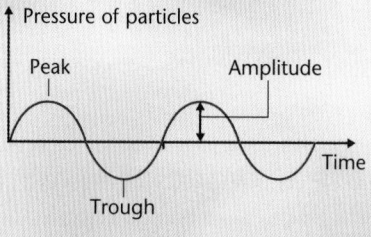

Wave frequency is measured in hertz (Hz). Sound waves with frequencies between about 20 and 20,000 hertz can be heard by the human ear and are commonly described as sound. Sound waves below this range are known as **infrasound**, and above it are **ultrasound**.

High sounds, such as birdsong, have high-frequency waves.

Low sounds, such as the rumble made by the engine of a heavy truck, have low-frequency waves.

LOUDNESS

Loud sounds are waves with a large amplitude. Soft sounds are waves with a small amplitude. As a sound travels further away from its source, the amplitude becomes smaller and so the sound becomes quieter.

The loudness of sound is measured in **decibels** (**dB**). The blue whale is the loudest animal in the world. It makes sounds of up to 188dB.

Aircraft make such loud sounds that ground crew wear ear protectors to avoid hearing damage.

SPEED OF SOUND

Sound waves travel at different speeds in different substances. They travel more quickly in solids than in liquids, and more quickly in liquids than in gases.

The speed of sound waves as they travel through dry air at 0°C is 331 metres per second. This speed increases if the air temperature goes up, and decreases if the temperature of the air goes down.

A speed that is faster than the speed of sound in the same conditions is known as a **supersonic speed**. One that is slower is a **subsonic speed**.

As it reaches supersonic speed, an aircraft makes a deafening bang called a **sonic boom**. In this photo, the sound waves can be seen as they disturb the misty air.

The sound of an aircraft landing measures about 120dB.

ECHOES

Echoes are sound waves that have reflected (bounced) off a surface and are heard shortly after the original sound. Echoes can be used to find the position of objects. This is done by timing how long the echoes take to return to their source.

Ultrasonic sound waves are most often used because waves of high frequency bend less around obstacles in their path. The waves spread out less than ordinary sound waves and give more accurate information about the surface reflecting them.

When animals such as bats and dolphins use echoes, it is called **echo location**. They use it to find their way around or to locate prey.

Sonar is the name given to the method used by ships to measure the depth of sea water, or to detect underwater objects, such as shipwrecks or shoals of fish. The echoes are detected by equipment on board the ship.

Ultrasound waves sent from the ship bounce off the wreck. A computer times the echoes to find the wreck's position.

Dolphins send out streams of over 700 ultrasonic clicks in a second. The time the echoes take to return can tell them how far away they are from shoals of fish.

Echoes are also used in **ultrasound scanning** to see inside the body – for example to check on the growth of an unborn baby inside its mother. Bone, muscle and fat all reflect ultrasonic waves differently. A computer uses this information to make a picture.

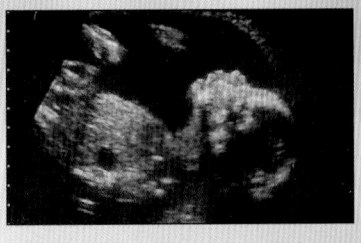

Ultrasound scan of an unborn baby

Internet links

To find out more about sound, go to **www.usborne-quicklinks.com** and type in the keyword "science".

There you'll find links to websites where you can:

- Learn about sound with online activities and experiments

Go to Usborne Quicklinks for links to hand-picked websites on hundreds of subjects.

MUSICAL INSTRUMENTS

Musical instruments work by making sound waves. The shape and size of the instrument and the material of which it is made affect the sound. Some instruments have a soundbox that **resonates**. This means that it vibrates at the same frequency as the air vibrations created by the original sound, making the sound fuller and richer.

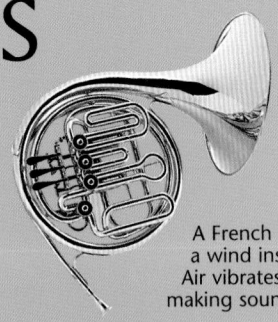

A French horn is a wind instrument. Air vibrates inside it, making sound.

TYPES OF INSTRUMENTS

Musical instruments can be divided into groups depending on the way they make sounds. **Stringed instruments**, such as harps and violins, have stretched strings that vibrate when you pluck or slide a bow across them. The strings inside a piano vibrate when they are hit by felt-covered hammers controlled by the keys. The more the strings vibrate, the louder the sound.

The bow strings are made of horsehairs. They slide across the strings, making them vibrate.

The bridge of this violin carries vibrations from the strings into the body of the instrument (its soundbox).

The soundbox resonates, making the sound fuller and louder.

Wind instruments work by making a column of air vibrate inside them. The vibrations are produced in different ways. For example in a trumpet, the player's lips vibrate in a cup-shaped mouthpiece. This sound is then made louder, or **amplified**, by the tube and the flared end of the instrument.

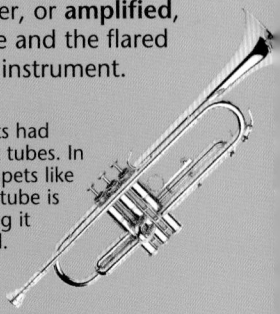

Early trumpets had long, straight tubes. In modern trumpets like this one, the tube is coiled, making it easier to hold.

Clarinets and oboes have a mouthpiece that contains one or two pieces of reed. These vibrate as air is blown past them.

Percussion instruments produce sound when they are beaten, scraped or shaken. A drum, for example, has a tight skin which you beat with your hand or a stick. The vibrations make the air inside the drum vibrate, and the hollow shape of the drum amplifies the sound.

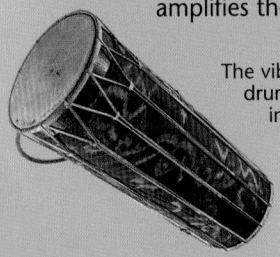

The vibrations of a drum skin resonate inside the drum and are amplified.

ELECTRIC INSTRUMENTS

In **electric instruments**, such as an electric guitar, small sound vibrations produced by the strings are amplified by an electronic amplifier instead of a soundbox. Special effects, such as echoes, can also be added electronically to the sound.

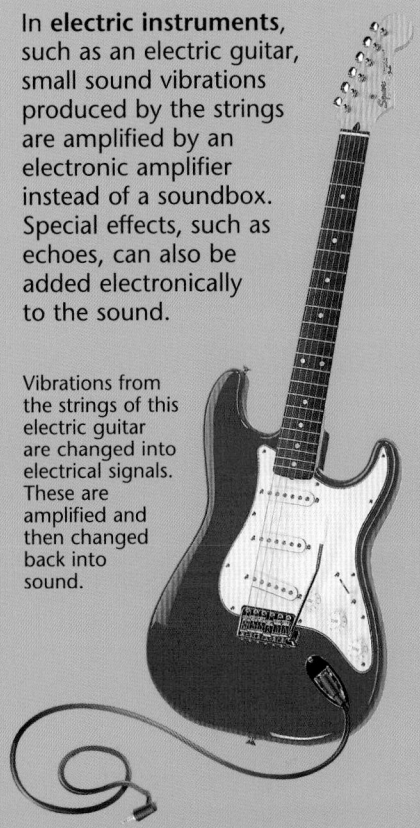

Vibrations from the strings of this electric guitar are changed into electrical signals. These are amplified and then changed back into sound.

SYNTHESIZED SOUND

A **sound synthesizer** is an instrument that stores sound waves as binary code* in its electronic memory. The synthesizer can reproduce a sound by converting the code for the sound into an electric current and sending it to a loudspeaker.

The sounds of musical instruments, as well as other noises, such as dogs barking, can be stored as binary code and reproduced by a synthesizer.

This keyboard synthesizer contains binary code for the sound waves of many different instruments.

PITCH

The highness or lowness of a sound is known as its **pitch**. Sound waves with a high frequency produce sounds of a high pitch, those with a low frequency, a low pitch. Musical sounds of a specific pitch are called **notes**. For example, the note known as **Middle C**, which is the C nearest to the middle of a piano keyboard, has a frequency of about 262 hertz*. The next C above it has a higher frequency – about 523 hertz.

The size of an instrument affects the pitch of the notes that can be played on it. For example, in a stringed instrument, the longer the string, the lower the pitch. This is why a double bass makes lower notes than a violin.

A harp has strings that vibrate as they are plucked. Strings of different lengths make notes of different pitches.

Players can change the pitch of the sounds an instrument makes. For example, a guitar or violin player presses down on the strings. This shortens the length of string that can vibrate, and so it makes higher notes. On a flute or recorder, the player covers and uncovers holes. This alters the length of the column of air that can vibrate inside it, and so changes the notes produced.

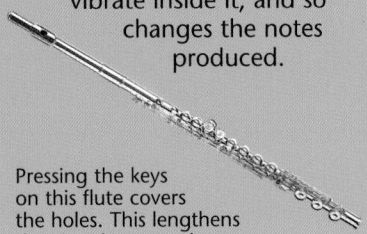

Pressing the keys on this flute covers the holes. This lengthens the air column, and so lowers the pitch of the note.

HARMONICS

Most instruments produce complex sound waves that have higher, quieter sounds mixed in. These sounds are called **harmonics**. They give an instrument its individual sound quality, or **timbre**.

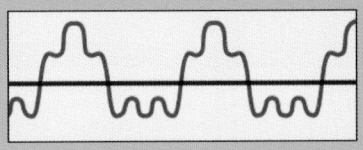

On a sound wave diagram, harmonics look like extra little waves. This diagram shows the waves made by an instrument.

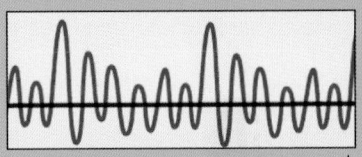

These are the sound waves of the same note played by a different instrument.

See for yourself

Try blowing across the top of an open, empty bottle. If you get it right, you will make the air column inside the bottle vibrate, producing a musical note. Now pour some water into the bottle and blow again. The water will have reduced the size of the air column, so the note that you produce will be higher.

Internet links

Go to **www.usborne-quicklinks.com** and type in "science" to find out more about musical instruments.

There you'll find links to websites where you can:

- Play music games online
- Conduct simple pitch experiments

Go to Usborne Quicklinks for links to hand-picked websites on hundreds of subjects.

** Binary code, 238; Hertz 203.*

SOUND REPRODUCTION

By changing sound energy into electrical energy, sounds can be recorded and stored, to be played back at another time. In this form, sounds can also be sent over long distances, for example, over the internet.

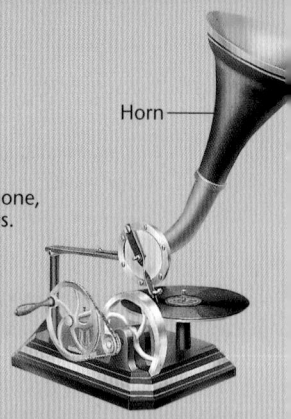

An early gramophone, made in the 1890s. Grooves on a disc made a needle vibrate, creating sound waves that were amplified (made louder) by the horn.

MICROPHONES

Sounds can be converted into an electric current by a device called a **microphone**. This contains a thin metal disc called a **diaphragm**, which is attached to an electromagnet*, that is, a coil of wire and a ring-shaped magnet.

When sound waves hit the diaphragm, it vibrates at the same frequency* as the waves. The diaphragm makes the wire coil vibrate. When the coil moves near the magnet, it creates an electric current which flows along the wire. The current produced varies according to the size and frequency of the sound waves.

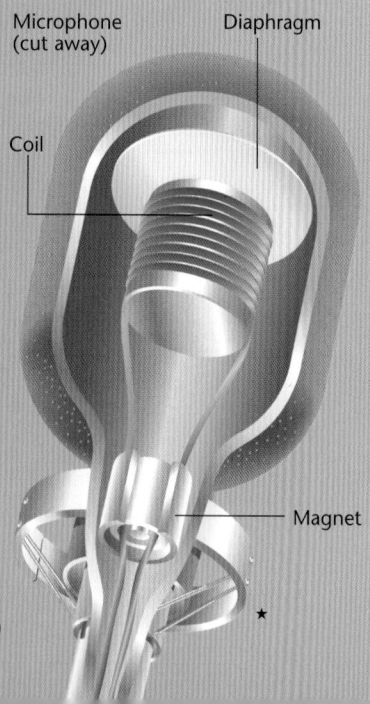

LOUDSPEAKERS

A **loudspeaker** turns an electric current from a source such as a microphone back into sound waves. Inside the loudspeaker there is an electromagnet. When an electric current flows through the coil in the electromagnet, it becomes magnetic. The coil is attached to a cone-shaped paper diaphragm.

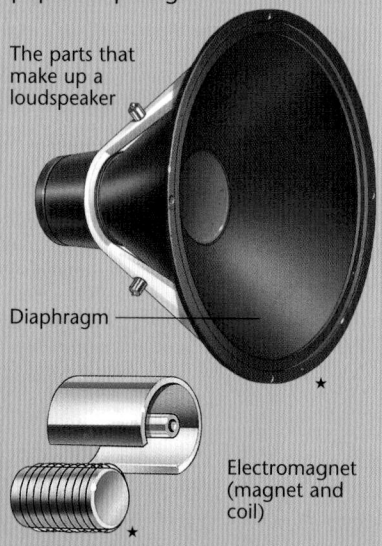

When a varying current produced from a sound wave flows through the coil, the force between the coil's magnetic field and that of the magnet makes both the coil and the diaphragm vibrate.

The air in front of the diaphragm vibrates to create sound waves of the same frequency as the original sound.

CASSETTE RECORDERS

In a **cassette recorder**, sounds are recorded as a pattern of magnetized particles of iron or chromium oxide on plastic tape.

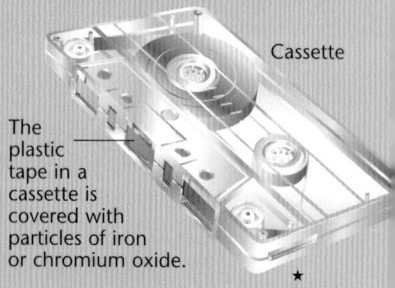

This is done by a part called the **recording head**, which is an electromagnet. A varying current produced from a sound wave passes from a microphone through a metal coil in the recording head. This causes variations in the head's magnetic field which arrange the metal particles on the tape into different patterns.

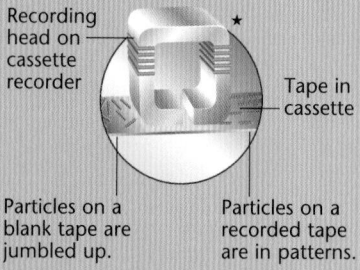

The patterns of particles on the tape can be read by a part called the **playback head**. It produces a varying current which is converted back into sound by a loudspeaker.

* *Electromagnet, 233; Frequency, 203.*

ANALOGUE RECORDING

The varying current from a microphone produces a varying pattern of magnetic particles on a cassette tape. This is a continuous record of the position of the microphone's diaphragm as it vibrates back and forth in response to the sound waves, and is an example of **analogue recording**.

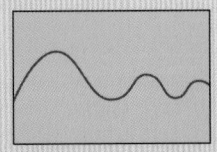

Original sound wave

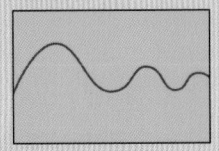

Recorded analogue sound wave

One problem with analogue recordings is that they can be changed by repeated use. For example, the playback heads on a cassette recorder gradually wear away the magnetic particles on the tape. This means that the sound heard becomes less like the original sound that was recorded.

See for yourself

You can hear the effect of magnetism on tape if you record something on a blank cassette. Wind the tape back to the start and take the cassette out of the machine. Unravel part of the tape and run a magnet over it a few times. Wind the tape back into the cassette and play it back. You will find that the magnet has rearranged the particles on the tape and has distorted the sound.

DIGITAL RECORDING

In **digital recording**, an electric current representing a sound is described by a code made up of the numbers 0 and 1 (binary code*). This is done by measuring the current at different points, a process called **sampling**.

The more points that are sampled, the closer to the original sound the recording is when played back. For example, in CD recording, 44,100 samples are taken every second. This produces a **high-fidelity recording** – one that sounds very similar to the original.

Analogue sound wave

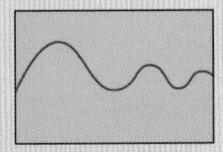

Low-fidelity digital sound wave

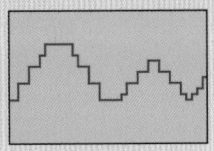

High-fidelity digital sound wave

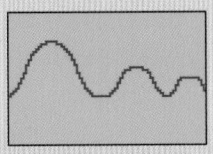

With a digital recording, the same series of numbers is used to make up the sound each time it is played back. This means that it always sounds the same as when it was first recorded and is known as **perfect sound reproduction**.

Digitally recorded information can be stored as a file on computer. It can then be used in many ways, for example it can be transferred onto a CD, or sent across the internet.

COMPACT DISCS

A **compact disc**, or **CD**, uses digital methods to store sound or other information. The binary code is represented by tiny **bumps**, and flat areas called **land**, on the surface of the disc.

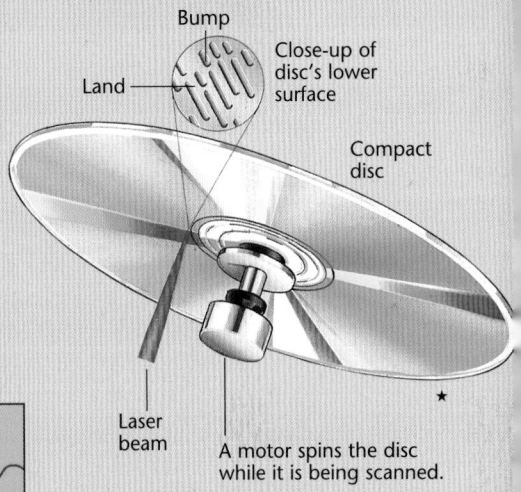

Inside a CD player, a laser beam scans the disc's shiny underside. As light hits the edge of each bump, a light detector reads an electric pulse as a binary 1. As light hits the flat areas on and between the bumps, this is read as a 0. The stream of pulses is turned into sound by a loudspeaker.

Internet links

Go to **www.usborne-quicklinks.com** and type in "science" to find out more about sound reproduction.

There you'll find links to websites where you can:

- See animated tutorials on electrical energy, CDs, DVDs and more
- Experiment with sound in a virtual recording studio

Go to Usborne Quicklinks for links to hand-picked websites on hundreds of subjects.

* *Binary code, 238.*

ELECTROMAGNETIC WAVES

Electromagnetic waves are transverse waves* made up of continually changing electric and magnetic fields. Like mechanical waves, electromagnetic waves can travel through most solids, liquids and gases. They can also travel through a **vacuum** – an empty space where there are no particles of air or any other matter. All electromagnetic waves are invisible, except for those that make up light.

ELECTROMAGNETIC SPECTRUM

The complete range of electromagnetic waves, arranged in order of their wavelength* and frequency*, is known as the **electromagnetic spectrum**. At one end are waves with a short wavelength and high frequency, and at the other are waves with a long wavelength and low frequency. They all travel at the same speed – approximately 300,000 kilometres per second. This is known as the **speed of light**.

GAMMA RAYS

Gamma rays are short, high-frequency waves. They can kill living cells and are used to sterilize medical equipment by destroying any germs on them.

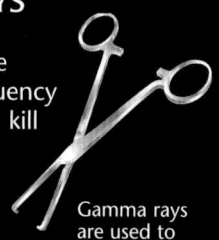

Gamma rays are used to keep these forceps free of germs.

X-RAYS

X-rays can travel through most soft substances but not hard, dense ones. X-rays are used in hospitals to make shadow pictures of parts of the body. They travel through soft tissue, such as skin and muscle, but not through hard bone. X-rays are also used for security at airports to check what may be hidden in people's luggage.

X-rays were used to create this image of a woman's foot in a shoe. The bones and metal shoe parts show up most clearly because the X-rays could not pass through them.

The electromagnetic spectrum

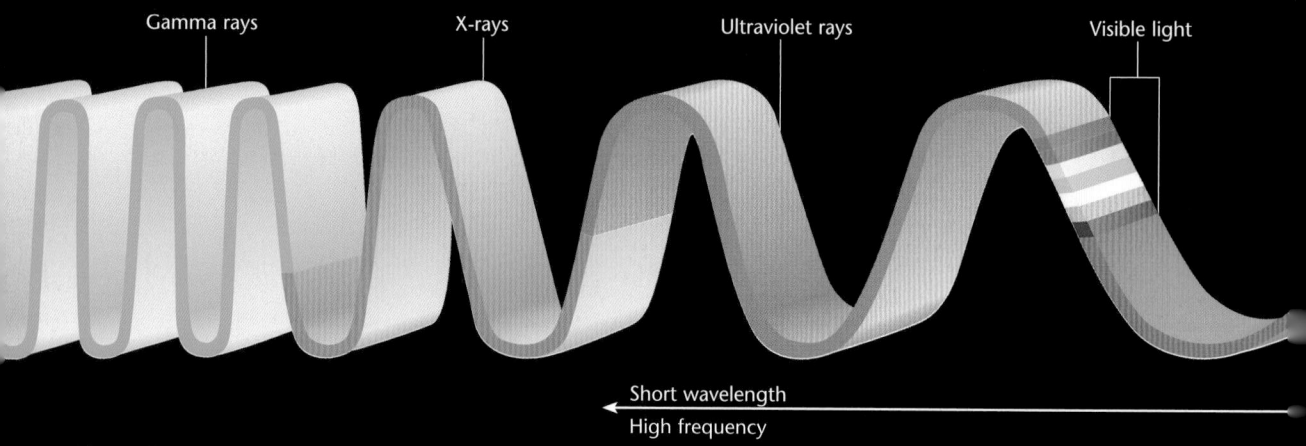

* *Frequency, Transverse waves, Wavelength, 203.*

UV RAYS

Ultraviolet (UV) rays have more energy than visible light (see below) and can cause chemical reactions to take place.

Suncreams protect skin by blocking out harmful UV rays.

For example, UV rays from the Sun cause the skin to increase its production of a brown chemical called **melanin**. This makes the skin tanned. Too much exposure to UV rays can result in high levels of melanin, and may lead to skin cancer.

VISIBLE LIGHT

There is a narrow section of the electromagnetic spectrum that humans can see. This is called the **visible light spectrum**. You can find out more about visible light and the way it behaves on pages 214-217.

INFRARED RAYS

Infrared rays are given out by anything hot. For example, heat from the Sun travels to the Earth as infrared rays.

RADIO WAVES

Radio waves are those with the longest wavelength and lowest frequency. You can read more about them on page 226.

Microwaves are radio waves with a relatively short wavelength. They are easy to control and direct, and have many different uses.

In an ordinary oven, heat is passed from molecules at the edge of the food to ones in the middle. Microwave ovens work by making all the molecules in a food substance vibrate at the same time. This heats and cooks the food more quickly.

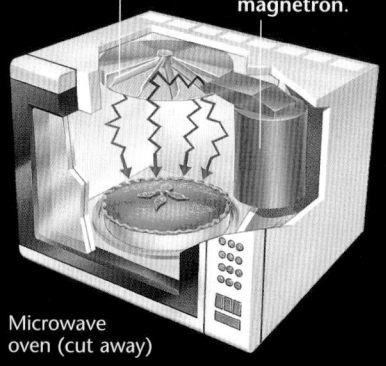

RADAR

Radar (which stands for **ra**dio **d**etection **a**nd **r**anging) uses microwaves to find the position of distant objects, such as ships and aircraft. A transmitter sends out a beam of microwaves that is reflected off a solid object and picked up again by a receiver. This information is transformed into a screen image that shows the distance and direction of the object.

Radio telescope dishes like this one can pick up microwaves that travel from distant stars and planets. They can detect things that are too dark or too far away to be seen with normal telescopes.

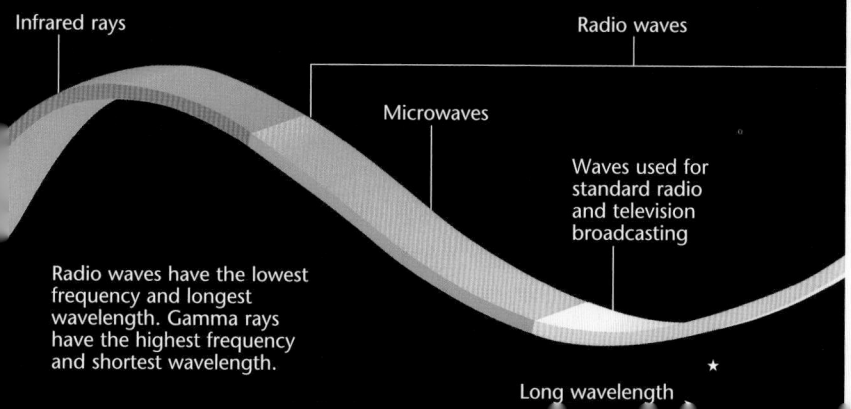

Radio waves have the lowest frequency and longest wavelength. Gamma rays have the highest frequency and shortest wavelength.

Internet links

Go to **www.usborne-quicklinks.com** and type in "science" to find out more about electromagnetic waves.

There you'll find links to websites where you can:

- Experiment online and learn more about electromagnetic waves
- Discover the uses and dangers of electromagnetic waves

Go to Usborne Quicklinks for links to hand-picked websites on hundreds of subjects.

LIGHT AND SHADOW

Light is a form of energy. It is made up of electromagnetic waves which are part of the electromagnetic spectrum*. This part is known as **visible light** because it can be seen.

The beacon in this lighthouse rotates, flashing with intense bright light that can reach ships many kilometres out at sea.

LIGHT

Light waves are a type of transverse wave*. Like other waves, they transport energy from a source to its surroundings.

Any object that gives off light, for example the Sun or a light bulb, is said to be **luminous**. Most objects are non-luminous and can be seen only because they are reflecting the light from something luminous. For example, the Moon can only be seen when light from the Sun bounces off it.

Light from the Sun reflects off the surface of the Moon, enabling it to be seen.

Some luminous objects give off more light than others. The level of brightness is called **intensity**. The further you are from a source of light, the less intense the light is. This is because light waves spread out as they travel away from the source.

The bright flashlight gives more intense light than the small candle.

The light fades as the vibrations of the light waves become gradually smaller.

SHADOWS

Different types of substance allow different amounts of light to pass through them. Substances through which light can pass fully, such as clear glass, are said to be **transparent**. Substances which only let some light through are **translucent**. Frosted glass is translucent.

When light shines on an **opaque** object, the waves cannot pass through, so a dark area, called a **shadow**, forms on the other side.

Light cannot pass through this ball, so a shadow is formed.

Opaque objects cast two types of shadow. If no light reaches an area, a dark shadow, called an **umbra**, is formed. If some light reaches an area, grey shadow is formed. This is called a **penumbra**, and it forms around the edge of the umbra. The smaller the light source, the more umbra and less penumbra it creates.

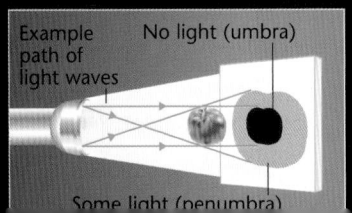

See for yourself

To see the two different kinds of shadow, hold a book over a piece of white paper under the light of a lamp. Notice the types of shadow it casts. If you move the book closer to the paper, you will see more umbra and less penumbra.

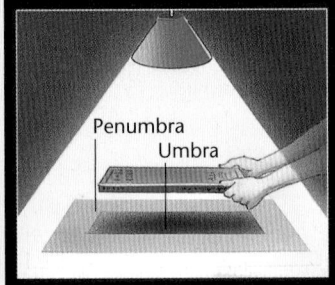

LASERS

Visible light is made up of several colours of different wavelengths* and frequencies*. Machines called **lasers** create beams of intense, pure colour of one wavelength and frequency.

In a simple laser, a ruby rod absorbs light energy from a bright lamp. Atoms in the ruby gain the energy and give off bursts of light of a certain wavelength and frequency. Each burst of light causes other atoms in the ruby to give off light waves of the exact same type. Together they form a **laser beam**.

In this laser, a rod of ruby absorbs light from a coiled flash lamp.

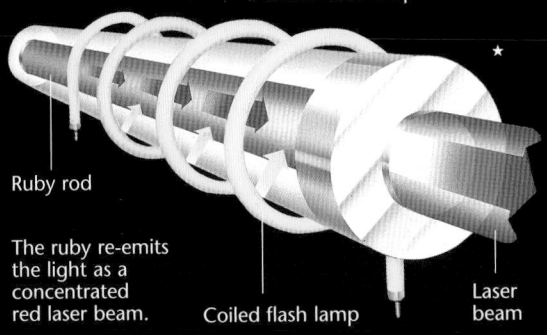

The waves in a laser beam are **coherent**. This means that they travel in step with each other as everything about them is exactly the same. They stay together in a narrow, concentrated beam, making them easy to direct.

Some powerful lasers produce extremely hot beams of infrared light*. These are used in industry for melting through metals, diamonds and other tough materials. Less powerful lasers are used in certain types of eye surgery, such as replacing a detached retina. The laser makes a small heat scar which welds the detached part back into place.

The drill (far left) makes a rough hole in the metal and produces waste shavings.

The powerful laser beam, by contrast, melts a clean hole.

FLUORESCENCE

Some substances can absorb energy, such as electricity or ultraviolet (UV) rays*, and give it out as light. They are described as **fluorescent** substances. They are widely used in advertising and paints as they make colours seem to glow.

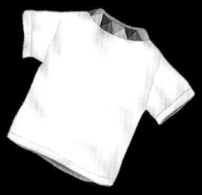

This T-shirt has been washed with a washing powder containing fluorescent substances that absorb UV rays from the Sun and make white clothes look whiter.

Fluorescent lights consist of a tube filled with a gas such as neon. When electricity is passed through the tube, it gives energy to particles in the gas, which give off their new energy as light. Fluorescent lights give off different colours, depending on the gas used.

These coloured lights are filled with fluorescent gases.

Internet links

Go to **www.usborne-quicklinks.com** and type in "science" to find out more about light and shadow.

There you'll find links to websites where you can:

- Discover more about lasers
- Investigate the properties of light
- Find out more about light and shadow with online activities

Go to Usborne Quicklinks for links to hand-picked websites on hundreds of subjects.

COLOUR

Rainbows, like this one, form when light hits tiny drops of water in the air and splits up into separate colours.

Visible light appears colourless. It is also known as **white light**. In fact, it is made up of seven different colours: red, orange, yellow, green, blue, indigo and violet. Each colour has a different wavelength* and frequency*. Together they make up the **visible light spectrum**. Colours of the spectrum are called **chromatic colours**.

DISPERSION

In 1666, scientist Isaac Newton discovered that white light could be divided into separate colours. This process is called **dispersion**. He dispersed light using a **prism** – a transparent solid with two flat surfaces at an angle to each other.

The picture below shows a prism. As light hits the first surface, the colours in it are bent (refracted*) by various amounts. This splits up the light into its separate colours. This dispersed light is refracted further when it hits the second surface. Colours with the shortest wavelengths, namely blue and violet, are refracted the most.

A rainbow is a result of dispersion that happens naturally. Water particles in the air act like prisms, separating sunlight into colours.

Rays of white light are separated into seven colours as they shine through this glass prism.

COLOUR OF THE SKY

The colour of the sky is a result of sunlight being scattered by small particles in the atmosphere. They reflect and diffract* sunlight, scattering high-frequency light waves, such as blue, most of all. When you look up at the sky, it appears blue because some of this scattered blue light reaches your eyes.

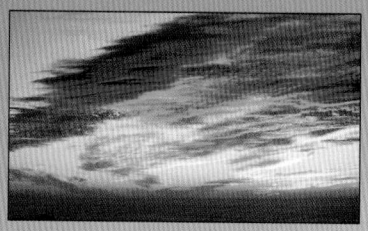

The different colours of this evening sky are caused by light scattering.

At sunrise and sunset, the light has to travel through more of the atmosphere before reaching your eyes. This means that the blue is scattered out before you can see it, leaving the sky with an orange or red glow. These are the colours of light with the lowest frequencies.

MIXING LIGHT

Almost any colour of light can be made by **additive mixing**, that is, by using different combinations of red, green and blue light. For this reason red, green and blue are known as the **primary colours** of light.

Red, blue and green are the primary colours of light.

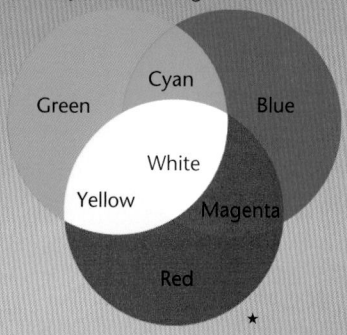

Cyan, magenta and yellow are the secondary colours of light.

When two primary colours are added together, the colour they make is called a **secondary colour**. Any two colours that can be added together to make white light, for example, red and cyan (opposite each other in the diagram above) are called **complementary colours**.

* Diffraction, 205; Frequency, 203; Refraction, 205; Wavelength, 203.

SEEING IN COLOUR

You can see colours when light reflecting off objects is detected by colour-sensitive cells in your eyes.

All coloured objects and paints contain **pigments**. These are substances that absorb certain colours and reflect others. You can see the colour of an object because it reflects only light of that colour. For example, a red flower reflects red light and absorbs all the other colours of the spectrum.

This bottle looks blue because it reflects only blue light and absorbs all the other colours.

White objects appear white because they reflect all the colours of light equally. Black objects absorb all the colours, so hardly any light is reflected, making the object look black. Black and white are known as **achromatic colours**.

The white feathers on this penguin reflect all the light that hits them.

The black feathers absorb all the light that hits them.

MIXING PIGMENTS

Pigments mix by a process called **subtractive mixing**. For example, the pigment in yellow paint absorbs blue light and the pigment in cyan paint absorbs red light. So when you mix yellow and cyan paints, the mixture can only reflect green light, making it look green. The primary colours of pigments are cyan, yellow and magenta. Red, blue and green are the secondary colours.

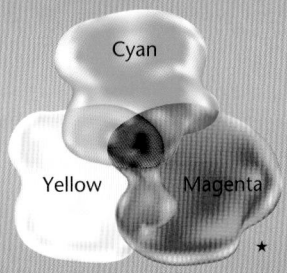

Yellow and cyan pigments mix to make green because they absorb blue and red light.

See for yourself

You can see the colours of the spectrum form white light by making a colour spinner. Draw around the bottom of a jar on some stiff cardboard. Cut out the circle, divide it into seven sections and paint them with the colours of the rainbow. Push a pencil through the middle and spin it on a table. As it spins, the coloured light reflecting off it merges to make white.

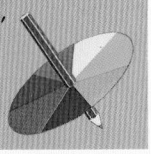

COLOUR PRINTING

Colour printing in books and magazines uses dots of magenta, yellow and cyan ink, along with black ink to make the pictures look sharper. This process is called **four-colour printing**.

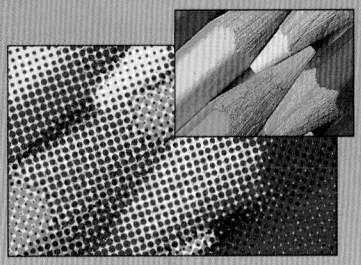

This magnified picture shows how all the colours are made up of tiny dots of magenta, yellow, cyan and black.

If you look through a magnifying glass at any picture in this book, you will see the dots which make up the image.

Colours used in four-colour printing

Cyan Magenta Yellow Black

Internet links

To find out more about colour, go to **www.usborne-quicklinks.com** and type in the keyword "science".

There you'll find links to websites where you can:

- Find an animated guide to how people see colour
- See amazing pictures of rainbows
- Mix colours online

Go to Usborne Quicklinks for links to hand-picked websites on hundreds of subjects.

LIGHT BEHAVIOUR

Like all electromagnetic waves, light travels incredibly quickly – about 300,000 kilometres per second when measured in a vacuum. The direction in which light waves travel is shown in diagrams by arrows. These are called **light rays**. Light waves usually travel in a straight path but may change direction when they meet an obstacle, or move from one substance into another.

The colours on the surface of soap bubbles are caused by light interference.

REFLECTION OF LIGHT

Light rays travelling towards an object are known as **incident rays**. If they hit the object and bounce off it, they are then called **reflected rays**. Each ray is reflected at the same angle as it hits the object.

When parallel light rays hit a smooth, shiny surface, they are reflected so that the reflected rays are also parallel. This is called **regular reflection**.

When parallel light rays hit a rough surface, the reflected rays are scattered in different directions. This is **diffuse reflection**. It is the most common type of reflection as most surfaces are rough (though they may not seem so unless seen with a microscope).

Regular reflection of light rays

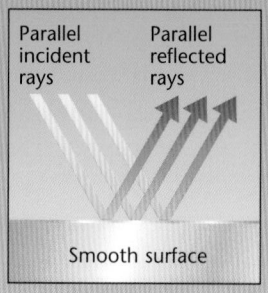

Diffuse reflection of light rays

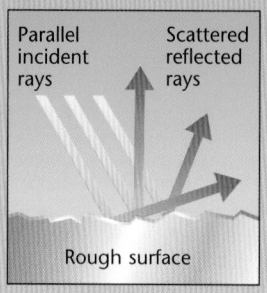

When you look at an object, the light that reflects off it goes directly into your eyes, so you see the object where it really is. If you look at an object in a mirror, the rays bounce off the object and then bounce off the mirror before entering your eyes. What you are looking at is the **image** of the object. In this case the image appears to be behind the mirror.

REFRACTION OF LIGHT

If light rays pass from one substance to another of a different density, their speed will change. If they are also bent, they are known as **refracted rays**. The amount of speed change and refraction depends on the change in density. Light rays speed up on moving into a less dense substance, and slow down on moving into a denser one.

For instance, light rays bouncing off objects in water can make the objects look distorted. This is because the rays are refracted as they pass out of the water into the less dense air. You can find out more about refraction on page 205.

See for yourself

To see light refraction, look at a straw in a glass of water from all sides. It seems to bend in different ways. The unbroken lines in the diagram show the real path of the light rays looking from above. But the brain assumes they travel straight, so it sees the end of the straw at X.

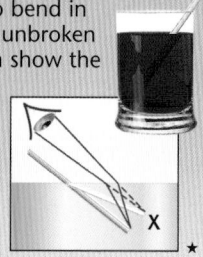

The rays of sunlight breaking through these clouds show that light travels in straight lines.

LIGHT DIFFRACTION

When light rays pass through tiny gaps, or meet the edge of an opaque object, they are diffracted, or spread out. For more about diffraction, see page 205.

LIGHT INTERFERENCE

When light rays are reflected or diffracted, their paths may cross, causing interference. See page 205 for more about interference.

As light rays interfere with each other, some wavelengths of light are strengthened and some are weakened, so certain colours become visible. The colours on a compact disc and on the surface of soap bubbles, for example, are caused by interference.

The metallic sheen on the wings of this butterfly is caused by light interference.

The shiny side of a compact disc has tiny bumps on it. When light enters the gaps between them, the waves are diffracted and interfere, so certain colours are seen at different angles.

Compact discs diffract white light, making its colours visible.

The rainbow colours on a soap bubble appear when light reflected off the outer surface of the bubble interferes with light reflected off the inner surface.

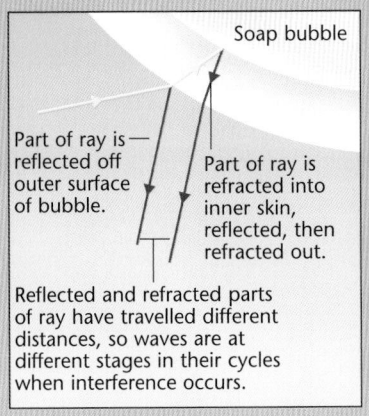

The colours are constantly changing, giving a shimmering effect called **iridescence**. This is also seen on the wings of some insects and birds.

POLARIZATION

Light waves are made up of vibrations in electric and magnetic fields. The vibrations change direction many millions of times per second, but are always at right angles to the direction the wave is travelling.

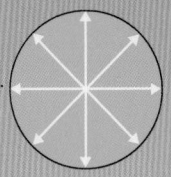

Imagine a normal light wave travelling directly into your eye. Its vibrations are in many directions, as shown here.

When light is **polarized**, the vibrations only occur in one direction, such as up and down.

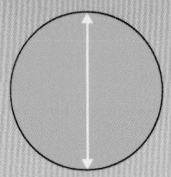

A polarized light wave is filtered so that its vibrations are in just one direction, as shown here.

Polarizing sunglasses work by filtering out all light wave vibrations that are not in a certain direction. This shields the eyes from excessive glare.

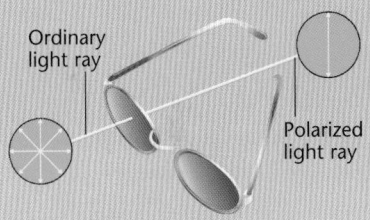

Polarizing sunglasses only allow light vibrations through in one direction.

Internet links

Go to **www.usborne-quicklinks.com** and type in the keyword "science" to find out more about light behaviour.

There you'll find links to websites where you can:

- Follow animated explanations of reflection and refraction
- Play games about light

Go to Usborne Quicklinks for links to hand-picked websites on hundreds of subjects.

LENSES AND MIRRORS

A **lens** is a piece of transparent substance with curved surfaces, that makes light passing through it bend in a particular way. A **mirror** is a shiny surface that reflects nearly all of the light that hits it. Lenses and mirrors have many uses, for example in cameras and telescopes.

This photograph of New York City was taken through a fish-eye lens. This curved lens creates a distorted, circular image, covering an angle of 180°.

LENSES

Lenses are shaped so that light passing through them is bent (refracted*) in a particular way. There are two main shapes of lens: convex and concave. In a **convex lens**, one or both surfaces curve outwards. In a **concave lens**, one or both surfaces curve inwards.

Types of convex lenses

Bi-convex | Plano-convex | Convex meniscus

Types of concave lenses

Bi-concave | Plano-concave | Concave meniscus

Lenses are described as converging or diverging lenses, depending how the light rays are refracted. For example, a glass convex lens in air acts as a converging lens and a glass concave lens in air acts as a diverging lens.

Any point where light rays come together or appear to come from is called a **focus**. A **converging lens** causes parallel rays of light passing through it to come together at a focus.

Converging lens

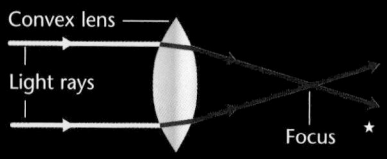

A **diverging lens** makes parallel rays of light spread out.

Diverging lens

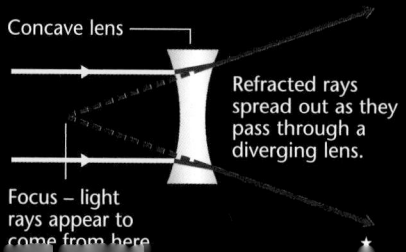

The size and position of an image seen through a converging lens depends how far the object is from the lens. If the object is very close to a converging lens, the image is upright and enlarged.

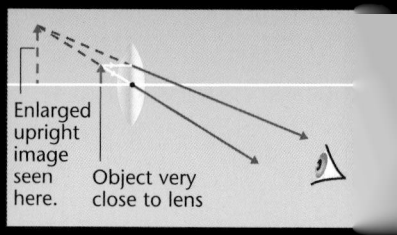

If the object is further away from a converging lens, the image is upside down.

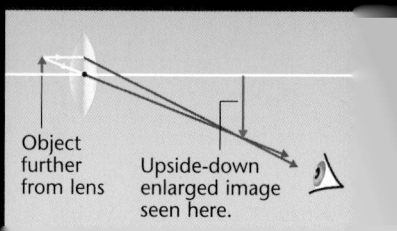

Our eye turns light reflected from an object into an image that can be recognized by your brain. The front part of the eye is a convex converging lens. It focuses the light rays so that they form an image on a layer called the **retina**, at the back of the eye. The image formed is upside down, but your brain then corrects this so you see things the right way up.

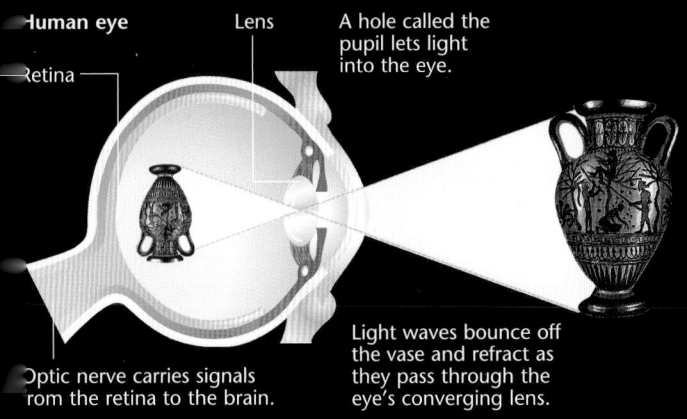

Distant objects are blurred for people with short sight. This is because the lenses in their eyes bend the light rays too much and the image forms in front of the retina.

Short sight

Rays from a distant object focus in front of the retina.

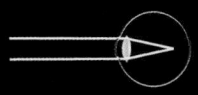

Diverging lens

A diverging lens corrects this, focusing rays on the retina.

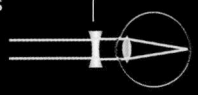

Long-sighted people can't see nearby objects well. This is because the lens does not bend the light rays enough so the rays focus behind the retina.

Long sight

Rays from a near object focus beyond the retina.

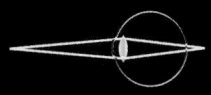

Converging lens

A converging lens corrects this, focusing rays on the retina.

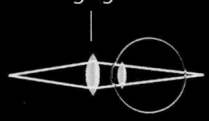

See for yourself

Look at your reflection in the bowl of a shiny metal spoon. If you hold the spoon very close to your face, the reflection will be enlarged. If you hold it a little further away, the reflection will be upside down. Look at the two diagrams at the bottom of the column on the right to see why this happens.

When light from an object hits a flat mirror straight on, it is reflected straight back. The image produced is the same size and same way up as the object but the left and right sides are swapped around. The image is the same distance behind the mirror as the object is in front of the mirror.

Curved mirrors bounce light off at an angle, producing different kinds of images. A **convex mirror** curves outwards. The image formed is upright and reduced in size.

Car wing mirrors are convex.

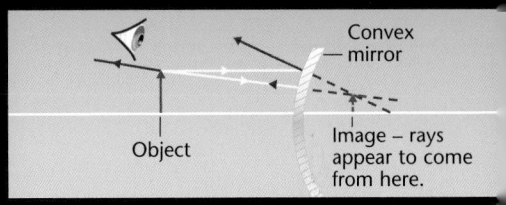

Concave mirrors curve inwards. If an object is very close to the mirror, an enlarged image is produced. If the object is further away, the image is upside down. The bowl of a shiny metal spoon acts like a concave mirror.

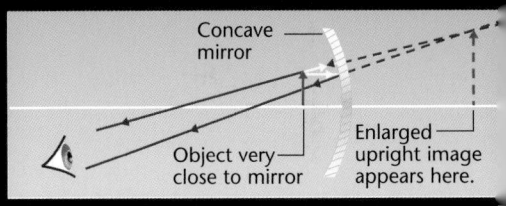

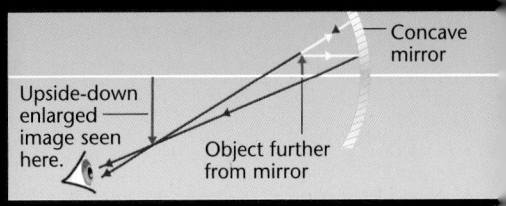

Internet links

Go to **www.usborne-quicklinks.com** and type in "science" to find out more about lenses and mirrors.

There you'll find links to websites where you can:

- See animations of how the human eye works

OPTICAL INSTRUMENTS

Optical instruments use combinations of lenses and mirrors to produce a particular type of image, for example, an image that appears larger than when viewed with the eye alone. These pages show some of the many kinds of optical instruments.

Binoculars use lenses to magnify objects.

OPTICAL MICROSCOPES

Optical microscopes use lenses to make small objects look bigger. Simple ones, such as a magnifying glass, have only one lens. More complex ones use two lenses or more.

Inside a **compound optical microscope**, the object is first magnified by the **objective lens**. It is further magnified by the **eyepiece**, which produces the final image. Some optical microscopes can magnify up to 2,000 times.

A compound optical microscope

1. **Eyepiece**. This refracts (bends) light from the objective lens, turns the image the right way up, and makes it look much bigger.

2. **Focusing knob**. This controls the sharpness and clarity of the image.

3. **Body tube**

4. **Nosepiece**. This holds three objective lenses, each giving a different magnification. It is swivelled round to change between them.

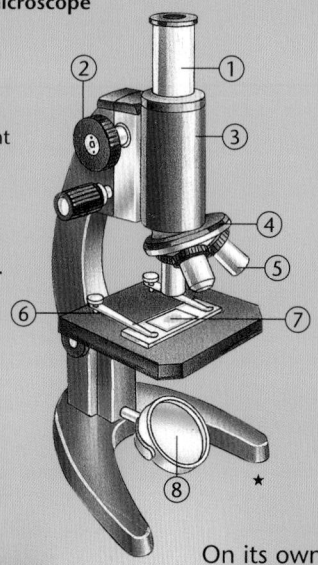

5. **Objective lens**. This refracts light from the object to form a larger, upside-down image. The eyepiece then further magnifies this image.

6. **Stage**. The object to be magnified goes on here.

7. **Object**

8. **Mirror**. This reflects daylight or lamplight through a hole in the stage onto the object.

Using magnifying lenses, scientists can learn about the structure of tiny living things, such as this ladybird.

On its own, the eye can only see small objects separately if they are at least a quarter of a millimetre apart. A microscope can show you objects separately that are up to 1,000 times closer together than this.

The tiny hairs on the ladybird's mouthparts are too small to be seen with the eye alone, but are easy to make out under a microscope's magnifying lens.

PERISCOPES

A **periscope** is an upright tube with prisms at each end. Prisms are glass shapes with two flat surfaces at an angle to each other. In a periscope they are used to reflect light around corners, which allows you to see something when you are far below it. For instance, periscopes are used in submarines to look above the surface of the water.

Diagram of a periscope

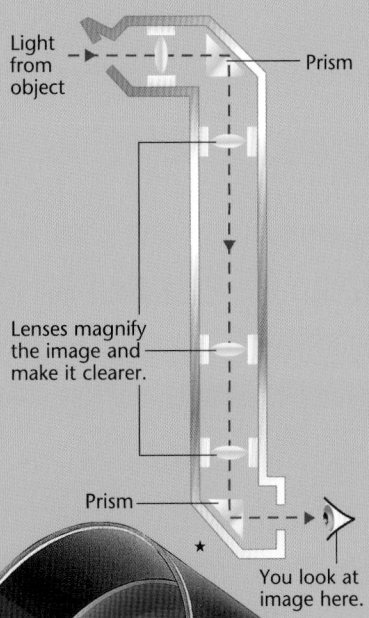

TELESCOPES

Telescopes are used to make distant objects appear closer and therefore larger. They are often used for looking at the stars. There are two main types: reflector and refractor telescopes.

A **reflector telescope** uses a curved mirror to collect light. The light then reflects off a second mirror and an image is focused in front of the eyepiece, which magnifies it.

This diagram shows the path of light rays in a reflector telescope.

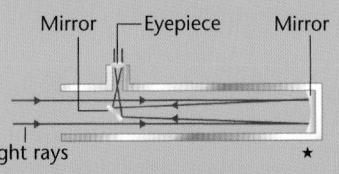

A **refractor telescope** uses lenses. The objective lens collects the light but, like the mirror in a reflector telescope, it does not magnify the object. This is done by the eyepiece.

This diagram shows the path of light rays in a refractor telescope.

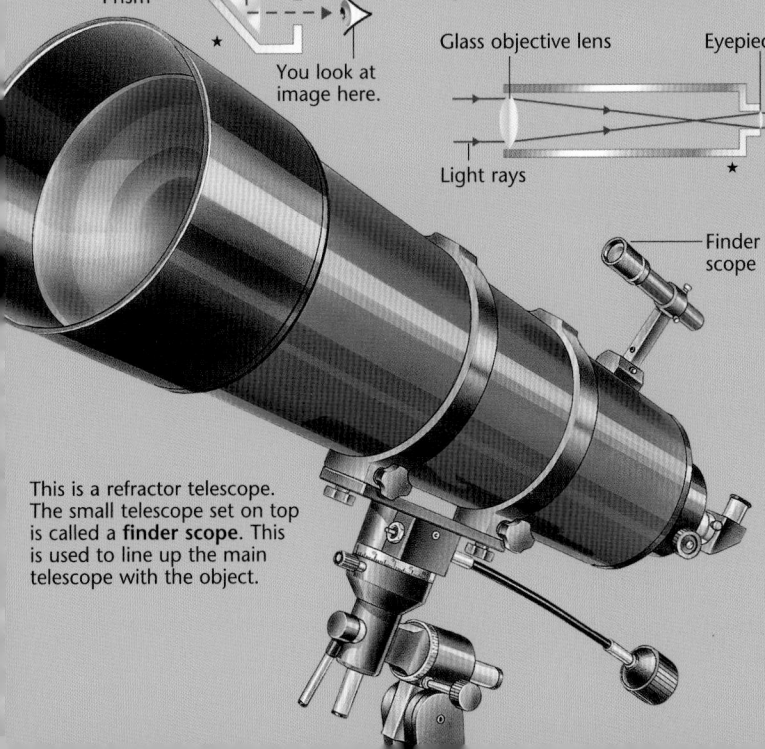

This is a refractor telescope. The small telescope set on top is called a **finder scope**. This is used to line up the main telescope with the object.

See for yourself

You could use a pair of binoculars to look at the stars.

Binoculars are made in various sizes and powers, shown by a pair of numbers, such as 7 x 35 or 10 x 50. The first number is the magnification. The second is the diameter, in millimetres, of the front, objective lenses. The larger the lenses, the more light they can collect, so the fainter the starlight they can pick out.

Stars seen with the eye alone are tiny pinpoints.

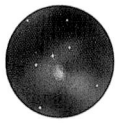

Seen through binoculars, more details are visible.

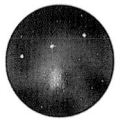

It is a good idea to rest your binoculars on a steady surface, such as a wall or fence. This will stop them shaking in your hand and give you a clearer view of the stars.

A good telescope can show the stars in even greater detail.

Many more distant stars can be seen through a good telescope.

Internet links

Go to **www.usborne-quicklinks.com** and type in "science" to find out more about optical instruments.

There you'll find links to websites where you can:

- Get instructions for making a simple kaleidoscope
- Find out about the inventor of the optical telescope, Galileo

Go to Usborne Quicklinks for links to hand-picked websites on hundreds of subjects.

CAMERAS

Cameras are optical instruments that record pictures. They use lenses to focus light onto film or some other device that saves the picture so that you can look at it again later. Early cameras stored pictures on sheets of glass or metal coated with light-sensitive substances. From the 1880s glass and metal were replaced with light-sensitive film. Digital cameras, invented in the 1990s, store pictures electronically.

This is an early Polaroid camera. Polaroid film develops rapidly, so you see the picture just after you take it.

CAMERA PRINCIPLES

Light enters a camera through a lens. The amount of light that is let in is called the **exposure**. Exposure is controlled by two things. First, an adjustable hole called an **aperture** determines how much light gets into the camera. Second, a flap called a **shutter** controls how long light is allowed to fall on the film.

Single-lens reflex (SLR) camera

In this type of camera, light entering the lens is reflected off a mirror and refracted through a prism to a little window called the **viewfinder**. This lets the photographer see exactly what the lens sees.

Photographer looks through the viewfinder, which is at the back of the camera.

Prism

Shutter release button

The film goes inside the main body of the camera.

Aperture adjuster

Winding mechanism pulls film into place behind the shutter.

The film is pulled across inside the back of the camera to a spool in here.

This mirror flips up to let light shine onto the film when the shutter is released.

A camera uses a combination of several different lenses to focus light from an object onto the film.

PHOTOGRAPHIC FILM

Photographic film is coated with silver nitrate, a light-sensitive chemical. How the film reacts depends on the amount of light that reaches it.

The exposed film is dipped into chemicals to produce the images and stop the film being sensitive to any more light. This process is called **developing**.

Positive film (also called **transparency** or **slide film**). This shows images with the correct colours.

Negative film. The light parts of the piano keyboard in the picture appear dark and the dark parts appear light.

Developed negative film is projected onto light-sensitive paper to make the final print.

MOVING PICTURES

Motion-picture cameras record images on very long strips of photographic film. They take 25 separate pictures, called **frames**, every second. The film is developed in the same way as film from a normal camera.

The film is held in a cassette which clips onto the camera.

To watch the film, it is wound through a projector at a rate of 25 frames per second. The frames move so fast that you see the next frame before the last one fades in your brain. This is called **persistent vision**.

See for yourself

You can demonstrate persistent vision by making your own "movie" flick book.

On the back page of a small pad of paper draw a simple character. Turn over the page and trace this image, making slight changes to show the character moving. Draw at least 20 more images, changing each one a little.

When you flick the pad, the images appear as one moving picture.

TELEVISION CAMERAS

Television cameras do not use film, but turn the light that enters them into a series of electrical signals. These signals are sent down a cable and are either transmitted as a live broadcast, or recorded onto tape or computer to be transmitted at another time.

A television studio camera is heavy and is supported by a stand.

CAMCORDERS

A **video camcorder** is a combined TV camera and video recorder. Lenses direct an image onto a tiny light-sensitive electronic part called a **charge-coupled device (CCD)**. The CCD produces electrical signals which are recorded onto videotape, a memory card or hard disk.

This small camcorder can fit in the palm of your hand.

DIGITAL CAMERAS

Digital cameras record images onto a CCD. The images are broken down into tiny coloured squares called **pixels**. Information about the pixels is stored in the camera's memory as binary code*. To print the picture or see it on a computer screen, the pixels recombine, forming a complete picture.

The degree of detail in a picture is called its **resolution**. The more pixels that a digital camera creates in an image, the higher the image's resolution.

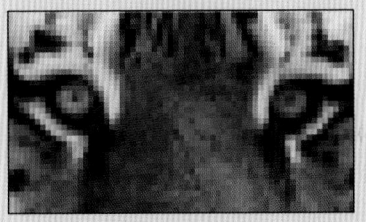

Low-resolution image

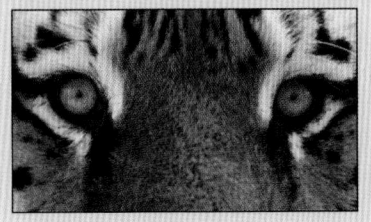

High-resolution image

Because digital images can be stored on a computer you can alter the photo after it has been taken. This can be very useful.

For example, if you take a photo when it is quite dark, the camera will use a flash to light up the target. The flash can make people's eyes look red, because it is lighting up the inside of their retina*. "Red eye" can spoil a photo, but with a digital camera you can use a computer programme to make the eye colour more natural again.

** Binary code, 238; Retina, 370.*

TV AND RADIO

The first radio transmissions were made about 100 years ago. Television was invented in 1926. The first signals could only be sent over very short distances, but today satellites can instantly broadcast clear signals around the world.

This early radio was invented by Marconi. It was called a marconiphone.

BROADCASTING

Most radio and television shows are broadcast as **radio waves**. These are a band of waves in the electromagnetic spectrum* with a range of different frequencies* and wavelengths*.

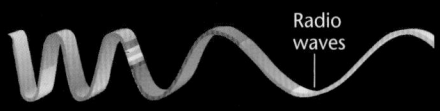

Radio waves are the longest waves in the electromagnetic spectrum.

Before broadcasting, sounds and images first have to be converted into electrical signals. Sounds are made into electrical signals by microphones. Cameras create electrical signals from images.

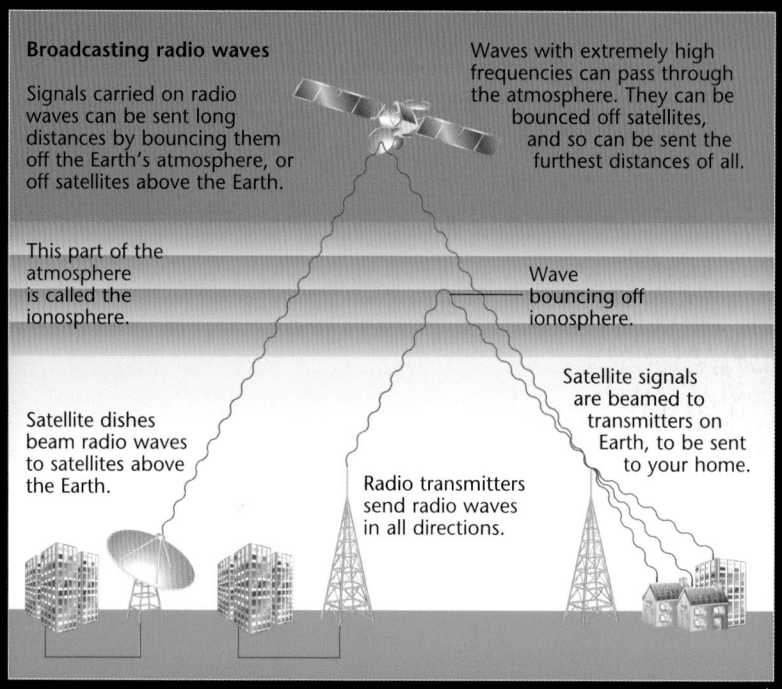

MODULATION

To enable them to be broadcast, electrical signals have to be altered, using a method called **modulation**. This is done by mixing the electrical sound and picture signals with radio waves, called **carrier waves**.

As a result of modulation, the shape of the carrier wave varies depending on the electrical sound and picture signals. The picture on the right shows an example of this.

With **frequency modulation (FM)** the electrical signals are altered to match the frequency of the carrier wave. With **amplitude modulation (AM)** the electrical signals are altered to match the amplitude* (strength) of the carrier wave.

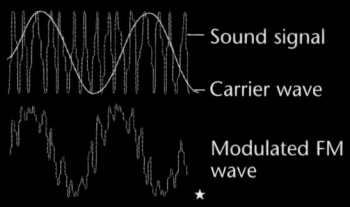

HOW A RADIO WORKS

A radio works by receiving modulated radio waves through its aerial, and then converting them back into very weak electrical signals.

Radio receives many different signals. Tuner is adjusted to select wavelength of broadcast required.

The signal is strengthened (amplified) and a loudspeaker turns it into a sound that can be heard.

* Amplitude, 203; Electromagnetic spectrum, 212-213; Frequency, Wavelength, 203.

HOW TV WORKS

Television signals are carried by radio waves. As well as the sound signals, the waves carry picture signals. A television converts these signals into sound and pictures. The sound is converted in the same way as in a radio. The picture signals are converted into pictures by a **cathode ray tube**. The pictures are built up from about 350,000 tiny shapes called **pixels** (short for picture elements).

A cathode ray tube

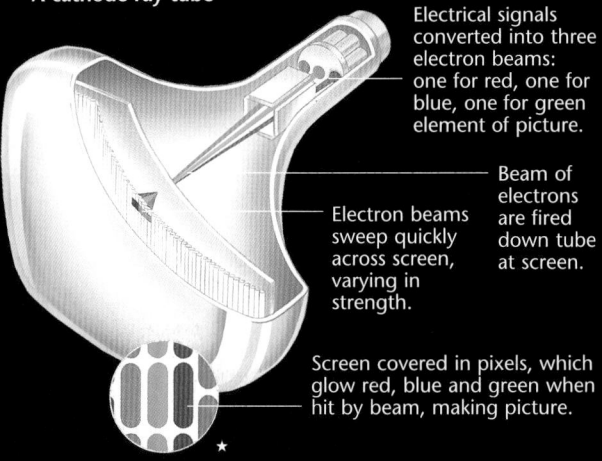

CABLE BROADCASTING

TV and radio signals can be carried along cables, too. The cables can convey more signals than when they are transmitted through the air, so more channels are available. A vast network of underground cables exists. These can also be used to carry phone signals.

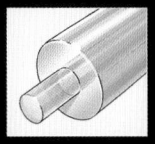

Fibre-optic cables are used for carrying television and radio signals.

DIGITAL BROADCASTING

In many countries, radio and television are broadcast **digitally**. Digital signals are electrical signals which carry information as a code made up of millions and millions of just two components: either "on" (1) or "off" (0).

The digital code is mixed onto – and then carried by – radio waves. Digital information can be compressed (see *Transmission Speed*, page 245, for an example) so far more can be sent. As a result, broadcasters can offer more channels than previously.

INTERACTIVE TV

Digital broadcasting makes it possible to communicate in two directions. As a result, you can send information back through your TV, to order programmes to watch whenever you want, or to buy things, or even to take part in games and competitions. This is called **interactive TV**.

This TV shows an interactive game to play during a football match.

Competitors predict the goalscorers and the match's outcome. Their predictions are registered with the TV company and if they are right they win instant prizes.

SATELLITE TV

Satellite TV companies bounce signals off space satellites, to be received directly by a small dish that is fixed to the side of your home.

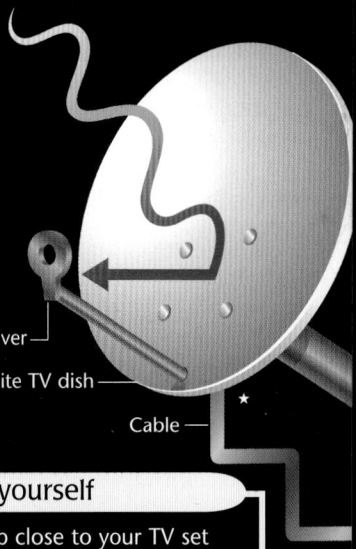

The dish focuses the TV signal onto a receiver. The signals travel along a cable to a television set.

See for yourself

Put a magnifying glass up close to your TV set while it is on. Look carefully and you'll be able to see the pixels that make up the picture.

Internet links

Go to **www.usborne-quicklinks.com** and type in "science" to find out more about TV and radio.

There you'll find links to websites where you can:

- Follow the journey of a radio sound wave

Go to Usborne Quicklinks for links to hand-picked websites on hundreds of subjects.

ELECTRICITY

Lightning is a form of electricity.

Electricity is a useful form of energy. It can easily be converted to other forms of energy, such as heat or light, and it can flow along cables, which makes it easy to transport. Electricity is used to power many devices, from kettles to computers, and to provide heat and light in homes, offices and factories.

ELECTRIC CHARGE

All matter is made up of tiny units called **atoms**. In the middle of each atom is a **nucleus**. This contains particles called **protons** which have a positive charge and neutrons which have no charge. Negatively charged particles called **electrons** whizz around the nucleus. Normally, the number of protons and electrons is equal. Their charges cancel each other out so the atom is electrically neutral.

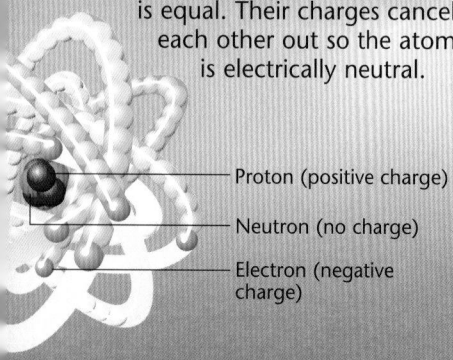

An atom can gain or lose electrons. If it gains electrons, it becomes negatively charged (–). If it loses electrons, it becomes positively charged (+).

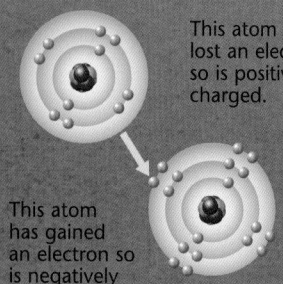

If charged particles are near enough to each other, they have an effect on each other known as an **electric force**. The area in which this force has an effect is called an **electric field**.

Particles with opposite charges (positive and negative charges) attract each other. Particles with the same type of charge, for example two positively charged particles, push each other away.

Atoms with opposite charges attract each other.

Atoms with the same charge push each other away.

Electricity is the effect caused by the presence or movement of charged particles.

ELECTRIC CURRENT

In certain substances, such as metals, some electrons are not held tightly by the atoms and can move between them. If they are made to move, there is a flow of electric charge called an **electric current**. Substances through which current can flow are called **conductors**. Those substances, such as plastic, which cannot conduct current, are called **insulators**.

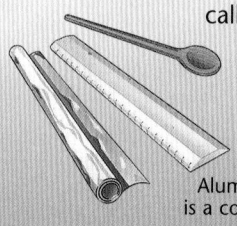

Insulated wires are electrical wires, usually made of copper, covered with plastic to insulate them.

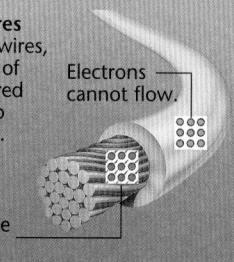

See for yourself

To see how charges affect each other, tape two equal lengths of nylon thread to the top of a door frame, spaced about 2.5cm apart. Tie a balloon to each thread, so that they touch and hang at the same height. Rub the balloons with a woollen scarf or sweater. The balloons become negatively charged and move away from each other. If you put your hand in between the balloons, they move towards your hand, which has a positive charge.

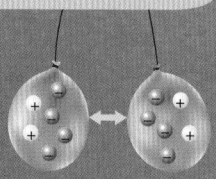

Matching charges repel each other.

STATIC ELECTRICITY

Some insulating materials become charged when rubbed. This happens because electrons from one material are transferred to the other. The charge cannot flow away because there is no conductor, so it builds up on the surface of the material. Electrical charge that is held by a material is called **static electricity**.

The diagrams below show how static electricity builds up if you rub a balloon on a wool sweater.

Before they are rubbed, the balloon and the sweater are electrically neutral.

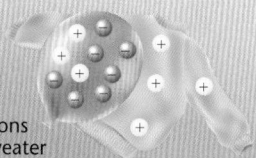

As they are rubbed, some electrons from the sweater move to the balloon. This becomes negatively charged, and the sweater becomes positively charged. They cling together because their opposite charges attract each other.

Equipment such as laser printers and photocopiers use static electricity as part of their printing process.

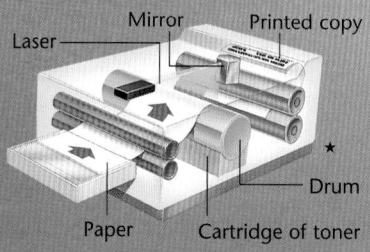

In a laser printer, a laser beam reflected by a mirror makes dots of static electricity on a drum. Toner clings to the dots of static and is pressed onto the paper.

LIGHTNING

Lightning is caused by static electricity that builds up when falling water droplets and rising ice crystals rub against each other in storm clouds.

Water droplets and ice crystals become charged as they rub against each other and the air.

Positive charges gather at the top of the cloud and negative charges in the base. As this happens, positive charges collect together on the ground beneath the cloud.

A giant spark, called a **leader stroke**, flashes out from the cloud, seeking a point with the opposite charge on the ground. When it finds it, it makes a path which is followed by a powerful stroke of lightning from the ground to the cloud. This is called the **return stroke**.

Lightning contains a vast amount of electrical energy, which is changed into light, heat and sound (thunder).

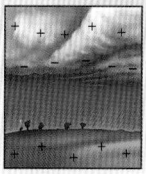

A build-up of negative charge at the base of a storm cloud causes a build-up of positive charge in the ground below.

When lightning strikes, an electric current flows between the cloud and the ground, leaving them both electrically neutral.

The air heated by the flashes of lightning expands very rapidly. This makes the noise that we hear as **thunder**. Light travels faster than sound, so unless the storm cloud is directly overhead, you see the lightning before you hear the thunder.

A stroke of lightning branches out in many directions as it seeks its way to the ground.

Internet links

To find out more about electricity, go to **www.usborne-quicklinks.com** and type in the keyword "science".

There you'll find links to websites where you can:

- Learn about lightning
- Try some electricity experiments
- Find out about conductors

Go to Usborne Quicklinks for links to hand-picked websites on hundreds of subjects.

The links at Usborne Quicklinks are regularly reviewed and updated, so you might find a slightly different selection of websites from the ones described here.

CIRCUITS

An electric current flows from one place to another as a result of something called **potential difference**. This is similar to the pressure difference that causes water to flow through pipes. Potential difference is measured in **volts (V)** and is also called **voltage**. Current is measured in units called **amperes (amps)**.

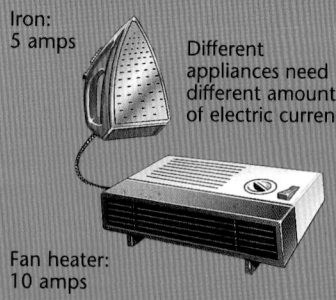

For an electric current to keep flowing there must be a power source, such as a battery (see opposite page), joined to an unbroken conducting pathway, such as a loop of copper wire. This pathway is called an **electric circuit**. The power source has two ends with opposite charges, called **poles** or **terminals**. These are where the circuit starts and finishes.

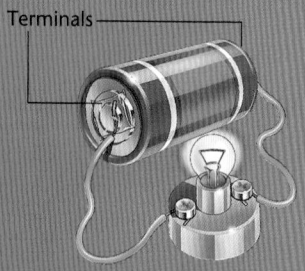

A potential difference exists between the terminals of a battery. When they are joined, a circuit is formed and a current flows.

Components, such as bulbs, can be added to a circuit. These convert the electrical energy carried by the current into other forms of energy such as light and heat. The components in a circuit can be arranged in two ways: in series or in parallel.

In a **series circuit**, the current passes through the components one after the other. If one component is not working, it breaks the circuit and no current flows.

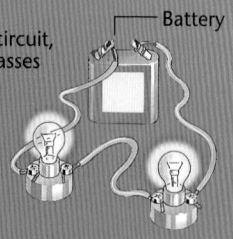

In this series circuit, the current passes through each component in turn.

A **parallel circuit** has more than one path for the current. If a component in one path does not work, current continues to flow through the other path.

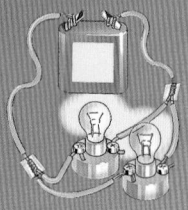

In this parallel circuit, the current passes through the components by different paths at the same time.

ELECTRICITY AT HOME

Household electricity is 240V in some countries and 110V in others. These large voltages can give you a deadly electric shock. Appliances are protected by **fuses** containing very thin pieces of wire. These melt, and cut off the current if it is too large.

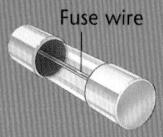

Electricity is carried to different parts of a house by parallel circuits. These circuits contain two wires called the **live** and **neutral wires**, which carry the current. In some countries there is also an **earth wire**. This is a safety device. It provides a path to the ground through which electric current can escape if the plug develops a fault.

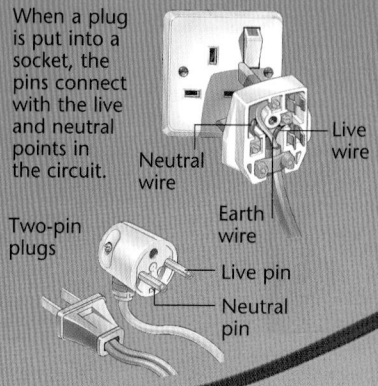

This electricity substation reduces to a lower level the massive voltage it receives from the main power station. The current travels along cables to homes and factories.

BATTERIES

A **battery** is a store of chemical energy that can be converted to electrical energy. The most common type of battery used at home is called a **dry cell**. It contains a paste called an **electrolyte** which contains charged particles that can move. Chemical reactions make the charges separate. Positive charges move to one terminal and negative ones move to the other.

Batteries produce an electric current that moves in a single direction. This is called **direct current** (**DC**).

Cutaway view of a dry cell

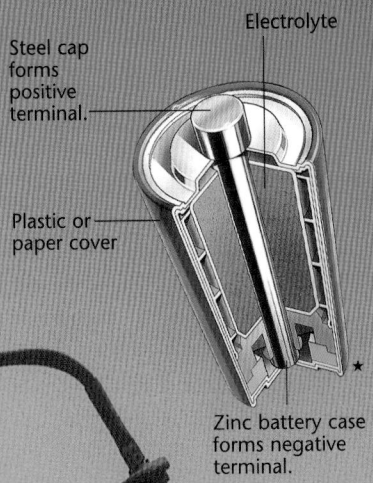

A 1.5V battery, such as the type used in a personal stereo, is called a **single cell**. Larger batteries are made up of several single cells.

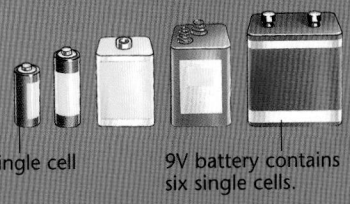

Dry cells are **primary cells**. When the chemicals in the electrolyte run out, the battery is finished. **Secondary cells**, or **accumulators**, are batteries that can be recharged. A car battery is a type of secondary cell. It is continually recharged with electric current generated from the car.

Cutaway view of a car battery

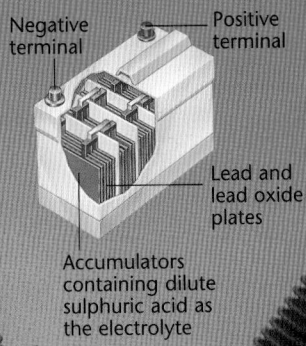

A **solar cell** converts the Sun's energy into electricity. Sunlight falling on the layers of silicon makes the electrons move, creating a potential difference between the two layers.

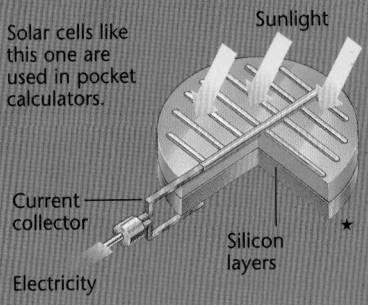

See for yourself

To make a simple battery, draw around a coin to make twelve circles each on a sheet of foil and a paper towel, then cut them out. Dampen the paper circles in a cup of water with ten teaspoons of salt stirred in.

You need 12 copper coins. Pile the circles in groups of three (a cell), made up of one foil, one paper and one coin. Tape the bare end of a piece of insulated copper wire to the bottom of the pile, and another wire to the top. Touch the other two ends together. In a dark room you should see a spark.

Internet links

To find out more about electricity, go to **www.usborne-quicklinks.com** and type in the keyword "science".

There you'll find links to websites where you can:

- Examine different types of circuit

MAGNETISM

Magnetism is an invisible force that attracts some metals, especially iron and steel. Materials that create this force are said to be **magnetic** and are called **magnets**.

Migrating terns like these may use the Earth's magnetic field to guide them.

POLES

If you float a magnet in water or hang it from a thread tied around its middle, it will always point in a north-south direction. The part of the magnet that points north is the **north** or **north-seeking pole**. The other is the **south** or **south-seeking pole**.

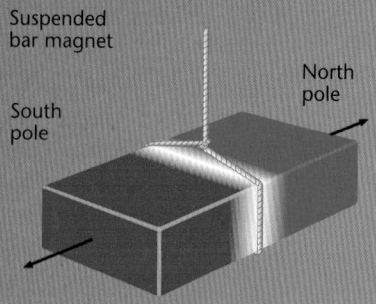

A north and a south pole of two magnets will pull toward or **attract** each other. Two north or two south poles will push each other away. This is called **repulsion**.

Like poles repel each other.

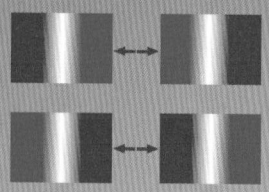

Unlike poles attract each other.

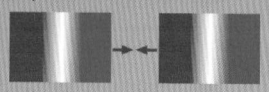

★

TYPES OF MAGNETS

Materials that can easily be magnetized (turned into magnets) are said to be **ferromagnetic**. They can be described as hard or soft.

Soft ferromagnetic materials such as iron quickly lose their magnetic properties. Magnets made from these materials are called **temporary magnets**. Hard ferromagnetic materials such as steel keep their magnetic properties for much longer. They are used to make **permanent magnets**.

Each paper clip in this chain has become magnetized by contact with the magnet. Each is a temporary magnet.

If the magnet is removed, the clips will lose their magnetism.

A compass needle is a permanent magnet. It points to the Earth's magnetic north pole.

DIPOLES AND DOMAINS

A ferromagnetic material has molecules which behave like tiny magnets. They are known as **dipoles** and are grouped in **domains**, in which they all point the same way. When the material is magnetized, all the domains become ordered and point the same way. The material loses its magnetism if its domains become jumbled up again.

When magnetic material is in a non-magnetized state, the domains are jumbled up.

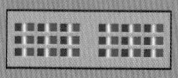

When it is magnetized, the domains line up, with their poles all pointing the same way.

★

Ordered dipoles collectively form a magnet, but individually, each one is trying to flip round, as its poles are attracted to the opposite poles of the whole magnet. As they turn, the magnet loses its magnetism.

A metal **keeper** across a magnet's ends helps it to stay magnetic. The keeper becomes magnetized and attracts the magnet's dipoles to its poles.

MAGNETIC FIELDS

The region around a magnet in which objects are affected by its magnetic force is called a **magnetic field**. The strength and direction of the magnetic field are shown by **magnetic flux lines**. The arrows on the lines show the direction. The magnetic field is strongest where the lines are close together.

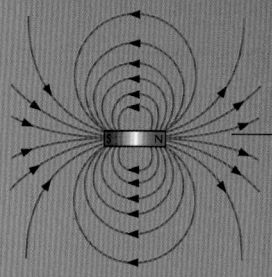

Magnetic flux lines showing the direction of the magnetic field around a bar magnet

The lines are closest near the poles, where the field is strongest.

The Earth itself has a magnetic field. It acts as though it has a giant bar magnet through its middle. The north pole of a compass points towards a point called **magnetic north**, its south pole points to **magnetic south**. These are different from the geographical North and South Poles.

These magnetic flux lines show the direction of the magnetic field around the Earth.

ELECTROMAGNETISM

When an electric current flows through a wire, it produces a magnetic field around it. This effect is called **electromagnetism**.

The magnetic field of the wire can be made stronger if the wire is wound in a coil. When a current is passed through the coil, the coil behaves like a bar magnet and is called a **solenoid**. The region inside the coil is called the **core**.

If a solenoid has a rod of a soft ferromagnetic material such as iron placed inside it, the rod is quickly magnetized and adds its own magnetic field to that of the solenoid. Together the solenoid and the ferromagnetic core make an **electromagnet**. You can find out more about the uses of electromagnets over the page.

A simple electromagnet

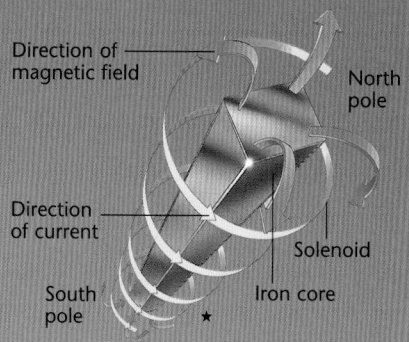

The position of the north and south poles in an electromagnet depends on the direction of the current flowing through the wire.

Viewed end-on, current flowing anticlockwise gives a north pole.

Current flowing clockwise gives a south pole.

See for yourself

To see magnetic flux lines, sprinkle some iron filings onto a sheet of clear plastic or a piece of white paper, then hold a magnet underneath. The iron filings will move to show the pattern of the magnetic field.

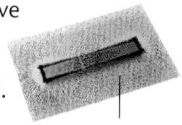

Clear plastic sheet

Internet links

To find out more about magnetism, go to **www.usborne-quicklinks.com** and type in the keyword "science".

There you'll find links to websites where you can:

- Find out how to make a compass
- Carry out magnetism experiments
- Investigate the many everyday uses of magnets

Go to Usborne Quicklinks for links to hand-picked websites on hundreds of subjects.

USING ELECTROMAGNETS

Electromagnets often contain iron, a soft ferromagnetic material. The iron loses almost all of its magnetism when the current through the electromagnet is switched off. For this reason, electromagnets have many uses, such as in switches, bells and buzzers.

When you press the button of an electric bell, for example, current flows through the coils of an electromagnet and attracts a metal arm. As the arm moves nearer to the electromagnet, it loses touch with the contact through which the current is flowing, breaking the circuit. The arm is pulled back by a spring, making a hammer hit a bell. This completes the circuit and the cycle begins again.

Electric bell

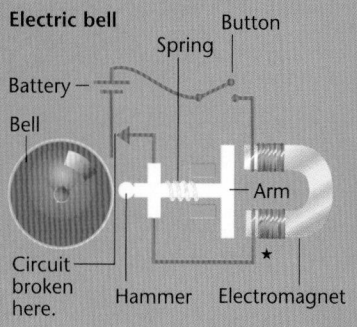

See for yourself

You can make an electromagnet using a 4.5V battery, a pencil, a large iron nail and some insulated copper wire. To make a solenoid*, wind the wire tightly around the pencil, and tape both ends to the battery. Your electromagnet should be strong enough to affect a compass needle, but too weak to pick anything up. If you replace the pencil with the nail, you will have an electromagnet that can pick up paper clips.

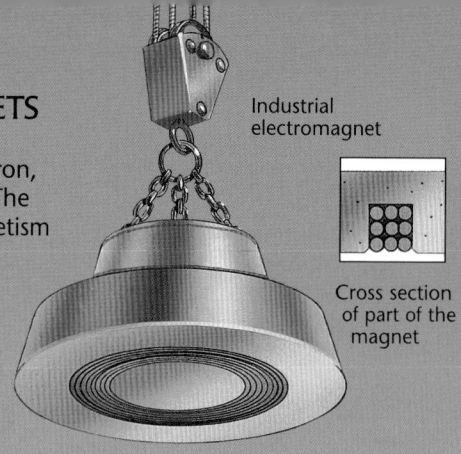

Very powerful electromagnets are used in steelworks to lift heavy loads. When current flows through the coil of wire, the iron becomes magnetized. It attracts steel, which can be moved from one place to another. When the current is switched off, the electromagnet releases its load.

Magnetic levitation (maglev) trains have electromagnets on the bottom. They run on tracks with electromagnets on them. The magnets repel each other, so the train hovers just above the track. This reduces the amount of friction between the train and the track, so the train needs less energy to make it move.

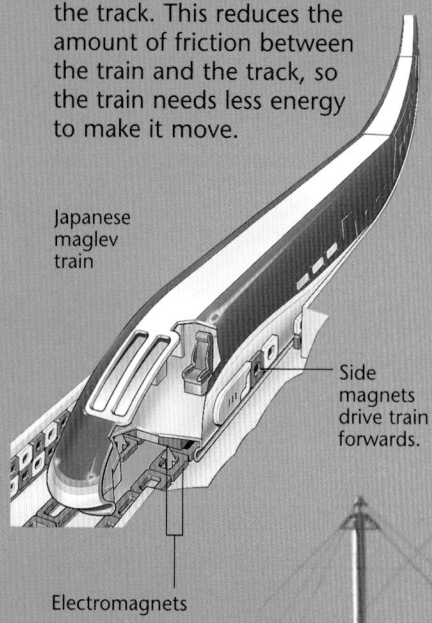

ELECTRIC MOTORS

Electric motors change electrical energy into movement. A simple electric motor (see picture below) contains a flat coil of wire called an **armature** between two magnets.

When current flows through the armature, the combination of the electromagnetic field of the armature and the magnetic fields of the magnets pushes one side of the armature up and the other side down.

A simple electric motor

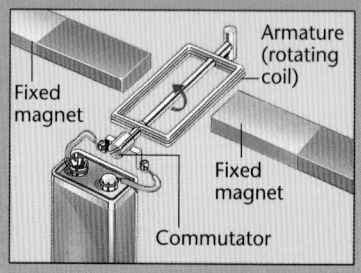

When the armature is in an upright position, a device called a **commutator** causes the direction of the electric current to be reversed, so the magnetic field of the armature is reversed. The side of the armature that was pushed up is now pulled down. The armature completes its circle and the cycle begins again.

* *Solenoid, 233.*

USES FOR MOTORS

Electric motors are used in all kinds of equipment, from washing machines and hairdryers to battery-driven toy cars and model trains. Tiny **micromotors** (see picture below) are being developed for use in microsurgery and space research.

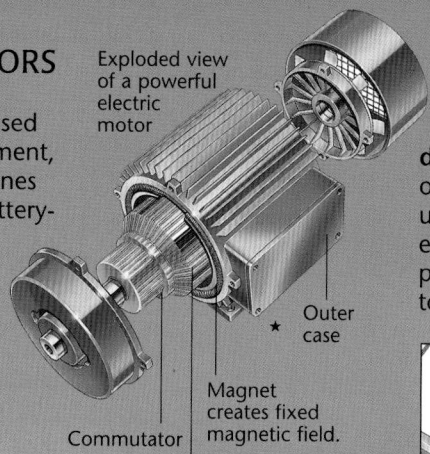

This Toshiba micromotor is 0.8mm wide – about the same as the eye of the needle next to it.

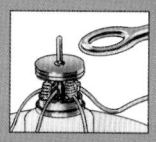

A **bicycle dynamo** is a type of generator. It uses the movement energy from a wheel to produce electric current to light a lamp.

GENERATING ELECTRICITY

A **dynamo** or **generator** is a machine for converting movement energy into electrical energy. It works rather like an electric motor in reverse. The diagrams below show how a generator produces electricity. As the armature turns between the two magnets, an electric current starts to flow. As the armature passes through its upright position, the direction of the current changes. This type of current is called **alternating current** (**AC**).

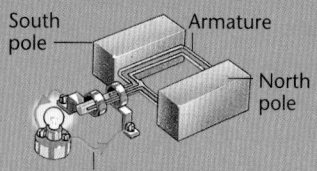

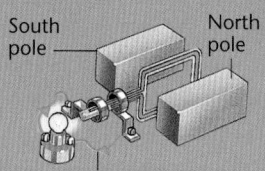

Electricity is generated on a larger scale in **power stations**. Many power stations use heat energy from burning coal to boil water and turn it to steam. The pressure of the steam is used to spin the shaft of a machine called a **turbine**. This then turns the shaft of a huge generator and produces alternating current.

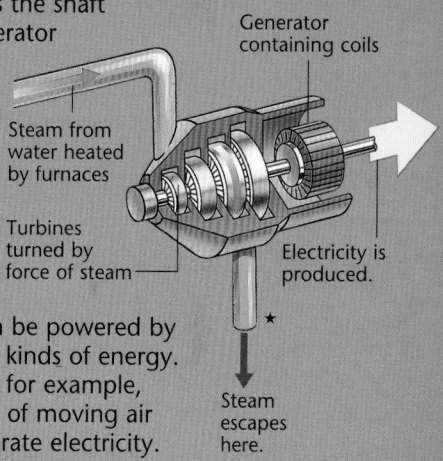

Cutaway of steam turbine

Generators can be powered by many different kinds of energy. Wind turbines, for example, use the energy of moving air (wind) to generate electricity.

The shafts of these wind turbines are made to spin by the wind. The movement energy is used to generate electricity.

Internet links

Go to **www.usborne-quicklinks.com** and type in the keyword "science" to find out more about magnetism.

There you'll find links to websites where you can:

- Find out how electric motors work
- Investigate electromagnets with animated diagrams
- Watch Maglev trains in action

Go to Usborne Quicklinks for links to hand-picked websites on hundreds of subjects.

ELECTRONICS

Electronics is the use of devices called **electronic components** to control the way electric current flows around a circuit, making it do particular tasks. A circuit controlled in this way is called an **electronic circuit**. All sorts of machines, such as TVs, robots and computers, use electronic circuits.

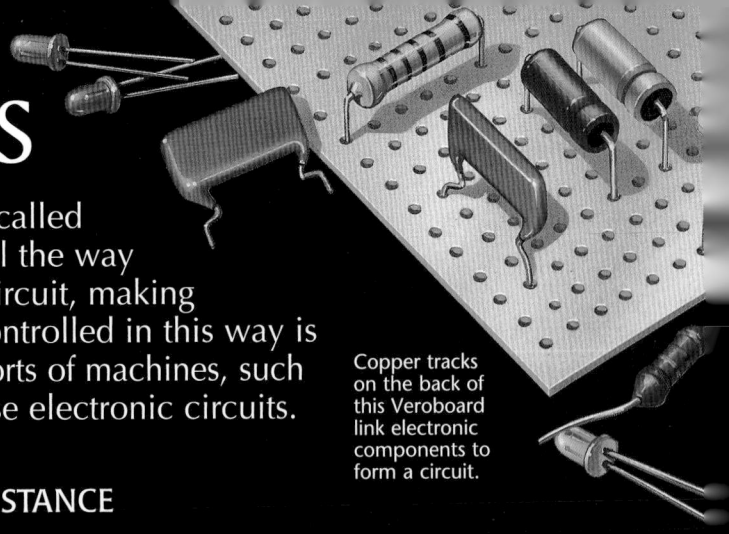

Copper tracks on the back of this Veroboard link electronic components to form a circuit.

BUILDING CIRCUITS

Electronic circuits can be made up using different components. The simple circuit below, for instance, contains a resistor (see right).

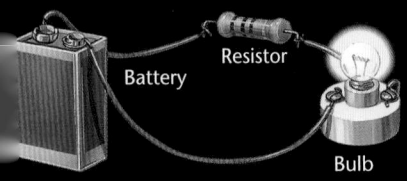

Circuits can be mapped out using diagrams like the one below. Each component is shown using a different circuit symbol. The main circuit symbols can be found together on page 409.

Circuit diagram of circuit above

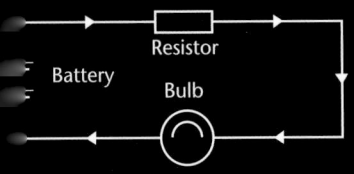

You can make simple circuits using **Veroboard**. This has rows of holes and copper tracks on the back. Components are pushed through from the front, then their legs are soldered onto the tracks to form a circuit. **Printed circuit boards (PCBs)** are plastic boards which are imprinted with metal tracks. They are used, for example, in televisions. **Integrated circuits** are tiny circuits engraved onto small slices of silicon.

RESISTANCE

The ability of a substance to restrict the flow of electric current is known as **resistance**. All the parts in an electric circuit have a certain amount of resistance, and this reduces the amount of current that is able to flow around it in a certain time. When a substance resists an electric current, it converts some of the electrical energy into heat or light.

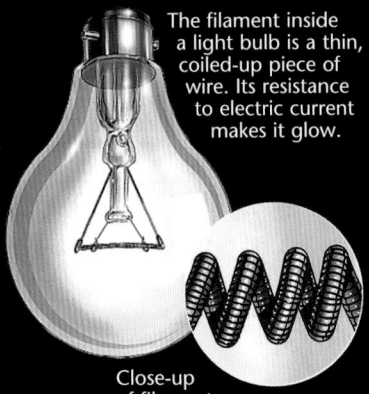

The filament inside a light bulb is a thin, coiled-up piece of wire. Its resistance to electric current makes it glow.

Close-up of filament

Resistance is measured in units called **ohms**, named after Georg Ohm, a nineteenth-century physicist.

The Greek letter omega is used as a symbol for ohms.

Resistors are electronic components which reduce the flow of current. Resistors have three or four colour-coded stripes on them which show how much resistance they give.

The first two stripes on a resistor stand for numbers. The third tells how many zeros to put on the end. The fourth stripe tells you the rating's range. The stripes on the resistor below, for example, are blue (6), red (2), black (0) and gold (±5%), so it has a resistance of 62 ohms, plus or minus 5%.

The stripes on this resistor show that it gives between 58.9 and 65.1Ω of resistance.

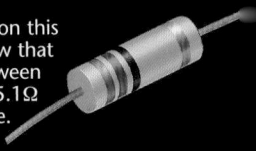

See for yourself

Using the colour code chart above, try to work out which of these two resistors has the highest ohm rating. (Answer on page 447.)

TYPES OF COMPONENTS

There are several types of electronic components. Each one is designed to do a different job in an electronic circuit. For example, different kinds of resistors are designed to resist current by greater or lesser amounts in different conditions.

A variable resistor, or **rheostat**, can be adjusted to give different amounts of resistance. The volume control on a radio uses a variable resistor to change the amount of current. This varies the amount of electrical energy that is converted to sound energy.

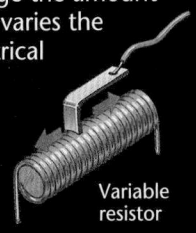

Variable resistor

A thermistor is a heat-sensitive resistor. Its resistance falls as the temperature rises, and rises as the temperature falls. They are used in some fire alarms to sense when a room is too hot.

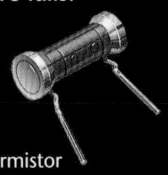

Thermistor

Diodes allow the current to flow through them in only one direction. A **light-emitting diode (LED)** glows when current flows through it.

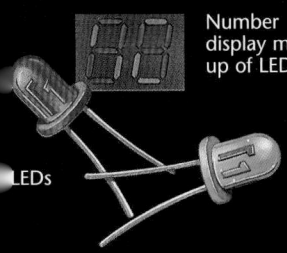

On this printed circuit board, the black oblong shapes contain integrated circuits. They are connected to each other and to other components by metal tracks.

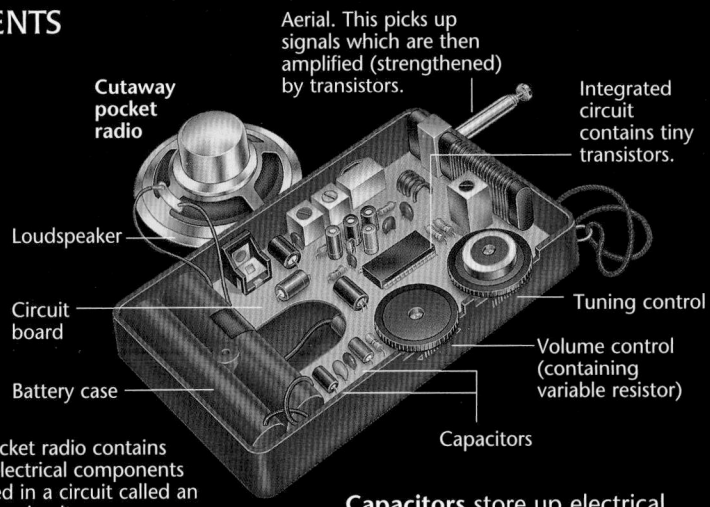

This pocket radio contains many electrical components arranged in a circuit called an amplifier circuit.

Transistors are electronic switches. A transistor has three legs, called the **base**, the **collector** and the **emitter**. When a small current flows into the base leg, the transistor allows a larger current to flow between the collector and the emitter. The transistor is then switched on. When no current flows to the base leg the transistor is off.

Transistor

This diagram shows the currents (white arrows) that flow through a transistor in a circuit.

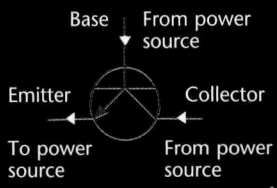

Capacitors store up electrical energy and release it when it is needed. A television uses capacitors to build up and store very high voltages.

Capacitors

There are different kinds of capacitors.

Internet links

To find out more about electronics, go to **www.usborne-quicklinks.com** and type in the keyword "science".

There you'll find links to websites where you can:

- Build and test simple circuits online
- Learn to recognize the symbols used on circuit diagrams

Go to Usborne Quicklinks for links to hand-picked websites on hundreds of subjects.

DIGITAL ELECTRONICS

Digital electronics is a form of electronics that uses pulses of electricity instead of continuously flowing, or **analogue**, electricity. All sorts of electronic equipment, from digital watches and calculators to computers, use digital electronics.

Pocket calculators contain digital electronic circuits.

DIGITAL CIRCUITS

In a **digital circuit**, the electricity exists in pulses at either high voltage* or low voltage. Tiny electronic components* change and redirect these pulses as they flow around the circuits.

In an analogue circuit, electricity flows continuously.

In a digital circuit, the electricity is broken up into a series of pulses.

A digital watch is controlled by digital circuits.

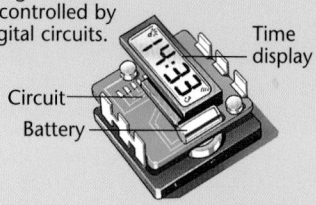

The pulses of electricity can be used to represent information in **binary code**. This expresses information using numbers made up of the digits 0 and 1. Words, sounds and pictures can be translated into binary, too. As there are only two options (0 and 1), devices that use digital electronics can process information very quickly.

Wave form of digital current

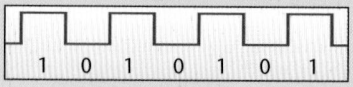

A pulse at high voltage represents a 1 and a pulse at low voltage represents a 0.

LOGIC GATES

A **logic gate** is an arrangement of transistors* used to carry out calculations in digital electronic circuits. Logic gates change or redirect the pulses that flow through them. Most logic gates have two **inputs**, which receive signals, and one **output**, which gives out a signal.

There are three main types of logic gate, and they are each represented by a different circuit symbol, as shown below.

AND gate

Input	Output
1, 1	1
0, 1	0
0, 0	0

An AND gate gives out a 1 if it receives two 1s. Otherwise, it gives out a 0.

NOT gate

Input	Output
1	0
0	1

A NOT gate has one input and one output. It changes a 1 to a 0 and a 0 to a 1.

OR gate

Input	Output
1, 0	1
1, 1	1
0, 0	0

An OR gate gives out a 1 if it receives a 1 in either of its inputs.

Logic gates have many uses. For example, an AND gate might be used in a security system, such as that used in a bank, where two officials must turn keys at the same time to open a safe. Only when both keys are turned would two 1s pass through the AND gate, and so open the lock.

This security circuit uses an AND gate so that the lock only opens when keys X and Y are both turned.

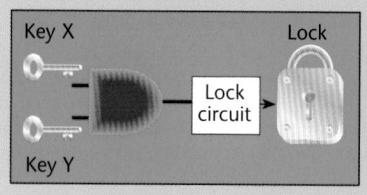

If the output is 1, current flows through the lock circuit and the lock opens.

FLIP-FLOPS

Logic gates are usually combined to make up more complex devices, such as **flip-flops**. Electric pulses circulate back and forth inside flip-flops in a process called **feedback**. This enables the flip-flops to "remember" pieces of binary information.

Integrated circuits in computers (see opposite) often contain many thousands of flip-flops. These are joined together to make the computer's memory.

* *Electronic components, 237; Transistors, 237; Voltage, 230.*

INTEGRATED CIRCUITS

An **integrated circuit**, also known as a **silicon chip** or **chip**, is a complete electronic circuit containing thousands of tiny components etched on a very small piece of an element called silicon.

Large cylinders of silicon are sliced into thin sections called **wafers**, and the tiny circuits are printed onto them. The wafer is then cut up with a diamond saw to make the individual chips.

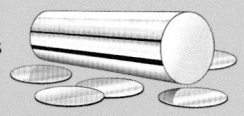

To make chips, silicon cylinders are sliced into thin wafers.

Many circuits are printed onto each wafer. The wafer is then cut up into individual chips.

This is a **CPU** (**Central Processing Unit**) chip, the main chip in a computer. It contains more than 28 million tiny transistors arranged into logic gates. The transistors are connected to each other by extremely fine aluminium threads.

Silicon is used because it is a **semiconductor** – a type of material that acts as a conductor* or an insulator*, depending on its temperature. The components that make up the circuits are also semiconductors, made of silicon mixed with tiny amounts of elements such as phosphorus or boron.

When the chips are made, they are mounted in plastic fittings which have wire feet to attach them to other components on a circuit board.

Wire feet link chips to other components.

The main circuit board in a computer is called the **motherboard**. It is made up of a piece of plastic with chips fixed onto it. The chips are connected by metal tracks printed onto the motherboard. Other components on the board control the amount of electricity flowing through the chips.

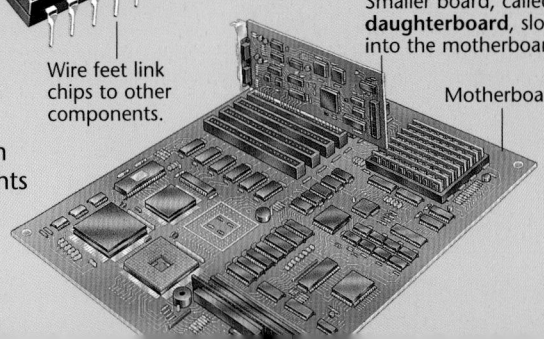

Smaller board, called a **daughterboard**, slots into the motherboard.

Motherboard

Internet links

Go to **www.usborne-quicklinks.com** and type in "science" to find out more about digital electronics.

There you'll find links to websites where you can:

- Watch an online demonstration of how logic gates work
- See microscope images of a microprocessor

Go to Usborne Quicklinks for links to hand-picked websites on hundreds of subjects.

The links at Usborne Quicklinks are regularly reviewed and updated, so you might find a slightly different selection of websites from the ones described here.

* *Conductor, Insulator, 228.*

COMPUTERS

At their most basic, **computers** are machines that do calculations and sort information. When they were invented in the late 1940s, computers were so big they filled whole rooms. Since then, they have been continuously improved and made smaller. Today, computers with more power than the early ones are no bigger than a book.

The Analytical Engine, a forerunner of the computer, built over a hundred years ago.

HARDWARE

The pieces that make up a computer are called **hardware**. Items of hardware that sit outside the case containing the computer's main electronic circuits are called **peripherals**. The screen, keyboard and mouse are all peripherals.

The type of computer shown below is called a **personal computer**, or **PC**.

This cathode ray tube* screen makes a picture in a similar way to a television.

Portable computers, called **laptops**, and handheld computers, called **palmtops**, have flat screens. They contain a thin layer of liquid crystal solution, which darkens to form an image when an electric current passes through it.

The keyboard is laid out like an old-fashioned typewriter, but it has some extra keys, called **function keys**. These make the computer do certain tasks.

With the mouse, you move a pointer around the screen and click on instructions. This can be quicker than using the keyboard.

Flat screen

Mouse

Keyboard. Function keys are lined up across the top.

Case contains computer's main circuits.

SOFTWARE

A computer won't work unless it has a set of instructions called a **program**, or **software**, loaded into its memory. Software that controls how the computer works is called the **operating system**. Windows®, made by Microsoft®, is an operating system.

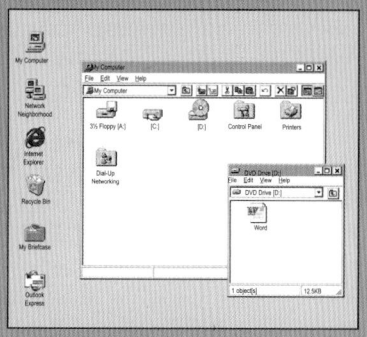

This screen shows files containing Windows software and documents.

Further software is needed to let you use the computer for particular activities such as playing games or connecting to the internet.

See for yourself

When you start up a PC, watch out for lines of information which flash past your eyes. This is the computer checking through its own hardware and software, making sure that everything is working correctly.

* *Cathode ray tube, 227.*

This stream of 0s and 1s gives an artist's impression of how digital information flows through a computer.

BITS AND BYTES

Computers do all their calculations using a code of only two numbers: 0 and 1. This is known as **binary code**. Each 0 or 1 is called a **bit** (short for **b**inary dig**it**). Binary code is easy to express by pulses of high (1) or low (0) electrical voltage through the computer's circuits.

A group of eight bits, called a **byte**, is used to represent a small piece of data (information). Lots and lots of bytes together can represent complex data.

01000010

This byte stands for the keyboard letter B.

PROCESSING

Calculations in a computer are done by **microprocessors**. In a personal computer, the most important is called the **central processing unit**, or **CPU**. CPUs can deal with several million calculations per second.

A microprocessor

Bytes travel around a computer along tiny electronic pathways, called **buses**. These take information between the CPU and other parts of the computer.

PROCESSING SPEED

How quickly a microprocessor can deal with information depends on two things:

- the number of bytes that it can process at once, called **bandwidth**;
- the number of instructions it can deal with in one second, called **clock speed**. This is measured in megahertz (MHz). A CPU that can process 500,000 calculations per second is said to have a clock speed of 500MHz.

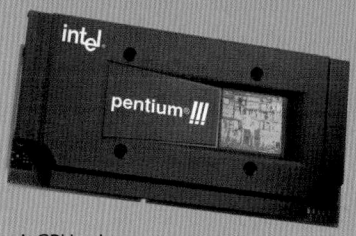

A CPU microprocessor made by Intel

Computer CDs look just like music CDs. All CDs store information in a similar way.

MEMORY

A computer stores information in its **memory**, on a set of disks called the **hard disk**. This information is retained when the computer is switched off. Information can also be stored for later use, or moved between computers, on floppy disks, CDs, DVDs or USB devices.

A computer's **RAM** (**random access memory**) stores data on silicon chips* while other calculations are done by the CPU. RAM is emptied when the computer is shut down.

USB flash drives can hold more information than a CD, and are much smaller.

Internet links

To find out more about computers, go to **www.usborne-quicklinks.com** and type in the keyword "science".

There you'll find links to websites where you can:

- See how a computer stores information in its memory
- Explore lessons and quizzes about computer hardware and software

Go to Usborne Quicklinks for links to hand-picked websites on hundreds of subjects.

* *Silicon chip, 239.*

SOFTWARE PACKAGES

There are hundreds of different types of software available. These range from simple programs that let you type letters, through to super-sophisticated packages that are used to design modern jets.

This picture of an Airbus was made using design software only. When the image was created, no real versions had been built.

There is software available for almost every type of work. In advertising and publishing, for instance, graphics software is used to manipulate pictures to create special effects.

Scanning this photo converted it into a mass of tiny squares, called **pixels**. Using graphics software, the pixels were altered to give the result on the right.

Close-up of pixels

Software comes loaded on floppy disks or, if it takes up a lot of memory, on CDs. These are downloaded (copied) onto the computer's hard disk.

See for yourself

Windows® contains simple graphics software called Paint®. Although it is not as powerful as the software used to create the images on these pages, you can use it to alter an image's colours and shapes.

A colour-selection panel from Paint®

HARDWARE CONTROL

How a piece of computer hardware, such as the screen, works is controlled by a set of microprocessors held on a small printed circuit board called a **card**.

A graphics card controls how pictures appear on the screen.

Each card slots into the computer's main circuit board. It is controlled in turn by software called a **driver**, which needs to be installed on the computer's hard disk.

You can often improve the performance of a computer by removing a card and installing a better one, and loading a new driver into the computer. This is called **upgrading**.

HOW THIS PICTURE WAS CREATED

This picture of a snowboarder was created using graphics software on a computer with a high-quality graphics card. First of all, the photo on the far left was scanned into the computer using a scanner (see opposite page).

Using the software, background colours were changed to make it more eye-catching. The snowboarder's left hand doesn't appear in the original photo, so the right hand was copied, reversed and added to the left arm. The picture was made to look blurred to give the impression of movement.

To make the background, lines were drawn in shades of yellow and orange. They were then mixed to create a spiral effect, before the figure was placed on top.

EXTRA HARDWARE

As well as basic hardware such as a screen, keyboard and mouse, other peripherals can be attached to a computer. These include printers, scanners and devices such as DVD recorders for storing lots of information.

Speakers let you listen to music or speech on software, or downloaded from the internet.

This steering wheel and foot pedal attach to the computer and make computer driving games more realistic and exciting.

A scanner turns text and pictures into digital information which can be stored in the computer.

How a scanner works

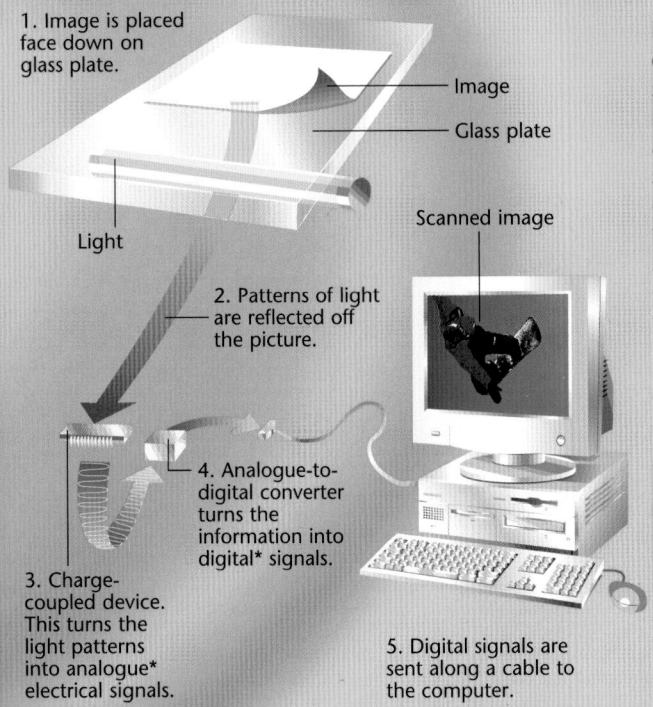

NETWORKS

Connecting computers to each other is called **networking**. It allows information to be shared easily. A network can consist of computers that are close to each other or thousands of miles apart.

The simplest LAN consists of just two computers in the same room.

A network consisting of computers that are close together, for example all in the same room, is called a **local-area network**, or **LAN**.

A network of computers that are far apart is called a wide-area network, or WAN.

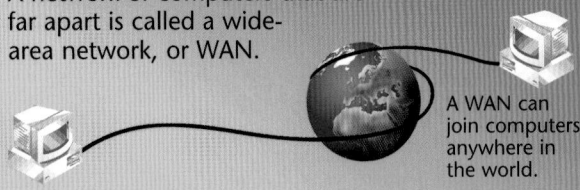

A WAN can join computers anywhere in the world.

TYPES OF NETWORK

The simplest kind of network is called **peer-to-peer**. This means that the network is not controlled by any one computer. Peer-to-peer networks are fairly easy to set up.

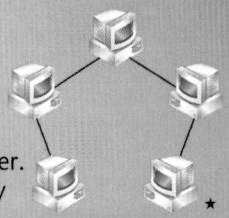

A peer-to-peer network setup

In **client/server** networks, one computer, called the **server**, has control of the network. Important programs and data are held on the server. Other computers (the **clients**) collect these from the server to work on. If the server is not working, the clients can't use the data, so the network doesn't function.

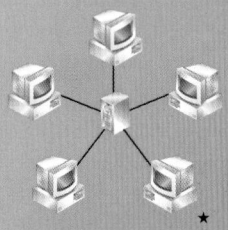

A client/server network setup

Client/server networks can process more information than peer-to-peer networks.

Internet links

Go to **www.usborne-quicklinks.com** and type in the keyword "science" to find out more about computers.

There you'll find links to websites where you can:

- Take a journey inside a computer
- Complete a computer quiz

** Analogue, Digital, 238.*

TELECOMS

Since the invention of the telephone in 1876, there have been continual improvements to telephone systems. Used with computers, there is now a whole range of ways that people can send and receive information. This branch of technology is called **telecommunications**, or **telecoms**.

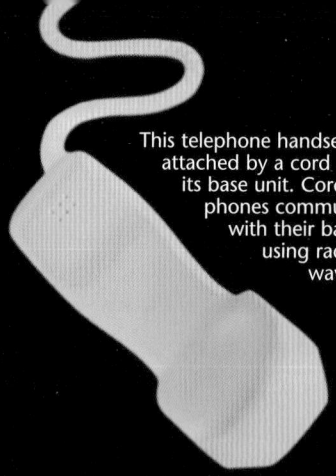

This telephone handset is attached by a cord to its base unit. Cordless phones communicate with their base unit using radio waves.

TELEPHONE LINES

Traditionally, telephone messages are carried by cables made of copper that are either buried underground or slung between poles.

Originally, these cables carried analogue* signals generated by the telephone. Many modern telephones send and receive digital information, which needs less power and takes up less room on the cable. As a result, more information can pass along the lines.

TELEPHONE SYSTEM

The **telephone system** consists of a complicated network of cables, switches and telephone exchanges.

If you make a long-distance call, your message may be bounced off a satellite in outer space, beamed between transmitter masts, or simply routed through huge lengths of cabling. Whichever route it takes, your call will reach its destination in a matter of seconds.

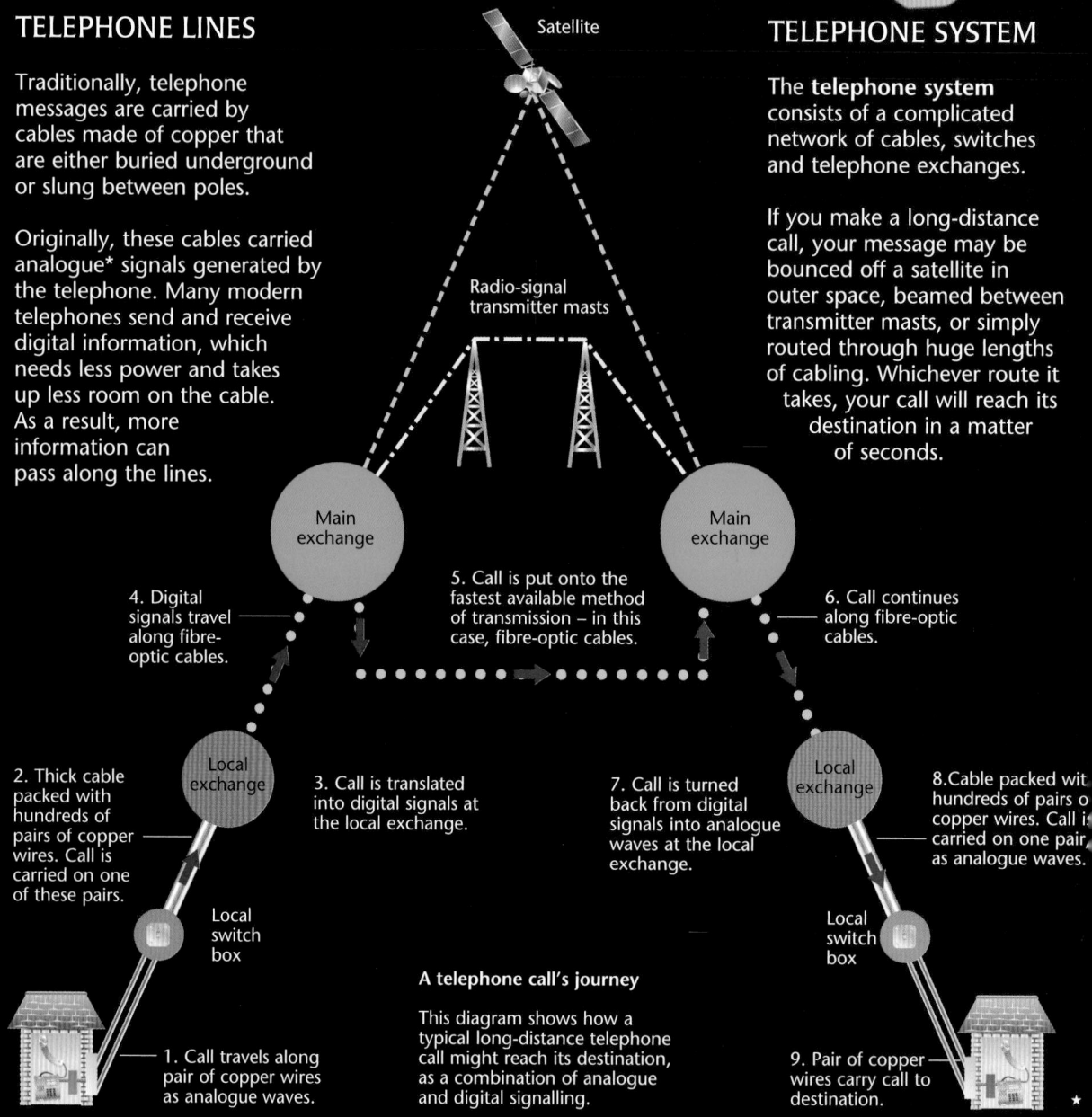

A telephone call's journey

This diagram shows how a typical long-distance telephone call might reach its destination, as a combination of analogue and digital signalling.

* *Analogue, 238.*

MODEMS

A **modem** allows a computer or fax to send and receive information along telephone lines. "Modem" stands for **mo**dulator-**dem**odulator.

The modem converts, or modulates, digital information produced by a computer or fax into analogue waves. The modem receiving the information demodulates (turns back) the waves into digital code which is understood by another computer or fax.

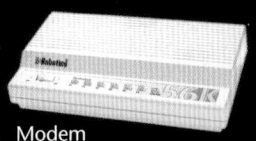

Modem

TRANSMISSION SPEED

The amount of information that can be sent by a modem is limited by the speed at which it can process information. **Data compression** can speed this up by cutting out any information that is not vital.

For example, music can be compressed using **mp3** software. This removes parts of sound that your ears can't detect. A stripped-down version is left, which is quicker to send.

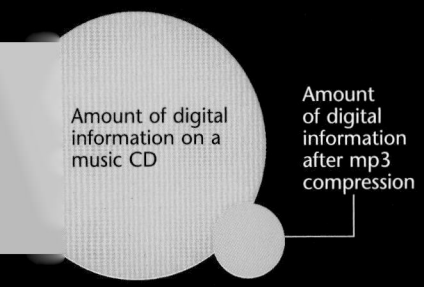

Mp3 software cuts out any very high or very low frequency soundwaves that are out of the range of sounds that you can hear. It also cuts out sounds that are masked by other sounds.

BANDWIDTH

The amount of information that can be processed each second by a telephone line is called its **bandwidth**. Copper cabling has a limited bandwidth. **Fibre-optic cables**, made of glass or plastic fibres, have a much greater bandwidth. However, they are expensive to install.

MOBILE PHONES

Mobile telephones do not make use of telephone lines. Instead, they send digital radio signals through the air to nearby transmitter masts, called **base stations**. These pass the signal on to the next station, and on and on, until they reach the phone that you are calling.

How a mobile phone works

1. You dial a number and press the call key.

2. Your phone chooses an available radio channel and sends a digital radio signal of the phone number to the nearest base station.

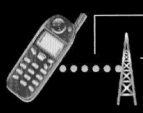

3. The base station sends the signal around the network of base stations, until it finds the phone you are calling.

4. The phone you are calling sends a message back via the base stations, saying whether it is available. Only now do you hear a ringing tone.

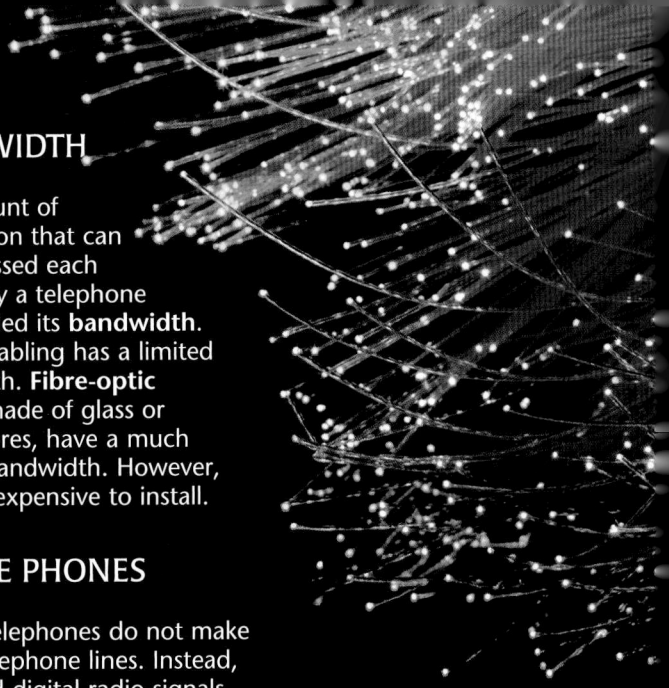

Here you can see light shining out of the ends of a bundle of fibre-optic cables. Fibre-optic cables carry digital information as pulses of light.

See for yourself

Try dialling a fax number from a telephone. When the fax answers your call, you will hear a high-pitched warbling sound. This is its internal modem sending a little message. The message is to establish whether a fax is calling it, and if so, to tell the other fax to start transmitting its information.

Internet links

To find out more about telecoms, go to **www.usborne-quicklinks.com** and type in the keyword "science".

There you'll find links to websites where you can:

- Play telecoms games
- Explore the history of the telephone
- Find out about telecom satellites

Go to Usborne Quicklinks for links to hand-picked websites on hundreds of subjects.

THE INTERNET

The **internet** is a vast computer network linking together millions of computers all over the world. It gives access to information put onto it by individuals, companies and organizations. The internet can also be used to exchange information, send messages and to buy things.

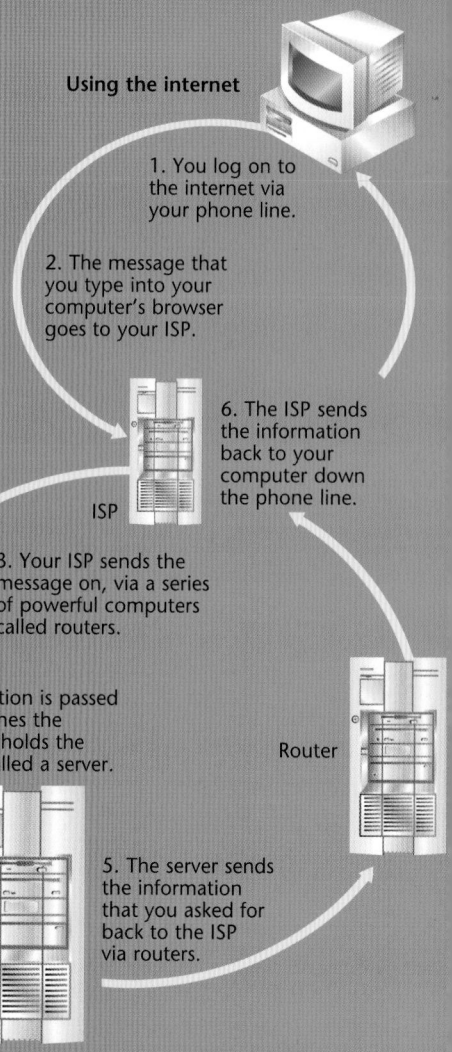

INTERNET BASICS

Most people connect, or **log on**, to the internet using software called a **browser**.

The basic structure of the internet is provided by telephone companies. Their phone lines carry the information that you send and receive when you use the internet.

Most home users use **internet service providers** (**ISPs**) to access the internet. When you are **online** (connected to the internet) messages go from your computer down the phone line to the ISP's powerful computers. The computers work like electronic post offices, automatically sorting and sending things on in a matter of seconds.

The World Wide Web is a huge network of websites that can be accessed from the internet.

WORLD WIDE WEB

The **World Wide Web** (**www**) is a huge information resource, arena for social networking, and place to conduct ecommerce (see opposite page). It consists of thousands of individual websites. Each site is made up of individual documents, called web pages.

HTML

Web pages are written using a computer language called **HyperText Markup Language** (**HTML**). If you are looking at a Web page, you can view the HTML code by clicking on the "View" button and then choosing "Source".

HYPERLINKS

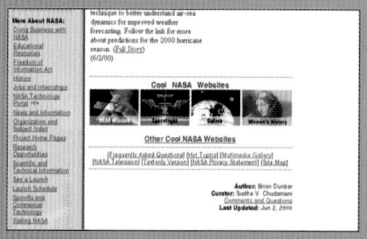

On web pages, some words or pictures are highlighted. Click on them and a new page with related information is shown, or **downloaded**. This is a **hyperlink**. These links enable you to jump really quickly from page to page all over the Web.

INTERNET NAMES

Each piece of information on the internet has an address, called a **URL** (**Uniform Resource Locator**). A URL enables you to call up the exact piece of information you want. It also defines the format (called the **protocol**) in which the messages are sent.

A URL

http://www.howstuffworks.com/web-server.htm

http:// This is the **protocol name**. "http" stands for **hypertext transfer protocol**.

www.howstuffworks.com/ is the **domain name**. This identifies the name of the site and the Web server it is held on.

web-server.htm is the **file path**. This is the name of the file in which the page is stored. The *.htm* part shows that the file is written in HTML code.

DOT COM

The final part of a domain name is called the top-level domain. Here are some examples and what they indicate:

- .com - commercial organization
- .edu - school or educational establishment
- .gov - government agency
- .org - non-profit organization (such as a charity)

Some domain names have an extra two letters to identify which country they are based in. For example:

- .es - Spain
- .th - Thailand
- .uk - United Kingdom

EMAIL

Email stands for **electronic mail**. It is a way of using your computer to send messages to other internet users. You write and read emails using specialist email software, such as Outlook Express®, made by Microsoft®.

Email is sent down the phone line to your ISP. It is sent on to the recipient's ISP via the internet, where it waits for delivery the next time the recipient logs on to the internet.

Email addresses have three parts. Here's a typical one:

joeschmo@slugpost.com

joeschmo is the name that the person has decided to use when sending and receiving emails.

@ stands for "at".

slugpost.com is the domain name. For home computer users, this is normally the name of your ISP.

ECOMMERCE

The internet can be used to buy and sell things. This is called **ecommerce**. Goods and services that are offered for sale on a website can be ordered directly by filling in an order form which appears on the web page.

Ecommerce enables people to shop for just about anything, at any time, and from anywhere. However, it means that you can't inspect the goods or try them out before you buy.

MOBILE INTERNET

There is a part of the internet that can be accessed by most mobile telephones. It displays web pages that are written in a different protocol and have few pictures.

These pages are designed to be simpler than regular internet pages because mobile phone lines can carry less digital information than a regular internet connection.

Most mobile phones can also be used to send emails.

See for yourself

To see just how quickly email zips from place to place, try sending yourself an email. Write your own address in the "To:" window and then click "Send". (You don't need to add a subject name, even if the email software asks for one.)

The email should come back from your ISP (which could be in another country) in seconds. However, it may take longer, depending on how busy the internet is at the time.

Internet links

To find out more about the internet, go to **www.usborne-quicklinks.com** and type in the keyword "science".

There you'll find links to websites where you can:

- Watch an animated introduction to the internet
- Find out how search engines work
- Quiz yourself on internet basics

Go to Usborne Quicklinks for links to hand-picked websites on hundreds of subjects.

PLANTS AND FUNGI

PLANT CELLS

Every living thing is made up of tiny structures called **cells**. A plant has a number of different types of cell, and each one plays an important part in keeping it alive, such as absorbing water and minerals or making food.

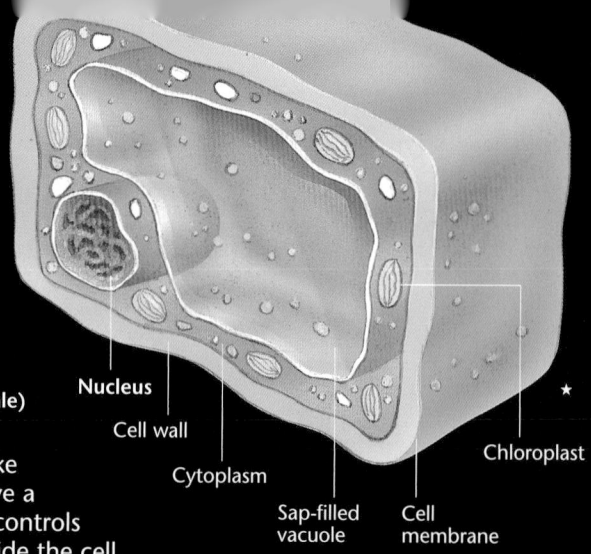

Typical plant cell (cutaway – not to scale)

CELL STRUCTURE

Plant cells have many features in common with animal cells*, but are generally larger. Plant cells also have a number of unique structures, most of which help the plant to make its own food.

Around each plant cell is a **cell wall**. This is made of a tough substance called **cellulose**, and helps the cell to keep its shape. Directly beneath the cell wall is a thin layer called the **cell membrane**. Animal cells also have a cell membrane, but they do not have a cell wall.

Vacuoles are fluid-filled sacs. Most plant cells have one large, permanent vacuole filled with a sugary liquid called **cell sap**, which is made up of water and dissolved substances.

* *Animal cells, 298-299.*

All plant cells, like animal cells, have a nucleus, which controls the activities inside the cell. The nucleus is surrounded by a gel-like fluid called **cytoplasm**, within which smaller structures, called **organelles**, are moved and arranged. These have different functions.

Chloroplasts, for example, are organelles which contain a green chemical called **chlorophyll**. These give plants their colour and help to make food.

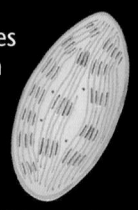

Chloroplast

Chromoplasts have a similar function. They give some flowers, and vegetables such as carrots, their particular colour.

See for yourself

You can use a microscope to look at plant cells. First, you need a slice of raw onion. Take one segment from the slice, and use tweezers to remove the thin membrane that covers it. Place the membrane on a glass microscope slide and look at it through a microscope, lighting it from beneath. You may be able to see the nucleus and the cell walls.

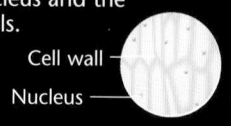

This is what leaf cells look like under a microscope. The dark spots inside the cells are the nuclei.

SPECIALIZED CELLS

Not all plant cells are exactly alike. Some have different shapes and structures, allowing them to do particular jobs. This is called **specialization**.

Palisade cells, for example, are found just beneath the upper surface of a leaf. They are column shaped, and contain a large number of chloroplasts.

Palisade cells

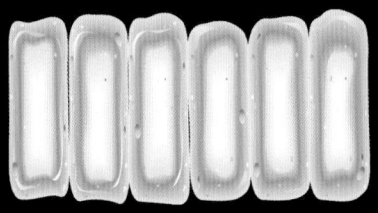

Spongy cells are found inside a leaf, beneath the layer of palisade cells. They have an irregular shape, which allows air spaces to form between them.

Spongy cells

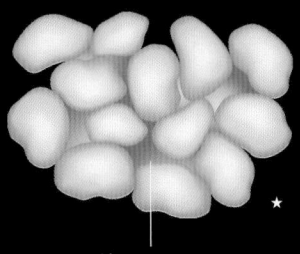

CELL DIVISION

Cells can divide to create new cells for growth or repair. Cell division happens in two stages. In the first stage, called **mitosis**, the nucleus divides into two parts, each becoming a new nucleus. Each of the two new nuclei, called **daughter nuclei**, are identical to the original.

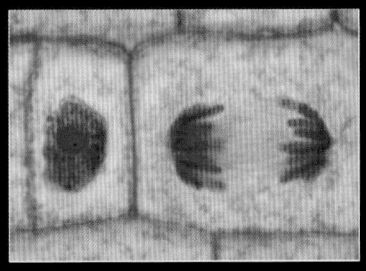

This microscope image shows the contents of a nucleus dividing in two.

In the second stage of cell division, called **cytokinesis**, a dividing line called the **cell plate** forms. This runs down the middle of the cytoplasm. New cell walls build up along the cell plate, to separate the two new cells.

Cytokinesis in a plant cell

Plant cell after mitosis has taken place

Cell plate forming

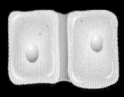

New cell wall forming

PLANT TISSUE

Cells of the same kind join together to form types of **tissue**. Most plants are made up of three types of tissue: dermal, ground and vascular.

Dermal tissue makes up the surface layer of most plants.

Dermal tissue

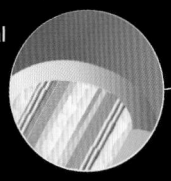

Ground tissue packs out most of the inside of younger plants.

Ground tissue

Vascular tissue is responsible for transporting food, water and other substances around the plant. For more about this, see page 254.

Vascular tissue

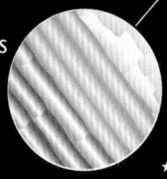

Internet links

To find out more about plant cells, go to **www.usborne-quicklinks.com** and type in the keyword "science".

There you'll find links to websites where you can:

- Watch an animated lesson on plant cells and try a quiz
- See plant cells under a virtual online microscope

Go to Usborne Quicklinks for links to hand-picked websites on hundreds of subjects.

STEMS AND ROOTS

A plant is mainly supported by its stem and roots. In most plants, these also play an important part in carrying fluids. The stem and roots are made up of various parts, which change as the plant gets older. You can find out more about these changes on pages 256-257.

STEM STRUCTURE

The **stem** is the major above-ground or **aerial** part of a plant. It supports the plant, usually growing upwards. Stems contain a system of **vascular tissue**, which carries water and minerals throughout the plant.

A **shoot** is a new stem which grows out of a seed or off the main stem of a plant. A **bud** is a small growth on a stem, which develops into either a new shoot or a flower. There are two different kinds of buds, called **terminal** and **axillary buds**. Axillary buds are also known as **lateral** or **secondary buds**.

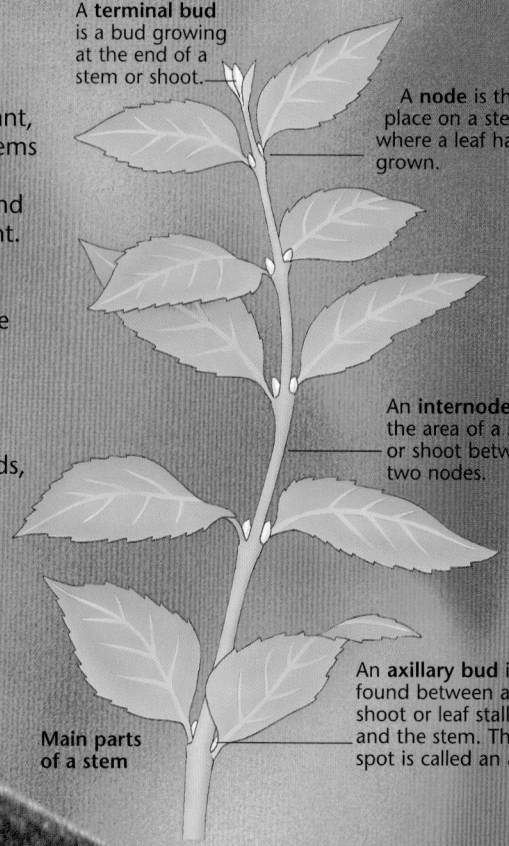

Main parts of a stem

This thick stem contains a system of tubes, which carry water and food through the plant.

GROWTH

A group of cells which divide to provide new growth is called a **meristem**. The main meristems are at the tip of the shoot and root. They are called **apical meristems**. A meristem formed in the main stem or a shoot is part of a terminal bud.

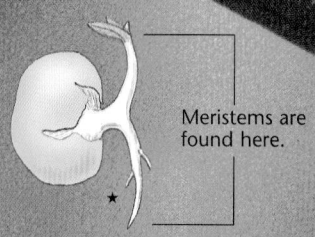

PARTS OF A ROOT

The **root** of a plant usually grows down into the ground. Its main purpose is to take in water and minerals from the soil. These are absorbed through tiny, tube-shaped cells called **root hairs**. The root also acts as an anchor, holding the plant firmly in the soil.

A root grows when cells just behind its tip divide. This area is called the **growing point**. The area of new cells produced is called the **zone of elongation**. The new cells have soft cell walls, which allow them to stretch lengthways as water is taken into the root.

As the new cells lengthen, they push the tip of the root further into the soil. A layer of cells called the **root cap** protects the root tip as it is pushed down into the ground.

Parts of a root

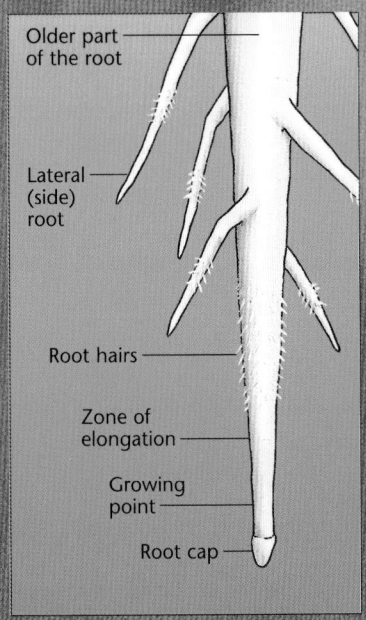

TYPES OF ROOTS

Roots can be many shapes and sizes, depending on the plant from which they grow. Some have particular tasks, such as allowing the plant to cling to other objects.

A **tap root**, or **primary root**, is a large root with smaller ones growing out of it. These small roots are called **lateral roots** or **secondary roots**. Many vegetables, such as carrots, are swollen tap roots and are known as **root vegetables**.

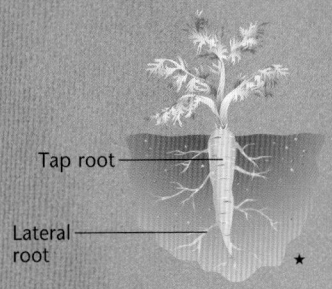

Fibrous roots are a system of many equal-sized roots, all of which produce smaller lateral roots.

Adventitious roots grow directly from a stem. They are produced from gardeners' cuttings, or grow out of a special kind of stem called a bulb*.

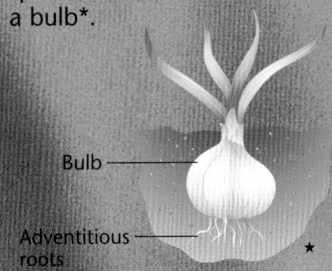

Aerial roots do not normally grow in the ground. Many can absorb moisture from the air. Some plants, such as ivy, also use them for climbing.

Aerial roots

Ivy

Prop roots are a particular kind of aerial root that grow outwards from a stem, then down into the ground. They support heavy plants, such as mangroves, which grow in ground which is often under water.

See for yourself

Look at a plant, and see how many parts of its stem you can identify. Notice what shapes and sizes they are. Be careful not to damage the plant.

Internet links

Go to **www.usborne-quicklinks.com** and type in "science" to find out more about stems and roots.

There you'll find links to websites where you can:

- Learn the parts of a plant, and test yourself with a plant parts game
- Investigate why soil is important for healthy plant growth

Go to Usborne Quicklinks for links to hand-picked websites on hundreds of subjects.

* Bulbs, 278

PLANT TISSUE

All plants, except for algae, mosses and liverworts, are known as **vascular plants**. This means that they contain a complex system of **vascular tissue**, which gives support and carries food and water through the plant.

TISSUE TYPES

Vascular tissue is made up of two main kinds of tissue, called xylem and phloem.

Water is carried up from the roots by **xylem**. In flowering plants, this is made up of short tubes called **vessels** and long, narrow tubes called **tracheids**. Long, thin cells called **fibres** help to provide support between them. Vessels are made up of column-shaped cells that have lost their dividing walls. Non-flowering plants have only tracheids.

Food made in the leaves dissolves in water and is carried to all parts of the plant by **phloem**. This is made up of fluid-carrying cells called **sieve tubes**. These have other cells packed around them for support.

Sieve tubes are arranged in long columns. They have cell walls*, and though they do not have a nucleus*, they are living cells with a thin layer of cytoplasm*. The end walls between the cells, called **sieve plates**, have tiny holes which allow liquids to pass through.

The first tissue formed by a new plant is called **primary tissue**. The xylem is **primary xylem** and the phloem is **primary phloem**.

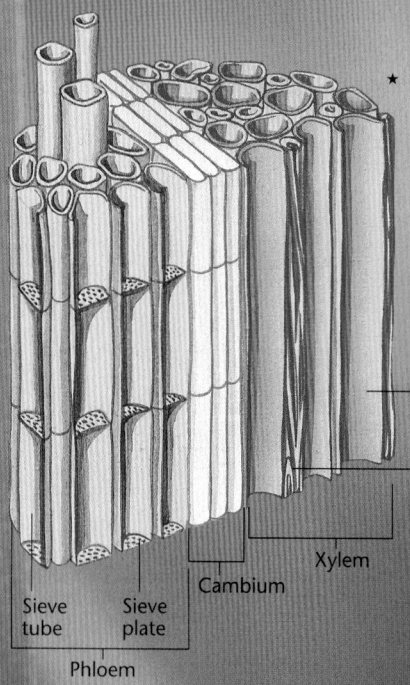

Section of vascular tissue in a flowering plant

Between the xylem and phloem is a layer of thin, narrow-walled cells called **cambium**. The cells in this layer are able to divide, making more xylem and phloem.

There is vascular tissue inside these tulip stems. It supports the plant and takes food and water around it.

** Cell wall, Cytoplasm, Nucleus, 250.*

INSIDE A STEM

In young stems, vascular tissue is usually arranged in groups called **vascular bundles**. These are surrounded by tissue called cortex. In plants known as dicotyledons*, the bundles are arranged in a regular pattern, as shown below.

Cross section of a young dicotyledon stem

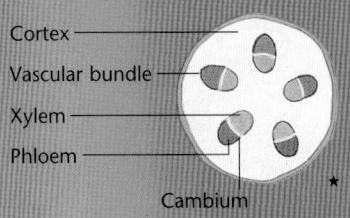

Cutaway of a young dicotyledon stem

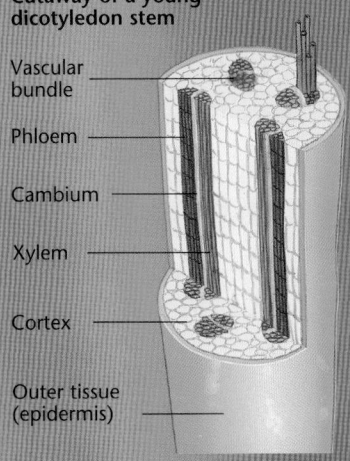

In older dicotyledon stems, the bundles join up to form a central core called the **vascular cylinder**. You can read more about vascular tissue in older plants on page 256.

In plants known as monocotyledons*, such as the tulip on the left, the vascular bundles are not arranged regularly in the stem.

INSIDE A ROOT

In a young root, the tissue is arranged in a different way from a stem. A central core forms as the plant gets older.

Cross section of a young dicotyledon root

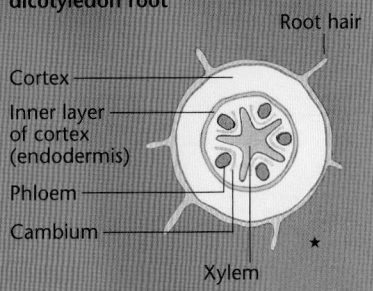

Cutaway of a young dicotyledon root

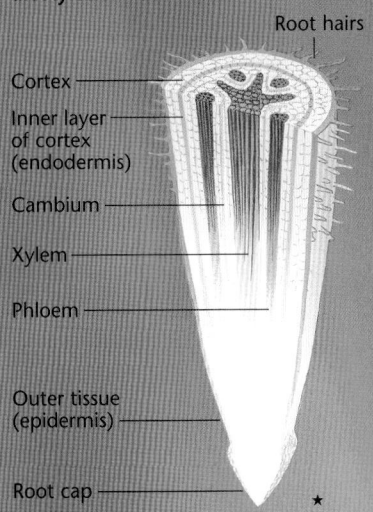

See for yourself

Try this experiment to see the xylem in a stick of celery. Fill a jar with about three centimetres of water, and add a few drops of ink or food colouring. Trim the end off a fresh celery stalk and stand it in the water. After a couple of hours, you can see the xylem as a pattern of coloured dots in the end of the stalk.

OTHER TISSUES

All parts of a young plant are surrounded by a thin layer of tissue called the **epidermis**. In older stems, the epidermis is replaced by bark. In older roots, it is replaced by a layer of hardened cells called the **exodermis**, then by bark. An outer tissue which encloses a plant, such as the epidermis, is known as **dermal tissue**.

The epidermis of stems and roots surrounds an area of **cortex**. In roots, this has an area called **endodermis** as its innermost layer. Cortex is made up mainly of **parenchyma**, a type of tissue with large cells and many air spaces. In some plants there is also some **collenchyma**, a type of supporting tissue with long, thick-walled cells. These are both types of ground tissue*.

The top layer of the epidermis is known as the **cuticle**. It is made of a waxy substance called **cutin**. The cuticle prevents a plant from losing or absorbing too much water.

Waxy cuticle gives these leaves their shiny appearance.

Internet links

To find out more about plant tissue, go to **www.usborne-quicklinks.com** and type in the keyword "science".

There you'll find links to websites where you can:

- Take a look at xylem and phloem under a microscope
- Try a plant tissues puzzle

Go to Usborne Quicklinks for links to hand-picked websites on hundreds of subjects.

** Dicotyledons, 295; Ground tissue, 251; Monocotyledons, 295.*

INSIDE OLDER PLANTS

Plants which live for many years, such as trees, form new tissue to support their original primary tissue. This process is known as **secondary thickening**. The new tissue is made up of more fluid-carrying tissue, formed towards the middle of the plant, and protective tissue, formed on the outside.

TISSUE GROWTH

The production of new tissue in young stems, called **secondary tissue**, happens in stages. The process is slightly different in roots, but the overall result is the same.

In a stem, secondary thickening starts when more cambium (growth tissue) forms between the vascular bundles*. This joins up to form a continuous cylinder of tissue.

The cambium starts to produce more xylem and phloem. These join up to form a **vascular cylinder**. Each year, new layers of xylem and phloem are produced.

Over time, the stem and roots thicken, and the plant becomes known as a **woody plant**. The new xylem is **secondary xylem**, and the new phloem is **secondary phloem**.

The core of vascular tissue, which is mostly xylem, gets bigger. By this stage, the xylem is also called **wood**. The phloem does not widen as much because the xylem pushes it outwards.

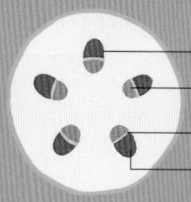

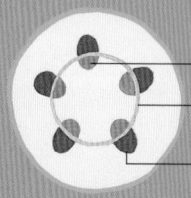

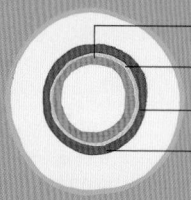

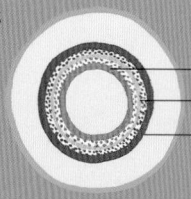

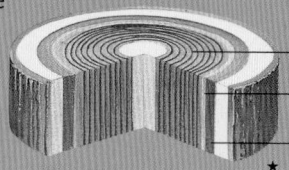

Giant sequoia trees may live for over 2,500 years. They develop lots of secondary tissue.

* *Vascular bundles, 255.*

TYPES OF WOOD

A single ring of xylem in a cross section of an older plant shows one year's growth and is called an **annual ring**. Each ring has two separate areas – **spring wood** and **summer wood**.

Soft spring wood (also called **early wood**) forms rapidly early in the growing season. It has large cells. Harder summer wood, or **late wood**, is produced later on. Its cells are smaller and more closely packed together.

Annual rings in a tree stump

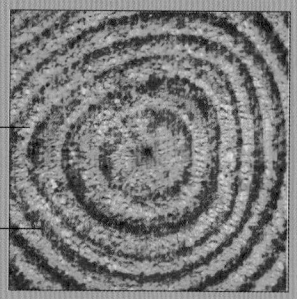

After a number of years, the annual rings themselves can also be divided into two separate areas. The area nearest the middle, where the rings are older, is called **heartwood**. Its vessels* have become solid and can no longer transport fluids, but they still provide the plant with support.

The outer area of rings is called **sapwood**. Its vessels are still able to carry fluid. Sapwood also helps to support the tree.

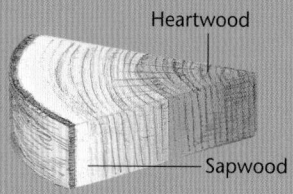

See for yourself

You can count the rings in a tree stump to discover the tree's age. For example, fifty rings show that the tree was fifty years old when it was cut down.

* *Vessels, 254.*

OUTER TISSUE

As well as new vascular tissue, an older plant also forms extra layers of protective tissue around its outside. These develop from a single layer of constantly dividing cells called **phellogen** or **cork cambium**.

As each new outer layer formed by the phellogen is pushed further out by new layers on its inside, it dies away to become waterproof **bark**. This contains tiny raised openings called **lenticels**, through which oxygen and carbon dioxide are exchanged. As a tree gets older, the layers of bark build up, making the trunk thicker and stronger.

Structure of bark in a mature tree

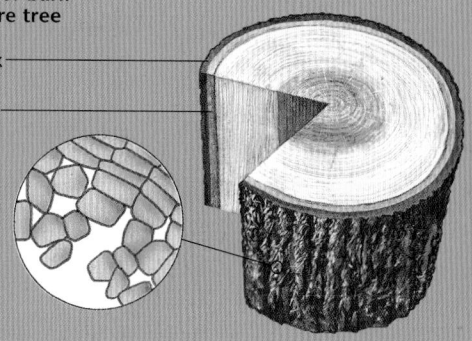

Bark stops the tree from drying out and helps to protect it from disease. It cannot grow or stretch, so it splits or peels as the trunk gets wider, and new layers of bark develop underneath.

Some types of bark

Silver birches have tough, papery bark.

English oak bark develops deep cracks.

Scots pine bark flakes off in small pieces.

Beech trees have very thin bark.

Internet links

Go to **www.usborne-quicklinks.com** and type in the keyword "science" to find out more about older plants.

There you'll find links to websites where you can:

- Find out how to read tree rings, then try a tree ring activity
- Discover more about roots, bark, twigs and leaves

LEAVES

The **leaves** of a green plant are its main food-making parts. They make food by a process called **photosynthesis**. A plant's leaves are collectively called its **foliage**. There are many different sizes and shapes of leaves, but only two main types: simple and compound leaves.

SIMPLE LEAVES

Simple leaves are made up of a single leaf blade, called a **lamina**. Lilies, elms and maples are examples of plants with simple leaves.

This fern's pinnate leaves have pinnate leaflets.

COMPOUND LEAVES

Compound leaves are made up of small leaf blades called **leaflets**, which grow from a central leaf stalk. Clovers and ferns are examples of plants with compound leaves. The number and arrangement of leaflets on a compound leaf vary from plant to plant.

Palmate leaves have five or more leaflets growing from a single point.

Trifoliate leaves have three leaflets growing from a single point.

Ternate leaves are a type of trifoliate leaf. Each leaflet is made up of three lobes.

In **pinnate leaves** the leaflets, called **pinnae**, are arranged in opposite pairs along the stalk.

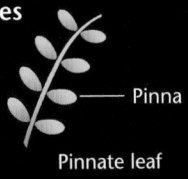

A **bipinnate** or **tripinnate leaf** is a pinnate leaf with pinnate leaflets.

LEAF ARRANGEMENTS

Leaves can be arranged on a stem in several ways. **Opposite leaves**, for example, are leaf pairs whose members grow from opposite sides of the stem. **Decussate leaves** are opposite leaves in which each pair is at right angles to the one before.

This box has opposite leaves.

This purple loosestrife has decussate leaves.

Perfoliate leaves are single or paired leaves. The bases of the leaves surround the stem.

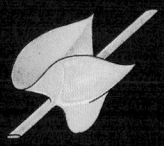

The leaves of this yellow-wort are perfoliate.

A **rosette** or **whorl** describes a circle of leaves which grow from one point. An example of this is a **basal rosette**, which grows at the base of a stem.

A primrose has leaves which form a basal rosette.

Alternate leaves grow individually from the stem, rather than in groups or pairs. **Spiral leaves** are alternate leaves which grow out from separate points that form a spiral around the stem.

This orpine has spiral leaves.

SPECIALIZED LEAVES

Some leaves are adapted to do particular jobs. They are usually found on plants that grow in a particular place or climate.

A **bract** is a leaf at the base of a flower stalk. It often protects buds.

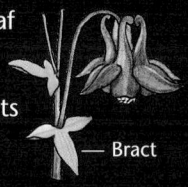

A pair of **stipules** grow at the base of a leaf stalk. They protect a bud as it forms.

A **tendril** is a special thread-like leaf or stem, which either twines around or sticks to a support.

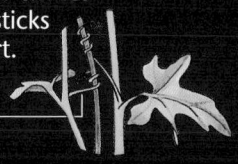

A **spine** is a modified leaf, which is thin and sharp. It has a much smaller surface area than most leaves, which prevents it from losing too much water.

This barrel cactus has many thin spines.

LEAF MARGINS

The edge of a leaf is known as the **leaf margin**. Some margins have a special shape, to help the plant's survival. For example, a leaf with a wavy margin allows more light to reach the leaves beneath. Some common leaf margins are described below.

An **entire** leaf margin has no indentation of any kind.

Lilac

A **serrate** leaf margin has tiny jagged teeth.

Lime

A **lobed** leaf margin forms sections, called **lobes**. It may also be serrate.

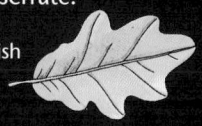

English oak

See for yourself

Collect some fresh leaves that have recently fallen from trees or other plants, and compare their shapes and arrangements. To preserve leaves, you can flatten them between sheets of tissue or blotting paper under some heavy books. Leave them for two weeks to dry out.

Internet links

To find out more about leaves, go to **www.usborne-quicklinks.com** and type in the keyword "science".

There you'll find links to websites where you can:

- Follow an animated guide to leaves and try a leaves quiz

LEAF STRUCTURE

Leaves are specially adapted to allow food production to take place. For example, most leaves have a broad, flat surface to collect sunlight, which is vital for making food. They also have areas which let out the waste substances created in the process.

INSIDE A LEAF

A leaf contains long strips of vascular tissue* called **veins**. These supply the leaf with water and minerals, and move the food made inside the leaf to other parts of the plant.

Some leaves, such as grasses, have long, parallel veins, but most contain one central vein called the **midrib**. This is an extension of the leaf stalk. The midrib branches into a number of smaller veins, called **side veins**. A leaf's whole vein system is called its **venation**.

Arrangement of leaf veins

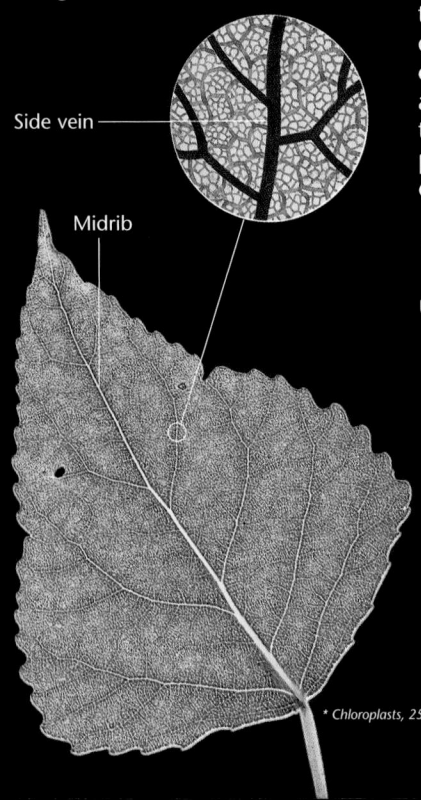

LEAF CELLS

A leaf is made up of layers of different types of cells. The **epidermis** is a layer of flat, waxy cells on the surface of the leaf. It prevents too much water from being gained or lost.

The **palisade layer** lies just beneath the epidermis, on the leaf's upper side. It is made up of column-shaped **palisade cells**, which contain many tiny green chloroplasts*. The contents of palisade cells are packed closely together, which helps them to absorb sunlight (see page 264).

Under the palisade layer is the **spongy layer**, made up of irregularly shaped **spongy cells** and air spaces. The spaces allow air to move around inside the leaf. The spongy layer and palisade layer together are called the **mesophyll**.

Cross section of a leaf

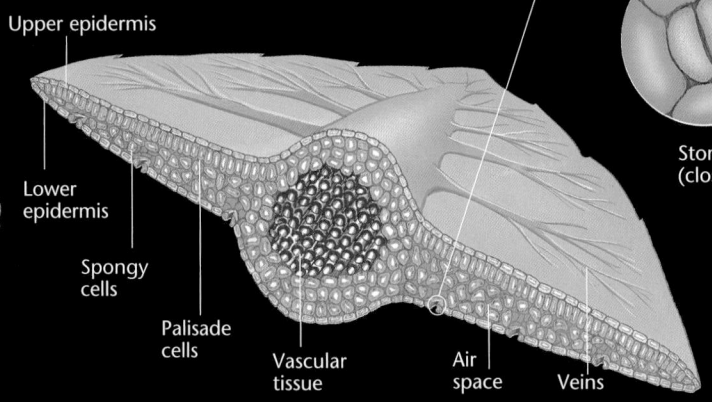

SURFACE OF A LEAF

On the underside of a leaf are tiny holes called **stomata**, each one called a **stoma**. These allow water and air to move in and out of the leaf.

On either side of each stoma is a crescent-shaped **guard cell**. These paired cells can change their shape to open and close the stoma, controlling how much air and water enters and leaves the leaf.

Close-up of stoma (cut in half)

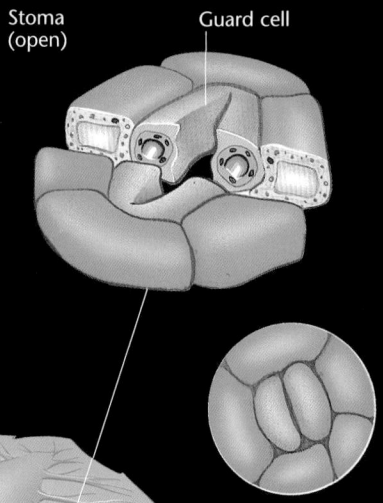

* *Chloroplasts, 250, 264; Vascular tissue, 254.*

When leaves are dying, their green chlorophyll breaks down to reveal other colours.

EAF STALKS

leaf stalk or **petiole** is a thin ructure which joins the main ody of a leaf to the stem. It ontains the **leaf trace**. This is n area of vascular tissue which anches off the vascular tissue a stem and becomes e leaf's central ein. This vein lows minerals be carried to the leaf.

efore a leaf dies, a layer of ells called an **abscission layer** rms at the base of its stalk. The oscission layer separates the leaf om the rest of the plant. The af then falls off, creating a **af scar** on the stem.

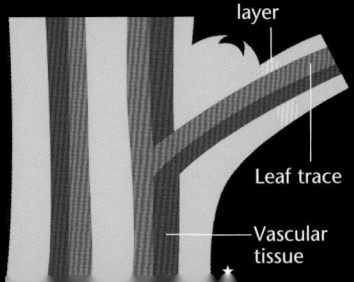

COLOUR IN LEAVES

Leaves get their colour from chemicals called **pigments**. Most leaves are green because they contain a green pigment called chlorophyll. **Variegated leaves** are patterned because they only have pigments in certain places on their surface.

Other pigments include **xanthophylls**, which produce yellow shades, and **carotene**, which makes leaves look red or orange. These pigments are present in many plants, but are usually masked by chlorophyll. After summer has ended, the chlorophyll in most plants breaks down, revealing the other pigments.

See for yourself

Collect leaves that have fallen from different trees and compare their colours. See if you can find a plant with variegated leaves, or one whose leaves are a colour other than green all year round. These contain pigments in addition to green chlorophyll.

Internet links

To find out more about leaf structure, go to **www.usborne-quicklinks.com** and type in the keyword "science".

There you'll find links to websites where you can:

- Discover more about why leaves change colour
- See microscope photos of leaves

Go to Usborne Quicklinks for links to hand-picked websites on hundreds of subjects.

MOVEMENT OF FLUIDS

Fluids, such as water, need to reach all the parts of a plant for its cells to stay healthy. A plant's fluids are carried by its **vascular tissue**, made up of xylem and phloem. The **xylem** carries water from the roots to the leaves, and the **phloem** carries dissolved foods from the leaves to all other areas. The movement of fluids inside a plant is called **translocation**.

WATER MOVEMENT

Water is taken into a plant by its roots, and travels up in the xylem, through the stem to the leaves. There, some of it escapes as vapour through tiny holes called **stomata** on the underside of the leaves. This type of water loss is called **transpiration**.

As the outer leaf cells lose water by transpiration, the concentration of minerals and sugars inside them increases. So water from the cells further in passes into the outer cells, to replace the water that has been lost.

The inner cells in turn take water from cells further down, and so on. Water is "pulled" up through the plant from the roots, which take in more from the soil. This upward movement of water is called a **transpiration stream**.

At certain times, such as at night or on a damp, humid day, the rate of transpiration slows down. However, water from the soil continues to enter the roots. This is because it still has a weak attraction to the xylem walls, which drags it upwards. This is called **capillary action**.

As water is taken into the roots, **root pressure** begins to build up. This is strong enough to push the water up the stem and into the stream.

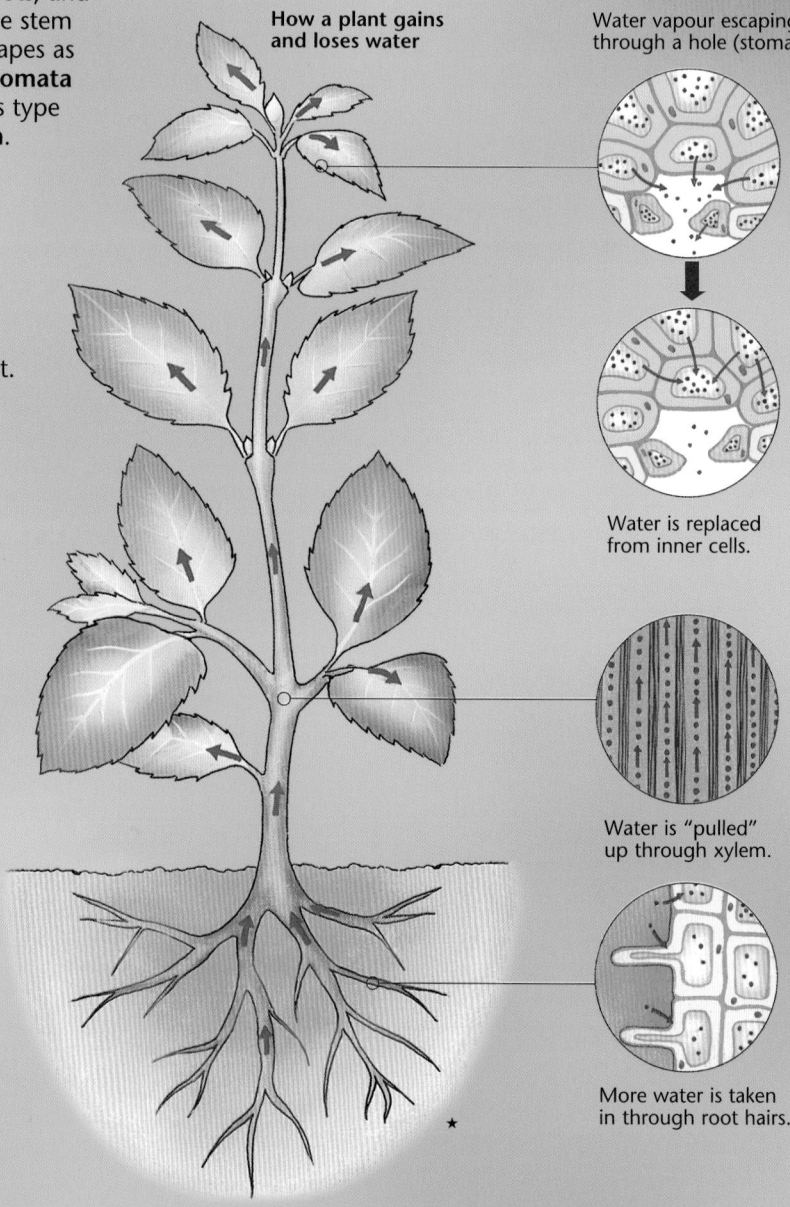

Here you can see water droplets oozing out of tiny holes around the leaf's edge.

LOSING LIQUID

If a plant does not lose enough water vapour by transpiration, and root pressure is still pushing water up the stem, the plant may also lose water in liquid form. Droplets are forced out of the plant through tiny holes at the tips or along the edges of leaves. This type of water loss is called **guttation**.

STANDING FIRM

Healthy plants usually stand firm and upright. This is because their vacuoles are full of cell sap, and push outwards against the cytoplasm and cell walls. Each cell is described as **turgid**, and the plant is in a state of **turgor**.

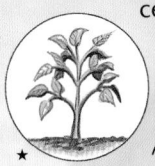

A healthy plant

WILTING

In hot or dry conditions, a plant may lose more water than it can take in. The pressure of water in its vacuoles drops to become less than that of the cell walls. This makes the cells limp. They cannot support the plant, so it droops. This state is known as **wilting**.

A wilting plant

In extreme cases, a plant may lose too much water through its leaves, and also through its roots into very dry or mineral-rich soil. Its cell vacuoles then shrink so much that the cytoplasm is pulled away from the cell walls. This state, called **plasmolysis**, may kill the plant unless it receives more water quickly.

A dying plant

Root cells of a healthy plant

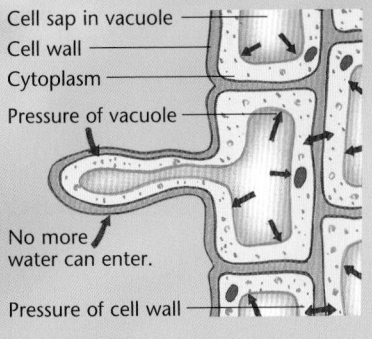

Root cells of a wilting plant

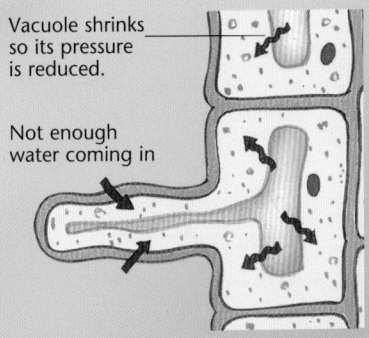

Root cells of a dying plant

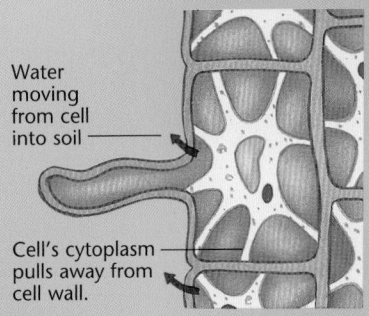

See for yourself

Water containing blue ink

To see how fluids move inside a plant, put some white flowers, such as carnations, into water containing blue ink. After a few days, their petals will have turned blue. This is because the inky water has been transported around the plants.

The lighter flowers in this picture have been in the dye for one day. The darker flowers have been in the dye for three days.

Internet links

Go to **www.usborne-quicklinks.com** and type in "science" to find out more about movement of fluids.

There you'll find links to websites where you can:

- Watch an animated online lesson about how plants transport fluids
- Review the structure of plants

PLANT FOOD

Unlike animals, most plants can make the food that they need. These plants are described as **autotrophic**. The process by which they make food is called **photosynthesis**. A small number of plants do not photosynthesize, but feed on living things. You can find out more about these over the page.

PHOTOSYNTHESIS

Photosynthesis uses water, sunlight, and carbon dioxide from the air. It takes place mainly in a plant's leaves, in the long, column-shaped **palisade cells**.

Palisade cells contain tiny structures called **chloroplasts**. These can move around inside the cell, according to how bright the light is and which direction it is coming from. Chloroplasts contain a green chemical called **chlorophyll** which absorbs the Sun's light energy. This is used to power photosynthesis.

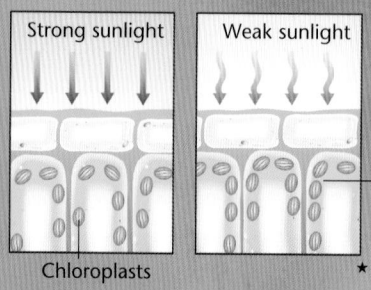

All green plants can make their own food, using sunlight.

Chloroplasts cluster together

The pictures above show how chloroplasts change position to make the best use of available light.

Carbon dioxide from the air is taken in through the surface of the leaves, and the roots take in water from the soil. The carbon dioxide and water are combined using energy taken in from sunlight by chloroplasts. This process produces chemicals called **carbohydrates** (the plant's food), and also oxygen.

Most of the food is used to produce energy for growth. The food that is not needed straight away is stored in the cells as a substance called **starch**.

The process of photosynthesis can be expressed in a word equation like this:

Carbon dioxide + Water + Energy (sunlight)

↓

Carbohydrates + Oxygen

Section of a leaf

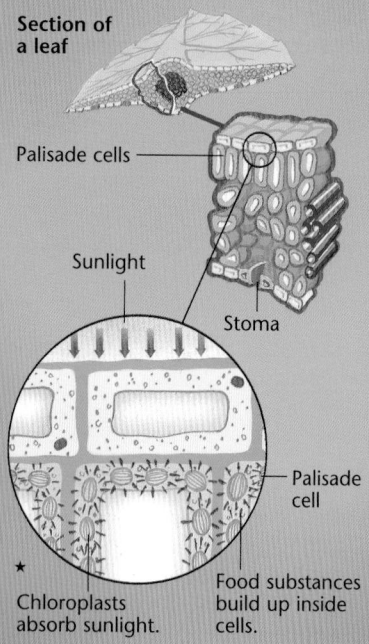

Photosynthesis in a green plant

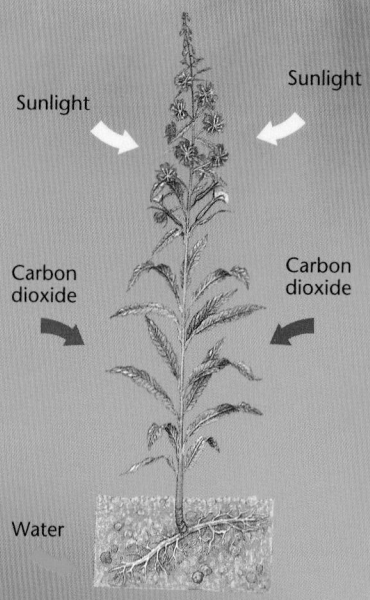

Nitrates and other minerals taken in by the roots are used to build new tissue.

INTERNAL RESPIRATION

Plants get energy from their food in a process called **internal respiration**. In most plants, carbohydrates are combined with oxygen to release energy, carbon dioxide and water.

The process of internal respiration can be expressed in a word equation like this:

Carbohydrates + Oxygen

↓

Carbon dioxide + Water + Energy

WORKING TOGETHER

The processes of photosynthesis and internal respiration are closely linked. Photosynthesis produces oxygen and carbohydrates, which are both needed for respiration. Respiration produces carbon dioxide and water, which are needed for photosynthesis.

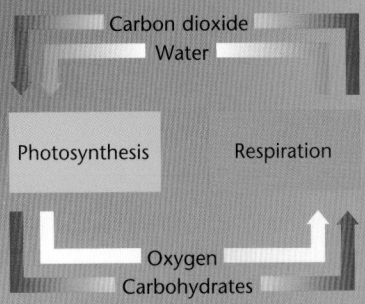

At most times of the day, one of the processes happens at a faster rate than the other. For example, in bright sunshine, photosynthesis happens faster. The plant produces more oxygen and carbohydrates than it can use for respiration. The unused oxygen is given off into the air and the carbohydrates are stored in the plant as starch.

COMPENSATION POINTS

At two points in a 24 hour period, normally at dusk and dawn, the processes of photosynthesis and respiration are exactly balanced. This means that photosynthesis produces just the right amounts of carbohydrates and oxygen for respiration, which produces the right amounts of carbon dioxide and water for photosynthesis. These times are called **compensation points**.

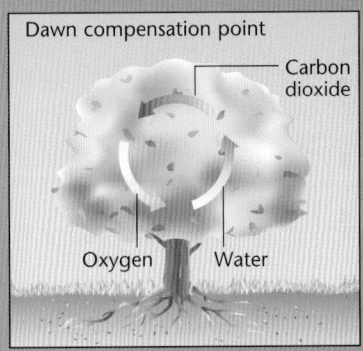

1. At dawn, rates of photosynthesis and respiration are equal.

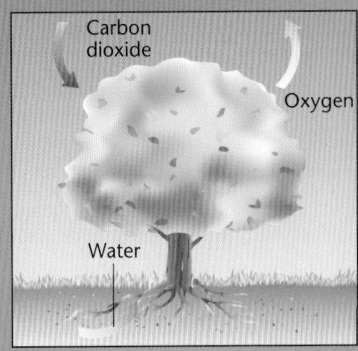

2. During the day the light is bright, so photosynthesis is faster.

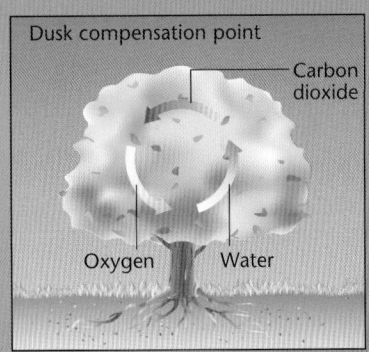

3. At dusk, rates of photosynthesis and respiration are equal.

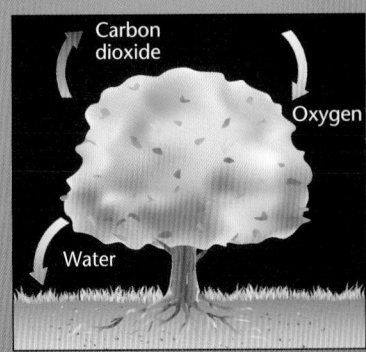

4. At night there is no sunlight, so no photosynthesis takes place.

See for yourself

You can do a simple test to show that sunlight is needed for photosynthesis. Take a houseplant with broad, light-green leaves and fold a piece of paper around one leaf. Secure it with a paper clip. Leave the plant in a sunny place for a few days, then remove the paper. The leaf will have a yellow strip, where it has been unable to photosynthesize.

Internet links

To find out more about plant food, go to **www.usborne-quicklinks.com** and type in the keyword "science".

There you'll find links to websites where you can:

- Take part in an interactive lesson on photosynthesis
- Find out why plants are important for life on Earth

Go to Usborne Quicklinks for links to hand-picked websites on hundreds of subjects.

PARASITES

A small number of plants are **parasites**. This means that they do not make their own food, but live and feed on other living things, called **hosts**. Some parasitic plants attack many different types of plants, and can be harmful to their host.

The dodder plant, for example, attaches itself firmly to its host plant by sinking thread-like structures called **haustoria** into it. Dodder stems then grow rapidly all over the host, which becomes completely covered and eventually dies.

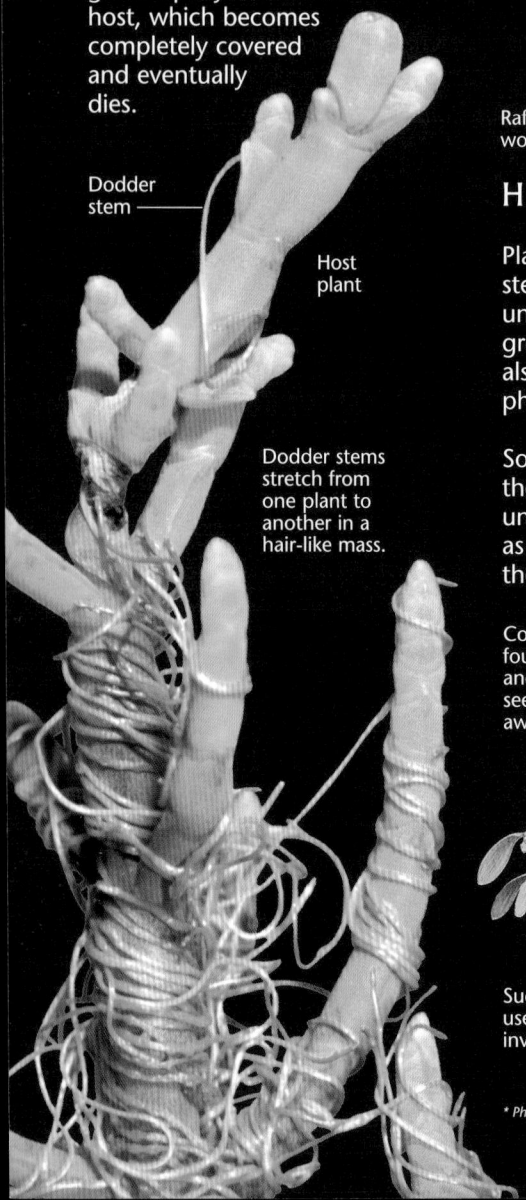

Some parasites can only live on one host. A rafflesia plant, for example, can only grow on a particular type of vine. The rafflesia lives in its host's roots as a mass of tangled threads, causing it little harm.

When conditions are right, the rafflesia produces a huge, foul-smelling flower, which attracts the flies needed to spread its pollen.

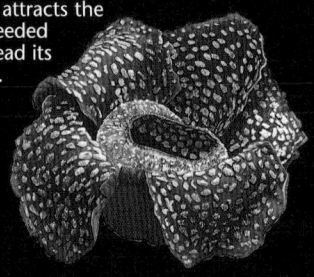

Rafflesia flowers are the largest in the world. They can weigh up to 7kg.

HEMIPARASITES

Plants called **hemiparasites** steal water and minerals but, unlike true parasites, they have green leaves and can therefore also make their own food by photosynthesis*.

Some hemiparasites attach themselves to their host's roots underground. Others, such as common mistletoe, attack them above ground.

Common mistletoe is a hemiparasite found on trees. It grows on branches, and spreads by producing sticky, seed-filled berries that are carried away by birds.

** Photosynthesis, 264.*

SAPROTROPHS

Some organisms feed on dead matter instead of living on a host or making their own food. They are known as **saprotrophic plants** or **saprotrophs**. The main body of most saprotrophs is found underground. Fungi and some orchids are saprotrophic.

The main part of a fungus is a mass of threads. These grow and feed under the ground, where it is dark and damp.

EPIPHYTES

Plants called **epiphytes** make their own food, but grow high up on other plants to catch water and get a better share of the light. Most epiphytes do not harm their host, although some, such as strangler figs, kill their host when they are fully grown.

Development of a strangler fig

Small fig plant starts to grow on a branch. It sends roots down the tree.

Roots start to take water and nutrients from the soil, and fig plant grows rapidly.

Fig plant takes all of host's light, water and nutrients. Host dies and rots away.

MEAT EATERS

Some plants, called **carnivorous plants**, can kill and digest small creatures, such as insects. Carnivorous plants lure their victims into deadly traps using particular smells or colours. Once inside, the insect is dissolved by powerful chemicals called **enzymes**.

Plants that feed in this way usually grow in soil which contains few minerals. They absorb what they need from the bodies of their prey by digesting them.

Pitcher plants, for example, catch animals in their jug-like leaves, called **pitchers**. Insects come to eat sweet nectar, which is made around the rim of the pitcher and under its lid. The insects fall down the pitcher's slippery walls, and die in a pool of liquid.

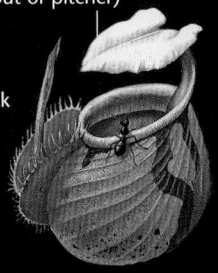

Sundews are carnivorous plants. Their leaves have hairs with sticky, gleaming drops at the end. These attract insects, which become trapped. As the insect struggles, the hairs start to curl over, wrapping up their prey tightly. The insect's body is then dissolved into a liquid and digested.

Fly trapped on a sundew leaf

The carnivorous Venus flytrap has pairs of leaves which snap shut like jaws to trap insects or other small animals. The leaves close when sensitive hairs on their surface are disturbed. Once trapped, the prey is slowly dissolved and digested by the plant.

This Venus flytrap will snap shut when the fly lands.

Internet links

To find out more about plant food, go to **www.usborne-quicklinks.com** and type in the keyword "science".

There you'll find links to websites where you can:

- Find lots of interesting information on carnivorous plants
- Watch a video clip of a Venus flytrap plant catching an insect

Go to Usborne Quicklinks for links to hand-picked websites on hundreds of subjects.

PLANT SENSITIVITY

All living things can react to changes in their environment. This is known as **sensitivity**, or responding to a **stimulus**. Unlike animals, plants do not have a specialized nervous system, but they are still able to react slowly to stimuli such as light, touch and temperature.

Vines have thread-like tendrils which are sensitive to touch. This lets them twine around a support.

PLANT RESPONSE

Most plants respond to a stimulus by growing towards or away from it. This response is called a **tropism**. Growing towards a stimulus is known as a **positive tropism**, and growing away from it is known as a **negative tropism**.

RESPONDING TO LIGHT

Almost all plants react to the amount of light available and the direction from which it is coming. This response is called **phototropism**. For instance, the leaves of most plants turn to face the Sun. This helps them to absorb as much light as possible for photosynthesis*.

Tropisms are controlled by **auxins**. These are growth hormones (chemicals) made in the plant's cells. Plant stems contain an auxin which collects in cells furthest from the light, causing these areas to grow more quickly. This makes the plant grow towards the light.

Plant growing towards light

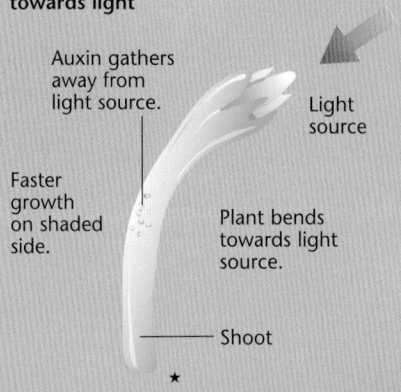

GRAVITY AND WATER

All roots respond to the pull of gravity. This is **geotropism**. The roots grow down into the soil to obtain water and minerals. Some roots also show a response to water, called **hydrotropism**. They may grow out sideways if more water lies in that direction.

Plant responding to gravity

The tips of roots and shoots produce growth hormones (auxins) which respond to gravity in different ways.

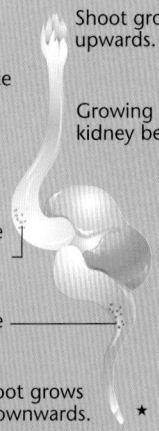

The sunflowers below respond to light by turning to face the Sun.

* Photosynthesis, 264.

RESPONDING TO TOUCH

Some plants are sensitive to touch. This response, which is known as **haptotropism** or **thigmotropism**, can help a plant in different ways. For example, meat-eating plants trap their food when it touches sensitive parts on their surface (see page 267).

Being able to respond to touch is also important to climbing plants, such as vines. When their thread-like tendrils touch something, it triggers a climbing and twining response.

This sweet pea's touch-sensitive tendrils help it to climb.

In some plants, touch causes a reaction which acts as a defence. For instance, the leaves of a mimosa (nicknamed the "sensitive plant") instantly close and droop when touched. This is because touch causes the pressure of water in its leaf cells to drop.

The leaves of this mimosa close up like fans when they are touched.

DAY AND NIGHT

Many plants will only grow during periods when light is available for a certain length of time. These periods are called **photoperiods**, and the plant's response is **photoperiodism**.

Long-night plants, such as chrysanthemums, only produce flowers at times of the year when the night is longer than a certain length, called its **critical length**. (These plants are also known as short-day plants.)

Short-night plants, such as larkspur, only produce flowers if the night is shorter than the critical length. (These plants are also known as long-day plants.)

It is thought that there is a growth hormone called **florigen** produced in the leaves, which makes a plant behave like this. When the correct amount of light is available, the florigen sends a "message" telling the plant to produce flowers.

Some plants, such as snapdragons, are described as **night-neutral** or **day-neutral**. Their flowering does not depend on the night's length.

Photoperiodism may be affected by the age of the plant, or the temperature of its surroundings.

Chrysanthemums flower when the nights are long.

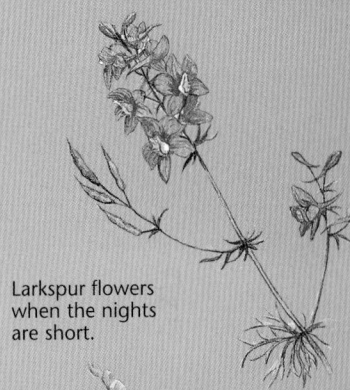

Larkspur flowers when the nights are short.

A snapdragon flowers whether the nights are long or short.

See for yourself

Leave a potted plant in a room with one window. Place it a little way from the window and water it as usual. After a few days, you will see that the plant's leaves are leaning towards the window. If you turn the plant around, after a few more days the same thing will have happened. This is because leaves always grow towards the nearest source of light.

Internet links

Go to **www.usborne-quicklinks.com** and type in "science" to find out more about plant sensitivity.

There you'll find links to websites where you can:

- Watch film clips of plants growing
- Discover more about plant growth
- Find out more with online activities

Go to Usborne Quicklinks for links to hand-picked websites on hundreds of subjects.

FLOWERING PLANTS

There are over 250,000 kinds of flowering plants, including grasses, wild flowers, shrubs and trees. Plants which produce flowers are known as **magnoliophytes**. Flowering plants have certain features in common. For example, they all produce seeds and contain tissue which transports fluid around the plant.

FLOWERS

Reproduction is the creation of new life. Flowers contain the parts of plants needed for reproduction. These produce male and female sex cells, called **gametes**, which join together to create new plants of the same kind. This type of reproduction is called **sexual reproduction**.

Flowers are made up of many specialized parts. These include petals, stamens (the male parts), and one or more carpels (the female parts). In most plants, the petals are arranged in a circle, around the male and female parts.

Just before a plant blooms, it produces a **bud**, which will eventually develop into a flower. It grows from the expanded tip of a stalk, called the **receptacle**. Buds are surrounded and protected by small, leaf-like **sepals**.

In some plants, such as buttercups, the sepals remain as a ring around the flower after the bud has opened. In others, such as poppies, they wither and fall off.

Petals are delicate, often brightly coloured, and surround the plant's reproductive parts. Many petals are scented or patterned and have areas of cells called **nectaries** at their base. These produce a sweet, sticky liquid called **nectar**, which attracts insects or other animals needed for pollination*.

Nectary at base of a buttercup petal

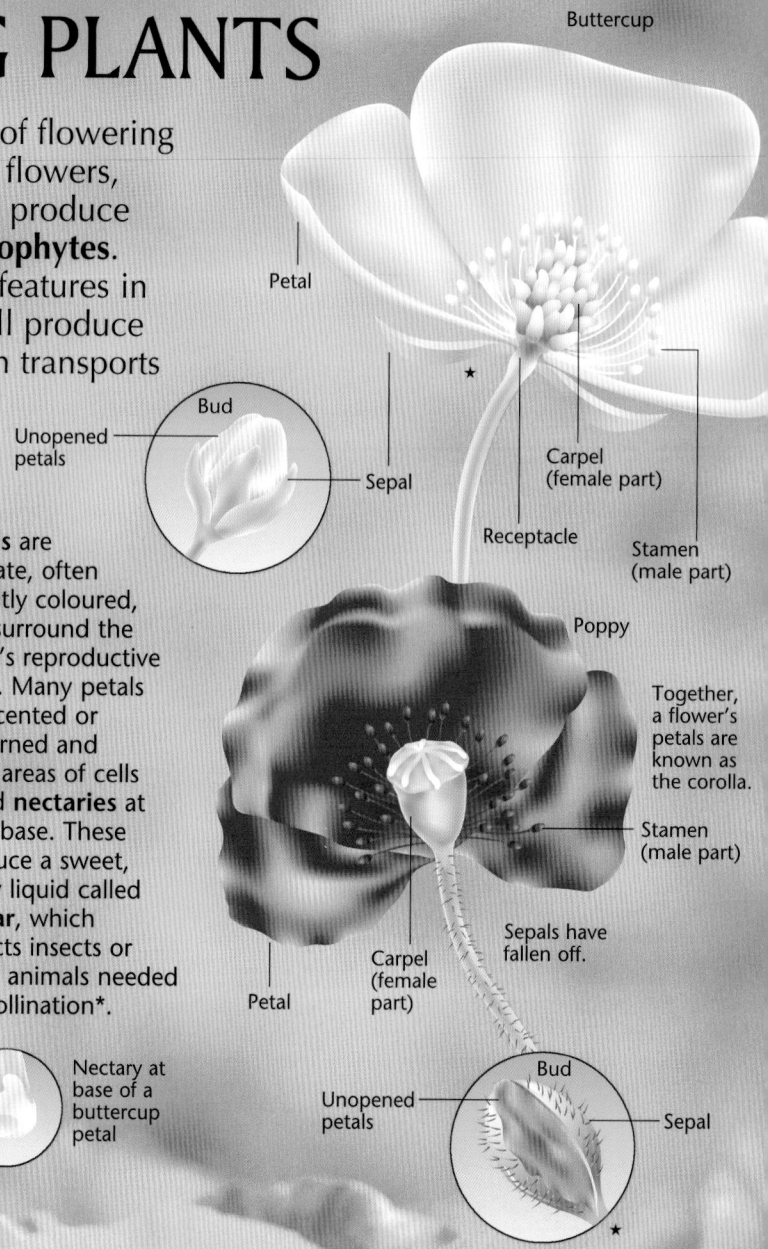

The petals of these Californian poppies surround their reproductive parts. Their sepals have fallen off.

* *Pollination, 272.*

MALE PARTS

A flower's male reproductive parts are called **stamens**. Each stamen is made up of a pod-like **anther**, at the end of a long stalk called a **filament**. Anthers contain **pollen sacs**, which split open to release grains of **pollen**, the male reproductive cells.

Male parts of a buttercup

(Not all stamens are shown here.)

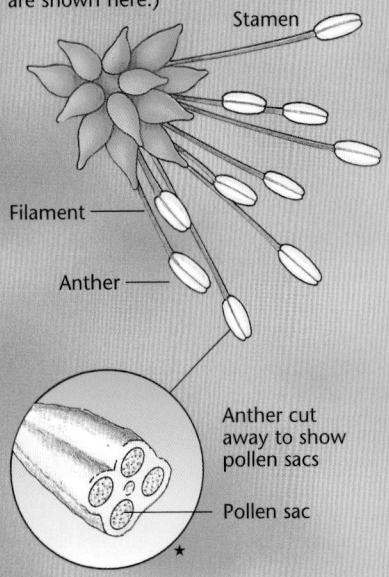

Pollen grains from different plants may be different sizes and shapes, but they do share some features. For instance, when they are mature, all pollen grains have a hard outer wall, making them very tough.

See for yourself

Look at different types of flowers and, using the pictures on these pages, try to identify their male and female parts.

You may find that not every plant has both parts together in the same flower. They may be on separate flowers or on separate plants.

FEMALE PARTS

A flower's female reproductive part is known as the **carpel** or **pistil**. It is made up of the stigma, style and ovary.

The **stigma** is the top part of a carpel. It has a sticky surface which traps grains of pollen that touch it. The stigma is joined to the ovary by a part of the carpel called the **style**. Each **ovary** holds one or more tiny eggs called **ovules**, which are the female reproductive cells. These develop into seeds after fertilization (see next page).

Female parts of a buttercup

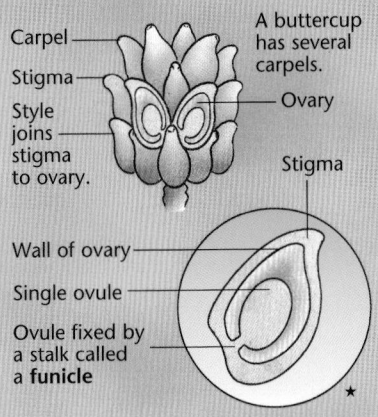

Some flowers, like the buttercup above, have several carpels clustered together. Others, such as the poppy below, have only one.

Female parts of a poppy

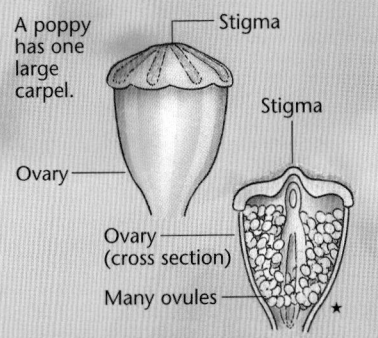

The styles of many flowers, such as daffodils, are easy to see. In others, such as poppies, the style is very short and almost impossible to see.

MALE AND FEMALE

Buttercups and tulips are examples of **hermaphrodite** plants. This means each flower has both male and female parts.

You can see the female carpel and the male stamens in the centre of this tulip.

Some plants, such as maize, have two types of flower on one plant: **staminate** flowers, which have only male parts, and **pistillate** flowers, which have only female parts. Plants with flowers of this kind are described as **monoecious**. Other plants, such as holly, have staminate and pistillate flowers on separate plants. They are described as **dioecious**.

Holly has its male and female parts on separate plants. Berries develop from the ovaries of the female plant.

Internet links

Go to **www.usborne-quicklinks.com** and type in the keyword "science" to find out more about flowering plants.

There you'll find links to websites where you can:

- Explore guides to flowers with online activities and quizzes

Go to Usborne Quicklinks for links to hand-picked websites on hundreds of subjects.

FERTILIZATION

In order for a flowering plant to reproduce, the male cell (pollen) and the female cell (ovule) need to join together. This is called **fertilization**.

When a pollen grain lands on the stigma of a plant of the same type, it forms a **pollen tube**. This grows down into the ovary and enters an ovule through a tiny hole called a **micropyle**. This process is called **pollination**.

Cross section of poppy ovary

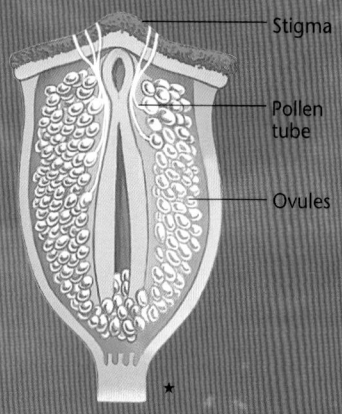

A pollen grain contains two male nuclei*. These travel down the pollen tube and join with the contents of the ovule. One forms a **zygote** – the first cell of a new organism. The other forms a layer of protective, nourishing tissue called the **endosperm**. Together these make a seed, and the ovary grows to become a fruit. After fertilization, the plant no longer needs the rest of its flower parts, so they wither and die.

Thousands of tiny pollen grains are being shed from stamens in the middle of this flower.

POLLINATION METHODS

Pollen may be carried from plant to plant by wind, water or animals. When pollen from one plant pollinates another plant of the same kind, it is described as **cross-pollination**. If the grains land on a different type of plant, they don't produce pollen tubes, so pollination can't take place.

Some types of plants are able to pollinate themselves. This is called **self-pollination**. For instance, a bee orchid tries to attract a certain type of bee, by looking and smelling like the female of its species. But if no bees come, the plant's stamens bend over and transfer pollen to its own stigma.

Unlike many flowers, a bee orchid does not produce sweet nectar. It attracts bees by looking and smelling like a female bee.

ANIMAL POLLINATION

Flowers have various ways of attracting animals to carry their pollen. Most have brightly coloured petals or sweet scents which attract insects, birds or bats. Many also produce a sweet liquid called nectar, or extra pollen, on which the animals feed. Some have patterns on the petals called **nectar guides**. These lead the insect into the middle of the flower, where the pollen or nectar can be found.

Nectar guides in the middle of these pansies lead insects to the nectar.

Plants pollinated by animals tend to produce spiky pollen grains. When an animal visits a plant, pollen grains stick to its body. The animal may then transfer these to another flower.

* *Nucleus, 250.*

WIND POLLINATION

Wind-pollinated plants rely on the wind to scatter their pollen. They do not need to attract animals, so their flowers are usually unscented, with very small petals and sepals. Some have their male and female parts on separate plants. The male parts hang outside the flowers, allowing their pollen to be scattered more easily.

Pollen from these birch tree catkins is scattered by the wind.

Plants which are pollinated by the wind produce huge amounts of pollen. This increases the chances of some landing on female flowers nearby. The pollen grains are usually smooth and light, allowing them to glide easily through the air.

FLOWER SHAPES

The shapes of many flowers help them to transfer pollen onto an animal. For example, the petals of some flowers are shaped like a bell. Animals such as the hummingbird on the right hover beneath the flower, and reach in to feed on the nectar. As they do so, pollen from the stamens sticks to them.

Lipped flowers, such as sage flowers, have paired petals. A bee lands on the lower petal to drink nectar from within the flower. As it does so, the stamens, which hang down from the top lip, transfer pollen onto its body.

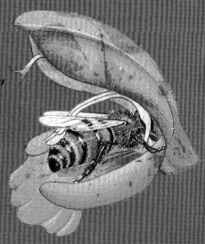

As the bee lands on this sage flower's lower "lip" to drink nectar, pollen is brushed onto its body.

Pollen rubs off on the hummingbird's head as it feeds with its long beak.

Most flowers have ways of keeping their pollen safe until they are visited by a certain kind of animal. For instance, evening primrose flowers remain closed all day. They open up at night, when the moths which pollinate them become active. Many flowers close up when it begins to rain, to keep their pollen dry.

See for yourself

If you have a garden, you can plant flowers to attract certain types of animals. For instance, butterflies tend to visit plants with purple or yellow flowers, such as buddleia or sedum. Bees are attracted to flowers with a strong scent, such as lavender.

Pollen sticks to this butterfly's body as it feeds from a daisy.

Internet links

Go to **www.usborne-quicklinks.com** and type in "science" to find out more about flowering plants.

There you'll find links to websites where you can:

- Explore some of the ways that flowers attract pollinators
- Play a pollination game
- Watch video clips and animations

Go to Usborne Quicklinks for links to hand-picked websites on hundreds of subjects.

SEEDS AND FRUIT

Fertilization in flowering plants leads to the production of a **seed**. Each seed contains a new developing plant and a store of food. Seeds are kept in a part of the plant called a **fruit**. When the seeds are ready, they are scattered and can grow into new plants if conditions are right.

INSIDE A SEED

Seeds are protected by a tough coat called a **testa**. Each has a mark called a **hilum** on its surface, showing where the ovule* was joined to the ovary*. The tiny hole (micropyle) through which the pollen grain entered the ovule can also still be seen. It lets in water.

Bean seed

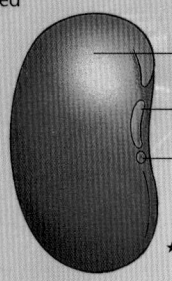

The developing plant inside a seed is known as an **embryo**. It has two parts: the **plumule**, which will develop into the first shoot, and the **radicle**, which will be the first root of the new plant.

Bean seed (cross section)

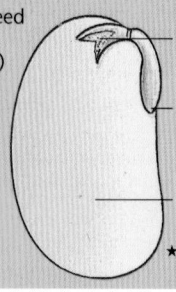

This orange fruit protects the seeds of the orange tree. Its flesh is made up of tiny hairs, each one swollen with juice.

Orange seed (pip)

TYPES OF FRUIT

Fruit protect the seeds they carry and help them to spread to a place where they can grow. Most fruit develop from a plant's ovary*. These are known as **true fruit**. Some, such as strawberries, develop from the receptacle* and the ovary. They are **false fruit**. Fruits can also be described as succulent or dry.

SUCCULENT FRUIT

Fruit with thick, fleshy layers that are often tasty to eat are known as **succulent fruit**. There are various kinds.

Succulent fruit with a single, hard-cased seed in the middle are called **drupes**. Plums and cherries are drupes.

Plum

Succulent fruit that contain many seeds are called **berries**. Oranges are berries. Fruit with a thick, fleshy outer layer and a core, with the seeds contained in a capsule, are false fruit called **pomes**.

Apples are pomes.

Raspberries and blackberries are examples of **aggregate** fruit or **compound fruit**. They form from many ovaries in one flower. Each fruit is made up of fleshy beads called **drupelets**, each containing a single seed.

Blackberries

* Ovary, Ovule, 271; Receptacle, 270.

DRY FRUIT

Dry fruit are dry cases that hold the seeds until they are ripe. There are several types. The main ones are described below.

Nuts are dry fruit with only one seed surrounded by a hard shell. Acorns and walnuts are nuts.

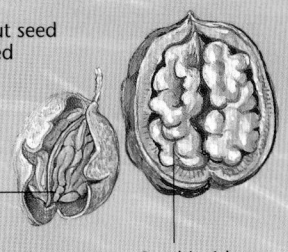

This walnut seed is protected by a hard shell.

Achenes are small, dry fruit with only one seed. An achene with papery wings, for example an ash or sycamore fruit, is called a **samara** or **key fruit**. Some achenes, such as ash achenes, grow in bunches.

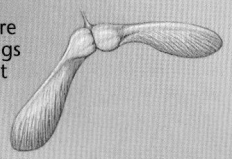

This sycamore fruit has wings which help it to float on the wind.

A dry fruit with seeds attached to its inside wall is known as a **legume** or **pod**. It splits along its length to open. The fruit of the pea plant are pods. The peas are the seeds.

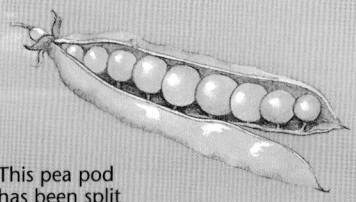

This pea pod has been split open to show the seeds attached inside it.

A **grain**, also called a **caryopsis** or a **kernel**, is a small dry fruit whose wall has fused with the seed coat. Wheat and barley are examples of plants with many grains.

The fruit of the wheat plant is called grain. Each stalk carries many grains.

CONES

The seeds of conifer trees are contained in **cones**, not fruit. These develop from the female flowers (conifers have male and female flowers). After pollination* the scales harden and close.

Atlas cedar cone

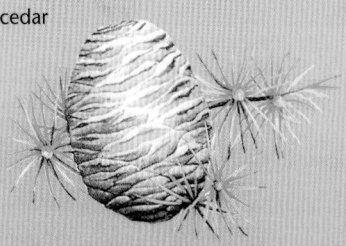

When the seeds are ripe and the weather is warm and dry, the scales of the cones open. The seeds flutter out on papery wings. Most cones stay on the tree for a year. Others take two years to ripen, and some remain long after the seeds have been dropped.

See for yourself

Look at as many different types of fruit as you can find. Notice whether they are succulent or dry fruit, and the number of seeds they contain. If you find a cone, you could make it open by placing it on a radiator. If you put it in a damp place, its scales will close up.

Internet links

Go to **www.usborne-quicklinks.com** and type in "science" to find out more about seeds and fruit.

There you'll find links to websites where you can:

- Print out seed, flower and leaf identification sheets
- Learn more about fruit and seeds
- Play a mystery seed game

Go to Usborne Quicklinks for links to hand-picked websites on hundreds of subjects.

* *Pollination, 272.*

SCATTERING SEEDS

Before seeds start to grow into new plants, they are usually carried away from the parent plant. This is called **dispersal**, and it helps to stop new plants from competing with their parents for space, light and water. Some seeds, such as peas, burst out of the fruit while it is still attached to the parent plant.

Ripe pea fruit explode and fling out their seeds.

Other seeds are carried away from their parent plant inside the fruit. Seeds can be spread by several methods, including by animals, water and wind.

ANIMAL DISPERSAL

Some seeds are tasty to animals or are held inside tempting, fleshy fruit. Animals eat them, and the seeds pass out in their droppings. Some animals, such as squirrels and jays, store away fruit and seeds. Sometimes they put them in a place that is ideal for new plants to sprout.

Not all animal-dispersed fruit are eaten. Some, such as those of burdock or goosegrass, have hooks on them which catch in the fur of passing animals. A fruit can be carried a long way from its parent plant before it falls off.

Burdock fruit have hooks that catch on animals' fur.

WATER DISPERSAL

Seeds or fruit that are dispersed by water, such as coconuts, have waterproof shells. Coconuts contain the seeds of coconut palm trees. They float in rivers o on seas until they are washed up on shore. Some have travelled u to 2,000km on ocean currents before reaching land.

The coconut fruit is held inside a large, waterproof outer shell, seen here.

WIND DISPERSAL

Fruit or seeds which are dispersed by the wind are very light. Some seeds, such as those of sycamore trees, are held in fruit with papery wings. Others, such as dandelions, have fruit with hairs that catch the wind.

Sycamore fruit, each containing two seeds

Parachute

Fruit with seed inside

Each dandelion seed is held inside a fruit attached to a parachute of very fine hairs. The lightest breeze catches the parachute and pulls the fruit off the parent plant.

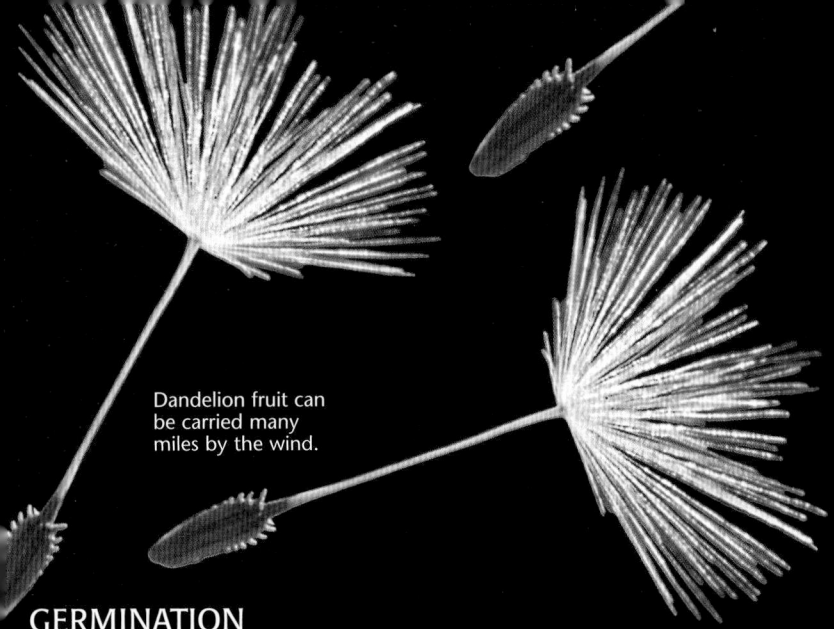

Dandelion fruit can be carried many miles by the wind.

GERMINATION

When conditions are right, a seed will begin to grow into a new plant. This is called **germination**. To germinate, a seed needs warmth, oxygen and water. The seed absorbs water and starts to swell. Its testa splits open and the first shoot and root (the **plumule** and **radicle**) grow.

Germinating pea seed

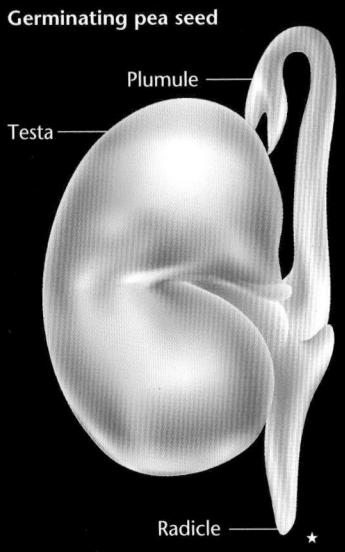

Many seeds that are scattered do not start to grow right away. Seeds that lie inactive for a long time before germinating are described as **dormant**.

The first leaves to grow are called **cotyledons** or **seed leaves**. They are often a different shape from later, true leaves. Some plants, such as grasses and tulips, have only one cotyledon. They are known as **monocotyledons**. Those with two cotyledons, such as peas, are **dicotyledons**.

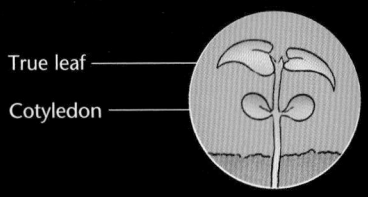

The young plant, called a **seedling**, lives off the food stored in its seed until it grows leaves. It then starts to make its own food by photosynthesis*. It grows and eventually flowers, ready to begin the cycle again.

See for yourself

To germinate seeds such as dried kidney beans or lentils, place them on a piece of paper towel in a saucer, and water them thoroughly every day. After a few days, they will have sprouted. If you like, you can then plant them in small pots.

GERMINATION TYPES

There are two main types of germination. In **hypogeal germination** the cotyledons stay below the ground inside the testa, and the plumule is the only part to come above the ground. Peas germinate in this way.

Germination of a pea plant

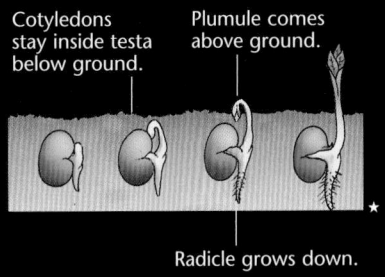

In **epigeal germination**, the cotyledons appear above the ground, below the first true leaves. Beans germinate in this way.

Germination of a bean plant

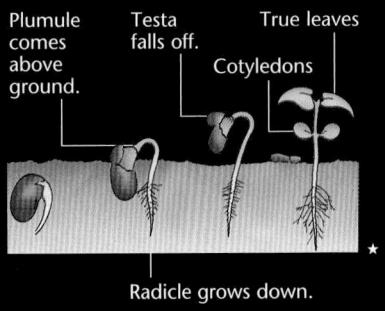

Internet links

Go to **www.usborne-quicklinks.com** and type in the keyword "science" to find out more about seeds and fruit.

There you'll find links to websites where you can:

- Learn more about seed dispersal
- Watch films of germinating seeds

Go to Usborne Quicklinks for links to hand-picked websites on hundreds of subjects.

* *Photosynthesis, 264.*

NEW PLANTS FROM OLD

As well as making seeds which grow into new plants, many plants can reproduce by a process in which part of the plant develops into a new one. This method, called **vegetative reproduction** or **vegetative propagation**, is a type of asexual reproduction, which means it does not involve a male and female sex cell. Some of the different plant parts that can grow into new plants are described here.

Each crocus has grown from a swollen stem called a corm.

BULBS

Plants such as garlic and tulips grow from bulbs. A **bulb** is a short, thick, underground stem surrounded by scaly leaves that are swollen with food. It stays alive over winter when the rest of the plant has died. Some bulbs can reproduce asexually by sprouting extra bulbs on the side.

See for yourself

Garlic bulbs are composite bulbs. This means that each swollen leaf, called a clove, can grow into a garlic plant.

Try planting a few cloves in a pot of potting compost, with the rounded end down. Keep them watered. After about two weeks, shoots of new garlic plants should appear.

Garlic bulb

Each clove of garlic can grow into a new plant.

CORMS

A **corm** is a short, thick stem base that is swollen with food. It can sprout extra corms each year.

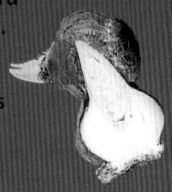

Crocus corms

RUNNERS

Some plants, such as spider plants and strawberry plants, can reproduce by forming long side shoots called **runners** or **stolons**.

When the runners touch the ground, they develop roots of their own, and start to grow into new plants. At first the new plant is fed by the parent, but once it can live on its own, the runner rots away.

RHIZOMES

Many plants grow from thick stems called **rhizomes** which grow horizontally underground. A rhizome produces roots along its length and also buds from which new shoots grow. Ferns, mint, irises and many grasses are plants that produce rhizomes.

TUBERS

A number of plants produce offspring from swollen underground stems called **tubers**. These develop from shoots which grow into the soil. Food is stored in the tuber. In winter the parent plant dies, but the tubers develop into new plants the following year.

Tulips like these grow from bulbs. Each year, market gardens provide thousands of tulips for the flower industry.

SPEED AND QUALITY

Vegetative reproduction produces new plants much more quickly than they can grow from seed. Also, the new plants are identical to the parent plant. Farmers and market gardeners often make use of a plant's ability to reproduce vegetatively. As well as producing more plants, they know that the new plants will be the same quality as the original plant.

Growers have also developed methods of removing parts from a plant to grow new plants. These are examples of **artificial propagation** as, left to themselves, plants do not usually reproduce in these ways.

Some varieties of fruit, such as this navel orange, do not have seeds. They can only be grown by artificial propagation methods.

TAKING CUTTINGS

One common method of artificial propagation is **cutting**. This involves taking a piece such as a side stem or leaf (known as the cutting) off a plant and planting it in soil where it grows into a new plant. The cutting may need to stand in water for a while to develop new roots before being planted in soil.

Growing a plant from a cutting

A piece of plant is cut from the parent plant.

The cutting is placed in water until roots begin to grow.

The cutting is replanted in soil, where it will grow into a new plant.

MICROPROPAGATION

Scientists can grow new plants from just a few cells taken from a meristem (growth area) of a plant. The cells are placed on a gel that contains chemicals which make the cells divide. Groups of cells are then moved to a second gel which contains growth chemicals that make the cells grow into shoots. This method, called **micropropagation**, can create hundreds of identical plants from one parent plant.

Internet links

To find out more about new plants, go to **www.usborne-quicklinks.com** and type in the keyword "science".

There you'll find links to websites where you can:

- Find out more about bulbs and how to grow them
- Read more about potatoes

Go to Usborne Quicklinks for links to hand-picked websites on hundreds of subjects.

African violet plants can be grown from leaf cuttings.

WATER PLANTS

Most plants grow on land, but there are also many aquatic plants – plants specially adapted to live in water. These are known as **hydrophytes**. They range from microscopic plants, which are found in groups of several million, to huge flowering plants over a metre across.

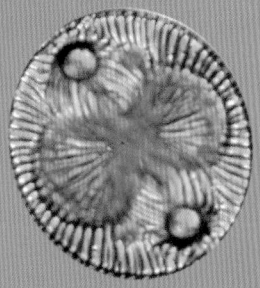

This is a microscopic water plant called a diatom.

A WATERY LIFESTYLE

Water plants are either emergent or submergent. **Emergent** plants, such as reed mace, grow well in very wet soils, or in soils which spend a lot of time covered in water. Most or all of their stems and leaves can be seen above the surface of the water.

Reed mace can often be seen growing out of the water by a river bank.

Submergent plants, such as water lilies, grow beneath the surface of the water. However, some of their parts, for instance large leaves, may float on the surface. Unless they are free-floating, their roots, or root-like parts, anchor them to the ground beneath the water.

Free-floating submergent plants, such as duckweed, are not attached to anything. They are found in large numbers in calm, sheltered water.

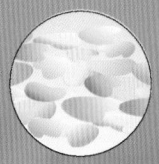

This duckweed floats freely on the water's surface.

SPECIAL FEATURES

Water-living plants have a number of special features. For instance, most underwater leaves, unlike leaves of other plants, do not have a waxy waterproof coating. This is because the whole leaf surface is needed for exchanging gases between the plant and the water. Many water plants also have very different leaves above and below the surface.

Above the water's surface, water crowfoot has broad, flat leaves.

Under the water, its leaves are thin and finely divided.

Some submergent plants develop gaps between the cells in their stems and leaves. These gaps trap air which helps the parts to float.

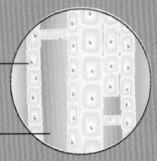

A water lily's stem and roots grow under water.

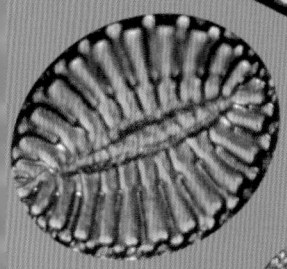

Diatoms, like these, are a type of algae.

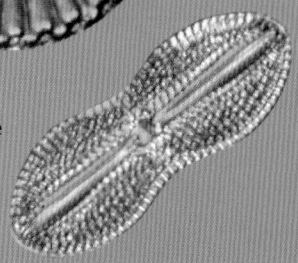

Each diatom is made up of two halves, which fit together like a lid on a box.

ALGAE

Algae form a large group of plants which have a very simple structure. Most types of algae are found in water, but they can grow in any suitably damp conditions, including in soil, on rocks, and even on living things.

One of the simplest types of algae are microscopic **diatoms**. Most are made up of a single cell, with a hard, glassy case. Each species of diatom has a differently patterned case.

Microscopic algae never have roots, stems or leaves, and don't contain true vascular tissue*. They can reproduce quickly and, like most plants, make their own food using the Sun's energy. Algae are an important source of food for many water creatures.

* Pigments, 261; Vascular tissue, 254.

SEAWEEDS

Seaweeds are types of many-celled algae. Most seaweeds have root-like **holdfasts** at their base, which anchor them to solid objects, such as rocks. Some have bubble-like **air bladders**, which keep them afloat. A seaweed's leaves, called **fronds**, often contain pigments* which allow them to take in light at different water depths.

Examples of seaweeds

Sea lettuce has very thin, crinkled fronds. These darken as the plant ages, because different tiny algae cover their surface.

Edible dulse grows in deep pools. The red pigment in its fronds helps it to capture light under water.

Knotted wrack has long fronds, which contain pockets of air called air bladders.

STUDYING ALGAE

Scientists study the types and numbers of algae in a water sample to find out how clean it is. Single-celled, freshwater algae called **desmids** are generally found growing in clean water.

Some types of algae, though, reproduce rapidly in water which contains high levels of nitrates (chemicals found in some fertilizers and sewage). This is called **eutrophication**. These algae use up oxygen that other living things in the water need, eventually killing them.

Eutrophication is mostly caused by sewage-dumping and by fertilizer being washed from the soil into the water.

Blue-green algae (called cyanobacteria) are starting to cover this polluted lake.

See for yourself

If you visit the coast, look for seaweed of different colours and textures. You may find it in rock pools, or washed up on the shore. Look for features like air bladders or a holdfast.

Internet links

To find out more about water plants, go to **www.usborne-quicklinks.com** and type in the keyword "science".

There you'll find links to websites where you can:

- Go on a virtual pond dip and examine microscopic algae

Go to Usborne Quicklinks for links to hand-picked websites on hundreds of subjects.

FLOWERLESS PLANTS

Liverworts, mosses, ferns, algae* and horsetails* are known as flowerless plants. They do not produce flowers or seeds, and in many cases reproduce at least some of the time by **asexual reproduction**. This is a type of reproduction in which only one parent is needed to produce a new living thing identical to itself. Many scientists believe that these plants were among the very first types of land plants on the Earth.

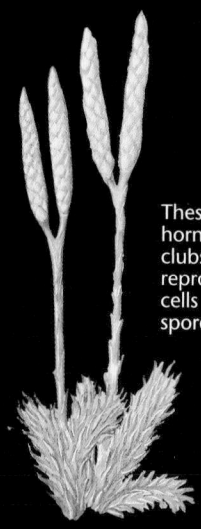

These paired, horn-shaped clubs contain reproductive cells called spores.

The leaves of this stag's horn club moss are packed tightly around the base of the stem.

LIVERWORTS

Liverworts are low-growing plants that live in damp places on soil or rocks. They do not have true roots, stems or leaves. The main part of a liverwort is called the **thallus**. It is held in the ground by simple root-like growths called **rhizoids**.

Liverworts do not contain vascular tissue* for transporting fluids. They also do not have a waterproof outer layer. This means that they can absorb all the water they need, but are also more likely to dry out.

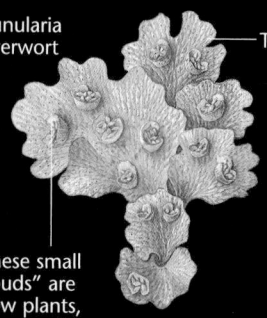

MOSSES

Mosses are low-growing plants that live in damp, shady places, for example on walls, rocks and tree trunks. Like liverworts, they do not have vascular tissue*. Instead, they absorb large amounts of water through their many tiny leaf-like structures, which are only one cell thick.

If conditions become too dry, the moss leaves curl up, shrivel, and turn brown. They remain inactive until conditions are damp enough for them to grow again.

The Mnium moss below grows on damp rocks and in shady woods.

CLUB MOSSES

Club mosses grow along the ground. They are not mosses at all, but are distantly related to ferns. They have narrow, scale-like leaves packed densely around stems that contain vascular tissue.

Club mosses get their name from their club-shaped growths called **strobili**, which contain reproductive cells called spores.

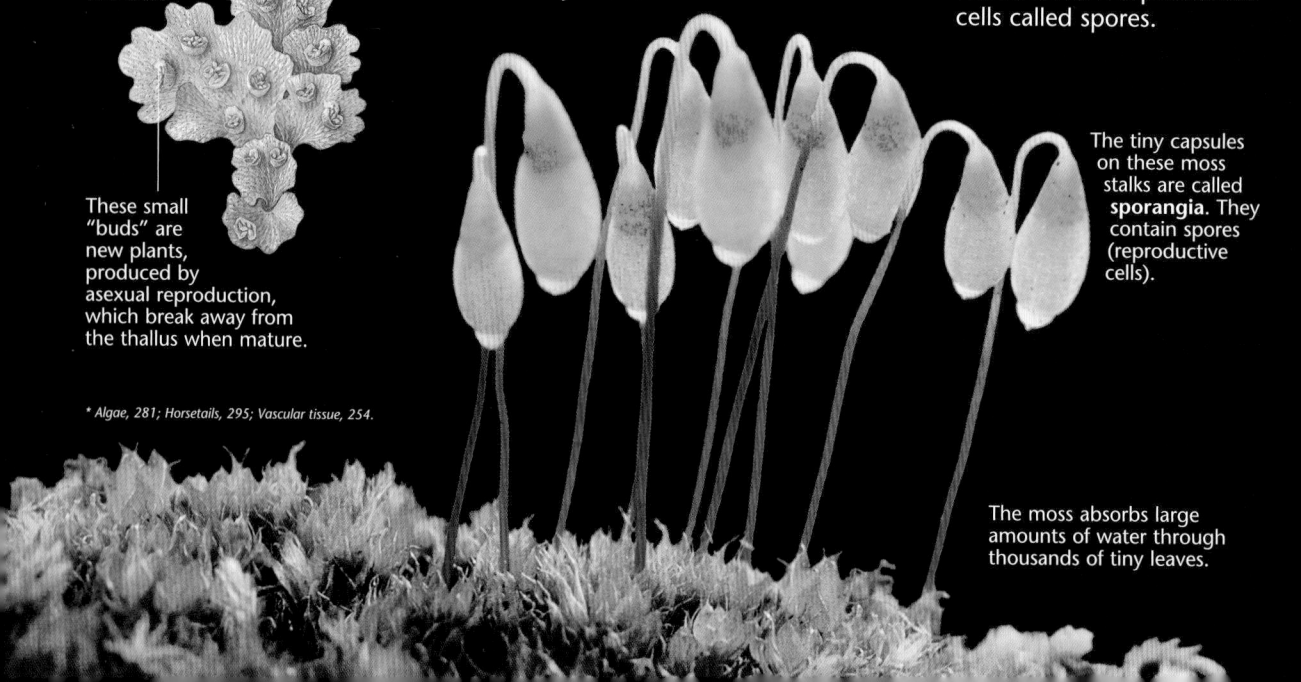

The tiny capsules on these moss stalks are called **sporangia**. They contain spores (reproductive cells).

The moss absorbs large amounts of water through thousands of tiny leaves.

** Algae, 281; Horsetails, 295; Vascular tissue, 254.*

FERNS

There are over 10,000 species of ferns. They grow in damp, shady places all over the world. Unlike mosses and liverworts, they have true leaves, stems and roots, with well-developed vascular tissue. This helps them to survive in drier conditions, and also to grow taller to get a better share of the light.

Most ferns have horizontal stems called rhizomes* that grow underground. Leaves known as **fronds** push out of the earth in tight coils which then unfurl. Fronds are different shapes depending on the type of fern.

This hart's-tongue fern has solid, leathery fronds.

Bracken fronds are made up of many leaflets.

Wall rue ferns have delicate fronds.

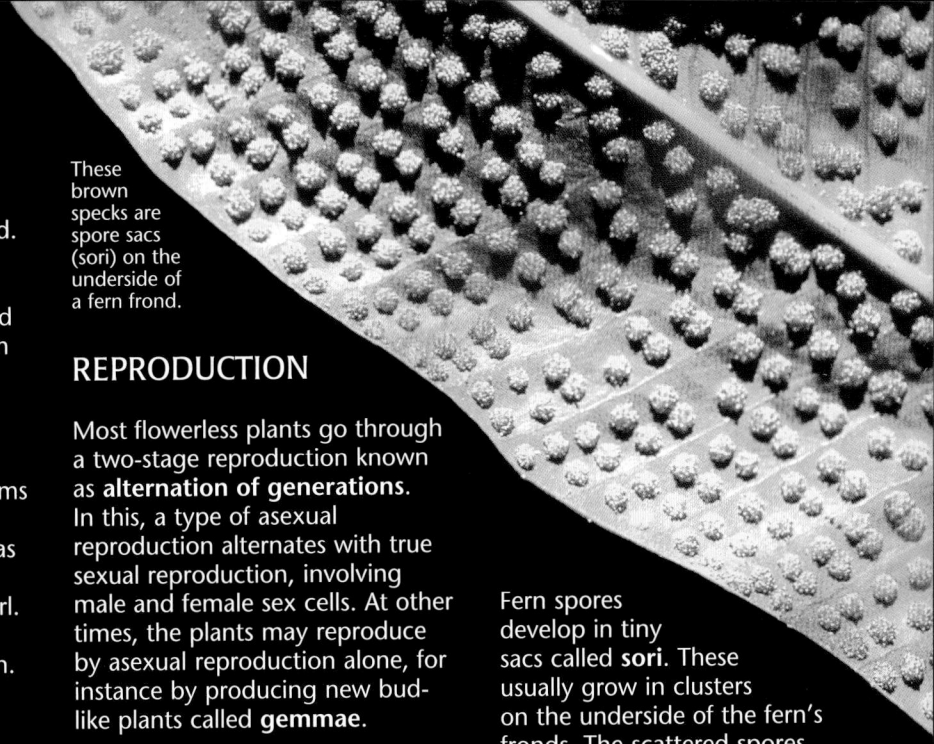

These brown specks are spore sacs (sori) on the underside of a fern frond.

REPRODUCTION

Most flowerless plants go through a two-stage reproduction known as **alternation of generations**. In this, a type of asexual reproduction alternates with true sexual reproduction, involving male and female sex cells. At other times, the plants may reproduce by asexual reproduction alone, for instance by producing new bud-like plants called **gemmae**.

The first stage of alternation of generations is sexual. The plant is called a **gametophyte**, because it produces male and female sex cells (gametes). A male cell travels through water to a female cell, and they join and grow into a plant body called a **sporophyte**. Mosses produce gametophytes and sporophytes on the same plant, but in liverworts, ferns and most algae they are on separate plants.

The second, asexual stage is called **sporulation**. The sporophyte produces reproductive cells called **spores**. Ripe spores are scattered, and grow into new gametophytes if they land in suitable conditions.

Fern spores develop in tiny sacs called **sori**. These usually grow in clusters on the underside of the fern's fronds. The scattered spores grow into flat, often heart-shaped gametophytes called **prothalli**.

Life cycle of a fern

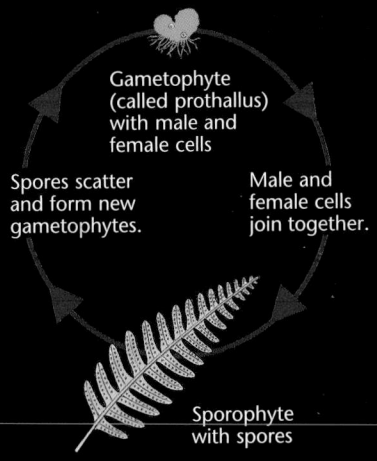

See for yourself

You may see small mosses growing on walls or on stones in a garden. Look closely at their texture and shape. If you live near a wooded area or even a garden centre, you may also find some ferns. Look for spore sacs on the undersides of their leaves.

Internet links

Go to **www.usborne-quicklinks.com** and type in the keyword "science" to find out more about flowerless plants.

There you'll find links to websites where you can:

- Explore pictures and information on mosses, ferns, liverworts and other flowerless plants
- Discover the life cycle of a fern
- Find out more with online activities and photographs

* Rhizomes, 278; Vascular tissue, 254.

FUNGI

Fungi are simple, plant-like organisms that never flower and do not have true leaves, stems or roots. They grow in damp, dark places, and do not contain the green chlorophyll needed to make their own food. Instead, they feed on either living things or dead matter. Moulds and yeast are types of fungi.

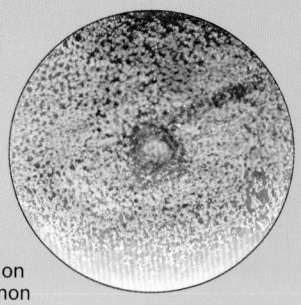

The mould on this lemon is a type of simple fungus.

STRUCTURE OF FUNGI

The main part of most fungi, called the **mycelium**, is found underground. It is a mass of tiny thread-like structures called **hyphae**, which spread out in the soil. These absorb food substances from dead matter or living roots in the soil. Fungi which live on roots are called **mycorrhizae**.

To reproduce, some of the hyphae pack densely together to form button-like growths. These push up through the soil and grow into **fruiting bodies**.

Growth of a fruiting body

Like mosses and ferns, fungi reproduce by producing tiny cells called spores. Fruiting bodies contain millions of spores. When the spores are ready, they are released and scattered by the wind. If they land in suitable conditions, they grow into new fungi.

The fruiting bodies of fungi grow and die very rapidly, but the spores and mycelium can continue to live underground for many years.

MOULDS AND MILDEWS

Moulds and **mildews** are simple fungi which do not produce large fruiting bodies. They grow in warm, damp and dark places, feeding on living or once-living matter, such as paper and wood.

You might see moulds or mildews in your own home or garden. For example, the small blue spots and green furry patches that grow on old bread or fruit are types of mould. Mildews often look like powdery white or black patches. They grow in damp areas, such as bathroom ceilings. Some grow on plants – roses, for example.

Fruiting body of a fungus

The flattened gills of this fungus have opened out to shed its spores.

This sulphur shelf fungus is a saprotroph. It lives and feeds on the wood of dead trees.

FUNGI FEEDING

Fungi that feed on dead matter are called **saprotrophs**. Dead matter contains useful substances such as carbon and nitrates. As they feed, fungi release powerful chemicals called **enzymes** which break down their food into simple substances.

Some substances are absorbed by the fungi, but others are returned to the soil, where they are used again by plants and animals. In this way, the fungi play an important part in the carbon and nitrogen cycles*.

Fungi that feed on living things are called **parasites**. Some are good for the plants that they feed on, providing them with water and minerals. This is called a **symbiotic relationship**.

See for yourself

You can look at spores by cutting the stalk off an ordinary cooking mushroom, and placing the cap on a piece of white paper. Cover it with an upturned bowl and leave it overnight. When you remove the bowl and mushroom cap, you will see that the mushroom has released its spores in a pattern on the paper.

Spore print

HELP AND HARM

Some kinds of fungi are useful to people. For instance, a medicine called **penicillin**, which kills the bacteria that cause various diseases, is made from a particular mould. The blue veins in some cheeses are also made from similar moulds. A single-celled fungus called **yeast** is used in bread-making and brewing some alcoholic drinks.

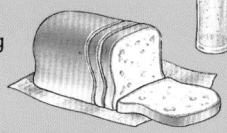

Bread, wine and beer are made using the fungus yeast.

Many fungi can harm living things. Some, for instance, produce fruiting bodies that are highly poisonous. Others, such as the mould which causes Dutch elm disease, grow on plants and slowly kill them. Some fungi can also grow on animals' bodies. For instance, athlete's foot and ringworm are human skin conditions caused by fungi.

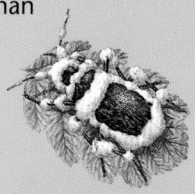

This beetle has a fungus feeding on its body.

Internet links

To find out more about fungi, go to **www.usborne-quicklinks.com** and type in the keyword "science".

There you'll find links to websites where you can:

- Find interesting facts about fungi
- See detailed microscope images of fungi

Go to Usborne Quicklinks for links to hand-picked websites on hundreds of subjects.

The links at Usborne Quicklinks are regularly reviewed and updated, so you might find a slightly different selection of websites from the ones described here.

* *Carbon cycle, Nitrogen cycle, 292.*

FIGHTING FOR SURVIVAL

Every living thing in nature struggles to survive. Most plants are threatened by animals and people, as well as by other plants, and may have to live in difficult conditions. Plants survive by adapting to life in different environments, and competing successfully with other living things.

NATURAL SELECTION

Over time, some plants develop features which help them to survive in particular conditions. Plants with helpful features are more likely to survive and reproduce. Plants without these features often die out. This process is called **natural selection** (see also page 339).

COASTAL PLANTS

The seashore is an example of an environment where conditions can be harsh. There is little firm soil or fresh water, and strong, salty winds often blow. Even so, some plants have adapted to life in these surroundings.

For instance, when a sand dune first forms, only grasses grow there. Their roots form a network which helps to bind together the loose, sandy ground, eventually creating a kind of soil that other types of flowering plants can grow in.

Grasses growing on sand dunes help to make the ground firmer.

Shingle beaches are made up of small rock fragments, mixed with sand. Only plants with long or sprawling roots, which hold the plant firmly in the shingle, can live in these areas. Long roots also help the plant to reach supplies of fresh water deep under the ground.

Yellow horned poppies are anchored firmly in the shingle by their long roots.

Areas called **salt marshes** form where a river joins the sea. Their soil is **saline** (salty), which means that most plants are not able to grow in it.

A group of plants known as **halophytes** can survive in saline areas. Some need salt in order to grow. Others are adapted to remove salt from water that they take in. For example, some halophytes have **salt bladders** on the surface of their leaves. These bladders burst to release salt. Other halophytes store the salt in old leaves, which they later shed.

Sea asters grow best in salty conditions.

This yucca is a desert plant. It has narrow, tough leaves, which lose little water.

DESERT PLANTS

Plants which grow in very dry areas, such as deserts, are called **xerophytes**. There are many ways in which they make the most of the limited water supply. For example, some have very small leaves, or needle-like leaves called spines, which lose very little water. Most desert plants have specially adapted cells which store water.

These cacti store water in their thick, fleshy stems.

ROCK PLANTS

Plants which live on the surface of rocks are called **lithophytes**. They are mostly found on walls, cliff-faces or mountainsides. Lithophytes usually have special roots which anchor them to rocks.

Mosses are one of the few types of plants that can survive on rocks.

See for yourself

You can easily keep cacti at home. A cactus will grow best in sandy soil with a covering of pebbles. It needs plenty of sunlight, but very little watering. When you water a cactus, you will notice that the water dribbles off its surface. This is because its skin is tough and thick, to keep in as much water as possible. A cactus gets all the water it needs through its roots.

PROTECTION

Plants are constantly under threat from animals that want to eat them. Some plants have special features which protect them from hungry animals and other dangers. These features are known as **protective adaptations**.

Some plants, such as this dog rose, have sharp thorns or prickles which make them difficult for animals to eat.

Tiny hairs on this nettle's leaves release a stinging chemical when they are touched.

Some types of plants use tricks and disguises to keep themselves safe. For instance, living stone plants have adapted to blend in perfectly with pebbles on the ground. Animals mistake them for real stones, and do not try to eat them. This type of disguise is called **camouflage**.

Living stones grow on the ground. They look like pebbles.

Many plants are damaged by hungry insect grubs, such as caterpillars. These hatch out of eggs laid on the plant's leaves.

Some passion flower vines protect themselves from this threat by developing small growths which look like butterfly eggs. Butterflies are less likely to lay eggs on a plant which looks as if it already has some on it. Only a small number of real eggs are laid on the plant, so it is attacked by few caterpillars.

This butterfly thinks the false eggs are real. It will not lay its own eggs near them.

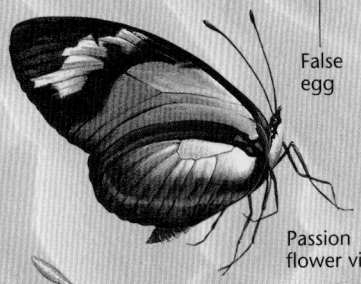

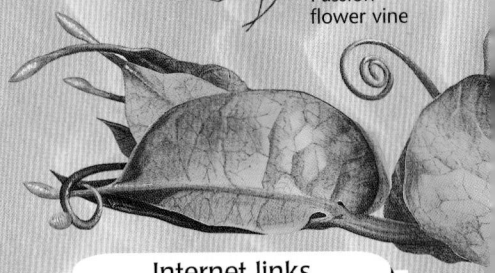

Internet links

Go to **www.usborne-quicklinks.com** and type "science" to find out more about plants fighting for survival.

There you'll find links to websites where you can:

- Discover more about how plants have adapted to survive
- Explore rainforest plants
- Take a look at how plants defend themselves

Go to Usborne Quicklinks for links to hand-picked websites on hundreds of subjects.

PLANT LIFESTYLES

The way a plant grows and reproduces depends on many things, such as climate, soil and weather conditions. Some plants live in areas where growth is impossible for some parts of the year, so they grow quickly and reproduce many times when conditions are right. Others may grow one year and reproduce the next. Each year in a plant's life is described as a single **growth season**.

These blue daisies are perennials. They bloom year after year.

ANNUALS

Flowering plants that live and die within a single year are called **annuals**. The entire process of growth, flowering and seed production may take place in as little as a few weeks. Annual plants have usually bloomed and died by the end of the summer. Their seeds remain inactive during the winter, ready to grow into new plants when spring comes.

This lobelia grows, flowers and dies within a single year.

BIENNIALS

Some flowering plants take two years to complete their life cycle. They are called **biennials**. During the first year, they grow and store up food. In the second year, the plant grows taller, blooms and produces seeds. After this, the entire plant dies.

Wallflowers grow and store food in one year, then flower and die in the next.

PERENNIALS

Plants that live for many years are called **perennials**. There are two types. **Herbaceous perennials** lose all the parts that are above ground each winter. Their roots become swollen with food and remain inactive until new shoots sprout from them the following spring.

Shrubs and trees are **woody perennials**. They may lose some parts, such as leaves, during the winter, but their stems or trunks stay alive, growing thicker each year.

EPHEMERALS

Plants with very short life cycles are called **ephemeral plants**. They are often found where the right growth conditions occur for a limited time, such as in deserts. The plants grow quickly from seeds which have been inactive in the ground. They bloom and produce seeds, which may also then grow, bloom and produce seeds, and so on, until conditions become unsuitable again.

During the brief rainy season, these desert plants have bloomed, creating a carpet of flowers.

TREE LIFESTYLES

Trees can be divided into two categories: deciduous and evergreen. **Deciduous trees** lose their leaves every year. Most deciduous trees have thin, soft leaves that dry out easily. These are shed just before winter, when the temperature drops. If the ground freezes, there is less water available. If deciduous trees kept their leaves at this time, too much precious water would be lost through them.

Leaves on deciduous trees change colour before they fall. New leaves grow in spring, when the temperature rises.

In some places, such as grasslands, there are two seasons: rainy and dry. The trees there shed their leaves at the beginning of the dry season, when the moisture level of the soil drops below a certain point. The leaves begin to grow back at the start of the rainy season, when water is available again.

Trees that do not shed their leaves all at once are known as **evergreen**. Unlike deciduous trees, they have tough, waxy leaves, which means they lose less water. They can survive and grow in places where little water is available. Keeping their leaves also means that they can continue to make food during the winter, even though there is less sunlight available.

Conifers such as these have narrow, waxy leaves with a small surface area. Little water is lost through them.

See for yourself

Next time you are in a wooded area, look closely at the trees. See if you can find examples of both deciduous and evergreen trees, and compare the leaves. Deciduous leaves are flat, with thin veins running through them. Evergreen leaves tend to be waxy and pointed.

Internet links

Go to **www.usborne-quicklinks.com** and type in the keyword "science" to find out more about plant lifestyles.

There you'll find links to websites where you can:

- Visit a virtual forest and identify lots of trees
- Observe seasonal changes with online film clips

Go to Usborne Quicklinks for links to hand-picked websites on hundreds of subjects.

PLANTS AND PEOPLE

The world can be divided into **biomes**. Each is a region with a unique climate and type of soil. A biome supports **ecosystems** – groups of plants and animals which interact with each other and their surroundings. Many ecosystems are damaged by the way people use the land.

Map showing main world biomes

Key to biomes

- Tropical rainforest
- Deciduous forest
- Mountains
- Coniferous forest
- Scrubland
- Temperate grassland
- Tundra
- Tropical grassland
- Desert
- Polar areas (little plant life)

Tropical rainforests contain a huge number of plants, which grow in layers. Treetops form the highest layer, and ground plants form the lowest. Each layer supports different forms of life.

Orchid

Deciduous forests generally grow in layers. At the top are tall deciduous trees*. Beneath is a layer of small trees and saplings, then a layer of shrubs. Next, there are a number of smaller plants, and finally a layer of mosses and lichens on the ground.

Oak leaf

Mountains are cold and bleak. Only low-growing plants such as mosses and shrubs grow on them.

Coniferous forests contain large numbers of conifers. They are usually found in areas where the soil is frozen for part of the year. This makes it difficult for plants to obtain water. Conifers have narrow, tough leaves called needles which reduce water loss.

Silver fir cone

Scrublands mainly contain shrubs. Many of these have small, leathery or needle-like leaves, which help to prevent water loss in the dry season.

Temperate grasslands (also known as **prairies** or **steppes**) contain many different types of grasses, but few trees. Their rich mixture of grasses is food for many different grazing animals.

Tundra regions are cold and windy. They contain low-growing plants, such as lichens, mosses and small shrubs. The temperature is too low for large plants such as trees.

Lichen

Tropical grasslands have a permanent cover of grasses, and sometimes also trees and shrubs. During the long dry season, there are many fires. These leave behind ashes which help to fertilize the soil.

Big bluestem grass

Deserts are hot and dry. Desert plants generally have a thick, waxy outer covering and slim leaves, to reduce water loss.

By clearing large areas such as this for farmland, there is a danger that we are losing too many natural habitats, including hedgerows and woodland.

* Deciduous trees, 289.

FOOD FOR ALL

For thousands of years, people have found ways of producing the food they need from the land around them. But as the human population grows, more and more food is needed. This means using more space to grow crops, or using existing farmland more efficiently. Some farming methods have a disastrous effect on ecosystems, though.

Here, a huge area of land has been cleared for growing crops, destroying the ecosystem which was there before.

Since farming began, people have identified plants with useful features, such as bigger fruit or better resistance to pests, and have used their seeds to grow better crops. This is called **selective breeding**. Overuse of selective breeding may lead to a loss of **biodiversity** – the huge variety of living things on Earth.

Intensive farming uses chemical fertilizers, pesticides, machinery and other methods to grow the most crops possible. But these methods return very few natural substances to the soil, and the chemicals can harm the land and animals living on it.

Intensive farming often uses machinery such as this to spray fields full of crops with pesticides or other chemicals.

GENETIC MODIFICATION

A living thing's characteristics are controlled by genes* in its cells. These are inherited from parents through reproduction, so cannot be passed naturally from one type of living thing to a different type.

Scientists, though, are able to take a gene for a certain useful feature from one organism and place it in another of a different kind. This is called **genetic modification**. Food produced like this is known as **GM food**.

It is possible, for instance, to take a gene which makes a fish resistant to the cold, and place it in a tomato plant. This creates tomato plants which can survive in cold weather.

These GM tomatoes look like ordinary tomatoes. Many people who want to avoid buying GM food think it should be clearly labelled.

Some people believe GM crops could help to solve the problem of food shortages around the world, but others think they could cause great damage to the environment. For example, maize can be genetically modified to be poisonous to insects. This means that less of the crop is destroyed, but some birds and other wildlife that normally feed on those insects will die of hunger.

ORGANIC FARMING

Organic farming works closely with nature by not adding artificial chemicals to the soil. For instance, instead of using chemical pesticides, some organic farmers plant onions among their crops. The strong smell of onions masks the smell of the crops, and pests are not attracted.

Organic farmers often use a method called **crop rotation**. Crops which use or replace certain minerals, such as nitrates, are planted in different fields each year. Manure and compost are used as fertilizers to help the crops to grow. This method keeps levels of natural substances balanced in the soil.

Example of crop rotation

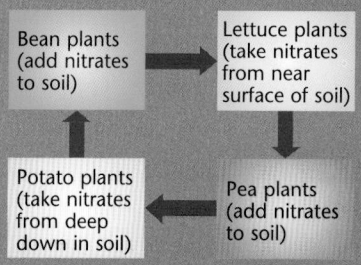

Some people prefer to eat organically grown food because they know it is entirely natural and better for the environment.

Internet links

Go to **www.usborne-quicklinks.com** and type in "science" to find out more about plants and people.

There you'll find links to websites where you can:

- Find more information on the major world biomes
- Investigate the arguments for and against GM crops

Go to Usborne Quicklinks for links to hand-picked websites on hundreds of subjects.

* Genes, 380.

NATURAL CYCLES

Plants and animals need carbon, nitrogen, oxygen and water to keep them alive. These vital substances are constantly recycled between the air, land and living things, which means that plants and animals need never run out of them. However, natural cycles are easily disturbed, especially by some human activities that release harmful substances into the environment.

Some fungi break down dead matter. This returns vital chemicals to the soil.

THE NITROGEN CYCLE

All living things need **nitrogen** to make essential chemicals called **proteins**. Before plants and animals can use nitrogen, it must be combined with oxygen to form **nitrates**. Lightning forms some nitrates from nitrogen in the air. Certain types of bacteria also form nitrates. They mostly live inside the roots of vegetables called legumes, for example peas and beans.

When a plant or animal dies, fungi and bacteria break it down. This releases nitrogen into the soil as a chemical called **ammonia**. **Nitrogen-fixing bacteria** in the soil change the ammonia into nitrates, which are taken in by plants. Animals gain these nitrates by eating plants, or animals that have eaten plants. (For more on the nitrogen cycle, see page 64.)

THE CARBON CYCLE

All living things need **carbon** to live and grow. Plants obtain it from carbon dioxide in the air. During photosynthesis*, they use carbon dioxide to make food substances called **carbohydrates**.

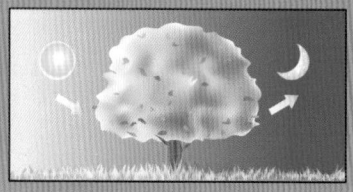

Plants take in carbon dioxide during the day to help them make food.

At night, they give out carbon dioxide when food is not being produced.

Inside living things, internal respiration* turns carbohydrates into energy, producing carbon dioxide as waste. Carbon dioxide is also released into the atmosphere when organic matter is burned or broken down in the soil. (For more on the carbon cycle, see page 52.)

THE WATER CYCLE

Water is constantly recycled through the air, rivers and seas. Water that falls as rain drains into rivers, then into the sea. It turns to vapour, forming tiny droplets in the air. These form clouds, and water falls back to Earth as rain.

Plants transpire (release water vapour) through their leaves. Most animals also release water when they breathe out. (You can find out more about the water cycle on page 74.)

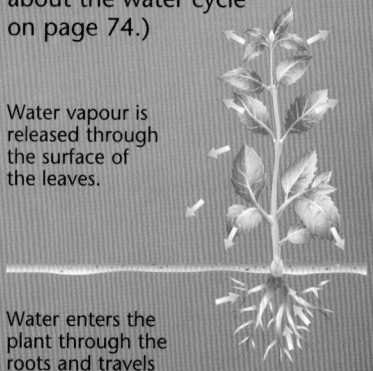

See for yourself

Plants that grow in towns may be harmed by particles of dirt from traffic exhaust. On a dry day, gather a few leaves from trees or bushes growing in a town where there is lots of traffic passing through.

Next, take a damp cloth, and rub the upper surface of the leaves. You may find that a layer of dirt from the polluted air rubs off. This blocks out light that the leaves need to make food for the plant, making it less healthy.

* *Internal respiration, 265; Photosynthesis, 264.*

UPSET BALANCE

People can upset the balance of natural cycles in various ways. For example, in some parts of the world, forests are burned down to make way for farming or building. Burning releases carbon, which forms carbon dioxide in the air.

The remaining plants do not remove this carbon dioxide fast enough during the process of photosynthesis*, so it builds up in the atmosphere.

The dense layer of carbon dioxide traps the Sun's heat around the Earth, creating what is known as the greenhouse effect. This is believed to cause global warming, a dangerous increase in the Earth's overall temperature.

Here, a large area of forest is being burned to make way for building and farming. Burning such as this increases the level of carbon dioxide in the atmosphere.

Pollution can also affect the growth patterns of living things. **Lichens** are simple living things made up of a fungus and an alga growing together. In areas with little or no pollution, shrubby lichens may be seen growing on trees. In very polluted areas, there are large amounts of green algae, but no lichens.

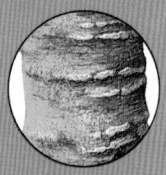

Green algae grow on trees in very polluted areas.

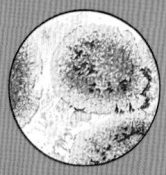

Leafy lichens grow on walls. They are found in areas with some pollution.

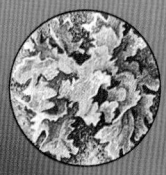

Shrubby lichens grow on trees in cleaner areas.

PLANTS UNDER THREAT

Some plants are directly threatened by human activities. For instance, golden barrel cacti are now very rare in Mexico, because they have been collected illegally and sold.

Golden barrel cactus

In Wales, seeds from the last tufted saxifrage plants in the country were grown into new plants. These were replanted in the wild to try to save the species from dying out. This was successful, but global warming is once again threatening the cold mountain areas in which they live.

Tufted saxifrage

Internet links

Go to **www.usborne-quicklinks.com** and type in "science" to find out more about natural cycles.

There you'll find links to websites where you can:

- View animated diagrams of the carbon, nitrogen and water cycles
- Find a guide to global warming

Go to Usborne Quicklinks for links to hand-picked websites on hundreds of subjects.

* *Photosynthesis, 264.*

CLASSIFYING PLANTS

In order to make living things easier to study, scientists organize them into groups with similar features. This process is called **classification**. Plants are usually classified by comparing the structure of their stems and leaves, as well as the arrangement and types of their reproductive parts.

THE KINGDOMS OF LIFE

The largest groups into which scientists divide living things are called **kingdoms**. There are six main kingdoms:

Eubacteria

Simple microscopic organisms often called simply "bacteria", which do not have a nucleus* in their cells.

Archaea

Microscopic single-celled organisms without nuclei*. Their cell walls* are different from those of eubacteria.

Protista

Mostly single-celled organisms, including many with animal-like features (such as amoeba) or with plant-like features (algae).

Bacteria

Amoeba

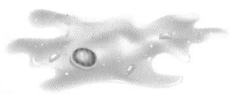

Plants

Living things such as trees and grass, which contain chlorophyll*. Most make their own food by photosynthesis*, but a small number digest other living things.

Yellow stargrass flowers

Fungi

Plant-like organisms that lack chlorophyll, and therefore cannot photosynthesize. Some break down dead matter, while others feed on living things.

Entoloma fungus

Animals

Creatures that can usually move around, and eat plants or other animals for food. Mammals and insects are examples of animals.

Pika

IDENTIFICATION

Scientists identify living things by comparing their main features and comparing them with those of similar species. One method used to compare features is called a **biological key**. A key is typically arranged in stages, with a choice of features at every stage. Each choice leads to another, until the organism is identified.

A key with two choices at each stage is called a **dichotomous key**. You can use the dichotomous key on the right to identify the six leaves above it. Pick one statement from each pair that describes the leaf you want to identify.

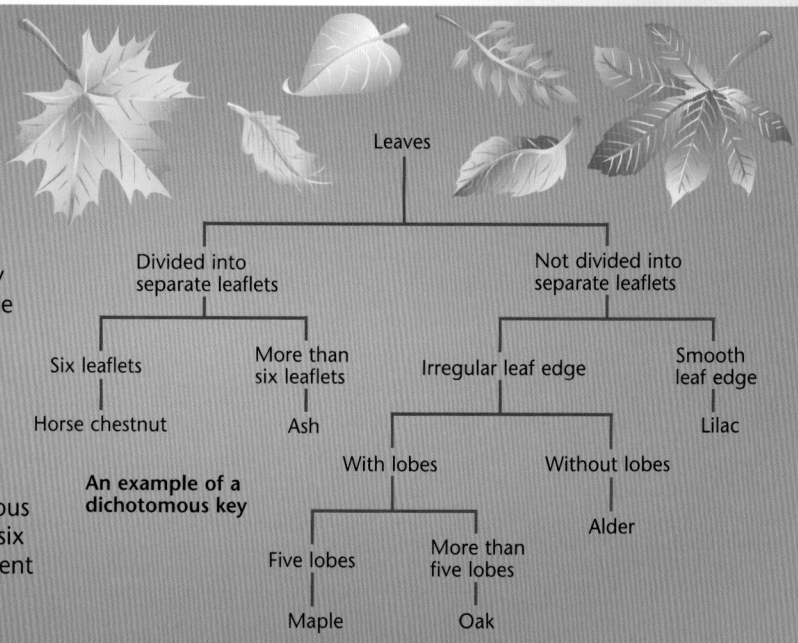

An example of a dichotomous key

* *Chlorophyll, 260; Nucleus, 250; Photosynthesis, 264, Cell wall, 250.*

THE PLANT KINGDOM

The plant kingdom has two main groups: those plants which contain fluid-carrying vascular tissue, and those which do not. These groups are broken into further divisions, based mainly on the plant's reproductive structures.

VASCULAR PLANTS

Not all vascular plants produce seeds, but those plants that do can be divided into five further groups.

In the first four groups (sometimes called **gymnosperms**), the seeds are not contained within a fruit. These groups are:

Conifers are usually tree-sized plants, with waxy needle-like or scaly leaves. They produce cones, which contain their seeds.

Larch cone

Cycads produce very large cones. These grow in the middle of a circle of spiky leaves.

Cycad cone

Ginkgoes are direct relatives of ancient seed-carrying plants. They produce fleshy cones and have soft, fan-shaped leaves.

Ginkgo leaf

Gnetophytes are a small group of plants that grow in very hot areas. They mostly have tough, leathery leaves.

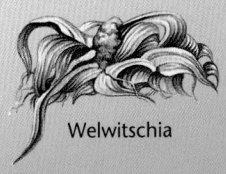

Welwitschia

The fifth group, **magnoliophytes** (or **angiosperms**) is the name given to all flowering plants. They produce seeds enclosed in a fruit of some kind. Flowering plants can be divided into two groups: monocotyledons and dicotyledons.

Monocotyledons have one cotyledon (simple first leaf). Their vascular bundles are scattered throughout the stem.

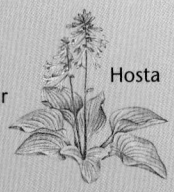

Hosta

Dicotyledons have two cotyledons. Their vascular bundles are arranged in a regular pattern inside the stem (see page 255).

Lesser celandine

Seedless vascular plants have a simple structure, and do not produce flowers. They reproduce using spores*.

Horsetails produce spores inside cones. Their leaves are arranged in rings around the stem.

Horsetail

Ferns reproduce either by producing rhizomes*, or by making spores. These are produced on the underside of the fern's leafy fronds.

Bracken

Club mosses are related to ferns. Their spores are carried in tight, club-shaped spirals at the end of their stalks.

Stag's horn club moss

NON-VASCULAR PLANTS

Plants without vascular tissue, such as mosses and liverworts, are known as **bryophytes**. They are usually small, with single-celled root-like structures, and simple leaves. They have no flowers and reproduce using spores. Most live in damp, shady places.

Mosses on a rock

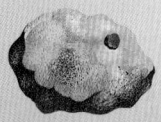

Liverwort

Summary of divisions in the plant kingdom

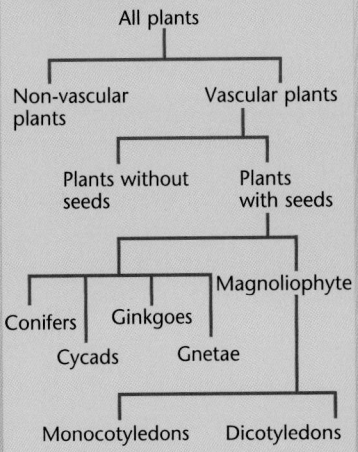

Internet links

Go to **www.usborne-quicklinks.com** and type in "science" to find out more about classifying plants.

There you'll find links to websites where you can:

- Identify trees with a plant key
- Play games to find out more about classification

* *Rhizomes, 278; Spores, 283.*

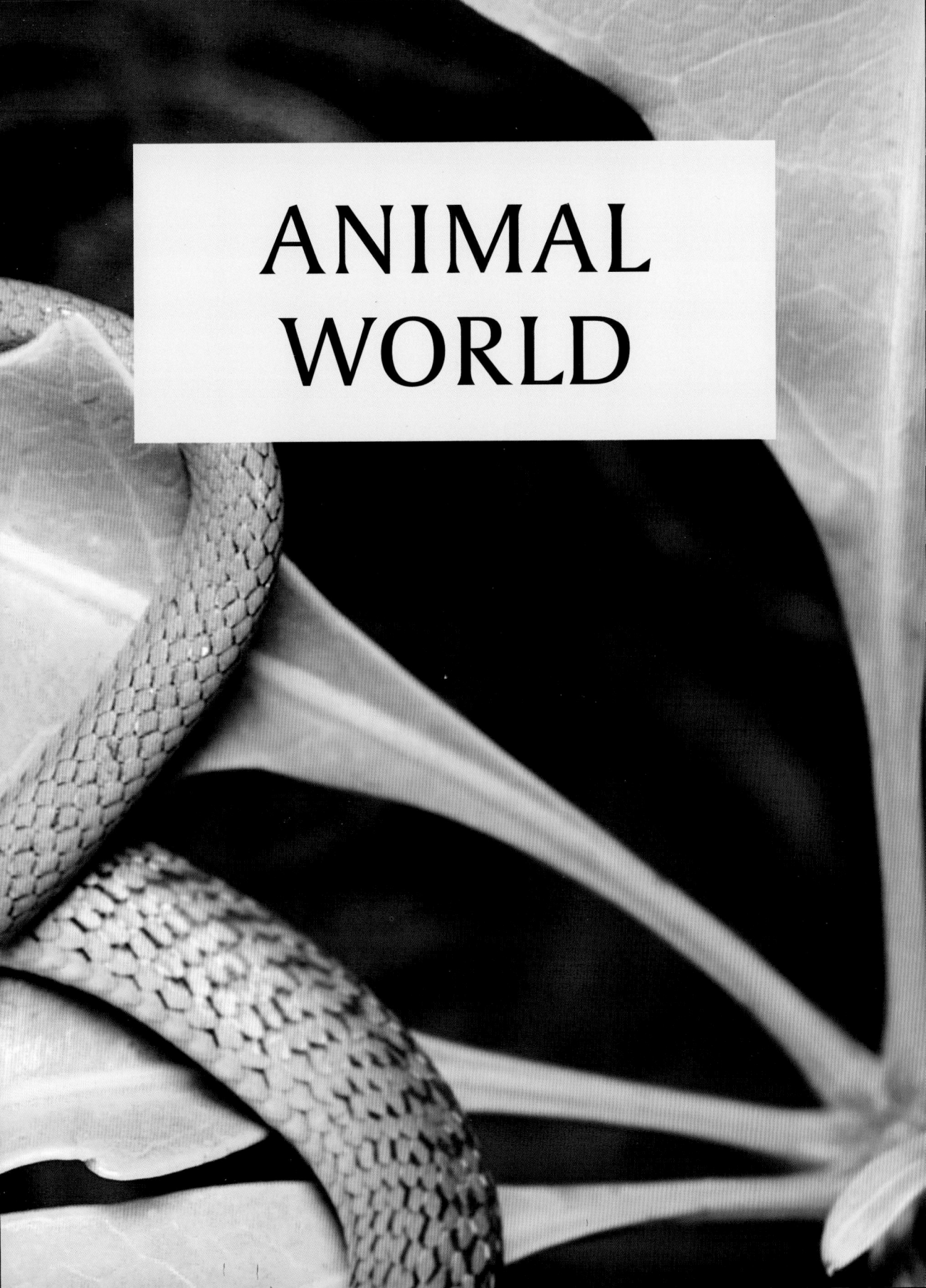

ANIMAL WORLD

ANIMAL CELLS

Every living thing is made up of one or more tiny units called **cells**. All the processes needed for life, such as producing energy from food and removing waste, take place inside cells.

PARTS OF A CELL

There are many different kinds of cell, each with a particular job to do, but most share certain features.

Cells contain a number of small parts called **organelles**, which have various functions. The largest and most important organelle is the **nucleus**. This controls everything that happens inside the cell. It has a double-layered outer skin, called the **nuclear membrane**, and a gel-like middle.

All cells are surrounded by a protective layer called the **cell membrane**, which holds together the contents of the cell. This layer is semipermeable, which means that it lets some substances pass through it, but not others.

The rest of the cell is called the **cytoplasm**. The cell membrane, nucleus and cytoplasm are collectively called the **protoplasm**.

Cluster of animal cells, shown at many thousand times its real size

Centrioles play a part in cell division.

Ribosomes help to build up substances called **proteins**, which are needed for all functions within the cell.

Lysosomes destroy invading bacteria* and parts of the cell which are no longer needed.

Organelles in a typical animal cell (not shown to scale)

The **Golgi complex** stores and distributes the substances made inside the cell.

Nucleus. The nuclear membrane has channels, called **nuclear pores**, which can open and close to let substances in and out of the nucleus. Inside the nucleus are chromosomes*, which contain DNA*.

The **nucleolus** makes the ingredients of ribosomes.

Mitochondria convert simple substances into energy for the cell.

Vacuoles are small, temporary sacs in the cytoplasm. They are used as storage areas for liquids or fats.

The **endoplasmic reticulum** is a series of channels used to transport materials around the cell.

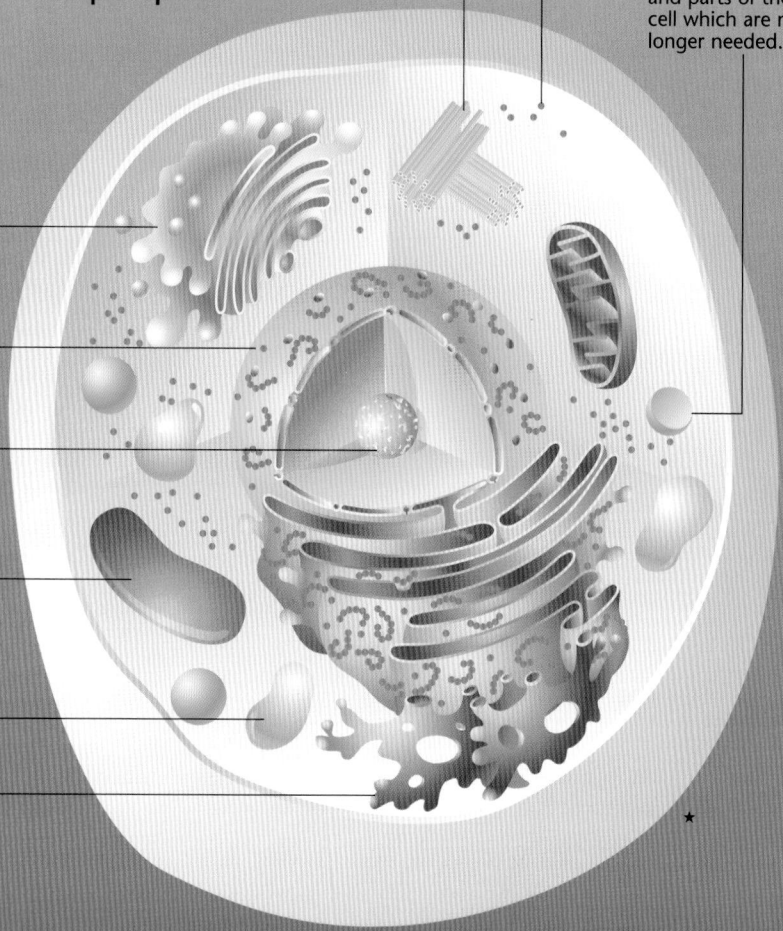

* *Bacteria, 341, 386; Chromosomes, 380; DNA, 382.*

These cells are growing and dividing. Many cells reproduce themselves to allow growth and to replace cells that wear out naturally.

CELL DIVISION

Cells are constantly dying or wearing out, so new ones need to be made. Cells make copies of themselves by splitting into two identical cells, called **daughter cells**.

Stages of cell divison

This single cell is about to start dividing.

The nuclear membrane disappears and the contents of the nucleus begin to pull apart.

The contents reform as two identical nuclei. The division of the nucleus is called **mitosis**.

A **cleavage furrow** forms, cutting through the middle of the cell.

Two daughter cells are formed. The division of the cytoplasm is called **cytokinesis**.

BUILDING WITH CELLS

Different cell types have different functions. This is called **specialization**. Animal cells come in a variety of shapes and sizes, depending on their job.

Cells of the same type combine to form **tissue**. For example, **columnar epithelial cells** are long and column-shaped, and allow substances to pass through them. They group together to make a tissue called **epithelium**. This is ideal for lining organs such as intestines, because gases and liquids can pass through it easily.

Columnar epithelial cells

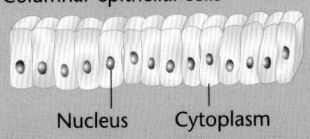

Several different types of tissue together form an **organ**, such as the stomach or intestines.

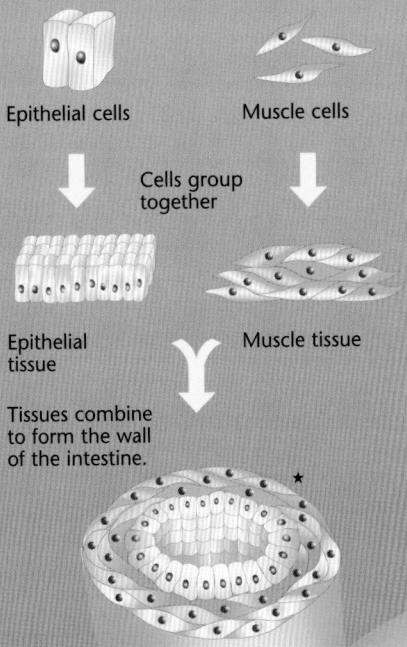

SYSTEMS

A group of organs which does a particular job is known as a **system**. For example, an animal's **digestive system** breaks down its food into simpler substances. The digestive system of the frog below contains four main organs: the stomach, liver, pancreas and intestine.

Organs in a frog's digestive system

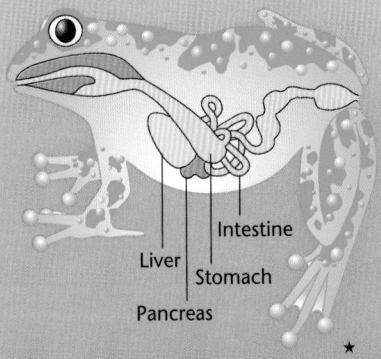

A frog has other systems, including a **skeletal system**, which supports its body, and a **circulatory system**, which transports blood around it. All the systems together make up a living individual called an **organism**, in this case a frog.

Internet links

To find out more about animal cells, go to **www.usborne-quicklinks.com** and type in the keyword "science".

There you'll find links to websites where you can:

- View cells through a microscope
- Learn more about cell division
- Explore a cell in detail

Go to Usborne Quicklinks for links to hand-picked websites on hundreds of subjects.

The links at Usborne Quicklinks are regularly reviewed and updated, so you might find a slightly different selection of websites from the ones described here.

BODY STRUCTURE

The structure of living creatures varies greatly. Animals with the simplest body structure are made of a single cell. More complex creatures are **multicellular**, which means that their bodies are made of hundreds, or even millions, of cells. Most animals have a fluid-filled body cavity and a skeleton.

The body of this starfish is made up of many parts. Its main organs are in the middle.

SIMPLE BODIES

Single-celled amoeba

Simple creatures have a **unicellular** structure. This means that their bodies are made up of a single cell. Some carry out processes common to all animals, such as feeding and moving. The internal parts of many, such as amoebas, are not fixed in place, but move around as the organism changes shape.

SEGMENTED BODIES

The bodies of some animals, such as worms and centipedes, are divided into separate areas called **segments**. A worm's segments are called **metameres**. Each one is almost identical. Segmentation of this type is called **metameric segmentation**. Walls of muscle tissue, each one called a **septum**, divide one metamere from the next.

Earthworm

Simplified cutaway view

Metamere

Septum

Parts of worm's nervous system can be seen in each segment.

Divisions between segments can be seen on the body's surface.

DIVIDED BODIES

Some more complex creatures, such as insects, have a segmented body structure, but the segmentation is not always clearly visible. Their bodies are divided into three parts: the **head**, **thorax** and **abdomen**. Each part is made up of a group of segments called **tagmata**. Unlike metameres, tagmata do not have dividing walls.

Body structure of a wasp

Head (carries main sense organs)

Thorax (upper body area, contains flight muscles)

Abdomen (contains most of insect's body organs)

Most insects have two pairs of wings and three pairs of legs, arranged symmetrically on either side of their thorax.

Paired legs (attached to thorax)

Wings (attached to thorax). This wasp's rear wings are hidden beneath its front wings.

BODY SYMMETRY

Most freely moving animals have **bilateral symmetry**. This means that one half of their body mirrors the other. Other animals, such as starfish, have **radial symmetry**. This means that there are two or more lines of symmetry, which radiate from one central point.

Bilateral symmetry

Only one division can produce two identical halves.

Radial symmetry

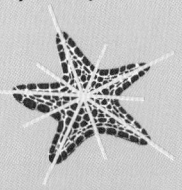

Many lines of symmetry produce identical halves.

BODY CAVITIES

Almost all animals have a fluid-filled body cavity called a **perivisceral cavity**, which acts as a cushion for the internal organs. Two types of perivisceral cavity are the coelom and the haemocoel.

A **coelom** is filled with fluid and contained by a membrane called the **peritoneum**.

Peanut worm

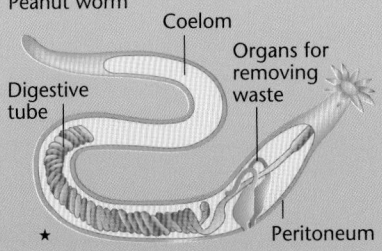

A **haemocoel** is a cavity filled with blood. It forms part of the animal's blood system.

Spider

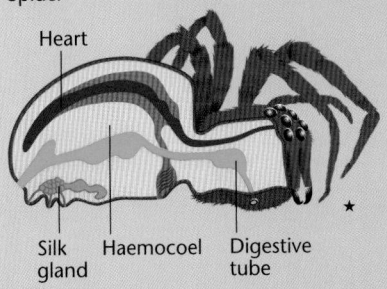

SKELETONS

A **skeleton** provides support for an animal's body, and protects its internal organs from damage. It helps the animal to move, by providing a surface for its muscles to pull on. There are three kinds of skeleton, described below.

An **endoskeleton** is a hard framework inside an animal's body. Endoskeletons are usually made of bone, but in **cartilaginous fish**, such as sharks and rays, they are made of a flexible substance called **cartilage**.

A rabbit's endoskeleton

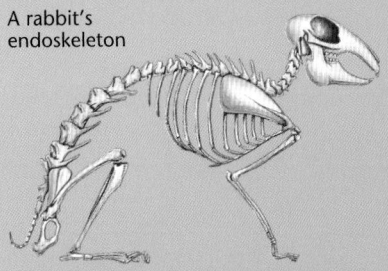

An **exoskeleton** is a hard body covering which supports and protects an animal with no internal skeleton. Crabs and insects are animals with an exoskeleton.

A crab's exoskeleton includes claws and leg coverings.

A **hydrostatic skeleton** is a system in which the fluid-filled body cavity provides pressure for muscles in the body wall to work against. Animals such as sea anemones, which have no hard framework for support, have hydrostatic skeletons.

A sea anemone's body is like a soft bag made up of two layers of tissue with a watery gel in between.

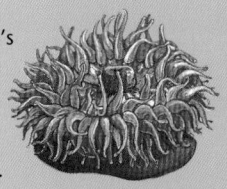

A sea anemone takes in water through its mouth. When the mouth shuts, its body becomes firm and solid, like a water-filled balloon.

Internet links

Go to **www.usborne-quicklinks.com** and type in the keyword "science" to find out more about body structure.

There you'll find links to websites where you can:

- Explore animal body structures
- Play games about body structure

Go to Usborne Quicklinks for links to hand-picked websites on hundreds of subjects.

BODY COVERINGS

All creatures have an outer layer to enclose their bodies. Some animals have a layer of skin, covered with feathers or fur. Others have a hard covering of some kind. In some cases, this covering also provides support for the animal's body.

A pangolin's body is covered with thick, sharp-edged scales. These stick out to defend it from enemies.

WATERPROOFING

Many soft-bodied animals have a waterproof outer layer called a **cuticle**, which is produced by the skin. In some animals, such as earthworms, the cuticle stays soft and waxy. In others, especially arthropods*, the cuticle hardens to form a supportive outer framework or **exoskeleton**.

An arthropod's cuticle prevents its body from drying out. It is tough, but also light enough to allow flight, for example in insects. It is made up of sections called **sclerites**, joined by flexible membranes. This arrangement allows the creature to move freely.

The ridged sections on an ant's body are its sclerites.

See for yourself

Look at a woodlouse under a magnifying lens. As it moves around, notice its sclerites. If it is alarmed, it may curl its flexible body into a ball. After you have finished looking at it, return the animal to where you found it.

Woodlouse

NEW COATS

A lot of animals shed their coverings in order to grow. An arthropod sheds its cuticle when it grows too big for it, and a new, larger one forms. This process is called **ecdysis**.

Crustaceans, such as crabs, have a protective cuticle which they shed. This hard, shield-like "shell" is called a **carapace**.

This crab's new hard covering, or carapace, is fully hardened.

Some other animals have a carapace which is not made of cuticle, and is not shed. Turtles and tortoises, for instance, are born with a carapace made of bony plates fused together, covered with a layer of horn. The carapace is connected to their body at the ribs, spine, shoulders and hips. As the animal grows, each plate in its carapace grows too.

Snails and other molluscs have a protective body covering called a **shell**. This is formed from a substance secreted by the animal's body. Like a tortoise's carapace, the shell grows with the animal and is not shed.

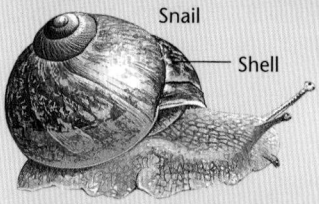

PROTECTIVE PLATES

Some animals are covered in hard plates called **scuta**. These can be made of horn, bone, or a substance called **chitin**. Scuta help to keep the animal safe from predators.

This armadillo's bony scuta are covered with horn.

* *Arthropods, 342.*

PRICKLY PROTECTION

Some mammals, such as porcupines and hedgehogs, have prickly body coverings made of **keratin**. This is the main ingredient of your hair and nails. The animal uses its prickles for protection.

When threatened, this porcupine raises its prickles, called **quills**, as a warning. If attacked, it moves backwards, stabbing the predator with its quills.

SCALY CREATURES

Many animals have a mosaic of **scales** covering their bodies. Scales tend to be thinner than scuta, and are often made from different substances. Many reptiles, for example, have scales made from hardened skin. Scuta are usually horny or bony, and are heavier than scales.

A butterfly's wings are protected by tiny overlapping scales made of chitin. These loose, powdery scales are very fragile, and can rub off if touched. Underneath their scaly coverings, the wings are thin and transparent, like those of a fly.

Close-up of a butterfly's wing

You can see a butterfly's scales under an ordinary microscope.

Small tortoiseshell butterfly

FISH SCALES

There are two main types of fish scales: dermal and placoid. **Dermal scales** are small, bony plates embedded in the skin. They grow out of a tough lower layer of skin called the **dermis**, and are covered by a thinner, slimy layer called the **epidermis**. Fish with bone skeletons have dermal scales.

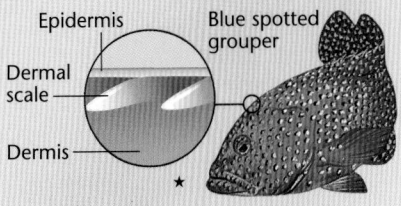

Placoid scales, also called **denticles**, are sharp, backward-pointing scales, which stick out from the skin. Cartilaginous fish*, such as sharks and rays, have placoid scales.

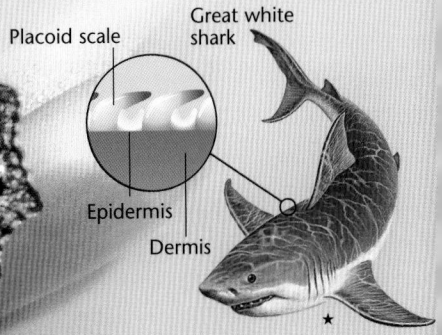

Internet links

Go to **www.usborne-quicklinks.com** and type in "science" to find out more about body coverings.

There you'll find links to websites where you can:

- Investigate the body coverings of various animals
- Learn about bird feathers
- See microscope images

Go to Usborne Quicklinks for links to hand-picked websites on hundreds of subjects.

* *Cartilaginous fish, 301.*

MOVING IN WATER

Most animals are capable of moving from place to place at some stage during their lives. This is called **locomotion**. Many animals have a particular body shape or specialized body parts which helps them to move around. For example, some creatures that live in water have flippers or fins.

The caudal fin (tail fin) propels the body forwards.

Anal fin. In some species, this is called the ventral fin.

A fish uses its fins to control balance and direction.

FALSE FEET

Some single-celled organisms, such as amoebas, do not have individual body parts for locomotion. Instead, they form extensions of their bodies called **pseudopodia** (meaning "false feet") which help them to move.

How an amoeba moves

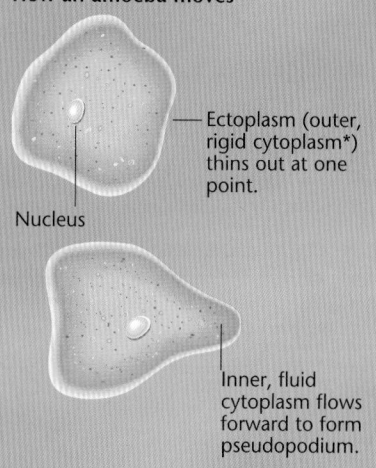

SIMPLE MOVEMENT

Many microscopic organisms are covered with tiny hairs called **cilia**. These flick back and forth like oars to "row" the creature through the water. Organisms with cilia are known as **ciliates**.

Paramecium

Some organisms have long, fine body threads called **flagellae**. These lash to and fro like whips to produce movement. An organism with flagellae is described as a **flagellate**.

Trichomonas

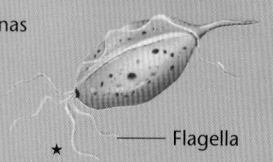

All species of bristleworms have paired projections called **parapodia** along the sides of their bodies. These are used for swimming. Each parapodium ends in bristles called **chaetae**.

Ragworm (type of bristleworm)

Parapodium

Chaetae

JET PROPELLED

Some animals, including squid, octopuses and jellyfish, move around by jet propulsion. Squid and octupuses do this by taking in water and forcing it out of their body through a funnel-shaped tube called a **hyponome**. The force of this water pushes the animal in the opposite direction.

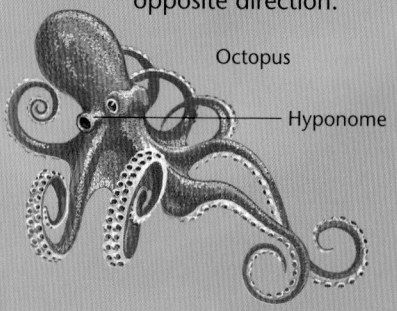

Jellyfish move by filling their bell-like bodies with water, then forcing it out. A jellyfish does this several times, moving itself up, and then drifts slowly down.

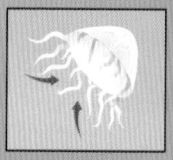

Jellyfish fills its hollow body with water.

Water is pushed out and the jellyfish moves.

* *Cytoplasm, 298.*

Dorsal fin

The dorsal fin and anal fin control changes of direction from side to side, and prevent rolling.

Pectoral fin

Pelvic fin

TYPES OF FINS

All fish have a number of projections called **fins**, which are used as stabilizers, and also to change direction. Fins are supported by fan-shaped **rays**. These are rods of bone or a tough, flexible substance called cartilage. Fish have two sets of fins: median and paired.

Median fins lie in a line down the middle of the fish's back or belly. They are divided into the **dorsal**, **caudal** (tail) and **anal** (or **ventral**) **fins**, shown in the picture above. **Paired fins** (**pectoral** and **pelvic**) stick out sideways from the body. They control movement up or down.

See for yourself

When you next see fish in a tank, look at how they use their pelvic fins. Many move them in a figure-of-eight shape. This helps them to swim very smoothly through the water.

POUCHES OF AIR

Some fish with bone skeletons have a long, air-filled pouch called a **swim bladder** inside their bodies. The fish can control the amount of air inside the bladder, so the density of its body can always be the same as that of the water. This means that the fish does not sink if it stops swimming.

Fish with cartilage skeletons, such as rays, do not have swim bladders. Their bodies are denser than the water, so they must control their position by other means.

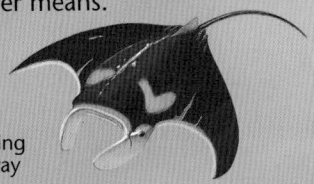

Swimming manta ray

FLIPPERS

Many animals, including some mammals and birds, are well suited to life in the water. They usually have a streamlined shape, and specialized body parts which allow them to swim. Animals such as dolphins, for example, have broad, paddle-like front limbs called **flippers**.

Dolphin

Penguins look clumsy on the land, but they are fantastic swimmers. Their flat, stiff wings are not suitable for flying, but are just the right shape to act as flippers in the water. A penguin can steer under water using its tail and webbed feet.

These penguins' streamlined bodies allow them to glide quickly and easily through the water.

Internet links

Go to **www.usborne-quicklinks.com** and type in "science" to find out more about moving in water.

There you'll find links to websites where you can:

- Watch video clips of dolphins and learn more about them
- See many sea animals swimming
- Learn more about penguins

Go to Usborne Quicklinks for links to hand-picked websites on hundreds of subjects.

FLYING AND GLIDING

Flying allows animals to escape from enemies on the ground, find new sources of food and, in some cases, travel long distances to find a partner. Only creatures with well-developed wings, such as bats, birds and insects, are able to fly, but some animals are able to glide for shorter distances.

This bat's leathery wings are made of skin, stretched over its arms and huge fingers.

Bats are the only mammals that can fly.

BIRDS AND FLIGHT

Birds that fly have many features to help them. These include smooth, light feathers, powerful wings and hollow bones.

BIRD BONES

Many birds have hollow bones, supported by thin, criss-cross structures. These make their bones strong as well as light.

Cross section of a bird's bone

FLIGHT MUSCLES

A bird's wings are attached to a large extension of its breastbone called the **keel**. They are joined by two pairs of large **pectoralis muscles**. These are used to move the wings.

Pectoralis muscles

Cutaway picture of an owl

Keel

FEATHERS

A bird's body and wings are covered with **feathers**. Each one is made up of a central **shaft**, with rows of thread-like **barbs** on either side. Tiny, hooked **barbules** lock the barbs together, creating a flat surface called a **vane**.

Structure of a feather

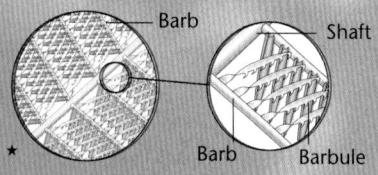

Contour feathers cover the bird's body, giving it a smooth and streamlined shape. **Flight feathers**, also called **remiges**, are long and stiff. They give the wing a large surface area, which is essential for flying.

Flight feathers

The wing can rotate freely at the shoulder, allowing a wide range of movement.

Contour feathers

Nerve endings at the base of each feather can detect tiny changes in air currents.

Gull in flight

FLYING INSECTS

Like birds, insects have light bodies and powerful muscles for flying. However, an insect's body is very large in relation to its thin wings, so it needs much more power than a bird to fly. Energy is stored in the insect's muscles, and is released rapidly as it flies.

Some insects, such as dragonflies, use two pairs of wings to fly. Many insects only use one pair, the other being modified in some way. For example, a beetle's front wings, called **elytra**, form a hard, protective casing made of hardened cuticle* for its rear wings.

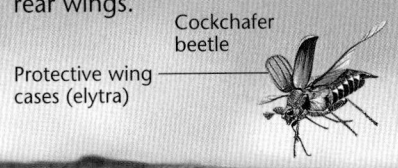

GLIDERS

Several animals have "flying" as part of their name, but they have no wings, so they cannot actually fly. Instead, they use a variety of methods to glide through the air.

The colugo on the right, for example, has flaps of skin between its front and hind legs. When it jumps, it spreads its limbs like wings. It moves its legs and tail to change direction as it glides from tree to tree.

A colugo gliding through the air

A flying lizard stretches out its long ribs to form broad, stiff flaps on either side of its body. When the lizard is resting, these flaps fold away against its body.

This flying lizard can glide up to 15m between trees.

Flying snakes live in rainforests. They climb trees and can glide up to 50m between branches. A flying snake does this by spreading out its ribcage, making its body into a flattened shape. As it glides, it twists its body through the air in S-shaped movements.

Flying snake

See for yourself

Stroke a feather from top to bottom. It will become ruffled as its barbs unhook. If you stroke the feather in the opposite direction, the barbs will join together to make the feather perfectly smooth again.

Internet links

Go to **www.usborne-quicklinks.com** and type "science" to find out more about flying and gliding.

There you'll find links to websites where you can:

- Investigate the principles of flight with games and activities
- Watch slow-motion film clips of birds in flight

Go to Usborne Quicklinks for links to hand-picked websites on hundreds of subjects.

The links at Usborne Quicklinks are regularly reviewed and updated, so you might find a slightly different selection of websites from the ones described here.

* *Cuticle, 302; Exoskeleton, 301.*

MOVING ON LAND

Animals that spend most or all of their lives on land are called **terrestrial animals**. They have many ways of moving around. Most of them use one or more pairs of legs to move. Animals without limbs, such as worms and snakes, move by changing the shapes of their muscular bodies.

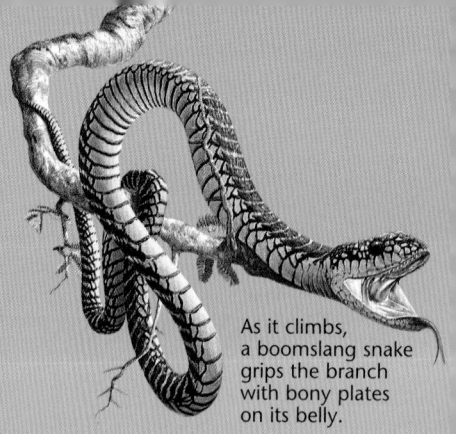

As it climbs, a boomslang snake grips the branch with bony plates on its belly.

CRAWLING

Earthworms, and some other soft-bodied creatures, move using muscles in the body wall. Fluid in the body provides pressure for the muscles to work against. As they expand and contract, different parts of the body move forwards.

How an earthworm moves

The movement of the muscles looks like a wave rippling along the body.

A snake has ribs and powerful muscles along the whole length of its body. Most snakes move by stretching forward and pushing back in S-shaped curves. Bony scuta* (plates) on their bellies help them to grip.

CREEPING

Some caterpillars move by arching their bodies, then stretching forwards. Only one end of the body moves forwards at a time, while the legs at the other end grip the surface. This is called **looping**.

How a caterpillar loops

Back legs grip the ground, and front of body stretches forwards.

Front legs grip the ground, and back of body moves forwards. This pulls body into tight arch.

SWINGING

Many jungle-dwelling primates*, such as gibbons and orang-utans, can climb or swing using their long, strong front limbs and curved gripping fingers. Most primates can also grip well with their toes.

Some primates have a very flexible tail which can be used like an arm, to grip branches. A tail that can grip is called a **prehensile tail**.

A black-handed spider monkey's tail is strong enough to support its whole body.

A cheetah's claws grip the ground like spiked running shoes.

Powerful muscles and a flexible body help the cheetah to move fast.

* *Scuta, 302; Primates, 342.*

USING LEGS

An animal's limbs are arranged symmetrically on either side of its body, and front limbs may look different from back limbs. Animals that walk upright on two legs, such as birds, are called **bipeds**. Most bipeds move one leg forwards with every step, but some birds hop on both legs.

Ostriches have extremely strong legs and they can run very fast.

A four-legged animal is called a **quadruped**. Typically, when walking, diagonally opposite legs move together, for example front left and rear right.

When running fast, most mammals stretch out their front and rear legs and then bring them together in powerful bounding movements.

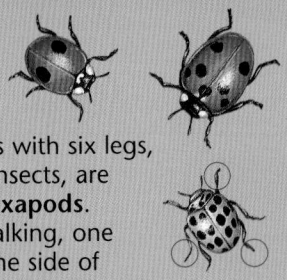

Creatures with six legs, such as insects, are called **hexapods**. When walking, one leg on one side of the body and two legs on the other side move forwards.

Circles show which of the ladybird's legs move together.

Many-legged creatures, called **myriapods**, can have up to 750 legs. These move in wave-like motions along the body.

LEAPING

Some creatures, such as frogs and fleas, can leap huge distances. They do this using powerful muscles in their back legs. Some other creatures, such as the springtail below, have different body parts which allow them to leap.

How a springtail leaps

Tail is folded under the body. Tail is quickly flicked onto the ground. Springtail is pushed into the air.

STANCE

Stance is the word which describes how an animal stands and moves. It is determined by the part of the foot on which the animal stands.

Unguligrade animals, such as horses, walk on hooves at the tips of the toes.

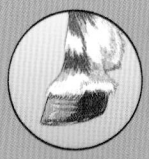

Digitigrade animals, such as dogs, walk on the undersides of the toes.

Plantigrade animals, such as bears, walk on the underside of the whole foot.

See for yourself

Look at different animals, and notice how many legs they have and what part of their feet they walk on. Also, do the animals move their legs differently when they are walking and running?

This Thompson's gazelle can run at up to 80 km/h (50mph).

Internet links

Go to **www.usborne-quicklinks.com** and type in "science" to find out more about moving on land.

There you'll find links to websites where you can:

- Watch a video clip of a cheetah chasing its prey
- Take a virtual trip to a zoo and watch animals via webcams
- Learn more with online activities

Go to Usborne Quicklinks for links to hand-picked websites on hundreds of subjects.

FEEDING

The structure of an animal's mouthparts depends on the kind of food it eats. Teeth, and the part they play in feeding, are described on page 312. Toothless creatures, called **edentates**, often have a beak or a flexible tongue for capturing their food.

A sea anemone's mouth (not visible here) is in the middle of its body.

SIMPLE FEEDING

Single-celled organisms, such as amoebas, do not have mouths. Instead, they feed by a process called **phagocytosis**. Their bodies flow around and engulf tiny food particles. The food is then digested in a chemical-filled area called a **vacuole**.

How an amoeba feeds

FEEDING IN WATER

Many animals **filter feed**, by sieving small creatures out of the water. Barnacles do this using bristly limbs called **cirri**.

Some whales feed using frayed plates of whalebone, called **baleen**, which hang down from their top jaw. Small animals called krill get caught in the baleen.

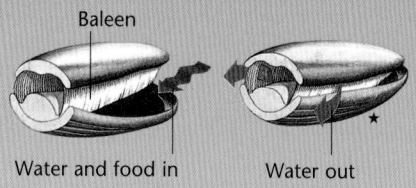

Grey whale filtering water

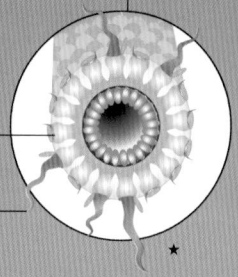

Cnidarians*, such as sea anemones, have tiny sac-like cells called **cnidoblasts** or **thread cells** on their tentacles for seizing food. Each cnidoblast contains a long, poisonous thread called a **nematocyst**. When a tentacle touches something, the threads shoot out to sting and paralyse it. The tentacles then pull the prey into the animal's mouth.

SCRAPERS

Almost all molluscs*, such as snails, have a rough tongue called a **radula**. It is used like a file to scrape plant matter into the animal's mouth. If you listen closely to a feeding snail, you may hear its radula scraping.

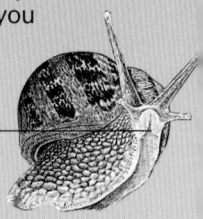

* *Cnidarians, Molluscs, 342.*

INSECT MOUTHPARTS

Insects' mouths are made up of a number of different parts: the mandibles, maxillae, labrum and labium. The appearance of these mouthparts varies from species to species.

A grasshopper's mouthparts ★

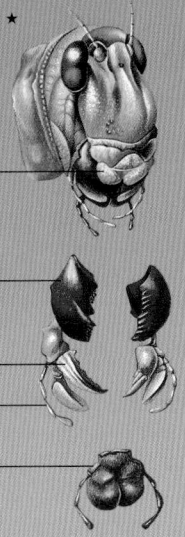

The labium of a housefly is an extended pad-like sucking organ. The fly dissolves its food using saliva, then mops up the liquid with its spongy mouthparts.

In some insects, the maxillae fit together to make a long tube called a **proboscis**. Female mosquitoes have a sharp, rigid proboscis for piercing skin. A butterfly has a flexible proboscis for sucking nectar from flowers.

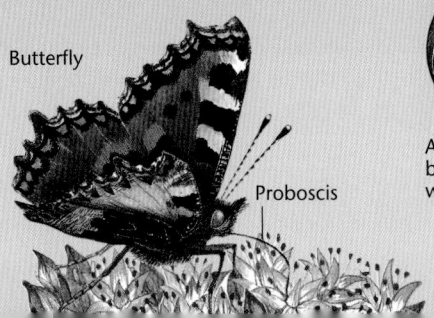

BEAKS

A bird's hard upper and lower jaws come together to form a **beak** or **bill**. The shape and size of a bird's beak depend on the kind of food it eats.

Types of beak

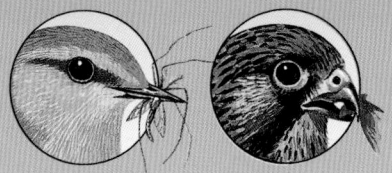

A wood warbler's thin, sharp beak catches insects.

A kestrel's sharp, curved beak tears meat.

A honey-eater's long, thin beak sucks from flowers.

A greenfinch's strong, chunky beak cracks seeds.

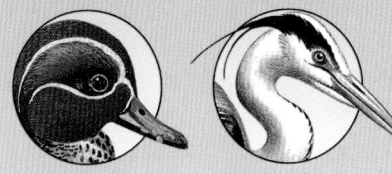

A teal's flattish bill scoops up water plants.

A heron's long, sharp beak stabs fish.

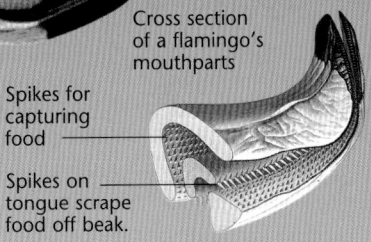

Flamingos have unusual beaks and tongues for sieving food. They feed by raking their beaks through the mud at the bottom of lakes. Tiny plants and animals stick to small spikes on the inside of the beak. The flamingo scrapes the food off its beak using larger spikes on its tongue.

Internet links

To find out more about feeding, go to **www.usborne-quicklinks.com** and type in the keyword "science".

There you'll find links to websites where you can:

- Watch videos clips showing how birds use their beaks
- Look at bugs in microscopic detail
- Find out more about whales

Go to Usborne Quicklinks for links to hand-picked websites on hundreds of subjects.

TEETH AND DIGESTION

Many animals have **teeth** to tear, chew or grind their food. Animals with teeth are described as **dentate**. After it is swallowed, an animal's food is broken down further by the **digestive system**, so it can be absorbed by the body. Animals have different sorts of teeth and digestive systems depending on the type of food they eat.

Like many plant eaters, a giraffe has flat, ridged teeth for grinding plants.

MEAT EATERS

Meat-eating animals, called **carnivores**, have sharp teeth for tearing meat. Dagger-like **canines** are used for piercing and killing prey. The large, jagged **carnassials** are used for slicing meat. Smaller front teeth called **incisors** come together to bite or scrape meat from bones.

Sharks' teeth grow in rows in their jaws. When they lose a tooth from the front set, another moves forwards to take its place. Almost all mammals have two sets of teeth during their lifetimes. The second set, called **permanent teeth**, cannot be replaced if lost.

This picture of a lioness shows the teeth of a carnivore.

Carnassials slide against each other to slice flesh.

Canines stab and pierce flesh.

Incisors scrape meat from bone.

PLANT EATERS

Plant-eating animals, called **herbivores**, have square cheek teeth (**premolars** and **molars**), for grinding plants. The incisors are long and chisel-shaped. In ruminants, such as cows and deer, these grip plants against a hard pad in the top jaw. A gap called the **diastema**, between the incisors and cheek teeth, allows space to move the tongue.

This deer's skull shows the teeth of a herbivore.

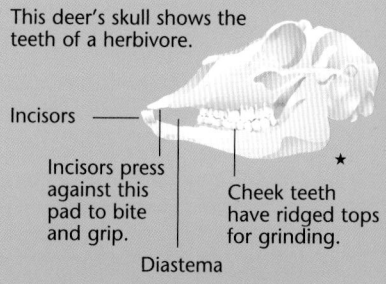

ALL-PURPOSE TEETH

Animals that eat both plants and meat are called **omnivores**. An omnivore's teeth can be many different shapes and sizes, depending on the kind of food it eats. For instance, a monkey has long canines to pierce flesh, and flat back teeth to grind plants.

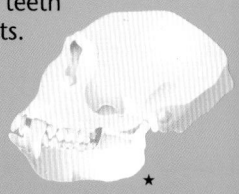

This monkey's skull shows an omnivore's varied types of teeth.

DIGESTING PLANTS

Plants contain a tough substance called **cellulose**, which is hard to digest. Herbivores therefore have more complex digestive organs than other animals. Most herbivores have a sac inside their body called a **caecum**, in which plant matter is broken down by bacteria*.

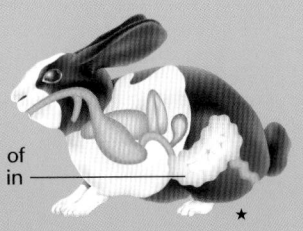

Ruminants, such as cows, sheep and deer, have four stomach-like chambers to digest their food: the rumen, reticulum, omasum and abomasum.

Digestive system of a cow

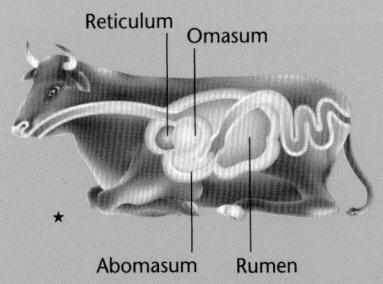

First, food passes unchewed into the **rumen**. There, bacteria start to break down cellulose. The partially-digested food is processed in the second chamber, or **reticulum**. It is then returned to the mouth to be re-chewed. Food at this stage is called the **cud**.

After chewing, the food is swallowed for a second time, and then broken down further in the remaining chambers, the **omasum** and the **abomasum** (true stomach).

DIGESTION IN BIRDS

Birds have no teeth to break up their food, so they have a digestive system specially designed to deal with solids.

After food has been swallowed, it is stored in a thin-walled pouch called the **crop**. It then travels to a thick, muscular-walled pouch called the **gizzard**. Here, the food is ground up by muscular ridges on the gizzard walls and small stones which the bird has swallowed.

Meat-eating birds, such as owls and hawks, swallow their prey whole. The parts which cannot be digested, such as bones and fur, form a compact **pellet** inside the bird's stomach. This is coughed back up and brought out through the mouth.

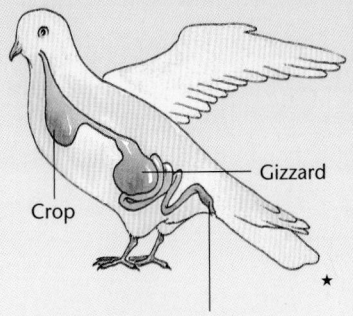

Waste is stored in a chamber called the **cloaca**, before being passed out of the bird's body.

Owls eat small animals, such as frogs and mice, in one piece.

This pellet came from a barn owl. An owl pellet may contain the skeletons of several small animals.

See for yourself

Next time you are in a wooded area, look for bird pellets. Use a stick to turn them over, and see what they are made up of. You are most likely to find pellets under trees and other places where birds roost. You can use a magnifying glass to look closely, but never touch a pellet with your hands.

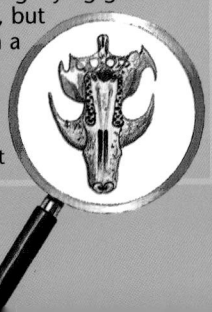

Bone from inside a pellet

Internet links

Go to **www.usborne-quicklinks.com** and type in "science" to find out more about teeth and digestion.

There you'll find links to websites where you can:

- Dissect a virtual owl pellet
- Investigate how animals feed and how their teeth and mouthparts have adapted over time

Go to Usborne Quicklinks for links to hand-picked websites on hundreds of subjects.

* *Bacteria, 341.*

BREATHING

Animals breathe in oxygen from air or water. They use it to release energy from digested food, breathing out carbon dioxide as a waste product. The process by which gases pass in and out of the body is known as **gaseous exchange**. This takes place in the **respiratory organs**. Gases travel to and from these organs in the blood.

You can see this shark's gill slits behind its head.

BREATHING IN WATER

Most water-dwelling animals take in oxygen through organs called **gills** or **branchiae**. There are two types of gills – internal and external.

Internal gills are found inside the bodies of many water creatures, especially fish. Most fish have four pairs of gills, with openings called **gill slits** between them. In bony fish, the gills are covered by a bony flap called the **operculum**. In cartilaginous fish*, they are open to the water at all times.

Breathing with gills

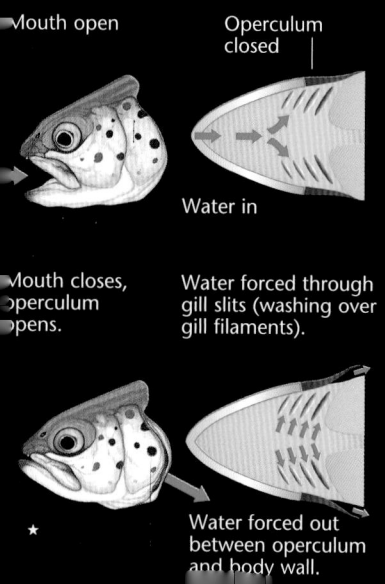

The water which washes over the gills comes in through a fish's mouth, and is pumped out through the gill slits. Each gill is made up of a curved rod called the **gill bar** or **gill arch**, which has many fine gill **filaments** radiating from it.

Each gill filament has even finer **gill lamellae** branching off it, like the branches of a feather. These all contain blood vessels. Oxygen is taken into the blood from the water, and carbon dioxide from the blood passes out to be washed away.

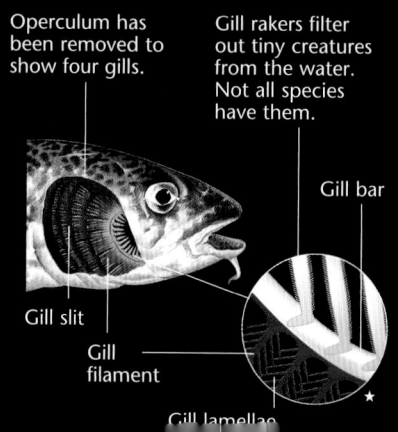

Many other water creatures, such as caddisfly larvae and tadpoles, have **external gills**. These are on the outside of the body. Their exact form depends on the type of animal, but in many cases they are frilly growths behind the head.

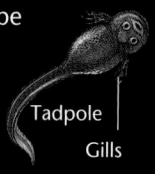

Some simple water creatures have tubes called **siphons**. These carry gases, which are dissolved in water, to and from their gills. A siphon that carries gases to the gills is described as **inhalant**, and one that carries them from the gills is described as **exhalant**.

Cutaway diagram of a whelk

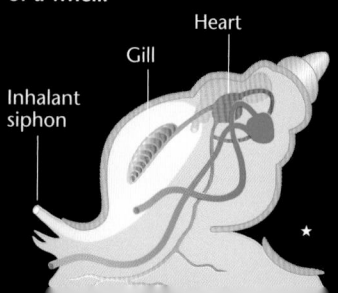

AMPHIBIANS

Amphibians* can spend time both in water and on land, and take oxygen from water or air. A frog, for instance, does this in a variety of ways. In water, dissolved oxygen passes in through its skin to the blood vessels beneath, and carbon dioxide passes out the same way.

On land, a frog breathes using a pair of light sacs called lungs. Gaseous exchange through the blood vessels inside these lungs works in the same way as in other vertebrate* lungs (see right). They are less efficient, however, because the frog uses a lot of energy actively pumping the gases in and out. So even on land, much gaseous exchange still happens through the skin.

The frog is also able to exchange gases directly through blood vessels in the lining of its mouth.

This frog's skin gleams with natural moisture. Gases dissolve in the moisture and are exchanged through the skin.

LUNGS

All reptiles, birds and mammals have a pair of **lungs** for exchanging gases. Their breathing is automatic and effortless. Air flows in and out of the lungs through a tube called the **trachea** or **windpipe**. This splits into two thick tubes, each one called a **bronchus**, which in turn branch into smaller **secondary** and **tertiary bronchi** inside the lung.

Tertiary bronchi branch into tiny tubes called **bronchioles**. Each bronchiole ends in a small sac called an **alveolus**. Gases are exchanged through tiny blood vessels on the surface of each alveolus.

Diagram of a mammal's lung

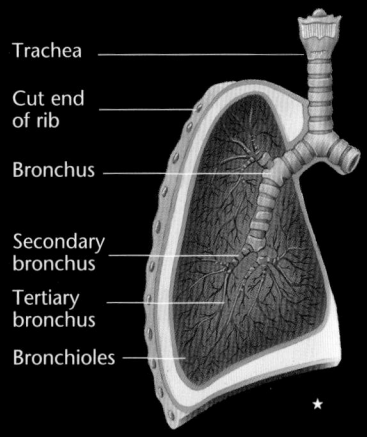

HOW INSECTS BREATHE

Gaseous exchange in insects takes place through small holes called **spiracles** in their bodies. Air enters the spiracles, and travels through a network of pipes called **tracheae**. These branch into tiny tubes called **tracheoles**, which carry gases to and from cells in the body.

Respiratory system of a flea

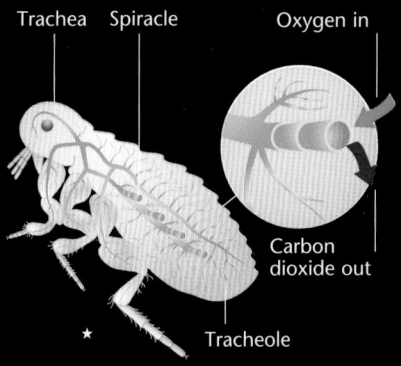

See for yourself

Certain large, active insects need a way of taking in extra oxygen. They do this by opening their spiracles and pumping their abdomen in and out. You may see a grasshopper or a large moth doing this when it is resting.

Internet links

To find out more about breathing, go to **www.usborne-quicklinks.com** and type in the keyword "science".

There you'll find links to websites where you can:

- See clips of whales and dolphins and find out how they breathe
- Investigate how animals breathe, with pictures and diagrams

Go to Usborne Quicklinks for links to hand-picked websites on hundreds of subjects.

** Amphibians, 342; Vertebrates, 322.*

INTERNAL BALANCE

In order to stay alive, an animal's temperature must remain within certain limits, and substances in its body, such as salts and water, need to be kept at the right level. Keeping the body and the chemicals inside it in a balanced state is called **homeostasis**. Solid and liquid waste must also be removed. The parts of the body that deal with this are known as the **excretory organs**. In most animals, they include the lungs, skin, liver and kidneys.

BODY TEMPERATURE

An animal cannot survive for long if it is too hot or too cold, because its organs cannot work efficiently. Keeping the body at the right temperature is called **thermoregulation**. The animal's skin and blood usually play an important part in this.

Mammals and birds can keep their body at the same internal temperature in most conditions. They are described as **warm-blooded**. All other animals are **cold-blooded**. This means that their body temperature is not under their internal control, and it changes with the temperature of their surroundings.

WARMING UP

When a warm-blooded animal needs extra heat, its feathers or hairs stand on end. These act like a blanket, trapping warm air next to its skin. The animal may also begin to shiver, which produces heat. Both of these actions happen automatically when an animal's body temperature becomes too low.

Cold-blooded creatures, though, have no way of using their bodies to keep warm. If their temperature is too low, they must bask in the Sun to raise it again.

Like all reptiles, green anoles are cold-blooded. They keep warm by sunning themselves.

These young owls have fluffy down feathers, which trap heat next to their bodies.

COOLING DOWN

Cold-blooded animals must find shade or water to cool their bodies. Warm-blooded animals can cool down in other ways. For example, some sweat when they are too hot. The evaporation of moisture from their skin cools them down. A hairy animal that is unable to sweat may pant instead. It loses moisture and heat from the tongue's surface and in air it breathes out. Many desert mammals, like this fennec fox, lose heat through the lining of their huge ears.

Fennec fox

WATER BALANCE

All creatures need to keep the amount of water in their bodies at the right level, or their organs will not work properly.

Single-celled creatures, such as Paramecium, do this using a tiny sac in their bodies called a **contractile vacuole**.

Paramecium

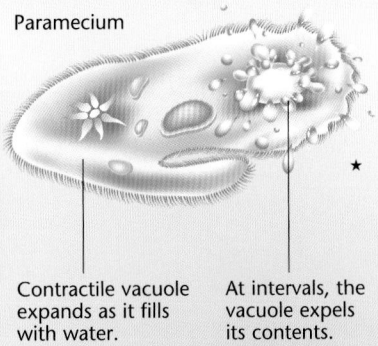

LIVER AND KIDNEYS

In many animals, most waste is removed from the body by the liver and kidneys. The **liver** breaks down amino acids from food, to produce a substance called **urea**. This is mixed with blood and taken to the **kidneys**. These filter the blood, removing the urea, along with water and harmful salts, which form a liquid called **urine**. This is stored in a sac-like organ called the **bladder**, which is emptied regularly.

Diagram of kidneys and bladder

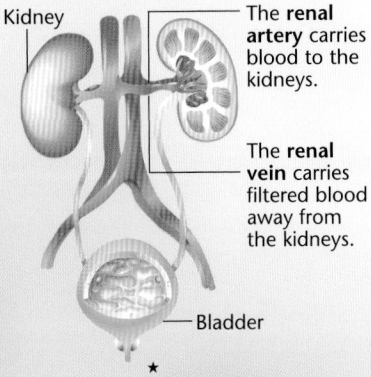

WASTE TUBES

Arthropods* do not have kidneys or a liver. Instead, they have tubes called **malpighian tubules**. These remove liquid waste from the body cavity (haemocoel*). The waste is turned into solid **uric acid** in the gut. Any water is reabsorbed into the blood. The uric acid leaves the body.

Excretory system of a spider

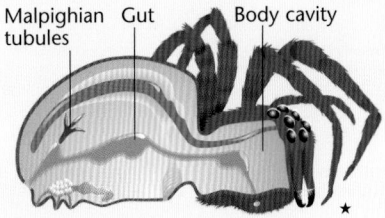

Some soft-bodied creatures, such as simple worms, have waste tubes called **protonephridia**. Waste enters these through hollow **flame cells** and leaves the body through tiny holes called **nephridiopores**.

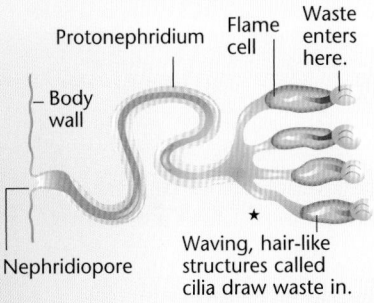

Birds have large, efficient kidneys, but no bladder. They excrete a solid waste called uric acid.

Internet links

Go to **www.usborne-quicklinks.com** and type in the keyword "science" to find out more about internal balance.

There you'll find links to websites where you can:

- Investigate how animals keep cool in hot climates
- Follow the life of a lizard

Go to Usborne Quicklinks for links to hand-picked websites on hundreds of subjects.

** Arthropods, 342; Haemocoel, 301.*

SENDING MESSAGES

The process of giving information that another creature can understand is called **communication**. Animals communicate with each other in many ways, using colours, sounds, movements and chemicals. Most of their messages are connected with finding a mate or giving a warning to other animals.

A skunk growls, stamps its feet and raises its tail to warn enemies to leave it alone, or it will spray a smelly liquid at them.

COLOUR CODING

Many animals respond to particular patterns or colours. A male European robin, for example, will become aggressive when a rival shows its red breast near its territory. A display like this that triggers a certain response is called a **sign stimulus**.

European robin displaying red breast

Creatures which are foul-tasting, poisonous, or have a painful sting or bite, often have brightly coloured bodies. Predators quickly learn to avoid any animals with these bright colours.

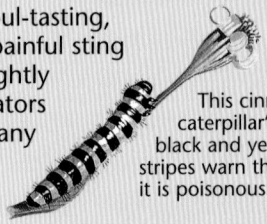

This cinnabar caterpillar's black and yellow stripes warn that it is poisonous.

A male frigate bird's throat sac is usually orange, but during the mating season it turns red and can be puffed out.

The frigate bird sits on a nest of sticks as he displays. If a female is interested, she offers him more sticks.

Some harmless animals have similar colours to poisonous ones. Predators think that these animals are dangerous and leave them alone. This copy-cat colouration is called **mimicry**.

Swallowtail butterfly

African monarch butterfly

Birds will not eat the non-poisonous swallowtail, because they mistake it for the poisonous African monarch.

Animals often display coloured body parts to attract a mate. For instance, a male frigate bird inflates his bright red throat sac to attract females. He also snaps his bill and holds his body in different poses.

The males of many other bird species, such as peacocks, develop fantastic plumage during the mating season. They raise their feathers and shiver them in a dazzling display.

BODY LANGUAGE

Many animals, especially those that live in groups, give out messages by the way they move or hold their bodies. Bees, for example, move in particular patterns, or **dances**, to show where food can be found. A dance can tell the other bees about the quality of the food, and where to find it.

The waggle dance of a bee

The bee follows a figure-of-eight path, waggling its abdomen in the middle of the pattern.

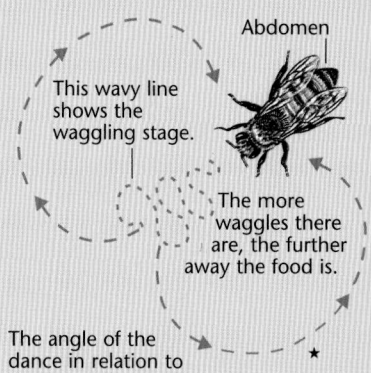

MAKING NOISES

Most animals use sounds to communicate a wide variety of messages. Sounds can be produced using different parts of the body.

When you hear a bird sing, it may be trying to attract a mate, or warning other birds not to come near its territory. The bird sings using a part of its windpipe called the **syrinx**.

Some insects, such as locusts, make sounds by **stridulation**. The insect rubs together two body parts, usually the legs and wings, to make a shrill chirp or whine. The noise attracts females.

A grasshopper rubs tiny pegs on its legs against its wings to make a noise.

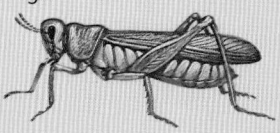

A female moth can release scent (pheromones) into the air.

A male moth can detect minute traces of the female's scent from over a mile away.

CHEMICAL MESSAGES

Many animals communicate by releasing chemicals called **pheromones** into the air. Some insects, for example, release incredibly powerful pheromones to attract a mate.

A number of male animals spray urine, or release other chemicals from glands on their bodies, to mark their territory. Other animals recognize these smelly areas as belonging to that male, and stay well away.

ORDER OF IMPORTANCE

Animals that live in groups are called **social** animals. In some social species, such as wolves, body language is used to show the importance of each animal. A more powerful wolf, called a **dominant** wolf, nips weaker wolves, called **subordinates**, on the neck. This shows that he is more important.

Wolf at the top of the pack

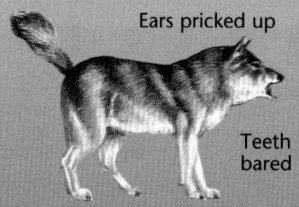

Tail and body held straight

Wolf at the bottom of the pack

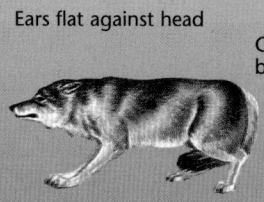

Tail tucked under body

Internet links

Go to **www.usborne-quicklinks.com** and type in "science" to find out more about sending messages.

There you'll find links to websites where you can:

- Listen to many different animal sounds
- Try an animal sounds quiz
- Identify different birdsongs

Go to Usborne Quicklinks for links to hand-picked websites on hundreds of subjects.

ANIMAL SENSES

Most bats have small eyes, but large, sensitive ears.

All animals need **senses**, that is, they must be able to take in information from around them and to respond. Sensitive cells called **receptors**, found on or just under the surface of an animal's body, collect this information and send messages to its brain. There, the messages are turned into **sensations**, such as sights and sounds.

HEARING

Most land animals hear by detecting air movements called **sound waves**. These hit a thin surface called the **tympanum**, which vibrates. Tiny bones pass the vibrations on inside, and messages are sent to the brain. In many animals, a channel, and often an outer body part, leads the sound waves into the body. In these cases, the whole thing is called an **ear**, and the tympanum is called the **eardrum**.

A mammal's ear ★

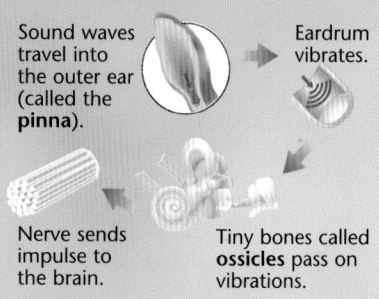

See for yourself

Stretch some plastic film tightly across the top of a tube, such as a cardboard tube from inside a roll of kitchen paper, and put a few grains of rice on it. Ask someone to clap beneath the tube. See how the air vibrations move the film, which moves the rice. This is how sound waves move the eardrum and ossicles.

Some animals have a simpler structure, with the tympanum on the body surface, and a less complex system inside. This is then usually called a **tympanal organ**. In some animals, such as frogs, the tympanal organ is on the head, but others, such as crickets, have them on their legs.

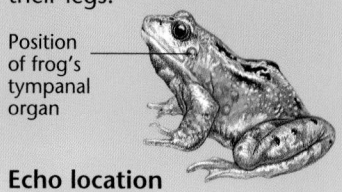

Echo location describes the way that some animals detect the size and position of objects around them. Bats, for example, give out very high-pitched sounds as they fly. The sound waves bounce off nearby objects, and return to the bat. These echoes help bats to avoid obstacles, and to find food in the dark.

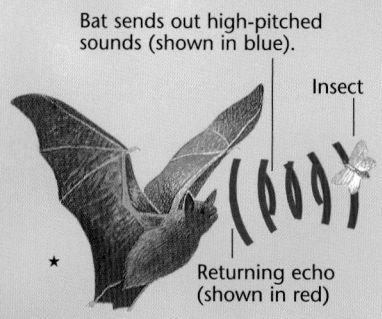

BALANCE

In many species, the brain keeps the body balanced using information from sensitive cells in the ears along with messages from the eyes. Some creatures, though, have specialized body parts which help them to balance.

Jellyfish, for example, have sac-like organs of balance called **statocysts**. These contain tiny grains called **statoliths** which move around as the animal swims. The grains touch sensitive cells, which tell the animal which way up its body is.

Floating jellyfish

Flies have small, modified back wings called **haltères**. These are used to keep the animal's body balanced as it flies.

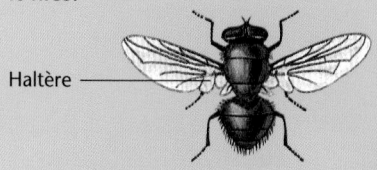

SIGHT

Many animals have eyes. These are the organs which allow them to see their surroundings. Eyes contain sensors called **photoreceptors**, which detect light.

Insects and some other creatures, such as crabs, have **compound eyes**. Each eye is made up of hundreds of tiny lenses. Each lens sees an individual image. The animal's brain puts together this information to make a complete **mosaic image**.

Compound eye

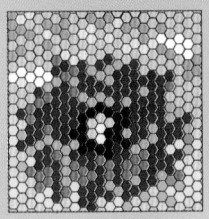

Mosaic image of flower as seen by an insect ★

Many animals' eyes have a slit in the middle called a **pupil**. This expands and contracts to let in different amounts of light. Animals which are active at night, called **nocturnal** animals, have large eyes, with pupils that can open very wide to let in as much light as possible.

Cat's eyes in bright light

Cat's eyes in dim light ★

Nocturnal animals and some deep-sea fish have a shiny layer at the back of their eyes called a **tapetum**. This acts like a mirror, collecting whatever light is available. When you see a cat's eyes shining in the dark, light is reflecting off its tapetum.

EYE POSITION

The area that an animal can see is called its **field of vision**. It depends on the position of the animal's eyes. Most plant-eating animals, for instance, have eyes on the sides of their head. This helps them to look out for predators while they are grazing. This kind of vision is called **lateral vision.**

This suslik can watch all around for predators.

Predators and tree-dwelling animals have eyes on the front of their head, which gives them **binocular vision**. This allows them to focus on objects in the distance, such as their prey.

Monkeys, apes and humans also have **stereoscopic vision**. Each eye views things from a slightly different angle. The brain joins the two views to form a 3D image.

The position of this orang-utan's eyes help it to judge distances when swinging from tree to tree.

See for yourself

You can do a simple test to show that humans have stereoscopic vision. Hold both hands at arm's length, with the index fingers extended and pointing towards each other. Close one eye and try to bring your two fingertips together. You will find this is harder to do without both eyes open.

Internet links

Go to **www.usborne-quicklinks.com** and type in "science" to find out more about animal senses.

There you'll find links to websites where you can:

- Investigate how nocturnal animals see in the dark
- Explore some amazing animal "super senses"

Go to Usborne Quicklinks for links to hand-picked websites on hundreds of subjects.

TOUCH

The sense of touch can help an animal to find its way around, or to bond with other members of its species. For example, some animals groom each other, or rub their body parts together.

Sensors called **tactile receptors** allow an animal to detect touch. Animals with backbones, called **vertebrates**, usually have tactile receptors covering most of their bodies. Animals without backbones, called **invertebrates**, only have them on particular parts.

TENTACLES

Tentacles are long, flexible structures found in many molluscs, such as snails, and some sea creatures. In most cases, the animal uses its tentacles to grasp food and feel its way around.

An octopus has eight sensitive tentacles.

WHISKERS

Most mammals, such as cats and mice, have long, stiff hairs, called **whiskers** or **vibrissae**, on their faces. These are very sensitive to touch.

Nerve endings at the base of this hamster's whiskers can detect the slightest movement.

ANTENNAE

Many animals, such as insects and crustaceans (crabs and related creatures), have whip-like, jointed structures called **antennae** or **feelers** on their heads.

Antennae help an animal identify smells and tastes. They can detect changes in air currents, and the texture of a surface. Some animals, such as barnacles, use antennae to attach themselves to something. Others may use them for swimming.

SENSITIVE BRISTLES

The hard body covering of most invertebrates, such as insects, is not very sensitive. For this reason, many invertebrates have bristles called **setae** which stick out of their bodies. At the base of each seta is a nerve which responds to vibrations or air movement.

A longhorn beetle's large antennae are jointed and very flexible.

This beetle's body has a covering of tiny, sensitive hairs (setae).

SMELL AND TASTE

Organs used for smelling and tasting contain sensors called **chemoreceptors**. These are usually in an animal's mouth, but can also be found on other parts of the body.

Some fish, for example, have taste and smell sensors all over their bodies. Many insects, though, have chemoreceptors only in certain places, such as on the ends of their legs. These allow the insects to taste their food simply by walking on it.

Sensors on the feet of this fly let it taste the substance it is walking over and help it to decide whether or not to eat it.

Many arthropods* also have feeler-like organs, called **palps**, formed from their mouthparts. Palps contain chemoreceptors which allow the animal to smell and taste. Some touch-sensitive organs are also called palps.

See for yourself

The senses of smell and taste often work together. This is why you may find it hard to taste food when you have a cold and your nose is blocked. Try pinching your nose while eating something, and see how well your sense of taste works.

A snake brings scents and tastes into its mouth by flicking its tongue out and in. Two pits called **Jacobson's organs** in the roof of its mouth can identify these scents and tastes. This helps the snake to track prey. In addition, some snakes have a **pit organ** on its head, which can detect their prey's body heat from a distance.

Coral snake flicking its tongue out and in to taste the air

OTHER SENSES

Fish and some amphibians* have two tube-like channels in their bodies called **lateral lines**. These lie along the sides of the body, just under the skin, and are filled with water. Lateral lines detect currents and pressure changes in the water caused by other animals.

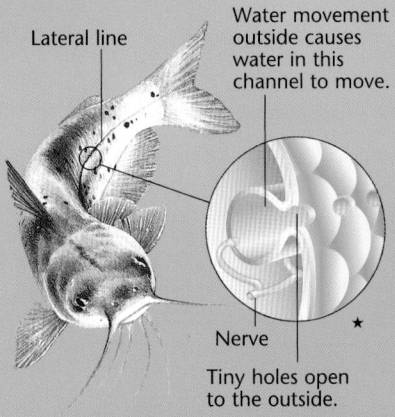

A shark can detect electrical pulses given off by creatures nearby. It does this using small chambers called **ampullae of Lorenzi** in its head. Sensitive hairs in these chambers connect to nerve cells which detect electricity. This sense is called **electroreception**.

Scientists are not certain what senses help a bird to migrate*, but they have many theories. It is possible that birds can sense the Earth's magnetic field and use it as a guide.

Arctic terns use many senses to find their way to the Antarctic and back.

Internet links

Go to **www.usborne-quicklinks.com** and type "science" to find out more about animal senses.

There you'll find links to websites where you can:

- Find out more about bug senses
- Investigate how animals use senses to find and choose food
- Learn more with online activities

Go to Usborne Quicklinks for links to hand-picked websites on hundreds of subjects.

* Amphibians, 315, 342; Arthropods, 342; Migration, 329.

CREATING NEW LIFE

Every living thing can create more of its own kind. This process is called **reproduction**. Most animals pair up to do this, in couples made up of one male and one female partner. Simple creatures, though, can **clone**, or copy, their own bodies, without needing a partner. This is called **asexual reproduction**.

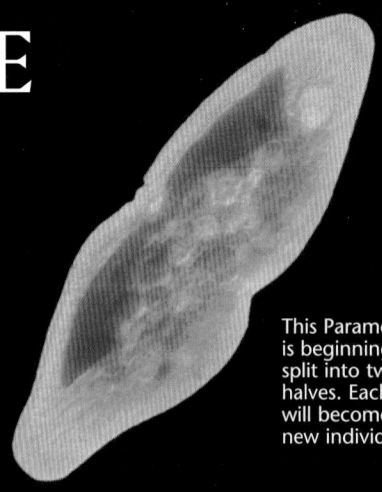

This Paramecium is beginning to split into two halves. Each one will become a new individual.

SPLITTING

Single-celled creatures, such as amoebas, reproduce asexually by dividing into identical halves. This is called **binary fission**.

Some tiny organisms reproduce many times by constantly splitting. This is called **multiple fission**. In this way, large numbers of new individuals, called **daughter cells**, are produced in a short time.

A few creatures, such as corals, remain joined to their parent after asexual reproduction has taken place. This is known as **incomplete fission**.

This coral reef is built up of many individual corals joined together.

BUDDING

Some simple animals, such as hydra, reproduce by forming growths or **buds** from their bodies. This is called **budding**. Each bud eventually breaks off and becomes a new individual.

Budding in a hydra

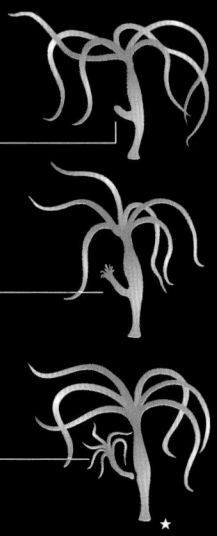

BREAKING DOWN

A small number of animals can produce new individuals from parts of their bodies. This is called **fragmentation**.

Fragmentation in a flatworm

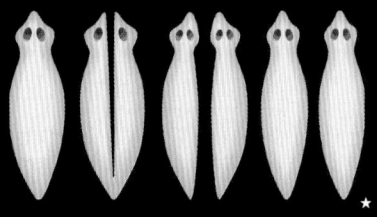

If a flatworm is split into pieces, each piece can become a new worm.

BUILDING UP

Some creatures, such as starfish, sea cucumbers and certain lizards, can re-grow parts of their body which have broken off. This is called **regeneration**.

Starfish

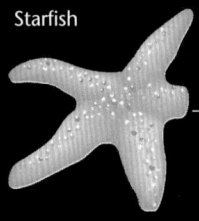

If an arm is broken off, a new one will grow to replace it.

MALE AND FEMALE

A result of asexual reproduction is that any weaknesses in the parent are always passed to the young. **Sexual reproduction***, by contrast, involves joining the sex cells of a male and a female. The young then inherit features, called **traits**, from both parents.

In most species, males and females are separate. However, some creatures, such as snails and earthworms, have both male and female sex cells in their bodies. These creatures are called **hermaphrodites**.

Snail with eggs

After fertilization has taken place (see below), a snail lays eggs which it buries in a hole.

The joining of male and female sex cells is called **fertilization**. Hermaphrodites generally do not fertilize themselves, but swap male sex cells to fertilize each other. The young inherit traits from both parents.

See for yourself

When two earthworms swap sex cells, a saddle-like body part called the **clitellum** makes a sticky substance which holds their bodies together. Next time you see a worm, look for its clitellum.

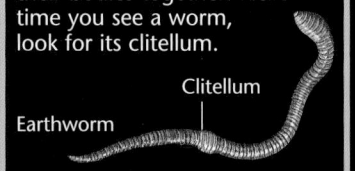

SEXUAL AND ASEXUAL

Tiny insects called aphids have a reproductive cycle which has both sexual and asexual stages.

During the warm spring and summer months, there is plenty of food to eat. The female aphids reproduce asexually. They produce many live female young, and later live male young. These all grow from the sex cells inside the females' bodies, without being fertilized by male sex cells. This is called **parthenogenesis**.

When the summer is over, the aphids reproduce sexually. After fertilization, the females lay eggs, from which new females hatch the following spring.

In a colony of bees, only the queen produces young. She reproduces sexually, receiving sex cells from the males and laying fertilized eggs. These develop into females called **workers**. The queen also lays eggs that have not been fertilized. These develop into males called **drones**.

Drone (male) | Queen bee | Worker (female)

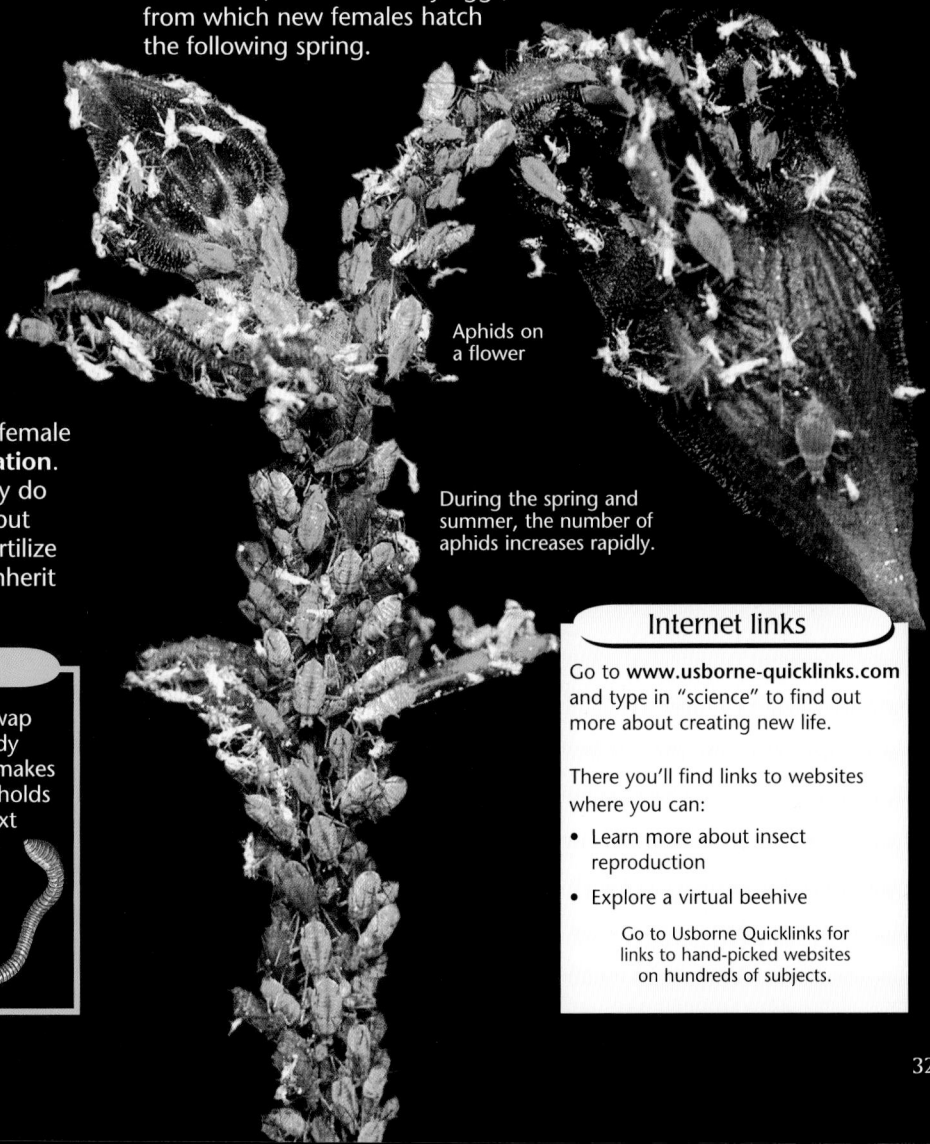

Aphids on a flower

During the spring and summer, the number of aphids increases rapidly.

Internet links

Go to **www.usborne-quicklinks.com** and type in "science" to find out more about creating new life.

There you'll find links to websites where you can:

- Learn more about insect reproduction
- Explore a virtual beehive

Go to Usborne Quicklinks for links to hand-picked websites on hundreds of subjects.

* *Sexual reproduction, 326-327.*

SEXUAL REPRODUCTION

Most animals pair up or **mate** with another member of their species to produce young. A male and a female come together in a process called **sexual reproduction**. A single sex cell from the male fertilizes a sex cell from the female to create a new individual.

FINDING A PARTNER

Many animals use sound, scents called pheromones*, visual displays (see page 318) or other devices to attract a mate. Once together, the two may go through a **courtship ritual** of some kind before mating. Usually, the male displays to the female, trying to impress her. In some species, especially certain types of birds, the two may "dance", or perform, together.

In most species, the male leaves the female after mating, but some pairs stay together for many years, producing new young each year.

FERTILIZATION

Fertilization takes place when a male sex cell, called a **sperm**, joins with a female sex cell, called an **ovum**. Each ovum can only be fertilized by one sperm. This creates the first cell of a new organism. As it grows, it is called an **embryo**.

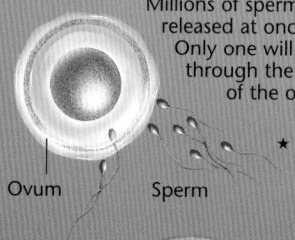

A female frog lays many soft eggs.

External fertilization takes place mostly in water-dwelling animals, such as fish and amphibians*. The female lays many eggs containing her ova, and then the male fertilizes them by covering them with sperm. The closer he is to the eggs, the more likely it is that his sperm will fertilize them. A male frog, for example, grasps the female's body and deposits sperm on the eggs as she lays them.

Internal fertilization takes place inside the female's body. Almost all land animals, such as mammals, are fertilized in this way. The male puts his sperm directly into the female's body, usually through a specialized organ called a **penis**.

A pair of swans will stay together for life.

* *Amphibians, 315, 342; Pheromones, 319.*

LAYING EGGS

Egg-laying animals are described as **oviparous**. Most reptiles, insects, birds and fish are oviparous. The eggs may be fertilized externally or they may result from internal fertilization. There are two main types of eggs.

Most fish and amphibians, such as the frog on the left, produce hundreds of tiny, soft eggs, called **spawn**. These often contain young which do not look like the adults at all.

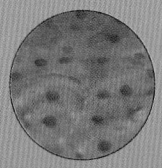

The tiny black dots in this frogspawn are the developing young.

Most land animals, such as birds and reptiles, produce a smaller number of **cleidoic eggs**. In these, the embryo is fed by a food store called a **yolk** and protected by a hard shell. When the eggs hatch, the young are usually miniature versions of the adults.

A cleidoic egg

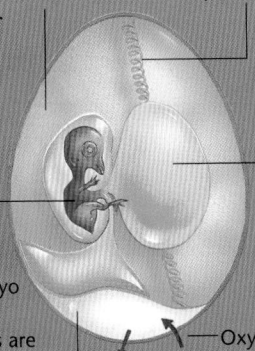

GIVING BIRTH

Animals that give birth to live young are described as **viviparous**. Many animals of this kind are mammals. The baby grows inside the female in a sac called the **womb** or **uterus**. An organ called the **placenta** feeds the baby inside the womb. After a period of time, muscles in the female's body contract and the baby is pushed out.

The length of time a baby spends inside the womb is called the **gestation period**. It varies from species to species.

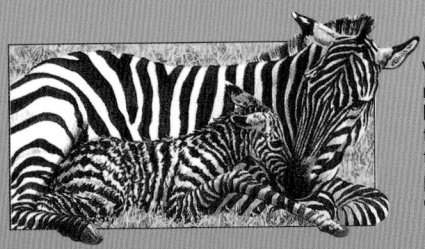

After giving birth, most mammals, such as this zebra, lick their young clean.

ANIMAL FAMILIES

Many baby animals are born helpless, and depend entirely on their mother to protect and feed them. A mammal feeds her young with milk from her **mammary glands**. The babies drink milk, or **suckle**, until they are old enough to eat solid food.

A gorilla gives birth to one baby every few years. The baby suckles until it is about three or four years old.

Almost all birds and some reptiles also feed and protect their young after they are born. In some species, both parents share these duties.

A female emperor penguin protects her chick while the male feeds at sea.

When the male returns, both parents take turns to feed and protect the chick.

See for yourself

In the springtime, look in ponds for clumps of frogspawn. Although there may seem to be lots of eggs, many of the young will be eaten by predators after they hatch. Very few will survive to become adult frogs.

Internet links

Go to **www.usborne-quicklinks.com** and type in "science" to find out more about creating new life.

There you'll find links to websites where you can:

- Watch video clips of chicks hatching
- Find out some of the ways that birds attract their mates

Go to Usborne Quicklinks for links to hand-picked websites on hundreds of subjects.

LIFE CYCLES

Many changes take place between the beginning and end of an animal's life: it grows, develops, and produces young. These patterns of growth and behaviour are called a **life cycle**. Some animal life cycles take many years to complete. Many insects, by contrast, complete their life cycle in a few months.

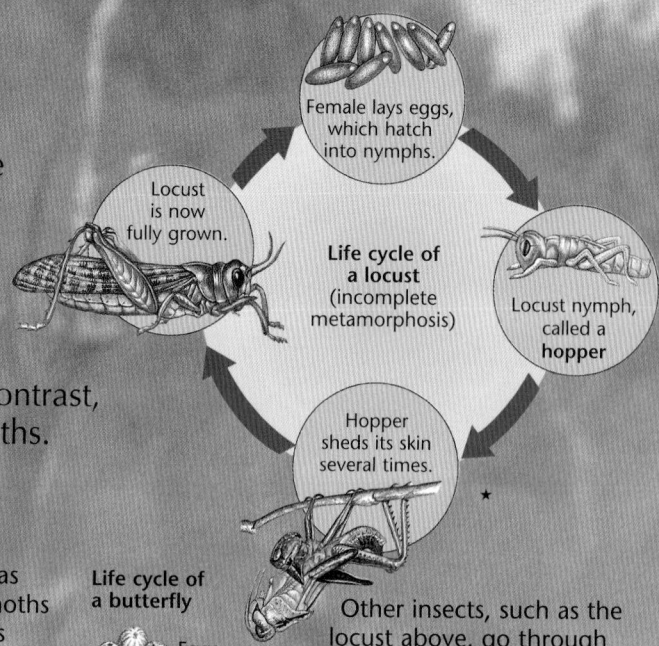

METAMORPHOSIS

Some animals, such as insects and frogs, change their form completely in the course of their life cycle. This is called **metamorphosis**. There are two kinds of metamorphosis: complete and incomplete. In **complete metamorphosis**, the young form looks very different from the adult form.

Insects such as butterflies, moths and ladybirds undergo complete metamorphosis. Their young, called **larvae**, feed and grow, then develop hard cases called **pupae**. Inside the pupae, they change into adults.

Life cycle of a butterfly

Eggs

Larva, called **caterpillar**

Pupa

Adult emerges from pupa.

Other insects, such as the locust above, go through **incomplete metamorphosis**. This means that the young, called **nymphs**, look similar to their parents, although some body parts, such as their wings, are not yet formed. Nymphs shed their skins several times as they become larger. As they grow, their wings and reproductive organs develop.

The adult form of an insect that has gone through either complete or incomplete metamorphosis is known as the **imago**.

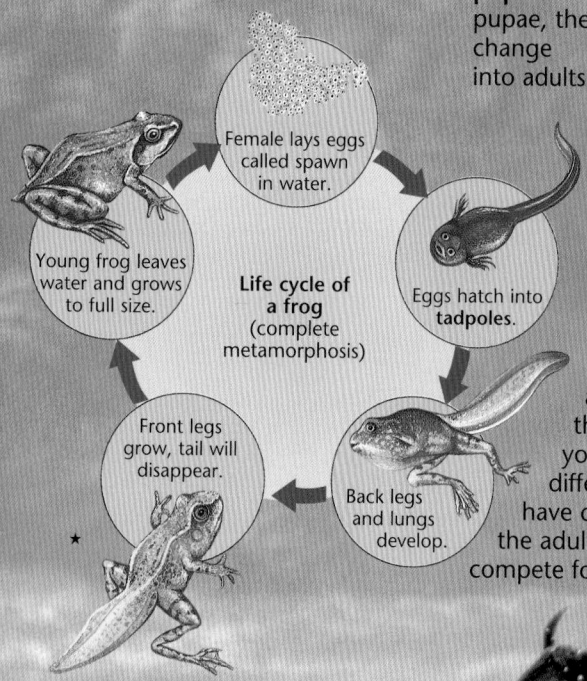

Complete metamorphosis often provides a form in which the animal can survive the winter. The young usually live in different habitats and have different diets from the adults, so they do not compete for food or space.

See for yourself

If you are able to find any frogspawn in a pond during the springtime, go back and look at the tadpoles every week after they hatch. After about eight weeks, you will notice their tiny legs starting to develop.

Migrating wildebeest crossing a river

These Canada geese, like almost all geese, migrate to their breeding grounds every year.

MAKING A JOURNEY

At some stage in their life cycles, many animals travel long distances in large groups, often to breed or find food. This journey is called **migration**.

Many birds migrate twice every year (to their breeding or feeding grounds and back). They use the position of the Sun, stars and features of the land to find their way. Many land animals, such as wildebeest, move with the seasons to find food. They may have to overcome obstacles, such as rivers.

MIGRATION IN WATER

Some animals, such as salmon and eels, may only migrate once in their lifetime. The journey is long and hard, and few fish survive to breed again.

Life cycle of a salmon

Salmon travel upstream to breed. They swim from the sea to the rivers where they were hatched.

When they arrive, the females lay eggs in the riverbed, in hollows dug out with their tails.

The young salmon, called **fry**, live in the rivers for about three years before swimming to the sea, where they remain until ready to breed.

A LONG REST

Many animals which do not migrate survive seasons of cold or drought in a sleep-like state called **dormancy**. Dormancy during a drought is called **aestivation**. Dormancy in winter is called **hibernation**.

Before hibernating, animals collect food. Some eat it all and develop a layer of body fat to keep them alive through the winter. Others store the food and wake occasionally to eat.

Hibernating animals, such as this dormouse, settle down in a safe, well-hidden place.

The animal's breathing and heartbeat slow down, and its body temperature drops. It becomes active again in the spring, when food is available.

Internet links

To find out more about life cycles, go to **www.usborne-quicklinks.com** and type in the keyword "science".

There you'll find links to websites where you can:

- Watch video clips of butterflies as they emerge from their cocoons
- Follow the migrations of birds and other animals

Go to Usborne Quicklinks for links to hand-picked websites on hundreds of subjects.

ECOLOGY

The world can be divided into different areas, each with its own plants and animals. All living things are suited to their surroundings, or **environment**, and they depend on each other for survival. The study of the relationships between plants, animals and their environment is called **ecology**.

ANIMAL HOMES

The natural home of an animal or group of animals is called its **habitat**. The plants and animals that live together in a particular habitat are called a **community**. A community, together with non-living parts of the environment such as air and water, form an **ecosystem**. Smaller ecosystems can be found within a larger one, for example a rotting log in a forest.

A single rainforest flower may be a habitat for frogs and many insects.

See for yourself

Lift up a stone and see what lives in the habitat beneath it. You will probably find creatures which like damp, dark places, such as slugs, earthworms and woodlice. Remember to leave everything as you found it.

SUCCESSION

Sometimes a habitat and its community are destroyed – for example in a forest fire. After the fire, different plants and animals replace each other as the habitat develops. This process is called **ecological succession**. Eventually, a community is established that will remain unchanged, as long as its environment is stable. This is called a **climax community**.

Succession in a disused field

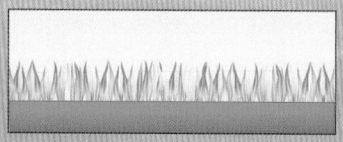

First or **pioneer community** is made up of grasses. This becomes a home for insects and small mammals.

Shrubs and bushes begin to grow. Mammals such as rabbits join the community.

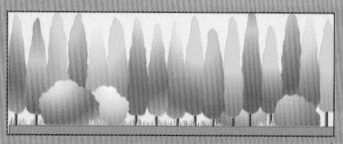

Climax community of trees can support a wide variety of animals, including foxes and badgers.

FOOD FOR ALL

The role of an animal in its community, including what it eats and where it lives, is called its **ecological niche**. Two species cannot live in the same niche at the same time. If they tried, one would die out or be driven away.

All of the animals below can survive together in the African grasslands, because their diets are slightly different, so they occupy different niches.

Grassland ecological niches

Giraffes reach up to feed on the top parts of trees.

Elephants stretch their trunks to browse on twigs, leaves and branches.

Gerenuks stand on their back legs to pluck leaves from bushes.

Rhinos eat leaves in the middle of bushes.

BIOMES

Biomes are the largest ecosystems into which the Earth's surface can be divided. Most are named after the main types of vegetation they contain. Each biome has its own unique combination of vegetation and wildlife. Below, you can see a type of animal that is normally found in each major biome.

Map showing main world biomes

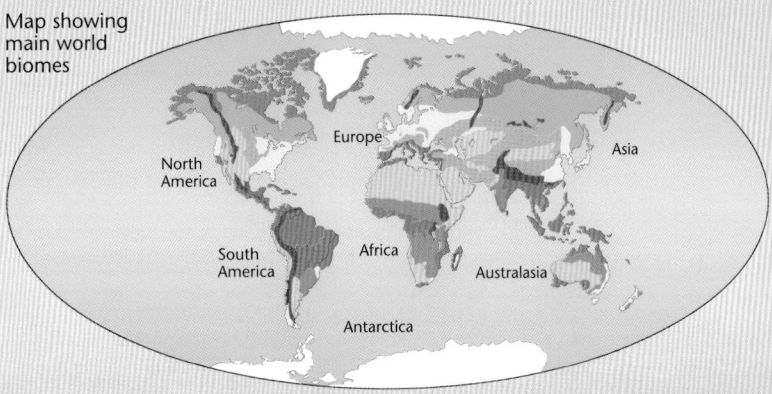

Tundra areas are very cold and windy. Few plants or animals can survive there.

Snowshoe hare

Tropical rainforests are hot and wet all year, and are rich in plant and animal life.

Morpho butterfly

Scrublands (called **maquis**) have hot, dry winds in the summer.

Chameleon

Coniferous forests contain evergreen trees and are cool all year round.

Black bear

Deserts are hot and dry and contain few living things.

Scorpion

Oceans contain a huge number of ecosystems and cover most of the surface of the Earth.

Ocean goldfish

Tropical grasslands are mostly made up of grasses and trees.

Lion

Temperate grasslands are open, grassy plains with few trees.

Prairie dog

Polar areas are covered in ice and snow. Few living things can survive there.

Walrus

Red squirrel

Deciduous forest areas have warm summers and cold winters.

Mountains are mostly cold and bare at the top, with vegetation at the foot.

Bighorn sheep

Polar bears can live in the Arctic because their thick skin and shaggy coat protect them from the cold.

Internet links

To find out more about ecology, go to **www.usborne-quicklinks.com** and type in the keyword "science".

There you'll find links to websites where you can:

- Take an interactive tour of the Amazon rainforest
- Take a look at some animal homes
- Find a map of world biomes, and a guide to the animals that live in each of them

Go to Usborne Quicklinks for links to hand-picked websites on hundreds of subjects.

FOOD AND ENERGY

Plants make their own food using water, carbon dioxide from the air and energy from the Sun. They are described as **autotrophic**. Animals, though, depend on other living things for food and are described as **heterotrophic**. Animals get energy by eating plants or other animals that have themselves eaten plants.

This dragonfly gets its energy by eating plant-eating insects.

FOOD CHAINS

All animals are part of a **food chain**. This is a series of living things, each of which is eaten by the next in line. The position of a living thing within a food chain is its **trophic level**, with plants at the first level. Plants are called **producers**, because they make food which provides energy. Animals in a food chain are called **consumers**.

A woodland food chain

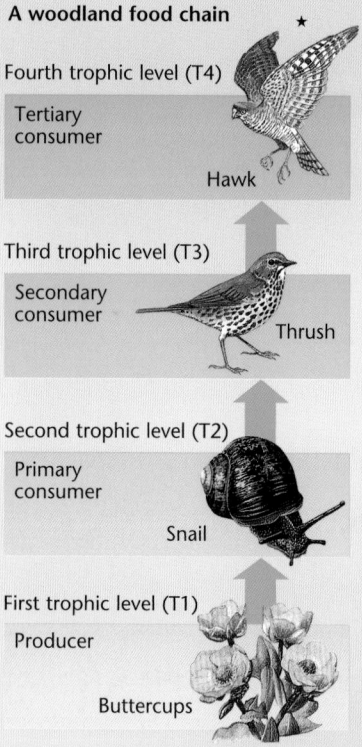

Within a food chain, a herbivore (plant-eating animal) is known as a **primary** or **first order consumer**. An animal that eats a primary consumer is called a **secondary consumer**, and so on. Many carnivores (meat eaters) eat both herbivores and smaller carnivores. They are therefore secondary consumers on some occasions and tertiary consumers on others.

Food chains also contain tiny organisms called **decomposers**. These include bacteria, fungi and many invertebrates. Decomposers break down dead plant and animal matter, and return minerals from them to the soil.

Fungi release chemicals that break down plant and animal matter into simpler substances.

ENERGY TRANSFER

Most of the food an animal eats is used up by its body, and some is stored. When that animal is eaten, the next consumer only gains the stored energy. Therefore, much less energy is available at the next stage in the chain.

Alligators eat animals from every level of their food chain to get the energy they need.

Each trophic level has far fewer consumers in it than the level below. This is because the animals have to eat more food to get the energy they need. This can be shown as a **pyramid of numbers**.

Pyramid of numbers

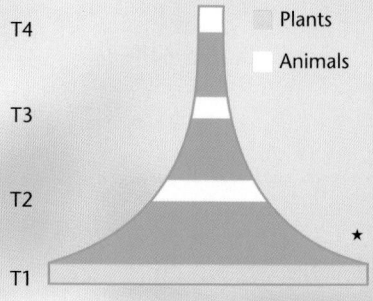

BIOMASS

Biomass is the combined weight of all living things in a habitat. The biomass of plants is much higher than that of any other living things in the same area. At each level of a food chain, there are fewer living things than in the level below, with a lower combined biomass.

This can be shown in a diagram called a **pyramid of biomass**.

Pyramid of biomass

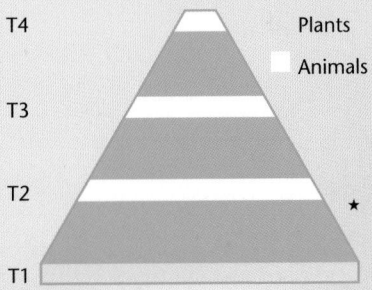

A meadow is an example of a habitat, and its biomass could be shown by a pyramid like the one above. The total biomass of plants at T1 in a meadow can be several thousand kilograms. Several hundred kilograms of insects at T2 may live on these plants.

The small mammals at T3, which eat the plants and insects, have a combined biomass of about 150kg. A single fox at T4, which feeds on the small animals, has a biomass of around 5kg.

See for yourself

Next time you eat, think about what trophic level you occupy. For instance, if you are eating vegetables, you are on the second trophic level. If you are eating meat, you are on a higher trophic level.

FOOD WEBS

A series of interlinked food chains is called a **food web**. Many food chains are linked because very few animals feed on just one thing. For example, most carnivores eat whatever small animals they can find. A herbivore might eat different types of plants depending on the season.

Interdependence describes a number of living things relying on each other and the environment to stay alive, for example in a food web.

A rainforest food web

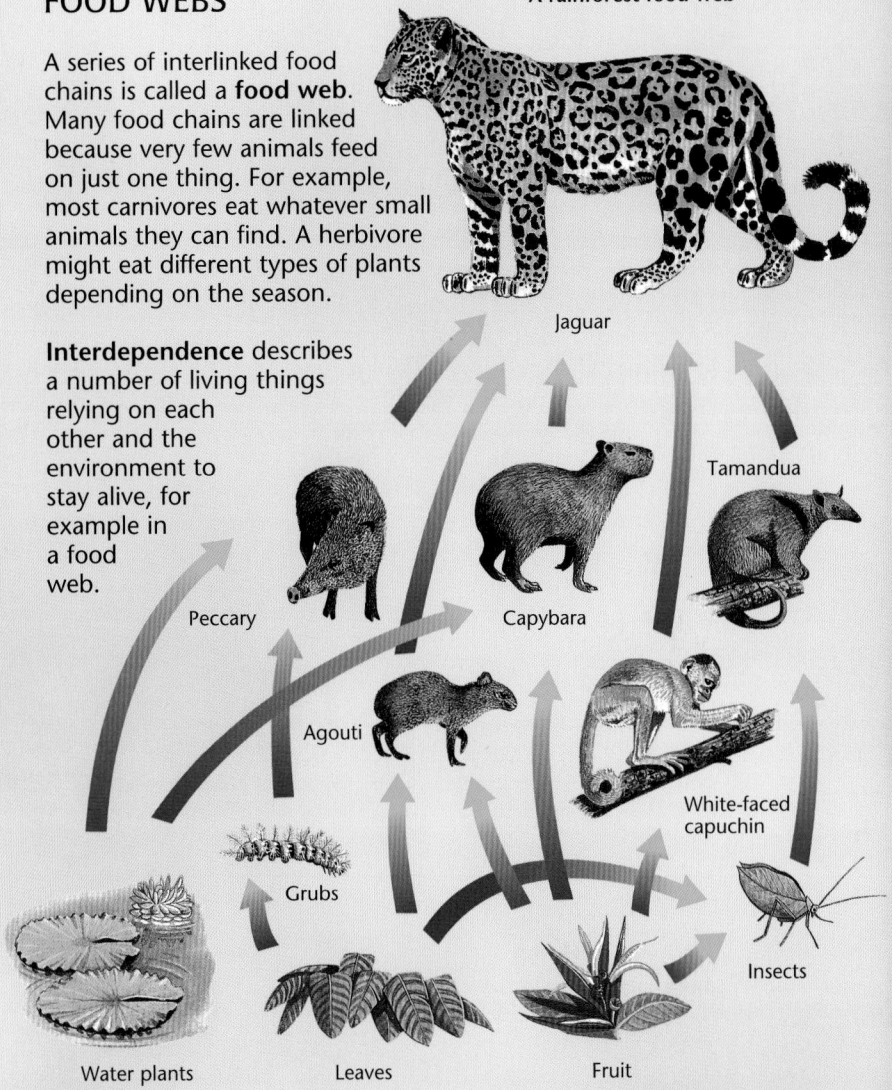

Food webs are easily damaged by humans. For instance, in 1910, wardens in the Grand Canyon Game Reserve tried to protect the deer population by shooting the animals that ate them. The numbers of deer increased, but there was not enough food for them all. Eventually, many starved to death.

Numbers of plant eaters, like these deer, can become too high without meat eaters to control them.

Internet links

Go to **www.usborne-quicklinks.com** and type in "science" to find out more about food and energy.

There you'll find links to websites where you can:

- Play a food web game
- Take part in an interactive tutorial
- Learn more with online activities

Go to Usborne Quicklinks for links to hand-picked websites on hundreds of subjects.

BALANCE IN NATURE

Animals and plants depend on each other, and on the **abiotic** (non-living) parts of the environment, to stay alive. Essential substances, such as carbon, nitrogen and water, constantly move through plants and animals, as well as through the land, sea and air. These circulations are called **cycles**. Many human activities, such as fuel burning, affect the delicate balance between living things and their environment, putting their lives in danger.

Many dolphins and other sea creatures are killed accidentally in commercial fishing nets.

THE NITROGEN CYCLE

The gas **nitrogen** is constantly recycled through the living world. Plants and animals need nitrogen-based substances to build chemicals called **proteins** in their bodies. Plants absorb nitrogen in the form of **nitrates** from the soil and use it to grow. Animals get nitrogen by eating plants, or plant-eating animals.

When living things die, bacteria and fungi break them down and nitrogen is released back into the soil in a chemical called **ammonia**. Other bacteria change this into nitrates, which are taken up by new plants. (For more on the nitrogen cycle, see page 64.)

These dung beetles bury balls of dung. Bacteria in the soil release nitrogen from the dung as they break it down.

THE CARBON CYCLE

Different forms of **carbon** are recycled through the living world. Plants take in carbon dioxide from the air and use it, along with water and sunlight, to make food. Animals eat plants, and their bodies break down the plant matter and use the carbon for growth and energy. (For more on the carbon cycle, see page 52.)

Plant eaters such as cows take in carbon from plants. Meat eaters gain carbon by eating plant eaters.

Chemical reactions inside animals and plants turn food into energy, and carbon dioxide is produced as waste. Animals release carbon dioxide into the air as they breathe out, and plants give it off at night when they are not making food. Carbon dioxide is also released back into the air when dead plant and animal matter breaks down.

THE WATER CYCLE

The water that falls as rain drains into rivers, then into the sea. It evaporates, rises, then forms tiny droplets of moisture in the air. These form clouds and fall again as rain. In this way, water is constantly recycled between the air and the earth. (For more on the water cycle, see page 74.)

The water cycle

Plants and animals also release water. For example, animals do this when they breathe out.

See for yourself

You can see water in the air you breathe out by breathing heavily on a mirror. The warm moisture in your breath cools as it touches the mirror's surface, and turns into tiny drops of water.

POLLUTION

Pollution is damage usually caused to the environment by human activities, such as garbage dumping. Waste chemicals from factories are pumped into rivers and seas, and fumes from burning fuels and vehicle exhausts pollute the air. Animals that live in a seriously polluted environment may become unable to breed, or fall sick and die.

This seabird is trapped on a seashore polluted with oil from a damaged oil tanker. This type of pollution can wipe out the sea life in an area.

DEADLY CHEMICALS

When dangerous chemicals are released into the environment, food chains* are often damaged. For example, **insecticides** are poisons used to kill insects that harm crops. These poisons are often taken in by other small creatures. When predators eat these animals, they also take in the poison, and so it is passed to animals at higher levels in the food chain.

This happened on a large scale in the 1950s and 1960s, when an insecticide called DDT was widely used. It entered some food chains, becoming more concentrated at each level. Eventually, it killed thousands of birds of prey at the top of these chains.

THREATENED SEA LIFE

Many species of fish and shellfish are becoming endangered* because too many have been caught to provide food for people. This is called **overfishing**. The remaining fish cannot produce enough young to replace the ones that have been caught.

Some fishermen are now using nets with larger holes. These allow young fish to escape and breed, so their numbers do not decrease too much.

Young fish can escape from a net with large holes.

This farmer is spraying his crops with insecticides. The insecticides kill pests, but they may also harm many useful creatures that live in the same place.

Internet links

Go to **www.usborne-quicklinks.com** and type in "science" to find out more about balance in nature.

There you'll find links to websites where you can:

- Explore an interactive guide to the water cycle
- Review the carbon and nitrogen cycles with quizzes

Go to Usborne Quicklinks for links to hand-picked websites on hundreds of subjects.

* *Endangered species, 336; Food chains, 332.*

CONSERVATION

Many animal species are in danger of dying out completely. This is known as becoming **extinct**. Some animals are hunted for useful body parts, such as fur, but most are threatened by loss of habitat. Nature **conservation** aims to protect animals and look after the Earth's natural resources to ensure the future of all living things.

Koalas were once faced with extinction, but conservation efforts have been successful and their numbers are increasing.

DISAPPEARING SPECIES

Since life on Earth began, many species have disappeared as a result of natural changes in the environment. This is called the **background rate of extinction**. More recently, human activity has led to a huge increase in the extinction rate. However, people are now taking action to protect disappearing species.

Tiger hunting has been banned since 1970, but tigers are still illegally killed by poachers.

An animal that is in danger of becoming extinct in the wild is described as an **endangered species**. If a species is likely to become endangered in the near future, it is described as **threatened**. In many countries, it is now illegal to kill, capture or sell animals which are threatened or endangered.

GUARDING ANIMALS

Although many laws have been passed to protect animals, it is hard to make people obey them. For instance, it is illegal to hunt elephants and rhinos, but poachers still kill them for their tusks and horns. In Africa, many rhinos and elephants are now kept under close guard.

This rhino has had its horns removed. In parts of Africa, people are trying to save rhinos by removing their horns, so poachers will have no reason to kill them.

NATURE RESERVES

To preserve the world's threatened wildlife, areas have been set aside as **nature reserves**, where plants and animals can live in safety.

Wherever possible, tourists are allowed to visit these reserves. With the proper control, tourism is harmless to wildlife, and can be an excellent source of money for poorer countries.

Kenya earns millions of dollars every year from tourists who come to see elephants in nature reserves.

SAVING HABITATS

Major ecosystems*, such as coral reefs and rainforests, play a vital role in supporting life on Earth. Coral reefs are home to huge numbers of living things, which recycle oxygen and minerals through the oceans. Many countries are trying to protect their reefs. For instance, Australia has a 2,250km stretch of protected coral reefs called the Great Barrier Reef Marine Park.

Many thousands of plant and animal species live in or around coral reefs. When a reef is damaged or destroyed, all these living things are affected.

Rainforests are vital to all life because they recycle large amounts of carbon and nitrogen, which plants and animals need to survive. Vast areas of rainforest have already been destroyed, but people are working together to preserve the areas that remain.

Over half of all plant and animal species on Earth live in rainforests. Without conservation efforts, many may die out.

CAPTIVE BREEDING

Sometimes, a species becomes so rare that it will certainly die out without human help. In such cases, scientists try to increase the animals' numbers by breeding them in captivity, such as in a reserve or a zoo. These animals are sometimes returned to the wild, but many lack the skills that they need to survive.

Golden lion tamarins are rare, but they breed successfully in captivity.

Some species are **slow breeders**, which means that they produce very few young at long intervals. Giant pandas, which are highly endangered, are slow breeders. A few have been born in captivity, but the panda's best chance for survival is to save its native bamboo forests from future harm.

Giant pandas cannot survive without a good supply of bamboo, as it makes up around 99% of their diet.

DANGER AREAS

The main threat to animals is loss of habitat, but they are also killed by pollution and hunting. Many species are also **endemic**. This means that they are found in only one place. Scientists can identify areas, called **hotspots**, which contain large numbers of an endemic species, and ensure that they are well protected.

Many birds, particularly parrots and macaws, are put in danger by the pet trade. Some are also killed for their striking feathers. Combined with habitat loss, this has led to a third of all parrot species becoming endangered in the wild. It is possible, though, that numbers can be increased through captive breeding.

Hyacinth macaws are highly valued as pets because of their striking appearance. They are now one of the rarest types of macaw.

Internet links

To find out more about conservation, go to **www.usborne-quicklinks.com** and type in the keyword "science".

There you'll find links to websites where you can:

- Read an online guide to endangered animals
- Find out what you can do to help
- Learn more with online activities

Go to Usborne Quicklinks for links to hand-picked websites on hundreds of subjects.

* *Ecosystem*, 330.

EVOLUTION

Scientists believe that life on Earth started with very simple creatures and developed gradually, through a long series of changes. This is called the **theory of evolution**. By studying existing organisms and prehistoric remains, scientists try to explain how and why living things have changed over time.

Fossils such as this ammonite shell allow scientists to learn more about ancient life.

EVOLUTION

Scientists believe that bacteria were the first organisms on Earth, and that they began to develop around 3,500 million years ago. They suggest that, over the course of many millions of years, these bacteria developed into the first animals, as shown here.

Evolution of main animal groups

500 million years ago
First fish evolved, with thick skin and no jaws. About 150 million years later, bony fish and cartilaginous fish* evolved.

Sacabambaspis

410 million years ago
First wingless insects appeared. About 110 million years later, winged insects evolved.

Meganeura

350 million years ago
Some water-dwelling creatures began to breathe air, and became the first amphibians*.

Ichthyostega

300 million years ago
First reptiles appeared. Dinosaurs evolved around 200 million years ago, and lived for 135 million years, before they rapidly died out.

Dimetrodon

200 million years ago
First small mammals appeared. After the dinosaurs died out, larger mammals started to evolve.

Megazostrodon

150 million years ago
First birds evolved from small species of dinosaurs.

Archaeopteryx

FOSSILS

When a plant or animal dies, its body rots away, but hard parts, such as the skeleton, may be preserved in sand and mud. Over millions of years, the sand and mud build up in layers, and eventually turn to rock with the preserved remains of the plant or animal, called a **fossil**, inside.

How a fossil forms ★

The animal's flesh rots away.

Layers of sand and mud cover the skeleton, and turn into rock with the shape of the skeleton inside.

See for yourself

Museums can often provide interesting information about fossils and dinosaurs. You could visit a local museum and find out if it has a fossil collection, or a dinosaur exhibit.

** Amphibians, 315, 342; Bacteria, 341; Cartilaginous fish, 301.*

MASS EXTINCTION

Many scientists suggest that there have been five events in the Earth's history during which huge numbers of living things died at once. They call such an event a **mass extinction**. This normally happens as a result of sudden, dramatic changes in the Earth's climate. Many organisms cannot adapt to these changes, and so they die out.

Dinosaurs may have been killed off by a change in climate caused by a meteorite hitting the Earth.

Large reptiles, such as this Deinonychus, have not lived on the Earth for over 65 million years.

NATURAL SELECTION

In the 1850s, a British scientist, Charles Darwin, put forward the **theory of natural selection** to explain how evolution takes place. He suggested that individual organisms with qualities that help them to survive in their environment tend to live longer and pass on these useful qualities to their offspring.

In this way, over a very long period of time, most of the members of a species will have the useful qualities and be well suited to their environment.

Features which offer protection increase an animal's chances of survival, and are therefore more likely to be passed on from one generation to the next. This is known as **protective adaptation**.

An example of this is when patterns on an animal's body allow it to remain hidden from enemies. This is called **camouflage**.

Peppered moth (dark variety)

A type of moth, called the peppered moth, is often used to show how natural selection takes place. During the nineteenth century, many trees upon which peppered moths rested became blackened by soot from factories.

Both dark and pale peppered moths resting on a soot-covered tree trunk

Moths with pale wings were seen and eaten by birds, but the rare moths with dark wings survived, bred and increased in numbers. Now, however, there is less pollution from soot and the moths with pale wings are increasing again.

Peppered moth (pale variety)

Internet links

To find out more about evolution, go to **www.usborne-quicklinks.com** and type in the keyword "science".

There you'll find links to websites where you can:

- Explore the history of life with timelines and activities
- Try some dinosaur activities
- Read some theories of why dinosaurs became extinct

Go to Usborne Quicklinks for links to hand-picked websites on hundreds of subjects.

CLASSIFICATION

To make living things easier to study, biologists organize them into groups with similar features. Fitting organisms into groups that can be divided to form smaller groups is called **classification**. For example, an elephant and a mouse both belong to the mammal group, because they have hair and produce milk for their young. Within the mammal group, though, they belong to different sub-groups.

A mouse and an elephant look different, but they both belong to the mammal group.

IDENTIFICATION

Scientists identify an organism by comparing its main features and deciding how these are different from those of a similar species. The method used is called a **biological key**. A typical biological key is arranged in branches, as in the example below. At each branch the scientist asks "Does the specimen have...?" and there is a choice between two or more features. Each response leads to another set of options until the organism is identified.

Branching key

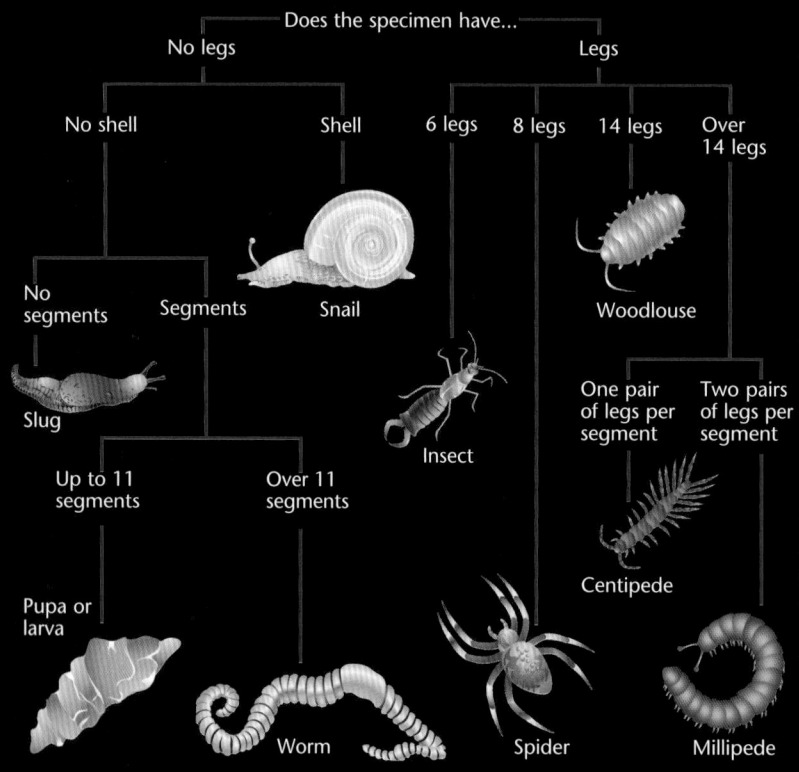

See for yourself

A key where you are given a choice of only two statements is called a **dichotomous key**. Try identifying the six creatures below using the key at the bottom of this box.

Look at each creature in turn and go through the dichotomous key, choosing one statement from each pair and following the instructions.

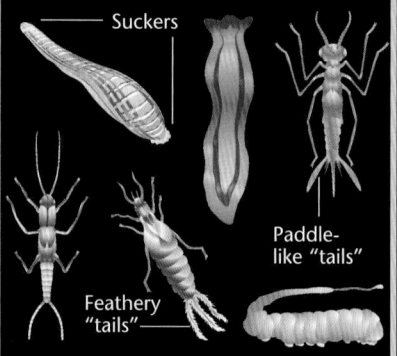

Dichotomous key

1. Six jointed legs	Go to 4
No legs	Go to 2
2. Segmented body	Go to 3
Body has no segments	Flatworm
3. Suckers at front and back	Leech
No suckers	Hoverfly larva
4. Two "tails"	Stonefly nymph
Three "tails"	Go to 5
5. Paddle-like "tails"	Damselfly nymph
Feathery "tails"	Mayfly nymph

HE SIX KINGDOMS

he largest groups into which iving things can be sorted are called **kingdoms**.

Scientists currently divide iving things into six main kingdoms: plants, fungi, animals, protista, archaea and eubacteria. This method of classifying organisms is called **classical taxonomy**.

Viruses are not included in classical taxonomy. Although they can grow and reproduce, they are only able to exist within the cells of living things.

he six kingdoms of living things

Plants

Organisms such as trees, grass and lowers, that make their own food using sunlight.

Rosy periwinkle

Fungi

Organisms that are plant-like, but cannot make their own food. Instead, they mostly feed on dead plants and animals. Yeast and toadstools are examples of fungi.

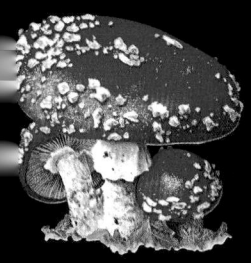

ly agaric

Animals

Creatures, such as fish, that have more than one cell, can usually move around, and eat plants or other animals for food.

Corkwing wrasse

Protista

Single-celled organisms, such as euglena, which share features with both plants and animals.

Euglena

Eubacteria

Microscopic organisms, such as bacteria, which do not have nuclei* in their cells.

Archaea

Microscopic single-celled organisms without nuclei*. Their cell walls* are different from those of eubacteria. Some of the oldest organisms yet discovered are archaea.

Salmonella bacterium (magnified many thousand times)

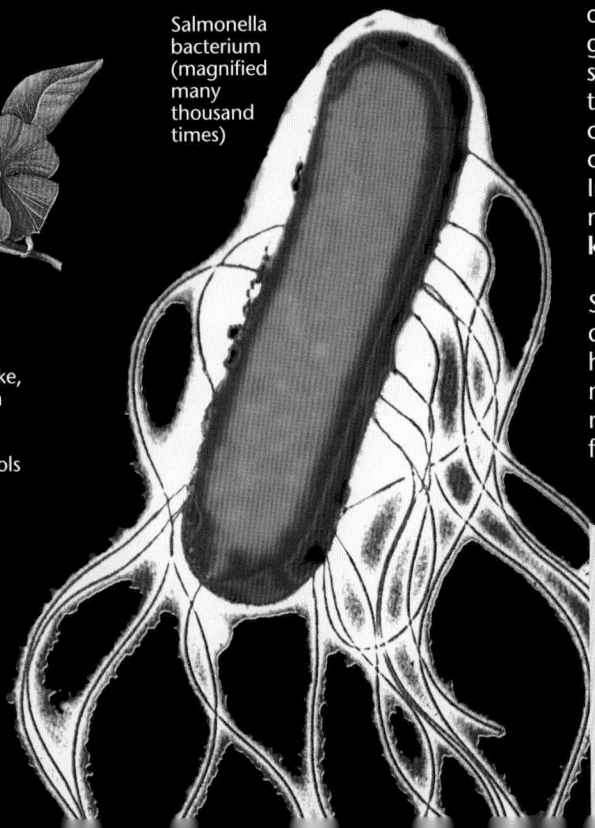

DIVIDING KINGDOMS

Each kingdom can be broken down into levels called **taxonomic ranks** or **taxa**. The first rank is called a **phylum**. Each phylum breaks down into groups called **classes**. Classes are divided into **orders**, then **families**, then **genera**.

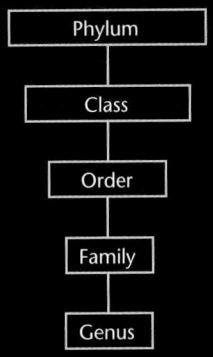

Each genus contains a number of **species**, which are individual groups of animals that are similar enough to breed together. Over the page, you can see how a single species can be traced from a phylum. In some cases, there are also mid-way groups, such as **sub-kingdoms** and **sub-phyla**.

Some phyla cannot be broken down in this way, because they have too few members. The next group after the phylum may therefore be an order, family, genus or even a species.

Internet links

To find out more about classification, go to **www.usborne-quicklinks.com** and type in the keyword "science".

There you'll find links to websites where you can:

- Take a classification quiz and find out how living things are related

THE ANIMAL KINGDOM

The animal kingdom contains a number of phyla, the main eight of which are shown below. These can be sorted further into classes, orders, families, genera and species (see previous page). Below, you can see how a single species, such as a northern wolf, can be traced from one of the phyla. Each step down becomes more specific and includes fewer animals than the one before.

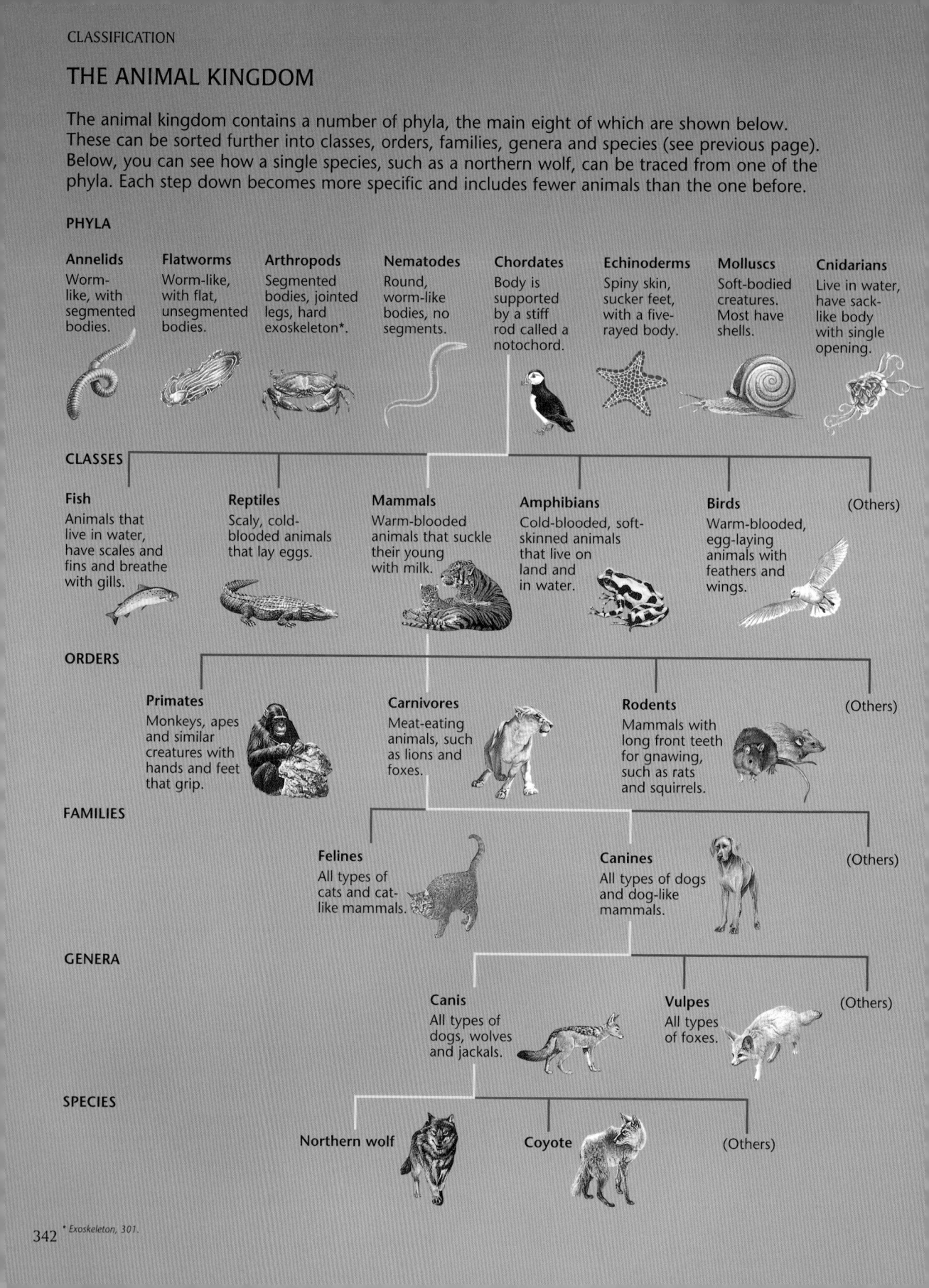

* *Exoskeleton, 301.*

NAMING THINGS

Living things are generally given one or more common names and a biological name. The **common name** is the one used by most people, such as tawny owl or red squirrel. A **biological name** is needed because an animal may have many common names, each one used in a different area. Biological names are usually in Latin. These names can be recognized by scientists all over the world.

These butterflies are so rare that they do not have common names, only biological names.

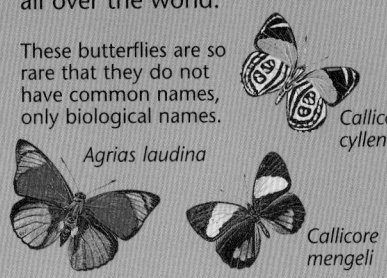

The biological name is created using the **binomial system**, which means that it is made up of two parts. The first part, called the **generic name**, is based on the organism's genus. The second part, called the **specific epithet**, identifies its species.

In many cases, a biological name refers to the animal's appearance, habitat or body features. For instance, a giraffe's biological name is *Giraffa camelopardalis*. *Giraffa* means "swift walker", *camel* means "camel-like", and *pardalis* means "marked like a leopard". So a giraffe is a swift-moving, camel-like animal with a patterned coat like a leopard.

SUB-SPECIES

In some cases, there are also **sub-species**, which have a third part added to their biological name. This can refer to the area in which the sub-species is found, or to a particular characteristic.

This tiger's name is *Panthera tigris sumatrae*. The third part of its name shows that it is a sub-species from Sumatra.

An animal's biological name often refers to a particular physical feature. For instance, *Giraffa* is based on an Arabic word meaning "swift walker".

INFORMAL GROUPS

Different species which share certain types of lifestyle can also be put together in informal groups, by using terms which describe this lifestyle. Social* and nocturnal* animals are two such terms, and there are other examples below.

An animal or plant which lives and feeds on another organism (called the **host**) is known as a **parasite**. Some parasites are harmful to their hosts.

Fleas are common parasites which feed on the blood of their host.

Mutualists are animals or plants which live close together in a situation where both gain. For example, birds called oxpeckers eat parasites that live on the hides of larger animals, such as buffalo and zebra. The larger animals benefit in turn from having the pests removed.

Two species in a relationship where one gains without affecting the other are called **commensals**. House mice, for example, live where humans are found, and feed on their scraps.

Internet links

To find out more about classification, go to **www.usborne-quicklinks.com** and type in the keyword "science".

There you'll find links to websites where you can:

- Explore an interactive family tree of the animal kingdom
- Read the latest ideas about classification

Go to Usborne Quicklinks for links to hand-picked websites on hundreds of subjects.

* Nocturnal animals, 321; Social animals, 319.

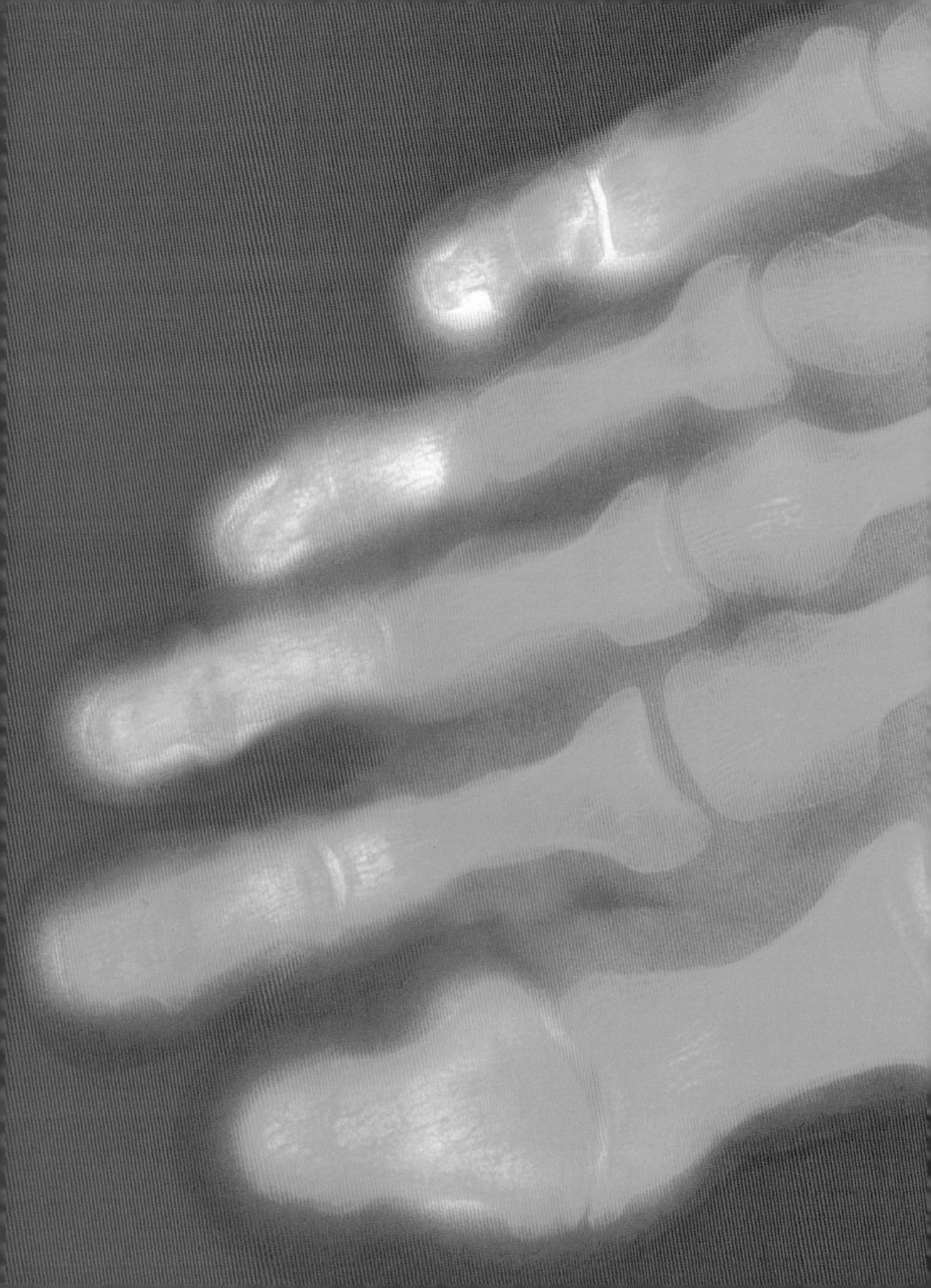

HUMAN BODY

THE SKELETON

Your **skeleton** is a framework of bones that supports your body and gives it shape. It protects delicate parts, such as the heart, and provides hard surfaces for muscles to pull on so you can move.

TYPES OF BONE

The bones in your body can be divided into four main types, depending on their shape.

Flat bones (such as your shoulder blades and ribs) give protection and provide surfaces to which muscles can attach.

Ribs

Short bones are knobbly nugget shapes, which are nearly equal in length and width. The bones in your wrists and ankles are short bones.

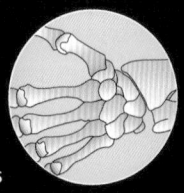

Wrist bones

Irregular bones have complicated shapes and do not fit into any of the other groups. The bones that make up your backbone are irregular bones.

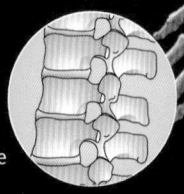

Backbone

Long bones are longer than they are wide. They are slightly curved to make them stronger. The bones in your fingers are long bones.

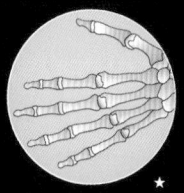

Finger bones

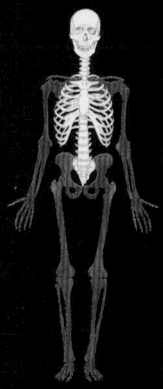

DIVISIONS OF THE SKELETON

A skeleton can be divided into two parts. The **axial skeleton** (shown in yellow) is made up of bones in the skull, backbone and rib cage. They all lie on or around an imaginary line down the middle of the body. The **appendicular skeleton** (shown in red) is made up of bones on either side of this line, namely those in the arms, legs, shoulders and pelvis.

This picture shows the main bones of the skeleton.

Cranium (skull). The adult cranium is made up of eight flat, bony plates, joined together.

Mandible (jawbone)

Clavicle (collarbone)

Scapula (shoulder blade)

Sternum (breastbone)

Humerus

Vertebral column (backbone or spine) made of 33 **vertebrae**

Rib

Radius

Ulna

Carpals (wrist bones)

Pelvis (pelvic girdle or hip girdle). Each side is made up of three bones – the **ilium**, **pubis** and **ischium**.

Coccyx

Metacarpals (hand bones)

Femur (thighbone)

Patella (kneecap)

Tibia (shinbone)

Fibula

Your fingers and toes are called **digits**. The bones in them are known as **phalanges**.

Metatarsals (foot bones)

Tarsals (ankle bones)

TYPES OF JOINTS

oints are places where bones meet. Some, such as those between the bones in your skull, are fixed, but most are movable. The most common types of freely movable joint are listed below. They are called **synovial joints** because they contain a lubricating liquid called **synovial fluid**.

Your hip joint is a **ball and socket joint**. It has a round-ended bone which fits into a fixed, cup-like socket. This lets you swivel your leg in many directions.

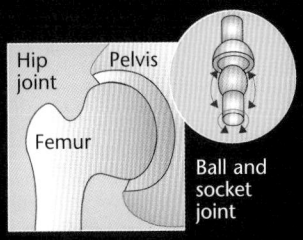

Your knee joint works like a hinge, so you can bend your leg in two opposite directions, such as up and down. This type of joint is called a **hinge joint**.

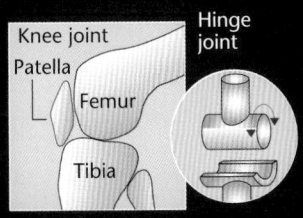

The joints in your wrist are **gliding** or **sliding joints**. The surfaces which touch are flat and the bones can move from side to side, and back and forth.

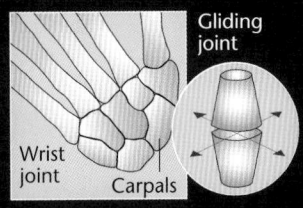

The **pivot joint** between your top two vertebrae allows you to turn your head from side to side. The rounded end of one bone twists around in a hole in the other.

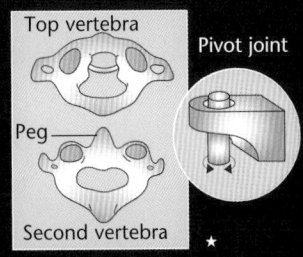

BABY SKELETONS

The skeleton of a newborn baby has over 300 parts. Most are not made of bone, but of a tough, flexible material called **cartilage**. Over time, this slowly turns into bone, in a process called **ossification**. As the baby grows, some of the bones join together to make bigger bones. By the time it is an adult, its skeleton contains only 206 separate bones.

INSIDE A BONE

Each of your bones is covered by a thin layer of tissue called **periosteum**, which contains cells for growth and repair. Inside this, the bone itself is made up of blood vessels, nerves and living bone cells called **osteocytes**, all held within a framework of hard, non-living material containing calcium and phosphorus.

Inside a femur

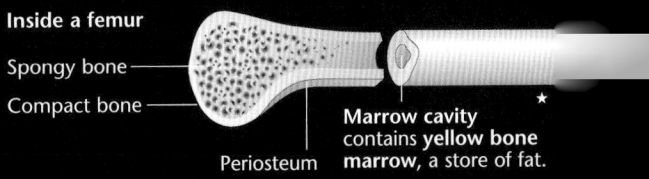

Spongy bone is a mesh of branches called **trabeculae**, with large spaces between them. This strong, light tissue is found in short, flat bones, and in the ends of long bones.

Spongy bone

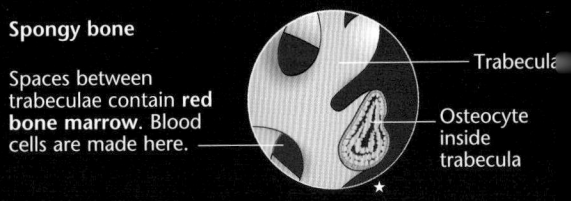

Compact bone is made up of dense, circular layers of bone called **lamellae**. Compact bone forms the outer layer of all bones.

Compact bone

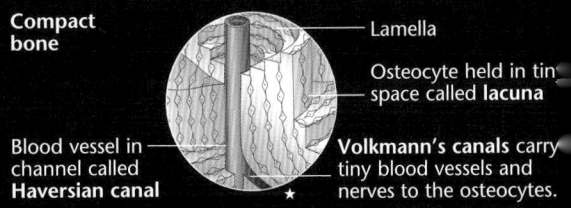

Internet links

To find out more about the skeleton, go to **www.usborne-quicklinks.com** and type in the keyword "science".

There you'll find links to websites where you can:

- Play games and watch video clips to find out what bones are made of
- Investigate the functions of the skeleton
- Find out more about joints

MUSCLES

Muscles are areas of stretchy tissue found all over your body. They are responsible for movement. Muscles that you can control, such as those which lift your arm, are called **voluntary muscles**. Muscles which work automatically, such as those which make your heart beat, are **involuntary muscles**. There are three types of muscles: skeletal, cardiac and visceral muscles.

SKELETAL MUSCLES

Your body contains about 640 **skeletal muscles**. These are voluntary muscles which are attached to the skeleton, usually by tough bands of tissue called **tendons**. Some skeletal muscles are attached to skin. The muscles in your face, for example, are skeletal muscles. They allow you to make different expressions.

When a muscle contracts, it shortens and tightens, pulling the bone (or skin) with it. Muscles cannot push, though, so you need another muscle to pull the part back to its original position. The muscle which contracts is called the **agonist**, and the one which relaxes is called the **antagonist**. Pairs of muscles that work in this way are known as **antagonistic pairs**.

See for yourself

The **biceps** and **triceps** muscles in your arm are an antagonistic pair. Place your hand gently around your upper arm while you bend and straighten your arm. You can feel your biceps and triceps working as a pair – one muscle tightens as the other relaxes.

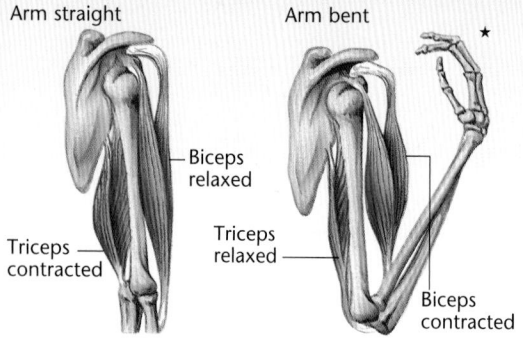

This picture shows the main skeletal muscles.

Frontalis raises eyebrows and wrinkles forehead.

Trapezius keeps shoulders straight.

Deltoid lifts shoulder.

Rectus abdominis (stomach muscles)

Sartorius bends leg.

Quadriceps straightens leg.

Vastus lateralis extends knee.

Gastrocnemius used in walking

Gracilis bends and twists leg.

Tibialis anterior used in walking

Soleus used in standing

CARDIAC MUSCLES

Cardiac muscles make up most of your heart. They are involuntary muscles, which never tire. They form two separate sets. The upper set contracts, filling the lower chambers of your heart with blood. The lower set then contracts and squeezes the blood out into your arteries*.

Cardiac muscles at work

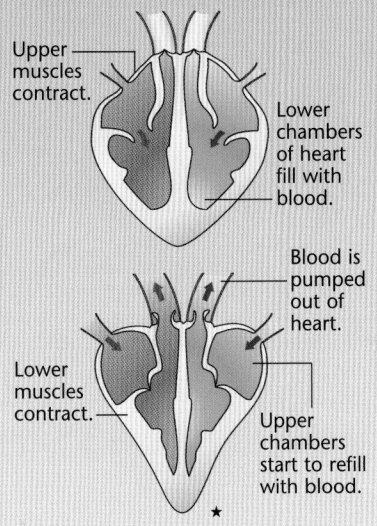

VISCERAL MUSCLES

Visceral muscles are found in the walls of many of the organs inside your body. They are involuntary muscles which contract slowly and rhythmically without becoming tired. This enables them, for example, to move food through your digestive system*.

Section of intestine

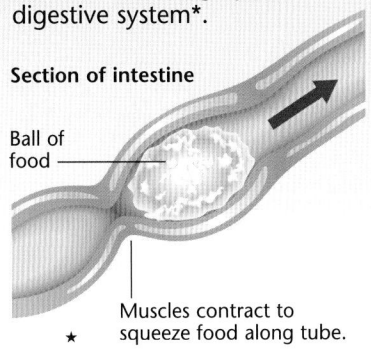

MUSCLE TISSUE

Skeletal muscles are made of **striated** or **striped muscle tissue**. This is made up of long, rod-shaped cells called **muscle fibres** or **myofibres**.

Myofibres are grouped into bundles called **fascicles**. Each fibre is made up of cords called **myofibrils**. These contain interlocking thick and thin threads called **myofilaments**. Thick myofilaments are made of a type of protein called **myosin**, and thin filaments are made of **actin**, another protein.

When a muscle contracts, its filaments slide past each other. This makes the muscle shorter and fatter.

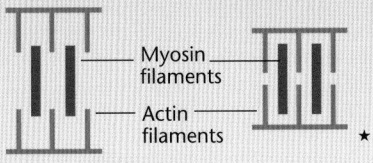

Filaments slide past each other.

Striated muscle fibres can be divided into two types. **Slow-twitch fibres** contract slowly and use relatively little energy. They can act for a long time without becoming tired. **Fast-twitch fibres** contract quickly, using more energy. They act in short, powerful bursts, but tire quickly.

The neck muscles which support your head contain many slow-twitch fibres.

Arm muscles used for throwing contain many fast-twitch fibres.

Structure of a skeletal muscle

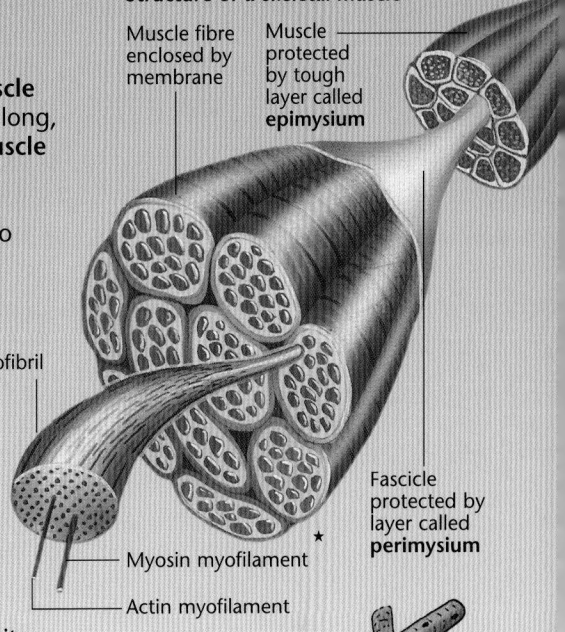

Cardiac muscle fibre

Cardiac muscles are made of a type of striated muscle tissue called **cardiac muscle tissue**. This is made of interlocking Y-shaped fibres.

Smooth muscle fibre

Visceral muscles are made of spindle-shaped fibres which join together to form **smooth muscle tissue**.

Internet links

To find out more about muscles, go to **www.usborne-quicklinks.com** and type in the keyword "science".

There you'll find links to websites where you can:

- Play a muscle game
- Test your reactions online
- Review different types of muscles

Go to Usborne Quicklinks for links to hand-picked websites on hundreds of subjects.

** Arteries, 351; Digestive system, 354.*

THE CIRCULATORY SYSTEM

Your **circulatory system** transports substances, such as food and oxygen, around your body, and collects some waste substances. It has three main parts: **blood**, a liquid which carries the substances to and from the cells; tubes called **blood vessels**, through which the blood travels; and the **heart**, which pumps blood to all parts of your body.

HEART

Position of heart

Your heart is a muscular organ which, unlike other muscles, never gets tired. It is divided into four parts called **chambers**. The two upper chambers are called **atria**. They are joined to two lower chambers, called **ventricles**.

One-way valves between the chambers keep your blood flowing in the right direction. The valves have flaps called **cusps**. As blood flows through the valves, it forces open the cusps. They then snap shut, to stop blood from flowing back. As the valves shut, they make the thumping "heart beat" sound.

How blood circulates around the heart

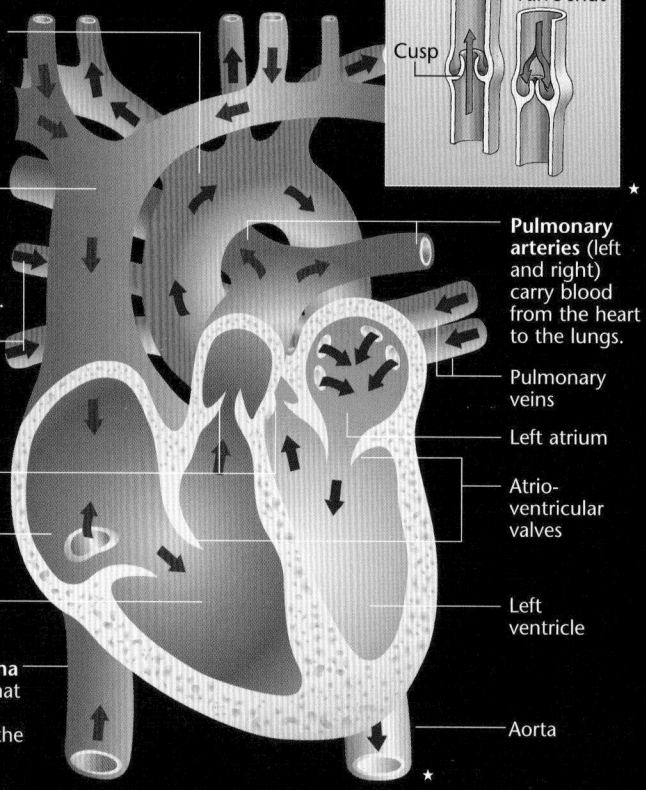

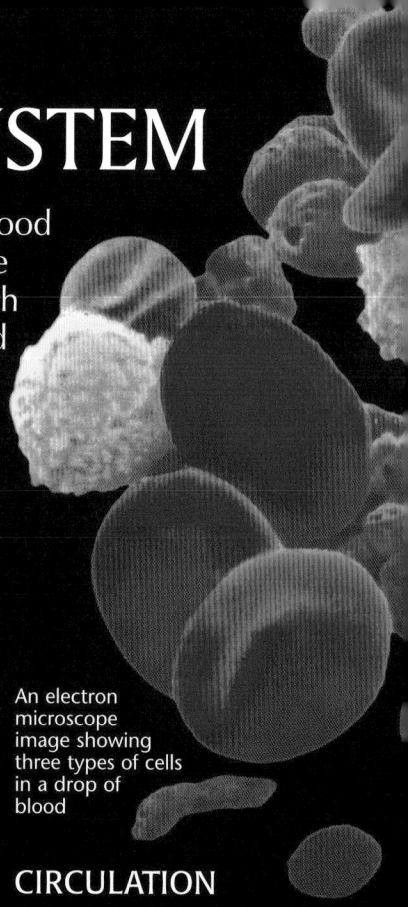

An electron microscope image showing three types of cells in a drop of blood

CIRCULATION

Blood passes through the heart twice during one complete circulation of your body. First, it is pumped from the right side of the heart to the lungs, where it picks up fresh oxygen you have breathed in. It then returns to the left side of the heart, from where it is pumped to the rest of the body to deliver the oxygen. Blood needing oxygen returns to the heart to begin the cycle again.

How blood travels around the body

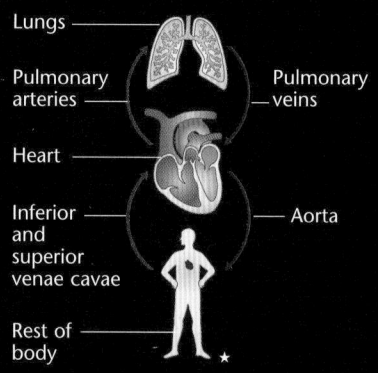

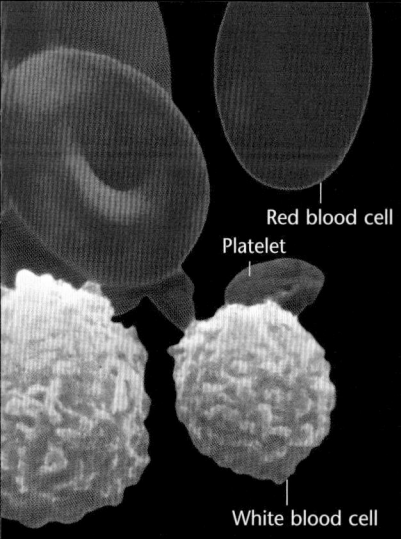

BLOOD VESSELS

Blood flows away from your heart along strong blood vessels called **arteries**. These branch off into ever smaller vessels, ending up with tiny tubes called **capillaries**. Their walls are only one cell thick, so oxygen and other substances needed by body cells can pass through easily into the **tissue fluid** around the cells.

Types of blood vessel

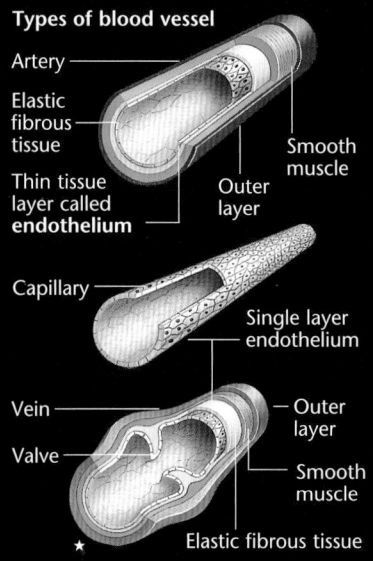

The tissue fluid takes substances between cells and the blood. Carbon dioxide and some waste pass into the capillaries, which eventually join up again into blood vessels called **veins**. These carry blood back to the heart.

BLOOD

Blood is made up of red and white blood cells and platelets, floating in a pale yellow liquid called **plasma**. The average adult has five litres of blood. As well as carrying substances around your body, blood helps to fight germs, heal wounds, and control body temperature.

Composition of blood

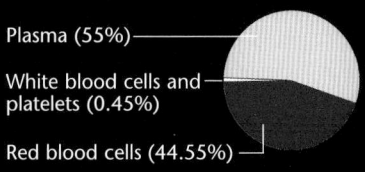

Red blood cells are disc-shaped cells, which contain a purple-red chemical called **haemoglobin**. As blood passes through the lungs, oxygen combines with the haemoglobin, forming **oxyhaemoglobin**, which is bright red. As the cells deliver oxygen around the body, the oxyhaemoglobin turns back into haemoglobin.

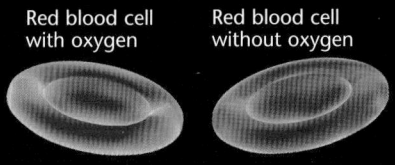

The cell's disc shape helps it to squeeze along inside tiny capillaries.

Red blood cells wear out every four months and are replaced by new ones. These are made in your bone marrow* at a rate of two million per second.

White blood cells are larger than red ones. They help your body to fight disease. You can find out more about this on page 387.

Platelets are tiny fragments of cells. They help to stop the bleeding if you cut yourself.

BLOOD CLOTTING

Most minor cuts bleed for a short time, then the blood turns into a gel-like mass called a **clot**. This is made up of sticky threads of **fibrin**, which form as a result of chemical reactions started by platelets. The clot stops more blood leaking out, and helps to prevent germs entering the wound.

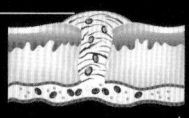

BLOOD GROUPS

Blood can be divided into four main groups – A, B, O and AB. They have different antigens* on the surface of the red cells, and different antibodies* in the plasma. In a blood transfusion, the type of blood you can be given depends on your blood group.

Blood group	Antigen	Antibody	Can be given
A	A	Anti-B	A and O
B	B	Anti-A	B and O
AB	A and B	None	All
O	None	Anti-A Anti-B	O only

Internet links

Go to **www.usborne-quicklinks.com** and type in "science" to find out more about the circulatory system.

There you'll find links to websites where you can:

- See animations of a heart beating
- Follow a red blood cell around the body
- Learn more with online activities

Go to Usborne Quicklinks for links to hand-picked websites on hundreds of subjects.

** Antibodies, Antigens, 387; Bone marrow, 347.*

TEETH

Your **teeth** help to prepare your food for digestion*. They cut and grind it up and make it easier for the rest of your body to absorb. Teeth contain living cells, nerves and blood vessels. You need to look after your teeth carefully, otherwise they will **decay** (rot away) or even fall out.

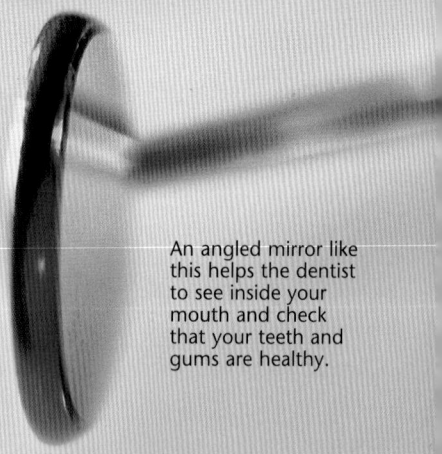

An angled mirror like this helps the dentist to see inside your mouth and check that your teeth and gums are healthy.

PARTS OF A TOOTH

A typical tooth has three main parts. The part of the tooth that can be seen is called the **crown**. Each tooth is fixed in a socket in the jawbone by one, two or three **roots**. The junction between the crown and root is called the **neck**.

Structure of a tooth

Gum or **gingiva**

Crown. The surface of the crown is made of **enamel**, the hardest material in your body. It contains the minerals calcium and phosphorus.

The second layer of a tooth is made of **dentine**. This is a substance similar to enamel, but softer.

Neck

The soft, central area of the tooth is called the **pulp cavity**.

Blood vessels and nerves enter the tooth at the base of the root, and run up to the pulp cavity inside **root canals**.

Jawbone

Tough fibres of **periodontal ligament** attach the root to the jawbone. They are flexible and act as shock absorbers during biting and chewing.

A bone-like substance called **cement** holds the root to the periodontal ligament.

Root

Blood vessels

Nerve

TYPES OF TEETH

There are four main types of teeth in an adult set. Each is shaped for the particular job it has to do.

Main types of teeth

Incisors are sharp front teeth, used for biting and scraping.

Chisel-shaped crown

One root

Canines or **cuspids** are cone-shaped teeth, used for piercing food.

Sharp point called a **cusp**

One root

Premolars or **bicuspids** are blunt, broad teeth, used for crushing and grinding.

Two cusps

One or two roots

Molars are broader than premolars, with more cusps. They crush and grind food.

Four or five cusps

Two or three roots

Wisdom teeth are the third and last molars to appear. They lie at the back of the jaw, one at each corner. They usually come through when you are 17-21.

* *Digestion, 354.*

This tool is called a **probe**. A dentist uses it to scrape away plaque and to check whether your teeth have holes.

TWO SETS OF TEETH

A set of teeth is called a **dentition**. During your life, you have two dentitions. The first begins to appear when you are around six months old. The teeth in this dentition are called **deciduous teeth**, **milk teeth** or **baby teeth**. There are 20 deciduous teeth in all.

Deciduous dentition (milk teeth)

- Incisors
- Canines
- Premolars

There are no deciduous molars.

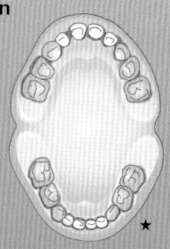

Between the ages of 6 and 12, the deciduous teeth fall out and are replaced by **permanent teeth**. There are normally 32 of these, although some people have one or two more or fewer.

Permanent dentition (adult teeth)

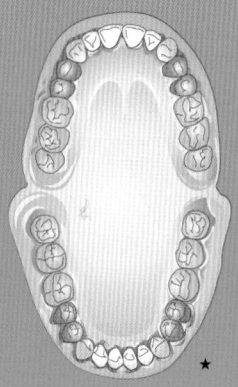

- Incisors
- Canines
- Premolars
- Molars

TOOTH DECAY

Everyone has tiny organisms called bacteria living in their mouth. These multiply very quickly if they have a supply of sweet foods. They form a sticky substance called **plaque**, which covers your teeth in a thin, white film.

As they feed on food lodged between your teeth, bacteria produce acid which dissolves the tooth. This can make your tooth ache, and eventually destroy it. The stages of tooth decay are described below.

1. Bacteria feed on sweet food stuck to a tooth. The acid they produce dissolves the enamel.

2. If the enamel is not repaired by a dentist, the acid will eat through the dentine.

3. If the decay reaches the pulp cavity and its nerve endings, your tooth will start to hurt.

4. Bacteria from the mouth can also enter the pulp cavity. This can cause an infection in the root which may result in a painful, pus-filled **abscess**.

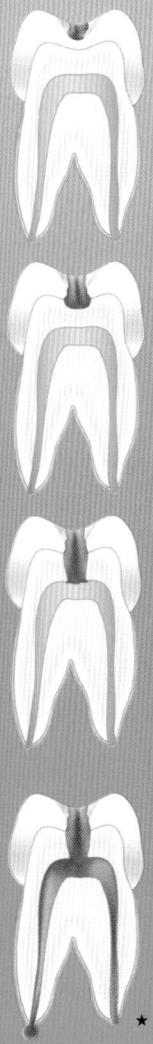

See for yourself

You can use disclosing tablets from a pharmacist or your dentist to see the plaque on your teeth.

Brush your teeth well, then use a disclosing tablet, following the instructions on the packet. The stained areas will show any food or plaque that you have not brushed away.

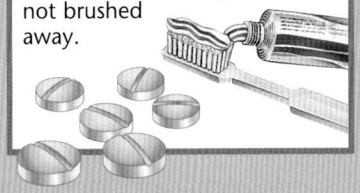

HEALTHY TEETH

Bacteria in your mouth also causes **gum disease**, or **gingivitis**. This makes the gums bleed and, if left untreated, affects the periodontal ligament and jawbone, making the teeth wobble or even fall out.

Cleaning your teeth twice a day is the best way to keep your teeth and gums healthy. Many toothpastes contain a mineral called **fluoride**. This strengthens teeth by making the enamel less soluble in acid and replacing minerals in enamel that has been attacked by acid. It also reduces the bacteria's ability to make acid.

Internet links

To find out more about teeth, go to **www.usborne-quicklinks.com** and type in the keyword "science".

There you'll find links to websites where you can:

- Play games to learn more about teeth and how to look after them
- Test your knowledge with an online quiz

Go to Usborne Quicklinks for links to hand-picked websites on hundreds of subjects.

DIGESTION

As food passes through your body, it is broken down into pieces small enough to be dissolved in your blood. This process, called **digestion**, takes place in the **digestive tract** or **alimentary canal** – a tube that runs from your mouth to a hole in your bottom called the **anus**. Food is broken down physically by chewing and churning, and chemically by the action of **digestive juices**, made by organs called **glands**.

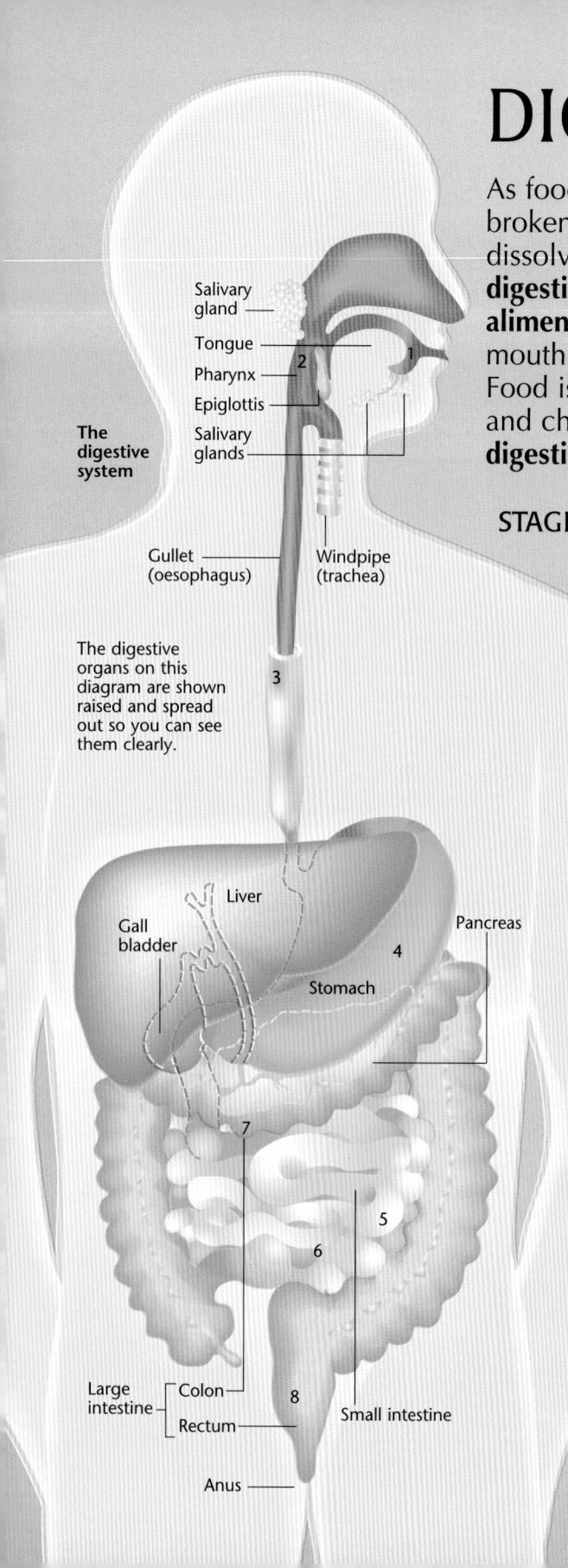

The digestive system

The digestive organs on this diagram are shown raised and spread out so you can see them clearly.

STAGES OF DIGESTION

1. Food is chewed in the mouth and mixed with a digestive juice called **saliva**, which is made in your **salivary glands**. Saliva moistens the food so it slides down your throat easily. It also starts to break down starch* in the food into a sugar called **maltose**.

2. Your throat muscles guide the food through the **pharynx** into a passage called the **gullet** or **oesophagus**. As you swallow, a flap called the **epiglottis** blocks off the top of your **windpipe** or **trachea**, so the food does not go down the wrong way.

How you swallow food

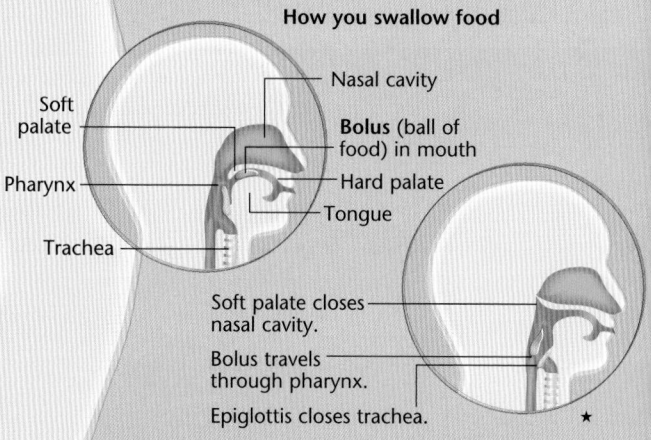

See for yourself

Put a piece of crusty bread in your mouth and notice the taste as you start to chew it. After a minute of chewing, you will find that the bread starts to taste sweeter. This happens as your saliva begins to turn the starch into sugar.

* *Starch, 356.*

3. Food travels down the gullet into your stomach. Muscles in the wall of the gullet contract to push the food along. This action, called **peristalsis**, takes place all along your digestive tract.

4. In the **stomach**, food is churned up with **gastric juices**. These start to digest protein*, and they also contain hydrochloric acid which kills germs in the food. Your stomach lining has folds called **rugae**, which flatten as it fills.

Stomach

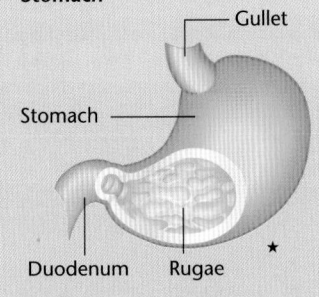

5. The food moves into a tube called the **small intestine**. This has three sections: the **duodenum**, the **jejunum** and the **ileum**. In the duodenum, digestive juices made by the liver and pancreas (see right) break down fats*, protein and starch*.

Small and large intestine

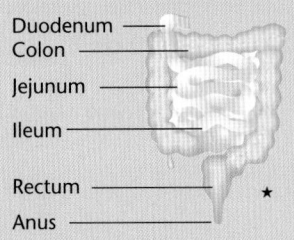

6. The small intestine, especially the ileum, is lined with tiny, finger-like projections called **villi** which increase its surface area. Each villus contains minute blood vessels, which absorb the digested food, and carry it to the liver for further processing before it is carried around the body.

Cross section of small intestine

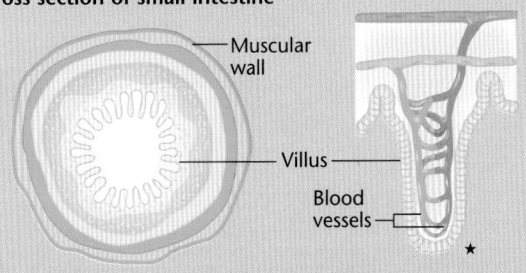

7. Water and any food, such as dietary fibre*, that cannot be digested move into the first part of the **large intestine**, called the **colon**. There water is absorbed into your bloodstream.

8. The semi-solid waste matter, called **faeces**, then passes into the second part of the large intestine, called the **rectum**. It is pushed out through the anus when you go to the toilet.

DIGESTIVE GLANDS

Your digestive glands make fluids needed for digestion. Many digestive juices contain chemicals called **digestive enzymes**, which help to break down your food. Some digestive glands are tiny, and set into the walls of digestive organs. For example, the wall of your stomach contains **gastric glands**. Other glands, such as your salivary glands, are separate organs.

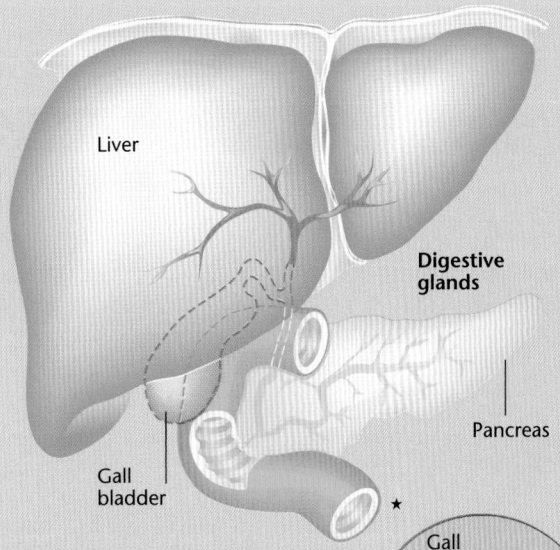

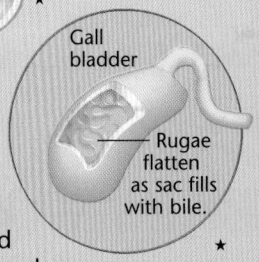

The largest digestive glands are the liver and pancreas. Your liver makes a green liquid called **bile**. This acts like a detergent, breaking up fats* into tiny drops so that enzymes can work on them. Bile is stored in a sac called the **gall bladder**. Your pancreas makes **pancreatic juice**. This contains enzymes which break down fats, protein* and starch*. Your liver and pancreas also have other important jobs to do, for example controlling the amount of glucose in your blood. You can read more about this on page 363.

Internet links

Go to **www.usborne-quicklinks.com** and type in the keyword "science" to find out more about digestion.

There you'll find links to websites where you can:

- Take a tour of a virtual digestive system
- Find lots of stomach-turning digestive information
- Follow an online lesson on digestion

** Dietary fibre, 357; Fats, Proteins, Starch, 356.*

FOOD AND DIET

The food and drink you take in are known as your **diet**. A healthy diet consists of a variety of foods, because different foods contain different things that your body needs. Carbohydrates, proteins and fats are vital for energy or growth. They are called **nutrients**. Vitamins, minerals and water are **accessory foods**. They help your body to work properly.

CARBOHYDRATES

Carbohydrates are energy-giving foods. There are two types: sugars and starch. **Sugars** are sweet and dissolve in water. Foods such as fruit and chocolate contain sugars. **Starch** is not sweet and does not dissolve in water. Bread, pasta, potatoes and rice are rich sources of starch.

Chocolate contains sugar, a carbohydrate.

During digestion, carbohydrates are broken down into simple sugars such as **glucose**. Your body uses these as fuel to produce energy. Some glucose is converted into **glycogen** and stored in the liver. Any remaining glucose is turned into fat, and stored under the skin.

Pasta is a healthy source of starch.

PROTEINS

Proteins are used for the growth and repair of body tissue, as well as other vital jobs. They are found in lean meat, fish, eggs, nuts, milk and beans.

Proteins are made up of simpler chemical units called **amino acids**. The type of protein depends on the order in which its amino acids are arranged. During digestion, proteins are broken down into individual amino acids. These are then rearranged to make different proteins needed by your body.

Examples of proteins in the body

Haemoglobin in these blood cells carries oxygen around the body.

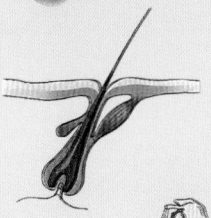

Keratin is the protein from which hair and nails are made.

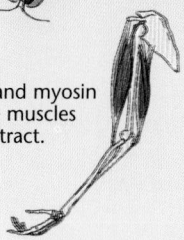

Actin and myosin enable muscles to contract.

FATS

Fats are needed by your body for energy and warmth. Unused fats are stored in various areas of your body, such as under the skin. There are two types of fats: saturated and unsaturated.

Saturated fats are found mostly in animal products, such as butter, lard and fatty meat. These foods also contain **cholesterol**, a fat-like substance. **Unsaturated fats** are found in non-animal products, including vegetable oils and nuts.

Junk food is often high in fat. Eating too much saturated fat and cholesterol may be linked to heart disease.

See for yourself

Look at the labels on the packaging of some of the foods that you eat. They tell you how much carbohydrate, protein and fat the foods contain. Some labels also include information about the vitamins and minerals in a particular food.

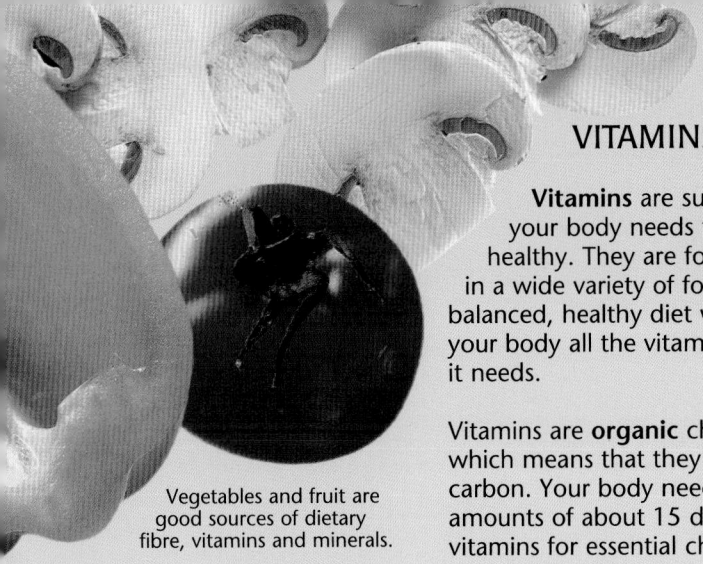

Vegetables and fruit are good sources of dietary fibre, vitamins and minerals.

VITAMINS

Vitamins are substances your body needs to remain healthy. They are found in a wide variety of foods. A balanced, healthy diet will give your body all the vitamins it needs.

Vitamins are **organic** chemicals, which means that they contain carbon. Your body needs tiny amounts of about 15 different vitamins for essential chemical processes to take place.

Sources and uses of vitamins

Vitamin	Good sources	Necessary for
A (retinol)	Milk, butter, eggs, fish oils, fresh green vegetables	Eyes (especially seeing in very dim light), skin
B (a group of several vitamins)	Wholemeal bread and rice, yeast, liver, soya beans	Energy production in all your cells, nerves, skin
C (ascorbic acid)	Oranges, lemons, blackcurrants, tomatoes, fresh green vegetables	Blood vessels, gums, healing wounds, preventing colds
D (calciferol)	Fish oils, milk, eggs, butter (and sunlight)	Bones, teeth
E (tocopherol)	Vegetable oils, wholemeal bread, rice, eggs, butter, fresh green vegetables	Not yet fully understood
K (phylloquinone)	Fresh green vegetables, liver	Clotting blood

MINERALS

Minerals are another group of substances needed by your body. They are **inorganic**, which means that they do not contain carbon. You need small amounts of about 20 different minerals in all. **Trace minerals**, such as iron, are minerals that are needed in extremely small quantities.

Sources and uses of some minerals and trace minerals

Mineral	Good sources	Necessary for
Calcium and **phosphorus**	Milk, cheese, butter, water in some areas	Strong bones and teeth
Sodium	Salt, milk and spinach	Blood, digestion, nerves
Fluorine (trace mineral)	Milk, toothpaste, drinking water in some areas	Healthy teeth and bones
Iodine (trace mineral)	Seafood, table salt, drinking water in some areas	Hormone* thyroxin
Iron (trace mineral)	Liver, apricots and green vegetables	Haemoglobin in red blood cells*

DIETARY FIBRE

Dietary fibre, also known as **roughage**, is a type of carbohydrate found in bran, wholemeal bread, fruit and vegetables. Fibre cannot be digested by humans. It is also bulky, which helps the muscles of your intestines to move food efficiently through your digestive system.

WATER

Water is vital for life. Without it, you would only survive for a few days. You need to take in water to replace what you lose, for example in urine* and sweat. There is water in what you drink, and also in some solid foods, such as lettuce, which is 90% water.

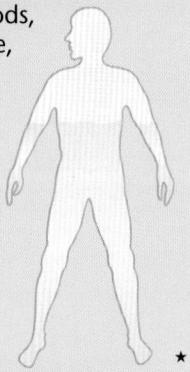

About 65% of your body is water. In very young children, up to 75% of their body weight is made up of water.

★

Internet links

Go to **www.usborne-quicklinks.com** and type in the keyword "science" to find out more about food and diet.

There you'll find links to websites where you can:

- Explore the food pyramid
- Play games to find out which foods are good for you
- Find tasty and healthy recipes

Go to Usborne Quicklinks for links to hand-picked websites on hundreds of subjects.

The links at Usborne Quicklinks are regularly reviewed and updated, so you might find a slightly different selection of websites from the ones described here.

** Hormones, 362, 363; Red blood cells, 351; Urine, 362.*

THE RESPIRATORY SYSTEM

The **respiratory system** is made up of your **lungs** and the passages that lead to them. You breathe air into your lungs, and oxygen from the air passes into the blood, which carries it around your body. Waste carbon dioxide passes from the blood into the lungs and is breathed out.

PARTS OF THE RESPIRATORY SYSTEM

When you breathe in, air is sucked through your nose or mouth and down a tube called the **windpipe** or **trachea**. The lining of your nose and trachea make a slippery liquid called **mucus**. This warms and moistens the air, so it can travel more easily along the passages. It also traps dirt and germs in the air. Tiny hairs called **cilia** waft the mucus away from your lungs towards your nose and throat.

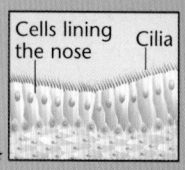

Your trachea divides into two tubes, each called a **primary bronchus**. One leads to each lung. There the bronchi branch off, to become **secondary** and **tertiary bronchi**, and eventually form narrow tubes called **bronchioles**.

Each bronchiole ends in a cluster of air sacs called **alveoli**. These are surrounded by capillaries*.

Oxygen passes through the thin walls of the alveoli into the network of capillaries. Carbon dioxide in the blood, produced by cells during internal respiration*, passes into the alveoli. It is removed from your body when you breathe out.

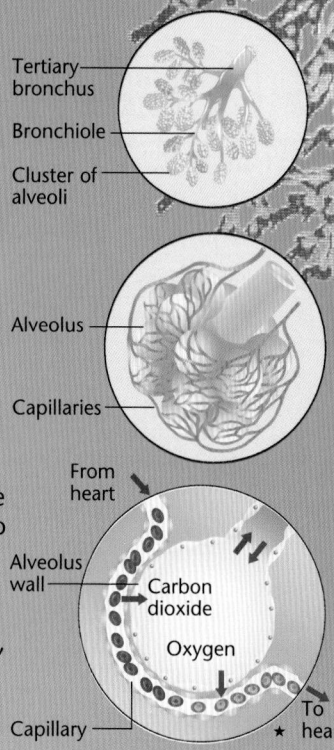

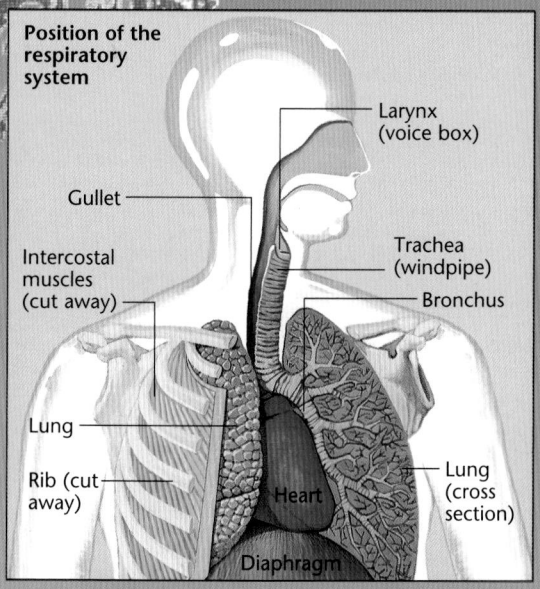

Primary bronchi

Secondary bronchi

Narrow tubes (bronchioles)

Tiny air sac (alveolus)

Lungs

Each lung contains many tubes, the smallest of which end in tiny air sacs (alveoli).

* *Capillaries, 351; Internal respiration, 360.*

BREATHING

Breathing, or **ventilation**, is the movement of air in and out of the lungs. It is controlled by the movements of muscles in your chest, called **intercostal muscles**, and a flat sheet of muscle called the **diaphragm**, which lies under your lungs.

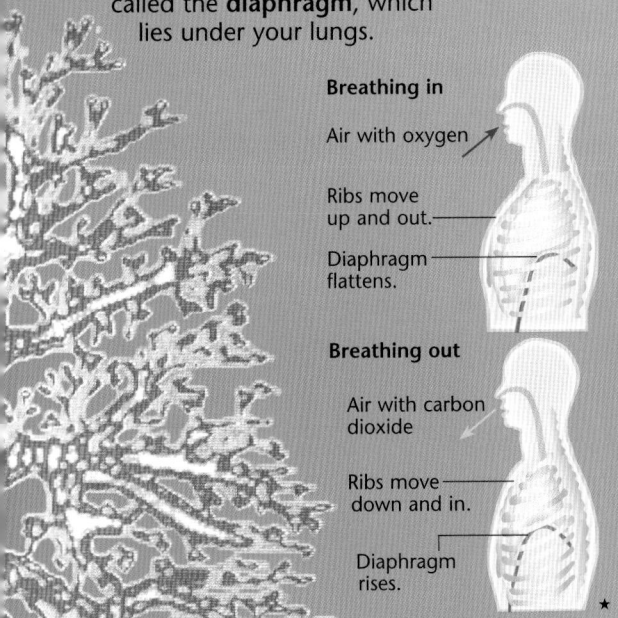

As you breathe in, your diaphragm flattens and your intercostal muscles contract, pulling your ribs up and out. The space inside your chest increases and makes the pressure of the air in your lungs lower than that outside your body. Air rushes in to fill the space. This is called **inhalation**.

As you breathe out, your diaphragm relaxes upwards, and your intercostal muscles relax, so your ribs move down and in. The space inside your chest gets smaller again, and air is squeezed out. This is called **exhalation**.

The normal rhythm of your breathing is sometimes interrupted. **Sneezing** clears irritating dust, pollen or germs from your nose. **Coughing** helps to clear such particles from your windpipe. **Yawning** raises the level of oxygen in your blood, and helps to rid your body of large amounts of carbon dioxide.

VOICE BOX

Your **voice box**, also called the **larynx**, is at the top of your trachea. Inside it are two bands of muscle called **vocal cords**. These open to let air past when you breathe, but when you speak or sing, muscles pull the cords together. The air passing up through the cords makes them vibrate. The vibrations can be heard as sounds.

Vocal cords as seen from above

See for yourself

Place your fingers lightly on the front of your neck while you talk, shout and sing. You will be able to feel the vibrations in your vocal cords, and the movement of your muscles as they relax and tighten.

The louder and lower the sound is that you make, the stronger the vibrations. Your muscles will tighten when you sing higher notes and relax as you sing lower ones.

The shorter your vocal cords are and the faster they vibrate, the higher the sound you will make. Women's vocal cords are short and vibrate about 220 times in a second, so their voices are high. Men's cords are longer and vibrate about 120 times a second. This is why men have deeper voices.

Internet links

Go to **www.usborne-quicklinks.com** and type "science" to find out more about the respiratory system.

There you'll find links to websites where you can:

- Find out why you yawn then try an experiment
- Investigate what happens when you breathe in and out

Go to Usborne Quicklinks for links to hand-picked websites on hundreds of subjects.

ENERGY FOR LIFE

Your body needs energy to keep alive and working. It releases energy from digested food in a series of chemical reactions. This process, called **internal respiration**, takes place in your cells, particularly in your muscles. All the processes in your body involved in producing energy, growth and waste are called **metabolism**.

A healthy diet provides this dancer with energy, and regular exercise keeps her strong and supple.

AEROBIC RESPIRATION

Internal respiration which uses oxygen is called **aerobic respiration**. Food, usually in the form of glucose*, is combined with oxygen breathed in from the air. The reaction releases energy, and its waste products are water and carbon dioxide. Chemicals called **enzymes** help to speed up the reaction.

Summary of aerobic respiration

Glucose + Oxygen

↓

Energy + Carbon dioxide + Water

Some of the energy is set free as heat in a process called **thermogenesis**. The rest is stored as a chemical called **ATP** (**adenosine triphosphate**). When energy is needed, ATP breaks down into **ADP** (**adenosine diphosphate**), releasing its stored energy.

METABOLIC RATE

The overall rate at which your body converts food into energy is called your **metabolic rate**. It varies from person to person.

People with a slow metabolic rate convert food into energy slowly. They may gain fat easily and often appear to have little energy. People with a fast metabolic rate often appear to have plenty of energy. They convert food to energy quickly and little is stored as fat.

Low metabolic rate	High metabolic rate
Food	Food
↓	↓
Energy	Energy
+	
Fat	

Regular exercise, such as swimming, can help to increase your metabolic rate and keep you fitter.

ENERGY VALUE

The amount of energy that can be released from food is called its **energy value**. This is usually measured in **kilojoules** (**kJ**). Energy value is sometimes given in **kilocalories**, also known as **Calories**. A kilojoule equals 0.238 kilocalories. Most pre-packed foods have labels showing the energy value both in kilojoules and kilocalories.

Swimming uses about 2,250 kilojoules (600 Calories) of energy per hour.

* *Glucose, 356.*

EFFECTS OF EXERCISE

Regular exercise is an important part of keeping healthy. It helps to keep your body fit in three ways, improving your strength, stamina and suppleness.

Strength is the amount of force a muscle or group of muscles can produce. **Stamina** helps you to exercise for longer without becoming tired. **Suppleness** describes how flexible your body is. Different types of activity help to develop these aspects of fitness. The effects of some types of exercise are shown in the table below.

BENEFITS OF EXERCISE

When you exercise, your muscles need more oxygen to release energy by aerobic respiration. You start to breathe more quickly to take in extra oxygen. This strengthens the chest muscles and increases the amount of air your lungs can hold.

Your heart beats faster to pump the oxygen-rich blood to your muscles. This strengthens the heart muscles. As blood rushes through your blood vessels, it helps to keep them clear of fatty substances that might build up and cause a heart attack.

Exercise	A	B	C
Badminton	★	★★	★
Cycling	★★★	★	★★
Dancing (energetic)	★★	★★★	★
Football	★★	★★	★★
Gymnastics	★	★★★	★★
Hill walking	★★	★	★
Horse riding	O	O	★
Jogging	★★★	★	★

Exercise	A	B	C
Judo	★	★★★	★
Roller blading	★★	O	★
Skipping (vigorous)	★★★	O	★
Swimming	★★★	★★★	★★★
Tennis	★	★★	★
Walking	★	O	O
Weightlifting	O	O	★★★
Yoga	O	★★★	O

Key **A** = Stamina **B** = Suppleness **C** = Strength
O = no effect ★ = beneficial effect ★★ = very good ★★★ = excellent

Swimming exercises all the muscles and is excellent for building strength, stamina and suppleness.

See for yourself

Take your pulse by using your first two fingers to press the artery on the inside of your wrist. Count how many beats you can feel in one minute. After a few minutes' exercise, take your pulse again. Your heart will be beating more quickly.

Feel for your artery in the dip on the thumb side of your wrist.

GETTING TIRED

Often during hard exercise, such as sprinting, your body cannot take in enough oxygen for aerobic respiration. The muscles then convert glucose to energy without using oxygen in a process called **anaerobic respiration**. A substance called **lactic acid** begins to build up. Your muscles ache and your body is said to have an **oxygen debt**.

By breathing deeply after hard exercise you take in extra oxygen to "pay back" the oxygen debt.

Summary of anaerobic respiration

Glucose → Energy + Lactic acid

Internet links

Go to **www.usborne-quicklinks.com** and type in "science" to find out more about energy for life.

There you'll find links to websites where you can:

- Find out more about the benefits of a healthy lifestyle
- Learn more about the human body's need for energy

Go to Usborne Quicklinks for links to hand-picked websites on hundreds of subjects.

BALANCING ACT

For your body to work properly, conditions inside it, such as temperature and the levels of water and other chemicals, need to be kept constant. This is known as **homeostasis**. An important aspect of this is **excretion** – the removal of waste substances from your body. Chemicals called **hormones** also help to control the levels of substances inside your body.

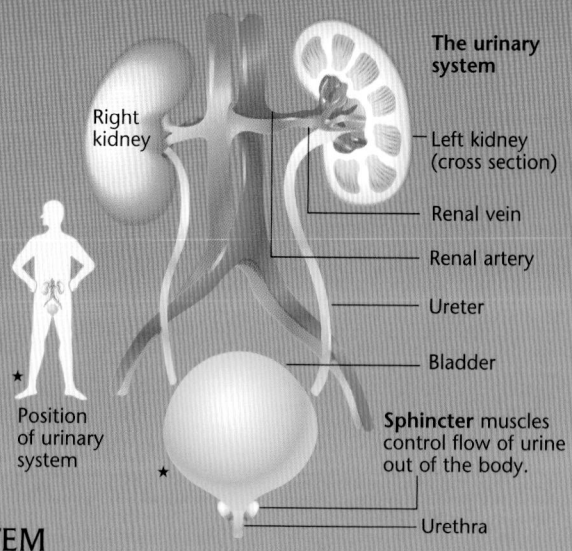

EXCRETORY ORGANS

Any part which removes waste from your body can be called an **excretory organ**. The main ones are your kidneys and liver, but there are others. Your lungs, for example, remove carbon dioxide and water when you breathe out, and your skin removes water and unwanted salts in the form of sweat.

This X-ray image shows the blood vessels inside a kidney.

URINARY SYSTEM

The **urinary system** controls the amount of water in your body. It is made up of two **kidneys**, a balloon-like sac called the **bladder**, and the tubes connected to them. Blood flows through **renal arteries** into the kidneys where it is filtered by about a million tiny units called **nephrons**.

Inside each nephron (see diagram, right), the artery splits into knots of capillaries* called **glomeruli**. High pressure inside the glomeruli forces glucose, water and salts to filter out of the blood into cup-shaped structures called **Bowman's capsules**.

The cleaned blood flows through the **renal vein** back to the body. The filtered liquid travels along a looping tube in the nephron, where some glucose, water and salts are reabsorbed.

Inside a nephron

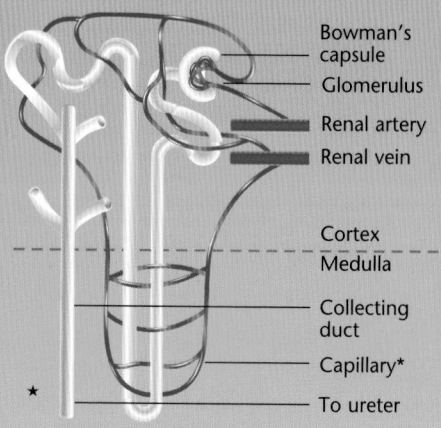

The remaining liquid, now called **urine**, passes into a **collecting duct**, which drains into an area known as the **renal pelvis**. From there the urine flows through a tube called the **ureter** into the bladder. The urine is stored until you go to the toilet, when it leaves the body through a hole called the **urethra**.

Inner part of kidney is called the **medulla**.

Outer part, where blood vessels branch out, is called the **cortex**.

The blood vessels can be seen clearly because they have been injected with a fluid which X-rays cannot pass through.

* *Capillaries, 351.*

HORMONES

Hormones are made in groups of cells called **endocrine glands** and are carried around the body by the blood. Your body makes over 20 types of hormone. Each type affects a different part of your body, known as its **target organ**. The main endocrine glands and some of the hormones they produce are shown in the table below.

Gland	Hormones made	Effect of hormones
Pituitary	Include growth hormone, prolactin	Control other endocrine glands, growth, mother's milk production.
Parathyroids	Parathormone	Controls calcium levels in blood and bones.
Adrenals	Adrenalin, aldosterone	Control blood glucose level, heart rate, body's salt level.
Thyroid	Thyroxin	Controls metabolism*.
Pancreas	Insulin, glucagon	Control use of glucose* by body.
Testes* (in scrotum*)	Testosterone	Controls sexual development in males.
Ovaries* (in abdomen)	Oestrogen, progesterone	Controls sexual development in females.

Endocrine glands

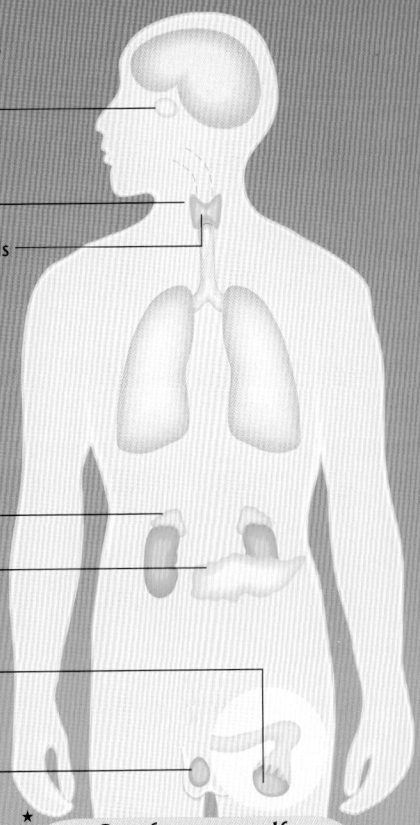

OPPOSITE EFFECTS

Many hormones work in pairs, producing opposite effects. They are known as **antagonistic hormones**. For example, the amount of glucose* in your blood is kept at a constant level by the hormones **insulin** and **glucagon**. These are made in the pancreas by clusters of cells called **islets of Langerhans**.

If your pancreas stops making enough insulin, it causes a condition called **diabetes**. People with diabetes need to control their intake of sugar. Many also take insulin tablets or injections of insulin.

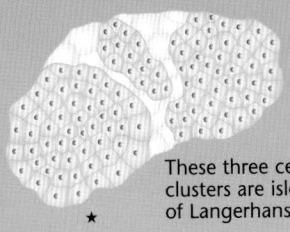

These three cell clusters are islets of Langerhans.

How insulin and glucagon control glucose

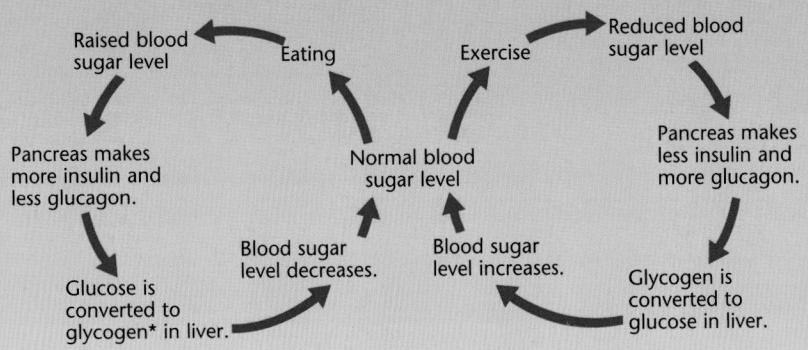

See for yourself

Some hormones act slowly, but others act very quickly. Notice the effect that the hormone adrenalin has on your body when you are excited, scared or angry. Your heart and lungs work faster to take more oxygen to your muscles. This helps to give you more power if you need to take action.

Internet links

Go to **www.usborne-quicklinks.com** and type in "science" to find out more about the body's balancing act.

There you'll find links to websites where you can:

- View interactive diagrams of the kidneys and urinary system
- Take a kidneys quiz

Go to Usborne Quicklinks for links to hand-picked websites on hundreds of subjects.

** Glucose, Glycogen, 356; Metabolism, 360; Ovaries, Scrotum, Testes, 376.*

THE NERVOUS SYSTEM

The **nervous system** is made up of the brain, spinal cord and nerves. Your brain and spinal cord are known as the **central nervous system**. They receive information from all parts of your body, process it, and send instructions to other body parts. The network of nerves that carries information to and from this central area is called the **peripheral nervous system**.

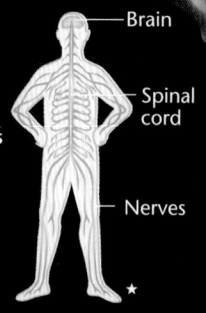

The nervous system

NERVE CELLS

The nervous system contains millions of nerve cells, called **neurons**. There are three types: sensory, association and motor neurons.

Sensory neurons have sensitive nerve endings called **receptors**. These respond to stimuli such as light, heat or chemicals, both inside and outside the body. Sensory neurons carry information about the stimuli from the receptors to the central nervous system.

Association neurons in the brain and spinal cord pick up and interpret information from the sensory neurons. They then pass instructions to **motor neurons** which carry them to other parts of your body, such as muscles and glands, where the instructions are obeyed.

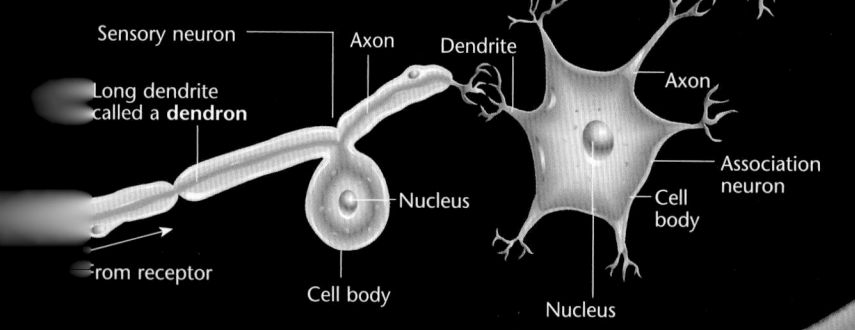

Dendrites and axons may be much longer than shown in this diagram.

PARTS OF A NEURON

Each neuron has a **cell body**, which contains the nucleus, and strands called **nerve fibres**. There are two types of fibres. **Dendrites** carry information towards the cell body, and **axons** carry information away from it. The axons of one cell join another cell's dendrites, or a muscle, to pass on information.

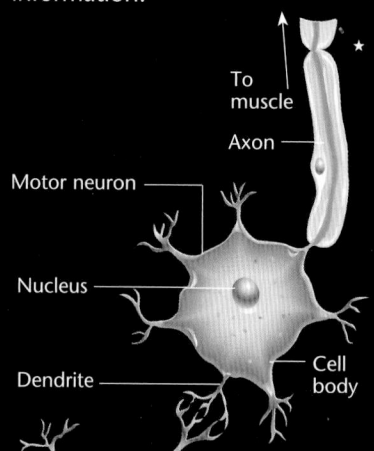

NERVES

Nerves are cords that contain bundles of nerve fibres. **Sensory nerves** have just the fibres of sensory neurons, and **motor nerves** have only those of motor neurons. **Mixed nerves** contain fibres from both.

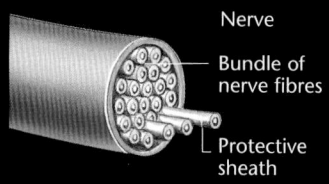

The **spinal cord** is a thick bundle of nerves, which runs from the brain down a tunnel of holes in your backbone. Impulses from all parts of the body pass through the spinal cord.

In this highly-magnified picture of nerve cells in the brain, the orange areas are cell bodies.

NERVE IMPULSES

Information travels along neurons in the form of electrical signals called **nerve impulses**. When an impulse reaches the junction between one neuron and the next, a chemical called a **neurotransmitter** is released. If enough of this chemical builds up in the next neuron, an impulse is sent on.

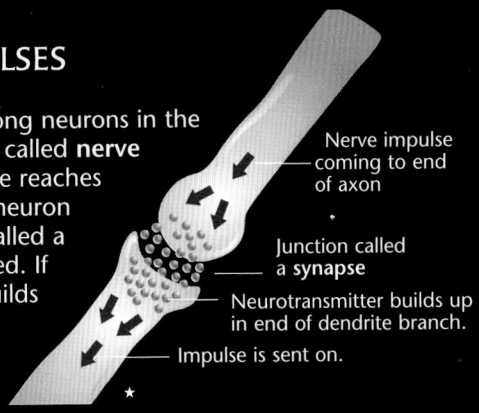

TYPES OF ACTIONS

There are two main types of actions carried out by your body. **Voluntary actions** are actions that your brain can control consciously, such as lifting a cup. Nerve impulses reach your brain and are analysed before you decide what action to take. **Involuntary actions** are those that your brain does not consciously control. For example, processes such as digestion, breathing and circulation are involuntary. The nerves which control involuntary actions are known as the **autonomic nervous system**.

REFLEX ACTIONS

Reflex actions are involuntary actions. They are usually sudden movements, such as pulling your hand away from something hot. Most reflex actions are directed by the spinal cord. You become aware of them because other impulses are sent to the brain to tell it what is happening. The route taken by impulses during a reflex action is called a **reflex arc**.

A reflex arc

This shows the path taken by nerve impulses when you prick your finger.

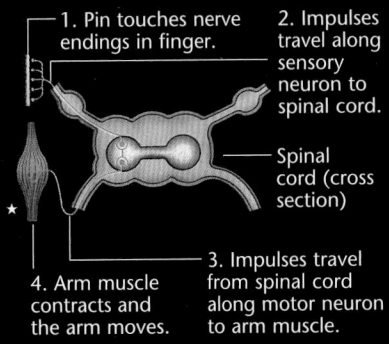

The tangled threads on the left are nerve fibres in the brain.

See for yourself

Try sitting on a chair with your legs loosely crossed, and tapping sharply just below your kneecap with the side of your hand. If you hit the right spot, your leg will jerk upwards. This is a reflex action.

Internet links

Go to **www.usborne-quicklinks.com** and type in "science" to find out more about the nervous system.

There you'll find links to websites where you can:

- Find out why it hurts when you hit your funny bone
- Learn more with online activities

Go to Usborne Quicklinks for links to hand-picked websites on hundreds of subjects.

THE BRAIN

Your **brain** controls everything that happens in your body. Information, in the form of nerve impulses*, travels to and from the brain along the thick bundle of nerves in your spinal cord. The brain is the only organ that can make decisions about actions, based on past experience (stored information), present events and future plans.

This computer image shows the position of the brain in the skull.

This main part of the brain is the cerebrum. It controls senses, intelligence and feelings. It also controls the cerebellum, which in turn controls movement.

Cerebellum

Your backbone protects a long string of nerve fibres, called the spinal cord. This runs from your brain down through a tunnel of holes in the backbone. Nerve impulses from all parts of the body pass through the spinal cord.

INSIDE THE BRAIN

Your brain is made up of millions of neurons*. It is protected by the skull and cushioned by a thin layer of liquid called **cerebrospinal fluid**. The brain has four main parts: the cerebrum, cerebellum, diencephalon and brain stem.

The **cerebrum** is the largest part of the brain. It controls most physical activities, and many mental activities, such as thinking and learning. It also controls the **cerebellum**, which in turn coordinates muscle movement and balance.

The **diencephalon** has two parts. The **thalamus** sorts impulses as they enter the brain, and directs them to other parts of the brain for processing. The **hypothalamus** plays a vital role in homeostasis*. It controls hunger, thirst, body temperature, and the release of hormones* from the pituitary gland.

The **brain stem** controls automatic functions, such as your heartbeat and breathing. It contains three parts: the **pons**, **medulla** and **midbrain**.

Cross section of the brain

Skull
Cerebrum
Corpus callosum
Cerebellum
Spaces filled with cerebrospinal fluid
Protective membranes called **meninges**
Thalamus
Hypothalamus
Midbrain
Pituitary gland
Pons
Medulla
Spinal cord

** Homeostasis, 362; Hormones, 362, 363; Nerve impulses, 365; Neurons, 364.*

AREAS OF CEREBRUM

The outer layer of the cerebrum is called **cerebral cortex**. It can be divided into three types of areas. **Sensory areas** receive information from all parts of your body, such as the eyes and ears. **Association areas** analyse the information and make decisions. **Motor areas** send orders for action to muscles or glands*.

Areas in the cerebrum

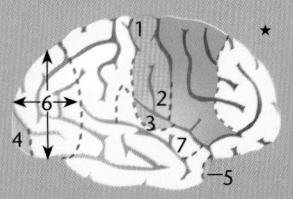

Sensory areas
1. Receives impulses from muscles, skin and inner organs.
2. Receives impulses from tongue.
3. Receives impulses from ears.
4. Receives impulses from eyes.
5. Receives impulses from nose.

Association areas include:
6. Produces sight.
7. Produces hearing.

Motor areas. Each tiny part sends out impulses to a specific muscle.

DIVIDED IN HALF

The cerebrum is made up of two halves called **cerebral hemispheres**. They are joined by the **corpus callosum**, which is a thick band of nerve fibres. Each hemisphere controls the opposite side of the body or deals with different skills.

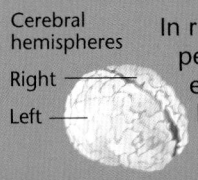

In right-handed people, for example, the left hemisphere controls the use of language, while the right side specializes in recognizing objects. In most left-handed people it is the other way round.

MEMORY

There are two different types of memory. Motor-skill memory helps you to remember how to do actions, such as walking or riding a bicycle. Factual memory enables you to remember specific pieces of information.

There are also two levels of memory. Short-term memory stores information for only a few minutes. Anything that you can remember for longer is in your long-term memory.

Information can be stored in your long-term memory for up to a lifetime.

See for yourself

Test your short-term memory by reading through the list of numbers below, then seeing how many you can write down in order. Most people cannot remember more than seven numbers.

3 0 9 7 1 2 8 5 4 1 6 9

BRAIN WAVES

The electrical impulses between nerve cells in your brain can be detected through your skull by sensor pads called **electrodes**. The patterns, or **brain waves**, are recorded on a chart called an **electroencephalogram** (**EEG**). Doctors use EEGs to find out if a person's brain is working normally.

Main types of brain waves

Alpha waves show when you are awake, but disappear during sleep.

Beta waves show when you are thinking, or receiving impulses from your senses.

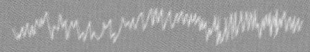

Theta waves show in EEGs of children, and adults suffering from stress or some brain disorders.

Delta waves show in EEGs of babies and sleeping adults. They can be a sign of brain disorder in an awake adult.

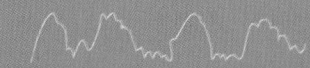

SLEEP

EEGs are also used to study brain activity during sleep. There are two kinds of sleep. One is known as **rapid eye movement** (**REM**) sleep, because your eyes move around even though they are closed. The other is called **non REM** (**NREM**) **sleep**. In REM sleep, the peaks and troughs (ups and downs) on the chart are close together, showing that the brain is very active. In NREM sleep, the peaks and troughs are further apart, so the brain is less active.

Internet links

To find out more about the brain, go to **www.usborne-quicklinks.com** and type in the keyword "science".

There you'll find links to websites where you can:

- Take a 3-D tour of the brain and examine the layers
- Play brain games
- Test yourself with online activities

Go to Usborne Quicklinks for links to hand-picked websites on hundreds of subjects.

* *Glands, 355, 363.*

SKIN, NAILS AND HAIR

The **skin** is the largest organ in your body. Along with your hair and nails, it makes up the **integumentary system**. This covers your body, protecting it against damage, infection and drying out. Your skin also helps to keep your body at a constant temperature, removes some waste, makes vitamin D and helps to collect information about your surroundings.

DIFFERENT LAYERS

Skin has two main layers: the outer **epidermis**, and the inner **dermis**. The dermis contains blood vessels, as well as structures such as receptors*. Under the dermis is a store of fat cells called the **subcutaneous layer**. This helps to keep your body warm.

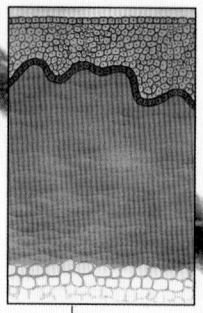

The epidermis has several layers. The top, **cornified layer**, is made of flat, dead skin cells, filled with a tough, waterproof protein called **keratin**. These cells are constantly being worn away and replaced by cells from a layer lower down.

INSIDE THE SKIN

As well as containing many blood vessels (which are not shown here), the dermis also contains other structures. These perform the skin's many jobs.

Key to structures in the skin

1. Touch receptors called **Meissner's corpuscles** send impulses to the brain when your skin touches an object.

2. **Sebaceous glands** produce an oil called **sebum**. This helps to keep your hair and skin waterproof and supple.

3. **Sweat glands** produce sweat.

4. **Hair erector muscles** make hairs stand on end, for example when your body is cold.

5. **Hair plexuses** are groups of nerve fibre endings. Each forms a network around the narrow tubes that contain hair, and sends impulses to your brain when the hair moves.

6. Pressure receptors called **Pacinian corpuscles** send impulses to your brain on receiving deep pressure.

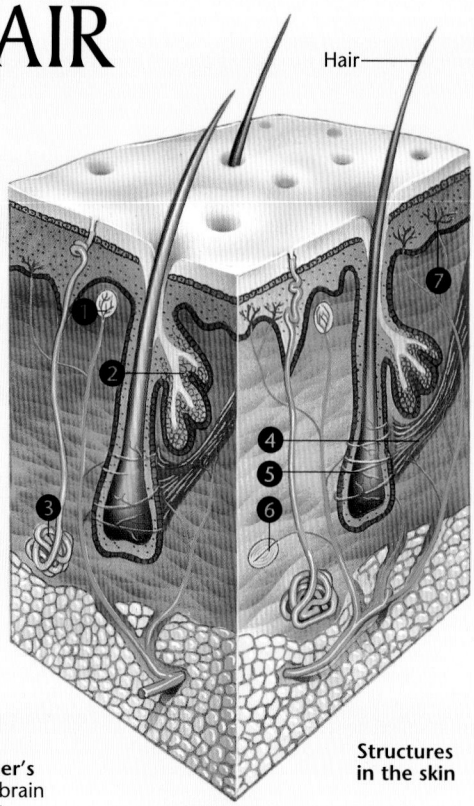

Structures in the skin

7. **Pain receptors** send impulses to the brain if any stimulation, such as heat or pressure, becomes too much. Your brain interprets such impulses as pain.

See for yourself

Gently press a piece of sticky tape onto the back of your hand, then pull it off and look at it carefully under a magnifying lens. You should be able to see tiny flakes of dead epidermal skin.

Hairs growing out of skin, shown magnified over 1,000 times

The flakes you can see here are dead skin cells from the top layer of the epidermis. They will fall off, and be replaced by cells from lower layers.

* Receptors, 364.

TEMPERATURE CONTROL

Your skin plays a vital part in keeping your body temperature constant, as shown below.

How skin cools down

Blood vessels widen, so more heat can be lost through the skin.

Hairs (only shown here at the surface) lie flat, so little warm air is trapped.

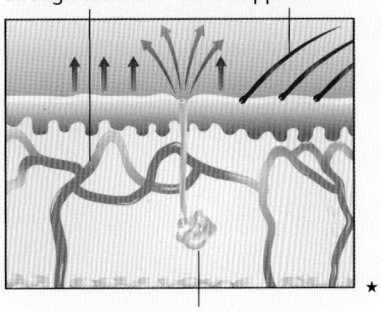

Sweat is produced. It escapes through holes called **pores**. As it dries, it uses heat from the skin, and cools you down.

How skin retains heat

Blood vessels narrow, so less heat escapes through the skin.

Erector muscles contract and make hairs stand up, trapping warm air.

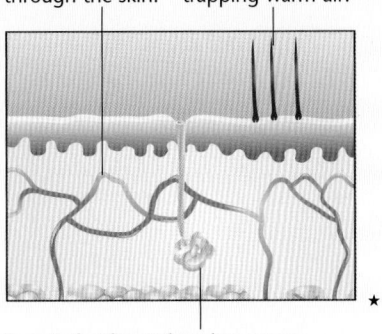

Sweat glands produce less sweat.

Your body also keeps warm by shivering. Your muscles jerk automatically, producing heat as they do so.

The outer surface of a hair is called the **cuticle**. It is made up of flat, overlapping scales of a tough substance called keratin.

NAILS

Nails help you to touch and feel things by forming firm pads to support your sensitive fingertips. Like skin, nails are mostly made from keratin. They grow from a row of dividing cells called the **nail root**.

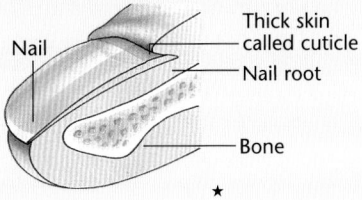

HAIR

Hairs grow out of deep pits, called **follicles**, in your skin. Cells at the base of each hair divide and push the hair up through the follicle. The hair you can see, called the **shaft**, is made of dead cells. This is why cutting your hair does not hurt.

How a hair grows

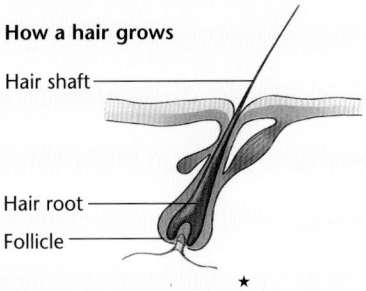

Hair types

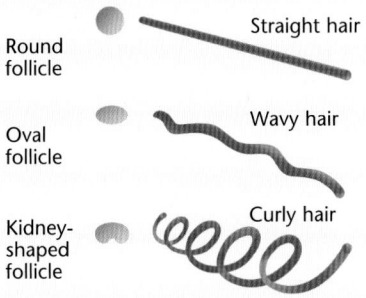

Whether your hair is curly or straight depends on the shape of each follicle.

DARK AND FAIR

Your skin contains cells called **melanocytes** which produce a brown substance called **melanin**. This absorbs some of the Sun's harmful ultraviolet rays, and so helps to protect your skin. The amount of melanin produced affects the colour of the skin.

Fair-skinned people have melanin in only the lower layers of the epidermis, but people with dark skin have larger amounts of it in all layers. Melanin mixed with an orange chemical called **carotene** gives skin a yellow tint. **Freckles** are small patches of skin which contain more melanin than the surrounding area.

The colour of hair is also due to melanin. Dark hair, for example, contains mostly pure melanin. Fair hair contains a type of melanin with sulphur in it, and red hair results from a type of melanin with iron in it.

Some variations in skin and hair colour

Internet links

Go to **www.usborne-quicklinks.com** and type in "science" to find out more about the skin, hair and nails.

There you'll find links to websites where you can:

- Take a closer look at the structure and function of skin
- Learn about goosebumps

Go to Usborne Quicklinks for links to hand-picked websites on hundreds of subjects.

The links at Usborne Quicklinks are regularly reviewed and updated, so you might find a slightly different selection of websites from the ones described here.

EYES

Your **eyes** are the organs of sight. You see things because light rays bounce off objects and enter your eyes. Light-sensitive cells at the back of your eyes send information to the brain, which interprets it as a picture, or **image**. Each eye sees objects from a different angle and your brain joins the two images to help you see in 3D. This is called **stereoscopic vision**.

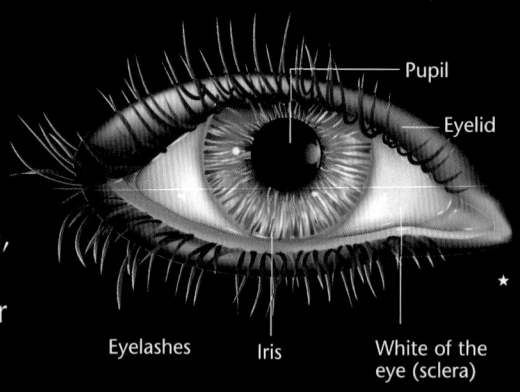

HOW EYES WORK

Light rays enter your eye through a hole called the **pupil**. They travel through a clear layer called the **cornea** and a disc called the **lens**. These bend the light rays so that they form an image on the **retina** at the back of the eye. The lens also turns the image upside down.

The retina contains light-sensitive receptors* called rods and cones. These convert the image into nerve impulses which travel to the brain along the optic nerve. Your brain interprets these impulses as an image, which it also turns the right way up again.

Cross section of an eye

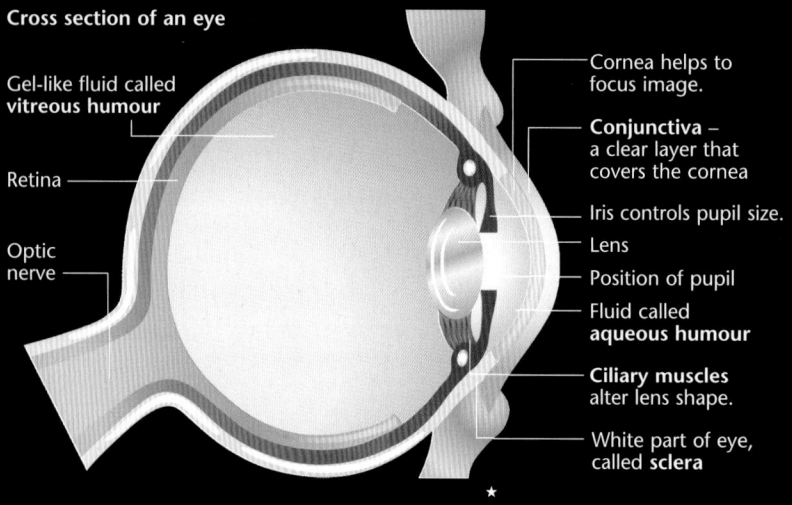

See for yourself

There are no rods and cones on the area where the optic nerve leaves your eye. If an image falls here, you cannot see it, so this area is called the **blind spot**. Test to find your blind spot by holding this page at arm's length. Close your left eye and stare at the square with your right eye. Slowly bring the page closer to your face and notice the circle disappear.

RODS AND CONES

Each eye has about 125 million rods and 7 million cones. Rods only detect black and white, but they work well in dim light. Cones see colours but need bright light to work. At night, you see mainly in shades of grey because only your rods are working.

Close-up of area of retina

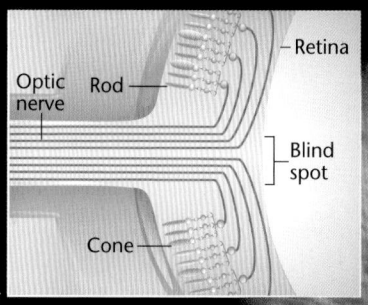

You have three types of cone, sensitive to red, green or blue light. Each type responds by a different amount depending on the colour you are looking at. For example, if you look at a purple object, the blue and red cones respond more strongly than the green ones. **Colour-blind** people cannot see colours well because some cones are faulty.

* Receptors, 364.

PUPIL SIZE

The coloured iris contains **radial** and **circular muscles** which control the size of the pupil and the amount of light entering the eye. In dim light, the radial muscles contract. This makes your pupils larger and allows in as much light as possible. In bright light, the circular muscles contract. Your pupils shrink to prevent you from being dazzled.

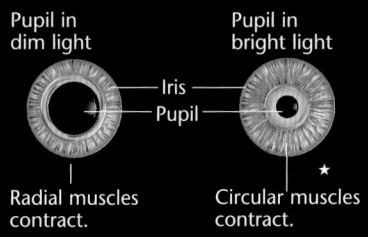

Iris and pupil

The fine threads are radial muscles. They help to control the size of the pupil.

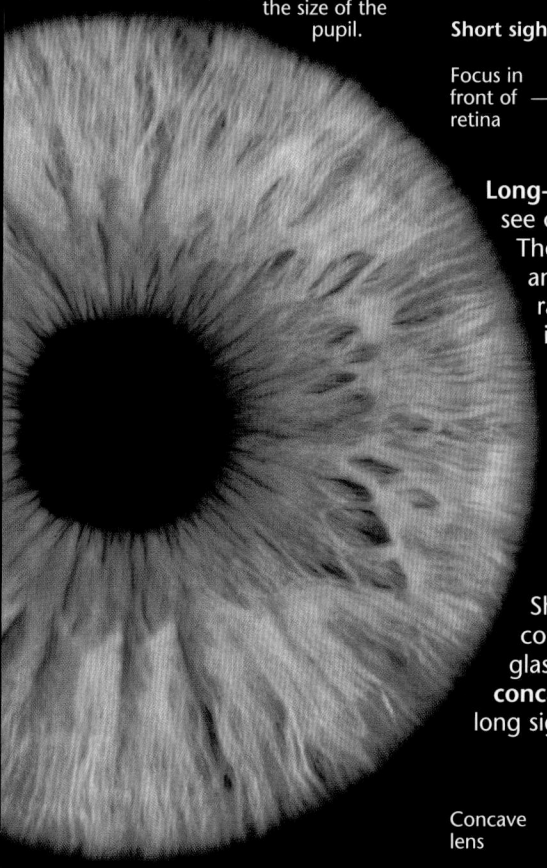

SEEING CLEARLY

As light rays from an object enter your eye, they are bent inwards by the cornea and lens. The point at which light rays meet is called the **focus**. If they focus on the retina, everything you see looks sharp and clear. The lens changes shape when looking at objects at different distances. This bends the light rays by different amounts, and keeps the image in focus.

Perfect sight

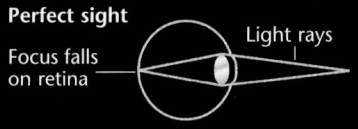

Some people cannot focus light properly. **Short-sighted** people cannot see distant objects clearly. They have long eyeballs, and the lens bends the rays too much, so they focus in front of the retina.

Short sight

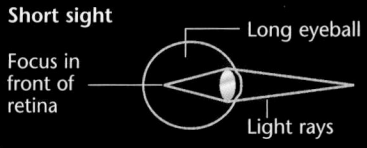

Long-sighted people cannot see close objects clearly. They have short eyeballs, and the lens bends the rays too little, so the image reaches the retina before it is in focus.

Long sight

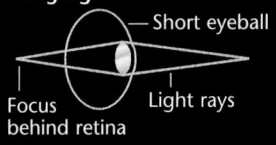

Short sight can be corrected by wearing glasses or contact lenses with **concave lenses**. People with long sight need **convex lenses**.

EYE PROTECTION

Eyes are very delicate. Most of the eyeball is protected by the bones of your skull. The front of the eye is protected by the thin layer of skin known as the **eyelid**.

Protecting the eyeballs

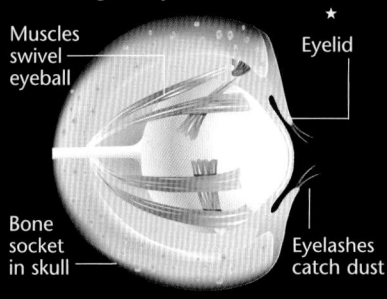

Eyelids keep dust and dirt out of your eyes. When you blink, your eyelids wipe **tears** over the eye, keeping it moist and clean. Tears contain chemicals which help to kill bacteria. They are made in **lachrymal glands** above each eye, and drain into your nose through two **lachrymal canals**.

Tear production in the left eye

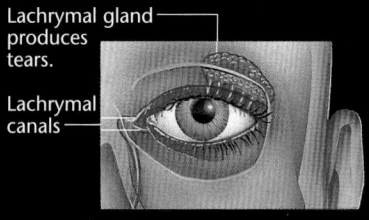

Internet links

To find out more about the eyes, go to **www.usborne-quicklinks.com** and type in the keyword "science".

There you'll find links to websites where you can:

- Watch an animated explanation of how eyes work
- Do an eye quiz
- Learn more with online activities

Go to Usborne Quicklinks for links to hand-picked websites on hundreds of subjects.

EARS

Your **ears** are the organs of hearing. All sounds are vibrations called **sound waves**. These enter your ears and stimulate receptors* in them to send nerve impulses* to your brain. The brain then interprets the impulses and identifies the sound. Your ears also help you to keep your balance, and give you information about the angle of your body.

As well as hearing sounds, your ears help you to keep your balance.

EARS AND HEARING

Your ear is divided into three areas: the **outer ear,** which is the part you can see, and the **middle** and **inner ear** which are the main working parts.

The ear flap, or **pinna**, funnels sound waves into a passage called the **ear canal**. The waves travel along this passage until they hit a thin layer of tissue called the **eardrum**, making it vibrate. The vibrations pass through three tiny bones (the **malleus**, **incus** and **stapes**) to the **oval window** – an oval hole covered by a thin membrane.

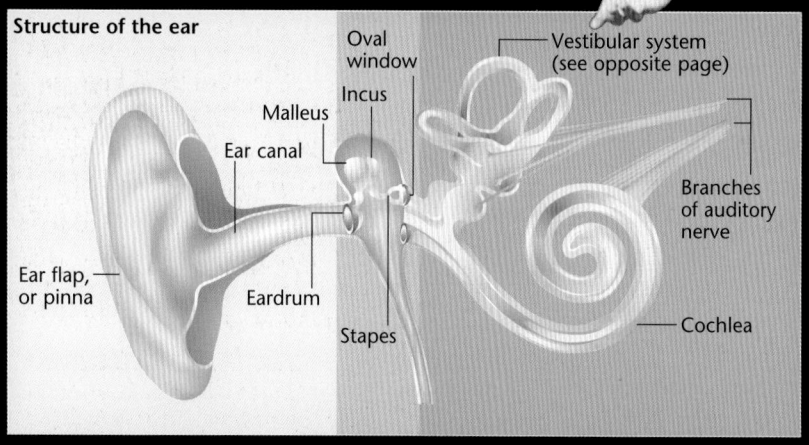

Outer ear (filled with air) Middle ear (filled with air) Inner ear (filled with fluid)

The oval window vibrates and the vibrations pass into a spiral-shaped tube called the **cochlea**.

The cochlea contains three chambers filled with fluid. The vibrations spread through the fluid and stimulate tiny **hair cells**. These are special nerve cells attached to a membrane, called the **organ of Corti**, that runs inside the cochlea. The hair cells change the vibrations into nerve impulses, which travel along the **auditory nerve** to the brain. Your brain interprets the impulses as sounds, so you can hear.

* *Nerve impulses, 365; Receptors, 364.*

KEEPING BALANCED

Many parts of your body help you to keep balanced. Your eyes tell you about the position of your body. So do sensitive cells known as **stretch receptors** in your muscles and tendons.

The **vestibular system** in your inner ear also has an important part to play in maintaining your balance. It has two main areas: three loops, called semicircular canals, and two sacs called the utricle and saccule.

The vestibular system

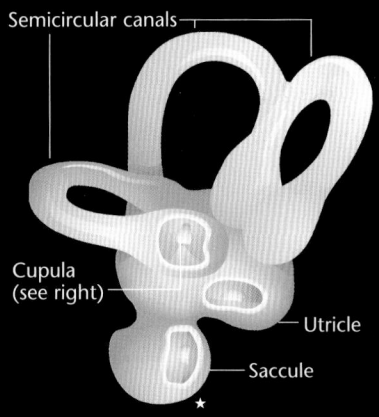

See for yourself

If you spin around very quickly, you will probably feel dizzy when you stop. This is because the liquid in your semicircular canals keeps on spinning after your body stops.

You can produce a similar effect by holding a glass of water in your hand and swirling it around.

The water in the glass will carry on swirling for a little while after you stop moving the glass.

The **semicircular canals** contain fluid-filled tubes called **semicircular ducts**. At the end of each duct is a small swelling which has a gel-like projection called a **cupula** inside it. When your head turns, the fluid moves more slowly than the head, bending the cupula back. Tiny **hair cells** at the base of the cupula send your brain information about rotation of the head.

How a cupula works

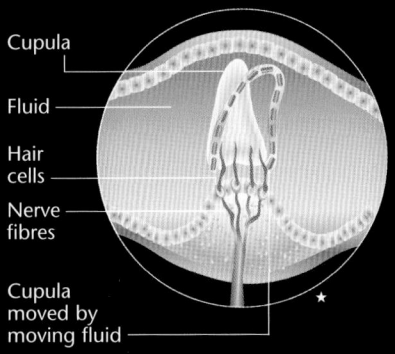

The **utricle** and **saccule** contain a small, gel-like patch called a **macula**. It contains tiny grains, called **otoliths**, and hair cells. When your head moves, gravity causes the otoliths to slide to one side, pulling with them the gel and the hairs. These send your brain information about the forward, backward, sideways or tilted position of the head.

How a macula works

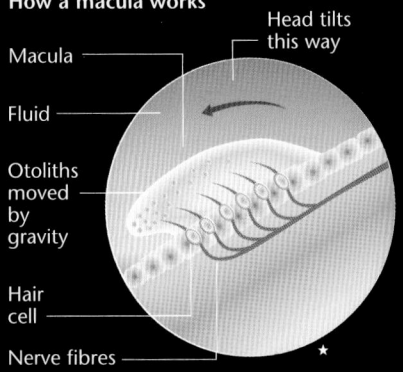

TWO EARS

Having two ears gives your brain two sources of information about sounds, movement and position. By combining this information, the brain finds out more than it would from one ear alone.

For instance, having two ears helps you to tell which direction a sound is coming from. A sound coming from the left will hit your left ear slightly earlier than your right and will produce stronger vibrations. If the sound is directly in front or behind, the sound arrives at each ear at the same time and volume.

See for yourself

You can use this test to find out how your brain locates a sound. Sit on a chair, blindfolded. Ask someone to make a sound by tapping together two pencils, in different places around and above your body. Say where you think the sound is coming from.

You will probably find it hardest to pinpoint the sound when it is coming from directly behind, above or in front of you, in line with the centre of your body. This is because the nerve impulses from your ears reach your brain at the same time.

Internet links

To find out more about the ears, go to **www.usborne-quicklinks.com** and type in the keyword "science".

There you'll find links to websites where you can:

- Learn how to fingerspell
- Watch an animation about hearing
- Try a balance experiment

Go to Usborne Quicklinks for links to hand-picked websites on hundreds of subjects.

THE NOSE AND TONGUE

Your **nose** and **tongue** are the organs of smell and taste respectively. Smells and tastes are chemicals. Cells called **chemoreceptors** in your nose and tongue detect these chemicals and send information to the brain, which identifies the smell or taste. Both organs also have other important jobs to do, for example the nose is part of the respiratory system and the tongue plays a role in digestion and speech.

This man is collecting rose petals to make into perfume. The human sense of smell can detect subtle variations in perfumes.

INSIDE THE NOSE

The two holes in your nose, called **nostrils**, open into a hollow space called the **nasal cavity**. As you breathe in, air is sucked into the lower part of the nasal cavity. Here, short hairs filter out large dust particles from the air, and mucus* in the cavity's lining warms and moistens the air before it travels into the lungs.

The roof of the nasal cavity has many tiny threads called **olfactory hairs** dangling through it. These hairs are the dendrites* of chemoreceptors called **olfactory cells**. Chemicals in the air, called **odorant molecules**, dissolve in the mucus and are absorbed by the hairs. The olfactory cells send nerve impulses* to the brain, which interprets them as a smell.

When you breathe in normally, only a small amount of air floats into your nasal cavity. When you sniff hard, you direct a stream of air towards your smell detectors. This is why things smell stronger if you sniff their scent.

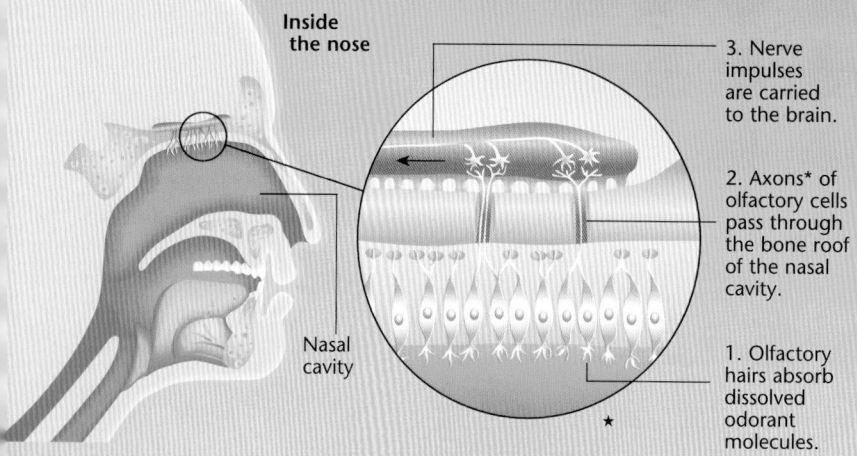

DIFFERENT SMELLS

Most humans are able to recognize thousands of different scents. For many years, scientists thought that all smells were made up of the seven basic scents listed below. More recent research, however, has led to the opinion that there are many more scents – perhaps hundreds.

Seven basic scents

Smell	Example
Camphor	Mothballs
Musk	Aftershave/Perfume
Floral	Roses
Peppermint	Mint toothpaste
Ether	Dry cleaning fluid
Pungent	Vinegar
Putrid	Rotten eggs

The sense of smell is strongly linked to memory. For example, the scent of mown grass might remind you vividly of a school sports day. This link probably happens because nerve impulses from the nose are analysed at the front of the cerebrum*. This part of the brain also deals with memory and feelings.

* *Axons, 364; Cerebrum, 366; Dendrites, 364; Mucus, 358; Nerve impulses, 365.*

TONGUE AND TASTE

The main purpose of your sense of taste is to tell you whether or not something is safe to eat. For example, rotten food and most poisonous plants taste revolting, so your immediate reaction is to spit them out.

The surface of your tongue is covered with tiny bumps called **papillae**. Many of these are lined with **taste buds**, which contain chemoreceptors called **gustatory receptor cells**. These are sensitive to chemicals from your food which dissolve in your saliva. The cells send nerve impulses to the brain, which interprets them as a taste.

Taste buds

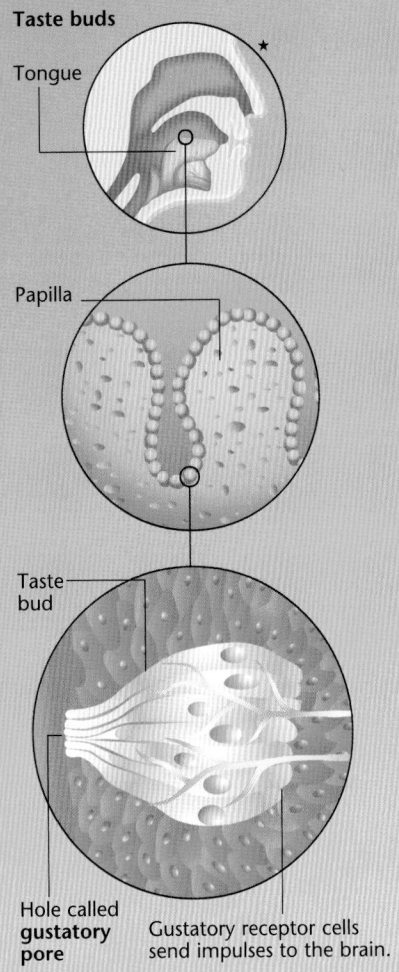

Taste-sensitive areas of the tongue

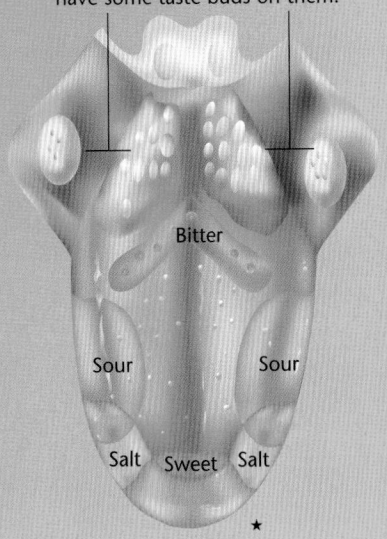

BASIC TASTES

Most of your taste buds lie at the sides and back of your tongue, although you have a few in other places around your throat. Buds in different areas of your tongue respond more strongly to different tastes. Scientists think that there are four main tastes: salt, sweet, sour and bitter. All flavours are made up of these basic tastes, plus smells detected by the nose.

Lemons taste sour.

Toffees taste sweet.

See for yourself

Wash your hands, and use your fingertip to place drops of cold, black coffee in different places on your tongue. Notice where your tongue is most sensitive to the coffee's bitter taste. Repeat the test using salty water, sugary water and lemon juice. Rinse your mouth with water and dry it with a piece of bread between each test.

See for yourself

You can use this test to show that the senses of taste and smell are closely linked. Grate a small amount of apple, pear and carrot into different bowls. Then shut your eyes tightly and hold your nose. Ask someone to feed you a spoonful of each food, one at a time. Try to identify the food. Repeat the experiment without holding your nose. You will probably find it easier to identify the food correctly.

TASTE AND SMELL

The senses of smell and taste are closely related. When you eat, odorant molecules from the food travel up the pharynx* into the nasal cavity, where the smell is detected in the usual way.

If you have a cold, you often lose your sense of smell and taste. This is because the lining of your nose swells, and makes thicker mucus than normal. This makes it harder for odorant molecules to reach the olfactory hairs. Your tongue can still detect the basic tastes, but you cannot identify the more subtle flavours.

Internet links

Go to **www.usborne-quicklinks.com** and type in "science" to find out more about the nose and tongue.

There you'll find links to websites where you can:

- Find animations, facts, experiments and quizzes on tasting and smelling

Go to Usborne Quicklinks for links to hand-picked websites on hundreds of subjects.

The links at Usborne Quicklinks are regularly reviewed and updated, so you might find a slightly different selection of websites from the ones described here.

* *Pharynx, 354.*

REPRODUCTION

The process of creating new life is called **reproduction**, and the parts of the body involved in it make up the **reproductive system**. A man's body makes male sex cells, which are called **sperm**, and a woman's body produces **ova**, which are female sex cells. When a sperm joins with an ovum, a new cell is formed. This will divide many times to form a baby.

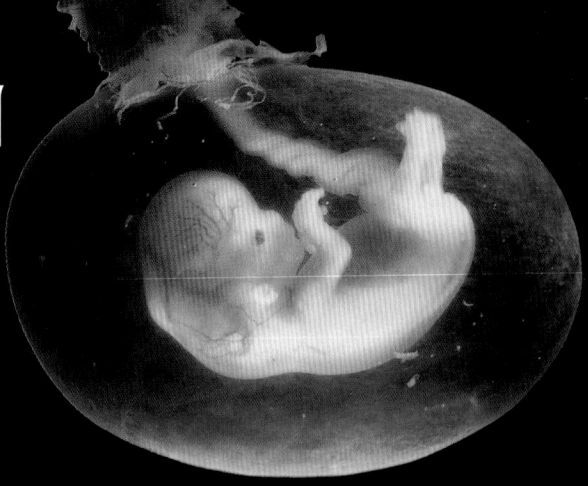

After eight weeks growing in its mother's womb, this developing baby is just over an inch long. It is floating inside a protective, fluid-filled sac called the **amniotic sac**.

MALE REPRODUCTIVE SYSTEM

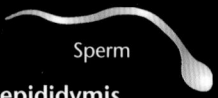

Sperm are made in two organs called **testes** and are stored in a comma-shaped organ called the **epididymis**, which lies over the back of each testis. The testes sit in a sac of skin known as the **scrotum**, which hangs outside the body. The temperature inside the body would be too high for sperm to survive.

Side view of the male reproductive system

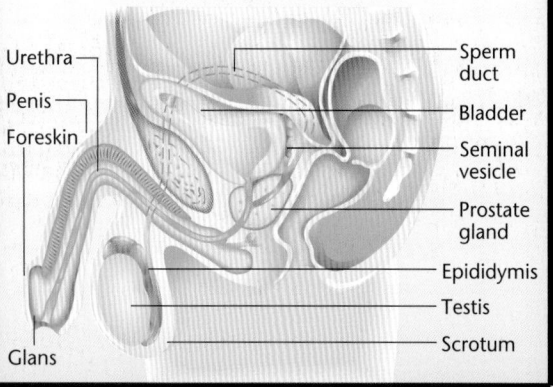

The **penis** is the organ through which sperm (and urine) leave the body. Its tip, called the **glans**, is very sensitive and is partly covered by a loose fold of skin called the **foreskin**. Sperm travel to the penis along two tubes called **sperm ducts**, which open into the urethra*. Several glands, including the **prostate gland** and **seminal vesicles**, make fluid in which the sperm swim. The mixture of sperm and fluids is known as **semen**.

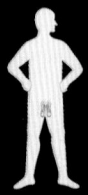

Position of male reproductive organs

FEMALE REPRODUCTIVE SYSTEM

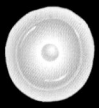

When a girl is born, she already has thousands of ova stored in two organs called **ovaries**. Every month, from the age of puberty*, one ovum is released from an ovary into one of the **Fallopian tubes**. This process, called **ovulation**, is described more fully on page 379.

Front view of the female reproductive system

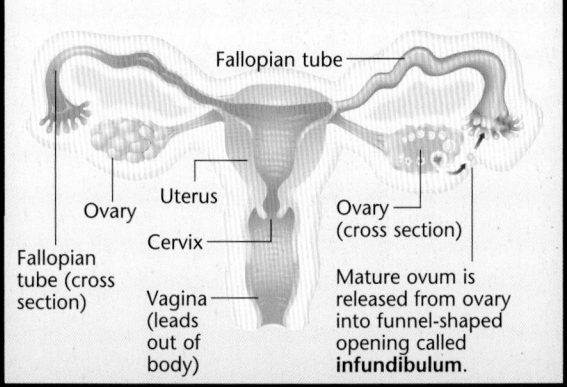

The Fallopian tubes lead to a hollow, pear-shaped organ called the **womb** or **uterus**. This is where a baby develops if an ovum has been fertilized (see right). At the bottom of the uterus is a muscular canal, called the **cervix**. This opens into a stretchy tube called the **vagina**, which in turn leads out of the body. The opening of the vagina lies behind that of the urethra*, and both are surrounded by two folds of skin called **labia**.

Position of fema reproductive organs

* *Puberty, 379; Urethra, 362.*

MAKING BABIES

During **sexual intercourse** (also known as **sex**), the penis becomes stiff and fits inside the vagina. Muscles around the male's urethra contract, squirting a small amount of semen out of the penis into the vagina. This is called **ejaculation**.

The sperm swim up through the uterus into the Fallopian tubes. If a sperm meets an ovum, they may join together to form a **zygote** – the first cell of a new baby. This event is called **fertilization** or **conception**. If no egg is present, then the sperm die within a few days.

Fertilization

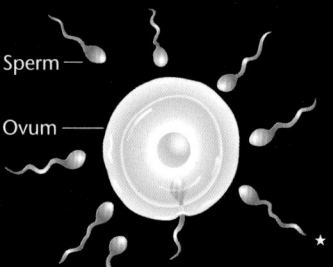

Only one sperm fertilizes each ovum: the others die.

There are several methods of preventing an ovum and a sperm from joining to make a baby. This is called **contraception**.

Internet links

To find out more about reproduction, go to **www.usborne-quicklinks.com** and type in the keyword "science".

There you'll find links to websites where you can:

- See how a baby grows from conception to birth
- Browse reproduction facts, animations and quizzes

Go to Usborne Quicklinks for links to hand-picked websites on hundreds of subjects.

HOW A BABY DEVELOPS

The zygote divides to form two identical cells. These divide several times to form a ball of cells, which embeds itself in the uterus lining. The cells continue to divide, and grow into different types, such as bone or blood cells. Cells of the same type join to form **tissue**, such as muscle. Different tissues make up **organs**, such as the heart, and organs group together to form **systems**, for example the digestive system. (For more about cells, tissues and organs, see pages 298-299.)

The future baby develops over nine months. For the first two, it is called an **embryo** and for the last seven, it is a **foetus**. The mother is said to be **pregnant**.

An unborn baby gets food and oxygen from its mother's blood through an organ called the **placenta**. Waste products from the baby go back in the opposite direction. Substances pass to and from the baby through a cord called the **umbilical cord**.

At the end of pregnancy, the baby moves so that its head is near the cervix. Muscles in the uterus contract strongly, squeezing the baby out through the mother's vagina. This process is known as **labour**.

At about 40 weeks, the baby is fully developed. Approximate size: 50cm

After the baby is born, its umbilical cord is clamped with a plastic clip, then cut. After about ten days, the stump falls off, leaving a navel.

Stages in the development of an unborn baby

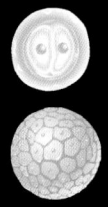

The new cell formed when the ovum and sperm join together, divides in two. These two cells divide to make four, then eight, sixteen and so on until a ball of cells forms.

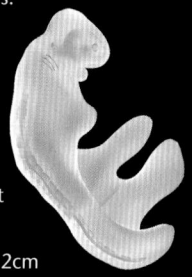

At six weeks, the backbone and brain are already forming. The heart starts to beat.

Approximate size: 2cm

Umbilical cord joins embryo to placenta.

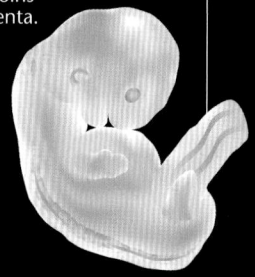

At seven weeks, tiny buds develop. They will become hands and feet.

Approximate size: 2.5cm

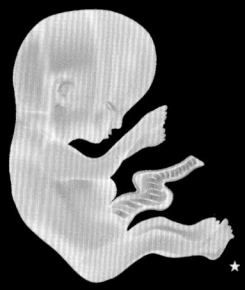

By 12 weeks, all the organs are formed. They will develop further over the next few months.

Approximate size: 7.5cm

GROWING AND CHANGING

During the first 20 years of life, a child gradually changes into an adult. The body grows in size and weight, and many new skills are learned. These processes are called **growth** and **development**. As you get older, your body continues to change, but more slowly. The rate at which you grow and develop depends on your genes*, as well as things such as diet and exercise.

GROWTH

Your body is made up of millions of different types of cells. To allow the body to grow, many of these divide in two to form new, identical cells. This type of cell division, called **mitosis**, also makes cells to replace many of those that wear out and die.

Parts of your body grow at different rates at different stages of life. This means that as your body grows, its proportions change. For example, a baby's head makes up one quarter of its height, but an adult's head makes up about one eighth of the height.

Your head also changes shape. A newborn baby has soft areas between its skull bones. Over the next few years, these are gradually replaced by bone and the head changes shape. Most parts of your body stop growing by the time you are 18, but some, such as your ears, continue to grow throughout life. Many other changes occur as you grow older, for instance your skin becomes less elastic (see photographs, right).

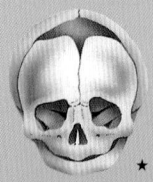

Child's skull ★

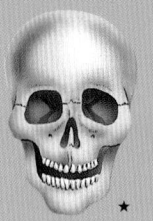

Adult's skull ★

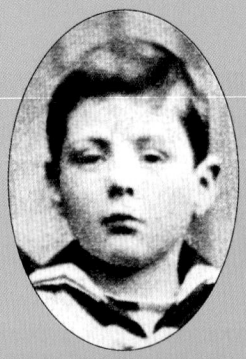

At the age of seven, Winston Churchill's face was round and his skin was smooth.

At 26, his face was longer. Frown lines started to appear on his brow as his skin became less elastic.

By his sixties, Churchill's skin had sagged, making his face look heavier.

Changes in body proportions from infancy to adulthood ★

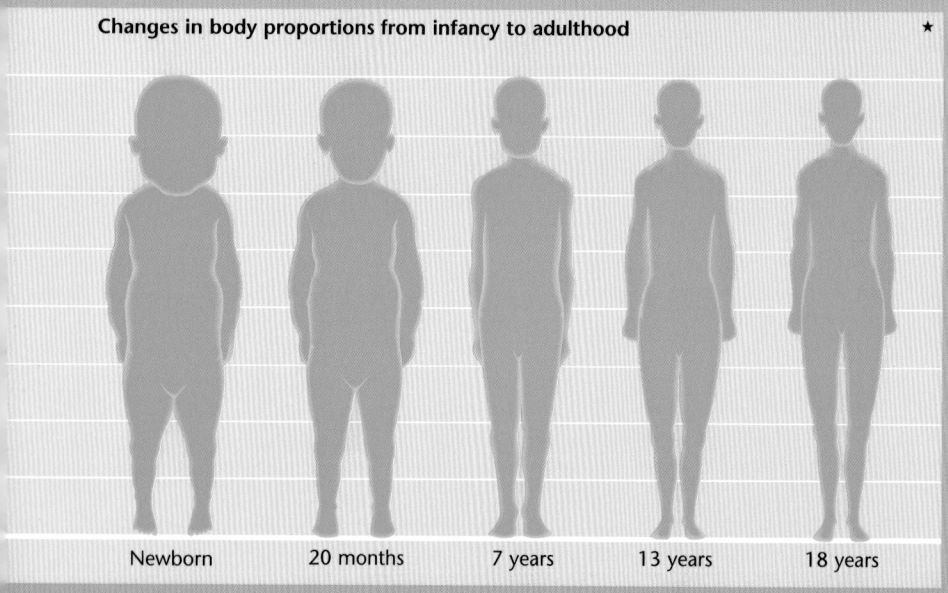

* *Genes, 380-385.*

PUBERTY

Between the ages of about 8 and 18, you change from a child into an adult. This time is known as **puberty** or **adolescence**. Changes to the body (known as **physical changes**) and to the mind and emotions (called **psychological changes**) prepare you for being an adult and a parent. These changes are triggered by hormones*.

Some of the physical changes that take place make it possible to have babies. For example, the reproductive organs* you were born with (called **primary sexual features**) become active. Other physical changes are not necessary for having babies. They result in **secondary sexual features** such as beards and other body hair.

Your feelings and emotions may change as you become more independent, explore new ways of thinking, and get used to your adult body. Changes in hormone levels in the body may also affect mood.

Physical changes at puberty

Boys	Girls
Height increases rapidly.	Height increases rapidly.
Hair grows on face; soft and downy at first, then coarser.	Fine covering of hair may grow on face.
Voice deepens.	
Hair grows under arms.	Hair grows under arms.
Shoulders and chest broaden.	Breasts start to develop.
Penis grows.	Hips widen.
Pubic hair grows around sex organs.	Pubic hair grows around sex organs.
Testes begin to make sperm.	Ovulation and periods start (see below left).

PERIODS

At birth, a girl's ovaries contain many thousands of immature ova. During and after puberty, one ovum matures about every 28 days and is released into a Fallopian tube. This is called **ovulation**. At the same time, the uterus develops a new inner layer, rich in blood vessels, ready to receive a fertilized* ovum.

If the ovum is not fertilized, this lining breaks down and leaves the body through the vagina. This is called "having a **period**" or **menstruating**. On average a girl has a period every 28 days, but it can vary. At some point between the ages of 40 and 55, the ovaries stop releasing ova and periods stop. This is the **menopause**.

A menstrual cycle

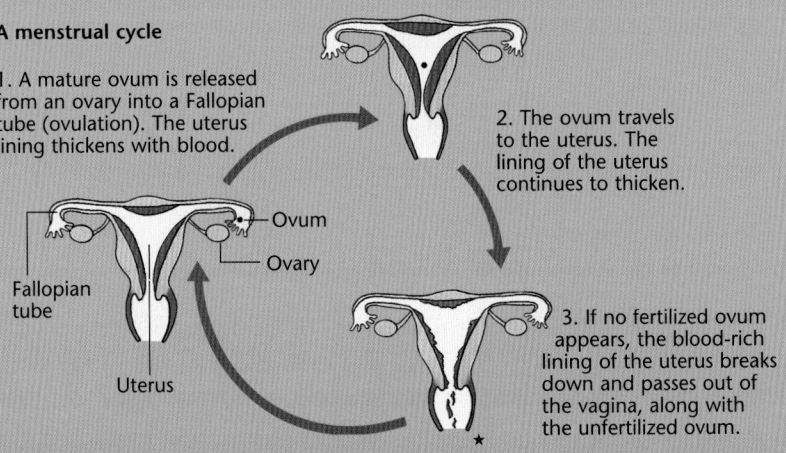

AGEING

After adolescence, the body becomes less efficient. This process, called **ageing** or **senescence**, starts slowly but speeds up later in life. The length of time you are likely to live is your **life expectancy**. It tends to be longer if you eat healthily, exercise sensibly, avoid smoking and drug misuse, and keep your mind active.

Internet links

Go to **www.usborne-quicklinks.com** and type "science" to find out more about growing and changing.

There you'll find links to websites where you can:

- Watch animated lessons on puberty and the menstrual cycle
- Find questions and answers on puberty and growing up

Go to Usborne Quicklinks for links to hand-picked websites on hundreds of subjects.

** Fertilization, 377; Hormones, 362, 363; Reproductive organs, 376.*

GENETICS

As soon as a sperm and an ovum join to make a new cell, that cell contains all the information needed to build a unique human being. The instructions that tell the body how to develop are **genes**, and the study of genes is **genetics**. Genes are sections of a chemical called **DNA** (**deoxyribonucleic acid**), which is packed in bundles called **chromosomes** inside a control unit called the **nucleus**. Human cells have 46 chromosomes. You inherit them from your parents.

These chromosomes are shown over 24,000 times their real size.

PAIRING UP

Your 46 chromosomes can be arranged in pairs called **homologous chromosomes**. These carry paired genes. Each gene, or gene group, on one chromosome has a partner on the paired chromosome (see opposite page).

Before cells divide for growth or repair (by mitosis*), all the chromosomes make copies of themselves, so each new cell has 46. But sex cells (ova and sperm) are made by a special type of cell division called **meiosis**. When this happens, the paired chromosomes move apart, resulting in only 23 chromosomes in each sex cell. They are ready to be paired up with new partners at fertilization*.

Inheriting chromosomes

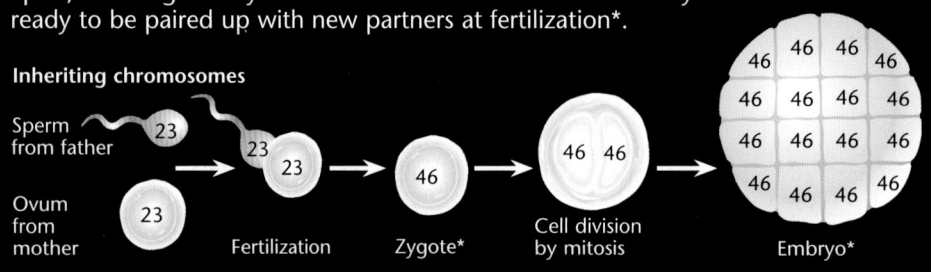

Before chromosomes split apart to make sex cells, a certain amount of swapping of gene pairs takes place. This means that every sperm is different from every other sperm produced by the same man, and every ovum is different from every other ovum produced by the same woman. So each new child from the same parents will be different, with different genes.

GIRL OR BOY

Two chromosomes, called **sex chromosomes**, determine whether a baby develops as a male or a female. These chromosomes are known as the **X** and **Y chromosomes**. Ova and sperm have one sex chromosome each. All ova have an X chromosome. Half the sperm have an X chromosome, and half have a Y. If a sperm with an X chromosome joins with an ovum, the baby will be a girl. If a sperm with a Y chromosome joins the ovum, the baby will be a boy.

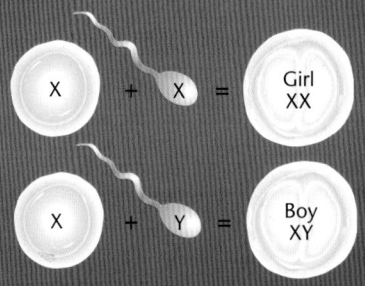

* *Embryo, Fertilization, 377; Mitosis, 378; Zygote, 377.*

HOW GENES WORK

You have 23 pairs of homologous chromosomes. Each gene, or gene group, on these chromosomes gives instructions to create or control one of your characteristics.

Genes for certain features, such as eye or hair colour, or blood group, have different forms, called **alleles**. So a gene pair might be made up of alleles giving identical instructions, or alleles giving different instructions.

One allele may order green eyes, for example, and the other blue eyes. In such cases, either one allele will be **dominant**, overruling the other, **recessive**, allele, or they will both have an effect, in which case they are called **co-dominant alleles**. For example, a green eye colour allele is dominant over a blue one, so if you have one of each, you have green eyes. You need two blue colour alleles to have blue eyes.

The diagram below shows how different pairs of blood group alleles result in different blood groups, depending on which allele is dominant.

The allele for blood group A is dominant, and the allele for group O is recessive. The two people on the right are blood group A.

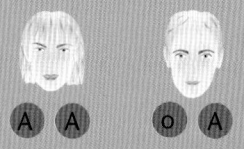

The allele for blood group B is dominant, and the allele for group O is recessive. The two people on the right are blood group B.

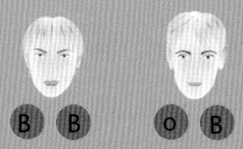

This person has two recessive O alleles, so is blood group O.

A and B are co-dominant so this person is blood group AB.

If the alleles in a pair are identical, as with the AA person, the person is **homozygous** for that characteristic, in this case blood group. If they are different, the person is **heterozygous**.

Some diseases, for example a disease called **cystic fibrosis** that affects the lungs, are caused by a recessive allele. A person who has a pair of these alleles will have the disease. Someone who has just one of them, paired with a normal (dominant) allele, will not be affected by the disease, but is said to be a **carrier**. The recessive allele can be passed to their children.

SEX-LINKED GENES

Some characteristics, for example colour-blindness, show up more often in males than females. This is because they are caused by recessive alleles found on the X chromosome which do not have partners on the Y chromosome to overrule them. Such characteristics are said to be controlled by sex-linked genes.

In genetics, alleles are represented by letters. A capital letter shows that an allele is dominant, and a small one that it is recessive. The diagram below shows what might happen if a female carrier of the recessive colour-blindness allele (c) has children with a man with a dominant normal sight allele (C).

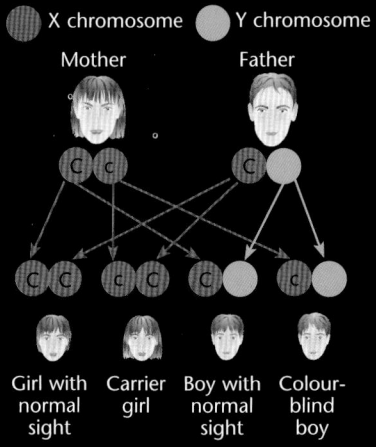

Internet links

To find out more about genetics, go to **www.usborne-quicklinks.com** and type in the keyword "science".

There you'll find links to websites where you can:

- Examine a 3-D model of DNA
- See how much DNA humans share with some other animals
- Learn more with online activities

Go to Usborne Quicklinks for links to hand-picked websites on hundreds of subjects.

GENE TECHNOLOGY

Genetic research took a great leap forward in the early 1950s, when James Watson and Francis Crick discovered the structure of DNA*. This knowledge has since helped scientists to find out much more about genes, and how living things are affected by them. New discoveries in genetics are being made all the time and these are put to a variety of uses, some of which are described here.

Watson and Crick with their DNA model

STRUCTURE OF DNA

Each molecule of DNA looks like a twisted rope ladder. This spiral shape is known as a **double helix**. The ladder's rungs are made up of four chemicals linked in pairs: adenine and thymine, guanine and cytosine. These chemicals are called **bases**, and are usually known by their initial letters, A, T, C and G.

The sides of the ladder are made up of strands of a sugar called **deoxyribose**, alternating with chemical clusters known as **phosphate groups**. One of each, together with a base, make up a unit called a **nucleotide**. A gene is a sequence of about 250 pairs of nucleotides. There are about 1,000 genes on an average DNA molecule.

This is part of a molecule of DNA. Its spiral shape is called a double helix.

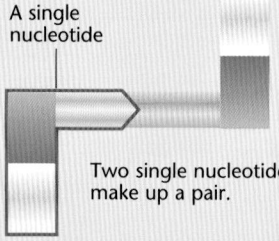

The sequence of bases in a gene forms a chemical code. Each gene has a different code, and contributes to a different characteristic.

GENOME RESEARCH

All the DNA in an organism is its **genome**. An ordered list of all the bases in a genome is called a **map**. The genome of the yeast cell was the first to be mapped.

A significant milestone in genetic research was reached in June 2000, when scientists announced that they had made a draft of the 3.2 billion base pairs that make up the human genome. The completed map will have many uses. For example, scientists may be able to use it to find out more about the links between genes and certain diseases, and develop new ways of treating or even preventing them.

Base A is always paired with base T.

Base G is always paired with base C.

A base always joins to a deoxyribose strand.

Key to DNA diagram

Bases

- Adenine
- Cytosine
- Deoxyribose
- Thymine
- Guanine
- Phosphate group

* DNA, 380.

GENETIC FINGERPRINTING

Unless you have an identical twin, the exact order of bases in your DNA is slightly different from everyone else's. A process called **DNA profiling** or **genetic fingerprinting** can be used to compare samples of DNA. If the DNA samples are identical, then they have probably come from the same person or from identical twins.

DNA profiling has various uses. Police scientists, for example, can extract DNA from a single strand of hair or drop of blood left at the scene of a crime. They can then use it to identify the guilty person.

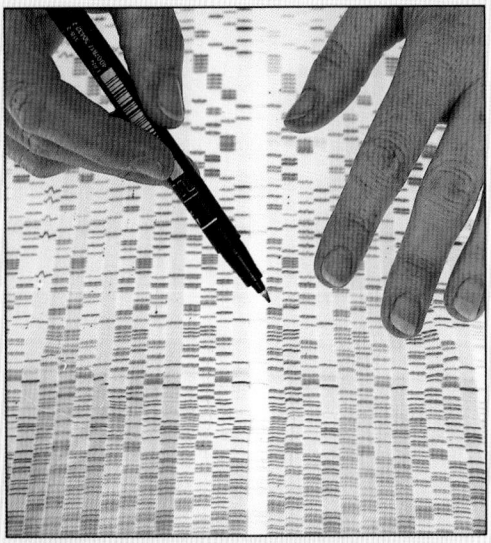

A scientist looking at DNA sequences. The bands depend on the order of bases. If the band patterns of two samples match exactly, they are likely to be either from the same person or from identical twins.

DNA samples from people who are related contain many more matching genes than samples from people who are not. Scientists can compare DNA samples to find out if and how people are related.

After the Russian Revolution in 1917, Tsar Nicholas II, his wife and three of their children were killed and buried in an unmarked grave. Bodies thought to be theirs were found in 1991. The Tsar was identified by comparing his DNA to his brother's. His wife's identity was proven by taking a DNA sample from Prince Philip, Duke of Edinburgh, who was a distant relation.

GENETIC ENGINEERING

Scientists have discovered how to extract genes and use them in different ways, for instance in medicine, farming and industry. This manipulation of genes is known as **genetic engineering** or **genetic modification**. You can read more about it over the page.

The main technique used in genetic engineering is called **gene splicing**. Chemicals called **restriction enzymes** are used to cut specific genes out of DNA. Other enzymes, called **ligases**, are used to splice, or join, the genes with DNA taken from a suitable organism.

This modified DNA, known as **recombinant DNA** (**rDNA**), can then be used in different ways. For example, it may be placed in a fast-breeding bacterium*. This reproduces very quickly to create lots of bacteria, each containing the target DNA with the specific gene.

A method of gene splicing

1. The gene that is needed (called the **target DNA**) is taken out of a cell's nucleus.

2. The target DNA is spliced with a **plasmid**, a special piece of DNA from a bacterium.

3. The recombinant DNA is then put into a **host bacterium** of a type which divides rapidly.

4. The host bacterium divides many times, creating many identical copies, each containing the target DNA (the desired gene).

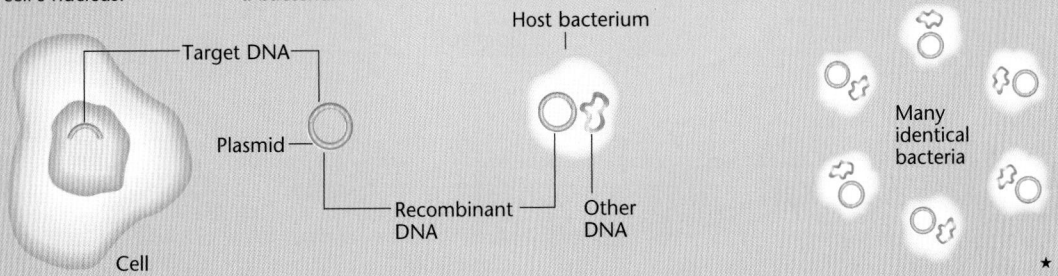

* *Bacteria, 386.*

BREEDING

Since earliest times, farmers have chosen their best animals and plants from which to breed. This is known as **selective breeding** or **artificial selection**. Some of the young of these animals or plants inherit the good qualities of their parents.

Breeding from two plants or animals of the same variety is called **pure breeding**. Using plants or animals of different varieties is **cross-breeding**. The offspring are a new, mixed breed called a **hybrid** or a **cross**, as shown in the example below.

MODIFYING GENES

More recently, scientists have found ways to produce plants and animals with a particular quality by altering their genes in some way.

Traditional selective breeding is only possible between breeds that belong to the same species. However, using genetic techniques, scientists can transfer genes between different species.

Organisms with genes from another source are described as **transgenic**.

Scientists are exploring ways of altering plants' genes to produce crops that are more resistant to disease, weather and chemicals used to kill pests or weeds.

Cotton plants such as these can be genetically modified to resist pests.

In Australia, for example, crops of cotton plants are often eaten by a particular species of caterpillar. Scientists have genetically engineered a cotton plant that makes a substance which is poisonous to the caterpillars or any other insect that tries to eat it.

The seedling shown below is being grown on a glass petri dish and given a nutrient fluid through a pipette. New types of genetically modified plants are grown and tested in a laboratory before they can be grown outside.

A method of cross-breeding
(The names in italic type are breeds of pig.)

Line 63 Synthetic boar. Very large, with good, lean meat.

Large White sow. Grows quickly.

Duroc boar. Strong, hardy outdoor breed.

Landrace sow. Produces large litters and is an excellent mother.

Pickboar cross-bred boar. Large and fast growing. An ideal meat pig.

Camborough 12 cross-bred sow. Has large litters of strong, hardy piglets and is an ideal mother.

The piglets selected are fast-growing, lean, strong and healthy, combining all the good features.

PHARMING

Genetic engineering has made it possible for plants and animals to produce proteins that are useful in medicine. This technique is known as **pharming**. For example, a sheep has been genetically modified to produce milk which contains **alpha-1 antitrypsin** – a drug used to treat cystic fibrosis patients.

Genetic modification of animals could have other medical uses. For example, by inserting certain human genes into the DNA of some pigs, it may be possible to breed pigs whose organs are suitable for transplanting into humans.

Heart transplants using a pig's heart could be possible, if a suitable human organ donor couldn't be found. After the operation, the patient would have to take medicines to stop the white blood cells attacking the new organ in the same way as they fight invading germs (see page 387).

ANIMAL CLONING

In nature, animals are born as a result of reproduction and they inherit genes from both parents. Genetic research has made it possible to breed **clones** – animals that are genetically identical to a single parent.

In 1996, scientists at the Roslin Institute in Edinburgh took an ovum* from a sheep and removed its nucleus* (with all its DNA). They fused the ovum with a cell from another sheep. After a week of growth in a laboratory, the ball of dividing cells was placed in the womb of a third sheep. After five months, a cloned lamb, named Dolly, was born.

How Dolly the sheep was cloned

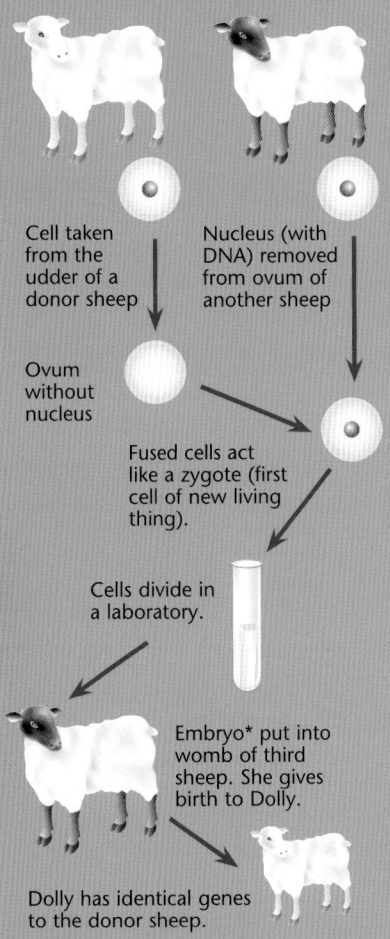

See for yourself

Gene technology is a very fast-growing area of science. Listen out for items about genetics on TV and radio news, and check in newspapers. You could also try searching the internet for up-to-the-minute information on genetic issues (see box below). Other uses of genetic technology you could find out about include:

- **Gene therapy** – treating certain genetic disorders with healthy genes.
- **Genetic screening** – looking for genes in a person's DNA that could cause a disease in them or their children.

GENETICS IN THE NEWS

Genetic engineering often makes sensational headlines. For example, the use of **genetically modified organisms (GMOs)** in food worries many people because the long-term effects are not yet known. Also, some people don't like the idea of eating "unnatural" food.

There are food companies, on the other hand, that see GMOs as a way of producing more food at a lower cost. You can read more about the genetic modification of food on page 291.

Internet links

Go to **www.usborne-quicklinks.com** and type in "science" to find out more about gene technology.

There you'll find links to websites where you can:

- Read a guide to GMOs
- Explore the rights and wrongs of genetic modification

Go to Usborne Quicklinks for links to hand-picked websites on hundreds of subjects.

** Embryo, 377; Ovum, 376; Nucleus, 380.*

FIGHTING DISEASE

Anything that stops all or part of your body from working properly can be called a **disease**. Some diseases are caused by harmful, microscopic organisms known as **germs**. Others can be caused by diet, lack of exercise, faulty genes*, old age, or poisonous chemicals, such as nicotine from cigarettes.

White blood cells such as this help to defend your body from infection.

GERMS

The scientific name for germs is **pathogens**. Two types of pathogens – bacteria and viruses – are responsible for many diseases in humans.

Bacteria are microscopic organisms found everywhere. Harmful ones may produce poisonous waste chemicals, called **toxins**, which can cause disease. Different bacteria cause different illnesses.

Viruses are strands of DNA* inside a protective coat. They cannot live on their own, but invade cells in your body and use them as factories to make more viruses. This eventually kills the cell. Diseases caused by viruses include colds, flu and AIDS.

A virus

Extension called a **pseudopodium** ("false foot") will engulf germs and trap them.

Main types of bacteria

Cocci are spherical. They cause most throat infections.

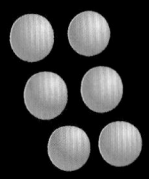

Bacilli are rod shaped. They cause tuberculosis and typhoid.

Vibrios are bent rod shaped. They cause diseases such as cholera.

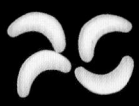

Spirilla are spiral. They cause diseases such as ratbite fever.

DEFENDING THE BODY

Germs are **infectious**, which means that they pass from one living thing to another. They can be spread in a number of ways, for example in air and water and by touch. They can also be carried by animals.

Germs stick to a fly's feet and hairy body as it feeds on dung or rotten matter. These germs can spread to food a fly lands on.

Your body has many ways of defending itself from germs. Firstly your skin tries to keep germs out. But if they do get inside, your body has several methods of fighting back. The main ones are shown in the table on the right.

Your body's defences	
Skin	Forms germ-proof barrier.
Nose	Hairs and mucus trap germs and dirt from the air.
Ears	Wax inside traps germs.
Eyelids	Keep germs out of your eyes.
Tears	Wash your eyes clean.
Stomach	Hydrochloric acid kills germs in food.
Tonsils and adenoids	Kill germs in your throat.
White blood cells	Destroy germs inside your body.
Spleen	Contains white blood cells which fight infection.

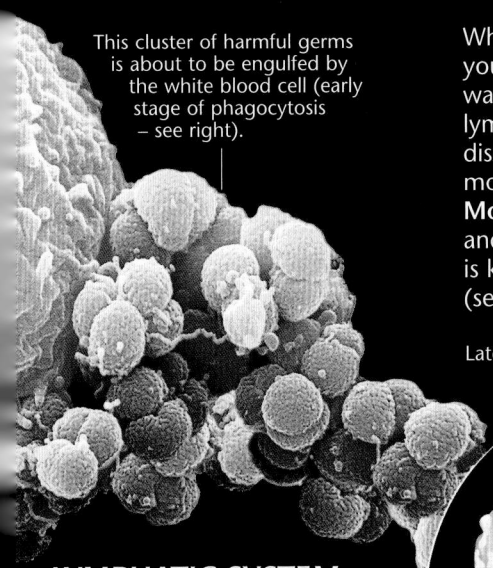

This cluster of harmful germs is about to be engulfed by the white blood cell (early stage of phagocytosis – see right).

LYMPHATIC SYSTEM

Your **lymphatic system** and your white blood cells form a disease-fighting partnership. The lymphatic system is a network of tubes and connected organs. The tubes contain **lymph**, a liquid made up of waste soaked up from tissue fluid* and white blood cells.

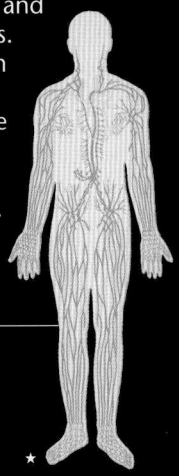

Lymph vessels carry lymph around your body.

Lymph drains back into your blood through two veins near your neck, recycling the white blood cells to begin again (see right). **Lymph nodes** are small organs found in clusters around the system (in your neck, armpits and groin). Many of your white blood cells are made in the lymph nodes, and many germs are trapped and destroyed there.

White blood cells move out of your blood (through capillary* walls) into tissue fluid* and lymph, and travel around fighting disease. There are two main types: monocytes and lymphocytes. **Monocytes** surround germs and digest them. This process is known as **phagocytosis** (see left and below).

Late stage of phagocytosis

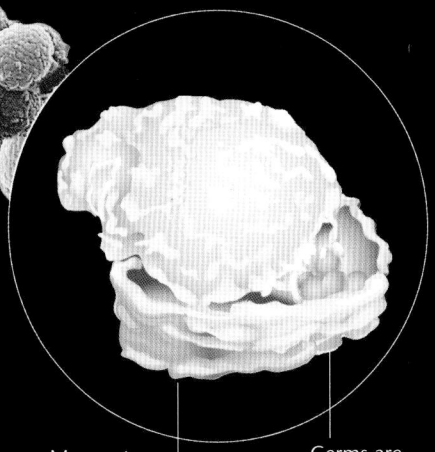

Some monocytes, called **wandering macrophages**, are constantly moving around. Others, called **fixed macrophages**, become fixed in a particular organ, such as a lymph node, and fight any germs that gather there.

Lymphocytes are mostly made in lymph nodes. They destroy germs with chemicals called **antibodies**. Each type of antibody is specially produced to attack a particular chemical, or **antigen**, carried on an invading germ.

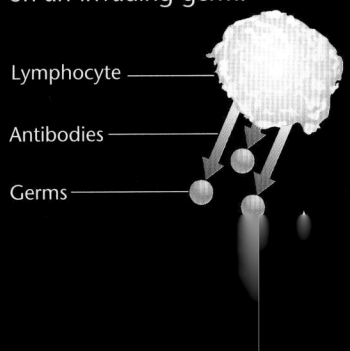

Once you have made an antibody against a particular germ's antigen, you can make it again very quickly if the same germ enters your body. This gives you **resistance**, or **active immunity**, to the disease.

You can also be made immune to diseases such as measles by being given a **vaccine**. This is a dose of the germ that is too weak to cause the disease, but has enough antigens to make you produce antibodies. These will protect you against future attacks by the germ. This process is called **vaccination**.

Vaccination methods

In some countries, drops of vaccine against the disease polio are given on lumps of sugar.

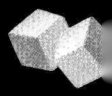

Most vaccinations are given by injection. This avoids them being destroyed by digestive juices*.

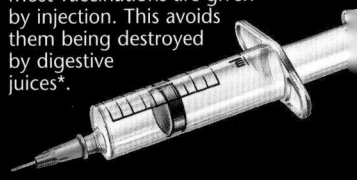

An injection of antibodies after a disease has developed will give you **passive immunity**. The harmful germs are killed, but the immunity does not last.

Internet links

Go to **www.usborne-quicklinks.com** and type in "science" to find out more about fighting disease.

There you'll find links to websites where you can:

- View an interactive lesson on how the human body fights microbes
- Find out how the polio vaccine was discovered

Go to Usborne Quicklinks for links to hand-picked websites on hundreds of subjects.

MEDICINE

Your body's defences are often strong enough for you to get better without seeing a doctor. If you do need help, though, there is a whole area of science that specializes in treating disease as well as keeping the body fit and healthy. This is called **medicine**. Major advances in medicine have helped to increase the life expectancy of many people.

DIAGNOSIS

When you visit a doctor because you are ill, the doctor will ask questions and examine you to find out what is wrong. This is called making a **diagnosis**. If the doctor needs more information, there are many tests that can be done. Some of these are simple and others involve expensive and complex equipment.

Chemical analysis of samples of body fluids such as blood and urine can reveal important clues. For example, glucose in urine can be a sign of diabetes. This can be tested for by dipping a chemical-soaked stick into a urine sample. Different amounts of glucose turn the tip of the stick particular colours.

A urine test chart

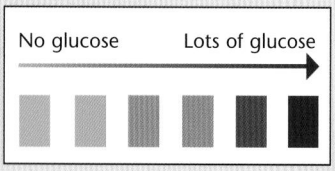

Various methods of **medical imaging** allow doctors to see inside a patient's body without cutting it open. For example, invisible rays of energy called **X-rays** can pass through soft tissue, but not through denser substances such as bone. X-rays are particularly useful for finding out if bones are broken.

Soft areas, such as the digestive tract*, can be examined by filling them with a **radio-opaque** liquid. This stops the X-rays passing through, and so any blockages or changes from the usual shape can be seen clearly.

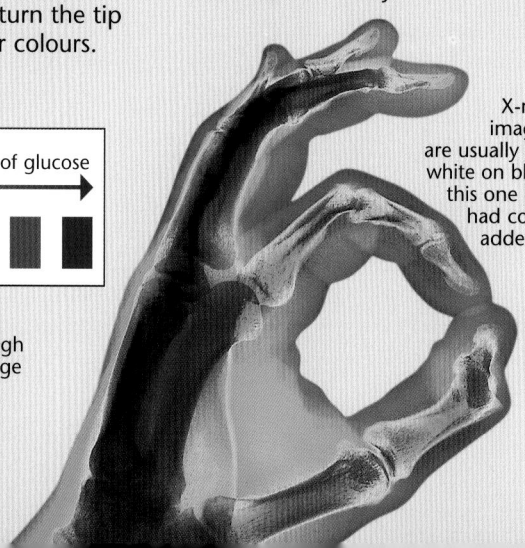

X-rays were passed through this hand to form an image on a photographic plate.

X-ray images are usually white on black: this one has had colour added.

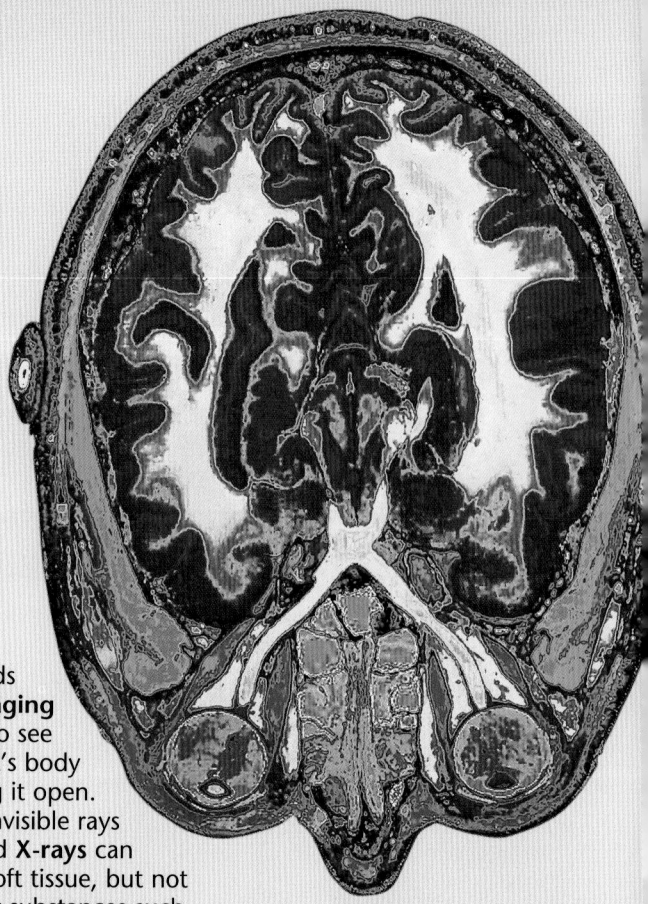

This MRI scan shows a section of the head. The walnut-shaped part is the brain and the pink blobs are eyeballs.

CT (computed tomography) scanners are special X-ray cameras that take detailed images of hard and soft tissues. The body is scanned in sections and the images are fed into a computer. Doctors look at the pictures to see if there are any unusual shadows or changes of shape that may be a sign of problems, such as abnormal growths called **tumours**.

Magnetic resonance imaging (MRI) scanners also scan sections of the body, but they use radio waves in the presence of a strong magnet. A computer builds up the images to create a 3-dimensional picture. MRI scans are used particularly to look for diseases of the nervous system, including the brain.

 * *Digestive tract, 354.*

TREATMENT

Treatments range from rest, exercises or changes of diet to medicines or other, more complex, methods. In some cases, for example, a doctor may perform an **operation**, cutting the body open to mend or take out a diseased part.

MEDICINES

Chemical substances called **medicines** or **drugs** are used to treat and prevent a wide variety of illnesses. Most medicines are made in laboratories. Many are based on substances in plants which have healing properties.

Foxglove leaves contain a substance called **digitalis**. This is now made artificially and is used to treat heart disease.

Medicines called **antibiotics** are used to treat many illnesses caused by bacteria*. They either stop the bacteria from multiplying, or destroy them completely. Antibiotics have no effect on illnesses caused by viruses*, such as colds and flu.

All medicines are dangerous and should not be touched without the advice of a doctor or pharmacist. Misuse of medicines could make you very ill or even kill you.

This green furry growth is a mould called *Penicillium*. In 1928, Scottish scientist Alexander Fleming discovered that it could kill bacteria. He used it to develop **penicillin**, the first antibiotic drug.

SURGERY

All operations are part of the area of medicine called **surgery**. They are usually carried out in hospital by specially-trained doctors called **surgeons**. There are many different fields of surgery, each with specialized techniques.

Laser surgery uses intense beams of light, called **laser beams**, to make clean, precise cuts and to carry out delicate surgery, such as eye operations. For example, if a patient's retina* has become detached, a laser can sometimes be used to weld it back in place with a tiny heat scar. Lasers were originally developed for non-medical purposes, such as cutting and welding in industry.

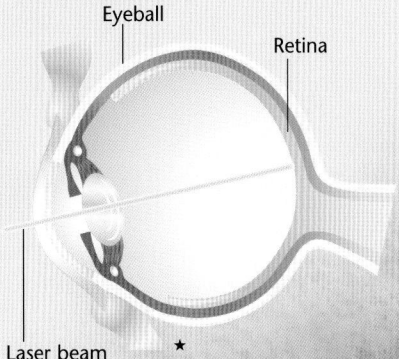

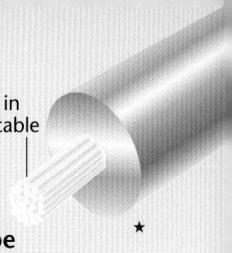

Lasers are often used with a tube called an **endoscope** which is pushed into a patient's body, often down the throat. Endoscopes are used to see and remove things, such as growths, inside the body.

Many endoscopes contain **fibre-optic cables**. These are made up of hair-like glass strands called **optical fibres**, through which light and laser beams can pass. Other types of cables have different jobs, such as sucking out samples for analysis.

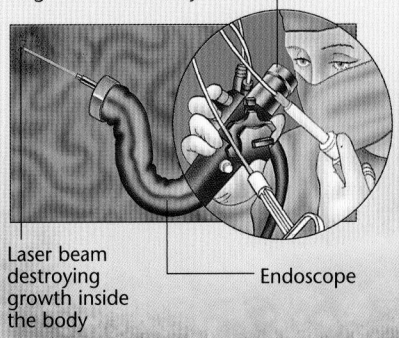

Internet links

To find out more about medicine, go to **www.usborne-quicklinks.com** and type in the keyword "science".

There you'll find links to websites where you can:

- Learn how technology is helping people with disabilities including paralysis, blindness and deafness
- Find out how the use of lasers has changed modern surgery

Go to Usborne Quicklinks for links to hand-picked websites on hundreds of subjects.

The links at Usborne Quicklinks are regularly reviewed and updated, so you might find a slightly different selection of websites from the ones described here.

* *Bacteria, 386; Retina, 370; Viruses, 386.*

OTHER TREATMENTS

There are many treatments, called **alternative treatments**, that have not traditionally been used by doctors. Some of these are now often used in addition to conventional treatments and are known as **complementary medicine**. Many people also use complementary treatments as part of a general healthy lifestyle.

HOMEOPATHY

Homeopathy was founded about 200 years ago by a German doctor named Samuel Hahnemann. It is based on the idea that a substance that causes certain symptoms in a healthy person can be used to cure the same symptoms in someone who is ill. Most scientists do not believe that homeopathic remedies are effective, but its supporters claim they work by stimulating the body's natural defences (see pages 386-387).

Homeopathic remedies are said to work best in very small doses. They are made from natural ingredients, such as herbs. Others contain minute amounts of conventional medicines.

These pink homeopathic pills are plain pills that have been soaked in very dilute solutions of a remedy.

ACUPUNCTURE

Acupuncture is an ancient Chinese treatment based on the idea that all things contain an energy force called **Chi**. Chi is said to flow along invisible channels in the body called **meridians**. On these channels are hundreds of invisible points known as **pressure points**.

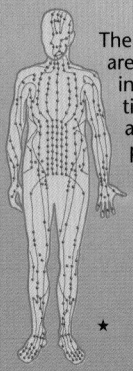

The meridians are shown in red. The tiny dots are pressure points.

An **acupuncturist** acts on these points mainly by sticking very fine needles into them. Acupuncture is used for many reasons, such as relieving pain and reducing stress.

PLACEBO EFFECT

Many scientists think that most successful alternative treatments are examples of the placebo effect. A **placebo** is a treatment that has no medicine in it, but works because the patient believes it will. Placebos work best on conditions with a large psychological element, such as mild depression or the experience of pain. They are also more effective when given by someone whom the patient trusts and respects, for example, a doctor or healer.

MANIPULATING JOINTS

Osteopathy and **chiropractic** are ways of treating physical problems by manipulating the joints, particularly the backbone. The treatments are often used for back problems, but osteopaths and chiropractors believe that other illnesses, such as headaches and rashes, can also be treated by their methods.

This pose is based on a yoga posture. Practising yoga can help to make your body more supple.

YOGA

Some people do **yoga** to help them to relax. It combines special movements and positions, called **postures**, with techniques of breathing and concentration called **meditation**. Many people find that yoga improves their general mental and physical health as well as helping to relieve aches and pains.

PREVENTATIVE MEDICINE

Preventing illness is just as important as treating it. Doctors, medical scientists and health officers spend much of their time looking for ways to control and wipe out illness. This is called **preventative medicine**.

One important way of preventing diseases is **vaccination** (see also page 387). Babies and children are usually given a series of vaccines against diseases such as polio and measles. If you go abroad you may need a vaccine against diseases not found in your country.

Regular medical check-ups to look for early signs of disease are carried out in schools and clinics. This is called **screening**, and helps because doctors may spot and be able to treat an illness before it develops.

HEALTH ADVICE

To help keep people healthy, doctors teach them about the benefits of regular exercise and a balanced diet. They also provide information about the harmful effects to the body of smoking, drinking too much alcohol, and misusing drugs.

DRUG INFORMATION

A **drug** is any substance that affects the way the body works. Different drugs have different effects. Medicines, alcohol, and nicotine in cigarettes are all drugs. These are available legally, though their use is controlled, for example by prescriptions or age restrictions. Other drugs, such as heroin, are only available illegally.

Too much of any drug, legal or illegal, can cause long-term damage or even death. Many drugs are **habit-forming**, so people feel that they need to take them. Some are **addictive**, which means that the body gets used to them and is disturbed without them. Below is a list of some drugs and their effects.

Substance	Description	Effect on the body
Alcohol	Clear liquid found in beer, cider, wines, spirits and alcoholic "soft drinks".	Relaxation, confidence or depression. Poor coordination and judgement, so drinking and driving is very dangerous. Addictive. Long-term effects of heavy drinking include serious liver damage.
Cannabis	Often dried leaves or brown solid lump. Usually mixed with tobacco and smoked.	Relaxation. Tired, dizzy or sick feeling and faster heart rate. Memory loss is a possible long-term effect. Effects of nicotine added if cannabis is smoked.
Cocaine Crack	Fine, white powder. Usually sniffed. A form of cocaine. Small lumps. Smoked.	Alert, excited or aggressive feeling. Destroys nasal passages and damages lungs. Highly addictive.
Ecstasy	Tablets or capsules. Swallowed.	Feelings of energy and confidence or sickness and anxiety. Damages liver and kidneys. Can kill without warning.
Heroin	Grey-brown powder, often sold mixed with bleach or talc. Smoked, sniffed or injected.	Feeling of well-being then depression. Very addictive. Body needs ever higher doses or suffers awful withdrawal pains. Death by overdose is common.
Inhalants	Include lighter fuel, glue, paint or varnish. Usually sniffed.	Fumes cause feeling of well-being and dizziness. Damage lining of nose and lungs. Can suffocate. Often addictive.
LSD	White tablet or on small pieces of paper. Usually swallowed.	Puts user in strange, sometimes terrifying world, called a **trip**. Causes mental problems and brain damage.
Nicotine	In tobacco, for example in cigarettes.	Enjoyment or sick feeling. Habit-forming and addictive. Damages lungs and cilia*. Causes heart disease and chest infections. Can lead to lung cancer.

Internet links

To find out more about medicine, go to **www.usborne-quicklinks.com** and type in the keyword "science".

There you'll find links to websites where you can:

- Take a quiz to test your knowledge of diseases and treatments
- Learn more about alternative medicine
- Explore facts and animations about drugs and how they affect the body
- Read about key medical discoveries

** Cilia, 358.*

SCIENCE FACTS AND LISTS

RESEARCH ON THE WEB

The internet is a fantastic resource, but finding information you can trust is sometimes tricky. If you want to find out more about subjects covered in this book, the tips below will help you find sites that you can use with confidence.

INTERNET RESEARCH

When using the internet for research, make sure the websites you visit can be trusted to provide accurate information. The websites recommended at the Usborne Quicklinks Website have been reviewed, but it is still a good idea to check the information for yourself. Here are some tips to help you:

• Check the name and url of the website you are visiting. If it is a well-known organization, museum or reference site, the information will probably (but not necessarily) be accurate.

• Look for signs that the website has been updated recently. If it contains old news and dates, the website may be out of date and contain inaccurate information.

• Look out for spelling mistakes, missing pictures and broken links. These may indicate that the website is not looked after and may contain information that is untrustworthy.

• It is always a good idea to use more than one source when doing your research. This way you can find out if a website is giving incorrect information. Remember, a book has to be checked for mistakes before it is printed, so it is less likely to contain errors than a web page; but if the book is old its details may be out of date.

USING INFORMATION

If you want to use information from a website for schoolwork – don't copy it word for word. Instead try to express the same ideas in your own words. At the end of your work, give the name and url of the website in your list of sources.

Many websites are happy for schools and students to use their information and pictures for educational purposes. But before downloading any pictures, check the website's "Terms and Conditions of Use" to make sure that downloading is allowed. You may use the downloadable pictures at the Usborne Quicklinks Website for school or personal use, but the pictures remain the copyright of Usborne Publishing.

INTERNET SAFETY

Never give out any personal information, such as your real name, address or telephone number when you are using the internet. You have no control over who gets hold of your details.

Never arrange to meet someone that you have only talked to over the internet. They may not be who they say they are, and could just be pretending to be your friend.

USEFUL WEBSITES

There are many superb science and technology sites on the internet. For each of the categories below you can find links to trustworthy and helpful websites by going to **www.usborne-quicklinks.com**, typing in the keyword "**science**" and then entering the page number "**395**".

General science

There are some huge general science websites available. They are a very useful accompaniment to this book, and many provide games and quizzes to test your knowledge. Some are so big that they have their own in-built search engine to help you find whatever it is that interests you.

Experiments

There are plenty of websites that suggest all kinds of scientific experiments you can try at home – from how to grow your own crystal to making a battery out of a lemon. Ask an adult to help you use any equipment you do not normally use.

Online magazines

Many magazines are also available online. Try searching for them yourself, or visit **www.usborne-quicklinks.com** for a selection of popular and useful titles.

Technology

The internet is a good place to find out about the latest technology, because new information is being added every day. Large organizations such as NASA will often post news of their latest discoveries on their websites. The Web is also an excellent source of computer information and upgrades that can be downloaded for free.

Environmental issues

Visit the websites of large organizations such as Greenpeace or Friends of the Earth to read up-to-date news on environmental issues, find out how you can get involved in working to protect the environment, and ask questions about the environmental issues that interest you. You can find these sites and others at **www.usborne-quicklinks.com**

Homework and revision

There are some sites that are designed especially to help you with homework or revision. For the most relevant information it is probably best to visit a site that is designed for your part of the world. Choose the level that applies to you and select the subject that you need to revise to get the best out of what the site has to offer.

Reference materials

There is a selection of online encyclopedias and other reference sites on the Usborne Quicklinks Website that you can use to find basic information on a subject, or to look up a scientific word or idea that you are unfamiliar with.

Image galleries

There are many superb scientific image galleries on the internet. Things to look for include:

- A huge variety of space photographs (try the NASA site for a database of free images)
- Amazing insights into cell biology
- Clickable photographic maps of the surface of the Earth

You can usually use the photos to illustrate your own work (but do check first what it says about this on the website offering the photos).

Online image galleries contain a wide range of useful pictures you can include in school projects.

REVISION QUESTIONS

You can use the revision questions on pages 396-403 to test yourself. There is one page of questions for each section of the encyclopedia. The answers can be found at the bottom of each page.

MATERIALS

1. Electrons are present
A. only in liquid or solid matter
B. only in electrical conductors
C. in all forms of matter *(Page 10)*

2. An atom usually has equal numbers of
A. neutrons and electrons
B. electrons and protons
C. protons and neutrons *(Page 11)*

3. The mass number of an atom of an element is the number of
A. protons and neutrons
B. protons
C. electrons *(Page 12)*

4. Atoms which have the same number of protons and electrons but a different number of neutrons are
A. isomers
B. isotopes
C. allotropes *(Page 13)*

5. The chemical symbol of iron is
A. F
B. I
C. Fe *(Page 15)*

6. The chemical symbol of gold is
A. Go
B. Au
C. Ag *(Page 15)*

7. The kinetic theory explains
A. energy changes
B. moving objects
C. the properties of solids, liquids and gases *(Page 16)*

8. Sublimation occurs when
A. solids change to gas
B. solids change to liquid
C. liquids change to gas *(Page 18)*

9. Condensation is when
A. gas changes to liquid
B. gas changes to solid
C. liquid changes to gas *(Page 19)*

10. A substance is classified as a solid, liquid or gas depending on its state at
A. 0°C
B. 20°C
C. 100°C *(Page 19)*

11. Gases have
A. definite volume and shape
B. no definite volume and shape
C. definite volume but can change shape *(Page 22)*

12. How many elements are there?
A. about 20
B. about 50
C. about 100 *(Page 24)*

13. Almost all non-metals are
A. liquids at room temperature
B. poor insulators
C. poor conductors *(Page 25)*

14. The most common element in the Earth's crust is
A. aluminium
B. oxygen
C. silicon *(Page 26)*

15. The periodic table is organized into periods of elements which are
A. arranged in columns
B. arranged in rows
C. arranged in clusters *(Page 28)*

16. The periodic table is also organized into groups which are
A. arranged in columns
B. arranged in rows
C. arranged in clusters *(Page 28)*

17. Metals are ductile, so they can be
A. beaten flat into sheets
B. pulled out to make a wire
C. polished *(Page 30)*

18. In a flame test, potassium gives
A. a red flame
B. an orange flame
C. a lilac flame *(Page 31)*

19. In water, alkali metals form
A. acidic solutions
B. alkaline solutions
C. neutral solutions *(Page 32)*

20. Noble metals are
A. always found in compounds
B. extremely reactive
C. very unreactive *(Page 32)*

21. Brass is a mixture of
A. copper and zinc
B. copper and tin
C. copper and nickel *(Page 35)*

22. Bronze is a mixture of
A. copper and zinc
B. copper and tin
C. copper and gold *(Page 35)*

23. Which gas is needed for corrosion to take place?
A. sulphur dioxide
B. carbon dioxide
C. oxygen *(Page 40)*

24. One of the oldest known metals is
A. aluminium
B. gold
C. zinc *(Page 42)*

25. The most abundant element in the universe is
A. aluminium
B. hydrogen
C. oxygen *(Page 46)*

26. Which element is not a halogen?
A. chlorine
B. iodine
C. phosphorus *(Pages 48-49, 55)*

27. Elements which exist in differently bonded forms are
A. alloys
B. allotropes
C. isotopes *(Page 50)*

28. Which of the following substances is not a form of carbon?
A. diamond
B. sulphur
C. graphite *(Pages 50-51, 54)*

29. One of the main uses of sulphur is
A. making sulphur dioxide
B. in food preservation
C. making sulphuric acid *(Page 54)*

30. Which of the following is not a form of phosphorus?
A. yellow
B. red
C. white *(Page 55)*

1.C 2.B 3.A 4.B 5.C 6.B 7.C 8.A 9.A 10.B 11.B 12.C 13.C 14.B 15.B 16.A 17.B 18.C 19.B 20.C 21.A 22.B 23.C 24.B 25.B 26.C 27.B 28.B 29.C 30.A

MIXTURES AND COMPOUNDS

1. Which of the following is not a mixture?
A. air
B. sea water
C. carbon dioxide *(Page 58)*

2. Dyes can be separated by
A. distillation
B. filtration
C. chromatography *(Pages 60-61)*

3. An insoluble solid can be separated from a liquid by
A. evaporation
B. filtration
C. chromatography *(Page 60)*

4. A soluble solid can be separated from a liquid by
A. evaporation
B. filtration
C. chromatography *(Page 61)*

5. The most abundant gas in the atmosphere is
A. carbon dioxide
B. nitrogen
C. oxygen *(Page 62)*

6. Ozone is a form of
A. nitrogen
B. oxygen
C. argon *(Page 65)*

7. The build-up of which gas causes the greenhouse effect?
A. carbon dioxide
B. oxygen
C. argon *(Page 65)*

8. What is formed when atoms of different elements combine?
A. a new element
B. a compound
C. a mixture *(Page 66)*

9. Which of the following is not an example of a compound?
A. citric acid
B. calcium carbonate
C. carbon *(Page 67)*

10. The forces holding atoms together are known as bonds. Which of these is not a type of bonding?
A. covalent
B. valency
C. ionic *(Pages 69-71)*

11. The second electron shell can hold up to
A. two electrons
B. eighteen electrons
C. eight electrons *(Page 68)*

12. Which statement is true? Many covalent substances
A. dissolve in water
B. conduct electricity
C. are liquids or gases at room temperature *(Page 69)*

13. An atom that has lost electrons is
A. an anion
B. a cation
C. an ionic lattice *(Page 70)*

14. Which statement is false?
A. the chemical name for water is hydrogen oxide
B. water can exist in three states: gas, liquid and solid
C. ice is more dense than water *(Page 72)*

15. Reactions in which heat is given out to the surroundings are
A. exothermic
B. endothermic
C. thermal *(Page 76)*

16. A catalyst
A. changes the rate of a reaction and is used up in the reaction
B. changes the rate of a reaction and is not used up in the reaction
C. is a substance that stops a reaction taking place *(Page 79)*

17. Combustion reactions need
A. carbon monoxide
B. carbon dioxide
C. oxygen *(Page 80)*

18. During reduction, a substance loses
A. oxygen
B. hydrogen
C. electrons *(Page 81)*

19. Which metal is extracted from bauxite by electrolysis?
A. aluminium
B. copper
C. iron *(Page 83)*

20. Which one of the following is not an example of a base?
A. toothpaste
B. tomato juice
C. wasp sting *(Pages 84-85)*

21. Which statement is incorrect? Acids are
A. compounds that contain hydrogen
B. corrosive
C. caustic *(Pages 84-85)*

22. The pH value of any acidic substance is
A. less than 7
B. 7
C. more than 7 *(Page 86)*

23. Salts contain
A. metals only
B. metals and non-metals
C. non-metals only *(Page 88)*

24. All organic compounds contain
A. silicon
B. oxygen
C. carbon *(Page 92)*

25. Saturated organic compounds are held together by
A. single bonds
B. double bonds
C. triple bonds *(Page 93)*

26. The most important product of the fermentation reaction is an
A. alkane
B. alkene
C. alcohol *(Page 94)*

27. Margarine is made by adding hydrogen to
A. alkane molecules
B. alkene molecules
C. ester molecules *(Page 97)*

28. The chemical process in which large molecules from crude oil are split into smaller molecules is
A. fractional distillation
B. hydrogenation
C. cracking *(Pages 97, 99)*

29. What type of organic compounds condense at 180°C?
A. residue compounds
B. gasoline compounds
C. kerosene compounds *(Page 99)*

30. Which of the following statements about thermoplastics is true?
A. Thermoplastics are easily recycled.
B. Thermoplastics can only be moulded once.
C. Thermoplastics are heat resistant. *(Page 101)*

1.C 2.C 3.B 4.A 5.B 6.B 7.A 8.B 9.C 10.B 11.C 12.C 13.B 14.C 15.A 16.B 17.C 18.A 19.A 20.B 21.C 22.A 23.B 24.C 25.A 26.C 27.B 28.C 29.C 30.A

ENERGY, FORCES AND MOTION

1. Energy is measured in units called
A. watts
B. joules
C. kilograms *(Page 109)*

2. The steam point (boiling point of water) is
A. 32°F
B. 100°C
C. 212°C *(Page 111)*

3. Which statement is true?
A. Conduction never occurs in solids.
B. Convection only occurs in liquids.
C. Convection cannot take place in solids. *(Pages 112-113)*

4. An alpha particle is made up of
A. two protons and two neutrons
B. two protons
C. a high-speed electron *(Page 114)*

5. Radioactive carbon-14 is written as $^{14}_{6}C$. This form of carbon has
A. six protons and six neutrons
B. six protons and eight neutrons
C. fourteen protons *(Page 115)*

6. A force's strength is measured in
A. kilograms
B. metres
C. newtons *(Page 119)*

7. A force is
A. a vector quantity
B. a scalar quantity
C. neither a vector nor a scalar quantity *(Page 119)*

Questions 8, 9 and 10 all refer to this diagram showing the forces acting on a wheelbarrow.

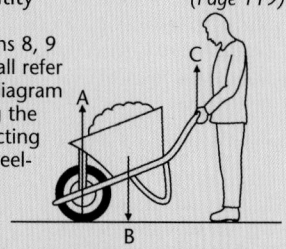

8. Which arrow represents the force of the ground on the wheelbarrow? *(Page 121)*

9. Which arrow represents the force of the man on the wheelbarrow? *(Page 121)*

10. Which arrow represents the weight of the wheelbarrow? *(Page 121)*

11. It is easier to turn something around a fulcrum if the force is applied
A. a long distance from the fulcrum
B. very close to the fulcrum
C. at the fulcrum *(Page 121)*

12. If no forces are acting on a moving object, the object will
A. slow down and stop
B. continue moving at the same speed in a straight line
C. change direction *(Page 122)*

13. Whenever you push an object you will always feel
A. a push in the opposite direction
B. a push in the same direction
C. no push at all *(Page 122)*

14. When a book slides across a table, the force that slows it down is called
A. lubrication
B. drag
C. friction *(Page 124)*

15. Average speed is equal to
A. distance multiplied by time
B. time divided by distance
C. distance divided by time *(Page 126)*

16. The difference between speed and velocity is that
A. speed is a scalar quantity whereas velocity is a vector quantity
B. speed is a vector quantity whereas velocity is a scalar quantity
C. they have different units *(Page 127)*

17. If an object accelerates, then its
A. speed and direction must change
B. speed or direction must change
C. speed must increase *(Page 127)*

18. An apple falling from a tree is pulled downwards because of
A. the pull of the Earth's gravity on the apple
B. the apple's low centre of gravity
C. the smooth skin of the apple, which reduces friction *(Page 130)*

19. Which statement is true?
A. The mass of an object depends on the pull of gravity on that object.
B. Mass is measured in newtons.
C. The weight of an object is due to the pull of gravity of the Earth on that object. *(Pages 130-131)*

20. Atmospheric pressure
A. is at its lowest near to the ground
B. is due to weight of air pressing down
C. increases as the height above ground increases *(Page 132)*

21. Which statement is true?
A. A force acting over an area exerts pressure.
B. The pressure of a needle is small due to the small area of the point.
C. Hydraulic machines are driven by gas pressure. *(Pages 132-133)*

22. When using a lever
A. the point about which the lever turns is called the fulcrum
B. the force you apply is the load
C. the force you need to overcome is called the effort *(Page 134)*

23. Which statement is correct?
A. Work is only done when a force makes an object move.
B. Work and power are both measured in watts.
C. If a man does work he gains energy. *(Page 137)*

24. Ships made of steel float because
A. steel is less dense than water
B. the hollow space inside the ship makes it less dense than water
C. the upthrust of the water on the ship is less than the weight of the ship *(Page 139)*

Questions 25-28 refer to this diagram which shows three of the four forces acting on an aeroplane.

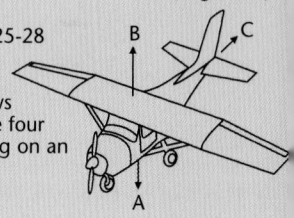

25. Which arrow represents the lift? *(Page 142)*

26. Which arrow represents gravity? *(Page 142)*

27. Which arrow represents the drag? *(Page 142)*

28. In the diagram above, the missing force is the
A. pull of the Earth's gravity
B. thrust provided by the engines
C. centripetal force *(Page 142)*

29. In level flight, lift is equal to the
A. speed of the aeroplane
B. pull of gravity
C. air resistance *(Page 142)*

30. Wings that are curved on top and flatter underneath are called
A. hydrofoils
B. aerofoils
C. ailerons *(Page 142)*

1.B 2.B 3.C 4.A 5.B 6.C 7.A 8.A 9.C 10.B 11.A 12.B 13.A 14.C 15.C 16.A 17.B 18.A 19.C 20.B 21.A 22.A 23.A 24.B 25.B 26.A 27.C 28.B 29.B 30.B

EARTH AND SPACE

1. At the centre of the Solar System lies
A. a moon
B. the Sun
C. the Earth *(Page 163)*

2. Planet Earth makes a complete orbit around the Sun once every
A. day
B. month
C. year *(Page 163)*

3. The four inner planets, which are all rocky and fairly small, are
A. Earth, Venus, Mercury, Mars
B. Pluto, Neptune, Saturn, Uranus
C. Venus, Mars, Saturn, Neptune *(Page 164)*

4. The Moon orbits the Earth once every
A. week
B. 28 days
C. year *(Page 167)*

5. The Moon shines at night because
A. it is made of pale, shiny rock
B. it reflects light from the Sun
C. it gives out its own light *(Page 167)*

6. Man-made devices that orbit the Earth, gathering information, are called
A. satellites
B. observatories
C. refractors *(Page 175)*

7. Spreading ridges are found at plate boundaries which are
A. constructive
B. destructive
C. sedimentary *(Page 181)*

8. High fold mountain ranges are formed when two continental plates
A. slide past each other
B. move apart
C. push together *(Page 181)*

9. When hot, molten rocks cool and harden, the rock formed is called
A. continental
B. metamorphic
C. igneous *(Page 181)*

10. The point directly above an earthquake's focus is its
A. seismic wave
B. epicentre
C. eruption *(Page 182)*

11. Magma in volcanoes which form above subduction zones has come from
A. a spreading ridge
B. the descending plate
C. a hot spot *(Page 183)*

12. About 540 million years ago there was a sudden increase in the number of animals with hard parts. This happened in the
A. Carboniferous Period
B. Cambrian Period
C. Permian Period *(Page 187)*

13. The world's largest ocean is the
A. Pacific Ocean
B. Atlantic Ocean
C. Southern Ocean *(Page 188)*

14. The ocean tides are caused mainly by the pull of gravity on the water by
A. the Moon
B. the Sun
C. the Solar System *(Page 189)*

15. In the USA tropical cyclones are called
A. depressions
B. typhoons
C. hurricanes *(Page 189)*

16. The source of a river is where it
A. starts
B. ends
C. meanders *(Page 190)*

17. In the middle and lower reaches of a river, wide loops often develop. These are called
A. sediments
B. deltas
C. meanders *(Page 190)*

18. A river's speed normally increases as it moves from the upper stage to the lower stage. This is mainly because
A. the river's width increases
B. a flood plain develops
C. the bed becomes smoother so there is less friction to slow down the water *(Page 190)*

19. All of the material carried by a river is called its
A. flood plain
B. load
C. gradient *(Page 191)*

20. When water vapour in the air changes into the tiny water droplets which form clouds, we say that it
A. disintegrates
B. evaporates
C. condenses *(Page 193)*

21. In July the northern hemisphere has its summer because
A. there are fewer clouds in the sky
B. the Sun gives out more heat in July
C. the northern hemisphere is tilted towards the Sun *(Page 193)*

22. In mountainous districts the climate changes mainly with
A. attitude
B. altitude
C. latitude *(Page 195)*

23. Air temperatures in cities are often higher than those in the surrounding countryside mainly because of the extra heat given out by
A. vehicle exhaust fumes
B. people walking around
C. concrete and buildings *(Page 195)*

24. Over the next 100 years the world's population is expected to
A. level off
B. decrease
C. continue increasing *(Page 196)*

25. The general movement of people from the countryside to settle in cities is called
A. commuting
B. urban migration
C. rural migration *(Page 196)*

26. For many people the main reason they move into cities is
A. to find a job
B. to farm the land
C. to build a home *(Page 196)*

27. The word which means all the materials needed by humans and provided by planet Earth is
A. resources
B. food
C. fuel *(Page 198)*

28. Oil and coal are examples of
A. fossil fuels
B. nuclear fuels
C. renewable fuels *(Page 198)*

29. Energy sources such as wind, waves and the Sun's rays, which do not rely on fossil fuels, are described as
A. temporary
B. renewable
C. non-renewable *(Page 198)*

30. One good way of using the Earth's resources so they last longer is
A. extracting
B. mining
C. recycling *(Page 199)*

Earth and space answers
1.B 2.C 3.A 4.B 5.B 6.A 7.A 8.C 9.C 10.B 11.B 12.B 13.A 14.A 15.C 16.A 17.C 18.C 19.B 20.C 21.C 22.B 23.C 24.C 25.B 26.A 27.A 28.A 29.B 30.C

LIGHT, SOUND AND ELECTRICITY

1. All waves are
A. vibrations and carry energy
B. vibrations in the same direction as the wave is travelling
C. vibrations at right angles to the direction the wave is travelling
(Pages 202-203)

2. The wavelength of a wave is
A. the number of complete waves that pass a point in one second
B. the distance between a peak and the next trough
C. the distance between a peak and the next peak *(Page 203)*

3. When a wave hits a surface and bounces off, it is
A. reflected
B. refracted
C. diffracted *(Pages 204-205)*

4. When a wave enters a new medium at an angle and changes direction, it is
A. reflected
B. refracted
C. diffracted *(Pages 204-205)*

5. Sound waves
A. are electromagnetic waves
B. can travel through a vacuum
C. travel more quickly in solids than in gases *(Pages 202, 206-207)*

6. Sound waves in air
A. always travel at the same speed
B. cannot be reflected off obstacles
C. are made up of vibrations of the air molecules *(Pages 206-207)*

7. The loudness of a note from a stringed instrument is increased by
A. plucking the string harder
B. lengthening the string
C. shortening the string *(Page 208)*

8. The pitch of a note from a stringed instrument is raised by
A. plucking the string harder
B. lengthening the string
C. shortening the string *(Page 209)*

9. Ultraviolet rays
A. have a shorter wavelength than visible light
B. have a longer wavelength than visible light
C. travel faster than visible light
(Page 212)

10. Light cannot pass through
A. transparent objects
B. translucent objects
C. opaque objects *(Page 214)*

11. The umbra is the
A. area where all the light falls
B. dark area of a shadow
C. grey area of a shadow *(Page 214)*

12. The penumbra is the
A. area where all the light falls
B. dark area of a shadow
C. grey area of a shadow *(Page 214)*

13. Which statement is not true?
A. White light can be split up into its various colours using a prism.
B. Blue light is refracted the least.
C. Different colours are refracted by different amounts. *(Page 216)*

14. Red, green and blue light are
A. primary colours
B. secondary colours
C. complementary colours *(Page 216)*

15. When red light and blue light are mixed, the resulting colour is
A. blue
B. red
C. magenta *(Page 216)*

16. When white light falls on a blue object, the object appears
A. blue
B. white
C. black *(Page 217)*

17. Light interference happens when light rays
A. travel parallel to each other
B. travel in opposite directions
C. cross *(Page 219)*

18. Polarized sunglasses reduce the glare in your eyes because they
A. filter out all light wave vibrations that are not in a certain direction
B. reflect light away from your eyes
C. bend light so that it does not all reach your eyes *(Page 219)*

19. A glass bi-convex lens in air
A. has surfaces which curve inwards
B. acts as a converging lens
C. acts as a diverging lens *(Page 220)*

20. A short-sighted person
A. cannot see nearby objects clearly
B. cannot see distant objects clearly
C. needs glasses with converging lenses *(Page 221)*

21. Small objects look larger using a
A. microscope
B. periscope
C. telescope *(Page 222)*

22. The aperture of a camera controls
A. how much light enters the camera
B. the time that light falls on the film
C. the size of the image *(Page 224)*

23. An electron has
A. a positive electrical charge
B. a negative electrical charge
C. no electrical charge *(Page 228)*

24. Two charged particles attract one another when
A. both are positively charged
B. both are negatively charged
C. one is positively charged and the other negatively charged *(Page 228)*

25. Which diagram correctly shows a circuit with two single cells, with the positive terminals to the right, connected to a bulb? *(Page 409)*

A. B. C.

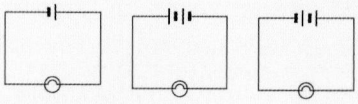

26. The diagram on the right shows a bulb, two single cells and a
A. resistor
B. transistor
C. diode *(Page 409)*

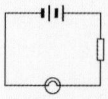

27. Which of the following magnetic poles will attract each other?
A. a north and a north
B. a north and a south
C. a south and a south *(Page 232)*

28. Soft ferromagnetic materials are
A. easy to magnetize and demagnetize
B. hard to magnetize and demagnetize
C. used to make permanent magnets
(Page 232)

29. A machine which converts energy of movement into electrical energy is
A. a generator
B. a motor
C. an armature *(Page 235)*

30. If the resistance of an electrical component in a series circuit increases, then the current
A. is increased
B. is reduced
C. stays the same *(Pages 230, 236)*

1.A 2.C 3.A 4.B 5.C 6.C 7.A 8.C 9.A 10.C 11.B 12.C 13.B 14.A 15.C 16.A 17.C 18.A 19.B 20.B 21.A 22.A 23.B 24.C 25.C 26.A 27.B 28.A 29.A 30.B

PLANTS AND FUNGI

1. Which of the following is found in plant cells but not animal cells?
A. a cell wall
B. a nucleus
C. cytoplasm *(Page 250)*

2. A carrot is
A. an aerial root
B. an adventitious root
C. a tap root *(Page 253)*

3. Water is taken into a plant through
A. its flowers
B. the root hairs in the soil
C. the surface of its leaves *(Page 253)*

4. The tissue in plants which carries water upwards is
A. xylem
B. phloem
C. cambium *(Page 254)*

5. In an older plant, xylem and phloem join up to form
A. lenticels
B. vascular bundles
C. a vascular cylinder *(Pages 256-257)*

6. Which tree has compound leaves?
A. horse chestnut
B. lime
C. oak *(Pages 258-259)*

7. Leaf stomata are found mainly on
A. both upper and lower surfaces
B. the lower surface
C. the upper surface *(Page 260)*

8. Water loss from the leaves through the stomata is called
A. transpiration
B. translocation
C. respiration *(Page 262)*

9. Chlorophyll is vital to a plant because
A. it colours it green
B. it provides food
C. it absorbs energy from the Sun *(Page 264)*

10. Photosynthesis can be expressed as
A. water + oxygen + energy →carbohydrates + carbon dioxide
B. oxygen + carbon dioxide + water →carbohydrates + energy
C. carbon dioxide + water + energy →carbohydrates + oxygen *(Page 264)*

11. Plants respire
A. all the time
B. only at night
C. when photosynthesis stops *(Page 265)*

12. A plant which feeds on dead matter is
A. a parasite
B. a saprotroph
C. an epiphyte *(Page 266)*

13. Which is a carnivorous plant?
A. mistletoe
B. strangler fig
C. sundew *(Pages 266-267)*

14. Male reproductive cells of a plant are called
A. anthers
B. pollen
C. pollen sacs *(Page 271)*

15. Female reproductive cells of a plant are called
A. ovaries
B. carpels
C. ovules *(Page 271)*

16. Pollination occurs when
A. a pollen grain connects with an ovule by a pollen tube
B. a pollen grain produces a pollen tube
C. a pollen grain lands on the stigma of another plant *(Page 272)*

17. Which statement is true?
Most wind-pollinated plants
A. have brightly coloured, sweet-scented flowers
B. have large sepals and petals
C. produce large quantities of smooth, light pollen grains *(Page 273)*

18. Which of the following is a true fruit?
A. strawberry
B. cherry
C. apple *(Page 274)*

19. Which plant has seeds dispersed by wind?
A. sycamore
B. goosegrass
C. pea *(Page 276)*

20. In order to germinate, seeds need warmth, oxygen and
A. water
B. light
C. food *(Page 277)*

21. The first root produced by a seed is called the
A. plumule
B. hilum
C. radicle *(Page 277)*

22. Long side shoots which run overground and can develop into new plants are called
A. tubers
B. rhizomes
C. runners *(Page 278)*

23. A plant adapted to living in water is called a
A. hydrophyte
B. lithophyte
C. halophyte *(Page 280)*

24. The rapid reproduction of algae in water which has a high level of nitrates is called
A. intoxication
B. eutrophication
C. adaptation *(Page 281)*

25. Which statement is true?
Ferns, mosses and liverworts
A. cannot grow in damp, shady places
B. produce large numbers of flowers
C. can reproduce by making spores *(Pages 282-283)*

26. The antibiotic medicine penicillin is made from a type of
A. alga
B. fungus
C. liverwort *(Page 285)*

27. A plant which takes two years to complete its life cycle is called
A. a perennial
B. an annual
C. a biennial *(Page 288)*

28. Plants which lose all their leaves once a year are called
A. xerophytes
B. evergreen
C. deciduous *(Page 289)*

29. Prairies and steppes are forms of which biome?
A. tundra
B. temperate grassland
C. tropical grassland *(Page 290)*

30. Plants take in nitrogen from their surroundings in the form of
A. ammonia
B. nitrogen gas
C. nitrates *(Page 292)*

1.A 2.C 3.B 4.A 5.C 6.A 7.B 8.A 9.C 10.C 11.A 12.B 13.C 14.B 15.C 16.A 17.C 18.B 19.A 20.A 21.C 22.C 23.A 24.B 25.C 26.B 27.C 28.C 29.B 30.C

ANIMAL WORLD

1. Protoplasm consists of
A. the nucleus
B. the nucleus and cytoplasm
C. the nucleus, cytoplasm and cell membrane *(Page 298)*

2. The liver is
A. a complex tissue
B. an organ
C. a body system *(Page 299)*

3. Most animals which actively move about are
A. asymmetrical
B. radially symmetrical
C. bilaterally symmetrical *(Page 301)*

4. The skeleton of an insect is
A. an endoskeleton
B. an exoskeleton
C. a hydrostatic skeleton *(Page 301)*

5. Hedgehog spines are made of
A. keratin
B. chitin
C. bone *(Page 303)*

6. A swim bladder can be found in
A. all fish
B. some fish with bone skeletons
C. fish with cartilage skeletons *(Page 305)*

7. Most beetles
A. cannot fly
B. fly by flapping both pairs of wings
C. fly by flapping one pair of wings *(Page 307)*

8. Dogs walk on
A. the tips of the toes
B. the undersides of the toes
C. the underside of the whole foot *(Page 309)*

9. Carnassial teeth are found in
A. herbivores
B. omnivores
C. carnivores *(Page 312)*

10. Animals which eat both plants and meat are called
A. omnivores
B. carnivores
C. herbivores *(Page 312)*

11. In a bird, food is stored in the
A. crop
B. gizzard
C. cloaca *(Page 313)*

12. Adult insects breathe using
A. gills
B. lungs
C. tracheae *(Page 315)*

13. Homeostasis is
A. keeping a constant body temperature
B. keeping a constant internal environment
C. keeping the external environment constant *(Page 316)*

14. Mimicry involves
A. copying the behaviour of another animal
B. copying the warning colours of another animal
C. copying the scent of another animal *(Page 318)*

15. Some snakes detect the body heat of their prey with
A. antennae
B. lateral lines
C. pit organs *(Page 323)*

16. The body of a hermaphrodite animal contains
A. only female sex cells
B. only male sex cells
C. both male and female sex cells *(Page 325)*

17. In cleidoic eggs the young are
A. fed by a yolk
B. called spawn
C. surrounded by a soft shell *(Page 327)*

18. A locust hopper is a stage of
A. complete metamorphosis
B. incomplete metamorphosis
C. migration *(Pages 328-329)*

19. A habitat is
A. the natural home for plants and animals
B. a group of animals
C. too cold to support life *(Page 330)*

20. An ecological niche can support
A. one species of animal
B. two species of animal
C. several animal species *(Page 330)*

21. The largest ecosystems are
A. habitats
B. communities
C. biomes *(Page 331)*

22. An organism which eats another organism is
A. autotrophic
B. heterotrophic
C. parasitic *(Page 332)*

23. At the second trophic level, an animal is a
A. producer
B. primary consumer
C. secondary consumer *(Page 332)*

24. An organism which breaks down dead plant and animal matter is a
A. decomposer
B. consumer
C. producer *(Page 332)*

25. A trophic level has
A. fewer consumers than the level below
B. more consumers than the level below
C. the same number of consumers as all other levels *(Page 332)*

26. The abiotic parts of an environment are made up of
A. living or organic matter
B. mineral or inorganic matter
C. dead matter *(Page 334)*

27. Endemic species of animals are those found
A. in many different places
B. in only one place
C. only on islands *(Page 337)*

28. The largest taxonomic ranks after kingdoms are
A. orders
B. classes
C. phyla *(Page 341)*

29. Biological names of living organisms are in
A. Greek
B. Latin
C. English *(Page 343)*

30. Animals which live closely together and both gain from the situation are
A. mutualists
B. commensals
C. parasites *(Page 343)*

1.C 2.B 3.C 4.B 5.A 6.B 7.C 8.B 9.C 10.A 11.A 12.C 13.B 14.B 15.C 16.C 17.A 18.B 19.A 20.A 21.C 22.B 23.B 24.A 25.A 26.B 27.B 28.C 29.B 30.A

HUMAN BODY

1. The knee is a type of
A. ball and socket joint
B. hinge joint
C. gliding joint *(Page 347)*

2. Which of these terms does not describe the biceps and triceps?
A. an antagonistic pair
B. cardiac muscles
C. skeletal muscles *(Pages 348-349)*

3. Oxygen-rich blood is carried from the heart around the body via the
A. aorta
B. pulmonary artery
C. pulmonary vein *(Page 350)*

4. Oxygen is given up to tissue fluid through the walls of
A. arteries
B. veins
C. capillaries *(Page 351)*

5. Oxygen is carried around the body in
A. white blood cells
B. red blood cells
C. platelets *(Page 351)*

6. The shape of molar teeth makes them particularly suitable for
A. tearing and stabbing food
B. crushing and grinding food
C. chopping food *(Page 352)*

7. A tooth starts to hurt when bacteria attack the
A. enamel
B. dentine
C. pulp cavity *(Page 353)*

8. The enzyme that is contained in saliva digests
A. starch
B. protein
C. fat *(Page 354)*

9. The organ in which bile is produced is the
A. pancreas
B. small intestine
C. liver *(Page 355)*

10. Absorption of digested food takes place in the
A. stomach
B. small intestine
C. colon *(Page 355)*

11. The main nutrient that is found in meat is
A. protein
B. carbohydrate
C. fat *(Page 356)*

12. Gas exchange takes place in
A. bronchi
B. bronchioles
C. alveoli *(Page 358)*

13. Internal respiration that uses oxygen is
A. anaerobic respiration
B. metabolism
C. aerobic respiration *(Page 360)*

14. Aerobic respiration is described as
A. glucose + oxygen + water →energy + carbon dioxide
B. glucose + carbon dioxide →energy + oxygen + water
C. glucose + oxygen →energy + carbon dioxide + water *(Page 360)*

15. Exercise
A. allows you to make do with less oxygen
B. increases the pulse rate
C. keeps the heart muscles beating at a steady rate *(Page 361)*

16. Chemical compounds which control the level of substances in the body are
A. glomeruli
B. hormones
C. nephrons *(Page 362)*

17. Receptors are the sensitive nerve endings of
A. motor neurons
B. association neurons
C. sensory neurons *(Page 364)*

18. The largest part of the brain is
A. the cerebrum
B. the cerebellum
C. the brain stem *(Page 366)*

19. Pacinian corpuscles are found in
A. the blood
B. the brain
C. the skin *(Page 368)*

20. The size of the pupil of the eye is controlled by
A. changing the shape of the lens
B. the iris
C. rods and cones *(Pages 370-371)*

21. A structure called the oval window is found in
A. the ear
B. the eye
C. the kidney *(Page 372)*

22. Taste buds that detect bitter tastes tend to be found in greater number at the
A. front of the tongue
B. back of the tongue
C. sides of the tongue *(Page 375)*

23. Conception is
A. ejaculation
B. another word for sexual intercourse
C. fertilization of an egg by a sperm *(Page 377)*

24. The organ that provides a baby with food and oxygen from the mother is
A. the placenta
B. the uterus
C. the vagina *(Pages 376-377)*

25. A woman's periods happen when
A. the uterus lining is lost
B. ovulation takes place
C. the uterus lining starts to thicken *(Page 379)*

26. The form of cell division that produces sperm is
A. fertilization
B. meiosis
C. mitosis *(Page 380)*

27. Which of the following does a measles vaccine contain?
A. lymphocytes
B. antibodies to the measles germ
C. a weak dose of the measles germ *(Page 387)*

28. Antibiotics are effective against
A. some viruses
B. some bacteria
C. all germs *(Page 389)*

29. Which of the following is not an alternative treatment?
A. laser surgery
B. homeopathy
C. acupuncture *(Pages 389-390)*

30. Which of the following is an example of an illegal drug?
A. nicotine
B. alcohol
C. heroin *(Page 391)*

Human body answers
1.B 2.B 3.A 4.C 5.B 6.B 7.C 8.A 9.C 10.B 11.A 12.C 13.C 14.C 15.B 16.B 17.C 18.A 19.C 20.B 21.A 22.B 23.C 24.A 25.A 26.B 27.C 28.B 29.A 30.C

UNITS OF MEASUREMENT

Measuring things is one of the most important parts of science. There are two main measuring systems: **imperial** and **metric**. The imperial system is very old, dating from the twelfth century or earlier. The metric system was introduced in France in the 1790s. This is easier to use because it is based on the system of counting in tens – the decimal system.

IMPERIAL MEASUREMENTS

Length and distance

12 inches (")	= 1 foot (')
3 feet	= 1 yard (yd)
1,760 yards	= 1 mile
3 miles	= 1 league

Area

144 square inches	= 1 square foot
9 square feet	= 1 square yard
4,840 square yards	= 1 acre
640 acres	= 1 square mile

Mass

16 drams (dr)	= 1 ounce (oz)
16 ounces	= 1 pound (lb)
14 pounds	= 1 stone
160 stone	= 1 ton

Volume and capacity

1,728 cubic inches	= 1 cubic foot (ft^3)
27 cubic feet	= 1 cubic yard (yd^3)
5 fluid ounces (fl oz)	= 1 gill (gi)
20 fluid ounces* (USA: 16)	= 1 pint (pt)
2 pints	= 1 quart (qt)
8 pints	= 1 gallon (gal)

* UK 1 fl oz = 0.0284 litres; USA 1 fl oz (liquid) = 0.0295 litres

METRIC MEASUREMENTS

Many metric measurements are spelled ending in "re" in British English and "er" in American English. For example, "metre" and "meter".

Length and distance

10 millimetres (mm)	= 1 centimetre (cm)
100 centimetres	= 1 metre (m)
1,000 metres	= 1 kilometre (km)

Area

100 square mm (mm^2)	= 1 square cm (cm^2)
10,000cm^2	= 1 square m (m^2)
10,000m^2	= 1 hectare (ha)
100 hectares	= 1 square km (km^2)

Mass

1,000 grams (g)	= 1 kilogram (kg)
1,000 kilograms	= 1 tonne (t)

Volume and capacity

1 cubic cm (cm^3/cc)	= 1 millilitre (ml)
1,000 millilitres	= 1 litre (l)
1,000 litres	= 1 cubic metre (m^3)

Scientists usually show numbers with up to four digits closed up, without commas, for example 9999. Numbers with more digits are shown with spaces to make them easier to read, for example 0.000 001. In non-technical writing, as in this book, numbers with over three digits are shown with commas.

CONVERSIONS

To convert between metric and imperial figures, use this table with a calculator.

To convert	into	multiply by	To convert	into	multiply by
cm	inches	0.394	inches	cm	2.54
m	yards	1.094	yards	m	0.914
km	miles	0.621	miles	km	1.609
grams	ounces	0.035	ounces	grams	28.35
kilograms	pounds	2.205	pounds	kilograms	0.454
tonnes	tons	0.984	tons	tonnes	1.016
cm^2	square inches	0.155	square inches	cm^2	6.452
m^2	square yards	1.196	square yards	m^2	0.836
km^2	square miles	0.386	square miles	km^2	2.59
hectares	acres	2.471	acres	hectares	0.405
litres	pints	1.76	pints	litres	0.5683

SI UNITS

SI units (short for the French *Système Internationale d'Unités*) are an internationally agreed system of units used for scientific purposes. The units have been defined very precisely in modern times. The metre, for example, is now defined as the distance light travels in a vacuum in $^{1}/_{299,792,458}$ of a second. Its measurement was originally based on a length of platinum alloy kept in Paris.

Quantity	SI unit
Length	metre (m)
Mass	kilogram (kg)
Time	second (s)
Temperature	kelvin (K)
Current	ampere (A)
Amount of a substance	mole (mol)
Light intensity	candela (cd)

DERIVED SI UNITS

These are derived from the units above using the equations shown.

Quantity	Derived SI unit	Equation
Area	square metre (m^2)	Depends on shape (see page 408)
Volume	cubic metre (m^3)	Depends on shape (see page 408)
Density	kilograms per cubic metre (kg/m^3)	$\frac{\text{Mass (kg)}}{\text{Volume (m}^3\text{)}}$
Velocity	metres per second (m/s)	$\frac{\text{Distance moved (m)}}{\text{Time taken (s)}}$
Momentum	(kg m/s)	Mass (kg) x velocity (m/s)
Acceleration	metres per second per second (m/s^2)	$\frac{\text{Change in velocity (m/s)}}{\text{Time taken for change (s)}}$
Power	watt (W)	$\frac{\text{Work done (J)}}{\text{Time (s)}}$
Force	newton (N)	Mass (kg) x acceleration (m/s^2)
Energy/Work	joule (J)	Force (N) x distance moved in direction of force (m)
Pressure	pascal (Pa)	$\frac{\text{Force (N)}}{\text{Area (m}^2\text{)}}$
Frequency	hertz (Hz)	Number of cycles per second
Electric charge	coulomb (C)	Current (A) x time (s)
Voltage	volt (V)	$\frac{\text{Energy transferred (J)}}{\text{Charge (C)}}$
Resistance	ohm (Ω)	$\frac{\text{Voltage (V)}}{\text{Current (A)}}$

TEMPERATURE SCALES

There are three main scales for measuring temperature: the Fahrenheit scale (imperial), the Celsius scale (metric) and the absolute temperature scale (SI), which is measured in kelvins.

The absolute temperature scale is seen as the most scientific because 0 kelvin (-273°C) is **absolute zero**: the temperature at which no more heat can be extracted from an object. Scientific theory holds that this point of absolute cold would be impossible to reach in practice.

Celsius (°C)	Fahrenheit (°F)	Kelvin (K)
110	230	383
100	212	373
90	194	363
80	176	353
70	158	343
60	140	333
50	122	323
40	104	313
30	86	303
20	68	293
10	50	283
0	32	273
-10	14	263
-20	-4	253
-30	-22	243
-40	-40	233
-50	-58	223
-60	-76	213
-70	-94	203
-80	-112	193
-90	-130	183
-100	-148	173
-110	-166	163

CONVERSIONS

Convert	into	calculation
°C	°F	x9,÷5,+32
°C	K	+273
°F	°C	-32,x5,÷9
°F	K	-32,x5,÷9,+273
K	°C	-273
K	°F	-273,x9,÷5,+32

MEASURING NATURE

It is not always easy to measure natural forces and substances precisely. The scales shown here work by measuring their effects or properties.

THE BEAUFORT SCALE OF WIND FORCE

The **Beaufort** Scale was developed in 1805 by Sir Francis Beaufort, a British Navy Commander, to estimate wind speed at sea. In the 1920s it was extended to include precise wind speeds and adapted for use on land. While it is now rarely used by **meteorologists** (weather scientists), it is still a popular means of calculating wind speed without using instruments.

Beaufort number	Kilometres per hour	Wind description	Observable effects on land	
0	Less than 1	Calm	Smoke rises vertically.	
1	1-5	Air moves slightly	Smoke drifts in direction of wind; weather vanes remain still.	
2	6-11	Slight breeze	Wind felt on face; leaves rustle; weather vanes move.	
3	12-19	Gentle breeze	Leaves and twigs keep moving; small flags unfurl.	
4	20-28	Moderate breeze	Dust and loose paper raised from ground; small branches move.	
5	29-38	Fresh breeze	Small trees in leaf begin to sway.	
6	39-49	Strong breeze	Large branches sway; umbrellas hard to use; whistling in telegraph wires.	
7	50-61	Moderate gale (or high wind)	Large trees sway; hard to walk against wind.	
8	62-74	Gale	Twigs and small branches break off trees; very hard to walk.	
9	75-88	Strong gale	Large branches break off trees; some damage to buildings.	
10	89-102	Storm	Trees are uprooted; severe damage to buildings.	
11*	103-117	Violent storm	Widespread damage to trees and buildings.	
12*	118 or more	Hurricane	Extreme widespread destruction.	

* Storms this strong usually only happen at sea.

MOHS HARDNESS SCALE

The hardness of minerals is measured on the **Mohs scale**, named after the German mineralogist, Friedrich Mohs (1773-1839). The scale has a sample mineral for each value, ranging from 1 – soft, crumbly talc, to 10 – diamond, the hardest mineral.

1. Talc
Very easily scratched with a fingernail.

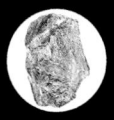

2. Gypsum
Can be scratched by a fingernail.

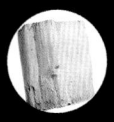

3. Calcite
Very easily scratched with a knife, and just with a copper coin.

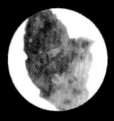

4. Fluorite
Easily scratched with a knife.

5. Apatite
Just scratched with a knife.

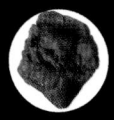

6. Orthoclase
Cannot be scratched with a knife. Just scratches glass.

7. Quartz
Scratches glass easily.

8. Beryl or topaz
Scratches glass very easily.

9. Corundum
Cuts glass.

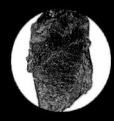

10. Diamond
Cuts glass very easily. Will scratch corundum.

MEASURING EARTHQUAKES

Seismologists (scientists who study earthquakes) measure the energy of the underground shock waves that cause them with a device called a **seismometer**. This uses the **Richter scale**. Every whole value on the Richter scale is equal to about 33 times the value below it. For example, an earthquake measured at 6 on the Richter scale has about 33 times the energy of one at Richter 5. The impact of an earthquake above ground, rated by its effects, is often measured on the **Mercalli scale**.

Mercalli	Effects	Richter	
1	Detectable only by seismometers.	0-2.9	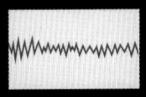
2	Only a few people on upper floors notice.	3-3.4	
3	Like a heavy truck passing by. Hanging lights may swing.	3.5-4	
4	Windows and dishes rattle. Like a heavy truck crashing into building.	4.1-4.4	
5	Almost everyone notices. Sleepers wake up. Small objects move and drinks spill.	4.5-4.8	
6	Many people frightened and run outdoors. Heavy furniture moves. Pictures fall off walls.	4.9-5.4	
7	Walls crack. Tiles and bricks fall from buildings. Difficult to stand up.	5.5-6	
8	Chimneys and some weaker buildings collapse. Mass panic may break out.	6.1-6.5	
9	Well-built houses collapse. Underground pipes damaged. Cracks open in ground.	6.6-7	
10	Landslides. Railway tracks buckle. Rivers overflow. Many stone buildings collapse.	7.1-7.3	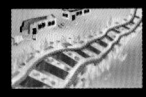
11	Most buildings destroyed. Large cracks in ground. Bridges destroyed.	7.4-8.1	
12	Ground moves in waves. Total destruction.	8.2+	

GEOMETRICAL SHAPES

There are two kinds of geometrical shape. **Planes** are flat shapes with only two dimensions – length and breadth. **Solids** have three dimensions – length, breadth and height.

PLANES

Polygons
A polygon is a plane with three or more straight sides.

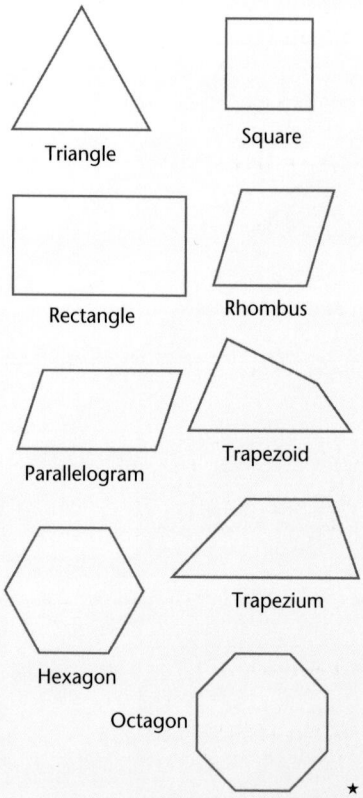

Triangles
A triangle is a three-sided polygon.

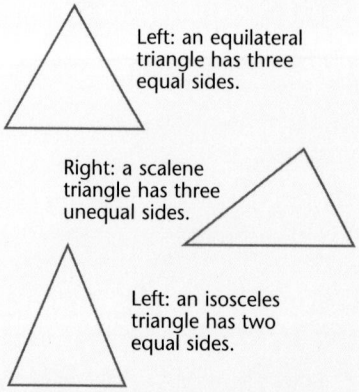

Circles
A circle is a curved line on which all points are equally distant from the centre. The parts of a circle are shown below.

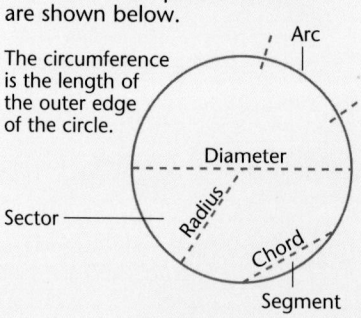

SOLIDS

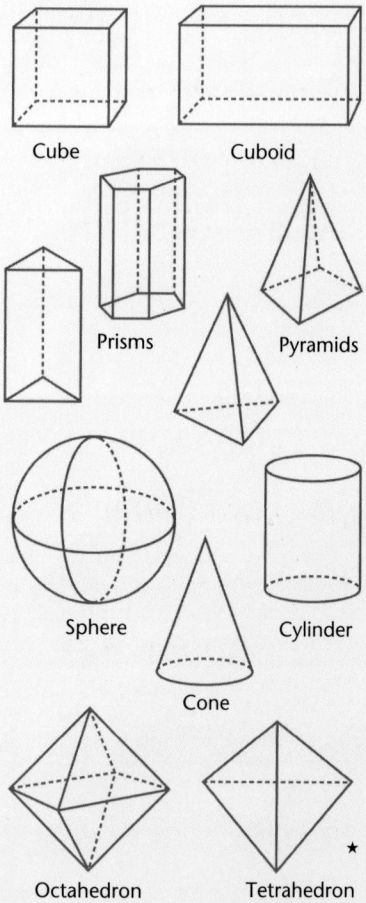

GEOMETRICAL FORMULAE

In these formulae, b = base, h = height, r = radius, π = pi (3.142), θ = an angle.

Area of circle = πr^2

Circumference of circle = $2\pi r$

Area of sector = $\frac{\theta \pi r^2}{360}$

Length of arc = $\frac{\theta \pi r}{180}$

Volume of cylinder = $\pi r^2 h$

Volume of cone = $\frac{1}{3} \pi r^2 h$

Volume of sphere = $\frac{4}{3} \pi r^3$

Surface area of sphere = $4\pi r^2$

Volume of pyramid = $\frac{1}{3}$ h x base area

Area of triangle = $\frac{1}{2}$ bh

Area of parallelogram = bh

LAWS AND SYMBOLS

SCIENTIFIC LAWS

Archimedes' principle The upthrust acting on an object is equal to the weight of the fluid that the object displaces.

Avogadro's law All gases of the same volume at the same temperature and pressure must contain the same number of molecules.

Bernoulli's principle When the flow of a fluid, for example air, gets faster, its pressure is reduced.

Boyle's law The pressure and volume of a gas at a constant temperature are inversely proportional.

Charles' law (or **law of volumes**) The volume of an ideal gas at a constant pressure is proportional to its kelvin temperature.

Hooke's law The extension of a material is proportional to the force stretching it.

Law of conservation of energy Energy cannot be created or destroyed. It can only be changed into a different form.

Law of conservation of mass Matter cannot be created or destroyed in a chemical reaction.

Law of conservation of momentum After two objects have collided, their combined momentum remains the same.

Newton's first law of motion (or **principle of inertia**) If an object is not being acted on by a force, it will either stay still or continue moving at a constant speed in a straight line.

Newton's second law of motion Any resultant force acting on an object will change its motion. How much the motion changes depends on the object's mass and the size of the resultant force.

Newton's third law of motion When an object A exerts a force on an object B, then B exerts an equal and opposite force on A.

Newton's law of universal gravitation There is a gravitational force of attraction between any two objects with mass, which depends on the masses of the objects and the distance between them.

Pythagoras' theorem The area of the square on the hypotenuse (side c in the diagram) of a right-angled triangle is equal to the sum of the areas of the squares on the other sides ($a^2 + b^2 = c^2$).

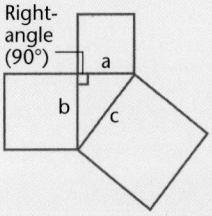

ELECTRICAL AND ELECTRONIC SYMBOLS

The symbols below are used to represent components found in electrical and electronic circuits. Different countries sometimes use alternative symbols.

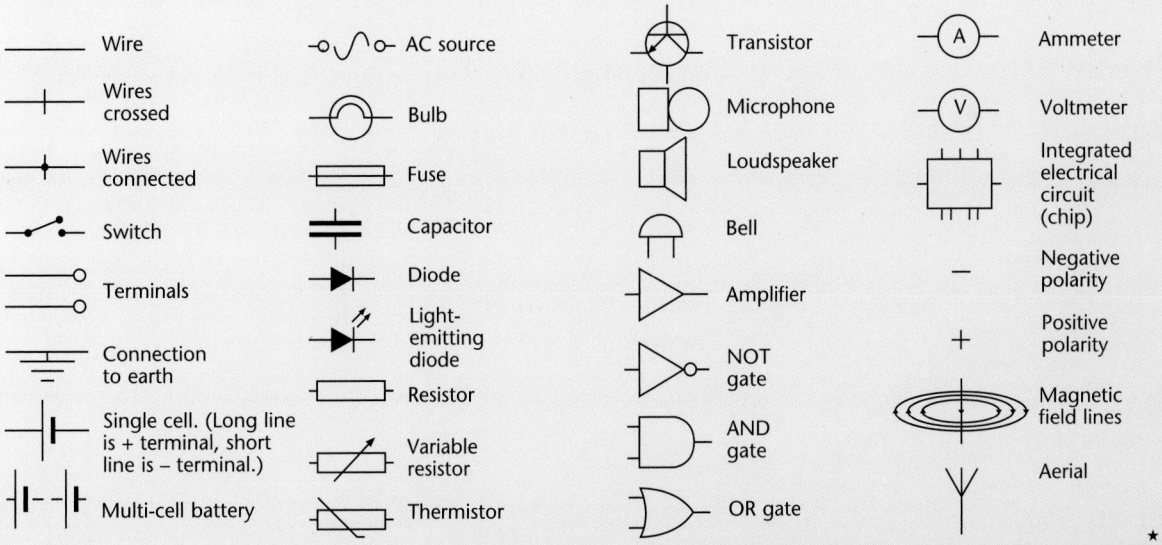

★

EARTH AND SPACE FACTS

These pages contain lists of some amazing facts about Earth, the planets, and space exploration. They are as accurate as possible, but there are different ways of measuring things, so you may find slightly different figures elsewhere.

THE CONTINENTS

Name	Area (km²)
Asia	43,608,000
Africa	30,335,000
North America	24,300,000
South America	17,611,000
Antarctica	13,340,000
Europe	10,498,000
Australasia	8,923,000

OCEANS AND SEAS

The largest ocean, the Pacific, is also the deepest. At one point in an area called the Mariana Trench, it is 11,022m deep.

Name	Area (km²)
Pacific Ocean	166,241,000
Atlantic Ocean	82,217,000
Indian Ocean	73,600,000
Southern Ocean	35,000,000
Arctic Ocean	12,257,000
Mediterranean Sea	2,505,000
South China Sea	2,318,000
Bering Sea	2,269,000
Caribbean Sea	1,943,000
Gulf of Mexico	1,544,000

LARGEST ISLANDS

Name(s)	Area (km²)
Greenland (Kalaallit Nunaat)	2,175,600
New Guinea	789,950
Borneo	751,100
Madagascar	586,376
Baffin Island, Canada	507,454
Sumatra, Indonesia	424,760
Honshu, Japan	227,920
Great Britain	218,896
Victoria Island, Canada	217,290
Ellesmere Island, Canada	196,236

GREATEST LAKES

The deepest lake, at 1,637m, is Lake Baikal in Russia. It also contains the most fresh water.

Name(s)	Location	Area (km²)
Caspian Sea	Europe/Asia	424,200
Lake Superior	USA/Canada	82,414
Lake Victoria	Tanzania/Uganda	69,215
Lake Huron	USA/Canada	59,596
Lake Michigan	USA	58,016
Aral Sea	Kazakhstan/Uzbekistan	40,500
Lake Tanganyika	Tanzania/Congo	32,764
Lake Baikal	Russia	31,500
Great Bear Lake	Canada	31,328
Lake Nyasa (Malawi)	Mozambique/Tanzania	29,928

LONGEST RIVERS

Name(s)	Location	Length (km)
Nile (Bahr-el-Nil)	North-east Africa	6,671
Amazon (Amazonas)	South America	6,440
Chang Jiang (Yangtze-Kiang)	China	6,276
Mississippi-Missouri-Red Rock	USA	6,019
Ob'-Irtysh	Asia	5,411
Yenisei-Angara	Russia	4,989
Huang Ho (Yellow River)	China	4,830
Amur-Shilka-Onon	East Asia	4,416
Lena	Russia	4,400
Congo (Zaïre; Lualaba)	Central Africa	4,380

HIGHEST MOUNTAINS

Some lists include Lhotse in fourth position at 8,501m, but we have regarded it as a peak of Everest rather than a separate mountain.

Name(s)	Location	Height (m)
Everest	Nepal/Tibet border	8,850
K2 (Chogori)	Pakistan/China border	8,611
Kanchenjunga	Nepal/Sikkim border	8,598
Makalu	Nepal/Tibet border	8,470
Cho Oyu	Nepal/Tibet border	8,201
Dhaulagiri	Nepal	8,172
Manaslu	Nepal	8,163
Nanga Parbat	Pakistan	8,126
Annapurna	Nepal	8,078
Gasherbrum	Pakistan/China border	8,068

PLANETARY FACTS AND FIGURES

Name of planet	Diameter of planet	Average distance from Sun	Time to orbit Sun	Time to rotate	Number of satellites
Mercury	4,879km	58 million km	88 days	58.7 days	0
Venus	12,104km	108 million km	224.7 days	243 days	0
Earth	12,756km	149.6 million km	365.2 days	23.9 hours	1
Mars	6,792km	228 million km	687 days	24.6 hours	2
Jupiter	142,984km	779 million km	11.9 years	9.9 hours	63
Saturn	120,536km	1,434 million km	29.5 years	10.7 hours	60
Uranus	51,118km	2,873 million km	84 years	17.2 hours	27
Neptune	49,528km	4,495 million km	165 years	16.1 hours	13
Pluto (dwarf)	2,390km	5,870 million km	248 years	6.4 days	3

SPACE MISSIONS

1957 Sputnik 1, the first artificial satellite, was launched into space on October 4 by the Soviet Union. On November 3, Sputnik 2 was launched into space, carrying a dog named Laika.
1959 The first space probes, Luna 1, Luna 2 and Luna 3, were sent to the Moon by the Soviet Union.
1961 Soviet cosmonaut Yuri Gagarin became the first person to travel into space. The flight lasted about 90 minutes.
1965 US astronomers detected weak signals, like radio noise, from space. Many people think that these prove the Big Bang theory.
1965 US space probe Mariner 4 took the first photos of Mars.
1966 Soviet space probe Luna 9 landed on the Moon, returning the first photos from its surface.
1967 Soviet Venera 4 became the first space probe to reach Venus. One day later, US probe Mariner 5 also reached Venus.
1968 The USA launched Apollo 8, the first manned space flight around the Moon.
1969 On July 20, the US Apollo 11 mission landed the first men on the Moon. They were Edwin "Buzz" Aldrin and Neil Armstrong, who was the first man to walk on the Moon. Another manned mission, Apollo 12, reached the Moon on November 14.
1970 US Apollo 13 Moon mission was aborted when an explosion destroyed the main module's power system.
1971 Manned Apollo 14 and 15 missions landed on the Moon.
1971 The Russians launched the first space station, Salyut 1.
1971 US Mariner 9 space probe returned the first close-up images of Mars.
1972 Manned Apollo 16 and 17 missions landed on the Moon.
1973 The USA launched Skylab, the first US space station.
1973 US Pioneer 10 probe returned the first close-up pictures of Jupiter.
1974 US Mariner 10 space probe returned the first photos of cloud-tops around Venus. It then went on to Mercury, sending back over 10,000 pictures of the planet.
1975 Soviet space probes Venera 9 and 10 took the first photos of Venus' surface.
1976 US space probes Viking 1 and Viking 2 landed on Mars. They took many photos and studied samples of Martian soil.
1979 US space probes Voyager 1 and Voyager 2 flew by Jupiter, sending back detailed pictures.
1980 US space probe Voyager 2 flew past Saturn, sending back detailed pictures.
1981 USA launched STS1, the first Space Shuttle flight.
1986 US probe Voyager 2 flew past Uranus, sending back detailed images.
1986 Soviet space station Mir was launched.
1986 US Space Shuttle Challenger exploded, killing seven astronauts.
1989 US space probe Voyager 2 flew by Neptune, sending back detailed pictures.
1991 The Hubble Space Telescope was launched from the USA.
1993 Spacewalking astronauts repaired the Hubble Space Telescope.
1993 US Galileo probe took the first close-up pictures of an asteroid, Gaspra.
1996 US Mars Global Surveyor was launched to study Mars while in orbit around the planet.
1997 US Mars Pathfinder reached Mars, releasing a small rover vehicle named Sojourner onto the surface.
1998 International Space Station construction began. Scheduled to finish in 2010.
2001 The Mir space station became the largest man-made object to be brought back to Earth. It broke up on re-entry into the atmosphere, before landing in the Pacific Ocean.
2001 US NEAR (Near Earth Asteroid Rendezvous) spacecraft landed on the surface of an asteroid, Eros.
2003 US Space Shuttle Columbia broke up on re-entry, killing seven astronauts.
2003-2004 US Mars Exploration Rovers, Spirit and Opportunity, began their mission to study its surface.

SCIENTISTS AND INVENTORS

These pages contain details of some of the people who have made important contributions to scientific discovery and invention across the centuries.

Key to historical dates

BC Before Christ. All other dates are **AD**, which stands for *Anno Domini*, Latin for "in the year of our Lord".
c. *Circa.* Latin for "about".

al-Haytham, Ibn (Alhazen) (965-1038) An Arab physicist who made great advances in optics, explaining refraction, and the role of reflection in vision.

Ampère, André Marie (1775-1836) A French mathematician and physicist who did pioneering work on electricity and magnetism. The unit of electric current, called the ampere, is named after him.

Anaxagoras (c. 500-428BC) This Greek philosopher was the first to explain the phases and eclipses of the Sun and Moon as the result of their movements.

Archimedes (c.287-212BC) A Greek mathematician and inventor who formulated the scientific principle that explains how a floating object displaces its own weight in water.

Aristotle (c.384-322BC) A Greek philosopher who made many contributions to physics, zoology and scientific theory.

Avogadro, Amedeo (1776-1856) This Italian chemist first theorized that all gases of the same volume at the same temperature and pressure must contain the same number of molecules. This is called Avogadro's law.

Babbage, Charles (1792-1871) An English mathematician and inventor who worked on a calculating machine called the Analytical Engine. The machine anticipated the modern computer.

Bain, Alexander (1811-1877) This Scottish clockmaker registered his design for the first fax machine (1843).

Baird, John Logie (1888-1946) A Scottish engineer who invented the television (1926).

Becquerel, Antoine (1852-1908) A French physicist who discovered radioactivity (1896).

Bell, Alexander Graham (1847-1922) A Scottish-American inventor who invented the telephone (1872-76).

Benz, Karl (1844-1929) A German inventor who designed the first car to be driven by an internal combustion engine.

Berliner, Émile (1851-1929) This German-American engineer invented the gramophone.

Berners-Lee, Tim (1955-) This English computer scientist invented the world wide web.

Biro, Lazlo (1900-1985) This Hungarian artist and journalist invented the ballpoint pen (1938).

Bohr, Niels (1885-1962) A Danish physicist who applied the quantum theory of physics to Rutherford's structure of the atom (1913).

Booth, Hubert (1871-1955) This British engineer invented the first successful vacuum cleaner.

Boyle, Robert (1627-1691) This Irish scientist proposed that matter is made up of tiny particles. He also formulated Boyle's law, which states that the pressure and volume of a gas are inversely proportional.

Braun, Wernher von (1912-1977) A German engineer who was a pioneer of rocket-building and space flight.

Brown, Robert (1773-1858) A Scottish biologist who noted the apparently random motion of particles suspended in liquids.

Brunel, Isambard Kingdom (1806-1859) This English engineer designed many great bridges and ocean-going steamships.

Cavendish, Henry (1731-1810) This English chemist and physicist discovered hydrogen, the chemical make-up of air and water, and estimated the weight of the Earth.

Celsius, Anders (1701-1744) This Swedish astronomer invented the first temperature scale to be divided into 100 degree units. It was named the Celsius scale.

Chadwick, James (1891-1974)
An English physicist who worked on radioactivity and discovered the neutron.

Charles, Jacques (1746-1823)
A French physicist who formulated Charles' law, which states the relationship between temperature and volume in gases.

Cockerell, Christopher (1910-1999) A British engineer who invented the hovercraft.

Copernicus, Nicolaus (1473-1543) This Polish astronomer developed the theory that the planets move around the Sun, not around the Earth (1530).

Crick, Francis (1916-2004)
This English biologist, along with his colleague, James Watson, discovered the structure of DNA. (See also *Franklin, Rosalind; Wilkins, Maurice.*)

Cugnot, Nicolas-Joseph (1725-1804) A French army engineer who in 1769 invented the steam tractor. This was the first vehicle to move on land by its own power.

Curie, Marie (1867-1934)
A pioneering Polish scientist who carried out work in radiation and discovered the radioactive material radium (1898).

Dalton, John (1766-1844)
This English chemist suggested that elements are made of atoms which combine to form compounds.

Darwin, Charles (1809-1882)
The English naturalist who first suggested that species evolve and change by natural selection.

Drew, Richard (1886-1956)
The American inventor of sticky tape (1928).

Edison, Thomas (1847-1931)
This American inventor made over a thousand devices including the phonograph, an early version of the gramophone.

Einstein, Albert (1879-1955)
A German-born physicist who published the Special Theory of Relativity (1905) and General Theory of Relativity (1915), revising previous ideas of time and space.

Fahrenheit, Gabriel (1686-1736) A German physicist who invented the mercury thermometer (1714) and devised the Fahrenheit temperature scale.

Faraday, Michael (1791-1867)
An English scientist who invented the dynamo, generating an electric current by spinning a coil of wire in a magnetic field.

Fermi, Enrico (1901-1954)
This Italian physicist was the first to control nuclear energy in a nuclear reactor.

Fleming, Alexander (1881-1955) This Scottish doctor discovered penicillin, a substance important in making antibiotics.

Ford, Henry (1863-1947) An American automobile engineer who built the Ford Model T and pioneered mass-production techniques in industry.

Franklin, Benjamin (1706-1790)
This American inventor and politician proved that lightning is a form of electricity.

Franklin, Rosalind (1920-1958) This English scientist, along with her colleague, Maurice Wilkins, carried out research crucial to the discovery of the structure of DNA. (See also *Crick, Francis; Watson, James.*)

Galilei, Galileo (1564-1642)
An Italian astronomer and scientist who made many discoveries. He proved that all falling bodies descend with equal acceleration. His studies of planetary motion supported the Copernican theory that the planets move around the Sun.

Gerbert (c.945-1003) This French monk invented the first mechanical clock. He became Pope Sylvester II in 999.

Gilbert, William (1544-1603)
This English physicist, also doctor to Queen Elizabeth I of England, founded the scientific study of magnetism. He was the first to suggest that the Earth itself is magnetic.

Hahn, Otto (1879-1968)
A German chemist who, together with Fritz Strassman, discovered nuclear fission. (See also *Meitner, Lise.*)

Halley, Edmund (1656-1742)
An English astronomer and mathematician who charted and predicted the orbit of a comet. Halley's Comet is named after him.

Harvey, William (1578-1657)
This English doctor discovered how blood circulates through the body.

Hawking, Stephen (1942-)
An English physicist who has advanced the understanding of the origin of the universe.

Herschel, William (1738-1822)
This British astronomer and telescope-maker mapped the stars of the northern hemisphere and, in 1781, discovered the planet Uranus. He also discovered infrared radiation in 1800. His sister, **Caroline (1750-1848)**, did important work in assisting him.

Hertz, Heinrich (1857-1894) This German physicist began the research that demonstrated the existence of radio waves.

Hooke, Robert (1635-1703) An English physicist and chemist who discovered the relationship between elasticity and force, as formulated by Hooke's law.

Hubble, Edwin (1889-1953) An American astronomer who proved the existence of galaxies beyond our own. The Hubble Space Telescope is named after him.

Huygens, Christiaan (1629-1695) This Dutch physicist and astronomer invented the first accurate pendulum clock, recognized Saturn's rings and was the first person to suggest that light travels in waves.

Jenner, Edward (1749-1823) This English doctor invented the first vaccine.

Joule, James (1818-1889) An English physicist who did important work on heat, and helped to establish the principle of the conservation of energy. The joule, a unit of measurement of work and energy, is named after him.

Kelvin, Lord See *Thomson, William.*

Kepler, Johannes (1571-1630) A German astronomer who discovered the laws of planetary motion.

Lavoisier, Antoine (1743-1794) This French lawyer and scientist named oxygen and hydrogen, and explained the role of oxygen in combustion.

Leeuwenhoek, Antony van (1632–1723) A Dutch scientist who was the first to examine bacteria, sperm and blood cells with a microscope.

Lemaître, Georges (1894-1966) A Belgian astrophysicist, mathematician and priest who first suggested the Big Bang theory of the origin of the universe.

Linnaeus, Carolus (Carl von Linné) (1707-1778) This Swedish botanist introduced the method of classifying living things into genus, species and other sub-divisions.

Lister, Joseph (1827-1912) This English surgeon was the first to carry out antiseptic operations.

Lovelace, Ada (1815-1852) An English mathematician, Lovelace worked on the Analytical Engine designed by Charles Babbage, devising "programs" which anticipated computer programming.

Maiman, Theodore (1927-2007) An American scientist who built the first laser.

Malpighi, Marcello (1628-1694) Using a microscope, this Italian physiologist discovered that arteries and veins are connected by tiny blood vessels now called capillaries.

Marconi, Guglielmo (1874-1937) This Italian physicist developed radiotelegraphy and succeeded in sending signals across the Atlantic (1901).

Maxwell, James Clerk (1831-1879) A Scottish physicist who established the presence of electromagnetic radiation.

Meitner, Lise (1878-1968) This Austrian physicist explained nuclear fission for the first time (1939). (See also *Hahn, Otto; Strassman, Fritz.*)

Mendel, Gregor (1822-1884) An Austrian monk and naturalist who developed the laws of heredity.

Mendeleyev, Dmitri (1834-1907) This Russian chemist devised the Periodic Table of Elements.

Mercator, Gerardus (1512-1594) This Flemish geographer and map-maker invented the Mercator projection: a way of accurately showing the Earth's round shape on a flat map.

Morse, Samuel (1791-1872) An American artist who invented a system of sending messages along electric telegraph wires by a coded system of dots and dashes (long and short electrical pulses) now called Morse code.

Newcomen, Thomas (1663-1729) An English inventor who built the first atmospheric steam engine.

Newton, Isaac (1642-1727) This English physicist and mathematician formulated fundamental laws of gravity and motion. He also discovered that light is made up of a spectrum of colours, and built the first reflecting telescope.

Nipkow, Paul (1860-1940) A German engineer and pioneer of television who invented the Nipkow disc, a mechanical scanning device.

Nobel, Alfred (1833-1896) A Swedish chemist who invented dynamite (1866), and founded the Nobel Prize scheme.

Ohm, Georg (1787-1854)
A German physicist who researched electrical resistance. The SI unit of electrical resistance, called the ohm, is named after him.

Pascal, Blaise (1623-1662)
A French mathematician and physicist who made contributions to hydraulics and the study of atmospheric pressure. The SI unit of pressure, called the pascal, is named after him.

Pasteur, Louis (1822-1895)
This French chemist showed that decay is caused by bacteria. He invented a process of preserving food by killing bacteria with heat, now called pasteurization.

Planck, Max (1858-1947)
This German physicist developed the quantum theory.

Priestley, Joseph (1733-1804)
A British chemist who discovered oxygen (1774). He also invented fizzy drinks.

Pythagoras (6th century BC)
A Greek scientist who made many discoveries, and devised Pythagoras' theorem, a formula for calculating the unknown length of one side of a right-angled triangle.

Röntgen, Wilhelm (1845-1923) This German physicist discovered X-rays (1895).

Ruska, Ernst (1906-1988)
A German engineer who invented the electron microscope (1933).

Rutherford, Ernest (1871-1937)
A New Zealand-born physicist who demonstrated the structure of the atom.

Savery, Thomas (c.1650-1715)
An English engineer who built the first steam engine.

Sikorsky, Igor (1889-1972)
A Russian-born American aeronautical engineer who built the first successful helicopter (1939).

Slipher, Vesto (1875-1969) An American astronomer who took the first clear photographs of Mars, and discovered the universe to be vastly bigger than was previously thought.

Stephenson, George (1781-1848) An English inventor who invented the first successful steam locomotive (1814) and, with his son Robert, built Stephenson's Rocket (1829) for the first passenger line.

Strassman, Fritz (1902-1980)
A German chemist who, with Otto Hahn, discovered nuclear fission (1938). (See also *Meitner, Lise.*)

Talbot, William Fox (1800-1877) This British scientist invented the method of reproducing photographs from a negative image.

Tesla, Nikola (1856-1943)
A Croatian electrical engineer who invented the AC motor and high-voltage electrical generation.

Thomson, William (Lord Kelvin) (1824-1907) A British mathematician and physicist who did important work in thermodynamics, and established the absolute temperature scale.

Tombaugh, Clyde (1906-1997)
An American astronomer who discovered Pluto in 1930.

Torricelli, Evangelista (1608-1647) An Italian physicist who devised the principle of the barometer (1644).

Turing, Alan (1912-1954)
This English mathematician was an important pioneer of computer science.

Vesalius, Andreas (1514-1564)
This Flemish medical researcher founded the modern science of anatomy (the study of the body).

Villard, Paul (1860-1934)
A French physicist who discovered gamma radiation (1900).

Volta, Alessandro (1745-1827)
An Italian physicist who built the first electric battery. The volt, which measures electric potential, is named after him.

Watson, James (1928-) This American scientist, together with Francis Crick, discovered the structure of DNA (1953). (See also *Franklin, Rosalind; Wilkins, Maurice.*)

Watt, James (1736-1819)
A Scottish inventor who improved the steam engine and introduced the sun-and-planet gear. The watt, a unit of electrical power, is named after him.

Wegener, Alfred (1880-1930)
A German meteorologist who first suggested the theory of continental drift.

Whittle, Frank (1907-1996)
An English inventor who devised the jet engine (1930).

Wilkins, Maurice (1916-2004)
This New Zealand-born British biologist and physicist, along with Rosalind Franklin, carried out research crucial to the discovery of the structure of DNA. (See also *Crick, Francis; Watson, James.*)

Wright, Orville (1871-1948) and **Wilbur (1867-1912)**
In 1903, these American brothers flew the first aircraft.

Yale, Linus (1821-1868)
This American inventor introduced the type of pin lock still used today.

KEY DATES IN SCIENCE

On these two pages, you can read about some of the most important dates in the history of scientific invention and discovery.

Key to historical dates

BC Before Christ. All other dates are **AD**, which stands for *Anno Domini*, Latin for "in the year of our Lord".
c. *Circa.* Latin for "about".

4241BC The Egyptian calendar was introduced, making this the first year in which events could be dated precisely.
c.4000BC The alloy bronze was first made in Mesopotamia.
c.3500BC The first wheels were made out of sections of tree trunks.
c.3000BC The Babylonians divided the day into 24 hours. They also invented the abacus, the first adding machine.
c.1600BC The first records were made of the study of astronomy.
c.1500BC Iron smelting was first developed in Asia Minor (Turkey).
c.700BC The *Ayurveda*, an early medical text, was written in India.
c.600BC The Greek philosopher Thales of Miletus described the magnetic properties of lodestone, a form of iron ore, later to be called magnetite.
c.530BC Pythagoras, a Greek mathematician, made various discoveries, including Pythagoras' theorem.
c.400BC The pulley was invented in Greece.
c.335BC The Greek philosopher Aristotle made many important scientific observations, including how levers work.
c.300BC Gears were first used in Egypt.
c.235BC Archimedes, a Greek scientist, invented the Archimedes' screw, which could move water upwards. It was used for bailing out water from flooded ships, and in irrigation systems for farming.
c.10BC The Roman architect Vitruvius described a crane.
c.200 The earliest known use was made of cast iron – to make a Chinese cooking stove.
c.635 Quill pens were used for writing.
c.700 The Catalan forge was used in Spain for smelting iron. It was an early version of the modern blast furnace.
c.950 Gunpowder was used by the Chinese to make fireworks and signals.
1000 The optical properties of lenses were first observed by the Arab physicist Ibn al-Haytham.
1088 The first known clock, which was powered by water, was invented in China by Han Kung-Lien.
1090 Compasses were first used by the Chinese and the Arabs to navigate at sea.
1202 The Italian scholar Leonardo Fibonacci published his *Liber Abaci*, the first European book to suggest the use of the Hindu-Arabic decimal number system.
1230 In China, gunpowder was first used as an explosive, to make bombs for attacking city walls.
1286 The first pair of glasses was made in Italy, probably by an Italian physicist named Salvino degli Armati.
1326 Early guns were in use in Italy.
1451 Johann Gutenberg invented the printing press in Germany.
1500 The Italian artist and scientist Leonardo da Vinci designed many devices, including a type of helicopter.
1540 The first artificial limbs were made for wounded soldiers by the French doctor Ambroise Paré.
1543 The Polish astronomer Copernicus published his theory that the planets revolve around the Sun, not the Earth.
1590 The microscope was invented in the Netherlands.
1592 The Italian astronomer Galileo invented the first thermometer based on the expansion and contraction of air.
1608 The telescope was first demonstrated in the Netherlands.
1610 Galileo used a telescope to make astronomical observations.
1616 The English doctor William Harvey lectured on the circulation of blood.
1618 A German astronomer, Johannes Kepler, published laws describing the planets' elliptical orbits around the Sun.
1623 The first mechanical calculator was invented in Germany by Wilhelm Schickard.
1644 Evangelista Torricelli, an Italian physicist, discovered the principle of the barometer.
1682 The English astronomer Edmund Halley described and charted the orbit of a comet, later named after him.
1687 The English physicist Isaac Newton published his book *Principia*, in which he proposed the laws of motion and gravity.
1704 Isaac Newton wrote *Opticks*, a book about prisms and light.
1712 The English inventor Thomas Newcomen built the first atmospheric steam engine.

1752 The American scientist Benjamin Franklin showed that lightning is a form of electricity.
1769 The Scottish inventor James Watt produced the first version of his improved steam engine.
1774 A British chemist, Joseph Priestley, discovered and isolated oxygen gas.
1783 The first flight in a hot-air balloon took place in Paris, France.
1789 Antoine Lavoisier, a French lawyer and scientist, published his *Elementary Treatise on Chemistry*, which became the basis for modern chemistry.
1796 In England, Edward Jenner performed the first vaccination.
1799 Alessandro Volta, an Italian physicist, built the first battery.
1808 The English chemist John Dalton published *A New System of Chemical Philosophy*, containing his theories of atomic structure.
1810 The first electric lamp was displayed in London, England.
1820 A Danish scientist, Hans Ørsted, noticed that a wire with an electric current running through it behaved like a magnet, an effect later called electromagnetism.
1821 An English scientist Michael Faraday invented the electric motor.
1831 Michael Faraday invented the dynamo.
1833-4 British mathematicians Charles Babbage and Ada Lovelace worked on the Analytical Engine, a forerunner of the computer.
1837 The electric telegraph, used to send messages along wires, was invented in England.
1839 In England and France, the invention of photography was announced.
1852 The first airship, powered by steam and filled with hydrogen, made its maiden flight in France.
1859 The internal combustion engine was invented in France.
1859 Charles Darwin, an English naturalist, published *On the Origin of Species by Natural Selection*. It contained his theories of evolution.
1862 The first celluloid plastic was exhibited in London, England.
1869 The Russian scientist Dmitri Mendeleyev developed the first periodic table of the elements.
1876 The first telephone message was transmitted by Alexander Graham Bell in Boston, USA.
1877 The first sound recording was made in America by Thomas Edison on his prototype phonograph machine.
1877 A German-American scientist, Émile Berliner, invented the microphone.
1879 Thomas Edison invented the first successful light bulb.
1881 The first power station was built in Surrey, England.
1884 The first artificial fibres, made from cellulose, were exhibited in London, England.
1885 The petrol-driven car was invented by the German Karl Benz.
1888 Heinrich Hertz, a German physicist, demonstrated the existence of radio waves.
1895 Moving pictures were first shown in public in France.
1895 X-rays were discovered by the German physicist Wilhelm Röntgen, and the first X-ray photograph was taken.
1895 The Italian physicist Guglielmo Marconi developed and demonstrated radio transmission.
1896 Antoine Becquerel, a French physicist, discovered radioactivity.
1903 The American Wright brothers made the first powered aircraft flight.
1905 German-born physicist Albert Einstein published scientific works including the Special Theory of Relativity.
1911 Marie Curie, a Polish scientist, won the Nobel prize for her work on radioactivity.
1911 A British scientist, Ernest Rutherford, showed that atoms have a central nucleus.
1926 John Logie Baird, a Scottish engineer, transmitted the first black and white television picture across the Atlantic.
1929 Edwin Hubble, an American astronomer, showed that galaxies are moving away from each other. This became the foundation of the Big Bang theory.
1936 The first helicopter flight was made in Germany by the Focke Fa-61.
1938 Nuclear fission was discovered by Otto Hahn and Fritz Strassman. Lise Meitner explained the discovery in 1939.
1941 Frank Whittle invented the turbojet aircraft engine in England.
1945 The USA tested the atomic bomb in New Mexico, USA, and used it on Hiroshima, Japan during WW2.
1948 Three American scientists, John Bardeen, Walter Brattain and William Shockley, invented the transistor, making miniature electronics possible.
1953 Francis Crick and James Watson discovered the structure of the DNA molecule which forms living cells, later proved by Rosalind Franklin.
1957 The first satellite, the Russian Sputnik I, was launched.
1959 The integrated circuit was invented in America.
1961 Vostok I, the first manned spacecraft, was launched. Yuri Gagarin became the first person to travel into space.
1969 An American astronaut, Neil Armstrong, became the first person to walk on the Moon.
1969 The Internet, in the form of ARPANET, an American military computer network, was born.
1975 The first home computer, the Altair, became available.
1981 The first reusable spacecraft, the Space Shuttle, was launched.
1990 The first transmission of high-definition television (HDTV).
1992 The World Wide Web, invented by the British computer scientist Tim Berners-Lee, went online for the first time.
2000 Scientists announced the completion of the first draft of the human genome sequence.

A-Z OF SCIENTIFIC TERMS

Abdomen 1. The region of a vertebrate's body between the diaphragm and the pelvis. 2. The rear part of an arthropod's body.
abiotic Non-living.
abscess A collection of pus in a cavity due to bacterial infection.
abscission layer A layer that forms at the base of a dead leaf's stalk, cutting it off from the body of the plant before it falls off.
absolute magnitude The actual brightness of a star in space.
absolute temperature scale The SI temperature scale, measured in kelvins (K), which are the size of degrees Celsius (°C).
absolute zero The complete absence of heat energy. Measured as 0K (-273°C).
abyssal zone The level of the ocean between 4,000m and 5,000m in depth.
AC See *alternating current.*
acceleration A change in the velocity of an object, that is, in its speed or direction.
accessory foods Substances which help the body to work properly, namely, vitamins, minerals and water.
accumulator See *secondary cell.*
acetic acid See *ethanoic acid.*
achene A small, dry fruit with one seed.
achromatic colours Black, white and the shades of grey between them.
acid A compound that contains hydrogen and dissolves in water to produce hydrogen ions.
acid rain Rain that has increased in acidity after absorbing polluting gases such as sulphur dioxide and nitrogen dioxide.
actinides (or **radioactive rare earth metals**) A sub-group of the inner transition metals with radioactive properties.
activation energy The minimum amount of energy needed to start off a chemical reaction.
active immunity Resistance to a disease coming from antibodies produced during past exposure to it.
addition reaction A chemical reaction in which the double or triple bonds of an unsaturated compound open up and new bonds are formed with different atoms.
additive mixing The process of adding different combinations of red, green and blue light to make light of almost any colour.
adhesion The attraction of the molecules of one substance to the molecules of another substance it is touching.
adolescence See *puberty.*
ADP (**adenosine diphosphate**) A chemical containing two phosphate groups, into which ATP breaks down, releasing energy.
adventitious root A plant root that grows directly from a bulb or gardener's stem cutting.
aerial root A type of plant root that does not usually grow in the ground, but absorbs moisture from the air.
aerobic respiration Internal respiration which uses oxygen.
aerodynamics The study of the way a gas, especially air, flows over moving objects.
aerofoil The special wing shape, curved on top, flatter underneath, that creates lift.
aeronautics The science of travel through the Earth's atmosphere.
aestivation A stage of some animals' life cycles when they enter a sleep-like state to survive drought.
aggregate (or **compound**) **fruit** Fruit, such as raspberries, which are made up of fleshy beads called drupelets, each with one seed.
agonist The contracting muscle in an antagonistic pair.
aileron A control surface on a plane's wing used to direct turning and tipping.
air bladders Bubble-like structures in seaweeds which help them to float.
air resistance See *drag.*
albumen The white of a cleidoic egg. It provides the embryo with water and proteins, and supports the yolk.
alcohols A homologous series of organic compounds with the general formula $C_nH_{2n+1}OH$. For example, ethanol is C_2H_5OH.
algae A large, varied group of simple water plants, ranging from diatoms to seaweeds.
alkali A base that is dissolved in water.
alkali metals The six very reactive metals, including potassium and sodium, that form group I of the periodic table.
alkaline earth metals The six metals, including magnesium and calcium, that form group II of the periodic table.
alkanes A homologous series of saturated hydrocarbons with the general formula C_nH_{2n+2}. For example, ethane is C_2H_6.
alkenes A homologous series of unsaturated hydrocarbons with the general formula C_nH_{2n}. For example, ethene is C_2H_4.
allele Any of the different forms in which a gene can occur. For example, an eye colour gene might have blue and green alleles.
allotrope One of the different forms in which certain elements, such as carbon, can exist.
alloy A mixture of two or more metals, or a metal and a non-metal.
alpha particle A cluster of two protons and two neutrons emitted from the nucleus of some radioactive substances.
alpha radiation A stream of alpha particles.
alternating current (AC) Electric current that changes direction many times a second.
alternation of generations A process, in many flowerless plants, where one generation reproduces sexually and the next asexually.
altitude Height above sea level.
alveoli Tiny sacs at the end of bronchioles in the lungs where gases are exchanged with the blood.
AM See *Amplitude Modulation.*
amino acids Fatty acids containing an amino group ($-NH_2$), which make up proteins.
ammonia (NH_3) A colourless, strong-smelling gas, used widely to make nitric acid.
ampere (A) The unit of electric current.
amphibians A class of cold-blooded, soft-skinned animals, which live both on land and in water, for example, frogs.
amplify To make something greater, for example, to increase the loudness of a sound.
amplitude The maximum distance of particles in a wave measured from their rest position.
Amplitude Modulation (AM) A type of modulation where the amplitude of the signals is altered to match the carrier wave.
ampullae Swellings in the ears' semicircular ducts, containing cupulae.
ampullae of Lorenzi Small chambers in a shark's head that allow it to detect the electrical pulses given off by other creatures.
anaerobic respiration Internal respiration, in which the muscles convert glucose into energy without using oxygen.
anal fin A median fin projecting from in front of a fish's anus.
analogue The term that describes a continuous signal which varies in proportion to the quantity it represents.
analogue circuit A circuit which uses a continuous current, rather than one broken into pulses. See also *digital circuit.*
anatomy The science of body structure.
AND gate A logic gate which gives an output of 1 only when both inputs are 1.
anhydrous The term describing a dry solid that has been separated from water.
aniline An organic compound found in coal tar, used to make dyes.
anion A negatively charged ion.
annelids A phylum of worms with round, segmented bodies.
annual ring A single ring of xylem in a cross-section of an older plant, showing one year's growth.
annuals Plants that live and die in one year.
anode In electrolysis, the electrode with the positive charge.
anodizing A method of coating a metal with a thin layer of its oxide using electrolysis.
antagonist The relaxing muscle in an antagonistic pair.
antagonistic hormones Pairs of hormones producing opposite effects, which work together to balance chemical levels.
antagonistic pair Two muscles which work together to move a body part, then return it to its original position. See *agonist*; *antagonist.*
antennae (or **feelers**) Whip-like jointed structures on the heads of creatures such as insects and crustaceans, used for smelling, tasting and feeling.
anther A pod-like structure at the end of a stamen which contains pollen sacs.
anthracite The purest form of coal, containing over 90% carbon.
antibiotics Medicines which are used to treat bacteria-caused illnesses.
antibodies Chemicals released by some white blood cells to destroy germs.
antigen The type of chemical, carried by a germ, that a specific antibody is specialized to destroy.
antiseptic A term describing any substance that destroys bacteria, or slows their growth.
anus The opening at the end of an animal's digestive tract through which waste is released.
aorta An artery which carries blood out of the heart, to be taken around the body.
aperture On a camera, the adjustable hole which, together with the shutter, controls the exposure.
apical meristems The main areas of growth on a plant, at the tips of the shoot and root.
apparent magnitude A star's brightness seen from the Earth.
appendicular skeleton The part of the skeleton made up of the bones in the shoulders, arms, pelvis and legs.
aqueous A term describing a substance that is dissolved in water.
aqueous humour A liquid, containing salts, sugars and proteins, which fills the cavity between the eye's lens and cornea.

archaea A group of simple microscopic organisms without cell nuclei
argon (Ar) A noble gas used to fill light bulbs.
armature A square, flat rotating coil in an electric motor.
arteries Strong vessels through which blood flows away from the heart.
arthropods A phylum of creatures with segmented bodies, jointed legs and a hard exoskeleton, for example, lobsters.
asexual reproduction Producing a new organism from a single parent.
association neurons Neurons in the brain and spinal cord which interpret information from sensory neurons, then pass instructions to motor neurons.
asterism Smaller patterns of stars within a constellation.
asteroids Large lumps of rock and metal that orbit the Sun in a region called the Asteroid Belt between Mars and Jupiter.
asthenosphere A weak, partly molten layer in the Earth's upper mantle, upon which the whole lithosphere moves.
astronomy The science of heavenly bodies.
astrophysics The science of the physical and chemical aspects of heavenly bodies.
atmosphere 1. The protective layer of air around the Earth that enables plants and animals to live. 2. A layer of gases around any planet. 3. (**atm**) A unit of pressure representing standard pressure at sea level, equivalent to 101,325 pascals.
atmospheric pressure The pressure caused by the weight of the air pressing down on the Earth's surface.
atomic number The number of protons in the nucleus of an atom.
atoms The tiny particles from which elements are made. Each atom has a positively charged nucleus, balanced by enough negatively charged electrons to make the atom electrically neutral.
ATP (adenosine triphosphate) A chemical containing three phosphate groups which stores energy released by aerobic respiration.
atria The two upper chambers of the heart.
auditory nerve See *organ of Corti*.
aurora A display of lights in the sky caused by particles from the solar wind trapped in the Earth's atmosphere near the poles.
autonomic nervous system The system of nerves which controls involuntary actions.
autotrophic A term describing organisms, such as plants, that make their own food from non-living materials.
auxins Growth hormones which control the responses of plants to stimuli such as light.
Avogadro number The number of atoms or molecules found in one mole of a substance, which is 6.023×10^{23}.
axial skeleton The part of the skeleton made up of the skull, backbone and ribcage.
axil The place on a plant between a shoot or leaf stalk and the stem.
axillary bud (also **lateral** or **secondary bud**) A bud which grows at an axil.
axons Nerve fibres which carry information away from a neuron's cell body.

Background rate of extinction The normal rate at which species die out, due to natural changes in the environment.
bacteria A varied group of microscopic organisms without cell nuclei, many of which cause disease.
baleen Frayed plates of horny whalebone in whales' mouths which they use to filter feed.
ball and socket joint A joint where a round-ended bone fits into a fixed, cup-like socket.
ball-and-spoke model A way of representing molecules showing atoms as balls and the chemical bonds joining them as sticks.
bandwidth The number of bytes a microprocessor can process at once.
barbs Thin filaments branching from the central shaft of a feather.
barbules Tiny, hooked projections on the barbs of feathers, which lock together to join the barbs into a flat surface.
barred spiral galaxy A galaxy with a central bar of stars with an arm at each end.
base 1. A substance that can accept the hydrogen ions of an acid and is the chemical opposite of an acid. 2. In genetics, any of the four compounds which combine in different ways to form the rungs of the DNA double helix. Known by their initials, they are: Adenine, Thymine, Guanine and Cytosine.
base station A mast used to transmit digital radio signals between mobile phones.
battery A source of electrical potential energy made up of two or more electrochemical cells.
bauxite The ore from which aluminium is extracted.
beta particles Radiation emitted as high energy electrons when a neutron turns into a proton in the nucleus of a radioactive substance.
beta radiation A stream of beta particles.
bicuspids See *premolars*.
biennials Plants that complete their life cycles within two years.
Big Bang theory The idea that all the matter in the universe came into being with a massive explosion known as the Big Bang.
Big Crunch theory The idea that gravity will slow down the expansion of the universe, pulling everything back until the galaxies crash.
bilateral symmetry A term describing the structure of an animal's body, in which only one division can produce identical halves.
bile A green liquid, produced by the liver, which breaks up fat into tiny drops so that enzymes can break it down.
binary code A method used to represent information using the digits 1 and 0.
binary fission A form of asexual reproduction by splitting into identical halves.
binary star Two stars orbiting each other.
binocular vision The field of view of animals with two eyes on the front of their head.
binomial system The system of giving organisms two-part biological names.
biodegradable The term used to describe matter that can be broken down into simpler substances by bacteria.
biodiversity The huge variety of living things on Earth.
biofuel Fuel made from fermented corn or sugar cane.
biological key A method of identifying the species of an organism by asking a series of questions about it, often shown as a tree diagram.
biological name A two-part Latin name used to classify organisms. The first part shows the genus; the second part shows the species.
biomass The combined weight of all the living things in a habitat.
biomes The largest ecosystems into which the Earth can be divided.
biped An animal that walks on two feet.
bit (binary digit) A single piece of information in binary code – a 0 or a 1.
black hole An area of such strong gravitational pull that no matter or energy can escape from it, thought to form after the largest supernovas.
bladder A balloon-like sac which stores urine until it is passed out of the body.
blast furnace A furnace used to smelt iron ore.
boiling point The temperature at which a substance turns from a liquid into a gas.
bolus A ball of swallowed food.
bond A force that holds together two or more atoms.
botany The science of plants.
Bowman's capsules See *glomerulus*.
bract A leaf at the base of a flower stalk which often serves to protect buds.
brain stem The part of the brain leading into the spinal cord. It controls automatic processes, such as breathing.
brain waves The patterns of nerve impulses that pass through the brain.
branchiae See *gills*.
brine A concentrated solution of common salt (sodium chloride) in water.
bronchi Two thick tubes into which the trachea divides, leading into the two lungs.
bronchioles Tiny tubes in the lungs, which branch off tertiary bronchi, ending in alveoli.
Brownian motion The movement of microscopic particles, such as dust, in liquids and gases, caused by constant collisions with rapidly moving molecules.
browser Computer software used to log on to the internet.
bryophytes Plants without vascular tissue, such as mosses and liverworts.
buckminsterfullerene An allotrope of carbon with spherical molecules (often called buckyballs) containing 60 atoms.
bud A small growth on a plant stem, which develops into a new shoot or flower.
budding A form of asexual reproduction, found in creatures such as hydras, which form growths called buds that fall off to become new individuals.
bulb A short, thick underground stem surrounded by scaly leaves swollen with food.
bus Electronic pathways that carry information between the CPU and the other parts of a computer.
byte A group of eight bits of information.

Caecum A chamber found in the bodies of most herbivores, containing bacteria which break down cellulose.
caldera A very large crater formed when the upper part of a volcano either blows off or collapses into the magma chamber below.
calorie A unit of heat energy, equivalent to the amount of energy needed to raise the temperature of a gram of water by 1°C. It is equal to 4.2 joules.
Calorie The common term for a kilocalorie.
cambium A layer of thin, narrow-walled cells that produces new xylem and phloem.
camouflage Patterning, or other features which help animals to conceal themselves.
canines (or **cuspids**) Dagger-like teeth used for piercing food.
capacitor An electronic component which stores up electrical energy until it is needed.
capillaries Tiny vessels where oxygen passes from the blood into the body, and carbon dioxide and waste are carried away.
capillary action The process by which a fluid is drawn up a narrow channel by adhering to its walls. See *adhesion*.
carapace The shield-like hardened cuticle of animals such as crabs.
carbohydrates Organic compounds, containing carbon, hydrogen and oxygen.
carbon An element found in all living things.
carbonado (or **black diamond**) An impure form of diamond used for cutting in industry.
carbonates A group of salts containing the carbonate ion (CO_3^{2-}).

carbon cycle The process by which carbon from the atmosphere enters the food chain through photosynthesis and returns to the atmosphere through respiration and decay.
carbon dating A method of calculating the time that has passed since living matter died by measuring the radiation of carbon-14 present in the sample.
carbon dioxide (**CO_2**) A gas with one carbon atom and two oxygen atoms in each molecule.
carbon monoxide (**CO**) A poisonous gas with one carbon atom and one oxygen atom in each molecule.
carboxylic acids Organic acids that contain a carboxyl group (–COOH).
card In computing, a printed circuit board which slots into a computer's main circuit board, and controls the way a certain piece of hardware, such as a monitor, works.
cardiac Relating to the heart.
cardiac muscle tissue A type of striated muscle tissue, made of Y-shaped fibres which interlock to make up the heart.
carnassials Large, jagged teeth found in carnivores, used for slicing meat.
carnivore 1. An animal that eats mainly meat. 2. An order of animals, such as lions and foxes, with teeth specialized for eating flesh.
carotene A natural pigment which produces red or orange colours.
carpals The wrist bones.
carpel (or **pistil**) The female reproductive organ of a plant.
carrier waves See *modulation*.
cartilage (or **gristle**) A tough, flexible white tissue which, in most mammals, cushions joints and makes up such body parts as the ears and trachea. It forms the skeletons of young vertebrates, and of fish such as sharks.
caryopsis (or **grain**, or **kernel**) A small, dry fruit, in which the wall has fused with the seed coat.
cataclysmic variable A close-together pair of stars between which a huge and sudden increase in brightness occurs when one star pulls material away from the other.
catalyst A substance that changes the rate of a chemical reaction but is itself left unchanged.
catalytic converter A device fitted to cars to remove toxic gases from their exhaust fumes.
cathode In electrolysis, the electrode with a negative charge.
cathode ray A continuous stream of electrons that travels from a cathode through a low-pressure gas or a vacuum.
cathode ray tube A glass tube, containing a vacuum, which is used in television to turn picture signals into beams of electrons. These sweep across the screen to build up images.
cation A positively charged ion.
caudal fin A fish's tail fin.
caustic A term used to describe a strongly alkaline substance that can burn or corrode.
cell 1. In biology, the smallest unit of an organism that can carry out chemical processes vital to life. 2. An electrochemical cell.
cell body The part of a neuron that contains the nucleus.
cell membrane A thin layer surrounding a cell's cytoplasm. In animal cells, it forms the outer layer. In plant cells, it lies beneath the cell wall.
cell plate The dividing line that separates the cytoplasm during cytokinesis.
cell sap A liquid found in plant cell vacuoles.
cellulose A natural polymer, made from glucose monomers, which forms the cell walls of plants.
cell wall The tough outer layer of a plant cell.
Celsius scale A temperature scale which places 100 degrees Celsius (°C) between the ice point (at 0°C) and the steam point (at 100°C).
Cenozoic Era See *eras*.
central nervous system The brain and spinal cord.
Central Processing Unit (**CPU**) The main integrated circuit, set of circuits or PCBs, controlling the operation of a computer.
centre of gravity The point where the whole weight of an object seems to act.
centrifuging Spinning a liquid around very quickly to separate out suspended solid particles.
centrioles Two X-shaped organelles that play an important role in cell division.
centripetal force A force that keeps an object moving in a circle.
cerebellum The part of the brain that coordinates muscle movement and balance.
cerebral cortex The cerebrum's outer layer.
cerebral hemispheres The two halves into which the cerebrum is divided.
cerebrospinal fluid A thin layer of liquid that cushions the brain in the skull.
cerebrum The largest part of the brain. It controls most physical, and many mental, activities. It also controls the cerebellum.
cervix A muscular passage at the bottom of the womb, which opens into the vagina.
CFCs Chlorofluorocarbons, that is, organic compounds of carbon, fluorine and chlorine, that are believed to damage the atmosphere.
chaetae Bristles found on the bodies of some invertebrates, or on the end of their parapodia, which they use to move along.
charge-coupled device (**CCD**) A light-sensitive electronic part, found for example in a camcorder, that produces electrical signals.
chemical energy Energy stored in a substance and released during a chemical reaction.
chemical formula A combination of chemical symbols showing the atoms of which a substance is made and their proportions.
chemical reaction An interaction between substances in which their atoms are rearranged to form new substances.
chemical symbol A shorthand way to represent a specific element in formulae and equations.
chemoreceptors Cells which sense the presence of certain chemicals.
chip See *silicon chip*.
chitin A sugar-based substance which forms the hard protective coverings of arthropods.
chlorides A group of salts made from hydrochloric acid.
chlorofluorocarbons See *CFCs*.
chlorophyll A green pigment found in many plant cells. It absorbs light for photosynthesis.
chloroplasts Organelles in a plant cell which contain chlorophyll.
cholesterol A fat-like substance found in animal cell membranes. Too much cholesterol in the body can cause arterial disease.
chordates A phylum of animals with bodies supported by a stiff rod called a notochord.
chromatic colours All the colours of the visible light spectrum.
chromatogram A pattern of coloured bands made on filter paper or in a tube by substances separated by chromatography.
chromatography Separating the substances in a mixture by the rate they move through or along a medium, such as filter paper.
chromoplast An organelle that contains pigment, so giving many plants, flowers, fruit and vegetables their characteristic colours.
chromosomes Bundles of DNA in a cell nucleus, which together contain all the information needed to develop an organism.
cilia 1. Tiny hairs on the bodies of some microscopic animals which they flick back and forth to propel themselves. . Tiny hairs in the bodies of larger creatures, such as those on the lining of the human nose which keep dust and mucus out of the lungs.
ciliary muscles Muscles in the eye which change the shape of the lens.
ciliate A microscopic organism with cilia.
circuit See *electric circuit* and *electronic circuit*.
circular muscles Muscles in the iris which contract in bright light, shrinking the pupil to avoid dazzling.
circulatory system The interconnected network of arteries and veins that carries blood around an animal's body.
cirri Bristly limbs used for filter feeding by creatures such as barnacles.
cirrus A high, wispy type of cloud.
class The largest subdivision of a phylum.
classical taxonomy The division of living things into five kingdoms: monera, protista, fungi, plants and animals.
classification In biology, a method of sorting organisms into groups, which are themselves divided into smaller groups.
clavicle The collarbone.
cleavage furrow A constriction around the middle of a cell that pinches it until it divides.
cleavage plane The boundary between the regular lines of particles in a crystal, along which it can be split.
cleidoic egg A hard-shelled egg, laid by animals such as birds and reptiles, in which the embryo is fed by a food store called a yolk.
client/server network A type of network where one computer (the server) holds essential data which can be accessed by the other computers (the clients).
climate A typical pattern of weather conditions.
climatic region A large area of the Earth in which the climate is generally the same.
climax community A community that survives in its habitat as long as its environment remains stable.
clitellum A saddle-like body part on an earthworm.
cloaca A chamber in a bird's body where waste is stored before being excreted.
clock speed The number of instructions a microprocessor can deal with in one second, measured in Megahertz (MHz).
cloning Making an identical copy of an organism. The copy is called a clone.
clotting The process by which blood flow is stopped in an injured area as a gel-like mass, called a clot, is formed.
cnidarians A phylum of water creatures, such as jellyfish, whose sack-like bodies have a single opening.
cnidoblasts (or **thread cells**) Specialized cells, on the tentacles of creatures such as sea anemones, used for seizing food.
cochlea A spiral-shaped tube in the inner part of the ear, filled with fluid which passes sound vibrations from the oval window to hair cells on the organ of Corti.
co-dominant genes A pair of genes, the instructions of which are both carried out.
coelom A type of perivisceral cavity that is contained by a peritoneum.
coherent The term that describes waves that have the same wavelength and frequency and travel in step with each other.
cohesion The attraction of molecules to each other rather than to the molecules of a substance they are touching.

cold-blooded A term describing animals, such as reptiles, whose internal temperature varies with that of their surroundings.
collenchyma A type of supporting plant tissue with long, thick-walled cells, found in cortex.
colloid A mixture of extremely small particles of a substance held in another substance in which it does not dissolve.
colon The first part of the large intestine.
combining power See *valency*.
combustion The scientific term for all forms of burning.
comet A chunk of frozen gas and dirt which orbits the Sun.
commensals Organisms living together where one benefits without affecting the other.
community In ecology, the plants and animals that live together in a certain habitat.
commutator A device that causes the direction of an electric current to be reversed.
compact bone A type of bone forming the outer layer of all bones, made up of lamellae.
compact disc (CD) A shiny disc on which information can be stored digitally as a series of bumps, and "read" by a laser beam.
compensation points The two points in every 24 hours when the processes of photosynthesis and respiration in a plant are exactly balanced.
complementary colours Any two colours that together make up white light.
complementary medicine Alternative medical treatments used alongside traditional methods.
complete metamorphosis The type of metamorphosis in which the young form is very different from the adult.
composite bulb A bulb made up of sections called cloves, each one able to produce an individual plant.
composites Synthetic materials, especially plastics, made up of different substances combined to improve their properties.
compound A substance made up of two or more elements that are chemically bonded.
compound eye An eye made up of many tiny lenses, such as is found in insects.
compound fruit See *aggregate fruit*.
compound leaf A leaf made up of more than one leaflet growing from a central stalk.
compound microscope A microscope with two or more lenses.
concave lens A lens with one or both surfaces curving inwards.
concave mirror A mirror with an inward-curving surface.
conception See *fertilization*.
condensation 1. The process of a gas cooling to form a liquid. 2. The droplets of liquid that form as a gas cools.
conduction 1. The way heat energy is transferred in a solid by the vibration of the solid's heated particles. 2. The way an electric current is transferred in a substance by the movement of free electrons.
conductor A substance through which an electric current can flow, or heat can flow easily.
cones Cone-shaped cells in the retina, which are sensitive to red, green or blue light.
conifers Trees or plants with waxy needle-like or scaly leaves, which bear cones containing their seeds. Most are evergreen.
conjunctiva A clear layer which covers the cornea and lines the eyelids.
conservation The efforts made to protect animals and natural resources in order to ensure the future of all living things.
constellation One of 88 recognizable patterns of stars in the night sky.
constructive boundary A plate boundary where new crust is formed.
constructive interference An increase in amplitude that may result when two waves meet.
consumers All organisms above the trophic level of the producers (plants) in a food chain.
contact forces Forces that require two or more objects to be touching to take effect.
continent Any of the seven large landmasses into which the Earth is divided: Asia, Africa, North and South America, Antarctica, Europe and Australasia.
continental drift The slow movement of the continents, caused by the gradual shifting of the Earth's plates.
contour feathers The feathers that cover a bird's body, making a streamlined surface.
contraception Methods of preventing an ovum and sperm joining to make a baby.
contractile vacuole A tiny sac in the body of a unicellular creature, which allows it to maintain its water balance.
control surfaces Hinged flaps on a plane's wings and tail used to control the direction of its movement.
convection The way heat energy in liquids or gases is transferred. The part of a fluid nearest the heat source expands, becoming less dense, and rises; the denser, cooler part sinks.
convection current A movement of a liquid or gas caused by convection.
convective zone The part of the Sun between the radiative zone and the photosphere.
converging lens A lens that causes parallel light rays passing through it to come together.
convex lens A lens with one or both surfaces curving outwards.
convex mirror A mirror with an outward-curving surface.
core 1.-The central part of an object, such as the Sun. 2.-The region inside a solenoid.
corm A short, thick plant stem base, swollen with food.
cornea A transparent covering protecting the front of the eye.
cornified layer The outer layer of the epidermis, made of dead skin cells.
corona A low-density layer of gas around the Sun, visible during a total solar eclipse.
corpus callosum A thick band of nerve fibres connecting the cerebral hemispheres.
corrosion The process by which a metal is worn away as its surface reacts with oxygen and other chemicals.
corrosive A term describing a substance, usually a strong acid, that burns away skin or the surface of an object.
cortex 1. The tissue that surrounds vascular tissue in a vascular plant. 2. The outer part of any animal organ.
cotyledon (or **seed leaf**) The first type of leaf to grow on a plant.
covalent bond A bond formed between two atoms, in which an electron from each atom is attracted to the other's nucleus, becoming shared by both.
CPU See *Central Processing Unit*.
cracking A method of changing organic compounds with large molecules into more useful compounds with smaller molecules.
cranium The skull bone.
crater 1. The hole in the top of a volcano. 2. The hole formed in a planet's surface by the impact of a meteorite.
crop In birds, a thin-walled pouch which temporarily stores swallowed food.
crop rotation A farming practice in which crops which use or replace certain minerals are planted in different fields each year.
cross-breeding Breeding together animals of different species.
cross-pollination Pollination in which one plant pollinates another plant of its own kind.
crown The visible part of a tooth.
crude oil A dark, thick oil made of a mixture of natural hydrocarbons, from which many useful fuels and other chemicals are obtained by fractional distillation.
crust A layer of rock between the Earth's outer surface and its mantle.
crystal A solid substance with a definite geometrical shape, straight edges and flat surfaces.
CT (computed tomography) scanner A special X-ray camera used by doctors which makes pictures of sections of the body and feeds them into a computer for viewing.
cumulus A fluffy, white type of cloud which appears high up in warm, sunny weather.
cupula A gel-like patch in an ampulla, containing sensitive hair cells. These send information to the brain about the rotation and tilting of the head.
currents 1. Huge bands of ocean water which flow in a certain direction. 2. See *electric current*.
cusps 1. Flaps on the valves between the heart's four chambers, which are forced open and shut, ensuring one-way circulation of blood. 2. Sharp points on certain types of teeth.
cuticle The protective, waterproof outer layer of the epidermis of a plant or animal.
cycads A group of gymnosperms which produce very large cones in the middle of a circle of spiky leaves.
cytokinesis The division of the cytoplasm that occurs after meiosis or mitosis.
cytoplasm The gel-like substance inside a cell in which organelles are suspended.

Data Information, especially that processed by a computer or used in scientific studies.
data compression Methods used to increase the speed at which data can be transmitted, by leaving out inessential information.
daughter cells Identical copies of a cell produced when it divides.
decantation A method of separating solid particles from a liquid by leaving the particles to settle and pouring off the liquid.
deceleration (or **negative acceleration**) A decrease in velocity.
decibel (dB) The unit of loudness.
deciduous (or **milk**) **teeth** The first set of teeth, which fall out to be replaced by permanent teeth.
deciduous trees Trees that shed their leaves in the autumn.
decomposers Tiny organisms, including bacteria and fungi, which break down dead animal and plant matter into minerals.
decomposition reaction A reaction in which a single compound breaks down into the substances that make it up.
deep time See *geological time*.
dehydrating agent A substance which removes water that is chemically combined in another substance.
dehydration The process by which water is removed from a substance, often by heating.
deionization A method of purifying water by filtering it through an ion exchange resin. The ions causing the impurity are removed by exchanging them for ions in the resin.
delta A flat area of land, usually roughly triangular in shape, built up of material deposited by a river as it flows into a sea.
deltoid The large shoulder muscle which allows movement of the upper arm.

dendrites Nerve fibres which carry information towards a neuron's cell body.
density A measure of the amount of matter in a substance compared to its volume.
dental amalgam An alloy of mercury and copper used for filling tooth cavities.
dentate A term describing an animal with teeth.
denticles See *placoid scales*.
dentine The substance that makes up the layer of a tooth below the crown.
dentition A set of teeth.
deoxyribonucleic acid See *DNA*.
deoxyribose A type of sugar that makes up part of the sides of the DNA double helix.
dermal Of or relating to the skin, or to the surface layer of a plant or animal.
dermal scales Small, bony plates embedded in the skin of a fish.
dermis The thick, lower layer of skin beneath the epidermis.
desert A climatic region that is very dry, with under 250mm of rainfall per year.
destructive boundary (or **subduction zone**) Plate boundary where an oceanic plate melts partially as it moves beneath a continental plate, forming a trench.
destructive interference A decrease in amplitude that may result when two waves meet.
detergent A substance that enables water to remove dirt.
diabetes A medical condition in which the pancreas does not make enough insulin.
diagnosis The process by which a doctor tries to identify a disease by examining a patient's symptoms.
diamond An allotrope of carbon with each atom linked to four others in a tight formation, forming extremely hard, four-sided crystals.
diaphragm 1. The flat sheet of muscle under the lungs. 2. In physics, the thin disc inside a microphone or speaker that vibrates at the same frequency as the sound waves hitting it.
diatoms Types of mostly single-celled algae with hard, glassy body cases.
dichotomous key A biological key in which there are only two choices at each stage.
dicotyledon A plant, such as a pea, that has two cotyledons.
diencephalon The central part of the brain, made up of the thalamus and hypothalamus.
diesel oil A fuel obtained from the fractional distillation of crude oil.
dietary fibre (or **roughage**) A carbohydrate contained in bran, wholemeal bread, fruit and vegetables. It is indigestible by humans, but helps their digestive system to work properly.
differential A part of a car's transmission which consists of gears on the axles which allow the wheels to go at different speeds.
diffraction The bending of a wave when it meets an obstacle or passes through a gap.
diffuse reflection Reflection in which parallel incident waves bounce off an object in many directions.
diffusion The spreading out of a gas to fill the available space.
digestive glands Glands found in the digestive system, which produce digestive juices.
digestive juices Fluids produced by digestive glands which contain enzymes that break down food into simpler substances.
digestive system A system of organs that breaks down food into simpler substances.
digestive tract (or **alimentary canal**) The tube in an animal, from the mouth to the anus, through which food passes.
digit 1. In anatomy, a finger or toe. 2. In mathematics, any numeral from 0 to 9.
digital The term that describes a signal made up of separate electrical pulses, used to represent the 0s and 1s of binary code.
digital circuit An electronic circuit that uses pulses of electricity. See also *analogue circuit*.
digital electronics Electronics which uses pulses of electricity.
digital TV Television broadcasting which sends programmes as electrical signals in binary code carried on radio waves.
digitigrade An animal, such as a dog, that walks on the underside of its toes.
diode An electronic component which allows current to flow through it in one direction only.
dioecious A term describing a plant species in which individuals have either staminate or pistillate flowers.
dipole (or **molecular magnet**) A molecule in a ferromagnetic material which behaves like a tiny magnet.
direct current (DC) Electric current that flows in one direction only.
dispersal In botany, the scattering of seeds away from the parent plant.
dispersion The splitting up of light into the colours of the visible light spectrum.
displacement reaction A chemical reaction in which one of the elements in a compound is replaced by a more reactive element.
distillation A method of obtaining a pure liquid from a solution by collecting the liquid as it evaporates, then allowing it to condense.
diverging lens A lens that causes parallel rays of light passing through it to spread out.
DNA (deoxyribonucleic acid) The acid, found in cell nuclei, that forms the genes and chromosomes of all living things.
DNA profiling (or **genetic fingerprinting**) A scientific process used to compare samples of DNA. It can be used, for example, to identify a person from a sample of their blood or hair.
domain An area in a ferromagnetic material in which the dipoles all point the same way.
domain name The part of a URL that identifies a particular website, for example, *www.usborne.com*.
dominant gene The member of a pair of genes which carries an instruction that overrules that of the other (recessive) gene.
dormancy Of some animals' life cycles, a stage when they enter a sleep-like state to survive cold or drought.
dorsal fin The fin on a fish's back.
double bond A covalent bond in which a pair of atoms shares two pairs of electrons.
double helix The shape of the DNA molecule, like a twisted rope ladder.
download To copy digital information from a main source to an external device, for example, from an internet server to a computer.
drag (or **air resistance**) The force of friction that slows down objects moving in air.
driver Software that controls the actions of a computer card (see *card*).
drug Any substance that affects the way the body works.
drupe A succulent fruit, such as a plum, with a single hard-cased seed in the middle.
drupelets The fleshy beads that make up aggregate fruit. Each contains one seed.
dry cell A type of electrochemical cell which contains an electrolyte paste, not a liquid.
dry fruit Dry cases that hold seeds until they are ripe. For example, a hazelnut.
ductile The term that describes a metal which can be stretched out to make wire.
duodenum The first part of the small intestine, where digestive juices break down fats, protein and starch.
dwarf planet A round space object not large enough to have cleared its orbit
dwarf star A star smaller than the Sun.
dyke A magma-filled channel that leads from a volcano's main vent to the surface.
dynamics The study of how forces affect movement.
dynamo See *generator*.

Ear canal The passage in the ear which channels sound waves towards the eardrum.
eardrum A thin layer of tissue in the ear which vibrates in response to sound waves.
earthquake A sudden movement of rock in the Earth's crust which releases pressure and shockwaves.
earth wire A safety device in an electric cable that provides a path for the current to flow to the ground.
ecdysis The process in which an arthropod sheds an outgrown cuticle and grows a new, larger one.
echinoderms A phylum of sea creatures, such as starfish, with spiny skin, suckered feet and five-part bodies.
echo A sound wave that has reflected off a surface and is heard after the original sound.
echo location Any method of locating an object by detecting the return of sound waves bouncing off that object. See also *sonar* and *ultrasound scanning*.
eclipse The total or partial disappearance of a heavenly body when another one moves between it and the viewer.
eclipsing variable A binary star which varies in brightness as one star eclipses the other.
ecological niche The role of an animal in its community, including where it lives and what it eats.
ecological succession The different habitats and communities that replace each other in an environment as it changes.
ecology The study of the relationship between living things and their environment.
ecommerce Buying or selling over the internet.
ecosystem A community of living things together with the non-living parts of its habitat, such as air and water.
EEG See *electroencephalogram*.
effort The force needed to operate a machine.
ejaculation The squirting of semen out of the penis, caused by the contraction of muscles around the urethra.
elastic The term describing something that can be stretched out of shape or size by a force, but returns to its original form when the force is removed.
elastic limit The point beyond which an elastic substance is altered permanently by stretching.
electric charge A property of matter which causes electric forces between particles.
electric circuit The path along which an electric current flows.
electric current A flow of electrically charged particles.
electric field The area in which an electric force has an effect.
electric force The effect that electrically charged particles have on each other.
electricity The effect caused by the presence or movement of electrically charged particles.
electric motor A device that changes electrical energy into movement.
electrochemical cell (or **cell**) A device which produces electric current from chemical energy using two electrodes in an electrolyte. Several cells joined together make a battery.

electrode In electrolysis, a conductor through which a current enters or leaves an electrolyte.
electroencephalogram (EEG) A chart used by doctors to record brain wave patterns.
electrolysis A method of splitting the elements in a compound by passing an electric current through it when it is molten or in a solution.
electrolyte A molten or dissolved substance that can conduct an electric current.
electromagnet A magnet (made of a solenoid with a ferromagnetic core) which can be switched on and off by an electric current.
electromagnetic spectrum The arrangement of electromagnetic waves in order of wavelength and frequency.
electromagnetic waves Transverse waves made up of continually changing electric and magnetic fields, for example, light.
electromagnetism The effect that takes place when an electric current flows through a wire, forming a magnetic field.
electron A negatively charged particle that exists around the nucleus of an atom.
electron cloud model A way of picturing electron shells as cloud-like regions (also called orbitals) in which an electron may be found anywhere at a given time.
electron configuration The number of electrons that exist in each of the shells around the nucleus of an atom.
electronic circuit An electric circuit that contains electronic components.
electronic components Devices that control the flow of a current in an electronic circuit.
electronics The use of electronic components to control the flow of a current around a circuit, making it do particular tasks.
electron shell A region around an atom's nucleus in which a certain number of electrons can exist.
electroplating A method of covering an object with a thin layer of metal by electrolysis.
electroreception The ability of an organism to sense electricity.
electrorefining A method of purifying metals using electrolysis.
element A substance made up of one type of atom and which cannot be broken down by a chemical reaction to form simpler substances.
elevator A control surface on a plane's tail used to direct movement up and down.
elliptical galaxy A galaxy, round or oval in shape, that contains many old, red stars.
elytra The hardened front wings of beetles and some bugs, which protect the rear wings.
email (electronic mail) A way of sending messages over the internet using a computer.
embryo 1. An organism developing inside a womb, egg or seed. 2. A human baby in the first two months of growth in the womb.
emergent plants Plants which flourish in wet or water-covered ground. Their leaves and stems are mostly visible above the water.
emulsifier A substance that helps two liquids, such as oil and water, to mix by breaking up one of the liquids into tiny drops.
emulsion A colloid of tiny particles of one liquid dispersed in another.
enamel The hard, white substance which forms the surface of a tooth's crown.
endemic A term describing a plant, animal or disease which is found only in one place.
endocrine glands Hormone-making glands.
endoplasmic reticulum A series of channels which transport substances around a cell.
endoscope A special medical camera, made of a flexible tube containing a fibre-optic cable, used to look inside patients' bodies.
endoskeleton A hard, bony skeleton that supports an animal's body from the inside.
endosperm A layer of tissue in a seed that surrounds and nourishes the growing plant.
endothermic reaction A chemical reaction that takes in heat energy.
energy chain A method, often pictorial, that shows how energy changes into different forms.
engine A machine which converts into movement the energy stored in fuel.
environment The surroundings in which an organism lives.
enzyme A catalyst that speeds up a chemical reaction in living things.
ephemeral The term used to describe organisms with very short life cycles, such as some desert flowers.
epicentre The point on the Earth's surface directly above the focus of an earthquake.
epidermis 1. The thin outer layer of tissue on a young plant. 2. An outer layer of skin.
epididymis A comma-shaped organ lying over the back of each testis, which stores sperm.
epiglottis A flap which closes the trachea during swallowing, to prevent choking.
epimysium A tough, protective layer around a muscle.
epiphyte An organism which makes its own food, but grows high up on other plants to get a better share of the light and water.
epithelium Any tissue which forms a surface covering or cavity lining.
equation In chemistry, a way of showing chemical reactions using chemical formulae. The reactants are written to the left of an arrow which points to the products on the right.
Equator An imaginary circle which runs around the middle of the Earth, dividing the northern and southern hemispheres.
equatorial A climatic region which is always hot and wet, often having rainforests.
equilibrium In physics, the state of an object when the forces acting on it are balanced.
eras The four main divisions of geological time: Precambrian: 4,600-545 million years ago (mya); Paleozoic: 545-250 mya; Mesozoic: 250-55 mya; Cenozoic: 55 mya to the present.
erosion The gradual wearing down of rock by wind or water.
eruption An explosion of magma onto the Earth's surface through a volcano.
esters A homologous series produced by carboxylic acids reacting with alcohols. They give fruit and flowers their fragrances.
ethane (C_2H_6) An alkane containing two carbon atoms, produced from petroleum.
ethanoic (or **acetic**) **acid (CH_3COOH)** A carboxylic acid found in vinegar.
ethanol (C_2H_5OH) A major alcohol, produced by fermentation or by reacting ethene with steam. Used in alcoholic drinks and as a solvent in perfumes.
ethene (C_2H_4) The first compound in the alkene series. A colourless, sweet-smelling gas which forms polythene by addition reactions.
eubacteria A group of simple microscopic organisms without cell nuclei
eutrophication An overgrowth of algae in a body of water due to high levels of nitrates and other compounds found in fertilizers.
evaporation 1. The process by which the surface molecules of a liquid escape into a vapour. 2. A method of separating a solute from a solvent by heating the solution until the solvent turns to vapour.
Evening Star Another name for the planet Venus, as it appears just after sunset.
evergreen A term describing trees that do not shed their leaves all at once.
evolution See *theory of evolution*.
excretion The removal of waste substances from the body.
excretory organs Organs that deal with the removal of waste from the body.
exhalation Breathing out.
exodermis A layer of hardened cells on the root of an older plant.
exoskeleton A hard body covering which supports and protects the bodies of animals with no internal skeleton.
exosphere The outermost layer of the atmosphere, which merges into space.
exothermic reaction A chemical reaction that gives off heat energy.
exposure In photography, the amount of light that is allowed in through a camera lens.
external combustion engine An engine which produces power from fuel burning outside its main body.
external fertilization Fertilization of ova by sperm that takes place outside the female's body.
extinct A term describing a species which has died out.
eyepiece The lens on an optical instrument that refracts light from the objective lens.

Facula A cloud of glowing gases that often surrounds a sunspot.
faeces The semi-solid waste left after digestion.
Fahrenheit scale A temperature scale which places 180 degrees Fahrenheit (°F) between the ice point (at 32°F) and steam point (at 212°F).
Fallopian tubes Tubes which carry the ovum into the uterus during ovulation.
false fruit Fruit, such as strawberries, which develop from the receptacle and the ovary.
family In classical taxonomy, the largest subdivision of an order.
fascicles The bundles into which muscle fibres are grouped.
fast-twitch fibres Striated muscle fibres which contract quickly, working in short bursts.
fats A group of solid esters found in living tissue and important as a reserve energy source.
fatty acids Carboxylic acids found in natural fats and oils.
faults Cracks in the Earth caused by the movement of its plates.
feedback In electronics, the process which returns part or all of an output signal to the input.
femur The thighbone.
fermentation A chemical reaction in which sugar is broken down by enzymes to produce ethanol and carbon dioxide.
ferromagnetic The term used to describe metals that can easily be magnetized.
fertilization (or **conception**) The joining of male and female sex cells to form the first cell of a new individual.
fibre-optic cable A cable made up of many glass or plastic fibres, used to transmit light.
fibrin A substance made up of sticky threads, produced by chemical reactions in platelets, which join to form a blood clot.
fibrous roots A system of many equal-sized plant roots, all of which produce smaller roots.
fibula The outer of the two lower leg bones. See also *tibia*.
field of vision The area an animal can see.
filament In botany, part of the stamen: the stalk which supports the anther.
file path The last part of a URL (for example, */index.html)* specifying the file in which a web page is stored.
filter feeding Feeding by sieving tiny plants or animals out of water.
filtrate The liquid that passes through a filter.

filtration A method of separating solid particles from a liquid by trapping them in a material that lets only the liquid pass through.
flagellae Long, fine threads on the bodies of some microscopic animals which they lash to and fro in order to propel themselves.
flagellate An organism that has flagellae.
flatworms A phylum of worms with flat, unsegmented bodies.
flight feathers (or **remiges**) Long, stiff feathers used for flying.
flip-flop A combination of logic gates often used to store binary information.
flood plain The wide, flat floor of a river valley, that is covered with water in a flood.
florigen A growth hormone in plants that signals them to flower only when the nights reach a certain length.
fluid Any liquid or gas.
fluorescence The ability of certain substances to absorb ultraviolet radiation, or other forms of energy, and give it out as light.
fluoride Any inorganic compound of fluorine.
FM See *Frequency Modulation.*
focus 1. Any point where light rays come together, or appear to come from. 2. The point where the rock first gives way in an earthquake.
foetus An embryo after the first stages of its growth in the womb. For example, an unborn human baby after two months.
fold mountains Mountain ranges formed where plates push together above ground.
follicles Deep pits in the skin from which hairs grow.
food chain A series of living things, each one of which is eaten by the next in line.
food web A network of linked food chains.
force A push or pull on an object.
force magnifier A machine which overcomes a load greater than the effort it uses.
force ratio The load a machine needs to overcome divided by the effort used.
foreskin A loose fold of skin which protects the sensitive tip of the penis.
formic acid See *methanoic acid.*
fossil fuel A fuel, such as coal, oil and natural gas, that is formed from the fossilized remains of plants or animals.
four-colour printing The use of dots of cyan, magenta, yellow and black ink to create the effect of printing in many different colours.
four-stroke combustion cycle The four-stage process by which the pistons in a vehicle's engine take in, compress, and ignite fuel, then release the exhaust.
fraction In fractional distillation, a mixture of compounds that separates out at a certain level of a fractionating column.
fractional distillation A process by which substances are separated from a mixture by boiling using a fractionating column.
fractionating column A piece of equipment used for the distillation from a mixture of substances with different boiling points.
fragmentation A form of asexual reproduction in a few animals, where new individuals can grow from parts of another.
frequency The number of waves passing a point in one second, measured in hertz (Hz).
Frequency Modulation (FM) A type of modulation in which the frequency of the signals is altered to match the carrier wave.
friction The force that tends to slow down moving objects that are touching.
frontalis The muscle which raises the eyebrows and wrinkles the forehead.
fruiting body The part of a fungus where spores are produced.
fulcrum (or **pivot**) The fixed point around which something is turned.
function keys Keys along the top of a computer keyboard which make the computer do certain tasks, such as opening a Help menu.
fundamental frequency The lowest frequency in a note.
fungi Plant-like organisms that cannot make their own food, so feed on dead or living plants and animals.
fuse A safety device with a thin piece of wire in it that melts and cuts off an electric current if it becomes too large.
fuselage The body of a plane.

Galaxy A vast collection of stars, held together by gravitational attraction.
Galilean Moons Jupiter's four largest moons: Ganymede, Io, Callisto and Europa.
gall bladder A sac in the body which stores bile until it is needed.
galvanizing A method of protecting steel by coating it with zinc.
gametes Male or female sex cells.
gametophyte A term describing a plant in the sexual stage of alternation of generations.
gamma radiation (gamma rays) Electromagnetic waves with the shortest wavelength and highest frequency. They are given off by radioactive substances.
gas A state of matter in which a substance has no fixed shape or volume.
gaseous exchange The process by which gases pass in and out of an organism's body.
gasoline (or **petrol**) An important liquid fuel made by the fractional distillation of crude oil.
gastric juices Acidic liquids in the stomach which break down food and kill germs.
gastrocnemius The calf muscle.
gas turbine engine See *jet engine.*
gears A system of two or more cogs interlocking so that the motion of one controls the speed and turning effect of the other.
gene A segment of DNA containing a specific instruction for building part of an organism. Genes are the simplest units by which parents' physical features are inherited by their offspring.
general theory of relativity A theory, developed by Albert Einstein, which related his special theory of relativity to gravitation.
generator (or **dynamo**) A machine that converts movement energy into electricity.
generic name The first part of a biological name, showing an organism's genus.
gene therapy Treating certain genetic disorders by giving patients healthy genes.
genetic engineering (or **modification**) The extraction of genes from organisms for various uses, for example, in creating new medicines. It can also be used to change an organism by inserting the gene for a desired feature from another organism. Food produced in this way is called GM (genetically modified) food.
genetic fingerprinting See *DNA profiling.*
genetics The study of genes.
genetic screening Looking for genes in a person's DNA that could cause disease in them or their children.
genome All the DNA making up an organism.
genus The largest subdivision of a family.
geological time (or **deep time**) A scale of millions of years used by geologists to measure the Earth's development.
geology The science of the Earth's origin and structure, and its rocks and minerals.
geostationary orbit The orbit of a satellite moving at the rate the Earth spins, so that it remains fixed over the same point.
geothermal energy Heat energy from underground rocks.
geotropism The response of roots to gravity, by which they tend to grow downwards into the soil, towards minerals and water.
germination The point in a seed's growth into a seedling when its first shoot and root break out of the seed case.
gestation period The length of time a baby animal spends in the womb before birth.
giant star A star larger than the Sun.
gills (or **branchiae**) The respiratory organs of most water creatures.
gill slits Openings in the sides of water creatures, such as fish, which allow water to pass across the gills and out of the body.
gingivae The gums.
gingivitis A gum disease, causing bleeding.
ginkgo An ancient gymnosperm species with soft, fan-shaped leaves and fleshy cones.
gizzard In birds, a thick-walled pouch which contains muscular ridges and small stones for grinding up solid food.
glacier A huge sheet of ice that moves slowly over land.
glands Organs which produce substances vital to the workings of the body.
glans The sensitive tip of the penis.
gliding (or **sliding**) joints Joints which allow flat bones to slide against each other.
global warming A rise in average temperatures around the world which scientists believe to be caused by the greenhouse effect.
globular cluster A densely packed, spherical collection of up to a million stars, moving at the same speed and in the same direction.
glomerulus A ball of coiled-up capillaries in a nephron, where high pressure filters glucose, water and salts out of the blood into cup-like structures called Bowman's capsules.
glucagon A hormone which raises the level of glucose in the blood.
glucose ($C_6H_{12}O_6$) A type of sugar used by most living things to obtain energy.
glycerol See *propane-1,2,3-triol.*
glycogen A form of starch into which glucose is converted, and stored in the liver.
GM See *genetic engineering.*
GMO Genetically Modified Organism
gnetae A small group of gymnosperms with tough, leathery leaves, that grow in hot areas.
Golgi complex A specialized area of the endoplasmic reticulum which collects and distributes the substances made in a cell.
gracilis An inner thigh muscle which allows the leg to bend and twist.
grain See *caryopsis.*
graphite A soft, flaky allotrope of carbon in which each atom is linked to three others in a layered formation.
gravitational field An area in which gravity has an effect.
gravity The pulling force that attracts objects to each other.
Great Red Spot A vast storm that rages constantly in Jupiter's atmosphere.
greenhouse effect The trapping of heat by carbon dioxide, ozone and other gases in the Earth's atmosphere.
group In the periodic table, a column of elements that have similar electron configurations, properties and valencies.
growth season One year of a plant's life.
guard cells Crescent-shaped cells, arranged in pairs around stomata, that control the amount of air and water entering or leaving a leaf.
gullet See *oesophagus.*
gustatory receptor cells See *taste buds.*

guttation Water loss, in liquid form, through tiny holes in leaf tips and edges.
gymnosperms Vascular plants in which the seeds are not contained in a fruit.
gyroscope A wheel that spins very fast inside a freely moving frame, creating a centripetal force which enables it to tilt steeply without falling over.

Haber process The method of producing ammonia by combining hydrogen and nitrogen.
habitat An organism's natural home.
haemocoel A type of perivisceral cavity which contains blood, and is connected to the circulatory system.
haemoglobin A purple-red chemical in red blood cells. It combines with oxygen in the lungs to form bright red oxyhaemoglobin.
hair erector muscles Tiny muscles in the skin that make hairs stand on end.
hair plexuses Groups of motion-sensitive nerve fibre endings around hair roots.
half-life The average time taken for half the radioactive atoms in a sample to decay.
halide A type of compound that contains one or more halogens.
halite (or rock salt) The mineral form of common salt (sodium chloride).
halogen Any of the poisonous and reactive non-metallic elements that make up group VII of the periodic table.
halophytes Plants that are specially adapted to live in salty areas.
haltères The tiny back wings of flies, modified for balancing the body in flight.
haptotropism (or **thigmotropism**) The response of a plant to touch.
hard disk A set of magnetic disks in a computer that continues to store information after the computer has been switched off.
hardware The pieces that make up a computer, such as the case and keyboard.
hard water Water which contains a lot of dissolved minerals from rocks it has flowed over. Temporary hard water contains minerals that can be removed by boiling. Permanent hard water contains minerals that cannot.
harmonics (or **overtones**) Sounds of higher frequency that mix with a note's fundamental frequency to give an instrument its timbre.
haustoria Thread-like structures used by some parasitic plants to attach to a host.
Haversian canal A channel in compact bone through which blood vessels pass.
heartwood The old wood at the core of a tree that has grown too solid to transport fluid.
heavenly body Any naturally-occurring object in space.
helium (**He**) A noble gas. The second lightest and least reactive element.
hemiparasite A plant which feeds off other plants, but can also photosynthesize.
herbaceous perennials Perennials which lose their visible parts in the winter, storing food in swollen roots until the spring.
herbivore An animal that feeds on plants.
heredity The transmission of genetic traits from one generation to the next.
hermaphrodite An organism that has both male and female sex cells.
hertz (**Hz**) The unit of wave frequency.
heterotrophic A term describing organisms that depend on other living things for food.
heterozygous A term describing a gene pair in which different genes for a characteristic have been inherited.
hexapod A six-legged animal.
hibernation A stage of some animals' life cycles when they enter a sleep-like state to survive the winter cold.
high-fidelity recording A sound recording that is very similar to the original.
hilum The mark on a seed which shows where the ovule was joined to the ovary.
hinge joint A joint allowing movement in two opposite directions, such as a knee joint.
homeostasis An organism's natural regulation of its internal conditions, such as temperature and chemical balance.
homologous chromosomes Pairs of chromosomes which work together to produce the features of an organism.
homologous series A group of organic compounds with the same chemical structure and properties.
homozygous A term describing a gene pair in which identical genes for a characteristic have been inherited from both parents.
hormones Chemicals which help to control the level of substances in the body.
horsetails Vascular plants which produce spores in cones, rather than seeds.
host An organism fed upon by a parasite.
hotspot 1. In geology, an area of the Earth where there is a great deal of volcanic activity. 2. In ecology, an area containing large numbers of endemic species.
HTML (**HyperText Markup Language**) A language used to create Web pages.
http (**HyperText Transfer Protocol**) The protocol used on the World Wide Web.
humerus The bone in the upper arm.
humidity The amount of water in the air.
hurricane See *tropical cyclone.*
hybrid (or **cross**) An organism produced by cross-breeding.
hydrated A term describing a substance which has undergone hydration.
hydration The process by which water combines chemically with another substance.
hydraulic Powered by liquid pressure.
hydraulics The study of liquids in motion.
hydrocarbon An organic compound that contains only hydrogen and carbon.
hydroelectric power Power generated by turbines that are driven by falling water.
hydrofoil A type of boat with stilts attached to underwater wings called foils, which reduce water resistance.
hydrogenation An addition reaction in which unsaturated molecules are saturated by adding hydrogen atoms.
hydrogen bomb A nuclear weapon that uses the power of nuclear fusion.
hydrogen oxide (**H_2O**) The chemical name for water.
hydrometer A device used to measure the density of a liquid.
hydrophytes Plants adapted for life in water.
hydrostatic skeleton A system supporting body structure, and sometimes movement, by muscles in the body wall working against pressurized fluid in a perivisceral cavity.
hydrotropism The response of roots to water, by which they grow towards it.
hydroxyl group (**–OH**) An oxygen atom linked to a hydrogen atom by a covalent bond.
hyperlink A piece of text or picture on a Web page that links to another page when clicked on.
hyphae White thread-like structures forming the mycelium of a fungus. They absorb food from dead matter in the soil.
hyponome A funnel-shaped tube, on the bodies of animals such as octopuses, from which they shoot jets of water to propel themselves.
hypopharynx A type of tongue in some insects, used for sucking up liquids.
hypotenuse The longest side of a right-angled triangle, that is, the side opposite the right-angle.
hypothalamus A part of the diencephalon controlling homeostasis and certain hormones.

Ice ages Periods of the Earth's history when much of its surface was covered in glaciers.
ice point The temperature at which pure ice melts (273K; 0°C; 32°F).
igneous rock A type of rock formed when molten rock cools and becomes solid.
ileum The last part of the small intestine.
ilium See *pelvis.*
image A view of an object formed by reflected or refracted rays.
imago The adult form of an insect that has undergone metamorphosis.
immiscible The term that describes two or more liquids that do not mix together easily.
incident wave A wave that is travelling towards a boundary between two media.
incisors Sharp front teeth which come together for biting or scraping.
incomplete fission A form of multiple fission, found in creatures such as corals, where the new individuals stay joined to the parent.
incomplete metamorphosis The type of metamorphosis in which the young look similar to the adults.
incus The second of three tiny earbones that pass sound vibrations to the inner ear. See also *malleus; stapes.*
indicator A substance that changes colour in the presence of an acid or alkali and is used to distinguish between them.
inertia The tendency of objects to resist a change in their movement.
inferior vena cava A vein which carries blood from the lower body to the heart.
inflammable Liable to catch fire.
infrared radiation (**infrared rays**) Electromagnetic waves that are given out by anything hot.
infrasound Sound waves with a frequency below 20 hertz.
infundibulum A funnel-shaped opening at the end of a Fallopian tube.
inhalation Breathing in.
inhibitor A catalyst that slows down the rate of a chemical reaction.
inner core The solid, innermost part of the Earth, which is about 1,250km in diameter.
inner planets Mercury, Venus, Earth and Mars.
inner transition metals A sub-group of the transition metals which share similar properties, such as high reactivity.
inorganic compound A compound that does not contain the element carbon.
input In electronics, the part of a circuit that receives an incoming signal, or the incoming signal itself.
insecticides Poisons used to kill insects that harm crops.
insolubility The quality of a substance that will not dissolve in a liquid.
instantaneous speed The speed of something at any particular moment.
insulator A substance that cannot conduct electric current, or does not conduct heat well.
insulin A hormone which lowers the level of glucose in the blood.
integrated circuit (or **silicon chip**) A complete electronic circuit etched onto a tiny piece of silicon.

integumentary system The skin, nails and hair, which, together, protect the body from damage, infection and water loss.
intensity The level of brightness of the light given off by an object. The SI unit of intensity is the candela (cd).
intensive farming Farming which uses machinery, chemical fertilizers and pesticides, in order to grow as many crops as possible.
interactive TV Digital television broadcasting which allows viewers to interact with the programmes they watch, for example, to arrange their own viewing schedule.
intercostal muscles Muscles between the ribs which contract on breathing in to expand the chest cavity, and relax again on breathing out.
interference The effect that occurs when two or more waves meet. See *constructive interference; destructive interference.*
internal combustion engine An engine which produces power by burning fuel in an enclosed space inside it.
internal energy The sum of the kinetic and potential energy of the particles in a substance.
internal fertilization The fertilization of ova by sperm that takes place inside the female's body.
internal respiration The process by which animals and plants use oxygen to break down their food, producing energy and releasing carbon dioxide.
internet A vast computer network linking together computers all over the world.
Internet Service Provider (ISP) A company which provides powerful computers, called routers, to give users access to the internet, along with other services, such as email.
internode The area of a plant stem or shoot between two nodes.
invertebrate An animal without a backbone.
involuntary actions Actions that are not consciously controlled by the brain, such as digestion.
involuntary muscles Muscles, such as the heart, which act automatically.
ion An atom or group of atoms that has become charged by gaining or losing one or more electrons.
ion exchange A method used to soften hard water by exchanging its dissolved calcium and magnesium ions for sodium ions.
ionic bond A strong bond caused by the attraction between ions of opposite charge.
ionic lattice The regular structure taken by an ionic compound.
iris The coloured part of the eye. It contains muscles which control the size of the pupil.
irregular galaxy A galaxy with no definite shape or arrangement.
irrigation Making dry land suitable for agriculture by watering it.
ischium See *pelvis.*
islets of Langerhans Clusters of cells in the pancreas that produce insulin and glucagon.
isotope An atom that has a different number of neutrons and so has a different mass number from the other atoms in an element.
ISP See *Internet Service Provider.*

Jacobson's organs Two pits in the roof of a snake's mouth, used for smelling and tasting.
jejunum The middle part of the small intestine, which absorbs digested food.
jet engine (or **gas turbine engine**) A powerful internal combustion engine, containing turbines, used to propel aircraft by forcing hot gases out of their exhausts at high speed.
joint A place where bones meet.
joule (J) The SI unit of energy and work.

Keel The extension of a bird's breastbone to which the wings are attached.
keeper A piece of metal placed across the end of a magnet to help it to stay magnetic.
kelvin (K) The SI unit of temperature.
keratin A waterproof protein of which animal horns, hair, nails and feathers are mostly made.
kernel See *caryopsis.*
kerosene A mixture of liquid alkanes obtained from the fractional distillation of crude oil, widely used as aviation fuel.
key fruit See *samara.*
kidneys Excretory organs which remove waste from the blood and regulate the body's fluid levels.
kilocalorie (or **Calorie**) A unit of heat energy, equal to 1,000 calories.
kilojoule (kJ) 1,000 joules.
kinetic energy The energy an object has when it is in motion.
kinetic theory The idea that all substances are made up of moving particles which have varying amounts of energy, giving rise to the different states of matter.
kingdom The largest group into which living things are classified.
krypton (Kr) A noble gas used in fluorescent tubes.

Labia Two folds of skin which surround the openings of the vagina and the urethra.
labium An insect's lower lip.
labour The series of strong contractions of muscles in the womb that push a baby out of the vagina during childbirth.
labrum An insect's hinged upper lip.
lachrymal canals Two channels that drain tears from the eye into the nose.
lachrymal glands Glands above the eyes that produce tears to keep them moist and clean, and to fight infection.
lactic acid An acid which builds up in the muscles during anaerobic respiration, making them ache.
lacunae Tiny spaces in bone which house the osteocytes.
lamellae Dense, circular layers of bone which form the structure of compact bone.
lamina See *simple leaf.*
LAN See *local-area network.*
lanthanides (or **rare-earth metals**) A sub-group of the inner transition metals that includes lanthanum.
large intestine The thick tube that receives water and waste from the small intestine.
larva A young insect before metamorphosis.
larynx (or **voice box**) The organ of speech, found at the top of the trachea.
laser (**l**ight **a**mplification by **s**timulated **e**mission of **r**adiation) A machine that creates beams of intense, pure colour of one wavelength and frequency (a laser beam).
lateral lines Two water-filled tube-like channels in the bodies of fish, and some amphibians, which help them to detect changes of pressure in water.
lateral root (or **secondary root**) A smaller root that grows from a plant's tap root.
lateral vision The field of vision of an animal with eyes on the sides of its head.
latex A natural polymer obtained as a milky fluid from rubber trees, used to make rubber.
lava Magma that has erupted onto the Earth's surface or the ocean bed.
LCD See *liquid crystal display.*
leader stroke A giant spark that flashes out from an electrically charged cloud, seeking a point with the opposite charge on the ground.
leaflets The small leaf blades that make up compound leaves.
leaf trace An area of vascular tissue which branches off that of the stem to become the leaf's central vein.
LED See *light-emitting diode.*
legume 1. A dry fruit with seeds attached to its inner wall. It is also called a pod, for example, a pea pod. 2. A pod-bearing plant.
lens A piece of transparent substance with curved surfaces, that makes light bend in a certain way.
lenticels Tiny openings in a tree's bark which allow it to exchange oxygen and carbon dioxide.
lichen An organism made up of an alga and a fungus living in a symbiotic relationship.
life cycle The stages of an organism's life.
lift The upward force created by an aerofoil shape such as that of an aircraft's wings moving through air.
ligament A tough band of tissue that holds together two bones at a joint.
light The electromagnetic waves that make all things visible.
light-emitting diode (LED) A diode which glows when an electric current flows through it.
lightning A brilliant flash seen when static electricity in storm clouds finds a conducting path to the ground. See *leader stroke; return stroke.*
light year The distance that light travels in one year – about 9.46 million million kilometres.
lignite (or **brown coal**) The least pure form of coal, containing 60-70% carbon.
liquid crystal display (LCD) A display made with compounds called liquid crystals used, for example, in digital watches. An electric current passing through the crystals makes them line up, blocking light and so forming patterns.
lithophytes Plants which live on the surface of rocks.
lithosphere The outer layer of the Earth, made up of the crust and upper mantle.
litmus A substance extracted from lichens that is used as an indicator.
liver A large organ that produces bile, breaks down amino acids from food into urea, filters some poisons, and stores glycogen, minerals and vitamins.
liverworts Low-growing plants without true roots, stems or leaves, that grow in damp, shady places.
live wire One of two current-carrying wires in an electric cable.
load 1. The force overcome by a simple machine. 2. The mud particles and other materials carried by a river.
local-area network (LAN) A network consisting of computers that are close together, for example all in the same room.
Local Group The group of about 30 galaxies that includes the Milky Way.
locomotion The process by which animals move around.
logic gate An arrangement of transistors used to carry out calculations in digital electronic circuits.
log on To connect to the internet, or to a network server.
longitudinal wave A wave in which the particles vibrate in the same direction as the wave is travelling.
long-term memory Memory that stores information for more than a few minutes.
loudspeaker A device that changes electric current from a source such as a microphone back into sound waves.

low surface brightness galaxy A large galaxy of loosely packed stars that does not give off much light.
lubricant A substance used to reduce friction.
luminous The term that describes any object that gives off light.
lunar eclipse The total or partial disappearance from view of the Moon due to the Earth's shadow.
lungs Sac-like respiratory organs found mostly in land-living vertebrates.
lymph A liquid made of waste soaked up from tissue fluid and white blood cells.
lymphatic system A network of tubes and organs containing lymph, which helps the body to fight disease.
lymph nodes Small organs that lie in clusters along the lymphatic system which produce white blood cells and trap germs.
lymphocyte A white blood cell that destroys germs by releasing antibodies.
lysosomes Organelles containing powerful enzymes to destroy bacteria invading a cell.

Macula A gel-like patch in a saccule, containing otoliths.
magma Molten underground rock.
magma chamber An area where magma gathers beneath a volcano.
magnet A magnetic material.
magnetic The term describing a material that shows the property of magnetism.
magnetic field The area around a magnet in which the magnetic force has an effect.
magnetic flux lines Lines which show the direction and strength of the magnetic field around a magnet.
magnetic north The point on the Earth towards which a magnet's north pole points.
magnetic south The point on the Earth towards which a magnet's south pole points.
magnetism An invisible force that attracts certain metals including iron.
magnitude (mag.) The scale on which star brightness is measured.
magnoliophytes (or **angiosperms**) Flowering plants. Their seeds are contained within some kind of fruit.
malleable The term used to describe metals that can be shaped by hammering.
malleus The first of three tiny bones in the ear: it picks up sound vibrations from the eardrum. See also *incus*; *stapes*.
malpighian tubules Excretory tubes in arthropods which remove liquid waste from the haemocoel.
mammals A class of hairy, warm-blooded animals that suckle their young with milk.
mammary glands Glands in a female mammal which produce milk for the young.
mandible 1. An insect mouthpart, used for gripping or biting. 2. The jawbone.
mantle The mostly solid part of the Earth that lies between its crust and its core.
marsupials A group of mammals, such as the koala, in which the females have no placenta and suckle their young in an external pouch.
mass The amount of matter in an object.
mass extinctions Five points in Earth's ancient past when huge numbers of living things died out in a very short time.
mass number The total number of protons and neutrons in the nucleus of an atom.
mass spectrometer A device used to help identify atoms by sorting them by mass.
mating Pairing up with a member of the same species to produce young.
maxillae Insect mouthparts used to push food into the mouth.
meander A wide loop in the course of a river.
mechanical wave A wave made up of vibrating particles in a solid, liquid or gas.
median fins Fins that lie in a line down the middle of a fish's back or belly.
medical imaging Methods of seeing inside patients without cutting them open, for example, by using X-rays.
meiosis The type of cell division by which a sex cell divides into two new cells, each containing half of its chromosomes.
Meissner's corpuscles Receptors in the skin that send touch sensations to the brain.
melanin The brown pigment in skin and hair. It absorbs harmful ultraviolet rays.
melanocytes Melanin-producing skin cells.
melting point The temperature at which a substance turns from a solid into a liquid.
menopause The time of life, usually between the ages of 40 and 55, when a woman's ovaries stop releasing ova and her periods stop.
menstruation (or **period**) The shedding of an unfertilized ovum, and the blood-rich inner layer of the womb, which occurs in girls after puberty about every 28 days.
meristem An area of cells on a plant which divide to provide new growth.
mesophyll The part of a leaf made up of the palisade and spongy layers.
mesosphere A layer in the middle atmosphere containing no clouds or ozone.
Mesozoic Era See *eras*.
metabolic rate The rate at which a body converts food into energy.
metabolism The collection of processes in the body involved in producing energy, growth and waste.
metacarpals The hand bones.
metallic bonding The way the atoms of metal elements bond – clinging together in a regular lattice of metal cations with free electrons flowing between them.
metalloid An element which shares some of the properties of metals and non-metals.
metallurgy The study of metals and their extraction.
metals The largest class of elements. Metals are mostly shiny, solid at room temperature, have high melting points, conduct electricity, and form cations.
metameres The near-identical segments into which the bodies of some animals, such as worms, are divided.
metamorphic rock The type of rock formed when another rock is changed by intense heat or pressure.
metamorphosis A stage in some animals' life cycles when their bodies are totally changed, such as when a caterpillar turns into a butterfly.
metatarsals The foot bones.
meteor (or **shooting star**) A meteoroid that starts to burn up as it enters the atmosphere.
meteorite The remains of a meteor that has survived the atmosphere and landed on Earth.
meteoroid A small piece of space debris.
meteorology The science of weather and climate.
methane (CH_4) The first compound in the alkane series. It is the main compound in natural gas and an important fuel.
methanoic (or **formic**) **acid** (**HCOOH**) A carboxylic acid found in ant stings.
microclimate The climate affecting a small, local area.
micromotor A tiny electric motor.
microphone A device that changes sounds into an electric current.
microprocessor An integrated circuit, or set of circuits, acting as a computer's Central Processing Unit.
micropropagation A method of cloning a plant from cells taken from a growth area.
micropyle See *pollination*.
microwaves Radio waves with a relatively short wavelength. Used in cooking and telecommunications.
midrib The central vein of a leaf.
migration A stage in some animals' life cycles when they travel a long distance to find food or to mate.
mildews Types of simple fungi, often appearing as powdery black or white patches.
milk teeth See *deciduous teeth*.
Milky Way The galaxy in which our Solar System lies.
millibar (mb) The unit of measurement of atmospheric pressure, equal to 100 pascals.
mimicry The colouration of some animals to resemble more dangerous animals, serving to defend them against predators.
mineral acid An acid which is produced from a mineral. For example, sulphuric acid is produced from sulphur.
minerals 1. The naturally occurring compounds of which rocks are made. 2. Inorganic compounds essential to the proper working of the body.
mining The removal of minerals from the ground.
miscible The term that describes two or more liquids that mix easily.
mitochondria Rod-shaped organelles which act as a cell's powerhouses, breaking down simple substances to provide energy.
mitosis A stage of cell division in which a nucleus divides into daughter nuclei, each containing the same number of chromosomes as the original nucleus.
mixture A combination of two or more elements or compounds that are not chemically bonded together.
modem (**mo**dulator/**dem**odulator) A device which allows a computer to send or receive information along telephone lines.
modulation A process by which sound and picture signals are mixed with radio waves (the carrier waves) so they can be broadcast.
molars Broad, blunt, square teeth set at the back of the jaw. Used for crushing and grinding, especially in herbivores.
mole The SI unit of the amount of a substance.
molecular lattice A regular structure of molecules held together by weak forces. It has a low melting and boiling point.
molecule The smallest particle of an element or compound that exists on its own and keeps its properties.
molluscs A phylum of soft-bodied creatures which mostly have shells, for example, snails.
moment The turning effect of a force, measured in newton metres (Nm).
momentum A measure of an object's tendency to carry on moving, equal to its mass multiplied by its velocity.
monoclinic sulphur An allotrope of sulphur with long, thin crystals.
monocotyledon A plant, such as a grass, that has only one cotyledon.
monocyte A type of white blood cell that destroys germs by phagocytosis.
monoecious A term describing a plant which has staminate and pistillate flowers.
monomers Small molecules that are joined together to make a polymer.
moon A natural satellite orbiting a planet or asteroid.
Morning Star Another name for the planet Venus, as it appears just before sunrise.

motherboard The main circuit board in a computer.
motor neurons Neurons which pass instructions from the central nervous system to the body, where they are carried out.
motor-skill memory Memory which recalls how to do actions such as walking.
moulds Types of simple fungi which form a furry growth on living or once-living matter.
mp3 A type of data compression software used to transmit music files over the internet.
MRI (magnetic resonance imaging) scanner A camera that uses magnetism and radio waves to make pictures of sections of the body.
mucus A slippery liquid, made by the lining of the nose and trachea. It warms and moistens air breathed in, and traps dirt and germs.
multicellular A term describing a living thing which is built up of many cells.
multiple fission A form of asexual reproduction in which a simple organism splits constantly into identical halves.
muscle fibres (or **myofibres**) Long, rod-shaped cells which make up muscle tissue.
mutualists Organisms that benefit each other by living closely together.
mycelium The main, underground part of most fungi, made up of a mass of hyphae.
mycorrhizae Fungi which feed on the roots of living plants.
myofibres See *muscle fibres*.
myofibrils Thin cords which join to make up muscle fibres.
myofilaments Thick and thin threads which interlock, making up myofibrils.
myriapod A creature with many legs.

Nanotechnology A field of technology that seeks to build devices at an atomic or molecular level.
nanotube A specially engineered microscopic fibre produced from graphite.
nasal cavity The hollow space inside the nose.
natural selection See *theory of natural selection*.
neap tides The lowest low tides, which occur at every half moon, when the Sun and Moon are at right angles to each other.
nebula A huge cloud of dust and gas where stars form.
nectar A sweet, sticky substance produced by plants to attract pollinating insects.
nectary An area of cells at the base of a petal which produces nectar.
negative film (or **reversal film**) Photographic film on which light parts of the picture appear dark and dark parts appear light.
nematocyst A poisonous thread, coiled inside a cnidoblast, which shoots out to paralyse prey.
nematodes A phylum of long, thin, round worms with unsegmented bodies.
neon (Ne) A noble gas used in electric lights.
nephridiopores Tiny holes at the end of protonephridia through which waste is ejected.
nephrons Tiny filtration units in a kidney.
nerve fibres Strands which make up the cell body of a neuron.
nerve impulses Pieces of information that pass through neurons electrical signals.
nerves Cords containing bundles of nerve fibres. Sensory nerves contain sensory nerve fibres, motor nerves contain motor nerve fibres, and mixed nerves contain both.
nervous system The nerves, brain and spinal cord.
network A group of computers connected together so that they can share information.
neurons Nerve cells.
neurotransmitter A chemical released when a nerve impulse reaches a synapse. If enough neurotransmitter builds up, the impulse crosses the synapse to the next neuron.
neutralization A reaction where one substance fully or partly cancels out the properties of another, for example, when an acid and a base react to produce a salt and water.
neutral wire One of two current-carrying wires in an electric cable.
neutron A subatomic particle with no electrical charge in the nucleus of an atom.
neutron star A small, spinning, exceptionally dense star that is left after a supernova.
newton (N) The SI unit of force.
newton metre (Nm) The unit of moment.
nitrates A group of salts produced from nitric acid. Nitrates occur naturally and are essential to plant growth.
nitrogen (N_2) A gas that makes up over 78% of the air. It is important to living things.
nitrogen cycle The natural process in which nitrogen is converted into nitrates in the soil, used by plants, and returned again to the air.
nitrogen-fixing bacteria Bacteria which convert ammonia in the soil into nitrates.
noble gas Any of six highly unreactive gases present in the atmosphere which together form group VIII of the periodic table. For example, argon and neon.
noble metal A metal, such as gold, that can be found naturally in a pure state.
nocturnal A term describing animals which are mostly active at night.
node The place on a plant stem where a leaf has grown.
nonchromatic colours Colours such as brown and magenta that are not in the visible light spectrum.
non-metal A class of element that forms anions. They are usually non-shiny solids or gases, with low melting and boiling points.
non-renewable fuels Fuels, such as coal and oil, which can be used only once.
northern hemisphere The half of the Earth's globe lying north of the equator.
north or **north-seeking pole** The part of a magnet that points north.
note A musical sound of a specific pitch.
NOT gate A logic gate from which the output is always the reverse of the input.
notochord See *chordates*.
nova A type of cataclysmic variable star which flares suddenly for a number of days or years, then fades back to its original brightness.
NREM (non-rapid eye movement) sleep Sleep in which the eyes remain still.
nuclear fission The splitting open of an atom's nucleus to form two or more new nuclei, releasing large amounts of energy.
nuclear fusion The joining of two small nuclei to form a larger one, releasing large amounts of energy.
nuclear membrane The double-layered outer skin of a cell's nucleus.
nuclear pores Holes in the nuclear membrane which allow substances to pass between the cytoplasm and nucleus.
nuclear reactor The part of a nuclear power station, or nuclear-powered vessel, in which controlled nuclear fission reactions occur.
nuclear weapons Bombs that cause devastating explosions by releasing the energy of uncontrolled nuclear reactions.
nucleolus An organelle in a cell's nucleus which produces the ingredients of ribosomes.
nucleotide The chemical unit of which DNA is built, itself made up of deoxyribose, a base and a phosphate group.
nucleus 1. The core section of an atom that contains protons and (except hydrogen) neutrons. 2. The part in a cell that controls all of its processes. 3. The main body of a comet, made up of frozen gases, ice, rock and grit.
nutrients Substances vital to energy or growth – carbohydrates, fats and proteins.

Objective lens A lens that refracts light from an object to form a larger, upside-down image.
observatory A building which houses a large telescope for studying stars.
odorant molecules Airborne chemicals absorbed by olfactory hairs in the nose, and interpreted by the brain as smells.
oesophagus (or **gullet**) The tube which carries food from the throat to the stomach.
ohm (Ω) The unit of electrical resistance.
oils A group of liquid esters made mostly of unsaturated carboxylic acids. They are insoluble in water and often flammable.
olfactory cells Chemoreceptors in the nose that send information about chemicals to the brain. The brain then interprets it as smell.
olfactory hairs Tiny hairs that dangle from the roof of the nasal cavity. They are dendrites of the olfactory cells.
omnivore An animal that eats both plants and meat.
online Connected to the internet.
opaque The term that describes an object through which light cannot pass.
open cast mining Mining in which minerals are extracted from near the Earth's surface, without digging tunnels or shafts.
open cluster A collection of between a few dozen and a thousand loosely scattered stars, moving in the same direction at the same speed.
operating system The software that controls how a computer works.
operculum A flap which covers the gills in bony fish.
optical instrument A device that uses combinations of lenses and mirrors to produce a particular type of image.
optical microscope An instrument that uses lenses to make small objects look bigger.
optical telescope An instrument that uses lenses and mirrors to make distant objects look closer.
optic nerve The nerve which sends impulses from the eye to the brain.
optics The science of light and vision.
orbit 1. To circle around an object. 2. The path in which one heavenly body moves around another. 3. The eye socket in the skull.
orbital See *electron cloud model*.
order The largest subdivision of a class.
ore A mineral from which useful substances, such as metals, can be extracted.
organ A part of the body with a special function, made of different types of tissue joined together. For example, the brain.
organelle Any of the small parts inside a plant or animal cell. Different types of organelle have different functions.
organic acid An acidic organic compound.
organic compound A compound that contains the element carbon.
organic farming Farming which tries to work with nature, by not using artificial fertilizers, weedkillers or pesticides.

organism Any living thing.
organ of Corti A membrane that runs inside the cochlea, containing hair cells which turn sound vibrations into nerve impulses. These are sent along the auditory nerve to the brain, enabling hearing.
OR gate A logic gate which gives an output of 1 if either of its inputs are 1.
oscillate To move back and forth regularly.
Oscillating Universe theory The idea that the universe expands and shrinks, in a repeating cycle of Big Bangs and Big Crunches.
osmosis The movement of molecules of a solvent through a semipermeable membrane, lowering the concentration of a solute on the other side of the membrane until the concentration on both sides is evened out.
ossification The process by which young cartilage skeletons turn into hard bone.
osteocytes Living bone cells.
osteopathy A medical treatment involving manipulation of the bones.
otoliths Tiny grains that move around in a macula, touching sensitive hairs. These send information to the brain about the position of the head.
outer core The molten outer layer of the Earth's core, which is about 2,200km thick.
outer planets Jupiter, Saturn, Uranus, Neptune and Pluto.
outgassing The process by which gases poured out of volcanoes, forming the Earth's early atmosphere.
output In electronics, the part of a circuit that gives out a signal, or the outgoing signal itself.
oval window An oval hole in the skull, covered with thin tissue, which passes sound vibrations from the stapes to the cochlea.
ovary A female reproductive organ which produces ova in animals, or ovules in a plant.
overfishing Fishing so much that the fish cannot produce enough young to replace those that have been caught.
oviparous Egg-laying.
ovulation The release of a mature ovum into a Fallopian tube.
ovules The female sex cells of a plant, which develop into seeds after fertilization.
ovum The female sex cell of an animal.
oxidation A chemical reaction in which a substance combines with oxygen, or loses hydrogen or electrons.
oxide A compound of oxygen and another element.
oxidizing agent A substance that provides oxygen or receives electrons or hydrogen in a redox reaction.
oxygen (O_2) A gas present in the Earth's atmosphere which is vital for aerobic respiration in plants and animals, and combustion.
oxyhaemoglobin A bright red chemical formed when haemoglobin in red blood cells combines with oxygen. As oxygen is released to the body, the oxyhaemoglobin turns back to haemoglobin.
ozone (O_3) A poisonous allotrope of oxygen. It forms the protective ozone layer, in the upper atmosphere, which absorbs harmful ultraviolet radiation from the Sun.

Pacinian corpuscles Pressure receptors sensitive to deep pressure in the skin.
paired fins Pairs of fins that stick out of the sides of a fish's body.
Paleozoic Era See *eras*.
palisade cells Column-shaped cells, containing many chloroplasts. They form the palisade layer on a leaf's upper side, beneath the epidermis.
palmate leaf A compound leaf with five or more leaflets growing from a single point.
palps Insect mouthparts used to taste food.
pancreas An organ which produces pancreatic juice and other important substances, such as insulin.
Pangaea A single giant landmass that began to split up about 225 million years ago, leading to the formation of the continents.
papillae Tiny bumps on the tongue, many of which contain taste buds.
parallel circuit An electric circuit with more than one path through which a current can flow.
parapodia Pairs of jointless projections on the sides of animals such as bristleworms which they flex to swim around.
parasite An organism which lives and feeds upon another, usually damaging, and never benefiting it.
parenchyma A type of plant tissue with large cells and many air spaces, found in cortex.
parthenogenesis Reproduction without fertilization by a male.
particle accelerator A machine which accelerates charged subatomic particles to a great speed, in order that new particles produced by their collisions may be studied.
pascal (**Pa**) The SI unit of pressure, equal to a force of one newton per square metre.
passive immunity A temporary resistance to a disease, gained by receiving antibodies against it after one has been infected.
pasteurization A process of preserving food, especially milk, by killing bacteria with heat.
patella The knee cap.
pathogen A microscopic organism, such as a virus or bacterium, that causes disease.
PCB See *printed circuit board*.
peak A point where a wave causes the greatest positive displacement of a medium, shown as a high point on a wave diagram.
pectoral fins Paired shoulder fins that project from just behind a fish's gills.
pectoralis muscles The breast muscles. Highly developed in birds for use in flight.
peer-to-peer network A type of network where no one computer is in control.
pellet A compact ball of indigestible parts, such as bones, regurgitated by birds that swallow their prey whole, for example, owls.
pelvic fins Paired fins that project from a fish's pelvic region.
pelvis (or **pelvic girdle** or **hip girdle**) The basin-like structure supporting the hip region. It is formed mainly by the two large hip bones, each of which is made up of three smaller bones: the ilium, pubis and ischium.
penicillin An important antibiotic made from a species of mould.
penis The organ with which a male passes sperm directly into a female's body. It also releases urine.
penumbra A pale shadow formed where an area is lit by only part of a light source.
perennials Plants that live for many years.
perfect sound reproduction A sound recording that always sounds the same as when it was first made.
perfoliate leaves Single or paired leaves with their bases fused to a plant's stem.
perimysium A protective layer around a fascicle in a muscle.
period 1. In chemistry, a set of elements sharing the same number of electron shells, shown as rows in the periodic table. 2. Subdivisions of geological Eras, each measuring several million years. 3. See *menstruation*.
periodic table A systematic arrangement of the elements in order of increasing atomic number.
periodontal ligament A bundle of tough fibres joining a tooth's roots to the jawbone.
periosteum A thin layer of tissue covering the bones that contains cells for growth and repair.
peripheral nervous system The network of nerves which carries information to and from the central nervous system.
peripherals Pieces of computer hardware, such as a keyboard or mouse, that sit outside the case containing the computer's main circuits.
peristalsis The contractions of muscles in the walls of the digestive tract which push food through it.
peritoneum A thin membrane which lines the body wall surrounding a coelom.
perivisceral cavity A fluid-filled body cavity cushioning the internal organs in most animals.
permanent magnet A magnet made from a hard ferromagnetic material such as steel that keeps its magnetic properties well.
permanent teeth The second, adult set of teeth, which does not regrow if lost.
permeable A term describing things which have holes or pores that let in water.
persistent vision The illusion of seeing movement when watching a quickly-changing series of still images, for example a movie.
petiole A leaf stalk.
petrol See *gasoline*.
pH The strength of an acid or base expressed as a number on a scale from 0 (strongly acidic) to 14 (strongly alkaline).
phagocytosis The process by which a unicellular organism digests food by changing its body shape to engulf it. Some white blood cells also act in this way to destroy germs.
phalanges The finger and toe bones.
pharming The genetic modification of organisms to produce chemicals useful in medicine.
phases The different shapes made by the sunlit portion of the Moon's near side as it orbits the Earth. For example, a crescent.
phellogen (or **cork cambium**) A single layer of cells on the outside of a tree which constantly divide, building up the bark.
pheromone A chemical released by an animal which sends a message to others, for example, to attract a mate.
phloem The food-carrying tissue in vascular plants.
phosphate groups Compounds of linked phosphorus, oxygen and hydrogen atoms essential to the body's energy processes.
phosphates A group of phosphorus salts containing oxygen and other elements.
phosphor A chemical that glows when it absorbs energy.
phosphorescence A fluorescence that continues after the source of energy producing it has stopped.
phosphoric acid (H_3PO_4) An acid made from phosphorus. Used in making fizzy drinks.
photochemical reaction A chemical reaction that gives off or takes in light energy.
photoelectric cell A device that turns light energy into electricity.
photon See *quantum theory*.

photoperiodism A plant response by which it will only grow if light is available for a certain length of time (the photoperiod).
photoreceptors Light-sensitive cells.
photosphere The surface of the Sun, made up of churning gases.
photosynthesis The process by which plants use energy from sunlight to make food from water and carbon dioxide.
phototropism The response of a plant in which it turns to face the light.
phylum The largest subdivision of a kingdom.
physiology The study of the life processes of plants and animals.
phytoplankton Microscopic plants that drift on the surface of seas and oceans.
piezoelectric effect The regular vibration produced by applying a voltage between the faces of a crystal such as quartz. It is used to measure time.
pigment A substance that absorbs some colours of light and reflects others, so making an object appear coloured.
pinnae 1. In animals, the outer part of the ears. 2. In plants, leaflets arranged along a stalk in opposite pairs.
pinnate leaf A leaf in which the leaflets are arranged in opposite pairs along the stalk.
pioneer community The first community in the process of ecological succession. It is made up of grasses which become the habitat for insects and small mammals.
pistil See *carpel*.
pistillate flower A flower which has only female reproductive parts.
piston A cylindrical part that moves up and down inside an engine's cylinder.
pitch 1. The highness or lowness of a musical note or other sound. 2. Of a plane, to move up or down.
pit organ An organ on a snake's head which allows it to detect its prey's body heat from a distance.
pivot joint A joint in which the rounded end of one bone twists around in a hole in another.
pixel Short for "picture element". A tiny dot or square that forms part of a picture on a TV screen or monitor.
placebo A treatment that contains no medicine
placenta An organ in the womb that provides an unborn mammal with food and oxygen from its mother during gestation.
placoid scales (or **denticles**) Sharp, backward-pointing scales which stick out of the skin of fish such as sharks.
plantigrade An animal, such as a bear, that walks on the underside of its whole foot.
plaque A thin, sticky white film that builds up on teeth, formed by bacteria.
plasma A pale yellow liquid which makes up over half the content of blood.
plasmolysis A shrinking of cell vacuoles away from the cytoplasm due to water loss.
plastic The term used to describe a substance which does not return to its original shape after stretching, and can hold a new shape. See also *thermoplastics*; *thermosetting plastics*.
plastics Easily-moulded synthetic polymers made from the organic compounds obtained from crude oil.
plate boundaries The areas where the edges of the Earth's plates meet.
platelets Cell fragments in the blood, with no nuclei, which gather together at an injured area to cause clotting.
plates Sections of the Earth's lithosphere, which move about on the asthenosphere.
plate tectonics The study of the movement of the Earth's plates, and its effects.
playback head The part of a cassette recorder that translates information stored on magnetized tape so it can be reproduced as sound.
plumule The part of a plant embryo which develops into the first shoot.
pneumatic Powered by the pressure of a gas, usually air.
polarized light Light in which the vibrations of electric and magnetic fields each only occur in one direction.
polar region A harsh climatic region with an extremely low temperature and little precipitation or plant life.
pole 1. The end of an axis, especially of the Earth. 2. An electrical terminal or electrode. 3. Either of the two points on a magnet where the force of attraction or repulsion is strongest.
pollen A plant's male reproductive cells.
pollination The process by which plants are fertilized. A pollen grain lands on the stigma and forms a pollen tube. This grows down into the ovary, entering the ovule through a tiny hole called a micropyle.
polymer A substance with long-chain molecules, each made up of many small molecules called monomers.
polymerization The process of joining monomers to make polymers.
polythene (or **polyethene**) A versatile plastic built up from ethene monomers.
polyvinyl chloride See **PVC**.
pome A false fruit, such as an apple, with a thick, fleshy outer layer and a core with seeds contained in a capsule.
poor metals A group of nine metals, including aluminium and lead. They are mostly quite soft, and are usually combined with other substances to make alloys.
population The total number of organisms of the same species living in a particular place.
pores Holes in the skin through which sweat escapes, cooling the body.
positive film (also **transparency** or **slide film**) Photographic film that shows images in the correct colours.
potential difference (or **voltage**) The work needed to push a certain amount of electric charge between two points on a conducting pathway. It is measured in volts (V).
potential energy The energy an object has because of its position in a force field such as a gravitational field.
power The rate that work is done or energy is used, measured in watts (W).
power station A site where electricity is generated on a large scale.
Precambrian Era See *eras*.
precipitate An insoluble solid that separates from a solution during a chemical reaction.
precipitation 1. Rain, sleet, snow or hail. 2. In chemistry, the formation of a precipitate.
prehensile A term describing part of an animal which is specially adapted for grasping.
premolars (or **bicuspids**) Blunt, square teeth between the canines and the molars, used for crushing and grinding.
pressure The force exerted over a given area by a solid, liquid or gas.
pressurized water reactor A nuclear reactor which uses nuclear energy to boil water. This makes steam that drives turbines.
primary cell Any electrochemical cell which has a limited life because the chemicals inside it are used up.
primary colours Colours from which all others can be made. The primary colours of light are red, green and blue. Those of pigments are magenta, yellow and cyan.
primary (or **first order**) **consumer** An organism that feeds on the producers (plants) in a food chain.
primary phloem The first food-carrying tissue formed by a new plant.
primary sexual features The male and female reproductive organs.
primary tissue The first tissue formed by a new plant.
primary xylem The first water-carrying tissue formed by a new plant.
printed circuit board (**PCB**) A plastic board imprinted with metal tracks used in electronics.
prism A transparent solid with two flat surfaces at an angle to each other.
proboscis A long feeding tube, in insects such as butterflies, formed from fused maxillae.
producers Organisms at the lowest trophic level of a food chain, that is, plants, which provide energy for all those above them.
product A new substance produced by a chemical reaction.
program A set of coded instructions telling a computer to carry out a certain task.
prominence A huge loop of flaming gas that leaps off the Sun's surface.
propane (C_3H_8) An alkane gas fuel with three carbon atoms in its molecules.
propane-1,2,3-triol (or **glycerol**) An alcohol which reacts with fatty acids to produce fats and oils.
prop root A type of aerial root which grows outwards from the stem then down into the ground, often found on plants that grow in ground that is under water.
prostate gland A gland surrounding the top of the male urethra which makes some of the fluid in semen.
protective adaptations Features, produced by natural selection, which help to protect creatures from danger.
proteins Natural polymers made up of amino acids. They are produced in cells and are essential to animal growth and tissue repair.
prothalli Flat, often heart-shaped gametophytes which grow from fern spores.
protista Single-celled organisms which share features with plants and animals.
protocol In computing, the format in which messages are sent between computers.
protocol name The first part of a URL, which tells the computer which protocol to use. See, for example, *HTTP*.
proton A positively charged subatomic particle in the nucleus of an atom.
protonephridia Waste-collecting tubes found in animals such as simple worms.
protoplasm The matter of which cells are made, consisting of the cell membrane, nucleus and cytoplasm.
pseudopodia Extensions formed temporarily in the bodies of single-celled animals to enable locomotion or feeding.
puberty (or **adolescence**) The stage of development, between the ages of about 8 and 18, when a child changes into an adult.
pubis See *pelvis*.
pulley A machine that lifts heavy loads with a system of ropes passing around grooved wheels.
pulmonary arteries Arteries which carry blood from the heart to the lungs.
pulmonary veins Veins which carry blood from the lungs to the heart.
pulp cavity The soft, central area of a tooth.

pulsar A neutron star that sends out beams of radiation which swing around as it spins.
pulsating variable A variable star that changes in brilliance as it changes in size and temperature.
pupa An insect during metamorphosis, when it is protected by a hard case.
pupil An opening in the centre of the eye which allows light to enter.
PVC (**polyvinyl chloride**) A hard-wearing plastic built up from chloroethene monomers (ethene monomers in which a hydrogen atom has been replaced with a chlorine atom).

Quadriceps A term often used to name the muscle at the front of the thigh, which straightens the leg.
quadruped An animal that walks on four feet, for example, a hippopotamus.
quantum theory The idea that energy comes in tiny "packets" called quanta, which helps to explain the properties of electrons in atoms and the relationship of energy to matter. Quanta of electromagnetic radiation, such as light, are called photons.
quarks Particles which scientists believe to make up protons and neutrons.
quartz The most common mineral in the Earth's crust, made of silica.
quills Long, protective prickles on the bodies of animals such as porcupines.

Radar (**radio detection** and **ranging**) The use of microwaves to find the position of distant objects.
radial muscles Muscles in the iris which contract in dim light to dilate (expand) the pupil, allowing more light to enter the eye.
radial symmetry A term describing the structure of an animal that can be divided into identical halves by two or more lines of symmetry radiating from a central point.
radiation Electromagnetic energy that travels in waves, or the energy given off by radioactive substances.
radiative zone The part of the Sun that surrounds its core.
radicle The part of a plant embryo which develops into the plant's first root.
radioactive decay The process by which a nucleus ejects particles through radiation, becoming the nucleus of a series of different elements, until stability is reached.
radioactive tracing A medical technique used to follow a substance through a patient's body by adding radioactive elements to it.
radioactivity The release of radiation from the nuclei of unstable atoms.
radioisotope A radioactive isotope.
radio telescope A telescope which detects distant stars by collecting their radio signals.
radiotherapy A medical technique which uses controlled doses of radiation to kill cancer cells.
radio waves Electromagnetic waves with the longest wavelength and the lowest frequency, including microwaves and those used for standard TV and radio broadcasting.
radius In anatomy, the shorter and wider of the two bones in the forearm. See also *ulna*.
radon (**Rn**) A radioactive noble gas.
radula A mollusc's rough tongue, used for scraping plant matter into the mouth.
RAM (**Random Access Memory**) A computer's memory, made up of integrated circuits.
rays 1. Straight arrows used in a diagram to show the direction in which light waves are travelling. 2. In a fish's fin, supportive rods of bone or cartilage arranged in a fan shape.
reactants The substances present at the beginning of a chemical reaction.
reactivity The tendency of a substance to react with other substances.
reactivity series A list of metals arranged in order of how easily they react with other substances.
receptacle The extended stalk tip from which a bud grows.
receptors Sensitive cells which send information about an animal's surroundings to its brain.
recessive gene The member of a pair of genes which gives an instruction that is overruled by the other (dominant) gene.
recording head The part of a cassette recorder that records sounds onto the tape.
rectum The final part of the large intestine, where the semi-solid waste matter (faeces) collects until it is released through the anus.
rectus abdominis The stomach muscles.
recycling Making materials, such as metals, reusable by treating them in various ways.
red blood cells Disc-shaped cells in the blood, containing haemoglobin, which deliver oxygen around the body.
redox reaction A chemical reaction in which both reduction and oxidation take place.
red phosphorus A dark red, powdery allotrope of phosphorus, used to make matches.
Red Planet A nickname of the planet Mars.
reducing agent A substance that takes oxygen from another substance during a redox reaction, or loses electrons or hydrogen.
reduction A chemical reaction in which a substance loses oxygen, or gains hydrogen or electrons.
reflection The change in direction of a wave due to its bouncing off a boundary between one medium and another.
reflector telescope A telescope that uses a mirror to collect light.
reflex action A type of involuntary action, usually a sudden movement, such as moving the hand away from something hot.
reflex arc The route taken by a nerve impulse in a reflex action.
refraction The change in direction of a wave due to its moving into a medium in which its speed is different.
refractor telescope A telescope that uses a lens to collect light.
regeneration The ability to regrow parts of the body which have been broken off.
regular reflection Reflection in which parallel incident waves have parallel reflected waves.
relative atomic mass The average mass number of the atoms in a sample of an element.
relative density The density of a substance in relation to the density of water.
relative velocity The velocity a moving object appears to have when viewed from another moving object.
relativity See *general theory of relativity* and *special theory of relativity*.
REM (**rapid eye movement**) sleep The type of sleep where the eyes move around.
remiges See *flight feathers*.
renal arteries Arteries carrying blood into the kidneys.
renal pelvis A cavity in the kidney where urine collects before it flows into the ureter.
renal veins Veins carrying filtered blood from the kidneys back to the body.
renewable energy resources Sources of energy, such as the Sun, wind or water, that can be used to generate power without themselves being used up.
reproduction The ability of living things to produce more of their own kind.
reproductive system The parts of an organism's body involved in reproduction.
repulsion The act of pushing an object away from something without the objects touching.
residue The solid particles that remain behind after filtration or evaporation.
resistance The ability of a substance to reduce the flow of electric current.
resistor An electronic component which reduces the flow of current.
resolution The degree of detail in an image.
resonate To vibrate at the same frequency as something else.
respiration (or **external respiration**, or **breathing**) The process of taking in oxygen and giving out carbon dioxide. See also *internal respiration*.
respiratory organs Organs concerned with breathing, for example, lungs or gills.
resultant force The total effect of all the forces acting on an object.
retina The light-sensitive layer at the back of the eye which sends nerve impulses to the brain.
return stroke The powerful lightning stroke from the ground to a cloud, following a leader stroke.
reversible reaction A reaction in which the products can, under the right conditions, react to form the original reactants.
rheostat See *variable resistor*.
rhizoids Short, hair-like organs that serve as roots in simple plants, such as liverworts.
rhizomes Thick stems which grow out horizontally underground, producing new buds and roots.
rhombic sulphur The commonest allotrope of sulphur, with closely fitting molecules.
ribosomes Tiny round organelles that help to produce proteins in a cell.
ridge A new, mountainous area of the Earth's crust, formed when plates move apart beneath the ocean.
rift valley The type of valley formed when the area of rock between two faults collapses as plates move apart.
Ringed Planet A nickname of the planet Saturn.
rock salt (or **halite**) The mineral form of common salt (sodium chloride).
rods Rod-shaped cells in the retina, which are sensitive to light, but not to colour.
root The part of a plant that grows into the ground, where it absorbs water and minerals and anchors the plant.
root canal The channel in the root of a tooth through which blood vessels and nerves enter the pulp cavity.
root cap A layer of cells that protects a plant's root as it is pushed into the ground.
root hair One of many tiny threads on a root through which water and minerals are absorbed.
root pressure The water pressure in a plant's roots, caused by osmosis and capillary action, which pushes water into the transpiration stream.
rosette (or **whorl**) A leaf arrangement in which a circle of leaves grows from one point.
router See *Internet Service Provider*.
rudder A control surface at the rear of ships and planes which directs turning to the left and right.
rugae Folds in the lining of some organs, such as the stomach, which flatten as the organ fills.
ruminant A mammal, such as a cow or camel, which has even-toed hooves, four digestive chambers, and chews the cud (regurgitated semi-digested food).

runners (or **stolons**) Long side shoots used for vegetative reproduction by plants such as strawberries.
rust A layer of oxide that forms on the surface of iron, or an iron alloy, leading to corrosion.

Saccule A sac in the inner ear between the utricle and the cochlea, housing a macula.
sacrificial metal A metal used to coat a less reactive metal, protecting it by corroding first.
saline Containing salt (sodium chloride).
saliva Spittle, which is produced by salivary glands in the mouth. It makes food easier to swallow, and contains enzymes which start to break it down.
salt 1. A compound of a metal and non-metal, produced when an acid reacts with a base. 2. The common name for sodium chloride (NaCl).
samara (or **key fruit**) An achene with papery wings, such as a sycamore fruit.
sampling In digital recording, the measuring of an electric current, representing an analogue sound wave, at different points, in order to build up a digital representation of the wave.
saprophyte See *saprotroph*.
saprotroph (or **saprophyte**) An organism which does not make its own food, but lives off dead plant or animal matter.
sapwood The soft outer area of a tree in which vessels transport fluid.
sartorius The long thigh muscle which allows the leg to bend.
satellite 1. Any object orbiting a star, planet or asteroid. 2. A man-made device orbiting the Earth used to gather scientific data or receive and transmit radio signals.
saturated compound An organic compound with atoms joined by single covalent bonds.
saturated solution A solution in which no more solute will dissolve.
scalar quantity A quantity that has magnitude but no direction.
scapula The shoulder blade.
sclera The tough, white coating of the eye.
sclerites The sections of an arthropod's cuticle, which are connected by flexible membranes.
scrotum The sac of skin hanging outside the body which protects the testes.
scuta Hard protective plates covering the bodies of some animals, such as armadillos.
search engine A computer program which searches for Web pages containing a particular word or group of words.
sebaceous glands Glands in the skin producing an oil (called sebum) that keeps it waterproof and supple.
secondary bronchi Smaller branches into which the bronchi divide inside the lungs.
secondary cell (or **accumulator**) An electrochemical cell or battery that can be recharged.
secondary colour A colour made by mixing two primary colours.
secondary sexual features Features different in males and females, but not essential to reproduction, such as facial hair.
secondary thickening The process by which long-living plants, such as trees, grow new tissue to support their original tissue.
sedimentary rock The type of rock formed when mineral particles are deposited, buried and squashed into layers.
seed leaf See *cotyledon*.
seismic waves Underground shockwaves that travel outwards from the focus of an earthquake.
seismologist A scientist who studies earthquakes.
selective breeding The controlled breeding of organisms to produce individuals with desired features, such as hardiness.
self-pollination A type of pollination in which a plant pollinates itself.
semen The mixture of sperm and fluids from the seminal vesicles and prostate gland which leaves the penis during ejaculation.
semicircular canals Three loops in the inner ear, positioned on the three different planes of movement. They contain semicircular ducts, and are involved in maintaining balance.
semicircular ducts Channels inside the semicircular canals, containing ampullae.
semiconductor A type of material that acts as a conductor or as an insulator depending on its temperature.
semi-metal An element which shares some of the properties of metals and non-metals.
seminal vesicles Two organs beneath the bladder that produce some of the fluid in semen.
semipermeable A term describing things which have holes or pores that allow some substances through, but not others.
senescence The process of ageing.
sensation A creature's awareness of its surroundings or internal state, as interpreted by the brain. For example, vision or pain.
senses The abilities of an organism which allow it to take in, and respond to, information from its surroundings. For example, sight.
sensory neurons Neurons ending in sensitive receptors. They carry information about stimuli from receptors to the central nervous system.
sepals Leaf-like structures that protect buds.
septum A wall of muscle tissue separating one metamere from the next.
series circuit An electric circuit in which the current passes through the components one after another.
serrate A term describing a leaf edge with tiny jagged teeth.
server See *client/server network*.
setae Bristles found on the bodies of many invertebrates, used to sense air movement.
sewage Water containing bodily waste.
sewage works A site where sewage is filtered to remove rubbish and treated with certain bacteria to break it down into harmless substances.
sex chromosomes The chromosomes, called X and Y chromosomes, which determine a child's gender. A girl has two X chromosomes; a boy has an X and a Y.
sex-linked genes Recessive genes found only on the X chromosome.
sexual intercourse (or **sex**) The joining of sexual organs, in which the stiffened penis fits into the vagina, squirting semen inside.
sexual reproduction Reproduction which involves joining male and female sex cells.
shell A region around an atom's nucleus in which a certain number of electrons can exist.
shoot A new stem which grows out of a seed or off the main stem of a plant.
shooting star See *meteor*.
short-term memory Memory that stores information for only a few minutes.
shutter A flap on a camera that controls the length of time light falls on the film.
sieve plates Tiny perforated cells that form the ends of the walls between sieve tubes.
sieve tube Fluid-carrying cells in phloem.
sign stimulus A visual display that triggers a set response from another creature, for example, when a robin displays its red breast to show aggression.
silica Silicon dioxide (SiO_2).
silicates A group of minerals containing elements combined with silica.
silicon chip (or **chip**) A small piece of silicon with an integrated circuit etched onto it.
simple leaf A leaf made up of a single blade, called a lamina, for example, a maple leaf.
single bond A covalent bond in which a pair of atoms shares one pair of electrons.
single cell See *electrochemical cell*.
siphon A tube that carries gases to or from the gills in many simple water creatures. An inhalant siphon carries gases to the gills; an exhalant siphon carries them away.
SI units An internationally agreed system of standard units used for scientific measurement.
skeletal muscles Voluntary muscles mostly connected to the skeleton by tendons.
skeleton The part of an animal, especially the framework of bones, or hard body covering, that supports an animal's body and protects its internal organs. See also *endoskeleton*; *exoskeleton*; *hydrostatic skeleton*.
slag Impurities present in iron ore, left over as waste after smelting.
Slowing Down theory The idea that the universe could expand continuously and gradually fade away.
slow-twitch fibres Striated muscle fibres which contract slowly, and can work for a long time without tiring.
small intestine The main section of the digestive system: a three-part coiled tube, made up of the duodenum, jejunum and ileum.
smelting The process of extracting a metal from its ore by heating to high temperatures, and reducing the ore.
smog A layer of pollution made up of smoke, fog and sulphur dioxide.
smooth muscle tissue A type of muscle tissue, made up of spindle-shaped fibres, which forms the visceral muscles.
sodium chloride (NaCl) The chemical name for common salt.
software The programs used by a computer, such as its operating system or the games one might play on it.
soil erosion The wearing away of topsoil by wind or rain.
solar cell In physics, a cell that converts the Sun's energy into electricity.
solar collector An array of black panels which absorbs the Sun's heat and uses it to warm water in a central heating system.
solar energy The Sun's heat and light energy.
solar flare A brief but violent explosion from the Sun's surface.
solar radiation Electromagnetic radiation emitted by the Sun, made up of ultraviolet rays, visible light and infrared rays.
Solar System The Sun together with all of the planets and other objects orbiting it.
solar wind A constant stream of invisible particles blown out into space from the Sun.
solenoid (or **coil**) A coil of wire that behaves like a magnet when an electric current passes through it.
soleus The flat leg muscle beneath the gastrocnemius.
soluble The term describing a substance that can dissolve in a liquid.
solute A substance dissolved in a liquid.
solution A mixture that consists of a substance dissolved in a liquid.
solvent 1. A liquid that can dissolve other substances. 2. The liquid in which a substance is dissolved.
sonar Echo location when used by ships or submarines.

sori Tiny sacs on the underside of fern fronds, where fern spores develop.
soundbox A box that resonates and so amplifies the original sound.
sound synthesizer An instrument that stores sound waves as binary code and can reproduce the original sound by converting the code into an electric current and sending it to a speaker.
sound wave (or **acoustic wave**) A longitudinal, mechanical wave that carries sound energy through a medium.
southern hemisphere The half of the Earth's globe lying south of the equator.
south or (**south-seeking pole**) The part of a magnet that points south.
space-filling model A way of representing molecules in which chemically bonded atoms are shown as balls clinging together.
space probe Unmanned spacecraft sent to explore the Solar System and beyond.
Space Shuttle A reusable manned spacecraft that is launched like a rocket, but lands on re-entry like a plane.
space station A large satellite orbiting the Earth where astronauts can live and perform scientific research over fairly long periods.
spawn The many tiny, soft eggs laid by most fish and amphibians.
specialization The developed suitability of cells and organisms for a particular function, environment or way of life.
special theory of relativity A theory, developed by Albert Einstein, which deals with the relationship of the speed of light to the measurement of time and space, and the relationship of matter to energy.
species The largest subdivision of a genus.
specific epithet The second part of a biological name, which shows an organism's species.
specific heat capacity The amount of heat needed to raise the temperature of 1kg of a substance by 1K.
spectral type The class of a star.
speed The measure of how fast an object is moving, calculated as the distance it travels in a certain amount of time.
speed of light The speed at which light travels in a vacuum – about 300,000 kilometres per second.
speed of sound The speed at which sound travels – usually quoted as 331 metres per second in dry air at 0°C.
sperm The male sex cells in animals.
sperm ducts Two tubes which carry sperm from the epididymis into the urethra.
spinal cord A thick bundle of nerves that runs from the brain down channels in the backbone. It carries impulses to and from all parts of the body.
spiracles Small holes in insects' bodies through which they breathe.
spiral galaxy A galaxy with a bright middle and two or more curved arms of stars.
spongy bone A strong, light type of bone made of a mesh of trabeculae and air gaps.
spongy cells Irregularly shaped cells which are spaced with air gaps to make up the spongy layer beneath a leaf's palisade layer.
spores Reproductive cells produced by a sporophyte, which grow into new gametophytes.
sporophyte A term describing a plant in the asexual stage of alternation of generations.
sporulation The asexual stage of alternation of generations, in which spores are released.
spreading ridge A ridge under the ocean that spreads out sideways as magma wells up along its centre.
spring balance A device which uses a spring to measure a force (in newtons).
spring tides The highest high tides, at the full and new moon.
spring (or **early**) **wood** The soft wood with large cells that grows rapidly in the spring.
stainless steel An alloy of steel and chromium that is both strong and resistant to corrosion.
stamens A plant's male reproductive organs.
staminate flower A flower which has only male reproductive parts.
stance A term describing how an animal stands or moves.
stapes The third of the three tiny earbones, it passes on sound vibrations from the incus to the oval window. See also *malleus*.
star A ball of tremendously hot gas which produces heat and light from nuclear reactions in its core.
starch A natural polymer, made up of glucose monomers, which plants use to store energy.
states of matter The different forms in which a substance can exist. The three basic states are solid, liquid and gas.
static electricity Electrical charge held by a material.
statocyst An organ of balance, found in creatures such as jellyfish, made up of a sac filled with receptors and tiny grains called statoliths.
steam engine The earliest kind of engine, based on external combustion, which boils water, producing steam that drives pistons.
steam point The temperature of steam above water boiling at atmospheric pressure (373K; 100°C; 212°F).
stem The main above-ground part of a plant. It contains vascular tissue and supports the plant.
stereoscopic vision The type of vision in which each eye gives a slightly different view, allowing the brain to form a 3D image.
sternum The breastbone.
stigma The sticky top part of a carpel, which traps pollen grains that touch it.
stimulus Anything that produces a response in an organism, for example, light.
stipules A pair of small, stalkless leaves at the base of a leaf stalk, which protect buds as they form.
stolons See *runners*.
stomata Tiny holes on a leaf's underside which let air and water move in and out.
strata Layers of sedimentary rock.
stratosphere A layer in the middle atmosphere containing the ozone layer.
stratus A type of cloud that forms low in the sky in flat, grey layers.
streamlining A way of designing vehicles so that air flows over them in smooth lines, reducing drag.
stretch receptors Sensitive cells in muscles and tendons which inform the brain about the position of the body.
striated (or **striped**) **muscle tissue** The tissue that makes up skeletal muscles.
stridulation The rubbing together of body parts to produce a shrill noise, as is done by crickets to attract a mate.
strong acid An acid in which most of the molecules separate to form hydrogen ions when in solution. For example, hydrochloric acid.
style Part of the carpel which joins the stigma to the ovary.
subatomic particles Particles smaller than an atom, especially those of which atoms are made: protons, electrons and neutrons.
subcutaneous layer A layer of fat cells beneath the dermis which helps to keep the body warm.
subduction zone See *destructive boundary*.
sublimation A change from solid to gas without going through liquid form.
submergent plants Plants, such as water lilies, in which most of the body grows underwater.
subsonic speed Any speed below the speed of sound.
sub-species A smaller division of a species.
substitution reaction A chemical reaction in which the bonds of some of the molecules in a saturated compound break open, and their atoms are replaced by atoms of another element.
subtractive mixing The process by which pigments are mixed, resulting from some parts of the visible light spectrum being absorbed by pigment while other parts are reflected.
succulent fruit Fruit with thick, fleshy layers that are often tasty to eat.
sucrose ($C_{12}H_{22}O_{11}$) The type of sugar found in sweets, a carbohydrate.
sugars A group of sweet-tasting carbohydrates which dissolve in water.
sulphates A group of salts produced from sulphuric acid.
sulphides A group of minerals made up of elements combined with sulphur.
sulphur dioxide (SO_2) A poisonous, polluting gas made of sulphur and oxygen. It mixes with rainwater to cause acid rain.
sulphuric acid (H_2SO_4) An acid produced from sulphur, important in making fertilizers.
summer (or **late**) **wood** The hard wood with densely packed cells which grows in summer.
sunless zone Level of the ocean, between 1,000m and 4,000m in depth, where no sunlight reaches.
sunlit zone The top 200m of the ocean, home to many animals and all sea plants.
sunspot A small, dark patch on the Sun which is slightly cooler than its surroundings.
superalloy An extremely strong, durable alloy that usually contains nickel, iron or cobalt.
supergiant star The largest size of star.
superior vena cava A vein which carries blood from the upper body to the heart.
supernova A colossal explosion that occurs when a giant star dies.
supersonic speed Any speed greater than the speed of sound.
supervolcano A huge, powerful volcano, the eruption of which would cause massive environmental damage.
surface tension A force that pulls together molecules on the surface of a liquid.
suspension 1. In chemistry, a mixture of solid particles floating in a liquid or gas. 2. In a car, a system of springs that absorbs the effects of an uneven road surface.
swim bladder An inflatable sac in the body of a bony fish. The fish varies the amount of air in the swim bladder to make its body rise or sink.
symbiotic relationship A relationship between two organisms which benefits both.
synapse The junction of two neurons.
synovial fluid A lubricating fluid produced in most freely-movable joints.
synovial joints Freely-movable joints containing synovial fluid.
synthesis (or **combination**) **reaction** A reaction in which substances combine to make a single new substance.
synthetic The term describing compounds that are made artificially by chemical reactions in a factory.
synthetic fibres Fibres, such as nylon, that are produced artificially by drawing out plastics into fine strands.
syrinx The part of a bird's windpipe with which it sings.

system In biology, a group of organs that work together for a certain purpose, for example, the digestive system.

Tactile receptors Cells on animals' bodies which allow them to detect touch.
tagmata Segments that make up the regions of an animal's body (such as the thorax) and are not divided by internal walls.
tapetum A reflective layer at the back of the eyes of nocturnal animals, and some fish, which collects light to help them to see.
tap root (or **primary root**) A large plant root with smaller ones growing from it.
tarsals The ankle bones.
taste buds Tiny structures in the papillae, containing gustatory receptor cells. These send signals about chemicals in food to the brain, which interprets them as tastes.
taxonomic ranks (or **taxa**) Subdivisions of a kingdom, ranging from phyla to species.
telecommunications (or **telecoms**) A branch of technology concerned with the transfer of information using telephone cables or satellites.
temperate region A climatic region with rainfall throughout the year and temperatures that vary with the seasons.
temporary magnet A magnet made from a soft ferromagnetic material, such as iron, that quickly loses its magnetism.
tendons Tough bands of tissue which attach muscles to bones.
tendril A special, thread-like leaf or stem which twines around, or sticks to, a support.
tentacles Long, flexible limbs found on many molluscs and some sea creatures. They are often used for grasping and feeling.
terminal A point on a source of potential difference, for example a battery, where wires are connected to make an electric circuit.
terminal bud A bud which grows at the end of a plant stem or shoot.
terminal velocity The maximum velocity reached by a falling object, at which point acceleration ceases, and velocity is constant.
ternate leaf A trifoliate leaf where each leaflet is made up of three lobes.
terrestrial animals Animals that live mostly on land.
tertiary bronchi Smaller branches into which the secondary bronchi divide.
testa A seed's tough, protective coat.
testes Two glands which produce sperm in a male animal.
thalamus Part of the diencephalon that sorts impulses entering the brain, then sends them to other areas for processing.
theory of evolution The idea that life on Earth began with very simple creatures, and developed gradually through a long series of changes.
theory of natural selection The idea that evolution occurs because individuals with qualities which aid survival tend to live longer, and pass them on to their offspring.
thermal capacity The amount of heat needed to raise the temperature of an object by one kelvin.
thermal decomposition reaction See *decomposition reaction*.
thermistor A resistor which gives different amounts of resistance, depending on the temperature.
thermodynamics The branch of physics which studies energy changes involving heat.
thermoplastics Plastics which can be melted and used again.
thermoregulation The process by which an animal keeps its body at the right temperature.
thermosetting plastics Plastics which can be moulded only once.
thermosphere An extremely hot layer of the upper atmosphere.
thermostat A device that switches an electric circuit on and off in response to a change in temperature.
thigmotropism See *haptotropism*.
thorax The upper region of an animal's body, between the head and the abdomen.
thread cells See *cnidoblasts*.
thrust The force that moves a plane or rocket forwards.
thunder The deep rumbling sound caused by air expanding rapidly as it is heated by flashes of lightning.
tibia The shinbone. See also *fibula*.
tibialis anterior A muscle that extends down the shin, used in walking.
timbre The individual sound quality of a musical instrument.
tissue Part of an organism that is made up of many cells of the same type.
top-level domain The last part of a domain name, showing the kind of organization which hosts a Web site, or the country it is based in. For example, *.com* refers to a commercial company.
total solar eclipse The masking of the Sun from view when the Moon passes in front of it.
trabeculae A criss-cross network of branch-like structures that make up spongy bone.
trachea (or **windpipe**) A tube through which air enters and exits the lungs.
tracheae Pipes in an insect's body, leading from the spiracles to the tracheoles.
tracheids Tubes that are part of the xylem of non-flowering vascular plants.
tracheoles Tiny tubes which carry gases to and from the cells in an insect's body.
traits Characteristics, such as eye colour, inherited genetically from a parent.
transgenic A term describing an organism which has been genetically modified.
transistor An electronic switch that uses a small current to control a larger one.
transition metals The largest group of metals, mostly hard and tough in nature.
translocation The movement of fluids inside a plant.
translucent The term describing substances that allow a little light to pass through them.
transmission In a car, a system of gears that transmits the engine's power to the wheels.
transparent The term used to describe substances through which light can pass.
transpiration The loss of water in vapour form through leaf stomata.
transpiration stream The upward movement of water in a plant, from the roots to the leaves.
transverse waves Waves in which the vibrations are at right angles to the direction of travel.
trapezius One of a pair of flat, triangular muscles, which cover the shoulders and back. It straightens the shoulder.
trench A long, deep, steep-sided pit in the ocean floor, formed at a destructive boundary.
tributary A river or stream that flows into a larger one.
trifoliate leaf A compound leaf with three leaflets growing from a single point.
triple bond A covalent bond in which a pair of atoms shares three pairs of electrons.
trophic level The position of an organism within a food chain.
tropical cyclone (or **hurricane** or **typhoon**) A fierce storm caused by warm ocean currents.
tropical region A climatic region that is warm all year with two seasons: dry and wet.
tropism The response of a plant to a stimulus. In positive tropism, a plant grows towards a stimulus; in negative tropism it grows away from it.
troposphere The lowest layer of the atmosphere, containing 80% of its gases and all of its weather.
trough The point where a wave causes the greatest negative displacement of a medium, shown as a low point on a wave diagram.
true fruit A fruit, such as the cherry, which develops from an ovary.
tuber A swollen underground stem that stores food for a plant through the winter, such as that of the potato.
tundra 1. A biome with harsh winds and low winter temperatures. Its underground soil is always frozen, so it has no trees. 2. A climatic region with these features.
turbine A machine with a shaft and blades, which are turned, for example, by the force of wind or steam. The movement energy is converted into electricity.
turbofan engine A type of jet engine with an extra-large fan. They are slower than turbojets, but quieter and more efficient.
turbojet engine The fastest type of jet engine, used in high-speed jet planes.
turboprop engine A jet engine that powers an aircraft by driving propellers.
turboshaft engine A jet engine that powers the rotor blades in a helicopter.
turgor The state of a plant when its cell vacuoles are full of sap, making it stand firmly upright.
twilight zone The level of the ocean, between 200m and 1,000m in depth, where very little sunlight reaches.
tympanal organ A simple hearing organ found in animals such as frogs, consisting of a tympanum on the body surface which passes vibrations into an air sac containing receptors.
tympanum A thin layer of tissue found in most land animals, which enables hearing by vibrating in response to sound waves.
typhoon See *tropical cyclone*.

Ulna The longer and thinner of the two bones in the forearm. See also *radius*.
ultrasound Sound waves with a frequency above 20,000 hertz.
ultrasound scanning The use of high-frequency sound waves to form a picture of the inside of the body.
ultraviolet radiation (**ultraviolet rays**) Electromagnetic waves that lie just beyond the violet end of the visible light spectrum.
umbilical cord A tube, containing arteries and a vein, which connects a baby to the placenta. It is cut at birth.
umbra A dark shadow formed where no light reaches an area.
unguligrade An animal that walks upon hooves at its toe-tips, such as a horse.
unicellular A term describing a living thing whose body is made of only one cell.
universal indicator An indicator made of a mixture of dyes that change colour according to the pH scale.
universe (or **cosmos**) The collection of all matter, energy and space that exists.

unsaturated compound An organic compound with at least one double or triple covalent bond.
upthrust The force pushing up on an object when it is placed in a fluid such as water or air.
urban migration The movement of people from country to city areas in search of work.
urea A waste substance produced in the liver from the breakdown of amino acids.
ureter A tube through which urine passes from the kidney to the bladder.
urethra An opening in the body through which urine is released from the bladder.
uric acid A weak organic acid excreted as solid waste by some animals, such as reptiles.
urinary system The system which controls the level of water in the body. It is made up of the kidneys, ureters, bladder and urethra.
urine A waste substance produced by the kidneys, made of urea, water and toxic salts.
URL (Uniform Resource Locator) The unique address of any individual internet document, such as, *http://www.usborne.com/index.html*
uterus (or **womb**) A sac inside the body of a female mammal in which the baby grows.
utricle A sac between the semicircular canals and the saccule, housing a macula.

Vaccine A dose of a germ too weak to cause disease in a person, but strong enough that they produce antibodies which will resist it in the future. The use of vaccines is called vaccination.
vacuole A fluid-filled sac inside a plant or animal cell. Most plant cells have a large, permanent vacuole; animal cells tend to have smaller, temporary vacuoles.
vacuum An empty space where there are no particles of air or other matter.
vagina The muscular passage which leads from a female's cervix out of her body. It receives the penis during sexual intercourse.
valency (or **combining power**) The number of electrons an atom must gain or lose to acquire a stable outer shell.
vane The flat surface of a feather, formed from interlocking barbs and barbules.
variable resistor (or **rheostat**) An electronic component that can be adjusted to give different amounts of resistance.
variable star A star that changes gradually in brilliance.
variegated leaf A leaf patterned with two or more colours.
vascular A term describing something made up of, or containing, conducting vessels. In plants, it means having xylem and phloem; in animals, it means having a blood supply.
vascular bundle One of the groups of xylem and phloem cells found in young stems.
vascular cylinder The ring of vascular tissue found in the stems of older dicotyledons, formed when the vascular bundles join up.
vastus lateralis A muscle above the knee which allows the lower leg to be lifted.
vector quantity A quantity that has magnitude and direction.
vegetative reproduction (or **vegetative propagation**) A type of asexual reproduction in which parts of plants grow into new plants.
veins Vessels carrying blood to the heart.
velocity The speed an object travels in a particular direction.
vent The main pipe through which magma flows up the middle of a volcano.
ventilation Breathing.
ventral fin A long anal fin that extends under a fish's belly.
ventricles The heart's two lower chambers.
Veroboard A board with rows of holes, and copper tracks on the back, used to make simple electronic circuits.
vertebrae 33 interlocking bones, which make up the vertebral column.
vertebral column (or **spine**) The backbone, made up of vertebrae.
vertebrate An animal with a backbone.
vessels Column-shaped cells with no dividing walls found in the xylem of flowering plants.
vestibular system A collection of organs in the inner part of the ear which help the body to keep its balance. See *semicircular canals*; *utricle*; *saccule*.
vibrissae Whiskers.
viewfinder The part of a camera that allows the photographer to see what will appear on the picture.
villi Tiny, finger-like projections on the lining of the small intestine which absorb digested food.
virtual image An image, made for example by reflection in a surface, from which rays of light only appear to come.
viruses Strands of DNA (or a related acid called RNA) in a protective coat. They cannot live on their own, but invade living cells in order to reproduce, often causing diseases, such as colds.
visceral muscles Muscles in the walls of internal organs such as the intestines.
visible light spectrum The narrow section of the electromagnetic spectrum that humans can see. It is made up of red, orange, yellow, green, blue, indigo and violet light.
vitreous humour A stiff, jelly-like substance that fills the central body of the eye behind the lens, keeping its shape.
viviparous A term describing animals which give birth to live young.
vocal cords Two muscles in the voice box which are pulled together during speech, vibrating to produce sound.
voice box See *larynx*.
volcanic bomb A lump of lava blasted into the air during a volcanic eruption.
volcano An opening in the Earth's surface formed by magma bursting out, usually taking the shape of a conical mound.
Volkmann's canals Tiny channels in bone which carry blood vessels and nerves to the osteocytes.
volt (V) The unit of potential difference.
voltage See *potential difference*.
volume The amount of space a substance occupies.
voluntary actions Actions, such as lifting a cup, which are consciously controlled by the brain.
voluntary muscles Muscles, such as the arm muscles, which can be consciously controlled.
VTOL Of a plane, **V**ertical **T**ake **O**ff and **L**anding. Such planes take off directly upwards and so do not need runways.
vulcanization A process used to strengthen rubber by heating it with sulphur.

Wafer A thin slice of a silicon cylinder which is cut up to make silicon chips.
WAN See *Wide-Area Network*.
warm-blooded A term describing animals who can keep their internal temperature constant under most conditions.
washing soda Hydrated sodium carbonate ($Na_2CO_3.10H_2O$). Used in bath crystals and as a water softener.
water cycle The natural process by which water is recycled between the Earth, the atmosphere and living things.
water of crystallization Water that has chemically bonded with another substance.
waterworks Site where water is filtered and chemically treated to remove mineral impurities and bacteria.
watt (W) The SI unit of power.
wavelength The distance between a point on one wave and the same point on the next cycle of the wave.
waxes A group of solid esters, many of which are produced by living things. They are usually glossy, easily moulded and insoluble in water.
weak acid An acid that contains relatively few hydrogen ions when in solution, for example, ethanoic acid (found in vinegar).
weight A measure of the strength of the pull of gravity on an object.
white blood cells Blood cells which help the body to fight against disease.
white light See *light*.
white phosphorus The most reactive allotrope of phosphorus, a poisonous white solid that ignites in air.
wide-area network (WAN) A network of computers that are far apart.
windpipe See *trachea*.
wisdom teeth The last set of molars to grow, set at the back of the jaw.
womb See *uterus*.
woody perennials Perennials, such as trees, that may lose some parts in the winter, but have protected stems which grow thicker each year.
work In physics, the distance an object moves multiplied by the force needed to move it.
World Wide Web (www) A vast information resource, and place to conduct e-commerce, consisting of thousands of Web sites linked together on the internet.
www See *World Wide Web*.

Xanthophylls Pigments which produce yellow colours in plants.
X chromosome The type of sex chromosome contained in all ova, and half of all sperm.
xenon (Xe) A noble gas used in high-speed flash photography.
xerophytes Plants such as cacti, which are specially adapted to live in very dry areas.
X-rays Short-wavelength, high-frequency electromagnetic waves that can pass through most soft substances but not hard, dense ones.
xylem Water-carrying tissue in vascular plants.

Yawing The turning movement of a plane, to the left or right.
Y chromosome The type of sex chromosome contained in half of all sperm.
yeast A single-celled fungus used in brewing and bread-making.
yolk sac A sac in a cleidoic egg that contains food, called yolk, rich in phosphorus and fat, which nourishes the embryo.

Zone of elongation The area of new cells produced by dividing cells just behind a plant's root tip.
zoology The scientific study of animals.
zooplankton Microscopic animals that drift on the surface of seas and oceans.
zygote The first cell of a new organism, formed when a male cell fertilizes a female cell.

INDEX

Where there is more than one page reference for a term in the index, you will find the main explanation on the page(s) shown in bold type. It may be useful to look at the other pages for further information.

1,2-dibromoethane **93**

A

abdomen **300**, 418
abiotic **334**, 418
abomasum **313**
abscess **353**, 418
abscission layer (leaves) **261**, 418
absolute
  magnitude **160**, 418
  temperature scale **111**, 405, 418
  zero **111**, 405, 418
abyssal zone **189**, 418
acceleration **127**, 128, 405, 418
accessory foods **356**, 418
accumulator **231**, 418
acetic acid **418**
achene **275**, 418
achromatic colours **217**, 418
acid rain 64, **65**, 86, 108, 418
acids 65, 78, **84**, 86-87, 88, 89, 94, 418
acrylic 101
actin **349**
actinides **29**, 418
actinium **28**
action specific (catalysts) **79**
activated charcoal **53**
activation energy **76**, 79, 418
active
  immunity **387**, 418
  volcanoes **183**
acupuncture **390**
addition reactions **93**, 97, 418
additive mixing (light) **216**, 418
adhesion **21**, 418
adolescence **379**, 418
ADP (adenosine diphosphate) **360**, 418
adventitious root **253**, 418
aerial root **253**, 418
aerobic respiration **360**, 418
aerodynamics **418**
aerofoil **142**, 418
aeronautics **418**
aerosol **93**, 185
aestivation **329**, 418
ageing **379**
aggregate fruit **274**, 418
agonist (muscle) **348**, 418
aileron **143**, 144, 418
air **62-65**, 113, 125, 132, 133, 138, 139, 142, 149, 192, 193, 358
  bladder **281**, 418
  pressure **132**, 133
  resistance **125**, **142**, 418
aircraft 35, 38-39, 103, 132, **142-145**, 207
albumen **327**, 418
alcohols **94**, 95, 111, 391, 418
Aldrin, Edwin "Buzz" **176**, 411
algae **281**, 282, 293, 418
al-Haytham, Ibn (Alhazen) **412**
alimentary canal **354**
alkali metals 29, **32**, 418
alkaline earth metals 29, **32**, 418
alkalis 32, 78, 84, **85**, 86, 87, 88, 94, 418
alkanes 92, **96**, 97, 99, 418
alkenes 92, 96, **97**, 100, 418
allele **381**, 418
allotrope **50**, 54-55, **71**, 418
alloy 33, **34-39**, 418
alpha
  particle **114**, 418
  radiation **114**, 115, 418
  wave **367**
alternate leaves **259**
alternating current (AC) **235**, 418
alternation of generations **283**, 418
alternative energy sources 185
altitude **130**, **195**, 418
alum **91**
aluminium 24, 26, 27, 29, 30, 33, 35, **38**, 39, 40, 42, 44, 45, 83, 91, 198
  oxide **83**
alveoli 315, **358**, 418
americium **28**
amethyst 90
amine 101
amino acids **356**, 418
ammonia 15, 47, 64, 178, 184, 292, **334**, 418
ammonium
  hydroxide **85**
  sulphate **87**
amoeba 294, 300, 304, 324
Ampère, André Marie **412**
amperes **230**, 418
amphibians 186, 187, 315, 326, 327, 338, 342, 418
amplification **208**, 226, 418
amplifier circuit **237**
amplitude **203**, 205, 206, 226, 418
Amplitude Modulation (AM) **226**, 418
ampullae **418**
  of Lorenzi **323**, 418
anaerobic respiration **361**, 418
anal fin **305**, 418
analogue
  electricity **238**, 244, 418
  recording **211**
anatomy **418**
Anaxagoras **412**
AND (logic gate) **238**, 418
Andromeda galaxy **156**
anhydrous **91**, 418
aniline **92**, 418
animal
  cells **298-299**
  kingdom **342**
  pollination **272**
anion **70**, 82, 418
annelids **342**, 418
annual ring **257**, 418
annuals **288**, 418
anode **82**, 83, 418
anodizing **83**, 418
antagonist (muscle) **348**, 418
antagonistic
  hormones **363**, 418
  pair (muscles) **348**, 418
antennae **322**, 418
anther **271**, 418
anthracite **52**, 53, 418
antibiotics **389**, 418
antibodies **387**, 418
antigens **387**, 418
antimony 25, **29**, 33, 43
antiseptic **418**
anus **354**, 418
aorta **350**, 418
apatite 55, **90**, 407
aperture (in camera) **224**, 418
apical meristem **252**, 418
Apollo
  asteroids **172**
  missions **176**, **177**
apparent magnitude **160**, 418
appendicular skeleton **346**, 418
aqueous **418**
  humour 370, **419**
archaea **294**, **341**
Archimedes **412**
Archimedes'
  principle **138**, 409
  screw **136**
area 404-405, **408**
Arecibo telescope 174
argon 14, 25, 29, **63**, 184, 419
Ariel (moon) **170**
Aristotle 13, **412**
armadillo 302
armature **234**, 419
Armstrong, Neil **176**, 411
arsenates **27**
arsenic 25, 27, **29**
artery **351**, 419
arthropods 187, 317, 342, 419
artificial
  propagation **279**
  selection **384**
ascorbic acid 84
asexual reproduction
  in animals **324**, 325, 419
  in plants 278-279, **282-283**
association
  area (in brain) **367**
  neuron **364**, 419
astatine 25, 29, 48, **49**
asterism **160**, 419
asteroid 163, 168, **172-173**, 419
Asteroid Belt 130, 163, **172**
asthenosphere **180**, 181, 419
astronauts 103, 130, **176**, 177
astronomers 168, 170, 171, 172, 173, 174, 175
astronomy **419**
astrophysics **419**
atmosphere **62**, 65, 166, 174, 177, **184-185**, 419
  atm unit **19**, 419
atmospheric pressure **19**, **132**, **192**, 419
atom **10-13**, 14, 15, 24, 34, 43, 50, 68-71, 76, 91, 114-115, 198, **228**, 419
atomic
  bomb **116**
  number **12**, 13, 28-29, 68, 115, 419
  theory (Dalton's) **13**
ATP (adenosine triphosphate) **360**, 419
atria **350**, 419
attraction (in magnets) **232**
auditory nerve **372**, 419
auroras (australis, borealis) **162**, 419
autonomic nervous system **365**, 419
autotrophic **264**, **332**, 419
auxins **268**, 419
Avogadro, Amedeo **412**
Avogadro number **77**, 409, 419
axial skeleton **346**, 419
axil **252**, 419
axillary bud **252**, 419
axon 364, **365**, 374, 419

B

Babbage, Charles **412**
babies 327
background rate of extinction **336**, 419
backward reaction **78**
bacteria 64, 74, 75, 292, 294, 313, 332, 334, 338, 341, 353, **386**, 419
Bain, Alexander **412**
Baird, John Logie **412**
balance 320, 372, **373**
baleen **310**, 419
ball and socket joint **347**, 419
ball and spoke models **15**, 419
ball bearings **125**
bandwidth
  in computers **241**, 419
  in telephones **245**
barb (in a feather) **306**, 419
barbule (in a feather) **306**, 419
barium **28**, 31, 32
bark (in trees) 255, **257**
barred spiral galaxy **156**, 419
basal rosette **259**
basalt 180
base
  in genetics **382**, 419
  in a transistor **237**
  station **245**, 419
  substance 84, **85**, 86, 88, 89, 419
batteries 39, 54, 106, **231**, 236, 409, 419
bauxite 38, 45, **83**, 419
beak **311**
Beaufort scale **406**
Becquerel, Antoine **412**
bee dances **319**
Bell, Alexander Graham **412**
belt (air pressure) **192**
Benz, Karl **412**
berkelium **29**
Berliner, Émile **412**
Berners-Lee, Tim **412**
Bernoulli's principle **142**, 409
berries **274**
beryl **27**, 407
beryllium 27, **28**
beta
  particle **114**, 419
  radiation **114**, 115, 419
  wave **367**
bicarbonate of soda **67**, 85, 87
biceps **348**
bicuspids **352**, 419
biennials **288**, 419
Big Bang theory **154-155**, **178**, 411, 419
Big Crunch theory **155**, 419
Big Dipper (asterism) **160**
bilateral symmetry **301**, 419
bile **355**, 419
bimetallic strip **110**
binary
  code 211, 238, **241**, 419
  fission **324**, 419
  star **159**, 419
binocular vision **321**, 419
binomial system **343**, 419

biodegradable **419**
biodiversity **291**, 419
biofuel **108**, **198**, 419
biological
key **294**, **340**, 419
name **343**, 419
biomass **333**, 419
biomes **290**, **331**, 419
biped **309**, 419
bipinnate leaves **258**
birds 186, 187, 306, 313, 317, 318, 323, 327, 329, 335, 338, 342
Biro, Lazlo **412**
birth control **197**
bismuth **29**, 33, 43
bit (computer) **241**, 419
bituminous coal **52**, 53
black
diamond **51**
hole **161**, 419
phosphorus **55**
bladder **317**, **362**, 419
blast furnace **36**, 42, 44, 419
blind spot **370**
blood 58, 61, 349, 351, 362
clotting **351**
groups **351**
vessels **351**
boats **140-141**
body
coverings **302-303**
structure **300-301**
Bohr, Niels 13, **412**
bohrium **28**
boiling **18**
point **18**, 19, 69, 70, 72, 419
bolus **354**, 419
bonding (atoms) 14-15, **68-71**, 76, 79, 91, 92-93, 96-97, 419
bone 55, 306, **347**, 419
marrow **347**
bones **346-347**
Booth, Hubert **412**
borates **27**
boron 25, 27, **29**, 239
botany **419**
Bowman's capsules **362**, 419
Boyle, Robert **412**
Boyle's law **409**
bract **259**, 419
brain 364, 365, **366-367**, 388
stem **366**, 419
waves **367**, 419
brakes 124, **133**, **151**
branchiae **314**, 419
brass 34, 35, **38**, 39, 82
breathing 62-63, **314-315**, 358, **359**
breeding 384
brine **89**, 419
bristleworm 304
broadcasting **226-227**
bromides **49**
bromine 22, 25, 29, 48, **49**, 93
bronchi **315**, **358**, 419
bronchioles **315**, **358**, 419
bronze 35, **38**, 39, 42
Brown, Robert 16, **412**
Brownian motion **16**, 419
browser (internet) 7, **246**, 419
Brunel, Isambard Kingdom **412**
bryophyte **295**, 419
buckminsterfullerene 50, **51**, **71**, 419
buckyballs 51
bud (in a plant) **252**, 270, 419
budding **324**
bulb,
light 63, 230, 236, 409
plant 253, **278**, 419
burning (See *combustion*)
fuels 63, 64, 185, 335
buses (computer) **241**, 419
butane **96**
byte (computer) **241**, 419

C

cable broadcasting **227**
cacti 194, 286, 293
cadmium **29**
sulphide 88
caecum **313**, 419
caesium **28**
calcite 32, **90**, 407
calcium 26, 28, 30, 31, 32, **38**, 73, 88, 357
carbonate 32, 67, 73, 76, 78, 86, 88
hydrogencarbonate **73**
hydroxide **86**
oxide **78**
sulphate **88**
calculator 238
calderas **183**, 419
californium **29**
Callisto (moon) **168**
Calories **360**, 419
cambium **254**, 256, 419
Cambrian Period **186**, **187**
cameras 170, 176, 220, **224-225**, 226
camouflage **287**, **339**, 419
cancer 115, 213
canines
dog family **342**
teeth **312**, **352**, 419
cannabis **391**
capacitor **237**, 409, 419
capacity **404-405**
capillary **351**, 419
action in plants **262**, 419
car 41, 44, 103, 127, 133, 134, 147, **150**
battery 231
carapace **302**, 419
carbohydrates **264**, **292**, **356**, 357, 419
carbon 12, 13, 15, 25, 27, 29, 35, 36, 37, 46, 48, **50-53**, 69, **71**, 81, 92-103, 115, **292**, **334**
cycle **52**, 285, 292, 334, 420
dating **115**, 420
dioxide 15, 18, 36, 52, 62, **63**, 65, 66, 69, 73, 78, 80, 81, 84, 85, 100, 147, 164, 178, 184, 185, 264, 265, 292, 332, 358, 360, 420
fibre **52**, 103
monoxide 36, 37, **64**, 79, 147, 420
carbonaceous (C-type) asteroids **172**
carbonado **51**, 420
carbonates **27**, 76, 84, 88, 420
carbonic acid **63**, **73**, 79, 88
Carboniferous Period **186**, **187**
carboxylic acids **94**, 95, 101, 420
card (in a computer) **242**, 420
cardiac **420**
muscle **349**, 420
carnassials **312**, 420
carnivores
eating habits **312**, 332, 420
order **342**
carnivorous plants **267**, 269
carotene **261**, 369, 420
carpals **346**, 420
carpel **271**, 420
carrier wave **226**, 420
cartilage **301**, **347**, 420
cartilaginous fish **301**
Cartwheel galaxy **156**
caryopsis **275**, 420
cassette recorder **210**
Cassini (Mars mission) 176
cataclysmic variable **159**, 420
catalyst 47, 51, 55, **79**, 147, 420
catalytic converter **79**, **147**, 420
cathode **82**, 83, 420
ray tube **227**, 240, 420
rays **420**
cation **70**, 82, 420
caudal fin **305**, 420
caustic **85**, 420
soda **85**, 89
Cavendish, Henry **412**
CD (See *compact disc*)
cell,
animal 250, **298-299**, 368, 420
body **364**, 420
electrochemical **231**, 420
plant **250-251**, 260, 420
cell
division in animals **299**
division in plants 251, 254
membrane **250**, 298, 420
plate **251**, 427
repair in plants 251
sap **250**, 420
wall **250**, 420
celluloid 102
cellulose **85**, **250**, **313**, 420
Celsius, Anders **412**
Celsius scale **111**, 405, 420
cement (in teeth) **352**
Cenozoic Era **186**, **187**, 420
central nervous system **364**, 420
Central Processing Unit (CPU) 239, **241**, 420
centre of gravity **131**, 420
centrifuging **61**, 420
centriole **298**, 420
centripetal force **128**, 129, 131, 420
cerebellum **366**, 420
cerebral
cortex **367**, 420
hemispheres **367**, 420
cerebrospinal fluid **366**, 420
cerebrum **366**, 367, 374, 420
Ceres (asteroid) **172**
cerium **28**
cervix **376**, 420
CFCs (See *chlorofluorocarbons*)
Chadwick, James 13, **413**
chaetae **304**, 420
chalk 32, 38, **86**, 88
Challenger (Space Shuttle) **411**
chambers (in heart) **350**
changes of state 16, **18-19**
charcoal 42, **52**, **53**
charge-coupled device (CCD) **225**, 243, 420
Charles, Jacques **413**
Charles' law **409**
Charon (moon) **171**, 411
chemical
energy **106**, 107, 420
equations **77**
formulae **15**, **66**, 420
reactions 13, **76-81**, 420
symbols 13, **15**, 28-29, 420
chemoreceptors **323**, **374**, 420
cherries 274
chiropractic **390**
chip (computer) **239**, 420
chitin **302**, 420
chlorides 66, **88**, 420
chlorine 19, 25, 29, **48**, 66, 67, 80, 89, 93, 96, 100
chloroethene **100**
chlorofluorocarbons (CFCs) 93, 96, **185**, 420
chlorophyll 32, **250**, 260, **261**, **264**, 284, 294, 420
chloroplast **250**, 251, 260, **264**, 420
cholesterol 97, **356**, 420
chordates **342**, 420
chromates **27**
chromatic colours **216**, 420
chromatogram **60**, 420
chromatography **60**, 420
chromium 28, 33, 34, 35, 37, **38**, 39, 82
chromoplast **250**, 420
chromosome 298, **380-381**,420
chrysanthemum 269
cilia **304**, **358**, 420
ciliary muscles **370**, 420
ciliates **304**, 420
circuits (electric/electronic) **230**, 231, **236-239**, 420
circular muscles **371**, 420
circulatory system 299, **350-351**, 420
cirri **310**, 420
cirrus cloud **193**, 420
citric acid **67**, 84, 100
class **341**, 420
classical taxonomy **341**, 420
classification,
animal **340-343**, 420
plant **294-295**, 420
clavicle **346**, 420
cleavage
furrow **299**, 420
plane **90**, 420
cleidoic egg **327**, 420
client/server network **243**, 420
climate 179, 187, 189, **194-195**, 198, 290, 339, 420
climatic regions **194**, 420
climax community **330**, 420
clitellum 325, **420**
cloaca **313**, 420
clock speed **241**, 420
clone **324**, **385**
cloning **385**, 420
clotting (blood) **351**, 420
clouds 74, **193**
clove (bulb) **278**
club mosses **282**, 295
cluster (star) **156**
cnidarians 310, **342**, 420
cnidoblast **310**, 420
coal 46, **52**, 53, 64, 107, 108, 198, 235
coastal
climate **195**
plants **286**
cobalt **28**, 35
cocaine **391**
coccyx **346**

cochlea **372**, 420
Cockerell, Christopher **412**
co-dominant genes **381**, 420
coelom **301**, 420
cogs **135**
coherent waves **215**, 421
cohesion **21**, 421
coke **36**
cold-blooded **316**, 421
collecting duct **362**
collector (in a transistor) **237**
collenchyma **255**, 421
colloid **421**
colon **355**, 421
colour **216-217**
  blindness **370**
  printing 217
columnar epithelial cells **299**
coma (of a comet) **173**
combination reaction **78**
combining power **71**, 421
combustion 62, 78, **80**, 146, 148, 421
comet 163, 170, 172, **173**, 421
commensals **343**, 421
communication **318-319**
communities **197**, **330**, 421
commutator **234**, 421
compact
  bone **347**, 421
  disc (CD) **211**, 219, 241, 421
compensation points **265**, 421
complementary
  colours **216**, 421
  medicine **390**, 421
complete metamorphosis **328**, 421
composite
  bulb **278**, 421
  volcano **182**
composites **103**, 421
compound 26, 58, **66-75**
  eyes **321**, 421
  fruit **274**, 421
  leaves **258**, 421
  optical microscope **222**, 421
computers 182, 236, 238-239, **240-243**, 246-247
computer
  graphics 242
  virus **7**
concave
  lens **220**, 371, 421
  mirror **221**, 421
conception **377**, 421
condensation **19**, 421
conduction
  of electricity 24, 25, 30, 31, 51, 421
  of heat 24, 25, 30, **113**, 421
conductors **113**, **228**, 239, 421
cone
  in the eye **370**, 421
  of a plant **275**
  of a volcano **182**
conifer 275, 289, 290, **295**, 421
coniferous forests **290**, **331**
conjunctiva **370**, 421
conservation **336-337**, 421
  of energy **107**, 409
  of mass **77**, 409
  of momentum **123**, 409
constellations **160**, 421
constructive
  boundary **181**, 421
  interference **205**, 421
consumer **332**, 421
contact force **118**, 421
continental
  climate **194**
  crust **180**
  drift **421**
  plate **181**
continents 179, 187, 410, **421**
  formation of **179**, 187
contour feather **306**, 421
contraception **377**, 421
contractile vacuole **317**, 421
control surfaces **143**, 421
convection **112**, 192, **421**
  current **112**, 192, 421
convective zone (Sun) **162**, 421
converging lens **220**, 221, 421
converter (in a furnace) **37**, 42
convex
  lens **220**, 371, 421
  mirror **221**, 421
Copernicus **413**
copper 29, 30, 31, 32, 33, 34, 35, **38**, 40, 42, 44, 78, 80, 83, 230, 244
  carbonate **27**
  oxide 81, **89**
  pyrites **54**
copper(II)
  chloride **82**
  sulphate 78, 83, 89, **91**
corals 324, 337
core,
  Earth's **180**, 421
  Sun's **162**, 421
core (in a solenoid) **233**, 421
Coriolis effect **192**
cork cambium 257
corm **278**, 421
cornea **370**, 421
cornified layer **368**, 421
corolla **270**
corona (of the Sun) **162**, 421
corpus callosum **367**, 421
corrosion 35, **40-41**, 65, 83, 84, 421
cortex
  in kidney **362**
  in plant tissue **255**, 421
cosmetics 67
cosmos **154**
cotyledon **277**, 421
Couch Adams, John 170
coughing **359**
courtship ritual **326**
covalent bonding 68, **69**, 92, 96, 97, 421
CPU (See *Central Processing Unit*)
crack (cocaine) **391**
cracking (molecules) **99**, 421
cranium **346**, 421
crater 167, 169, 170, 172, **182**, 183, 421
crawling **308**
Cretaceous Period **187**
Crick, Francis **382**, 413
critical length **269**
crop
  in a bird **313**, 421
  rotation **291**, 421
cross-breeding **384**, 421
cross-pollination **272**, 421
crown (of a tooth) **352**, 421
crude oil 96, **98-99**, 100, 421
crust, Earth's 26, 166, **180**, 181, 183, 421
cryolite 83
crystals 19, 26, 50, 87, 88, 89, **90-91**, 421
CT (computed tomography) scanners **388**, 421
cud **313**
Cugnot, Nicolas-Joseph **413**
cumulus cloud **193**, 421
cupronickel **38**
cupula **373**, 421
Curie, Marie **413**
curium **29**
current,
  electric 210-211, **228**, 230-231, 421
  water **188**, 421
cusp
  (heart valve) **350**, 421
  of a tooth **352**
cuspids **352**
cuticle
  in animals **302**, **369**, 421
  in plants **255**, 421
cutin **255**
cutting (plants) **279**
cyanobacteria 184, 281
cycads **295**, 421
cycle (wave) **203**
cyclotron **12**
cylinder **146**, **148**, 150
cytokinesis **251**, **299**, 421
cytoplasm
  in animal cells **298**, 304, 421
  in plant cells **250**, 251, 254, 263, 421

D

Dalton, John 13, **413**
Darwin, Charles **339**, 413
data **421**
  compression **245**, 421
daughter cell **299**, **324**, 421
daughterboard (computer) **239**
day-neutral plants **269**
days (planetary) **163**
decane **99**
decantation **60**, 421
decay (in teeth) 48, **352**, 353
deceleration **127**, 421
decibels (dB) **206**, 421
deciduous
  forests **290**, **331**
  teeth **353**, 421
  trees **289**, 290, 421
decimal system 404
decomposers **332**, 421
decomposition reaction **78**, 421
decussate leaves **259**
deep
  current **188**
  time **179**, **186**, 421
dehydrating agent 87, **91**, 421
dehydration **91**, 421
Deimos (moon) **165**
deionization **75**, 422
delta 190, **191**, 422
  wave **367**
deltoid **348**, 422
dendrites **364**, 374, 422
dendron **364**
density **17**, 72, **138**, 139, 141, 405, 422
dental amalgam **33**, 422
dentate **312**, 422
denticles **303**, 422
dentine **352**, 422
dentition **353**, 422
deoxyribonucleic acid (See *DNA*)
deoxyribose **382**, 422
deposition (in a river) 191
dermal **422**
  scales (on a fish) **303**, 422
  tissue 251, **255**
dermis
  in fish **303**, 422
  in human skin **368**, 422
desert
  climate **194**, 422
  plants **286**
deserts 289, **290**, **331**, 422
desmids **281**
destructive
  boundary **181**, 422
  interference **205**, 422
detergents 75, 87, **94**, 95, 422
developing (film) **225**
development (human) **378-379**
Devonian Period **186**, **187**
diabetes **363**, 422
diagnosis **388**, 422
diamond 27, **50**, 51, **71**, 90, 407, 422
diaphragm
  in the chest 358, **359**, 422
  in sound equipment 206, **210**
diastema **312**
diatom **281**, 422
dichlorodifluoromethane 93, **96**
dichotomous key **294**, **340**, 422
dicotyledon **255**, 277, 295, 422
diencephalon **366**, 422
diesel
  engine **148**
  oil **99**, 422
diet **356-357**
dietary fibre 355, **357**, 422
differential **151**, 422
diffraction **205**, 216, 219, 422
diffuse reflection **218**, 422
diffusion **22**, 422
digestion 79, **313**, **354-355**
digestive
  enzymes 79, **355**
  glands 354, **355**, 422
  juices **354**, 355, 422
  system 299, **312**, **354**, 422
  tract **354**, 422
digit,
  numerical 238, **422**
  skeletal **346**, 422
digital **422**
  broadcasting **227**
  cameras 224, **225**
  circuits **238**, 422
  electronics **238-239**, 422
  recording **211**
  TV **422**
digitalis 389
digitigrade **309**, 422
dinosaurs 186, 187, **338-339**
diode **237**, 409, 422
dioecious **271**, 422
dipoles **232**, 422
direct current (DC) **231**, 422
disease **386-387**
dispersal (of seeds) **276**, 422
dispersion **216**, 422
displacement **138**, 139
  reaction **78**, 422
distance (units) **404**, **405**
distillation **61**, 75, 422
diverging lens **220**, 221, 422
divisions (plant kingdom) **295**
DNA (deoxyribonucleic acid) 15, **380**, **382-385**, 422
  profiling **383**, 422

dodecanoic acid 94
dolerite 180
domain
in a magnet **232**, 422
name (in a URL) **247**, 422
dominant
animal **319**
gene **381**, 422
dormancy **329**, 422
dormant
seed **277**
volcano **183**
dorsal fin **305**, 422
double
bond **69**, **92**, 93, 97, 422
helix 15, **382**, 422
downloading 6, **246**, 422
drag **125**, **142**, 422
dragonfly 307
Drew, Richard **413**
drills 51, 134, **136**
driver (computer) **242**, 422
drug **391**, 422
drupe **274**, 422
drupelet **274**, 422
dry
cell **231**, 422
fruit **275**, 422
dubnium **28**
duckweed 280
ductility **30**, 422
duodenum **355**, 422
duralumin **35**
dwarf planet **163**, 171
dwarf star **159**, 161, 422
dyes 49, 86, 87, 92
dyke (in a volcano) **182**, 422
dynamics **122**, 422
dynamo **235**, 422
dysprosium **29**

E

Eagle Nebula **158**
ear canal **372**, 422
eardrum **320**, **372**, 422
early wood **257**
ears **320**, **372-373**
Earth 26, 46, 65, 128, 130, 131, 154, 157, 163, 164, **166-167**, **178-199**, 233, 411
earth wire **230**, 422
earthquake **182**, 202, 407, 422
earthworm 300, 308
ecdysis **302**, 422
echinoderms **342**, 422
echo **207**, 422
location **207**, 320, 422
eclipses 162, **422**, 427, 434
eclipsing variable **159**, 422
ecological
niche **330**, 422
succession **330**, 422
ecology **330-331**, 422
e-commerce **247**, 422
ecosystem **290**, **330**, 337, 422
Ecstasy (drug) **391**
edentates **310**
Edison, Thomas **413**
effort **134**, 422
eggs (ova) 327
Einstein, Albert 16, **413**
einsteinium **29**
ejaculation **377**, 422
elastic **121**, 422
limit **121**, 422
potential energy **106**
elasticity **121**
electric
arc furnace **37**
bell 234
buzzer 234
charge 11, **228**, 229, 407, 422
circuit **230**, 231, 422
current 210-211, **228**, 230-231, 422
field 212, 219, **228**, 422
force **118**, **228**, 423
instruments **209**
motor **234**, 423
electrical
energy **107**, 228
components 230
symbols 236, **409**
electricity 24, 25, 30, 31, 51, 53, 108, 109, 117, 198, 210, 215, **228-231**, 423
electrochemical cells **231**, 423
electrodes 51, **82**, 367, 423
electroencephalogram (EEG) **367**, 423
electrolysis 38, **82-83**, 423
electrolyte **82**, 83, **231**, 423
electromagnet 44, 210, **233**, **234**, 423
electromagnetic
spectrum **212**, 226, 423
waves 113, 114, 202, **212-213**, 214-215, **218-219**, 423
electromagnetism **233**, 423
electron 10, 11-14, 28, 43, **68**, 70, 71, 75, 80, 81, 92, 113, 114, **228**, 423
cloud model 11, 423
configuration **68**, 423
shells **10-11**, 14, 28, **68**, 71, 92, 423
electronic
circuit **236-239**, 423
components **236-239**, 423
electronics 38, 39, **236-239**, 423
electroplating **82**, 423
electroreception **323**, 423
electrorefining **83**, 423
elements 13, **24-33**, 46, 50, 58, 66, 82, 115, 423
elevator **143**, 144, 423
elliptical galaxy **156**, 423
elytra **307**, 423
email **247**, 423
embryo,
animal **326**
human **377**, 423
plant **274**, 423
emerald 90
emergent plant **280**, 423
emitter (in a transistor) **237**
emulsifier **59**, 423
emulsion **59**, 423
enamel **352**, 423
Enceladus (moon) **169**
endangered species 335, **336**
endemic **337**, 423
endocrine glands **363**, 423
endodermis (in plants) **255**
endoplasmic reticulum **298**, 423
endoscope **389**, 423
endoskeleton **301**, 423
endosperm **272**, 423
endothelium **351**
endothermic reaction 76, **78**, 423
energy **106-117**, 228, **332-333**, 360-361, 405
chain **107**, 423
efficiency **109**
value **360**
engines 141, 142, **146-151**, 423
entire leaf margin **259**
environment **330-331**, 423
enzymes **79**, 94, **267**, 285, 355, **360**, 423
ephemeral **423**
plants **289**
epicentre **182**, 423
epidermis
in fish **303**, 423
in human skin **368**, 423
in plants **255**, **260**, 423
epididymis **376**, 423
epigeal germination **277**
epiglottis **354**, 423
epimysium **349**, 423
epiphytes **266**, 423
epithelium **299**, 423
equations **77**, 423
equator 188, **192**, 193, 423
equatorial regions **194**, 423
equilibrium **120**, 423
eras **186**, 423
erbium **29**
Eros (asteroid) **173**
erosion **191**, **197**, 423
eruption **182**, 183, 423
esters **95**, 423
ethane **92**, 97, 423
ethanoic acid 84, 85, **94**, 423
ethanol **94**, 423
ethene 92, 93, 94, **97**, 99, 100
eubacteria **294**, **341**
euglena 341
Europa (moon) **168**
European Space Agency 175
europium **28**
eutrophication **281**, 423
evaporation **20**, **61**, 423
Evening Star **164**, 423
evergreen trees **289**, 423
evolution **338-339**, 423
excretion **362**, 423
excretory organs 316, 317, **362**, 423
exhalant siphon **314**
exhalation **359**, 423
exhaust fumes 79, **147**
exodermis **255**, 423
exoskeleton **301**, 302, 423
exosphere **185**, 423
exothermic reaction 76, 77, **78**, 79, 423
exposure (in a camera) **224**, 423
external
combustion engine **146**, 423
fertilization **326**, 423
gills **314**
extinct volcano **183**
extinction **187**, **336**, 339, 423
eyelids **371**
eyepiece **222**, 423
eyes 221, **321**, **370-371**

F

factual memory **367**
faculae **162**, 423
faeces **355**, 423
Fahrenheit, Gabriel **413**
Fahrenheit scale **111**, 405, 423
fallopian tubes **376**, 423
false fruit **274**, 423
families **341**, 423
Faraday, Michael **413**
farming 197, **291**
fascicles **349**, 423
fast-twitch fibres **349**, 423
fats **95**, 355, **356**, 423
fatty acids **94**, 423
fault **182**, 423
feathers **306**
feedback **238**, 423
feelers **322**
felines **342**
female reproductive system **376**
femur **346**, 423
fermentation **94**, 423
Fermi, Enrico **413**
fermium **29**
ferns 258, 278, 282, **283**, 295
ferromagnetic **232**, 234, 423
fertigation **197**
fertilization
animal **325**, **326**, **377**, 423
plant **272**, 423
fertilizer 38, 47, 54, 55, 64, 75, 87, **89**, 281, 291
fibre-optic cables 227, 244, **245**, **389**, 423
fibres (in plant tissue) **254**
fibrin **351**, 423
fibrous root **253**, 423
fibula **346**, 423
field of vision **321**, 424
filament **271**, 424
file path (websites) **247**, 424
filter feeding **310**, 424
filtrate **60**, 424
filtration **60**, 89, 424
fin (of a fish) 304, **305**
finder scope (in a telescope) **223**
fireworks 30, **80**
fish 186-187, 303, 305, **314**, 323, 326-327, 329, 335, 338, 342
fish-eye lens 220
fission **116**
flagellae **304**, 424
flagellate **304**, 424
flame
cell **317**
test **31**
flare (solar) **162**
flat bone **346**
flatworm **342**, 424
Fleming, Alexander 389, **413**
flight
of aircraft **142-145**
in animals **306-307**
feathers **306**, 424
flip-flop **238**, 424
flippers 304, **305**
floating **138-139**
flood plain **190**, 424
floppy disk 241, 242
florigen **269**, 424
flower shapes 273
flowering plants 187, **270-281**
flowerless plants **282-283**
fluid 133, **424**
movement in plants **262-263**
fluorescence **215**, 424
fluorides **48**, **353**, 424
fluorine 25, 29, **48**, 68, 71, 93, 96, 357
fluorite **48**, 407
fluorocarbons **48**

focus
of earthquake **182**, 424
of light **220**, **371**, 424
focusing knob (microscope) **222**
foetus **377**, 424
fold mountains **181**, 424
foliage **258**
follicle **369**, 424
food 291, **332-333**, **356-357**
chain **332**, 335, 424
production in plants 250-251, 258, 260-261, **264-266**
web **333**, 424
force
magnifier **134**, 424
ratio **134**, 424
forces **118-143**, 424
Ford, Henry **413**
foreskin **376**, 424
forests 186, 290
formic acid **84**, 424
formulae, chemical **15**, **66**
forward reaction **78**
fossil fuels 46, 52, 54, 64, **98**, **108**, **198**, 424
fossils 179, 186, 187, **338**
four-colour printing **217**, 424
four-stroke combustion cycle **148**, 424
fraction (oil) **99**, 424
fractional distillation **62**, 98, **99**, 424
fractionating column **99**, 424
fragmentation **324**, 424
frame (in photography) **225**
francium **28**
Franklin,
Benjamin **413**
Rosalind **413**
Frasch process **54**
freckles **369**
freezing **19**
point of water 72
frequency, wave **203**, 205, 206, 209, 212, 213, 215, 216, 226, 405, 424
Frequency Modulation (FM) **226**, 424
friction 51, 118, **124-125**, 424
frog 299, 314, 326, 328
frond 281, **283**
frontalis **348**, 424
fruit 84, 194, **274-277**
fruiting body **284**, 424
fuel 46, 47, 64, 80, 96, 98, 106, **108**, 198, 199
fulcrum **121**, **134**, 136, 424
function keys **240**, 424
fundamental frequency **424**
fungi 94, 266, **284-285**, 293, 294, 332, 334, 341, 424
funicle **271**
fuse **230**, 409, 424
fuselage **144**, 424
fusion **116**, 162

G

gadolinium **29**
Gagarin, Yuri 176, 411
galaxies 154, 155, **156-157**, 174, 175, 424
Galaxy M100 175
galena **38**
Galilean Moons **168**, 424
Galilei, Galileo 168, 174, 413
Galileo space probes 168, 169, 172, 176, 411
gall bladder **355**, 424
gallium **29**, 33
galvanizing 39, **41**, 424
gamete (of a plant) **270**, 424
gametophyte **283**, 424
gamma
radiation **114**, 424
rays (See *gamma radiation*)
Ganymede **168**
garlic 278
gas 16-19, **22-23**, 58, 79, 110, 112, 124, 128, 132, 133, 148, 149, 158, 173, 184, 185, 424
giants 168
turbine engines **149**, 424
gaseous exchange **314**, 424
gasoline **99**, 424
Gaspra **172**
gastric
glands **355**
juices **355**, 424
gastrocnemius **348**, 424
gears 41, **135**, 136, 148, **151**, 424
gemmae **283**
gemstones **199**
gene
splicing **383**
therapy **385**, 424
genera (sing. genus) **341**, 424
general theory of relativity **424**
generators **107**, 108, **235**, 424
generic names **343**, 424
genes 291, **380-385**, 424
genetic
engineering **383**, 384-385, 424
fingerprinting **383**, 424
modification **291** (See also *genetic engineering*)
screening **385**, 424
genetically modified organisms (GMOs) **385**
genetics **380-385**, 424
genome **382**, 424
geological time **178**, **186**, 424
geologists **179**
geology **424**
geometrical
formulae **408**
shapes **408**
geostationary orbit **175**, 424
geothermal energy **198**, 424
geotropism **268**, 424
Gerbert **413**
germanium 25, **29**
germination **277**, 424
germs 212, **386**
gestation period **327**, 424
geyser 16, **18**
giant
molecules **69**
stars **159**, 161, 424
Gilbert, William **413**
gills
in fish 62, **314**, 424
in fungi **284**
gingiva **352**, 424
gingivitis **353**, 424
ginkgo **295**, 424
gizzard **313**, 424
glacier **179**, **190**, 424
gland **354**, 363, 424
glans **376**, 424
glider (aircraft) 112, **142**
gliding
animals **307**
joints **347**, 424
Global Surveyor **165**
global warming 63, **65**, **185**, **293**, 424
globular cluster **156**, 424
glomeruli **362**, 424
glucagon **363**, 424
glucose 80, 81, 356, 360, 363, 388, 424
glycerol **95**, 424
glycogen **356**, 424
GM food **291**
gnetae **295**, 424
gold 15, 26, 27, 29, 30, **32**, 33, 35, **38**, 42, 43, 44, 45, 82
Golgi complex **298**, 424
gracilis **348**, 424
gradient (of a river) **190**
grain **275**, 424
granite 27, 180, 181, 191
graphite 25, 50, **51**, **71**, 83, 424
grasses 260, 286, 290, 294
gravitation (Newton's law) 409
gravitational field **130**, 424
gravity 118, 120, 127, 128, 129, **130-131**, 142, 155, 161, 162, 177, 180, 188, 424
Great
Bear (constellation) **160**
Dark Spot **170**
Red Spot **168**, 424
greenhouse effect 63, **65**, 108, **185**, **293**, 424
ground tissue **251**
group (in periodic table) **28**, 425
growing point (in a root) **253**
growth
in humans **378-379**
in plant cells 252, 256-257
season **288**, 425
guard cell (in a leaf) **260**, 425
gullet **354**, 358, 425
gustatory
pore 375
receptor cell **375**, 425
guttation **263**, 425
gymnophyte **295**, 425
gypsum **73**, 407
gyroscope **129**, 425

H

Haber, Fritz **47**
Haber process **47**, 425
habitats 187, 290, **330**, 337, 425
haematite **27**, **36**, 38, 199
haemocoel **301**, 425
haemoglobin **351**, 425
hafnium **28**
Hahn, Otto **413**
hair **368-369**
cells 372, **373**
erector muscles **368**, 425
plexuses **368**, 425
Hale-Bopp (comet) **172**
half-life **115**, 425
halides **27**, 425
halite 27, **89**, 91, 425
Halley, Edmund **413**
Halley's comet 173
halogens 27, 29, **48-49**, 425
halophytes **286**, 425
haltères **320**, 425
haptotropism **269**, 425
hard
disk **241**, 425
palate **354**
water **73**, 88, 94, 425
hardware **240**, 242-243, 425
harmonics **209**, 425
Harvey, William **413**
hassium **28**
haustoria **266**, 425
Haversian canal **347**, 425
Hawking, Stephen **413**
hearing 320, **372-373**
heart **350**, 361
heartwood **257**, 425
heat 16, 18, 24, 25, 30, 76, 78, 106, 107, 108, 109, **110-113**, 125
heavenly body 172, **425**
helicopter 142, 144, **145**
helium 25, 29, 46, 51, **63**, 114, 139, 154, 162, 184, 425
hemiparasites (plants) **266**, 425
herbaceous perennials **288**, 425
herbivores **312**, 332, 425
heredity **425**
hermaphrodites **271**, **325**, 425
heroin **391**
Herschel,
Caroline **413**
William **170**, 413
hertz **203**, 206, 209, 425
Hertz, Heinrich 203, **414**
heterotrophic **332**, 425
heterozygous **381**, 425
hexapods **309**, 425
hibernation **329**, 425
high
pressure 192
tides **131**, **189**
high-fidelity recording **211**, 425
hilum **274**, 425
hinge joint **347**, 425
Hipparcos (satellite) 175
holdfast **281**
holly 271
holmium **29**
homeopathy **390**
homeostasis **316**, 317, **362**, 425
homologous
chromosomes **380**, 425
series **92**, 94, 96, 97, 425
homozygous **381**, 425
Hooke, Robert **414**
Hooke's law **119**, 121, 409
hopper 328
hormones 362, **363**, 425
Horse's Head Nebula **158**
horsetails 282, 295, 425
host **266**, 343, 425
hot spots (geology) **183**
hotspots (ecology) **337**, 425
hovercraft **140**
HTML (HyperText Markup Language) **246**, 425
http (HyperText Transfer Protocol) **247**, 425
Hubble, Edwin **414**
Hubble Space Telescope (HST) 161, 170, 171, **175**, 177, 411
humerus **346**, 425
humic acid **86**
humidity 192, **425**
hurricane **189**, 425
Huygens, Christiaan **414**
hybrid **384**, 425
hydra 324
hydrated **91**, 425
hydration 89, **91**, 425
hydraulic machine **133**, 425

hydrocarbons 79, **92**, 96, 97, 98, 425
hydrochloric acid 48, **84**, 88, 89
hydroelectric power **108**, 425
stations 198
hydrofoil **140**, 425
hydrogen 14, 15, 24, 25, 28, 32, **46-47**, 52, 64, 68, 69, 72, 73, 75, 80, 81, 83, 84, 85, 86, 88, 92, 93, 94, 96, 97, 98, 100, 154, 162, 178, 184
bomb **116**, 425
oxide 66, **72**, 425
hydrogenation **97**, 425
hydrometer **17**, 425
hydrophytes **280**, 425
hydrostatic skeleton **301**, 425
hydrotropism **268**, 425
hydroxide ions **85**
hydroxyl group **94**, 425
hylonomus 187
hyperlink (internet) **246**, 425
hyphae **284**, 425
hypogeal germination **277**
hyponome **304**, 425
hypopharynx **311**, 425
hypotenuse 409, **425**
hypothalamus **366**, 425

I

ice 18, 19, **72**, 110, 173, 178, 179, 184, 229
ages **179**, 425
point 111, **425**
igneous rock **181**, 425
Ikeya Seki (comet) 173
ileum **355**, 425
ilium **346**, 425
image **218**, 220-221, 425
imago **328**, 425
immiscible (liquids) **59**, 425
immunity **387**
imperial system **404**
incident
ray **218**
wave **204**, 425
incisors **312**, **352**, 425
inclined plane **135**, 136
incomplete
fission **324**, 425
metamorphosis **328**, 425
incus **372**, 425
indicator **86**, 87, 425
indium **29**, 33
inertia **122**, 425
inferior vena cava **350**, 425
inflammable **425**
infrared
radiation **113**, 185, **213**, 215, 425
rays (See *infrared radiation*)
infrasound **206**, 425
infundibulum **376**, 425
inhalant siphon **314**
inhalants **391**
inhalation **359**, 425
inhibitor (catalyst) **79**, 425
inner
core of Earth **180**, 425
ear **372**
planets **164-166**, 425
transition metals **29**, 425
inorganic **357**, 425
input **238**, 425
insecticides 54, **335**, 425
insects 186, 187, **300**, 307, **309**, 315, 319, 321, 325, 328, 330, 338
insolubility **58**, 88, 425
instantaneous speed **126**, 425
insulated wire **228**, 230
insulator,
electrical **25**, **228**, 239, 426
heat 25, 103, **113**, 426
insulin **363**, 426
integrated circuit 25, 236, 237, **239**, 405, 426
integumentary system **368**, 426
intensity, light **214**, 426
intensive farming **291**, 426
interactive TV **227**, 426
intercostal muscles **359**, 426
interdependence **333**
interference **218**, 219, 426
internal
combustion engine **146-147**, 150, 426
energy **110**, 426
fertilization **326**, 426
gills **314**
respiration 52, **80**, 81, **265**, 358, **360**, 426
International Space Station (ISS) **177**, 411
internet 6-7, **246-247**, 426
Internet Service Provider (ISP) 7, **246**, 426
internode **252**, 426
invertebrates 187, **322**, 426
intestines 355
involuntary
actions **365**, 426
muscles **348**, 426
Io (moon) **168**
iodine 25, 29, 48, **49**, 70, **357**
ion **70**, 71, 73, 75, 82, 83, 84, 85, 86, 88, 94, 426
exchange **73**, 75, 426
ionic
bonding **70**, 426
compound **70**, 73, 88
lattice **70**, 426
ionosphere 226
IRAS Araki-Alcock (comet) 173
iridescence **219**
iridium **28**
iris 370, **371**, 426
iron 15, 26, 27, 28, 30, 33, 34, 35, **36-37**, **38**, 40, 42, 43, 44, 45, 54, 66, 77, 78, 80, 81, 89, 90, 178, 180, 199, 210, 232, 234, **357**
ore **36**, 81
oxide 27, 40, 81
pyrites 54, **90**
sulphide **66**, 77, 89
irregular
bone **346**
galaxy **156**, 426
irrigation **197**, 426
ischium **346**, 426
islands (largest) **410**
islets of Langerhans **363**, 426
isotope **13**, 49, 426
Ithaca (valley) 169

J

Jacobson's organs **323**, 426
jejunum **355**, 426
Jenner, Edward **414**
jet 35, 38-39, 96, 127, 143, **144**, 149, 185
engines 35, 39, 142, **149**, 426
jet, jump **145**
joints **347**, 426
Joule, James 110, **414**
joules **109**, 110, **137**, 405, 426
Jupiter 163, **168**, 169, 172, 176, 411
Jurassic Period **186**

K

Keck observatories 174
keel (in a bird) **306**, 426
keeper (of a magnet) **232**, 426
Kelvin, Lord **414**
kelvins **111**, 405, 426
Kepler, Johannes **414**
keratin **303**, 356, 368, 426
kernel **275**, 426
kerosene **96**, **99**, 149, 426
key fruit **275**, 426
kidneys **317**, **362**, 426
kilocalories **360**, 426
kilojoules (kJ) **109**, **360**, 426
kimberlite **27**
kinetic
energy **106**, 107, 110, 426
theory **16**, 426
kingdoms **294**, **341**, 426
Kohoutek (comet) 173
krypton 25, 29, **63**, 184, 426

L

labia **376**, 426
labium (in an insect) **311**, 426
labour **377**, 426
labrum **311**, 426
lachrymal
canal **371**, 426
gland **371**, 426
lactic acid **361**, 426
lacuna 347, **426**
lakes (greatest) **410**
lamellae **347**, 426
lamina **258**, 426
landmasses 179
lanthanides **29**, 426
lanthanum **28**
laptop **240**
large intestine **354**, **355**, 426
larvae **328**, 426
larynx **359**, 426
laser 51, 182, **215**, 426
printer **229**
surgery 215, **389**
late wood **257**
lateral
buds **252**
lines **323**, 426
roots **253**, 426
vision **321**, 426
latex **101**, 426
lattices **70**
lauric acid **94**
lava **182**, 426
Lavoisier, Antoine **414**
law of volumes (Charles' law) **409**
lawrencium **28**
lead 29, 30, 33, **38**, 39, 43, 44, 64, 75
leader stroke **229**, 426
leaf
margin **259**
trace **261**, 426
leaflet **258**, 426
leaping **309**
leaves 251, 254, **258-261**, 294
Leeuwenhoek, Antony van **414**
legumes **275**, 276, 292, 426
Lemaître, Georges **414**
length (units) **404**, **405**
lenses 174, **220**, 222-223, 224, 426
lenticel **257**, 426
lettuce 291
LeVerrier, Urbain Jean 170
levers **134**, 136
lichens 86, 290, **293**, 426
life
cycles **328-329**, 426
expectancy **379**
lift **142**, 145, 426
ligases **383**
light 78, 106, 107, 108, 154, 159, 212, **213**, **214-219**, 370, 426
years **154**, 426
light-emitting diode (LED) **237**, 426
lightning 64, 228, **229**, 292, 426
light-sensitive film 224
lignite **52**, 53, 426
limestone 32, 36, 38, **73**, 76, 78, 79, 86, 88, 180, 181
Linnaeus, Carolus (Carl von Linné) **414**
lipped flower **273**
liquid crystal **90**, 111, 240
display (LCD) **90**, 426
liquids **16-21**, 58, 59, 79, 110, 112, 124, 128, 132, 133, 138
Lister, Joseph **414**
lithium **28**
lithophytes **287**, 426
lithosphere **180**, 426
litmus **86**, 88, 426
live wire **230**, 426
liver **317**, 355, 362, 426
liverworts 254, **282**, 295, 426
load **134**, 426
of a river **191**, 426
lobes (of a leaf) **259**, 294
Local Group (galaxies) **156**, 426
local-area network (LAN) **243**, 426
locomotion **304-309**, **426**
log on (internet) **246**, 427
logic gate **238**, 426
long
bone **346**
sight 221, **371**
longitudinal wave **203**, 206, 427
long-night plants **269**
long-term memory **367**, 427
looping (in caterpillars) **308**
loudspeaker 206, **210**, 226, 409, 427
Lovelace, Ada **414**
low
pressure **192**
surface brightness galaxy **156**, 427
tide **131**, **189**
lower stage (of a river) **190**
LSD **391**
lubricant 51, **125**, 427
luminous **214**, 427
Luna 9 space probe 176, 411
lunar eclipse **427**
lungs **315**, **358**, 427
lutetium **28**

lymph **387**, 427
node **387**, 427
lymphatic system **387**, 427
lymphocyte **387**, 427
lysosome **298**, 427

M

machines 109, 124, 125, 133, **134-136**, 140-151
macrophage **387**
macula **373**, 427
Magellan space probe **165**
Magellanic Clouds **156**
magma **26**, **180**, 181, 182, 183, 427
chamber **183**, 427
magnesium 28, 30, 32, 35, **38**, 41, 68, 73, 78, 80, 88
chloride 80
hydroxide **85**
oxide **78**, 85
magnet **232-233**, 427
magnetic **232**, 427
field 210, 212, 219, **233**, 427
field of Earth 180, **233**
flux lines **233**, 427
levitation (maglev) **234**
north **233**, 427
south **233**, 427
magnetism 30, 45, 118, **232-235**, 427
magnetite **36**
magnetron **213**
magnifying glass 222
magnitude **160**, 427
magnoliophyte **270**, **295**, 427
Maiman, Theodore **414**
malachite **27**, 88
male reproductive system **376**
malleability **30**, 427
malleus **372**, 427
Malpighi, Marcello **414**
malpighian tubules **317**, 427
maltose **354**
mammals 186, 187, 338, **342**, 427
mammary glands **327**, 427
manganese **28**, 34, 35
mangrove 253
mandible (in humans) **346**, 427
mandibles (in insects) **311**, 427
mantle **180**, 181, 427
maquis **331**
Marconi, Guglielmo 226, **414**
margarine **97**
Mariner space probe **165**, 411
maritime climate **195**
marrow cavity **347**
Mars 19, 163, 164, **165**, 172, 176, 411
Global Surveyor 411
Pathfinder 411
marsupials **427**
mass **17**, 77, 122, 123, **130**, 138, 404, 405, 427
extinction **186**, **339**, 427
number **12**, 13, 29, 115, 427
spectrometer **12**, 427
mating **326**, 427
maxillae **311**, 427
Maxwell, James Clerk **414**
meandering (river) **190**, 427
mechanical wave **202-203**, 427
median fin **305**, 427
medical imaging **388**, 427
medicine **388-391**
Mediterranean climate **194**
medium **202**, 204-205
medulla
in brain **366**
in kidney **362**
megahertz (MHz) **241**
meiosis **380**, 427
Meissner's corpuscles **368**, 427
Meitner, Lise **414**
meitnerium **28**
melamine **101**
melanin 213, **369**, 427
melanocyte **369**, 427
melting 16, **18**
point **18**, 19, 69, 70, 427
memory,
computer **241**
human **367**
Mendel, Gregor **414**
Mendeleyev, Dmitri **414**
mendelevium **29**, 43
meninges **366**
menopause **379**, 427
menstruating **379**, 427
Mercalli scale **407**
Mercator, Gerardus **414**
mercury (element) 19, 29, 30, 33, **38**, 43, 55, 75, 111
Mercury (planet) 163, **164**, 411
meristem **252**, 427
mesophyll **260**, 427
mesosphere **185**, 427
Mesozoic Era **186**, **187**, 427
metabolic rate **360**, 427
metabolism **360**, 427
metacarpals **346**, 427
metallic
(M-type) asteroid **172**
bonding **70**, 427
lattice **70**
metalloids **25**, 29, 427
metallurgy 35, **427**
metals 24, 29, **30-45**, 82, 83, 88, 89, 113, 427
metamere **300**, 427
metameric segmentation **300**
metamorphic rock **181**, 427
metamorphosis **328**, 427
metatarsals **346**, 427
meteor **173**, 185, 427
meteorite **173**, 427
meteoroid **173**, 427
meteorologist **406**
meteorology **427**
methane 15, 47, 92, 93, **96**, 178, 184, 427
methanoic acid 84, **94**, 427
metric system **404**
microclimate **194**, 427
micromotor **235**, 427
microphone **210**, 409, 427
microprocessor **241**, 427
micropropagation **279**, 427
micropyle **272**, 427
microscope **222**, 250
microsurgery 235
microwave **213**, 427
oven **213**
midbrain **366**
middle
C **209**
ear **372**
stage (of a river) **190**
midrib (in a leaf) **260**, 427
migration 323, **329**, 427
mildew **284**, 427
milk teeth **353**, 427
Milky Way 154, 156, **157**, 427
millibars **132**, 427
Mimas **169**
mimicry **318**, 427
mimosa 269
mineral acids **87**, 427
minerals **26-27**, 73, 90, **199**, 253, 260, 262, **357**, 407, 427
mining **199**, 427
Mir (space station) 177, 411
Mira **159**
Miranda **170**
mirrors 174, 218, **220-221**, 222-223
miscible (liquids) **59**, 427
mistletoe 266
mitochondria **298**, 427
mitosis **251**, 299, **378**, 427
mixture **58-61**, 62-65, 427
mobile phone **245**, 247
modem 7, **245**, 427
modulation **226**, 427
module **177**
Mohs scale **407**
molar **312**, **352**, 427
mole (unit) **77**, 427
molecular lattice **70**, 427
molecule **14-15**, 16, 20, 21, 22, 23, 69, 70, 76, 79, 91, 94, 99, 100, 213, 427
molluscs **342**, 427
molten **180**
molybdates **27**
molybdenum 27, **28**
moment **121**, 427
momentum **123**, 407, 427
monoclinic sulphur **54**, 428
monocotyledon **255**, **277**, 295, 428
monocyte **387**, 428
monoecious **271**, 428
monomer **100**, 428
Moon (Earth's) 128, 130, 131, 163, **167**, 176, 188, 214
landings 176
orbit **167**, 189
moons **163**, 165, 168-171, 428
Morning Star **164**, 428
Morse, Samuel **414**
mosaic image **321**
mosses **282**, 287, 295
motherboard **239**, 428
motion 122, 123, 124, **126-129**
Newton's laws of **122**, 409
motion-picture cameras **225**
motor
area (in brain) **367**
nerve **364**
neuron **364**, 428
motorbike 80, **151**
motor-skill memory **367**, 428
moulds **284**, 428
mountain climate 195
mountaineers 185
mountains 166, 181, **290**, **331**, 410
mp3 245, **428**
MRI (magnetic resonance imaging) scanner **388**, 428
mucus **358**, 374, 375, 428
multicellular **300**, 428
multiple fission **324**, 428
muscle fibre **349**, 428
muscles **348-349**
musical instruments **208-209**
mutualists **343**, 428
mycelium **284**, 428
mycorrhizae **284**, 428
myofibre **349**, 428
myofibril **349**, 428
myofilament **349**, 428
myosin **349**
myriapod **309**, 428

N

nails **369**
nanotechnology **428**
nanotube **51**, 428
NASA (National Aeronautics Space Administration) 171, **175**, 176
nasal cavity **374**, 428
native elements **27**
natural
fibre 100, **101**
gas 96, 98, 108
polymer 100, **101**
selection 286, **339**, 428
nature reserves **336**
neap tide **189**, 428
NEAR (Near Earth Asteroid Rendezvous) spacecraft **173**, 411
near-Earth asteroid **173**
Near Infrared Camera 170
nebulae **158**, 428
neck (of a tooth) **352**
nectar **270**, 428
guide **272**
nectaries **270**, 428
needles (of conifers) **290**
negative
acceleration **127**
film **225**, 428
tropism **268**
nematocyst **310**, 428
nematode **342**, 428
neodymium **28**
neon 25, 29, **63**, 68, 184, 215, 428
nephridiopore **317**, 428
nephron **362**, 428
Neptune 163, **170-171**, 411
neptunium **28**
Nereid (moon) **171**
nerve
fibre **364**, 428
impulse **365**, 374, 428
nerves **364**, 366, 428
nervous system **364-365**, 428
networking **243**, 246-247, 428
neuron **364**, 428
neurotransmitter **365**, 428
neutralization reaction **78**, 85, 428
neutral wire **230**, 428
neutron **10**, 11-13, 114, 115, 116, 117, **228**, 428
stars **161**, 428
Newcomen, Thomas 146, **414**
New Horizon (space probe) 171
Newton, Isaac 119, 122, 216, **414**
newton metres **121**, 428
Newton's laws of motion **122**, 409
newtons **119**, 137, 405, 428
nickel **29**, 30, 33, 34, 35, 38, 180
nicotine **391**
night-neutral plants **269**
niobium **28**
Nipkow, Paul **414**
nitrates 27, **64**, **88**, 89, 291, **292**, **334**, 428

nitric acid 64, **84**, 88
nitrogen 15, 25, 27, 29, 47, 52, 62, **64**, 68, 147, 166, 184, 292, **334**, 428
cycle **64**, 285, **292**, **334**, 428
dioxide 65, 78
monoxide **78**
oxide 147
nitrogen-fixing bacteria **292**, 428
Nobel, Alfred **414**
nobelium **29**
noble
gases 29, 62, **63**, 428
metals **32**, 42, 428
nocturnal **321**, 428
node **252**, 428
non-chromatic colours **428**
non-metals 24, **25**, 29, 88, 428
non-renewable fuels **108**, 428
non-vascular plants **295**
North American plate 182
North Pole 179, 188
northern
hemisphere **193**, 428
lights **162**
north-seeking pole **232**, 428
nose **374**
NOT (logic gate) **238**, 428
notes (musical) **209**, 428
notochord **342**, 428
nova **159**, 428
NREM sleep **367**, 428
nuclear
energy 39, 108, **114**, 116, 198
fission **116**, 428
fusion **116**, 428
membrane **298**, 428
pores **298**, 428
power **116-117**
reaction **116-117**, 158, 159, 162
reactor 38, **117**, 428
weapons 38, 39, **116**, 428
nucleolus **298**, 428
nucleotide **382**, 428
nucleus
in animal cell **298**, 299, 428
in atom **10**, 11-13, 114, 115, 116, 117, **228**, 428
of a comet **173**, 428
in plant cell **250**, 251, 254, 294, 428
nut **275**
nutrients **356**, 428
nylon **100**, 101, 103
nymph **328**

O

Oberon (moon) **170**
object (in microscopy) **222**
objective lens **222**, 428
observatories **174**, 428
obsidian **26**
ocean trench **189**
oceanic
crust **180**
plate 181
oceans 184, **188-189**, 331, 410
octane **99**
octopus 304, 322
odorant molecules **374**, 428
Odysseus (crater) 169
oesophagus **354**, 428
Ohm, Georg 236, **415**
ohms **236**, 428
oil
platform **98**
rig (See *oil platform*)
oils 46, 59, **95**, 96, **98-99**, 100, 108, 125, 428
olfactory
cells **374**, 428
hairs **374**, 428
omasum **313**
omnivore **312**, 428
online **246**, 428
opaque **214**, 428
open
cast mine **199**, 428
cluster (stars) **156**, 428
operating system **240**, 428
operculum **314**, 428
Opportunity (Mars mission) 165
opposite leaves **259**
optic nerve **370**, 428
optical
instruments **222-225**, 428
microscope **222**, 428
telescope **174**, **223**, 428
OR (logic gate) **238**, 429
orbitals **428**
orbits **163-171**, 179, 428
order **341**, 342, 428
Ordovician Period **186**
ores 26, 36, 42, 44, 45, **199**, 428
organ **299**, 377, **429**
Organ of Corti **372**, 429
organelles **250**, **298**, 429
organic 357
acids **84**, **94**, 429
chemistry **92-97**, 98-103
compounds 52, **67**, **92-93**, 94-103, 429
farming **291**, 429
organism 299, **429**
Orion (constellation) **160**
Orion (space capsule) 177
Oscillating Universe theory **155**, 429
oscillation **429**
osmium **28**
osmosis **429**
ossicles **320**
ossification **347**, 429
osteocyte **347**, 429
osteopathy **390**, 429
otolith **373**, 429
outer
core (of Earth) **180**, 429
ear **372**
planets **168-171**, 429
outgassing **184**, 429
output **238**, 429
ova (sing. ovum) **326**, **376**, 377, 379, 380, 429
oval window **372**, 429
ovary **271**, 272, 363, **376**
overfishing **335**, 429
oviparous **327**, 429
ovulation **376**, **379**, 429
ovule **271**, 274, 429
ovum (See *ova*)
owl 306, 313
oxidation **80**, 81, 94, 429
oxides **27**, 40, 66, 80, **83**, 85, 89, 429
oxidizing agent **80**, 87, 429
oxygen 15, 25, 26, 27, 29, 30, 36, 37, 40, 41, 43, 46, 47, 52, **62**, 65, 69, 72, 73, 75, 78, 80, 81, 83, 94, 149, 166, 178, 184, 264, 265, 292, 350, 358, 360, 371, 429
debt **361**
oxyhaemoglobin **351**, 429
ozone layer 65, **185**, 429

P

Pacific plate 182
Pacinian corpuscles **368**, 429
pain receptors **368**
paint **59**, 88, 215
paired fins **305**, 429
Paleozoic Era **186**, 429
palisade
cells 251, **260**, **264**, 429
layer **260**
palladium **29**, 32
palmate leaves **258**, 429
palmtop **240**
palps **311**, **323**, 429
pancreas 354, **355**, **363**, 429
pancreatic juice **355**
panda 337
Pangaea (landmass) **179**, 429
papillae **375**, 429
parachutes 177
parallel circuit **230**, 429
Paramecium 304, 317, 324
parapodia **304**, 429
parasites **266**, 343, 429
parenchyma **255**, 429
parthenogenesis **325**, 429
particle accelerator **43**, 429
Pascal, Blaise 132, **415**
pascals **132**, 405, 429
passive immunity **387**, 429
Pasteur, Louis **415**
pasteurization **429**
patella **346**, 429
Pathfinder (Mars mission) 411
pathogens **386**, 429
PC (personal computer) 7, **240**
peak (wave) **203**, 206, 429
pectoral fin **305**, 429
pectoralis muscles **306**, 429
peer-to-peer network **243**, 429
pellet **313**, 429
pelvic fin **305**, 429
pelvis **346**, 429
penicillin **285**, **389**, 429
penis 326, **376**, 429
penumbra **214**, 429
percussion instrument **208**
perennial **288**, **429**
perfect sound reproduction **211**, 429
perfoliate leaves **259**, 429
perimysium **349**, 429
period
in geology **186**, 429
(menstruation) **379**, 429
in periodic table **28**, 429
periodic table 24, **28-29**, 429
periodontal ligament **352**, 429
periosteum **347**, 429
peripheral nervous system **364**, 429
peripherals **240**, 429
periscope **223**
peristalsis **355**, 429
peritoneum **301**, 429
perivisceral cavity **301**, 429
permanent
magnet **232**, 429
teeth **312**, **353**, 429
permeable 190, **429**
Permian Period **186**, **187**
persistent vision **225**
personal computer (See *PC*)
pesticides 55, **75**, 291
petal **270**
petiole **261**, 429
petrol **96**, 98, 99, 429
engine **148**, 150
pewter **39**
pH numbers **86**, 429
phagocytosis 310, **387**, 429
phalanges **346**, 429
pharming **385**, 429
pharynx **354**
phases (of the Moon) **167**, 429
phellogen **257**, 429
pheromones **319**, 326, 429
phloem **254**, 256, **262**, 429
Phobos (moon) **165**
phosphates **27**, **55**, 75, 87, 89, 429
phosphor **429**
phosphorescence **429**
phosphoric acid 40, **55**, 430
phosphorus 12, 25, 27, 29, **55**, 71, 89, 239, 357
photochemical reactions **78**, 429
photocopier 229
photoelectric cell **430**
photographic film 39, 45, 49, **225**
photon **430**
photoperiod **269**, 430
photoreceptor **321**, 430
photosphere (of Sun) **162**, 430
photosynthesis 52, 78, **81**, 258, **264**, 265, 266, 277, 293, 294, 430
phototropism **268**, 430
phylum **341**, 430
physical states **16-19**, 77
physiology **430**
phytoplankton **189**, 430
Pi (π) 408
Piazzi 172
piezoelectric effect **91**, 430
pig iron **36**
pigments 67, **217**, **261**, 281, 430
pinna **320**, **372**, 430
pinnae **258**
pinnate leaves **258**, 430
Pioneer space probes 169, 176, 411
pioneer community **330**, 430
pistil **271**, 430
pistillate flowers **271**, 430
pistons **146**, **148**, 150, 430
pit organ **323**, 430
pitch **209**, 430
pitcher plant 267
pitching **143**
pivot **121**
joint **347**, 430
pixel **225**, **227**, 242, 430
placebo **390**
placenta **327**, **377**, 430
placoid scales **303**, 430
Planck, Max **415**
planes 35, 38-39, 96, 132, **142-145**
planets 163, **164-171**
plankton **98**
plant
cells **250-251**, 260
food **264-267**
lifestyles **288-289**

plant
  sensitivity **268-269**
  tissue 251, 252, **254-255**
plantigrade **309**, 430
plaque **353**, 430
plasma (in blood) 61, **351**, 430
plasmid **383**
plasmolysis **263**, 430
plaster of Paris 88
plastic (plasticity) **121**, 430
plastics 12, 97, **100-103**, 430
plate
  boundary **181**, 182, 430
  tectonics **181**, 430
platelets 61, **351**, 430
plates (Earth's) 166, 181, 183, 430
platinum 29, 30, 32, **38**, 44, 45, 79
playback head **210**, 430
Pleiades (stars) **156**
Plough (asterism) **160**
plug (electrical) **230**
plug-ins **7**
plum 274
plumbago **51**
plumes **183**
plumule **274**, **277**, 430
Pluto 163, 168, **171**, 173, 411
plutonium 28, **38**, 115, 116
pneumatic machines **133**, 430
polar
  cap 171, **331**
  climate **194**, 430
polarization **219**, 430
polarizing sunglasses **219**
polaroid camera **224**
poles, magnetic **232**, 430
poles (power source) **230**, 430
pollen 16, **271**, 272-273, 430
  tube **272**, 430
pollination 270, **272-273**, 275, 430
pollution 53, 63, **64**, 65, **75**, 117, 174, 187, 293, 335
polonium 25, **29**, 33
polycarbonate **103**
polyester 94, **101**, 103
polymer **100**, 101, 430
polymerization **100**, 430
polypropene **102**
polystyrene 100, 101, **103**
polytetrafluoroethene (PTFE) 48
polythene 97, **100**, 101, **102**, 430
polyurethane 103
polyvinyl **103**
polyvinylchloride (PVC) 48, 93, **100**, 103, 430
pome **274**, 430
pons **366**
poor metals **33**, 430
poppy 270, 272, 286
population **196-197**, 430
pore **369**, 430
positive
  film **225**, 430
  tropism **268**
potash **89**
potassium 15, 28, 30, 31, 32, **38**, 68, 89, 91
potato 278
potential
  difference **230**, 430
  energy **106**, 110, 430
power 108, **109**, **137**, 405, 430
  stations 53, 107, 117, **147**, 230, **235**, 430
prairies **290**
praseodymium **28**
Precambrian Era **186**, 430
precipitate **89**, 430
precipitation **192**, 430
prehensile **308**, 430
prehistoric life **338-339**
premolars **312**, **352**, 430
pressure 18, **19**, 20, 23, **132-133**, 142, 405, 430
pressurized water reactor (PWR) **117**, 430
prevailing winds **188**
preventative medicine **391**
Priestley, Joseph **415**
primary
  bronchi **358**
  cells (battery) **231**, 430
  colours **216**, **217**, 430
  consumer **332**, 430
  phloem **254**, 430
  root **253**
  sexual features **379**, 430
  tissue (plant) **254**, 430
  xylem **254**, 430
primates 308, 312, 321, 327, 342
printed circuit board (PCB) **236**, 237, 430
prism **216**, 223, 430
proboscis **311**, 430
producer **332**, 430
products **76**, 77, 78, 430
program (computer) **240**, 430
promethium **28**
prominence, solar **46**, **162**, 430
prop root **253**, 430
propan-1,2,3-triol **95**, 430
propane 92, **96**, 430
propellers 34, **136**, 140, 141, 142, 149
propene **97**
prostate gland **376**, 430
protactinium **28**
protective adaptation **287**, **339**, 430
proteins 64, 101, **292**, 298, **334**, 355, 356, 430
prothalli **283**, 430
protista **294**, 341, 430
protocol **247**, 430
proton **10**, 11-13, 68, 70, 114, 115, **228**, 430
protonephridia **317**, 430
protoplasm **298**, 430
Proxima Centauri (star) **158**
pseudopodia **304**, 430
PTFE (See *polytetrafluoroethene)*
puberty **379**, 430
pubis **346**, 430
pulleys **135**, 430
pulmonary
  arteries **350**, 430
  veins **350**, 431
pulp cavity **352**, 431
pulsar **161**, 431
pulsating variable **159**, 431
pupae **328**, 431
pupil 22I, **321**, **370**, 371, 431
pure breeding **384**
PVC (See *polyvinylchloride)*
pyramid
  of biomass **333**
  of numbers **332**
pyrite 54, **90**
Pythagoras **415**
Pythagoras' theorem **409**, 415

Q

quadriceps **348**, 431
quadruped **309**, 431
quantum theory **431**
quark **10**, 431
quartz 27, **66**, 90, 91, 407, 431
  crystals **91**
Quaternary Period **187**
quicklime **78**
quill **303**, 431

R

radar **213**, 431
radial
  muscles **371**, 431
  symmetry **301**, 431
radiation 33, 38, **113**, 114-115, 117, 178, 431
radiative zone (Sun) **162**, 431
radicle (in seeds) **274**, 277, 431
radio 175, 213, **226-227**, 237
  telescope **174**, 213, 431
  wave 203, **213**, **226**, 244, 431
radioactive
  decay **115**, 431
  rare earths **29**
  tracing **115**, 431
  waste 198
radioactivity 38, 39, 49, **114-115**, 116-117, 198, 431
radioisotope **431**
radio-opaque **388**
radiotherapy **115**, 431
radium **28**, 115
radius (bone) **346**, 431
radon 25, 29, **63**, 431
radula **310**, 431
rafflesia plant 266
rainbow **216**
rainwater 64, 65, **73**, 79, 87
RAM (random access memory) **241**, 431
rare earths **29**
rayon 87
rays (fish fins) **305**, 431
reactants **76**, 77, 78, 431
reactions,
  chemical 13, **76-79**, 80-81
  nuclear **116-117**, 158, 159, 162
reactivity **30**, 32, 33, 40, 41, 46, 48, 79, 82, 83, 431
  series **30**, 40, 431
reactors (nuclear) 38, **117**
receptacle **270**, 274, 431
receptors **320**, **364**, 431
recessive genes **381**, 431
recombinant DNA **383**
recording head **210**, 431
rectum **355**, 431
rectus abdominis **348**, 431
recycling **44-45**, 101, 199, 431
red
  blood cells 61, **351**, 431
  bone marrow **347**
  giant 159, **161**
  phosphorus **55**, 431
  supergiant **161**
Red Planet **165**, 431
redox reactions **80**, 431
reducing agent **81**, 431
reduction 36, 42, 80, 81, 431
reed mace 280
refinery gases **99**
reflected
  ray **218**
  wave **204**, 207
reflection **204**, 207, 216, 217, **218**, 431
reflector telescope **174**, **223**, 431
reflex
  actions **365**, 431
  arc **365**, 431
refracted
  ray **218**
  wave **205**
refraction **205**, 216, **218**, 220, 431
refractor telescope **174**, **223**, 431
refrigerator 185
regeneration **324**, 431
regular reflection **218**, 431
relative
  atomic mass **29**, 431
  density **139**, 141, 431
  velocity **127**, 431
relativity **431**
REM sleep **367**, 431
remiges **306**, 431
Remote Manipulator System (Space Shuttle) **176**
renal
  arteries 317, **362**, 431
  pelvis **362**, 431
  veins 317, **362**, 431
renewable energy **108**, **198**, 431
reproduction
  in animals 324-327, 431
  in humans **376-377**
  in plants **270-279**, 282-283, 431
reproductive system **376**, 431
reptiles 186, 187, 316, 332, 338, 339, 342
repulsion (magnetic) **232**, 431
reservoirs,
  oil and gas **98**
  water 74
residue **60**, 431
residue compounds (oil) **99**
resistance,
  air **125**, **142**
  disease **387**
  electrical **236**, 405, 431
resistance (force) **128**
resistor **236**, 237, 409
resolution (of image) **225**, 431
resonance **208**, 431
respiration, internal 52, **80**, 81, **265**, **360**, 431
respiratory
  organs **314**, **358-359**, 431
  system **358-359**
restriction enzymes **383**
resultant force **120**, 431
reticulum **313**
retina **370**, 431
return stroke **229**, 431
reversible reaction **78**, 431
rhenium **28**
rheostat **237**, 431
rhizoids **282**, 431
rhizomes **278**, 283, 295, 431
rhodium **28**, 79
rhombic sulphur **54**, 431
rib **346**
ribosome **298**, 431
Richter scale **407**
ridge **181**, 431
rift valley **182**, 431
Rigel (star) **159**
Ringed Planet **169**, 431
rings, planetary 168, 169, 170
rivers **190-191**, 410

rock 168, 169, 173, 179, **180-181**, 182, 183, 186, 190-191, 198-199
plants **287**
salt 27, **89**, 431
rocket engines 35, 47, **149**
rockets 47, 149, 177
rodents **342**
rods (in eye) **370**, 431
rolling **143**
Röntgen, Wilhelm **415**
room temperature **19**
root
canal **352**, 431
cap **253**, 431
hairs **253**, 431
of plant 89, **253**, 431
of tooth **352**
pressure **262**, 431
vegetables **253**
rosette (leaves) **259**, 431
roughage **357**
router (computer) **246**, 431
rubber **101**, 124
rubidium **28**
rudder **140**, **143**, 144, 431
rugae **355**, 431
rumen **313**
ruminants **313**, 432
runners **278**, 432
Ruska, Ernst **415**
rusting **40**, **80**, 82, 432
ruthenium **28**
Rutherford, Ernest 13, **415**
rutherfordium **28**

S

saccule **373**, 432
sacrificial metal **41**, 432
sails 103, 140, **141**
salicylic acid **84**
saline **286**, 432
saliva **354**, 432
salivary glands **354**
salt
bladder **286**
marsh **286**
salt, common 48, 66, 70, 88, **89**, 432
salts 84, 85, **88-89**, 90, 91, 94, 432
Salyut I (space station) **411**
samara (fruit) **275**, 432
samarium **28**
sampling **211**, 432
San Andreas fault 182
sandstone 180, 191
saprophyte **432** (See also *saprotrophs*)
saprotrophic plants **266**
saprotrophs **266**, **285**, 432
sapwood **257**, 432
sartorius **348**, 432
satellite 174, **175**, 177, 185, 226, 244, 432
dish 226, 227
TV **227**
saturated
compounds **93**, 96, 97, 432
fats 356
solutions **73**, 432
Saturn 163, **169**, 170, 176, 411
Savery, Thomas **415**
scalar quantities **119**, 126, 432
scales (on animals) **303**
scandium **28**
scapula **346**, 432
sclera **370**, 432
sclerites **302**, 432
screening **391**
screw **135**
scrotum **376**, 432
scrublands **290**, 331
scum **73**, 94
scuta **302**, 308, 432
sea 188-189, 410
anemone 301
breezes 111
planes **144**
slugs **84**
salt **89**
water 49, 58, 59, 72, 74, 88, 89
seaborgium **28**
search engine 395, **432**
seasons **193**
seaweed 49, **281**
sebaceous glands **368**, 432
sebum **368**, 432
secondary
bronchus **358**, 432
bud **252**
cell (in a battery) **231**, 432
colours **216**, **217**, 432
consumer (food chain) **332**
phloem **256**
roots **253**
sexual features **379**, 432
thickening **256-257**, 432
tissue **256**
xylem **256**
sediment islands **191**
sedimentary rock **181**, 432
seed
crystal **91**
leaves **277**, 432
seed-carrying plants 187
seedling **277**
seeds **274-277**, 295
segment (in animal body) **300**
seismic waves **182**, 432
seismologists **182**, 407, 432
seismometer **407**
selective breeding **291**, **384**, 432
selenium 25, **29**
self-pollination **272**, 432
semen **376**, 432
semicircular
canals **373**, 432
ducts **373**, 432
semiconductor **25**, **239**, 432
semi-metals 24, **25**, 29, 432
seminal vesicles 376, **432**
semipermeable **432**
senescence **379**, 432
sensation 320, **432**
senses **320-321**, 364, 365, **368-375**, 432
sensory
area (brain) **367**
nerve **364**
neuron **364**, 432
sepals **270**, 432
septum **300**, 432
series circuit **230**, 432
serrate leaf margin **259**, 432
server **243**, 246, 432
setae **322**, 432
sewage **74**, 432
works **74**, 432
sex **377**
cells 325
chromosomes **380**, 432
sex-linked genes **381**, 432
sexual
features **379**
intercourse **377**, 432
sexual reproduction 432
(in animals) **325**, **326-327**
(in humans) **376-377**
(in plants) **270-272**
shadows **214**
shaft
of a feather **306**
of a hair **369**
shanty towns **196**
shark 301, 303, 312, 314, 323
shell, electron **10-11**, 14, 28, **68**, 70, 71, 92, 432
shell
models of atoms **68**
of a mollusc **302**
Shepherd Moons **169**
shingle beaches **286**
ships 41, 44, 139, **140-141**
shoot (plant stem) **252**, 432
shooting star **173**, 432
short
bone **346**
sight 221, **371**
short-night plant **269**
short-term memory **367**, 432
shutter (on a camera) **224**, 432
SI units **405**, 432
side vein (on a leaf) 260
sieve
plates **254**, 432
tubes **254**, 432
sight (See *vision*)
sign stimulus **318**, 432
Sikorsky, Igor **415**
silica **27**, 432
silicaceous (S-type) asteroid **172**
silicates **27**, 432
silicon **25**, 26, 27, **29**, 68, 239
chip **239**, 432
dioxide **69** (See also *silica*)
Silurian Period **186**
silver 27, **29**, 30, 32, 33, 35, **39**, 42, 43, 44, **45**
bromide **49**
nitrate 225
simple leaves **258**, 432
single
bond **92**, 93, 96, 432
cell (in battery) **231**, 409, 432
single-celled organisms 186
single-lens reflex (SLR) camera **224**
siphon **314**, 432
skeletal
muscles **348**, 432
system **299**, **346**
skeleton **301**, **346-347**, 432
skin 362, **368-369**
cancer 213
skis 48, **124**
sky (colour) **216**
Skylab (space station) 177, 411
slag **36**, 432
slaked lime **86**
sleep **367**
slide film **225**
sliding joints **347**
Slipher, Vesto **415**
slow breeders **337**
Slowing Down theory **155**, 432
slow-twitch fibres **349**, 432
small intestine **355**, 432
smell 323, **374**, 375
smelting **36**, **81**, 432
smithsonite **27**
smog **64**, 432
smoke 58, 64, 185
smooth muscle tissue **349**, 432
snakes 182, 307, 308, 323
sneezing **359**
soap 73, 84, 85, **94**
bubbles 94, 219
social animals 319
socket (electrical) **230**
sodium 14, 28, 30, 31, 32, **39**, 66, 67, 68, 71, 357
aluminium silicate 73
carbonate **73**, 88, 89, 91
chloride 48, 66, 67, 70, 88, **89**, 432
ethanoate **85**
hydrogencarbonate **67**
hydroxide 85, 88, 89, 94
hypochlorite 48
iodate 48, 49
phosphate 55
software **240**, 242, 432
soil 86, 292
erosion **197**, 432
solar
cell **109**, **231**, 432
collector **109**, 432
eclipse 162, 434
energy **109**, 162, 432
flare **162**, 432
panel 109, 177, **198**, 432
power 185, **198**
prominence **46**, **162**
radiation **192**, 432
wind **162**, **173**, 432
Solar System 154, 156, 157, **163**, 173, 176, 432
solder **39**
solenoid **233**, 432
soleus **348**, 432
solids **16-19**, 58, 79, 110, 113, 124, 132
solubility **58**, 88, 432
solute **58**, 432
solutions **58**, 59, 60, 61, **73**, 89, 432
solvents **58**, **73**, 433
sonar **207**, 433
sonic boom **207**
sori **283**, 433
sound 106, **206-207**, **210-211**
synthesizer **209**, 433
waves **206-207**, **320**, **372**, 433
soundbox **208**, 433
source (of a river) **190**
South Pole 179, 188
Southern Cross (asterism) 161
southern
hemisphere **193**, 433
lights **162**
south-seeking pole **232**, 433
space 103, 125, 130, 149, **154-177**, 411
exploration **174-177**, 411
probes 165, 168, 170, 171, 172, **176**, 177, 411, 433
stations **177**, 411, 433
telescopes 174, 411
travel 176, 411
Space Shuttle 24, 125, 176, **177**, 185, 411, 433
spacecraft 39, 103, 411
space-filling models **15**, 432
spawn **327**, 433
special theory of relativity **433**
specialization
in animal cells **299**, 433
in plant cells **251**, 270, 433

species **341**, 342, 433
specific
epithet **343**, 433
heat capacity 111, **433**
spectral type (star) **160**, 433
speed **126**, 127, 433
of light **212**, 433
of sound 144, **207**, 433
sperm **326**, **376**, 433
ducts **376**, 433
sphalerite **27**
sphincter **362**
spinal cord **364**, 366
spine (in a leaf) **259**, **286**
spiracle **315**, 433
spiral
galaxy **156**, 158, 433
leaves **259**
Spirit (Mars mission) 165
spongy
bone **347**, 433
cells 251, **260**, 433
layer **260**
sporangia **282**
spore **283**, 284, 295, 433
sporophyte **283**, 433
sporulation **283**, 433
spreading ridge **181**, 183, 433
spring
balance **119**, 433
tide **189**, 433
wood **257**, 433
springs 190
Sputnik 1 (satellite) 175, 411
stability
of atoms 42, **68**, **114-115**
of objects **131**
stage (on a microscope) **222**
stainless steel 34, 35, 38, **39**, 433
stalk (leaf) **261**
stamen **271**, 433
stamina **361**
staminate flowers **271**, 433
stance **309**, 433
standard pressure **19**
stapes **372**, 433
starch 46, 100, **264**, 354, **356**, 433
stars 46, 154, 156, 157, **158-161**, 162, 223, 433
states of matter **16-19**, 77, 433
static electricity **229**, 433
statocyst **320**, 433
statolith **320**
steam 16, 18, 47, 107, 117, 146, 147
engines **146**, 433
point 111, **433**
turbine **235**
steel 34, 35, **36-37**, 38, **39**, 40, 41, 44, 55, 82, 232
stem **252**, 433
Stephenson, George **415**
steppes **290**
stereoscopic vision **321**, **370**, 433
sterilization 212
sternum **346**, 433
stigma **271**, 433
stimulus 268, **433**
stipules **259**, 433
stolon **278**, 433
stomach **355**
stomata **260**, **262**, 433
strain energy **106**
Strassman, Fritz **415**
strata **433**
stratosphere **185**, 433
stratus **193**, 433
strawberries 274
streamlining **125**, **142**, 433
strength **361**
stretch receptors 373, **433**
striated muscle tissue **349**, 433
stridulation **319**, 433
stringed instruments **208**
striped muscle tissue **349**
strobili **282**
stromatolite **186**
strontium **28**, 80
style **271**, 433
subatomic particles **10**, 11-13, 433
subcutaneous layer **368**, 433
subduction zone **181**, 183, 433
sub-kingdoms **341**
sublimation **18**, 433
submarine **141**, 223
submergent plants **280**, 433
subordinates **319**
sub-phyla **341**
subsonic speed **207**, 433
sub-species **433**
substation **230**
substitution reactions **93**, 433
subtractive mixing **217**, 433
succession **330**, 422
succulent fruit **274**, 433
suckle **327**
sucrose **46**, 433
sugars 46, 52, **356**, 363, 433
sulphates 27, **88**, 433
sulphides **27**, 433
sulphur 24, 25, 27, 29, 36, 52, **54**, 66, 71, 77, 87, 89, 90, 101
dioxide **54**, **64**, 65, 433
trioxide **76**
sulphuric acid 39, 54, 76, 83, 84, **87**, 88, 89, 91, 164, 433
summer wood **257**, 433
Sun 46, 65, 106, 107, 108, 109, 112, 113, 128, 154, 158, 159, **162-163**, 167, 173, 178, 179, 183-186, 189, 192, 213
sundews 267
sunless zone **189**, 433
sunlight 260, 264-265
sunlit zone **189**, 433
sunspot **162**, 433
superalloys **35**, 433
supergiant star **159**, 161, 433
superior vena cava **350**, 433
supernova **161**, 433
supersonic speed **207**, 433
supervolcanoes **183**, 433
suppleness **361**
support
in animals 302-303
in plants 252, 253, 254, 255, 256-257
surface
currents **188**
tension **21**, 433
surgery **389**
survival **286-287**
suspension
in vehicles **151**, 433
in mixtures **58**, 61, 433
swamps 187
sweat 316, 357, 362, 369
glands **368**, 369
swim bladder **305**, 433
swinging (primates) **308**
switches 234, 244, 409
sycamore 275
symbiotic relationship **285**, 433
symbols, chemical 13, **15**
synapse **365**, 433
synovial
fluid **347**, 433
joints **347**, 433
synthesis reactions **78**, 433
synthetic **434**
compounds **93**, 100-103
fibres 87, 97, 100, **101**, 103, 434
syrinx **319**, 434
system **299**, 434

T

tactile receptors **322**, 434
tadpole 328
tagmata **300**, 434
Talbot, William Fox **415**
talc 407
tantalum **28**
tap root **253**, 434
tapetum **321**, 434
target
DNA **383**
organ **363**
tarnishing **40**
tarsals **346**, 434
taste **323**, **375**
buds **375**, 434
taxa **341**
taxonomic ranks **341**, 434
tears **371**
technetium **28**
teeth 33, 55, **312**, **352-353**
telecommunications **244-245**, 434
telephone 175, 227, 244-245
system **244**
telescopes 174-175, 220, **223**
television 90, 175, 213, **226-227**, 236
cameras **225**
tellurium 25, **29**
temperate
climate **194**, 434
grasslands **290**, **331**
temperature 18, 19, 20, 23, **110**, 111
control **316**, 369
scales **111**, **404**
temporary magnets **232**, 434
tendon **348**, 434
tendril **259**, 434
tentacle **322**, 434
terbium **29**
terminal
bud **252**, 434
velocity **128**, 434
terminals **230**, 409, 434
ternate leaves **258**, 434
terrestrial animals **308-309**, 434
tertiary bronchus **358**, 434
Tertiary Period **187**
Tesla, Nikola **415**
testa **274**, 434
testes 363, **376**, 434
Tethys (moon) **169**
thalamus **366**, 434
thallium **29**, 33
thallus **282**
theory
of evolution **338**, 434
of natural selection **339**, 434
thermal
capacity **111**, 434
thermal
decomposition reactions **78**, 434
thermistor **237**, 409, 434
thermodynamics **434**
thermogenesis **360**
thermometers **111**
thermoplastics **101**, 434
thermoregulation **316**, 434
thermosetting plastics **101**, 103, 434
thermosphere **185**, 434
thermostat **110**, 434
theta wave **367**
thigmotropism **269**, 434
Thomson, William (Lord Kelvin) **415**
thorax **300**, 434
thorium **28**, 115
thread cell **310**, 434
threatened species **336**
thrust **142**, 145, 434
thulium **29**
thunder **229**, 434
tibia **346**, 434
tibialis anterior **348**, 434
tides **131**, 189
timbre **209**, 434
tin 29, 30, 33, 35, **39**, 42, 43, 44, 82
tissue,
animal **299**, 377, 434
plant 251, **254-257**, 434
tissue fluid **351**
Titan (moon) **169**
Titania (moon) **170**
titanium 28, 33, 35, **39**
oxide 87
Tombaugh, Clyde 171, 415
tongue **375**
tonsils **375**
top-level domain **247**, 434
Torricelli, Evangelista **415**
tortoise 302
touch **322**, **368**
toxins **386**
trabeculae **347**, 434
trace minerals 357
trachea 315, **358**, 434
tracheae 354
tracheid **254**, 434
tracheole **315**, 434
Tracking and Data Relay Satellites (TDRS) 175
trains 234, 235
traits **325**, 434
transgenic **384**, 434
transistor 25, **237**, 409, 434
transition metals 29, **33**, 434
translocation (plants) **262**, 434
translucent **214**, 434
transmission 148, **151**, 434
transmitter 213
transparency film **225**
transparent **214**, 434
transpiration **262**, 263, **292**, 434
stream **262**, 434
transportation (in a river) **191**
transverse waves **203**, 212, 214, 434
trapezius **348**, 434
treeline **195**
trees **256-257**, 288
trench **181**, 434
Triassic period **186**
tributary **190**, 434
triceps **348**
trichomonas 304

Trifid Nebula **158**
trifoliate leaves **258**, 434
trilobite 187
tripinnate leaves **258**
triple bonds **92**, 93, 434
trisodium phosphate **55**
Triton (moon) **171**
Trojans (asteroids) **172**
trophic level **332**, 434
tropical
  climate **194**, 434
  cyclone **189**, 434
  grasslands **290**, **331**
  rainforests **290**, **331**, 337
tropism **268**, 434
troposphere **185**, 434
trough (wave) **203**, 206, 434
true fruit **274**, 434
tsunami (wave) **204**
tuber **278**, 434
tufa tower **76**
tundra **194**, **290**, **331**, 434
tungstates **27**
tungsten 27, 28, **39**
turbines 107, 108, 117, **147**, 149, **235**, 434
turbofan engine **149**, 434
turbojet engine **149**, 434
turboprop engine **149**, 434
turboshaft engine **149**, 434
turgid **263**
turgor **263**, 434
Turing, Alan **415**
turning forces **121**
turquoise **27**, 55
twilight zone **189**, 434
tympanal organ **320**, 434
tympanum **320**, 434
typhoon **189**, 434
tyre 101, **124**

U

ulna **346**, 434
ultrasound **206**, 434
  scanning **207**, 434
ultraviolet (UV) rays 65, 178, 184, 185, **213**, 215, 434
umbilical cord **377**, 434
umbra **214**, 434
Umbriel (moon) **170**
unguligrade **309**, 434
unicellular **300**, 434
universal indicator **86**, 435
universe **154-155**, 435
unsaturated
  compounds **93**, 97, 435
  fats **356**
ununbium **29**
ununhexium **29**
ununnilium **29**
ununoctium **29**
ununquadium **29**
unununium **29**
upgrading (a computer) **242**
upper stage (of a river) **190**
upthrust **138**, 139, 435
uranium 28, 38, **39**, 115, 117
Uranus 163, **170**, 173, 411
urban migration **196**, 435
urea **317**, 435
ureter **362**, 435
urethra **362**, 376, 435
uric acid **317**, 435
urinary system **362**, 435
urine 317, 357, **362**, 435
URL (Uniform Resource Locator) **247**, 435
Ursa Major (constellation) **160**
USB device 241
uterus **327**, **376**, 377, 435
utricle **373**, 435

V

vaccination **387**, **391**, 435
vaccine **387**, 435
vacuoles
  in animal cells **298**, 310, 317, 435
  in plant cells **250**, 263, 435
vacuum **113**, 206, **212**, 218, 435
vagina **376**, 435
valency **71**, 435
valves (in the heart) **350**
vanadates **27**
vanadium 27, 28, 35, 37, **39**
vane **306**, **435**
variable
  resistor **237**, 409, 435
  star **159**, 435
variegated leaves **261**, 435
vascular **435**
  bundle **255**, 256, 435
  cylinder **256**, 435
  plants **254-255**, 295
  tissue **251**, **252**, **254-255**, 260, **262**, 281, 282, 283, 295
vastus lateralis **348**, 435
vector quantities **119**, 435
vegetative
  propagation **278**, 435
  reproduction **278**, 435
veil (in fungi) **284**
vein
  (blood vessel) **351**, 435
  in a leaf **260**
velocity 123, **127**, 128, 405, 435
venation **260**
Venera (space probes) **165**, 411
vent (in a volcano) **182**, 435
ventilation **359**, 435
ventral fin **305**, 435
ventricle **350**, 435
Venus 163, **164-165**, 411
  flytrap 267
vermilion 88
Veroboard **236**, 435
vertebrae **346**, 435
vertebral column **346**, 435
vertebrates 187, **322**, 435
Vesalius, Andreas **415**
vessels (plants) **254**, 257, 435
vestibular system **372**, 435
vibrissae **322**, 435
video camcorder **225**
viewfinder (camera) **224**, 435
Viking space probe **165**, 411
Villard, Paul **415**
villi **355**, 435
vinegar 40, **84**, 85, 87, 94
virtual image **435**
virus 341, **386**, 435
  computer 7
visceral muscles **349**, 435
visible light spectrum **213**, 214-215, **216-219**, 435
vision 220, **321**, **370-371**
vitamins 93, **357**
vitreous humour **370**, 435
viviparous **327**, 435
vocal cords **359**, 435
voice box **359**, 435
volcanic gases **23**
volcanoes 112, 168, 178, **182-183**, 184, 435
Volkmann's canals **347**, 435
Volta, Alessandro **415**
voltage 230, 405, **435**
volts **230**, 405, 435
volume 16, **17**, 23, 404-405, 408, 435
voluntary
  actions **365**, 435
  muscles **348**, 435
Voyager space probes 168, 169, 170, 411
VTOL (Vertical Take Off and Landing) **145**, 435
vulcanization **54**, **101**, 435

W

wafers (silicon chip) **239**, 435
warm-blooded **316**, 435
washing soda **73**, 88, 89, 91, 435
waste substances 260, 350
water 15, 16, 19, 20, 21, 46, 47, 60, 61, 66, 69, **72-75**, 76, 83, 91, 94, 110, 125, 138, 139, 166, 184, 187,188, 198, 216, 250-251, 252-253, 254-255, 259, 262-263, 357
  cycle **74**, 75, **292**, 334, 435
  of crystallization **91**, 435
  plants **280-281**
  purification **75**
  softening **73**
  vapour 19, **72**, 74
waterworks **74**, 435
Watson, James **382**, 415
Watt, James 137, 146, **415**
watts **109**, **137**, 405, 435
wavelength **203**, 205, 212, 215, 216, 226, 435
waves **202-205**, **212-213**, **214-215**
waxes **435**
weather 65, 132, 166, 185, **192-193**
websites 6-7, 246-247, **394-395**
wedges **136**
Wegener, Alfred **415**
weight **17**, **130**, 134, 135, 138, 139, 435
wheel **134**, 151
whiskers **322**
white
  blood cells 61, **351**, **387**, 435
  dwarf (star) **161**
  light **216**, 435
  phosphorus **55**, 435
Whittle, Frank **415**
whorl (leaves) **259**
wide-area network (WAN) **243**
Wilkins, Maurice **415**
wilting **263**, 435
wind 111, 112, 173, **192**, 198, **406**
  instruments **208**
  pollination 273
  power **108**, 185
  turbines 108, 198, 235
windpipe **315**, 354, **358**, 435
wings
  on aircraft 142-145
  on animals **306**
wisdom teeth **352**, 435
womb **327**, **376**, 435
wood 52, 108, 113, **256-257**
woody
  perennials **288**, 435
  plants **256**
work **137**, 405, 435
World Wide Web (www) **246**, 394-395, 435
worms 300, 301, 324, 325
Wright brothers **145**, 415

X

X chromosomes **380**, 435
xanthophylls **261**, 435
xenon 25, 29, **63**, 184, 435
xerophytes **286**, 435
X-rays 33, 38, **212**, **388**, 435
xylem **254**, 256, **262**, 435

Y

Y chromosomes **380**, 435
Yale, Linus **415**
yawing **143**, 435
yawning **359**
year (planetary) **163**, 411
yeast 94, 284, **285**, 435
yellow bone marrow **347**
yoga **390**
yolk **327**
  sac **327**, 435
ytterbium **29**
yttrium **28**

Z

zeolite **73**
zinc 27, 29, 30, 34, 35, 38, **39**, 41, 42, 70, 231
  blende (sphalerite) **39**
  carbonate **27**
zirconium **28**
zone of elongation **253**, 435
zones (in oceans) **189**
zoology **435**
zooplankton **435**
zygote **272**, **377**, 435

See for yourself answers

68 Bonding

Element	Atomic number	Electron configuration
Magnesium	12	2, 8, 2
Argon	18	2, 8, 8
Nitrogen	7	2, 5
Potassium	19	2, 8, 8, 1
Silicon	14	2, 8, 4

236 Electronics

The red (2) red (2) blue (6) silver (±10%) resistor has the highest rating, with a value of between 19,800,000Ω and 24,200,000Ω. The green (5) green (5) black (0) silver (±10%) resistor is worth between 49.5Ω and 60.5Ω.

ACKNOWLEDGEMENTS

Every effort has been made to trace the copyright holders of the material in this book. If any rights have been omitted, the publishers offer to rectify this in any future edition, following notification. The publishers are grateful to the following organizations and individuals for their contribution and permission to reproduce material. Microsoft® Windows® and Microsoft® Internet Explorer are either registered trademarks or trademarks of Microsoft Corporation in the United States and other countries. Java and all Java-based trademarks and logos are trademarks or registered trademarks of Sun Microsystems Inc in the United States and other countries. Dacron®, Kevlar®, Mylar® and Nomex® are DuPont registered trademarks.

PHOTO CREDITS (t = top, m = middle, b = bottom, l = left, r = right)

Corbis: **8-9** Gary Braasch; **12** (bl) Jim Sugar Photography; **14-15** (main) Digital Art; 16-17 W. Perry Conway; **18** (tl) Fukuhara Inc; **19** (m) Keren Su; **22-23** Roger-Ressmeyer; **24** (bl) Jim Zuckerman; **26-27** Ric Ergenbright; **30-31** Buddy Mays; **32** (tr) Phil Schermeister; **34** Dan Guravich; **36-37** Dean Conger; **40-41** Roger-Ressmeyer; **42-43** (main) Charles E. Rotkin; **43** (tr) Roger Ressmeyer; **45** (tr) James L. Amos; **48-49** (main) Charles O'Rear; **52-53** (main) Charles O'Rear; **55** (main) Owen Franken; **62-63** (main) Jonathan Blair; **64-65** (main) Ted Spiegal; **72-73** (b) Peter Johnson; **74-75** (b) Wolfgang Kaehler; **76-77** (main) Randy Faris; **87** (b) Jonathan Blair; **89** (tr) Science Pictures Limited; **95** (main) Michael Freeman; **98** (tr) Science Pictures Limited; **102** (b) Tecmap Corporation/Eric Curry, Eric Curry; **108-109** Sean Aidan, Eye Ubiquitous; **112-113** (main) Gary Braasch; **115** (b) Owen Franken; **116-117** (main) Bettmann; **119** (main) Robert Landau; **147** (main) Richard Hamilton Smith; **166** (mr) NASA/Roger-Ressmeyer; **174-175** (b) Roger Ressmeyer; **184-185** (main) Galen-Rowell; **192-193** (t) L. Clarke; **196-197** (main) Hans Georg Roth; **198-199** (b) Roger Ressmeyer; **204-205** (b) Peter Johnson; **206-207** (b) George Hall; **214-215** (t) Stuart-Westmorland; **216-217** (t) Joseph Sohm, ChromoSohm Inc; 218-219 (b) Steve Austin, Papilio; 220 (tr) Charles E. Rotkin; **222**-(bl) Jamie Harron, Papilio; **228-229** Kennan Ward; **230-231** (b) Peter Hardholdt; **232** (t) The Purcell Team; **234-235** (b) Lowell Georgia; **237** (br) Charles O'Rear; **250-251** (b) Science Pictures Limited; **251** (m) Lester V. Bergman; **252** Richard Hamilton Smith; **254-255** Richard Hamilton Smith; **257** (ml) Bill Varie; **258** (t) Paul-A.-Souders; **259** (b) Scott T. Smith; **260-261** (t) Paul A. Souders; **266** (l) Kevin Schafer; **267** (main) Bill Ross; **268-269** (b) Ron Watts; **270-271** (b) Ralph-A.-Clevenger; **271** (br) Lee Snider; **272** (t) Darrell Gulin; **273** (b) Philip Marazzi, Papilio; **274** (t) Marko Modic; **275** (b) Australian Picture Library; **276** (r) Kevin Schafer; **278** (bl) Marlen Raabe; **278-279** (t) Richard Hamilton Smith; **279** (bl) Ed Young; **283** (tr) Raymond Gehman; **284** (t) Sally Morgan, Ecoscene, (b) Buddy Mays; **285** (tr) Kevin R. Morris; **286-287** (main) Joseph Sohm/ChromoSohm Inc; **287** (l) Richard Cummins; **288-289** (t) W. Wayne Lockwood M.D; (b) Joseph Sohm, ChromoSohm Inc; **290-291** (main) Galen Rowell; **291** (l) Hulton-Deutsch Collection; **292-293** (b) Raymond Gehman; **304-305** (t) Stephen Frink; **306-307** (main) David A. Northcott; **308-309** (b) Tom Brakefield; **312** (t) Michael Lewis; **314-315** (t) Amos Nachoum; **316-317** (main) W. Perry Conway; **318** (bl) Jim Zuckerman; **321** (r) W. Perry Conway; **322** (bl) Stuart Westmorland; **324** (tr) Lester V. Bergman, (bl) Robert Yin; **325** (main) Robert Pickett/papiliophotos.com; **328-329** (main) Yann Arthus-Bertrand; **330-331** (b) Kennan Ward; **332** Peter Johnson; **335** (b) Jim Sugar Photography; **336-337** (main) Annie-Griffiths Belt; **338** (t) James L. Amos; **372** (b) Hulton-Deutsch Collection; **374** (t) Michael Freeman; **377** (br) Jenny Woodcock, Reflections Photo Library; **378** (tr) Bettmann, (mr) Bettmann, (br) Corbis; **384** (tr) Richard Hamilton Smith; **389** (br) Science Pictures Limited; **390-391** (main) Bill Ross.

© **Digital Vision**: **19** (tm), (b); **20** (l); **22** (tr); **24-25**; **25** (m); **32** (br); **33**; **35** (ml); **37** (mr); **38** (tr); **38-39**; **41** (tr), (m), (mr); **44** (bm); **44-45**; **46** (t), (b); **48** (l); **52** (bl); **53** (tl); **56-57**; **58-59**; **59** (ml); **64** (tl); **65** (t); **72** (tr); **75** (tr); **78**(b); **80** (br); **81** (r); **82** (t), (br); **85** (tl); **87** (l); **96** (b); **98-99**; **99** (tl); **101** (m); **102** (tr); **103** (br); **104-105**; **106** (t), (b); **107** (bl); **110** (l); **112** (l), (bm); **113** (tr); **117** (ml); **118** (tr); **120**; **123** (tm), (tr); **124**; **126** (t), (br); **128** (t), (b); **132** (tr), (bl);

138-139 (t); **140-141**; **142-143**; **152-153**; **154** (bl); **156** (tr), (br); **158** (l); **161** (mr); **162** (t), (b); **163** (t); **164** (tr); **165** (tm); **166** (tr), (ml), (m), (b); **167** (t); **170-171** (t); **173** (l); **175** (tr); **176** (br); **176-177**; **177** (mr), (bl); **178** (tr); **179** (ml); **180-181**; **182-183**; **185** (t), (m), (ml); **187** (mr); **188-189**; **188** (tr); **190-191**; **192** (b); **193** (l), (m); **194** (m), (bm); **194-195** (b); **196** (tr), (ml); **197** (m); **199** (m); **202-203**; **204** (tr); **207** (tr); **208** (tr), (mr), (bl); **214** (ml); **216** (m); **225** (mr); **233** (tr); **238** (tr); **242** (b); **244** (tr); **245** (tr); **248-249**; **271** (tr); **284** (tr); **286** (bl); **289** (m), (r); **294** (tr); **296-297**; **303** (tl); **309** (tl); **323** (ml); **335** (l); **336** (l); **337** (l); **343** (m); **360-361**.

NASA: **Cover**; **51** (bm); **125** (l); **161** (tl), (bl); **164-165** (b); **165** (mr); **168** (tl); **170** (bl), (br); **171** (bl); **175** (m); **178** (b); **246** (bl), (bm), (br); **395** (br).

Science Photo Library: **Cover**; **1-3** Phil Jude; **58** (ml) Tek Image; **60-61** (main) Geoff Tompkinson; **61** (r) Tek Image; **71** (br) Ken Eward; **93** (br) Steve-Horrell; **101** (br) Eye of Science; **130** (b) Science Photo Library; **133** (tr) Will & Deni McIntyre; **135** (main) Jeremy Walker; **212** (tr) Hugh Turvey; **280-281** (t) Jan-Hinsch; **298-299** (t) Dr Yorgos Nikas; **341** (b) UDSA; **344-345** Mehau Kulyk; **346-347** (main) Manfred Kage; **348** (r) John Daugherty; **350-351** (t) National Cancer Institute; **352-353** (t) Tek Image; **358-359** (t) Alfred Pasieka; **362** (b) Biophoto Associates; **364-365** CNRI; 366 Mehau Kulyk; **368-369** (b) Prof. P.-Motta/
Dept of Anatomy/University "La Sapienza", Rome; **370-371** (b) David Parker; **376** (t) Dr G. Moscoso; **380-381** Biophoto Associates; **382** (tr) A. Barrington-Brown; 383 (tm) Simon Fraser; **384-385** Tek Image; **386-387** (t) Juergen Berger, Max-Planck Institute; **388** (t) Mehau Kulyk, (b) Hugh Turvey; **390** (bl) BSIP Boucharlat.

Telegraph Colour Library: **80-81** (main); **256-257** (main); **267** (tr); **282** (b); **303** (b); **322-323** (main); **326** (b).

Airbus Industrie 242 (tl); **Alamy 140-141** (m); **Allsport UK Ltd 227** (tr); **American Government 207** (ml); **Arriflex 255** (bl); **Stuart Atkinson 172** (tr); **British Telecom 247** (tr); **Britstock-IFA 262-263** (t), 268 (t); **Bruce Coleman 311** (t) John Cancalosi; **Crown copyright: Historic Royal Palaces 50** (Reproduced by permission of Historic Royal Palaces under licence from the controller of Her Majesty's Stationery Office); **Dell 240** (m); **Diamond Multimedia 242** (tr); **Epson** Perfection 610 Scanner **243** (l); **Ford Motor Co Ltd 125** (tr), **134** (r), **147** (ml), **148** (m), **150-151**; **Gateway 240** (bl), **243** (t); **Goodyear GB Ltd 124** (l); **Guillemot 243** (ml); **Honda UK 152** (tr); **Intel 239** (tr), (ml), **241** (m), (ml); **Karrimor International Ltd 101** (ml); **Lawson Mardon Star Ltd, Bridgnorth 24** (bm); **41** (l); **Microsoft 240** (mr), **242** (bl) (Screen shot reprinted with permission from Microsoft Corporation); **Susan Middleton & David Liittschwager 320** (t); © **Charles Michael Murray 215** (br); **NHPA 312** (b); **Nokia Mobile Phones 102** (m); **Northern Lites 132** (m); **Opera-North/Richard Moran 359** (mr) Roderick Williams as Figaro in Opera North's production of *The Barber of Seville*; **Philips 227** (tr), (m); **Planet Earth Pictures 326** (tr); **Porsche Cars Great Britain 127** (bm); **Powerstock/Zefa 276-277** (main); **Robert M. Reed 27** (bm); **Robert Pickett 85** (main); **Sony 225** (bm); **Snow and Rock 124** (br); **Still-Pictures 260** (bl) Klein/Hubert, **316** (b) John Cancalosi; **The Royal Festival Hall Gamelan Programme, London 208** (bl); **The Stock Market 264, 280** (bl); **Charlotte Tomlins 207** (mr); **Two Way TV 227** (tr); © **akg-images/Ullstein 47** (bm); **Undersea Research Programme (NURP) 281** (mr), **300-301** (t); **www.trekbikes.com 52** (m); **Yamaha-Kemble Music (UK) Ltd 209** (bl); **3Com 245** (ml).

ILLUSTRATORS

Simone Abel, Graham Allen, Sophie Allington, Rex Archer, David Ashby, Iain Ashman, Craig Austin (The Garden Studio), Graham Austin, Alan Baker, Bob Bampton (The Garden Studio), Jeremy Banks, John Barker, David Baxter, Andrew Beckett, Joyce Bee, Stephen Bennett, Mark Bergin, Roland Berry, Andrzej Bielecki, Gary Bines, Derick-Bown, Isabel Bowring, Trevor Boyer, Wendy Bramall (Artist Partners), John Brettoner, Paul Brooks, Gerry Browne, Peter Bull, Derek Bunce, Mark Burgess, Hilary-Burn, Andy Burton, Terry Burton, Liz Butler, Terry Callcut, Martin Camm, Sue Camm, Lynn Chadwick, Kuo Kang Chen, Peter Chesterton, Jeane Colville, Stephen-Conlin, Dan Courtney, Frankie Coventry, Patrick Cox, Steve Cross, Lindy Dark, Christine Darter, Gordon Davies, Kate Davies, Sarah De Ath (Linden Artists), Kevin-Dean, Peter Dennis, Richard Draper, Brin Edwards, Michelle Emblem, Malcolm English, Sandra Fernandez, Denise Finney, Don Forrest, John Fox, Sarah Fox-Davies, John Francis, Mark Franklin, Nigel Frey, Judy Friedlander, Sheila Galbraith, Stephen Gardiner, Peter Geissler, Nick Gibbard, Peter Gibson, Tony Gibson, William Giles, Victoria Goaman, Jayne Goin, David Goldston, Peter Goodwin, Victoria Gordon, Teri Gower, Phil Green, Coral Guppy (John Martin Artists), Terry Hadler, Alan Harris, Brenda Haw, Tim Hayward, Bob Hersey, Nicholas Hewetson, Philip Hood, Chris Howell-Jones, Christine Howes, Carol Hughes (John Martin Artists), David Hurrell, Gillian-Hurry, John Hutchinson, Ian Jackson, Frank Kennard, Roger Kent, Aziz Khan, Colin King, Deborah King, Stephen Kirk, Kim Lane, Jonathon Langley, Richard Levington, Jason Lewis, Mick Loates (The Garden Studio), Rachel Lockwood, Mark Logworth, Kevin Lyles, Chris Lyon, Kevin Maddison, Alan Male, Janos Marffy, Andy-Martin, Josephine Martin, Lucia Mattioli (Inklink at Firenze), Nick May, Rob McCaig, Joseph McEwan, David McGrail, Malcolm McGregor, Doreen McGuiness, Christina McInerney, Caroline McLean, Dee McLean, Annabel Milne, David More, Dee Morgan, Robert Morton, David Mostyn, Paddy Mounter, Patricia Mynott, David-Nash, Susan Neale, Jan Nesbitt, Tricia Newell, Martin Newton, Barbara Nicholson, Louise Nixon, David Nockels (The Garden Studio), Richard Orr, David Palmer, Patti Pearce, Justine Peek, Jack Pelling, Liz Pepperell, Francesco Petracchi (Inklink at Firenze), Roger Phillips, Julie Piper, Gill Platt, Maurice Pledger, Mick Posen, Cynthia-Pow (Middletons), Isaac Quaye, David Quinn, Charles Raymond, Kim Raymond, Barry Raynor, Luis Rey, Phillip Richardson, Jim Robins, Allan Robinson, Andrew-Robinson, Bernard Robinson, Eric Robson, Michael Roffe, Michelle Ross, Simon Roulstone, Graham Round, John Russell, Evie Safarewicz, Michael Saunders, Philip-Schramm, John Scorey, Coral Sealey, John Shackell, Chris Shields, John Sibbick, Sara Silcock, Penny Simon, Gwen Simpson, Gabrielle Smith, Tony Smith, Annabel-Spenceley, Peter Stebbing, Ian Stephen, Roger Stewart, Sue Stitt, Ralph Stobart, Rod Sutterby, Alan Suttie, Treve Tamblin, Myke Taylor, George Thompson, Joan-Thompson, Sam Thompson, Stuart Trotter, Joyce Tuhill, Sally Voke, Ian Wallace, Sue Walliker, Robert Walster, Peter Warner, David Watson, Ross Watton, Phil Weare, David Webb, Hans Wiborg-Jenssen, Sean Wilkinson, Adrian Williams, Adam Willis, Roy Wiltshire, Ann Winterbottom, Gerald Wood, James Woods, Zöe Wray, David Wright, John Yates.

With thanks to Dr Keith Taber, Simon Barnett, Simon Tudhope, Sarah Khan, Nayera Everall and Keith Furnival